W9-AHE-921

10 Jampa Lhakhang A five-day Drubchen festival is held in this geomantic temple, founded by Songtsen Gampo

11 Tamzhing Lhundrub Choling Rare murals depict Pema Lingpa's visionary teachings

12 Rodang La Trek Experience the cultural sites of Bumthang and the rural life of Lhuntse and Tashi Yangtse

13 Mebartso Gorge Pema Lingpa extracted treasures from the murky waters here, with a burning lamp in his hand!

14 Shingar Cobblestone streets, shingled houses and sheepskin shawls

15 Thrumzhing La National Park The natural habitat of the red panda

16 Drametse Monastery The largest monastery in Eastern Bhutan, founded by Pema Lingpa's great-granddaughter

17 Chorten Kora Modelled on the Great Stupa of Bodhnath in Nepal, at the entrance to the Bomdeling Wildlife Sanctuary

18 Royal Manas National Park Home to the one-horned rhino, the Bengal tiger and the golden langur

Paro Valley
One of the most prosperous rural landscapes in western Bhutan.

A foot in the door

The small Himalayan kingdom of Bhutan, wedged between the vast territories of Tibet to the north and India to the south, straddles an important continental divide, where the Buddhist culture of the temperate highlands encounters the predominantly Hindu and Nepalese culture of the sub-tropical duars – the low-lying canyons through which south-flowing tributaries of the Brahmaputra emerge on to the Bengal and Assamese plains.

Acutely aware of the linguistic, ethnic and social problems that this culture clash has engendered in neighbouring Sikkim and in distant Ladakh, the successive kings and royal governments of Bhutan have sought to maintain national unity by preserving their unique cultural heritage. Economic development was for long regarded as secondary and the country only began to emerge slowly from its self-imposed isolation following the rude awakening of the Sino-Indian border war in 1962.

Slightly larger than Switzerland and only one third the size of Nepal, Bhutan is known in the local language (Dzongkha) as 'Drukyul', which means 'land of the Drukpa Kagyu school', a reference to the tradition of Tibetan Buddhism that has come to dominate Bhutanese spiritual life since the 17th century. However, since the word *Druk* also means dragon, the country is often poetically known as the 'land of the thunder dragon' (the emblem portrayed on the national flag). The English name 'Bhutan' probably derives from the Sanskrit *bhotanta*, meaning 'extremity of Tibet'; while in Tibetan language, the country is most frequently known as 'Lhomon', or 'Southern Mon' – harking back to the seventh and eighth centuries when Bhutan was firmly entrenched within the orbit of Tibetan imperial power.

1 Traditional costume of the Laya region of northern Bhutan. ▸▸ See page 145.

2 The Ura Yakcho festival is celebrated with traditional dancing in the Bumthang District of Central Bhutan. ▸▸ See page 193.

3 Located on a sheer cliff above the Paro valley, Taktsang hermitage is one of 13 'tiger lairs' visited by Guru Padmakara. According to legend, he flew here on the back of a tigress to subdue negative spiritual forces. ▸▸ See page 115.

4 An archer eyes the target, using the traditional bamboo long bow. Archery is the most popular sport in Bhutan. ▸▸ See page 45.

5 Chotse Dzong is the largest and most impressively situated dzong in Bhutan, perched high on a cliff above the deep Mangde-chu gorge and dominated by a double winged watchtower ('Ta Dzong'). ▸▸ See page 163.

6 Masks, similar to those worn by performing monks during the tsechu and drubchen dances, are available in handicraft stores in Paro. ▸▸ See page 122.

7 Buddhist monks watch the dancing at Thimphu's tsechu festival. ▸▸ See page 75.

8 Golden langur in its natural habitat, the Royal Manas National Park. ▸▸ See page 195.

9 An astrological chart in Rinpung Dzong, Paro, depicts the apparent motion of planets and stars. ▸▸ See page 109.

10 Rice fields create a carpet of green in the lower reaches of the Punatsang-chu Valley in Punakha district. ▸▸ See page 137.

11 King Jigme Dorji Memorial Chorten in Thimphu is a fine example of a modern nine-storey stupa. ▸▸ See page 70.

12 Green wheat is one of the few crops to be cultivated in the Mo-chu river gorge. ▸▸ See page 140.

Land of mystery

Isolationist tendencies and a relatively undeveloped infrastructure have ensured that Bhutan remains the most mysterious country in South Asia, notwithstanding recent moves towards modernization. The first motor roads were constructed only in the 1960s, cable television was introduced in the late 1990s and a mobile phone network has only recently been established. Guesthouses and hotels offer simple accommodation, as the first international hoteliers are only now beginning to establish a presence in the country. Most foreign exchange is, in fact, generated by the export of hydroelectric power to India and, unlike Nepal, the county has little economic dependence on tourism. Affluent foreign visitors are therefore charged inordinately high daily rates for the privilege of internal travel and backpackers or independent travellers without guides and drivers are unable to enter the country. Such policies ensure that the number of visitors is self-limiting and that the negative impact of mass tourism can be avoided.

The beauty of Bhutan

This is without doubt a country of unmistakable natural beauty, where ecological issues are at the forefront of everyday concerns and where pristine forests extend from the Himalayan snow massifs of the north through the precipitous mid-mountain belt to the plantations and nature reserves of the southern plains. The dramatic changes in terrain and vertical climatic zones sustain a rich diversity of flora and fauna, characteristic of both Central and South Asia.

Moreover, Bhutan may be regarded as a microcosm of Tibetan culture, preserving intact traditions, lifestyles, art and architecture that have been subjected to periods of revolutionary change and devastation in Tibet itself

A yak caravan crosses the Loju La Pass (4,940 m) on the descent to Sephu in central Bhutan.

over the previous 50 years. Equally, it is important to recognize that Bhutan has evolved its own distinctive national identity over the last 350 years, while resolutely maintaining its independence from both Tibet and India.

North, south, east and west

The north and the more remote central and southerly parts of Bhutan are even now only accessible by trekking, which offers not only spectacular scenery but also a chance to see the village people maintaining their ancient skills and crafts. Several of the fast-flowing rivers are suitable for whitewater rafting. The bleak pastures of the high Himalayan ranges are grazed by nomads (*drokpa*), the decorative farm houses of the central valleys are inhabited by Drukpa, Monpa and Sharchokpa communities; and the jungle terrain of the south bordering India has been largely settled by the Lhotsampa of Nepalese origin. Relentless winding roads, exposed to landslides in the rainy season and snow drifts in winter, tenuously link the west of the country with the centre and the east, as well as with the trading towns of the south, such as Phuntsoling, where decorative Bhutan Gates demarcate the Indian border crossings.

Facing the future

Bhutan can claim much success in carrying its traditional culture into the modern world, however, with multinational companies and the forces of globalisation now on the verge of penetrating this Himalayan enclave, there are several major challenges that lie ahead.

Communications are slowly improving, but with such a fragile road and air network, affordable public helicopter services linking remote central and eastern areas of the country are surely a priority.

The assimilation of South Asian culture presents other dilemmas. The demographic and nationality issues associated with Nepalese migration still have to be resolved, as does Assamese insurgency in the south. The recent introduction of cable television, dominated by Bollywood movies, combined with a lack of investment in indigenous programming, has already started to undermine traditional ways of life.

Bhutan's protracted isolation from its Trans Himalayan roots has raised other contentious issues: Buddhist rituals and meditative practices have certainly been well maintained in some monasteries and hermitages, but most of the population are now unable to read their own classical literature, since schools emphasise only colloquial Dzongkha at the expense of the classical written language (cho-ke).

Pending resolution of the Sino-Indian border disputes, the northern trade routes with Tibet, which have been closed for half a century, are likely to reopen in the near future. In the interests of both economic prosperity and cultural heritage landlocked Bhutan will then have to forge a new relationship with its culturally dominant neighbour.

Contents

Footprint features

Planning your trip

Navigating Bhutan using this guide

The detailed description of Bhutan in this book is divided into four parts: Thimphu City (the capital), Western Bhutan, Central Bhutan and Eastern Bhutan. It would also have been possible to present the country according to its well-defined climatic zones (alpine, temperate and sub-tropical), which correspond respectively to the northern Himalayas, the central mountains and the southern borderlands, but for the purposes of this guide, the country has been divided into western, central and eastern regions, which continue to have profound cultural, linguistic, logistical and geographical significance for the peoples of Bhutan.

The country is divided into 20 administrative districts (*dzongkhag*). Of these Thimphu, Paro, Ha, Samtse, Chukha, Punakha, Gasa, Wangdu, Tsirang and Tarkar (Dagana) all fall within Western Bhutan. Trongsar (Tongsa), Zhemgang, Sarpang and Bumthang comprise Central Bhutan. The remainder – Mongar, Lhuntse, Tashigang, Tashi Yangtse, Pema Gatsel and Samdrub Jongkhar – are in Eastern Bhutan. Each of these districts is described in turn, highlighting places of historical and touristic importance in close proximity to the main roads, as well as the lesser jeep tracks, trekking routes and more remote sites. Practical information on services, including hotels, restaurants, transport and road conditions, has been updated in this edition, but the main emphasis continues to be placed on Bhutan's cultural heritage – the monasteries, local history, festivals and the spectacular terrain – given that many key destinations offer very little choice of accommodation or meals.

The maps at the end of the book clearly show the county-level subdivisions (*dzongkhag* and *gewok*), along with the main towns and villages, the major rivers and roads, and the important 4,000-m contour, which broadly divides sedentary from nomadic communities.

NB While Bhutanese Dzongkha is nowadays officially regarded as a language distinct from Tibetan for sound political, social and cultural reasons, its affinity with the dialects of Tibetan spoken in the neighbouring Khangmar and Dromo counties of Tibet cannot be ignored. Speakers of standard modern Tibetan can understand some 65-70% of modern Dzongkha, while natives of Khangmar and Dromo have a much fuller understanding. Tibetan and Dzongkha share the same classical language and literature (known as Choke in Bhutan) and a script that is largely identical (but for a few symbols that have been recently introduced to represent distinctive sounds and elisions in Dzongkha). The English transliteration used in this guide and in the companion Tibet guide corresponds closely to the standard orthography. Whenever local pronunciation diverges radically, these variants are included in parenthesis. The variant romanised spellings that are in use for some Bhutanese names are given at the end of this book (see page 280).

Organized travel

If you are visiting Bhutan as a tourist, your travel arrangements will be made by an international or Bhutanese tour operator. Expatriates working in Bhutan will have their arrangements made by an appropriate government department, acting as a host organisation. There is almost no scope for independent travel in Bhutan, except in cases where individuals have received a personal invitation from well-connected friends or relatives. Volunteer project workers based in Bhutan are permitted to extend two such invitations per year. Tour operators can make arrangements for large groups, small parties or even individuals, travelling with their own guide and driver.

▸▸ *For visa entry and permit procedures see page 25.*

⁑ Words and phrases

Pronunciation and spelling

The spelling adopted for the representation of Bhutanese Dzongkha, Tibetan and Sanskrit names in this guide is designed with the general reader in mind, rather than the specialist. Exact transliterations have therefore been avoided. Nonetheless, spellings have been chosen which are broadly consistent with the orthography rather than local pronunciation. For a comparison with the many variants in use for romanised Dzongkha, see page 329.

Bhutanese Dzongkha and Tibetan

A final e is never silent, but pronounced in the manner of the French é. Ph is never pronounced like an English f, but like a p with strong aspiration. Among the important regional variants, in some parts of the country, ky or khy may be pronounced as ch, gy as j, b as w, dr as b and ny as hmy. Also suffixes may be elided and the basic vowel sounds may change, such that u becomes i, and so forth.

Sanskrit In the absence of diacritics to represent Sanskrit letters, the following simplified conventions have been used throughout: palatal c̄ is rendered as c (but to be pronounced as in Italian ch); palatal s is rendered sh, and retroflex s as a simple s. The names of all deities are given, wherever possible, in their Sanskrit rather than Tibetan or Dzongkha forms. For a correspondence between the Sanskrit and Tibetan names see page 312, and the iconographic guide, page 280.

Essentials Planning your trip

Sustainable tourism

Tourism in Bhutan has either a cultural or a trekking focus, although it is possible to arrange an itinerary that combines both aspects. All flights, transportation, meals, accommodation, camping support, guiding and specified admission fees will be provided by the tour operator as a package. There is nowadays no limitation on the number of visitors to Bhutan imposed by the government, but in practice the high rates charged for package services, in excess of US$200 per day, naturally have an impact upon the number of visitors. The policy of the government is to encourage sustainable and manageable tourism, compatible with the available facilities, that will not disrupt or intrude upon the traditional way of life. No doubt the number of visitors will continue to increase as international hotel chains like the Singapore-based **Aman Resorts** expand within the country.

Preparing your itinerary

Visa clearance for Bhutan is issued on the understanding that you will have pre-paid for a guaranteed itinerary provided by a bona fide tour operator. It is essential to prepare an itinerary before entering Bhutan, since there is hardly any flexibility to alter the programme once you are in the country, except in cases of unforeseen flight cancellations or landslides.

When preparing an itinerary, visitors to Bhutan should take into account the restrictions imposed on visits to many sacred temples, monasteries and *dzongs*. These restrictions were imposed in 1988 in order to minimise disruption to the spiritual life of the country and to protect sacred artefacts from desecration and theft. Bona fide Buddhists may still apply for permission to visit specific restricted sites through the Ministry of Culture if they supply their tour operator with a supporting letter from a recognised international Buddhist organisation. Tour operators can also provide tailor-made itineraries for Buddhist groups, photographers, cyclists, botanists, ornithologists, art historians, musicologists and ethnologists. Permits are required for trekking and visiting the national parks of Bhutan, but access to some southern areas, such as the Manas Wildlife Park, is not currently permitted, as the Bhutanese Army grapples with the problems of Assamese insurgency.

Where to go

Keeping all these restrictions in mind, it is perfectly possible to spend three or four days in the **Paro-Thimphu** area of Western Bhutan, or to extend this trip to one week by including **Ha** and **Punakha**. Two weeks in the country would enable you to visit the main sites of **Bumthang**, **Trongsar** and **Wangdu Phodrang** in Central Bhutan, while a three-week option would provide sufficient time for the long drives required to visit **Mongar**, **Lhuntse**, **Tashi Yangtse** or **Tashigang** in Eastern Bhutan. It is also worth remembering that standards of accommodation and meals are simpler and more spartan in Central and Eastern Bhutan, once the Black Mountains have been crossed. **Trekking** itineraries can also be of varying length. It is possible to add a short three-day trek to a Western Bhutan itinerary, a short Bumthang trek to the two-week option, or to undertake longer specialised treks in Gasa, Lunana and Lhuntse districts. Details on all these trekking routes will be found under the respective districts, and for practical information on trekking, see page 47.

The areas of greatest importance for Bhutanese culture are to be found in the mid-mountain belt. **Kyerchu Lhakhang** in Paro and **Jampa Lhakhang** in Bumthang are revered as seventh-century geomantic temples, reputedly dating from the reign of the Tibetan king Songtsen Gampo, whose empire included Bhutan. **Lhakhang Karpo** in Ha and **Taktsang hermitage** in Paro, along with the temples of **Kurje Lhakhang** and **Konchoksum Lhakhang** in Bumthang, are all associated with Guru Padmakara and the establishment of Tibetan Buddhism throughout the Yarlung empire during the eighth century. From **Gangteng Monastery** in the Black Mountains through to the central valleys of **Bumthang**, there are several important sites associated with the three great Nyingmapa masters, Longchen Rabjampa, Dorje Lingpa and Pema Lingpa (13-16th centuries), who sojourned in Bhutan. Among them, the temples of **Bolu**, **Tharpaling**, **Trakar**, **Tamzhing** and **Rimochen**, along with the monasteries of **Kungzang Drak** and **Thowadrak**, are particularly renowned.

Bhutan's most striking cultural resonance is probably found in the strategic fortifications (*dzong*) founded by the Drukpa Kagyu hierarchs from the mid-17th century onwards. Constructed in a distinctively Bhutanese style, these buildings combine administrative and religious functions, as did the Potala Palace in Lhasa. The best known are **Tashi Chodzong** in Thimphu, **Rinpung Dzong** and **Drugyel Dzong** in Paro, and **Dechen Phodrang Dzong** in Punakha, but those of Wangdu Phodrang, Trongsar, Jakar, Lhuntse and Tashigang are also architecturally impressive and culturally significant.

When to go

While selecting a suitable itinerary for your visit to Bhutan, there are two other factors that will influence your decision: the weather conditions and the festival season. **Autumn** (late September-November) is the best season for mountain panoramas, photography and trekking. **Spring** (March-May) is somewhat dustier and more overcast, but ideal for botanists and bird-watchers. The extraordinary diversity of Bhutanese plants and flowers is best appreciated at this time. **Winter** (December-February) is fine for visits to the Paro-Thimphu area of Western Bhutan, although passes leading to Central and Eastern Bhutan can be closed by snow. The days can be warm and sunny, and the light is superb, but the nights are very cold, so warm clothing will be essential for any winter visitors. **Summer** (June-early September) is the rainy season. Although it can rain in Bhutan at any time of the year and you should always carry an umbrella, the monsoon deluge in summertime obscures mountains and valleys, flooding the narrow roads, and sometimes causing landslides. The areas of Eastern Bhutan bordering Assam have some of the highest levels of rainfall in the world, and the countryside is infested with leeches! Nonetheless, the cultivated fields and forests are more verdant at this time than in any other season.

The colourful pageantry and religious dances of the **tsechu** and **drubchen** festivals held throughout Bhutan in the district towns have in recent years attracted the interest of foreign visitors in ever-increasing numbers. *Tsechu* dances commemorate the enlightened activities of Guru Padmakara (Pema Jungne), an Indian master of the eighth century who is revered as the 'second Buddha' (Sangye Nyipa) and the 'precious teacher' (Guru Rinpoche), throughout the Tibetan Buddhist world. In each lunar month of the year, the '10th day' (*tse-chu*) is associated with a different facet of Guru Padmakara's extraordinary career in ancient India, Nepal, Tibet and Bhutan, and special feast-offering ceremonies will be held, particularly in monasteries of the Nyingma tradition, and those affiliated to it which have a special reverence for Padmakara's lineage. At some monasteries, such as Katok in East Tibet, sacred dances depicting his life will be held on or around the 10th day of the sixth lunar month, commemorating his birth in the kingdom of Oddiyana. In Bhutan the sacred festivals of the 10th day were choreographed by the great treasure-finder Pema Lingpa, among others, and they are held at different times in different locations throughout the months of the lunar calendar, particularly in the spring and autumn months, even as late as December.

Drubchen are elaborate ritual ceremonies in which the participants mentally visualise their identity with a particular assembly of meditational deities, and enact the liturgies and sacred dances symbolising the activity of these deities. For a detailed description of the sacred dances in Bhutan, see page 273. It is possible to plan your itinerary to coincide with a stay in any of the district towns or their outlying monasteries during a local *tsechu* festival or *drubchen*. For the schedule of these festivals in 2005, see page 42. Druk Air flights are often overbooked during the high season (autumn) and especially at times coinciding with the *tsechu* festivals. Hotels may also be overbooked during these periods.

> ✽ *Since flights in and out of Paro Airport operate only under visual flight rules, obscure or dangerous weather conditions can cause serious flight delays during the rainy season in particular.*

Recommended cultural tours and itineraries

The following tours encompass all parts of the country and they will assist you when preparing an itinerary; but they are by no means exclusive. A number of them overlap and it is obviously possible to combine parts of one with another.

Cultural tour of Western Bhutan

This short itinerary is ideally suited for those who dislike long journeys on winding mountain roads, in that the cultural centres of Paro, Ha, Thimphu and Punakha are all within easy reach, and the roads are in good condition. Starting from one of the gateway cities (Kathmandu, Bangkok, Delhi, Kolkata or Dhaka), fly to **Paro Airport** and find overnight accommodation here. Spend day two exploring **Paro** itself and remain here for a further night. On day three, travel by four-wheel drive or minibus to **Ha** and return to Paro for the night. Leave for **Thimphu** on day four and remain here overnight before progressing to **Chime Lhakhang** on day five. At the end of day five, overnight accommodation should be found at Punakha from where the following three days can be spent returning through Thimphu on day six and Paro on day seven before exiting Bhutan from Paro on day eight. Exit by road through Phuntsoling is also possible.

Cultural tour of Western and Central Bhutan

This is a slightly longer itinerary, combining the highlights of Western Bhutan with the culturally diverse Bumthang valleys of Central Bhutan. Starting from one of the gateway cities (Kathmandu, Bangkok, Delhi, Kolkata or Dhaka), fly to **Paro** and spend the following two nights here. On day three travel by four-wheel drive or minibus to **Thimphu** and remain here for a couple of days to explore. **Chime Lhakhang** should be the next destination on day five but overnight accommodation should be found in **Punakha**. On day six, travel to **Wangdu Phodrang** and spend the night in **Gangteng** before moving on to **Trongsar** on day seven. Find accommodation in **Jakar** for the next three nights in order to visit firstly the **Chukhor Valley** on day eight, the **Tang Valley** on day nine and the **Chume Valley** on day 10. From the Chume Valley return to Trongsar for the night as a means of visiting **Zhemgang Dzong** on day 11. Once again it is necessary to return to Trongsar for the night before spending day 12 in **Wangdu Phodrang**. From here move to **Phuntsoling** for the night and cross the border to **India** from here on day 13. Exit by air through Paro is also possible.

Grand cultural tour of Bhutan

This is a three-week option, including the eastern districts of Bhutan, as well as the main sites of western and central Bhutan. Starting from one of the gateway cities (Kathmandu, Bangkok, Delhi, Kolkata or Dhaka), fly to **Paro Airport** where accommodation should be found. Spend the following day and night here before using a four-wheel drive or minibus to get to **Thimphu** on day three. Explore Thimphu on days three and four and then progress to **Chime Lhakhang** on day five. Accommodation should be found in **Punakha** as this gives relatively easy access to **Wangdu Phodrang** on day six. Having spent the night in **Gangteng**, the next destination is **Trongsar** on day seven followed by an overnight stay in **Jakar**, from where it is possible to visit the **Chukhor Valley** on day eight and return to Jakar the same evening. On day nine visit **Ura** and **Dramitse** en route to an overnight stop in **Mongar**. Move to **Lhuntse** the following day before returning to Mongar on day 11. Day 12 should be spent in **Tashigang** while day 13 should be used to explore **Tashi Yangtse**, although accommodation should be found in Tashigang. Return to Mongar on day 14 and from here go to the **Tang Valley** on day 15 before staying the night in Jakar. Remain here for a further day before passing through the **Chume Valley** on day 17 and seeking accommodation in Trongsar. From Trongsar visit **Zhemgang Dzong** on day 18 and Wangdu Podrang on day 19 before spending the night in Thimphu. It is now possible to move to **Phuntsoling** on day 20 from where you can cross the border into **India** the following day. Exit by air through Paro is also possible.

International tour operators

A number of overseas operators run tours in Bhutan. Tours vary in price, depending upon the number of days, the number of persons in a group, the remoteness and distance covered by the itinerary, and the package arrangement. Prices are slightly higher than comparable tours of Tibet, sometimes exceeding US$200 per day. Bhutan travel arrangements may be made by any of the following international operators, some of which have a worldwide client base.

Trans Himalaya

Trans Himalaya, under the direction of Dr Gyurme Dorje, a Tibetologist whose published works include this Footprint Tibet Handbook, organise travel throughout the Tibetan plateau, as well as in Mongolia, China and the Himalayas (Bhutan, Sikkim, Nepal, and Ladakh).

Whether you are a first-time visitor to Central Tibet looking for a simple itinerary, or an experienced Tibet traveller planning an overland journey, trek or expedition in Ngari, Kham or Amdo, Trans Himalaya are the specialists, with a strong client base in the Americas, Europe, SE Asia, Australia and South Africa.

Accompanied by knowledgeable guides, you will be exposed to the diverse cultural heritage of Tibet, its distinctive Buddhist and Bon monasteries, and the life-styles of its people. Trans Himalaya's eco-tourism programme also enables you to participate directly in rural development or art restoration, working as a guest alongside Tibetan monks, villagers or nomads.

Circumambulate sacred Mts Kailash, Kawa Karpo & Amnye Machen!
Ride horseback through the rolling grasslands of Amdo!
Witness the horse festivals and masked dances of Kham!
Explore the wilderness and wildlife of the Jangtang & Kunluns!
Appreciate the rich diversity of Tibetan art & architecture!

For details and booking contact:

Trans Himalaya
4 Foxcote Gardens, Frome, Somerset, BA11 2DS, UK
Tel: +44-1373-455518 Fax: +44-1373-455594
Email: info@trans-himalya.com
Website: www.trans-himalya.com

Trans Himalaya Chengdu Office:
18 North Shuangqing Lane, Bldg 2, Suite 2A,
Chengdu, Sichuan, 610072, China
Tel/Fax: 0086-13540484871

UK

Abercrombie and Kent, Sloane Square House, Holbein Place, London SW1W 8NS, T0207730-9600, www.abercrombiekent.co.uk
KE Adventure Travel, 32 Lake Rd, Keswick, Cumbria, CA12 5DQ, T017687-73966, F017687-74693, www.keadventure.com, specialise in trekking.
Himalayan Kingdoms, Old Crown House, 18 Market St, Wotton-under-Edge, Gloucester, GL12 7AE, T01453-844400, F01453-844422, www.himalayankingdoms.com
Limosa Holidays, Suffield House, Northrepps, Norfolk, NR27 0LZ, T01263-578143, F01263-579251, limosaholidays@compuserve.com, specialise in escorted ornithological tours.
Steppes East, 51 Castle Street, Cirencester, Gloucestershire, GL7 1QD, T01285-651010, F01285-5885888, www.steppeseast.co.uk, specialise in small group travel throughout the Himalayas.
Trans Himalaya, 4 Foxcote Gardens, Frome, Somerset, BA11 2DS, T01373-455518, F01373-455594, www.trans-himalaya.com, specialise in cultural tours and Buddhist pilgrimages.

North America

Bhutan Travel, 120E, 56th St, Suite 1430, New York, NY 10022, T212-8386382, F212-868-1601, www.bhutantravel.com
Excellent Adventures, 5013 Needmore Road, Bryson City, NC 28713, T828-488-6785, www.excellent-adventures.net, specialise in river-rafting and kayaking.

Geographic Expeditions, 2627 Lombard St, San Francisco, CA 94123, T415-9220448, F415-3465535, www.geoex.com.
Himalayan Road Runners, PO Box 1402, Waitsfield, Vermont 05673, T908-236-6870, F908-236-8972, www.ridehigh.com. Offer motorcycle trips through Bhutan.
Mountain Travel, 6420 Fairmount Ave, El Cerrito, CA 94530, T415-5278100, www.mtsobek.com

Australia

Peregrine Adventures, 258 Lonsdale St, Melbourne, Victoria 3000, T03-9663-8611, F03-9663-8618, www.peregrine.net.au

Continental Europe

Terres d'Adventure, 6 rue Saint Victor, 75005 Paris, France, T1-53-73 77 73, F33-140-46 95 22, www.terdav.com.
Hauser Exkursionen, Marienstrasse-17, D-80331, Munchen, Germany, T089-235-0060, F089-291-3714, www.hauser-exkursionen.de
Horizons Nouveaux, Centre de l'Etoile, Case postale 196, 1936 Verbier, Switzerland, T027-771-7171, F027-771-7175, www.horizonsnouveaux.com

Nepal

President Travels & Tours, Durbar Marg, Kathmandu, T977-1226744.
Shambhala Travels and Tours, Durbar Marg, Kathmandu, T977-1225166, F977-1227229.

India

Malbros Travels, 415 Antriksh Bhawan, 22 Kastruba Gandhi Marg, New Delhi, T91-113722031, F91-113723292.
Stic Travel Pvt Ltd, 6 Maker Arcade (GF), Mumbai 400005, T9122-2181431.
Stic Travel Pvt Ltd, 142 Nungambakkam Sigh Rd, Chennai 600034, T91-44475332.

Bangladesh

Vantage Tours & Travels Ltd, L-270 Office Arcade, Sonargaon Hotel, Dhaka, T880-2326920.

Thailand

Oriole Travel & Tour Co Ltd, Skulthai Surawong Tower, 141 Surawong Rd, Bangrak, Bangkok 10500, T02-237-9201, F02-237-9200, oriole@samart.co.th

Bhutanese tour operators

Travel arrangements may also be made through an approved Bhutanese tour operator. A full listing of all 134 Bhutanese tour operators and travel agents may be found at the website of the Department of Tourism (www.tourism.gov.bt). A selection of the best of these now follows - almost all of them with offices in Thimphu. They include large operators such as **Etho Metho Tours** and the **Bhutan Tourism Corporation** (BTCL), as well as small-scale operators who provide a more personalised service, such as **Bhutan Travel Service, Chhundu Travels,** and **Yu Druk Tours and Treks. Yangphel Adventure Travel** is an important trekking company.

About Bhutan Tours & Treks, dwpenjor@druknet.bt
Baeyul Excursion, PO Box 437,

T975-2-324355, F975-2-323728, baeyul@druknet.bt
Bhutan Dorji Holidays, PO Box 550,

Essentials Planning your trip

T975-2-322192, F975-2-325174, dorji@druknet.bt

Bhutan Expeditions, T975-2-326266, F975-2-326689, tsewangnidup@yahoo.com

Bhutan Heritage Travels, PO Box 293, T975-2-324407, F975-2-326666, hishey@druknet.bt

Bhutan Himalaya Tours & Treks, PO Box 236, T975-2-323793, F975-2-323145, tshomo@druknet.bt

Bhutan Holidays, PO Pox 522, T975-2-326899, F975-2-323248, info@drukholidays.com

Bhutan Kaze Tours & Treks, PO Box 715, T975-2-326623, F975-2-326624, wings@druknet.bt

Bhutan Lhayul Tours & Travels, PO Box 483, T975-2-325073, F975-2-325035, lhayul@druknet.bt

Bhutan Mandala Tours & Treks, PO Box 379, T975-2-323676, F975-2-323675, mandala@druknet.bt

Bhutan Mystical Tours & Adventures, bmta@druknet.bt

Bhutan Nature & Culture Adventure, bnca@druknet.bt

Bhutan Nature Expeditions, bne@druknet.bt

Bhutan Scenic Tours, chodex@druknet.bt

Bhutan Tours & Travels, T975-2-325769, F975-2-325771, bttpu@druknet.bt

Bhutan Travel Bureau, PO Box 959, T975-2-321749, F975-2-325100, btb@druknet.bt

Bhutan Travellers, wladventures@druknet.bt

Bhutan Travel Services, PO Box 919, T975-2-325785, F975-2-325786, www.bhutantravel.com.bt

Bhutan Travel & Tourism, T975-2-325825, F975-2-322036, btt@druknet.bt

Bhutan Vacation Inc., PO Box 334, T975-2-323990, F975-2-326440, btvac@druknet.bt

Bhutan Wonderful Tour & Travels, wonderfulbhutan@druknet.bt

Bhutan Yak Adventure Travel, yaktravel@druknet.bt

Bhutan Yodsel Tours & Treks, PO Box 574, T975-2-323912, F975-2-323589, dawa@druknet.bt

Bonsem Tours & Travels, T975-2-324728, F975-2-323731, bonsem@druknet.bt

BTCL, PO Box 159, T975-2-322647, F975-2-323392, btcl@druknet.bt

Bumree Tours & Treks, bumree@druknet.bt

Changshe Norbu Tours & Treks, changshe@druknet.bt

Chhundu Travels & Tours, PO Box 149, T975-2-322592, F975-2-322645, chhundu@druknet.bt

Dechen Cultural Tours & Trekking Co., PO Box 818, T975-2-321358, F975-2-324408, dechen@druknet.bt

Discovery Bhutan, PO Box 825, T975-2-322457, F975-2-322530, discovery@druknet.bt

Dragon Trekkers & Tours, PO Box 452, T975-2-323599, F975-2-323314, dragon@druknet.bt

Druk Himalayan Expeditions, drukhimla@druknet.bt

Eagle Tours & Treks, PO Box 949, T975-2-326763, eagle@druknet.bt

Etho Metho Tours & Treks, PO Box 360, T975-2-323162, F975-2-322884, ethometo@druknet.bt

Exotic Destination Tours & Treks, PO Box 682, T975-2-327406, F975-2-326171, exotic@druknet.bt

Gangri Tours & Treks, PO Box 607, T975-2-323556, F975-2-323322, Gangri@druknet.bt **Gems Tours & Travels**, gem@druknet.bt

Geo-Cultural Tours & Treks, chhophelt@yahoo.com

Himalaya Adventures, Bhutan, PO Box 258, T975-2-351051, F975-2-351051, himalaya@druknet.bt

Himalayan Kingdom Tours, T975-2-326102, F975-2-324449, hktours@druknet.bt

Insiders Bhutan Tours & Travels, insider@insidersbhutan.com

International Treks & Tours, PO Box 525, T975-2-326591, F975-2-324963, intrek@druknet.bt

Jamphel Tours & Treks, PO Box 289, T975-2-322204, F975-2-324152, jamphel@druknet.bt

Jeroma Tours & Travels, jeroma@druknet.bt

Karmic Tours and Treks, kgayley@karmictours.com

Lhomen Tours & Treks, PO Box 341, T975-2-324148, F975-2-323243, lhomen@druknet.bt

Lingkor Tours & Treks, PO Box 202, T975-2-323417, F975-2-323402, lingkor@druknet.bt

Lotus Adventures, PO Box 706, T975-2-322191, F975-2-325678, info@bhutanlotus.com

Masagang Tours & Travels, T975-2-323206, F975-2-323718, masagang@druknet.bt

Namsay Tours & Adventures, PO Box 549, T975-2-325616, F975-2-324297, namsay@druknet.bt

Nature Tourism, T975-2-321273, nattouri@druknet.bt

Nima Tours & Treks, nimacomp@druknet.bt

Nirvana Expeditions, info@nirvanaexpeditions.com

Osang Tours & Treks, PO Box 304, T975-2-322733, F975-2-323541, ott@druknet.bt

Passage to Himalayas, T975-2-321726, F975-2-321727, lekid@druknet.bt

Pristine Druk-Yul Tours & Treks, T975-2-325455, F975-2-325455, pristine@druknet.bt

Rabsel Tours & Treks, PO Box 488, T975-2-324165, F975-2-324918, rabsel@druknet.bt

Rainbow Tours & Treks, PO Box 641, T975-2-323270, F975-2-322960, rainbow@druknet.bt

Ratna Tours & Treks, PO Box 420, T975-2-325006

Rinchen Tours & Treks, PO Box 550, T975-2-324552, F975-2-323767, dorji@druknet.bt

Sakten Tours & Treks, PO Box 532, T975-2-325567, F975-2-325574, sakten@druknet.bt **Sengey Karm Tours & Treks**, travelsktt@druknet.bt

Shangrila Bhutan Tours & Treks, PO Box 541, T975-2-321189, F975-2-324410, shangrila@druknet.bt

Silver Dragon Tours and Treks, silverdragon@druknet.bt

Sky Travels, T975-2-326994, F975-2-325605, sky@druknet.bt

Snow Leopard Trekking Co., PO Box 954, T975-2-321822, F975-2-325684, snowlprd@druknet.bt

Snow White Treks and Tours, snowwhite@druknet.bt

Sophun Tours & Treks, T975-2-324376, F975-2-321319, sophun@druknet.bt

Takin Tours, PO Box 454, T975-2-223129, F975-2-223130

Taktsang Tours & Travels, T975-2-322102, F975-2-323284, taktsang@druknet.bt

Tara Tours & Treks, T975-2-329149, F975-2-326149, tt_tour@druknet.bt

Tashi Tours & Travels, PO Box 423, T975-2-323027, F975-2-323666, tasitour@druknet.bt

Thimphu Tours & Treks, PO Box 465, T975-2-325469, F975-2-321346, ttt@druknet.bt

Thoesam Tours & Treks, PO Box 629, T975-2-324857, F975-2-323593, thoesam@druknet.bt

Thunder Dragon Treks, PO Box 303, T975-2-323699, thunder@druknet.bt

Wangchuk Tours & Treks, PO Box 507, T975-2-326233, F975-2-326232, mailto:wchuktt@druknet.bt

White Lake Adventures, wladventures@druknet.bt

White Lotus Tours & Treks, T975-2-324499, F975-2-326070, khorlo@druknet.bt

White Tara Tours & Travel, T975-2-322446, F975-2-324152, wtara@druknet.bt

Wind Horse Tours, Treks & Expeditions, PO Box 1021, T975-2-326026, F975-2-326025, windhor@druknet.bt

Yangphel Adventure Travel, PO Box 236, T975-2-323293, F975-2-322897, kamlots@yangphel.com.bt

Yarkay Tours & Treks, PO Box 336, T975-2-322628, F975-2-323894, Yarkay@druknet.bt

Yeti Tours & Treks, PO Box 456, T975-2-323941, F975-2-323508, yeti@druknet.bt

Yu Druk Tours & Treks, PO Box 140, T975-2-323461, F975-2-322116, yudruk@druknet.bt

Booking procedures and costs

Having worked out an itinerary, it will be simplest for most overseas visitors to Bhutan to make their arrangements through an international tour operator, who (if they have specialist knowledge) can make helpful suggestions regarding the proposed route. Otherwise, if you enter into a contract directly with a local operator, you should know that government regulations ensure that certain services and standards are provided in recognition of the high daily rates for travel in Bhutan. The local operator will require that the full payment for a pre-arranged itinerary should be made in advance of the trip to the Bhutanese Department of Tourism. Payments should be wired in US$ currency to the **Bhutan National Bank** ⓘ *The address is: Citibank, 111 Wall St, 19/F, New York, NY10043, credited to the Bhutan National Bank, ABA no 0210-0008-9, account number 36023474, Swift Code: Citius 33, Chips Routing No. 008,* specifying the local operator of your choice as the beneficiary.

It is important to fax a copy of the bank transfer form to the local operator as soon as possible in order to facilitate your visa clearance.

Tariffs As of January 2004, the daily tariffs charged by local operators for cultural tour and trekking packages to Bhutan (minimum group size four) are as follows: High Season (Feb-May, Oct-Nov): US$200, Peak Festivals (early April and late September): US$250, Low Season (Dec-Jan, June-August): US$165. Daily surcharge for two-person groups: US$30, Daily surcharge for one person: US$40.

Discounts The following discounts are also available: 100% for one member of a group exceeding 15, 50% for all children aged 5-12 (under-fives go free), 50% for one member of a large group (11-15 in size), 25% for bona fide students booking through a local operator, 25% for accredited diplomats, and an incremental 10-20% for long treks (excluding the first 10 days). Unspecified discounts may also be available for international tour operators or travel agents on FAM trips.

Cancellation charges Local tour operators are obliged to charge cancellation fees if you cancel a prepaid tour or trek before your departure. The following rates apply: no charge (above 30 days prior notice), 10% (within 21 days), 15% (within 14 days), 30% (within seven days), 50% (less than seven days). Refunds are generally paid by bank transfer.

Exemptions Expatriates working in Bhutan, whether employed by the Bhutanese Government, the United Nations, the European Union or various NGOs, are exempted from payment of the visa fee and the high daily tariffs (as is their quota of invited guests). Indian visitors to Bhutan require no visa at all, and can travel independently in the country. All those who have such exemptions can pay local rates for accommodation, food and transportation. However, they all require permits for internal travel on the lateral highway beyond the Paro and Thimphu valleys, and are strongly advised to make arrangements through a local Bhutanese tour operator.

Finding out more

Department of Tourism ⓘ *PO Box 126, Thimphu, T975-223251, F975-223695, www.tourism.gov.bt* acts as a regulator, a conduit for payments made to local operators, and an information service. Some 40% of all revenues received by local operators are taken by the Department of Tourism. Since the privatisation of the Bhutan Tourism Corporation in 1991, all other travel companies have functioned as private enterprises. The government of Bhutan has no tourism office overseas, but information on travel to Bhutan can be obtained directly from the Department of Tourism.

Friendship associations In the United Kingdom, information is available from **The Bhutan Society**, Unit 23, 78 Marylebone High Street, London W1U 5AP, T/F020-75802648, www.bhutansociety.org. It holds regular Bhutan-related events and publishes a quarterly newsletter. Their website has a number of useful links. There is a virtual exhibition of Bhutanese culture at www.bhutan.at, based on a 1997-8 exhibition – Bhutan: Fortress of the Gods – which was held in Vienna.

Embassies abroad

General information (but not visas) can also be obtained from the following Bhutan embassies and missions overseas:

Bangladesh: Royal Bhutanese Embassy, F5

(SE), Gulshan Ave, Dhaka, 1212, T02-882-6863, F02-882-3939.

India: Royal Bhutanese Embassy, Chandragupta Marg, Chanakyapuri, New Delhi, 11021, T011-6889807, F011-6876710, New Delhi 11021; Royal Bhutanese Consulate: 48 Tivoli Court, 1A Ballygunge Circular Rd, Kolkota.

Kuwait: PO Box 1510, Safat 13016, T533-1506, F533-8959.

Switzerland: Permanent Bhutanese Mission

to the United Nations, Palais des Nations, 17-19 Chemin Du Champ D'Anier, Ch-12209 Geneva, T022-7990890, F022-7990899.

Thailand: Royal Bhutanese Embassy, 375/1 Soi Ratchadanivej, Pracha-Uthit Road, Samsen Nok, Huay Kwang, Bangkok, T02-274-4740, F02-274-4743.

USA: Permanent Bhutanese Mission to the United Nations, 2 UN Plaza, 27th floor, New York, NY 10017, T212-826-1919, F212-826-2998.

Useful websites

Wide-ranging information on Bhutanese cultural organisations throughout the world may be found at **www.bhutan.org**. The national service provider, which offers chat-room and pen-pal facilities, and has some colourful downloads, is **www.druknet.bt**. Several Bhutanese government departments also have their own information sites, including the national newspaper *Kuensal* at **www.kuenselonline.com**, the national air carrier at **www.drukair.com.bt**, the Bhutan Planning Commission at **www.pcs.gov.bt**, and the Department of Information Technology at **www.dit.gov.bt**. An online version of the *Journal of Bhutan Studies* is available at **www.bhutanstudies.com**, and the National Library of Bhutan offers a concise presentation of Bhutanese history and government at **lcweb2.loc.gov/frd/cs /bttoc.html**. A useful non-governmental source is **www.bhutannewsonline**. For an interesting travelogue, see **www.bluepeak.net/bhutan**.

The following internet lists provide general information and discussion forums on Buddhism from either scholastic or practical perspectives: **www.budhscol.com, www.BuddhaL.com, www.dharmanet.org, and www.edharma.com**.

In addition, there are various websites representing specific Buddhist organizations and schools or monasteries of Tibetan Buddhism. Those relevant to Bhutan include: Nyingmapa sites such as **www.dudjomba.org, www.shechen.12pt .com** and **www.nyingma.org**. Kagyupa sites include: **www.karmakagyu.org** and **www.drukpa-kargyud.org**. ▶▶ *Information on NGOs which are active inside Bhutan may be found under Working and Studying in Bhutan, page 25.*

Language

Since the Drukpa of Bhutan share a common heritage of culture, language and religion with Tibet, the written language, here known as 'cho-ke', employs the classical Tibetan script. The colloquial form that is spoken in Western Bhutan nowadays has assumed the status of Bhutan's national language, and is known as Dzongkha. The teaching of the national language is compulsory at all levels of education, although English is the primary medium of instruction. ▶▶ *For further details on the languages of Bhutan, see under background, page 259 and our Dzongkha phrasebook, page 329.*

Specialist travel

Disabled travellers

Apart from the airport and the major hospitals where wheelchairs can be provided, there are no hotels in Bhutan with proper access facilities for disabled travellers. Our advice would be to carry portable equipment (such as wheelchairs) from home, and ensure that a travelling companion is always at hand to assist when climbing steps and staircases. There are no tour operators offering guided tours in Bhutan specifically for disabled people, but several international operators and their local agents will ensure that additional support is provided for clients who are disabled.

Gay and lesbian travellers

In Bhutan public expressions of affection are frowned upon, whether heterosexual or homosexual in nature. The language is full of sexual innuendo and much teasing takes place, but overt displays of bodily contact will not be appreciated, regardless of what happens behind closed doors. Gay or lesbian travellers who make their travel arrangements through international tour operators and local agents should expect to be treated like other clients.

Student travellers

Organisations like STA in the UK provide cheap flights to India and Thailand, and an international student card will give the holder access to slightly cheaper domestic flights, trains and buses within these countries, but you should not expect such concessions in Bhutan, where individual travel is virtually non-existent. Nonetheless, bona fide students who make travel plans through a local Bhutanese tour operator can obtain a 25% discount on ground arrangements. Expatriates working and studying in Bhutan or visiting Bhutanese friends may be able to use public transport on occasions, having obtained the necessary internal travel permits from the police.

Travelling with children

The Bhutanese are very fond of children, and travellers who take their children to Bhutan can expect to make new friends more easily. Discounts are generally available on intercontinental flights to India, Nepal and Thailand, and the national carrier Druk Air charges 10% for children under two and 67% for children aged 2-12. Ground arrangements and services provided in Bhutan can be discounted for children aged 5-12 years of age by as much as 50%. Younger children go free. Most children travel well at high altitude and they can be more resilient than their parents. It is always wise to carry a suitable supply of children's medications, including calpol, liquid paracetamol, rehydration powders and remedies for gastritis. If your child has to consult a doctor outside the gateway cities, the best medical facilities can be found in Thimphu. ▶▶ *Please also refer to the section on Health, page 52.*

Women travellers

Traditional Bhutanese society has many matriarchal elements, including rights of property inheritance that are passed on from grandmother to mother to daughter and grand-daughter. For information on health, educational and training projects geared towards Bhutanese women, contact the **National Women's Association of Bhutan** (T975-2-322910). Common-law marriage and divorce are relatively commonplace, and consequently women display a high degree of independence. Bhutan must be regarded as one of the safest destinations in Asia for foreign women travellers. Dress sensibly, wearing long skirts, trousers or the local *kira*, when travelling in the countryside. Shorter knee-length skirts may be worn in larger towns like Thimphu and Paro, during the summer months. Intimate friendships between younger Bhutanese men and foreign women are not unusual, and in certain circumstances it may be important to send the right signals in order to avoid any misunderstanding. However, there are very few reports of foreign women being sexually harassed. Local women are frequently teased and taunted in Bhutanese society and sexual repartee and innuendo are commonplace. However, the unwelcome attention paid to western female travellers in the subcontinent has largely bypassed Bhutan, where the sparsely populated terrain provides a greater sense of personal space and dignity.

Working and studying in Bhutan

Most foreigners working in Bhutan are employed either in the health or language teaching sectors, in some cases by government departments, United Nations organisations or academic institutions, and in others by NGOs that are active within Bhutan. Please note that Christian missionary activity is proscribed in Bhutan, where the government is naturally concerned to protect the country's Buddhist values. This means that several foreign charities, including a number of well-known US organisations, are unable to participate. However, there are limited opportunities for foreign experts to collaborate on Bhutanese cultural projects. Visas are arranged by the host organisation, and a two-week induction or cultural-orientation course will be provided by the Royal Institute of Management. For Information on working opportunities and volunteer service within Bhutan, the following organisations could be consulted.

Voluntary organisations

Save the Children, 17 Grove Lane, London, SE5 8RD, T0845-606-4027, www.savethechildren.org.uk
The Consulting Committee for International Voluntary Service, Unesco House, 1 rue Miollis, 75732, Paris, France, T0033-1-45 68 49 36, www.unesco.org/ccivs
Danish Agency for Development Assistance, Udenrigsministeriet, Asiatisk Plads DK-1448, Copenhagen, Denmark, T0045-33920000, www.un.dk
Deutsche Gesellschaft fur Technische Zusammenarbeit (GTZ), Buro Berlin, Reichpietschufer 20, 10785 Berlin, Germany, T030-726140, www.gtz.de
Synovus Finan (SNV), Bezuidenhoutseweg 161, 2594 AG The Hague, Holland, T0031-703440244, www.snvworld.org
Helvetas, St Moritzstrasse 15, 8042, Zurich, Switzerland, T0041-1-3686500, www.helvetas.ch
Australian Volunteers International, PO Box 350, Fitzroy, Vic 3065, Australia, T03-9279-1788, F03-9419-4248, www.ozvol.org.au
Japan International Corporation Agency, 6-13F, Shinjuku Maynds Tower, 1-1, Yoyogi 2-Chone, Shibuya-Ku, Tokyo 151-8558, T03-53525311, www.jica.go.jp

Studying Dzongkha language in Bhutan is also a possibility at institutions such as the **Simtokha Institute** in Thimphu, and **Sherabtse College** at Kanglung. For details and application procedures, please contact Lopen Lungtaen Gyatso, The Principal, Institute for Language and Cultural Studies, PO Box 158, Simtokha, Thimphu, Bhutan, T0975-1-351066, F0975-1-351064, ilcs@druknet.bt.

Before you travel

Visas and immigration

Visas

A valid passport, preferably with at least six months' validity, is essential. Unusually, visas cannot be obtained at Bhutanese embassies overseas. Instead a visa clearance number has to be obtained by your host organisation through the Ministry of Foreign Affairs. If you are travelling to Bhutan as a tourist, your tour operator will make all the necessary arrangements. You will have to fax or email details including your name, permanent address, occupation, nationality, date and place of birth, along with your passport number, its date and place of issue, and the expiry date to your tour operator. If you are contracting with a local Bhutanese operator directly, you will also have to fax your bank's confirmation that you have prepaid for your trip (see page 26). The tour

> ‡ Visas cannot be obtained at Bhutanese embassies overseas.

operator will first obtain an approval for the visa application from the Department of Tourism and then apply directly to the Ministry of Foreign Affairs, which will send a visa clearance number to the tour operator and to Druk Air. Otherwise Druk Air will not be allowed to issue flight tickets. Your tour operator will notify you of the visa clearance number. This whole procedure is currently very efficient and takes about two weeks.

Armed with a visa clearance number and an approved itinerary, you should then contact your designated Druk Air office in the gateway city from which you will leave for Bhutan (eg Kathmandu, Delhi, Bangkok, Kolkata or Dhaka). Druk Air will be able to trace your visa clearance number on their computers, and issue the flight tickets accordingly. On arrival at Paro Airport you will have to pay US$20 for the visa and submit a passport-size photograph with your passport number written on the reverse side. A visa stamp will then be entered in your passport, for the exact validity of your prepaid trip. The same procedures apply for those entering Bhutan by road at Phuntsoling.

The regulations are simpler for Indian nationals who require no visa for Bhutan. If you are an Indian national, you will have to carry some ID (such as a passport or driving licence) and three to five passport-size photographs. You will then be issued with a two-week permit for Bhutan on your arrival at Paro Airport or Phuntsoling land border. The document may be extended in Thimphu.

You are advised to carry photocopies of your passport, visa clearance number and insurance policy when you travel to Bhutan. If your passport is lost or stolen, you will have to travel stateless to a third country (such as India) to have it replaced and the photocopies will facilitate your passage.

Visa extensions A maximum visa extension of six months can be issued in Thimphu (cost: Nu 510), but this service is only available for expatriates working in Bhutan or long-term foreign residents. Tourists whose stay is unavoidably extended due to flight delays or landslides on the border road will not have to apply for a visa extension.

Restricted Area permits

If you intend to travel outside the Paro and Thimphu valleys, you will require a Restricted Area permit listing all the places on your itinerary. Tour operators will automatically make this arrangement on behalf of their clients. The permit will be endorsed by the police as you travel around the country at various roadside immigration checkpoints. Currently there are 13 such checkpoints (daily opening hours 0500-2100): Rinchending (above Phuntsoling), Chudzom (between Phuntsoling and Paro), Chukha (between Phuntsoling and Thimphu), Lhongtso (between Thimphu and Dochu La), Wangdu Bridge (between Dochu La and Wangdu Podrang), Chanchi Bridge (between Wangdu and Tsirang), Dinghibi (near Tsirang), Tago Pela (between Tarkar and Kalikhola), Trongsar (between Trongsar and Zhemgang/Bumthang), Mongar (between Mongar and Lhuntse/Tashigang), Hongrom Chakzam (west of Tashigang), Wamrong (between Tashigang and Samdrub Jongkhar) and Dewathang Checkpoint (4 km north of Samdrub Jongkhar, near the Assamese border). A Restricted Area permit will have to be returned to the police in Thimphu at the end of your trip.

Special Access permits

Most of the sacred sites in Bhutan have been closed to tourism since 1988. In 2001 regulations were slightly relaxed, enabling escorted tourists to visit the courtyard and one specified temple within each *dzong* throughout the country. Access to these courtyards is easier during the *tsechu* festivals, when they are generally open to the public, and otherwise they will have to be visited during regular opening hours. In addition the following sites are accessible: Ta Dzong, Drugyel Dzong and Takstang viewpoint (in Paro); Tashi Chodzong, Memorial Chorten, Changlingmethang and Jigmeling temples (in Thimphu); Kamji, Chasilakha, Zangdokpelri and Kharbandi temples (in Phuntsoling); Dramphu and

It is important to give tour operators sufficient time to process Special Access applications.

Lamidara temples (in Tsirang); Punakha Dzong (in Punakha); Wangdu Choling Dzong (in Wangdu Podrang), Mebartsho gorge and Ura temple (in Bumthang); Mongar Dzong (in Mongar); Chorten Kora (in Tashi Yangtse); Kanglung Zangdokpelri temple (in Tashigang); and Zangdokpelri temple (in Samdrub Jongkhar).

Bona fide Buddhists may be granted special access to other specified temples or hermitages by applying in writing to the National Commission for Cultural Affairs. Tour operators are accustomed to handling such applications, which should ideally include a supporting letter from an international Buddhist organisation.

Driving permits

Expatriate workers wishing to drive in Bhutan will have to apply for a driving licence from the Road Safety and Transport Authority. International driving licences are not accepted, with the exception of Indian driving licences, which are valid under a reciprocal agreement. Two-week vehicle permits can be issued at the Phuntsoling land border if you are driving from India, but the paperwork and bureaucracy are formidable. All pre-arranged tours in Bhutan will have an assigned driver and guide, so in most cases such problems are unlikely to arise. If you have to drive you should take extra care on the narrow, winding mountain roads.

Customs

On arrival at Paro Airport or Phuntsoling land border you will be given a customs declaration form, on which you should list all valuable electrical equipment (computers, cameras etc). Eight mm cameras are allowed, but special permits and fees are required for professional filming equipment (including High Eight and 16 mm cameras). For the relevant regulations and restrictions, contact the **Department of Tourism**, www.tourism.gov.bt, well in advance. The declaration form will have to be surrendered when leaving Bhutan, and the items you listed at the time of entry will have to be shown, so you should keep it safe with your passport at all times. Duty-free allowance: 2 litres of spirits and 400 cigarettes.

You may not export antiquities, religious artefacts, plants or animal products. Items resembling antiques and new religious artefacts (including *tangkhas*) may be taken out but will have to be cleared prior to your departure by the **Division of Cultural Properties** (T02-322284, F02-323286). All sales receipts should be kept for inspection.

Vaccinations

The only vaccination certificate required for entry to Bhutan is for yellow fever in the case of visitors arriving from infected areas of the world, such as equatorial Africa and Latin America. However, immunisation against typhoid, polio, tetanus and hepatitis is strongly recommended (see under Health, page 52). It would be best to consult your doctor to arrange immunisations well in advance. Try ringing a specialist travel clinic if your own doctor is unfamiliar with health in Bhutan.

If you are trekking in remote nomadic areas of northern Bhutan you might consider immunisation against rabies. Malaria prophylaxis is certainly recommended for visitors to low-lying sub-tropical parts of southern or eastern Bhutan, but since the particular course of treatment for a specific part of the world can change from time to time, you should seek up-to-date advice from the **Malaria Reference Laboratory,** T020-7760-0350 (recorded message, premium rate) or the **Liverpool School of Tropical Medicine,** T0151-7089393. In the USA, try **Centers for Disease Control, Atlanta,** T404-3324555.

What to take

An experienced traveller carries as little luggage as possible. Remember that you are allowed no more than the normal weight (20 kg in economy class and 30 kg in business class) and that you may be liable to pay for excess baggage. You should also carry essentials, medication, reading material, cameras, flashlights and other necessities (eg toilet paper) at all times in your flight bag or, as many prefer, in a lightweight backpack. It is always best to keep luggage to a minimum, and if you are on an all-inclusive package tour to Bhutan, you will need to carry fewer items than you otherwise would. A sturdy rucksack or a hybrid backpack/suitcase, rather than a rigid suitcase, covers most eventualities and survives bus boot, roof rack and plane/ship hold with ease. Serious trekkers will need a framed backpack and zip-fastening duffel bag.▶▶ *A complete checklist of items required for long treks or overland journeys is given below under Trekking, page 47. See also Health, page 52.*

Clothing

Cottons and light woollens should be worn in summer (June-September), and heavy woollens and jackets the rest of the year. Since it may rain at any time of the year, take an umbrella (not only for the monsoons), and a pair of comfortable walking shoes (remember that footwear over nine and a half British size, or 42 European size, may be difficult to obtain). The air temperature in Bhutan can change very quickly with a passing cloud and the coming of the night. A flexible system of 'layered' clothing is recommended: thermal underwear, cotton shirts and cotton undershirts with short-sleeves, cotton trousers or skirts, a warm pullover and windproof jacket, and lightweight or Goretex rain-gear, as well as a sun-hat, sun glasses designed for intense sunlight, and a scarf or face-mask to ward off the dust. Flip-flop sandals are useful for hotel bathrooms, and swimming costumes for pools, stone baths and hot springs. For short hikes, strong but lightweight walking boots and thick socks should be worn. Down jackets, warm gloves and woollen hats will be needed in the winter months. Shorts should not be worn when visiting towns. Casual clothes may be generally worn while travelling in Bhutan, but there are occasions when you will have to dress up, wearing a suit and tie (gentlemen) or a smart dress or trouser suit (ladies). These occasions will include visits to *tsechu* or *drubchen* festivals, when all the Bhutanese wear their finest clothes, meetings with senior government officials (which can happen here with surprising ease) and invitations to private homes.

Toiletries and cosmetics

Indian brands are widely available, but you will find few well-known international toiletries and cosmetics, even in Thimphu. You should consider bringing your own shampoo, shaving cream, toothpaste, mouthwash, dental floss, wet wipes, cotton buds, sunscreen with a high protection factor, lip-salve, insect repellent containing DEET, contact lens cleaning fluid, perfume, deodorant, face cream, manicure set, condoms, tampons (as these can be hard to find in remote areas) and even toilet paper. A small first-aid kit will also be useful.

Other useful items

You would do well to carry a water bottle (with purification tabs), flashlight, multi-headed electrical adaptor, an electrical recharger (to take power from an electric-light socket), batteries (for electrical appliances), pocket calculator, electric shaver (rechargeable type), inflatable pillow, hot water bottle (for winter months), ear plugs, sewing kit, Swiss army knife, bottle opener, corkscrew, tin-opener, pocket-size screwdriver, sheet sleeping bag and pillow case, folding umbrella, alarm clock, shoe polish, nail brush, pocket mirror, velcro or string, vacuum flask, light waterproof nylon shopping bag, clothes line, and a universal bath- and basin plug of the flanged type that will fit any waste-pipe. If you are visiting the sub-tropical areas of southern Bhutan, a mosquito net will also be useful, along with a straw hat which can be rolled or flattened and reconstituted after 15 minutes soaking in water. Remember not to throw away spent batteries containing mercury or cadmium; take them home to be disposed

of, or recycled properly. Never carry knives, scissors or other blunt objects in hand
baggage, and never carry firearms. Their possession could land you in serious trouble.

Insurance

In view of the Bhutanese regulations concerning pre-payment for tours and inflexible cancellation clauses, it is essential to take out an appropriate insurance policy. Before you travel make sure that your medical and cancellation insurance is adequate, and that you are covered for theft or loss of property. One standard insurance policy, available through Trailfinders' outlets in the UK, covers most requirements for travel in Bhutan. If you are river-rafting or undertaking some other 'dangerous' sporting activity, you may require additional cover.

Money

Currency

The national currency is the **Ngultrum** (Nu), which has the same monetary value as the Indian rupee. Indian currency circulates freely in Bhutan, alongside the Ngultrum. One Ngultrum is divided into 100 Chetrum. Bhutanese currency notes come in denominations ranging from one to 500, and they depict historically important *dzongs*. There are also coins minted in Bhutan, some of them carrying interesting Buddhist motifs. A useful currency converter can be found at www.oanda.com/converter/classic.

Exchange

Bhutanese currency is issued by the Royal Monetary Authority, and there are two clearing banks. The **Bank of Bhutan** (founded 1968) has 26 branches throughout the country, with its head office at Phuntsoling (open Mon-Fri 0900-1300, Sat 0900-1100 except in Thimphu where the opening hours are longer). The branches in Trongsar, Mongar and Tashigang close on Tuesdays and open on Sundays. The **Bhutan National Bank** (founded 1997) is computerised and more efficient, but only operates out of Thimphu, Phuntsoling, Paro, Gelekphuk and Tashigang. These banks will change travellers' cheques and hard currency (US dollars, GBP, euros, yen, Swiss francs, Singapore and Hong Kong dollars, and Danish kroner). In general it will be easier to change money at the airport, in Thimphu or one of the larger towns. Major purchases in craft and textile stores may also be made in US dollars. Even if you are a tourist travelling on an all-inclusive prepaid itinerary, you will still need some Ngultrum in hand for unforeseen contingencies and for incidentals (drinks, laundry, souvenirs, phone calls, donations to monasteries, photographic fees, tips etc). This is particularly important for long overland drives or treks. On leaving Bhutan by air you will also have to pay Nu 300 airport tax.

Travellers' cheques and credit cards

Currency-exchange outlets generally prefer travellers' cheques to currency notes — the banks charge 1% for cashing travellers' cheques, whatever the issuing bank. Credit cards (Amex, Visa, Mastercard) can be used only in a few large shops, such as the Handicrafts Emporium in Thimphu, and in the biggest hotels, but the card-processing surcharge is high and verification can only be

> ‡ *Only Amex travellers' cheques can be replaced when lost or stolen in Bhutan.*

 The current exchange rate (August 2004) is US$1 = Nu 45.25, 1 euro = Nu 54.78 and 1 GBP = Nu 81.29.

made during office hours (0900-1700). At the time of writing there is only one ATM machine in Bhutan, at the Bhutan National Bank in Thimphu.

Cost of living and travelling

Some 85% of the population are engaged in subsistence farming and the lifestyle is predominantly rural (the per capita income was only US$656 in 2000). But since the population is still relatively small, there are fewer economic pressures than in other parts of the subcontinent. Most manufactured commodities are imported – from India and elsewhere – and so they are priced slightly higher than they would be in neighbouring India. If you are an Indian national or expatriate worker in Bhutan you may pay for hotels, restaurants and transportation services directly at local prices. In such cases it is perfectly possible to select a cheaper or more expensive hotel or restaurant. However, tourists on prepaid itineraries who are charged a standard daily rate will not have to make such decisions. Instead they will only have to budget for incidental expenses and personal purchases.

Getting there

Air

Flights to neighbouring gateway cities

Since Bhutan is landlocked and presently has no transcontinental or long-haul flight connections, the air traveller will first have to reach one of the five neighbouring gateway cities: Delhi, Kathmandu, Bangkok, Dhaka or Kolkata. The most competitive airfares are usually available to Delhi or Bangkok, whether your journey begins in Europe, North America, South America, Australia or New Zealand. Kathmandu can be an important hub for travellers visiting central parts of Tibet as well as Bhutan, while Kolkota (and Bagdogra Airport) is closer to the land border at Phuntsoling. The following information is a brief list of the major airline schedules to the gateway cities from across the globe. Travellers should contact the various airline websites for updated price and schedule information.

Flights to Kathmandu Qatar Airways (www.qatarairways.com) have daily flights from London and Munich via Doha. **Gulf Air** (www.gulfairco.com) have flights from London, Paris, Frankfurt, Milan and Rome connecting through Abu Dhabi on Monday, Wednesday and Saturday, while **Aeroflot** and **Austrian Airlines** both have flights from European cities on Thursday connecting via Moscow and Vienna respectively. For travellers from Europe, Southern Africa, and the east coast of North America there are also onward connecting flights from Delhi (on **RNAC** or **Indian Airlines**), Karachi (**PIA**), Dhaka (**Biman**), and Bangkok (**Thai** and **RNAC**). For those originating in Australia, New Zealand and the west coast of the United States there are onward connecting flights from Hong Kong (**RNAC**), Kuala Lumpur (**Qatar**) and Singapore (**Singapore** and **RNAC**). Bangkok (**Thai** and **RNAC**), Osaka (**RNAC**), and Shanghai (**RNAC**). For reservations and price information, contact the relevant airline website.

Flights to Delhi Regular flights are available from many world destinations. From Europe, **Air India** (www.airindia.com) offers daily flights from London while **Virgin** (www.virgin-atlantic.com) has direct flights on the same route on Sunday, Wednesday and Friday. **Lufthansa** (www.lufthansa.com) has flights daily from Frankfurt and Munich. If travelling from the Middle East, **Emirates** (www.emirates.com) has direct flights from Dubai on Tuesday, Thursday, Saturday and Sunday. **Gulf Air**

(www.gulfairco.com) flies from Bahrain via Muscat every day and **Kuwait Airways** (www.kuwait-airways.com) offers a daily, direct service from Kuwait International Airport. Flights from Australasia and the Far East are also easy to find, **Singapore Airlines** (www.singaporeair.com) offers daily flights from Australia and New Zealand to Delhi via Singapore. **Malayasian Airlines** (www.malaysianairlines.com) has a direct service from Kuala Lumpur on Monday, Wednesday, Friday and Sunday. All flights from North America go to Delhi via another desitnation. Among these, **Air India** has flights from New York via London, Monday to Friday while **British Airways** (www.britishairways.com) offers flights on the same route every day. For reservations and price information, contact the relevant airline website.

Flights to Kolkata Worldwide direct flights to Kolkata are not as prevalent as those to New Delhi. **British Airways** (www.britishairways.com) is one of the few major providers of a direct service from Europe, departing from London on Tuesday, Thursday and Saturday. **Air India** (www.airindia.com) offers a service from London via Mumbai on Friday. Direct flights from the Middle East are available with **Singapore Airlines** (www.singaporeair.com) who offer a daily service via Singapore, and with **Royal Jordanian** (www.rja.com) who have a direct service from Amman every Saturday. **Gulf Air** (www.gulfairco.com) have a service from Bahrain via Muscat on Tuesday and Friday. **Singapore Airlines** are also the major provider of flights from Australia and New Zealand with daily services via Singapore. There are no direct flights from North America but **Air India** have flights from New York via London and Mumbai Monday to Friday and **British Airways** have flights from New York via London on Monday, Wednesday and Friday. For reservations and price information, contact the relevant airline website.

Flights to Bangkok There are direct flights available from most major cities in Europe. **British Airways** (www.britishairways.com) and **Quantas** (www.quantas.com) both have daily, direct services from London. **THAI** (www.thaiair.com) has daily, direct flights from London, Germany and Holland while **Lufthansa** (www.lufthansa.com) also flies directly from Germany on a daily basis. From Australasia, **Quantas** has daily flights direct from Sydney and Melbourne and **THAI** offers direct flights on Monday, Wednesday, Thursday and Sunday. **Air India** (www.airindia.com) flies direct from Delhi on Tuesday, Thursday, Friday and Sunday; **THAI** have a direct, daily service leaving from Delhi and also a direct service from Mumbai on Tuesday, Thursday and Saturday. **Singapore Airlines** fly direct to Bangkok from Singapore everyday. Flights from North America are provided mainly by **THAI** who offer a daily service from New York via London and also a one-stop direct flight from Los Angeles on Tuesday, Wednesday, Friday and Sunday. **British Airways** have daily flights from New York via London. For reservations and price information, contact the relevant airline website.

Flights to Dhaka Dhaka is supported by relatively few airlines. If travelling from Europe, **British Airways Airways** (www.britishairways.com) provides a direct service on Wednesday, Friday and Saturday. **Biman Bangladesh Airways** (www.bimanair.com) flies direct from London Monday to Thursday, Saturday and Sunday. It also has direct flights from Paris on Sunday and Frankfurt on Thursday. **Emirates** (www.emirates.com) has a daily service from London via Dubai. **Biman Bangladesh Airways** offers a direct service from many destinations in the Middle East and South East Asia. It flies from Dubai Monday to Saturday; from Singapore Monday Wednesday, Friday and Saturday; from Delhi Monday to Thursday; and from Kuala Lumpur Tuesday, Thursday and Saturday. **THAI** (www.thaiair.com) has a direct, daily service from Bangkok and also daily flights from Australia and New Zealand that go via Bangkok. **Dragon Air Airways** (www.dragonair.com) has a direct service from Hong Kong on Wednesday, Saturday and Sunday. Flights from North America are mostly provided by **Biman Bangladesh Airways** who have a service from New York via

Brussels on Tuesday and Saturday, and **Emirates** who fly daily from New York via Dubai. **British Airways Airways** also has a regular weekly service that goes via London. For reservations and price information, contact the relevant airline website.

Flights into Bhutan

The only civilian airport in Bhutan is presently the one at Paro, and the national carrier **Druk Air** has a monopoly on all flights in and out of Bhutan. The airline has both Airbus A-319 and Bae 146-100 aircraft, seating 100 and 72 passengers respectively. Druk Air flight tickets can only be issued to non-Bhutanese and non-Indian nationals on receipt of a valid visa clearance number (see page 25). Having received a visa clearance number and made your way to the gateway city designated in your prepaid itinerary, you will then have to contact Druk Air. The website, www.drukair.com.bt, has details of flight schedules from gateway cities to Paro. Druk Air recently announced that it will soon be extending the frequency of its flights to Kathmandu and adding other Indian destinations, such as Gaya, Varanasi and Chennai, but this expansion is yet to be implemented.

There are frequent delays due to inclement weather conditions during the rainy season and sometimes due to strong winds in the spring. Always check the day and time with your travel agent before departure. Visitors to Bhutan should try to avoid tight onward flight connections from any of the gateway cities, and if you are planning to visit India, Bangladesh or Burma on a Druk Air flight from Bhutan you should arrange the visa for your onward destination before leaving home. In 2004, the following flights were available (all prices are one-way only):

Delhi–Kathmandu–Paro Delhi–Paro costs approximately US$ 315, while Kathmandu–Paro costs approximately US$190.

Bangkok–Yangon–Dhaka–Paro Bangkok–Paro costs approximately US$360 and the Dhaka–Paro flight costs approximately US$190.

Bangkok–Kolkata–Paro Bangkok–Paro costs approximately US$360 and the following Kolkata–Paro flight costs approximately US$190.

Bangkok–Paro This flight should cost approximately US$360.

Druk Air offices and agents

Flight tickets can be issued from the following outlets: **Delhi** Druk Air Corporation, Indira Gandhi International Airport, T91-11-5653207.
Kathmandu Malla Treks, Lekhnath Marg, PO Box 5227, T977-1-4410089, drukair@mallatreks.com. **Bangkok** Druk Air Corporation, Room 3237, Central Block, Bangkok International Airport, T66-2-535-1960, drukair@loxinfo.co.th.
Kolkata Druk Air Corporation, 51 Tivoli Ct, Ballygunge, Circular Road, T91-33-2402419/569976, F91-33-2470050. **Yangon** Druk Air Corporation, Grand Meeyahta Executive Residence, Ground Floor, Room 6, 372 Bogyoke Aung San St, Pabedon Township, T95-1-371993, F95-1-371992.

Somewhat inconveniently, **Druk Air** has its head office in Paro rather than Thimphu: T975-8-271856, F975-8-271861, www.drukair.com.bt. However, since December 2002, the Thimphu office (T975-2-322215, F975-2-322775, drukairthimphu@druknet.bt) has been appointed as general sales agent for Thai International in Bhutan. This means that Thai International flight tickets to worldwide destinations can now be purchased in Thimphu. Other designated ticketing agents within Bhutan include: **Atlas Travel Service**, T2-326241; **Tsenden Travel**, T2-323027; **Tashi Tours**, T2-323027; **Norda Travel**, T2-326818; **Bhutan Travel Bureau**, T2-324421 and **World Travel Service**, T2-321866.

There are also a few designated travel agents in the gateway cities:

Oriole Travel, 5/F Skulthai Suriwong Tower, 141 Suriwong Rd, Bangkok, T66-2-237-9201, oriole@samart.co.th
Kamini Express, 241 Lake Rd, Kolkota, 700029, T91-11-4665472, F91-11-4663918.

Unique Air Travels, G2, Circular Centre, 222 AJC Bose Rd, Kolkota, T91-33-2474333.
Mams Travels, 33 Gulshan Ave Rd No 45, Gulshan-2, Dhaka.

Price and excess baggage

Druk Air flights are rather highly priced, although Bhutanese and Indian nationals are offered preferential rates. Children have discounts: 10% for under twos, and 33% for children aged 2-12. In most cases you will not have to go to the trouble of purchasing these tickets directly – your international or Bhutanese tour operator can accept payment in advance. Druk Air charges excess baggage on all routes into Bhutan at US$2.5-US$ 5 per kg.

Road

Tourists are obliged to use Druk Air on either the inbound or outbound sector of their trip to Bhutan. However, it is still possible to enter or exit via the only open land border at Phuntsoling. Bagdogra is the nearest Indian airport with connecting flights to Delhi and Kolkata. The road from Bagdogra passes through Siliguri, exits India at Jaigaon and enters Bhutan at Phuntsoling. The distance from Siliguri to Phuntsoling is 150 km (three to four hours' drive). Local Bhutanese tour operators can send vehicles to receive clients at Bagdogra Airport, Siliguri or New Jalpaiguri Railway Station (in the case of those taking the train from Delhi or Kolkata). **Taxis** and public **buses** also run between Siliguri and Phuntsoling. The taxi fare is Rs 650. The buses depart Siliguri Bus Station at 0800 and 1400 (price Rs 55). If you start driving from Darjiling or Gangtok via Siliguri, it will take about seven hours to reach Phuntsoling. The border gate crossing remains open each day until 2200.

Immigration procedures

After leaving India (with a proper exit stamp in your passport), your Bhutanese visa will then be issued at the local government office near the east end of the town. You will have to pay the US$20 fee and provide two passport-size photographs. If you are not travelling beyond Phuntsoling, you may come and go across the border during the day, and even stay over in Phuntsoling without having previously prepaid for a tour. However, if you are going further into Bhutan, you will have to have a visa clearance number and a prepaid itinerary with internal travel permits which your local guide will be carrying (see page 25). These documents will all be checked at the Rinchending immigration checkpoint on the road above Phuntsoling, and your passport will be endorsed there for travel within Bhutan as a bona fide tour member. Indian nationals can travel more freely through to Thimphu, just by presenting their passports or voter cards at Rinchending. It takes a further six hours to negotiate the winding 179 km road from Phuntsoling through to Thimphu (or Paro). Public transport is available for Indian nationals and some expatriates working in Bhutan. See the bus schedule information given under Phuntsoling, page 135.

Touching down

For foreign nationals, other than Indians, there are only two possible points of entry: Paro airport and Phuntsoling land border. Exit is currently possible only from these

⦂ Touching down

→ **IDD code** Bhutan's international dialing code is +975. Dial 00 to call an international number from Bhutan.

→ **Official time** Bhutanese time is 30 minutes ahead of Indian National Time or GMT +6 hours.

→ **Voltage** 230 volts, 50 cycles AC. The current is variable and supply sometimes erratic. A stabiliser will be useful to protect computers and other electrical devices from power surges or power cuts. Electrical sockets have two round-pin holes, but you should carry an adapter if possible.

→ **Weights and measures** The metric system is in use, as it is in neighbouring India. In some rural areas the traditional *sang* weight and *dre* (or *gasekhorlo*) dry measure are still used.

same locations, because the Samdrub Jongkhar border crossing with Assam is closed on account of its proximity to jungle areas occupied by Bodo and ULFA insurgents (see page 247). Indian nationals require no visa for Bhutan, and may also enter through the other southern border gates at Sarpang, Gelekpuk, Samtse, Ranibagan and Samdrub Jongkhar. As is the case with other foreign nationals, they require special permits to move around the country (see page 26). The high passes linking Tibet with Bhutan are traditional trade routes, but they have mostly been closed since the 1950s, following the Chinese occupation of Tibet. As a result, most districts that share a border with Tibet (Ha, Paro, Thimphu, Gasa, Bumthang, Lhuntse, Tashi Yangtse and Tashigang) can presently be accessed only from the lateral highway.

Airport information

Airport tax Nu 300 per person is payable at the time of departure from Paro Airport.
Airport security It would be best to carry all film in a lead bag that offers protection from x-rays, or at least in a plastic bag that can be removed for manual inspection when checking-in. Never leave film in checked baggage, which will also be x-rayed.
Airport transportation After completing immigration and customs formalities at Paro Airport, your ground arrangements will normally be provided by your host organisation, and in most cases this will be your local tour operator. Public coaches and taxis also run from the airport to Thimphu, at US$1 and US$9 respectively. The 55-km journey takes about one and a half hours.

Local customs and laws

Since the Bhutanese are acutely conscious of the need to preserve their distinctive cultural traditions and physical environment amid the pressures of globalisation, they have an established code of conduct, known as *Driklam Namzhag*, which, though based on traditional values, was published in 1999 to commemorate the present king's silver jubilee. The text runs to 423 pages, and its 23 chapters concern a wide range of issues, including correct motivation, dress code, physical demeanour, honorific modes of speech, the prescribed etiquette for dining, sitting and leave-taking, the importance of hierarchy and rank in processions or public gatherings, appropriate gestures of respect, and the conduct required while visiting *dzongs*, as well as correct procedures for funerals, births, inaugurations, festivals and

Himalayan Environment Trust Code of Practice

→ **Campsite** Leave it cleaner than you found it.

→ **Deforestation** Make no open fires and discourage others making one for you. Limit use of water heated by firewood in conservation areas (use of dead wood is permitted elsewhere). Choose accommodation where kerosene or fuel-efficient wood-burning stoves are used.

→ **Litter** Remove it. Burn or bury paper and carry away non-degradable litter. If you find other people's litter, remove theirs too! Pack food in biodegradable containers. Carry away all batteries/cells.

→ **Water** Keep local water clean. Do not use detergents and pollutants in streams and springs. Where there are no toilets be sure you are at least 30 m away from the water source and bury or cover waste. Do not allow cooks or porters to throw rubbish in nearby streams and rivers.

→ **Plants** Do not take cuttings, seeds and roots in areas where this activity is illegal.

→ **Giving to children** This encourages begging. Donations to a project, health centre or school are more constructive.

→ Respect **local traditions** and cultures.

→ Respect **privacy** and ask permission before taking photographs.

→ Respect **holy places**. Never touch or remove religious objects. Remove shoes before entering temples if required to do so.

→ Respect local **etiquette**. Dress modestly, particularly when visiting temples and shrines and while walking through villages; loose, lightweight clothes are preferable to shorts, skimpy tops and tight-fitting outfits. Avoid holding hands and kissing in public.

consecration ceremonies. The code applies to all sections of society: the monarchy, nobility, ministers, monastic body, married *mantrins* (*gomchen*), civil servants and private citizens. The Bhutanese are required to wear their national dress during working hours and in most other situations, although the code has been slightly relaxed for evenings out in Thimphu.

As a visitor you will not be expected to familiarise yourself with the myriad nuances of this code of conduct, but there are certain basic guidelines that will ensure your stay is happy and inoffensive: 1) You should remain polite and courteous in social relationships regardless of the difficulties which arise. Loss of self-control will not bring about your desired response. 2) Dress modestly and according to the occasion – casual clothes for everyday use, formal wear for special events, visiting *dzongs* and work. Tight or revealing clothes, including sleeveless shirts and T-shirts are not suitable. Shorts may only be worn by men when hiking in the countryside, and never by women. 3) You should remember to show respect for the monarchy and for all Buddhist institutions. Avoid killing animals or insects. Fishing in certain rivers can only be done under licence, and you should never pollute or swim in a lake. 4) You may take photographs of the exterior of a building, but not inside a temple or monastery. There are some limited opportunities to photograph the *dzong* courtyards. Do not block the view when filming during *tsechu* festivals or public gatherings. Always ask people for permission to take their photograph. 5) You should never point your fingers or feet towards anyone, and you should avoid public displays of intimacy. 6) At the time of arrival or departure, it is customary to exchange white offering scarves (*katak*), or gifts. Small gifts (such as bottles of wine, duty free spirits and cigarettes, etc) will be appreciated, particularly by your guide and driver, or by a host if you are invited to a Bhutanese home. Men also appreciate long argyle woollen socks, while photographs of important lamas from the various Buddhist traditions are revered throughout the monasteries, villages and towns of Bhutan.

Visiting a monastery or temple You will have to remove shoes, as in India. Cameras and umbrellas should be left outside, as well. Remember to remove your hat, to abstain from smoking, and to proceed around or through sacred shrines in a clockwise manner. You can bow or prostrate in the local manner towards the central images, and, if requested, you may even roll the sacred dice-cup indicative of good fortune that is found near the entrance. If you make an offering in a shrine you will probably be given a sip of consecrated water from a sacred vase. The water is taken in the palm of the right hand and after drinking you would wipe the remainder on the crown of your head. Never sit down pointing your feet towards the images of a temple or its inner sanctum. Never interrupt prayers or on-going ceremonies. You may feel privileged to bear witness to the survival of this ancient culture, which maintains the spiritual heritage of the Tibetan Buddhist world intact.

Tipping, bargaining and tax

Tipping is officially frowned upon, but an acknowledgement of good service is always appreciated in hotels, and by local guides, drivers and trekking staff. Bargaining will only be possible at the handicraft section of the weekend Changlimethang market in Thimphu and at the souvenir stalls on the ascent to Taktsang hermitage in Paro. Hotels and larger restaurants can charge 10% government tax and 10% service charge above their advertised prices, but these charges are absorbed if you are on a prepaid tourist itinerary.

Responsible tourism

Most visitors to Bhutan appreciate the need for the restricted access to temples and monasteries, as well as the established code of conduct. It will be important to follow the guidelines outlined above, and ensure that your visit is not intrusive. While trekking follow the Himalayan Code of Practice (see box page 35).

Safety

Traditionally crime levels in Bhutan have been remarkably low. It is worth noting however that since the introduction of television in 1999 the crime rate in Thimphu and other towns has begun to soar. Nonetheless, as a visitor, you will be received courteously throughout the length and breadth of the country. Theft and begging are still quite rare. Some remote village communities may be suspicious of passing strangers, but you are more at risk from dangerous hairpin bends than from the country's inhabitants. Though safety issues hardly ever arise, travellers are still advised to lock precious belongings and money inside a suitcase or a bag before leaving their hotel room. Some of the larger hotels have safety deposit boxes. The **Royal Bhutan Police Force** monitor traffic, crime, Restricted Area checkpoints and frontier immigration posts.

 If you are stranded on mountain roads, the following number plate information might be useful: BT-1 = Thimphu or Paro; BT-2 = Phuntsoling, Chukha and Samtse; BT-3 = Trongsar, Bumthang, Gelekphuk, Sarpang, Zhemgang and Tarkana; BT-4 = Mongar, Tashigang, Tashi Yangtse, Pema Gatsel, Samdrub Jongkhar and Lhuntse.

Getting around

Road

There is no domestic air or rail infrastructure. The road network is not extensive since construction only began in the 1960s. The main lateral highway links Thimphu with Tashigang (1965-85); and there are now four main roads linking the mountain areas with the plains: Thimphu–Phuntsoling (1982); Wangdu Phodrang–Sarpang; Trongsar–Gelekphuk; and Tashigang–Samdrub Jongkhar (1963-65). The principal means of road transport is by public **bus**, which is a crowded and uncomfortable way to travel. Public transport is accessible to all travellers in open areas, but in Restricted Areas it is largely reserved for locals, and hitchhiking is discouraged. For fares and schedules, see under Thimphu and the other main district towns.

Tourists travelling on prepaid itineraries will have all transportation provided, and there are even some companies that offer specialist motorcycling and mountain biking itineraries. Contact **Himalayan Roadrunners** (www.ridehigh.com) or the **Bhutan Mountain Biking Club** (www.bhutanmtb.com). For expatriate workers, four-wheel drive vehicles and Japanese cars are available for hire, invariably with a driver. In fact, four-wheel drive vehicles are essential for journeys through Central and Eastern Bhutan in the rainy season and in the winter months. Most roads are dusty and delays can occur in summer due to landslides. For such reasons, truly independent travel over long distances is not easy. Even if you are an expatriate working in Bhutan, you may prefer to hire a driver who has familiarity with the narrow, winding mountain roads.

Within Phuntsoling and Thimphu **taxis** are also available at fixed meter rates. There is an initial boarding charge of Nu 12 (0400-2100) or Nu 20 (2100-0400), and an incremental charge for mileage (range: Nu 8-10 per km). The average charge for a short ride is Nu 30-50.

Hitchhiking is officially discouraged in Bhutan, and since most foreign visitors have all arrangements provided on their behalf, they will seldom have occasion to try their luck, except in the event of road breakdowns or landslides. Some drivers who decide to stop will expect to receive payment.

Maps

The best, widely available English-language maps of the area are ITMB's 2001 fold-out *Map of Bhutan* (1:380,000), and the *Bhutan Himalaya Map* (1:390,000), published by the Himalayan Map House in 2000. There is a larger 1:125,000 colour map showing the district and county boundaries, published in 1994 by the Land Use Planning Section of the **Bhutanese Ministry of Agriculture**, in association with the Danish organisation Danida. A companion atlas based on this map, and on the same scale was published in 1997 by the Ministry of Agriculture. The **Survey of Bhutan** has published a composite Landsat map (1:125,000), and some interesting topographic maps (1:50,000) in 1995, as well as administrative maps for each district (1:540,000) in 1996. The Department of Tourism has published a series of detailed trekking maps (1:50,000), including the well-known Jomolhari Trek, and town plans of Thimphu and Paro. For readers of Tibetan, the *Tibetan Language Map of TAR*, published in Lhasa, and the *Map of Tibet and Adjacent Regions*, published in Dharamsala by the Amnye Machen Institute in 1996 both include Bhutan, Sikkim, Nepal and adjacent areas of northern India.

⁞ Hotel price codes explained

AL	Over US$120	C	US$30-US$70
A	US$100-US$120	D	US$20-US$30
B	US$70-US$100	E	Under US$20

Prices refer to the cost of a double room, not including service charge or meals, unless otherwise stated.

Other English-language maps include the *Operational Navigational Charts* (ONC) and the *Joint Operations Graphic Series* (JOG), both published in the United States. These maps are more useful for their topography but they are remarkably weak on place name data. Along with French-language maps and the Cyrillic Karta Mera series, they may be purchased from **Stanford's Map Centre**, 12-14 Long Acre, London WC2E 9LP (T020-78361321).

Sleeping

While the neighbouring gateway cities such as Kathmandu, Kolkata, Bangkok, Delhi and Dhaka offer the full range of luxury to budget accommodation, Bhutan has only been accepting foreign visitors since 1974 and the infrastructure is not yet well developed. The first international hotel chains in Bhutan (Aman Resorts and Como Hotels) opened their doors in Paro in 2004 and other branches will soon follow in Thimphu, Punakha, Gangteng, Trongsar and Jakar. These establishments are set to charge highly inflated rates for an all-inclusive package, in the range US$600-$1,000 per day. Apart from them, the best hotels, approved by the Department of Tourism, are to be found in Thimphu, Paro and Phuntsoling – they all have electricity, telephone connections, television, attached bathrooms with intermittent hot water supply, business centre facilities, restaurants and bars. Standard and deluxe rooms are available, as well as suites. If your visit is pre-arranged by the travel services, you will most likely be allocated a standard room, and may well have to pay extra to upgrade. On the other hand, you will not have to pay the additional taxes (20%) that such hotels have to charge – these costs will be absorbed by your tour operator. If you are an expatriate worker in Bhutan, you will be able to pay the local rates for accommodation and may have greater choice. The rooms are well decorated, often in traditional Bhutanese design, and there are electric or oil heaters, although a hot water bottle will be a useful asset in the colder months of the year. In the Bumthang area the hotels and guesthouses all have wood-burning stoves (*burkhari*). During the festival season, the best accommodation is frequently overbooked, and the larger tour companies, such as BTCL, which owns a number of its own hotels, may have a distinct advantage over some of the others. Accommodation in the towns of Central and Eastern Bhutan, including Trongsar, Jakar, Mongar and Tashigang, is simpler but the lodges in these parts still mostly have modern plumbing and helpful staff (water and electricity supply can be erratic). Most towns have simpler guesthouses (often called hotels) where the guests are predominantly Bhutanese, Indian and Nepalese. These establishments can be noisy, often with shared toilet and bathroom facilities. If you end up staying in such accommodation, you are advised to bring your own disinfectant and toilet paper.

Apart from the larger tourist hotels and major towns, no laundry or dry-cleaning service is available. If you wish to avoid the do-it-yourself option, it is sometimes possible to find a private arrangement for laundry services with local guesthouses.

⁞ Restaurant price codes explained

$	Cheap	Under US$5
$$	Mid-range	US$5-US$10
$$$	Expensive	Over US$10

Prices refer to the cost of a two-course meal for one person, including drinks and tax.

Hotel prices vary considerably from in excess of Nu 40,000 per night at the new Amankora Hotel in Paro, to Nu 2,000 for the upmarket hotels in Thimphu and Paro and Nu 800/1,000 for the smaller ones. In other towns the prices range from Nu 450 to Nu 1,000. Breakfast is generally excluded. For further details of the hotels in each city or town, see the relevant Sleeping sections.

Eating and drinking

Organized tours in Bhutan usually include a full package with three meals per day. The meals served in the best hotels provide both buffet and á la carte services. The buffet is generally the better option, in that there is usually a wide selection of dishes (Bhutanese, Nepalese and some Continental cuisine). Á la carte service can be very slow by comparison. You may also have the option of dining outside your hotel on certain occasions at downtown restaurants. International cuisine is only offered at a small number of hotels in the Thimphu and Paro areas. A few specialist restaurants will offer Tibetan, Indian, Nepalese, Thai or Chinese dishes. Otherwise the standard cuisine offered in restaurants throughout the country is Bhutanese.

Food

Bhutanese cuisine, for the most part, is pretty basic. In the central hills of Bhutan, **red rice** is the staple, eaten with spicy and hot vegetables and meat curries. The national dish *emadatse* consists of hot chillies and melted cheese, served with rice. Other spicy alternatives include beef with spinach, pork with rice noodles, and chicken in garlic butter. Buckwheat **pancakes** (*kule*) and **noodles** (*puta*) are popular in the Bumthang area, **corn** (*gesasip*) in Tashigang, and roasted **barley** or **wheat** (*tsampa*) in the nomadic *drokpa* areas of the northern mountains. The nomads also have **yak** meat and some mutton (fresh or dried), and dairy products – delicious yoghurt, butter, milk, buttermilk, as well as cheese which comes in many varieties: hardened cubes which must be carefully sucked to avoid damaging the teeth, and soft whisps which are easy to digest.

Roasted barley is also the staple of the Tibetan diet. Other **Tibetan dishes** are found on the menu of many restaurants. The famous *momo* – a steamed meat dumpling which resembles the Chinese *jiaoze* – or Tibetan country-style noodles (*then-thuk*), and noodle soup (*thukpa*) are great favourites.

In the south of Bhutan **Nepalese cuisine** is predominant, and some dishes such as *dhal bhat* (rice and lentils) and *alu takari* (potato curry) can be found in restaurants throughout Bhutan.

Pork and beef are the most commonly available meats, but both can be suspect, particularly during the rainy season. Fish is not generally eaten by the Bhutanese, and will not be fresh– usually it will be imported from neighbouring West Bengal in India. Mutton is rare, unlike in India. Chicken is becoming increasingly popular and is generally regarded as a safer option. Yak meat is a favourite during the winter season. Vegetarian fare is widely available and exotic: nettles, asparagus, taro, orchids and various types of mushroom are found, invariably seasoned with hot chillies and sometimes with a hot cheese sauce. Desserts are not generally served but delicious apples, apricots, peaches and walnuts are available in season. Indian snacks, such as *masala dosa* and *samosa*, are quite popular in urban areas of Bhutan. The Indian habit of chewing paan or doma, a mixture of powdered lime, palm nuts and tobacco rolled up in a betel leaf, is widespread. The habit is discouraged in some official quarters because of the links between *paan* and oral cancer, and because the red stains left on the pavements where *paan* eaters have spat out the remains are considered unseemly.

Packed lunches are provided by the tourist hotels and local operators for day-long hikes and longer drives, but you would do well to stock up on a few dietary supplements of your own before heading up country. Instant soups, cheeses, pâtés, biscuits, chocolates, real coffee and fresh bread rolls or pastries can be very welcome if the weather suddenly turns nasty, or if you have stomach trouble. Organised trekking expeditions which include camping will have a cook who can prepare a full campsite meal, or take over the kitchen of a roadside restaurant.

Drink

Sweet, Indian-style milk **tea** (*ngar-ja*) is very popular in Bhutan, as are the Tibetan-style dri-butter tea (*so-ja*) and clear salted tea (*ja-dang*). Butter tea is often consumed in Bhutanese homes on special occasions. Lipton tea bags are commonly served, but good quality teas are surprisingly hard to find. Only instant Nescafé is available in Bhutan, and if you are looking for real **coffee** or an alternative instant brand, you will have to bring your own. Soft carbonated drinks are imported from India and Pepsi Cola is even bottled at Phuntsoling. A variety of locally produced fresh **fruit juices** are available in cans and cartons: apple, mango, orange, pineapple and tomato, among them. Local and Indian brands of bottled **mineral water** are widely available. Indigenous **beer**, such as the Bumthang brews Red Panda and Weissbeer are available, as are imported beers, including Indian brands (Golden Eagle, Black Label, Kingfisher and Dansberg), and SE Asian brands (Tiger, Sinha and San Miguel).

‡ *No alcohol can be served before 1300, and none at all on Tue, which is considered a dry day.*

Expensive imported **wines** are available at the Duty Free Shop in Thimphu. Locally produced alcoholic drinks include traditional home brews, such as wet fermented barley or wheat ale (*pang-chang*), dry fermented millet, wheat or rice (*tomba or sin-chang*), and distilled rice liquor (*arak*). Indigenous brands of whisky, rum, brandy and gin are distilled by the military for commercial purposes, and these are widely consumed. Local **whiskies** include CSJ Coronation, Royal Supreme, Special Courier and Black Mountain. Local **rums** include Dragon and Triple X, brandies include Rockbee and Jachung and **gins** include Snow Lion, Crystal Dry and Pucham. Spice Liqueur is also made in Bhutan.

Entertainment

The Bhutanese have a great passion for seasonal outdoor **picnics** at which traditional performances of music, song and dance feature prominently. **Spectator sports** (see page 45) are increasingly popular, and there are also a large number of secular and religious **festivals** held throughout the country. In the capital city and in the larger towns (Paro, Phuntsoling), there are several **bars** and **discotheques**, which come to

Lunar calendar festivals

1st day of 1st lunar month
Bhutanese New Year (*Losar*)

15th day of 1st lunar month
Day of Miracles (*Chotrul Duchen*)

12th day of the 3rd lunar month
Anniversary of Zhabdrung Ngawang
Namgyel (*Zhabdrung Decho*)

1st day of the 4th lunar month
Monastic body leaves Thimphu
for Punakha

7th day of the 4th lunar month
Birth of Shakyamuni Buddha
(*Trungkar Duchen*)

15th day of 4th lunar month
Enlightenment of Shakyamuni
Buddha (*Sangye Duchen*)

15th day of 5th lunar month
World Incense Day (*Dzamling Chisang*)

4th day of 6th lunar month
Dharmacakra Day (*Chokor Duchen*)

10th day of 6th lunar month
Birth of Padmasambhava
(*Guru Trungkar*)

30th day of 7th lunar month
Bathing Festival/ Blessed Rainy
Day (*Tru*)

1st day of 8th lunar month
Harvest Festival (*Onkor*)

30th day of 8th lunar month
Start of Dasain

22nd day of 9th lunar month
Descent from Tusita (*Lhabab
Duchen*)

1st day of 10th lunar month
Monastic body leaves Punakha
for Thimphu

7th day of 11th lunar month
Ten Auspicious Omens (*Zangpo
Chudzom*)

16th day of 11th lunar month
Nine Bad Omens (Ngenpa Gudzom)

7th day of 12th lunar month
Agricultural New Year (*Sonam Losar*)

29th day of 12th lunar month
Averting negativity of old
year (*Gutor*)

Essentials Festivals & events

life late on Friday and Saturday nights. *Caram* is a table-top or board game in which draughts are flicked with the fingers into corner pockets. Card games are also a popular pastime, particularly among civil servants and staff working in the travel services. **Cinemas** are few in number and invariably crowded. Bollywood movies are the most popular, and a few old Hollywood films are also shown. **Video lounges** are quite commonplace in the towns; the latest blockbusters are imported on DVD and shown here, particularly those with a high degree of violence.

Festivals and events

Traditional Bhutanese festivals

The lunar calendar is calculated each year by astrologers versed in Tibetan or Bhutanese astrology. The years are calculated according to a sexagenary cycle rather than in centuries, and each of the 60 years comprising a cycle is named after one of the 12 animals (mouse, ox, tiger, hare, dragon, snake, horse, sheep, monkey, bird, dog and pig), and one of five elements (wood, fire, earth, iron, water) in combination. For example, 2004 is called the wood monkey year. A calendrical year normally contains 12 months, but the addition of an extra intercalary month for astrological reasons is not uncommon. Each lunar month has 30 days but certain days are occasionally doubled or omitted to compensate for discrepancies between the duration of the solar day and the sidereal day. The lunar month runs about two months behind the western calendar.

There are various systems of calendrical reckoning within the Tibeto-Bhutanese world, and these have their origins in different schools of Buddhism. They include the Phakpa system of Sakya, the Old and New Phukpa systems of Central Tibet, the Tsurphu system of the Karmapas, and the Drukpa system, based on the astrology of Drukchen IV Pema Karpo (1527-92). It was this last system that was introduced to Bhutan by Zhabdrung Ngawang Namgyel in the 17th century, but the nuances of the different calculations effectively result in only minor variations. For more detail on this subject see *Tibetan Elemental Divination Paintings* (Eskenazi and Fogg, 2001). The Zhabdrung also introduced an idiosyncratic method of calculating each day of the week.

Many festivals are traditionally held throughout the lunar calendar – some are nationwide and others applicable to a certain area only. They are primarily Buddhist in character, but have incorporated a number of secular elements as well. Major events in the Bhutanese calendar are shown below. The next year's calendar is prepared in the late autumn or winter and only then can the dates be matched to the western calendar. In addition, the 10th day of every month is dedicated to Guru Padmakara who introduced the highest Buddhist teachings from India in the eighth century. The 25th day of each month is a Dakini Day, associated with the female deities who are the agents of Buddha-activity. The 29th day of each month is dedicated to the wrathful doctrinal protector deities, while the 15th and 30th are associated with the Buddha, and the eighth with the Medicine Buddha.

National holidays

There are also a few important national holidays tied to the western or solar calendar. They include the birth and death anniversaries of the third king, Jigme Dorji Wangchuk, which are commemorated respectively on 2 May and 21 July. The coronation of the present king, Jigme Senge Wangchuk, is commemorated on 2 June, and his birthday on 11 November. National Day (commemorating the founding of the monarchy) falls on 17 December, and the Black-necked Crane Festival at Phobjika on 12 November.

Tsechu and drubchen festivals

The *tsechu* and *drubchen* festivals rank among the most important events of the Bhutanese calendar, and they are well-known for their sacred masked dances and pageantry. For a description of the sacred dances of Bhutan, see page 273. Most of these festivals take place in the spring and autumn months, and the dates for the following year's festivals will be calculated in the autumn of the previous year. Listed below are the most important authorised festival dates for late 2004 and tentative dates for 2005. Tour operators are usually sent a list by the Bhutanese Department of Tourism, well ahead of time.

Thimphu Drubchen 8-12 Sep 2005. Tsechu 13-15 Sep 2005.
Paro Tsechu 21-25 Mar 2005.
Chukha Tsechu 18-20 Mar 2005.
Punakha Dromcho 13-17 Feb 2005. Serda 12 Feb 2005.
Wangdu Phodrang Tsechu 11-13 Sep 2005.
Trongsar Tsechu 20-22 Dec 2004, 8-10 Jan 2006.
Bumthang Ura Tsechu 19-23 Apr 2005.

Nyimalung 15-17 Jun 2005. Kurje Tsechu 17 Jun 2005. Tamzhing Phala Chopa 12-14 Sep 2005. Tangbi Manicham 17-19 Sep 2005. Prakhar Tsechu 18-20 Oct 2005. Jampa Lhakhang Drubchen 17-21 Oct 2005. Nalakhar Tsechu 26-28 Nov 2004, 15-17 Dec 2005.
Pemagatsel Tsechu 18-21 Nov 2004, 7-10 Dec 2005.
Mongar Tsechu 18-21 Nov 2004, 7-10 Dec 2005.

Lhuntse Tsechu 20-22 Dec 2004, 8-10 Jan 2006.
Tashigang 18-20 Mar 2005. Tsechu

19-22 Nov 2004, 8-11 Dec 2005.
Tashi Yangtse Chorten Kora 23 Feb and 10 Mar 2005.

43

Shopping

There are 13 traditional forms of arts and crafts in Bhutan, which have been passed down through generations since the 15th century, and which are actively maintained at the present day. They are painting, carpentry, carving and engraving, masonry, sculpture, metal casting and metal work, rattan work, weaving and embroidery, leather-work and paper-making. Consequently, many of the interesting items available in the markets are traditional arts and crafts. ▸▸ *For a more detailed description of the Bhutanese artistic heritage, see below, 263.*

The only opportunities you will have for bargaining will be at the handicraft section of the Changlingmethang weekend market in Thimphu and the roadside stalls on the ascent to Taktsang Viewpoint in Paro. You should know that some artefacts on sale here, including Buddhist images, silver offering bowls and ritual objects, have in fact been imported from Nepal. According to government regulations you cannot export such artefacts without obtaining clearance from the Division of Cultural Properties in Thimphu. The export of antiquities is illegal, and clearance is hard to obtain for most Buddhist statues, whether new or old. ▸▸ *See also Thimphu Shopping, page 80.*

What to buy

Books

Books are available at outlets in Thimphu and Paro. Most publications are in English, Dzongkha, Tibetan, Nepali or Hindi. The National Library has its own bookshop in Thimphu, where texts in the traditional loose-leaf and modern bound format can be purchased. This shop also has a catalogue of published works.

Buddhist artefacts

Ritual objects for sale in the main market places of Thimphu and Paro include traditional loose-leaf style woodblock printed books, offering materials (incense, butter lamps, water-offering bowls, libation cups) and ritual instruments such as bells, vajras, cymbals, shin-bone trumpets (*kangling*), skull-drums, oboes (*gyaling*) and horns (*radong/dongchen*).

Clothing

In Paro, Thimphu and Phuntsoling there are a number of stores selling ready-to-wear Bhutanese garments in traditional patterns. The *gho* worn by men is a loose-fitting coat, similar to a dressing gown, which is tied at the waist by a narrow cumber band (*kera*) and worn knee-length, with a long-sleeved shirt and short pants underneath, and long woollen socks. The *kira*, worn by women, is a tighter fitting garment, secured to the shoulders by a pair of silver brooches and bound at the waist by a wide belt. It is worn ankle-length, with a long-sleeved blouse (*wangju*) underneath and a short-length jacket outside. Formal dress code requires both men and women to wear a ceremonial scarf over the left shoulder. The male version, known as the *kabney*, and the female version, known as the *rachu*, are both made of silk. The colours of the ceremonial scarves worn by men have a particular significance (see page 261).

Silk and cotton scarves (*katak*), usually white in colour but also red, blue, yellow or green, are sold to pilgrims and devotees for offering in temples or to important teachers, as well as to the public for important secular events, including marriage ceremonies, departures and arrivals.

Some intricately woven handmade silk textiles from Kurto in Lhuntse district are very highly priced. Woollen fabrics, best purchased at Zung-ne in the Chu-me valley of Bumthang, are used to make sweaters, blankets and scarves.

Traditional headwear made of bamboo, yak hair, brocade and felt is also for sale. Ready-to-wear monastic robes are available for itinerant monks and nuns.

Crafts

The round bamboo picnic baskets with colourful geometric patterns (*bangchung*) are common. Larger square baskets (*zhim*) are used for trekking and can easily be secured to the back of a pack-animal. Long bamboo cylinders are used for holding alcohol.

Indigenous carpets are made at recently established factories in Phuntsoling and Phobjika. Traditionally, most carpets were imported from Tibet.

Masks similar to those worn by performing monks during the *tsechu* and *drubchen* dances are available in handicraft stores.

The best traditional metalworking forges and foundries in Bhutan are recognised to be in the lower Thimphu valley at Kharbi. Some of the best items available include intricately carved swords and knives with elegant scabbards and hilts, which are almost impossible to export, even in checked baggage, following the events of 9/11. Cast metal images cannot be exported, and the best of these are in any case imported to Bhutan from Patan in Nepal.

Modern painted scrolls (*tangkha*) sewn in brocade are available from the National Handicraft Centre in Thimphu, and other shops. Prices vary according to the size and complexity of the subject, and the larger *tangkhas* can cost in excess of US$500. Generally speaking, it is better to commission a painted scroll from one of the more reputable artists at the National Institute for Traditional Arts & Crafts, in order to ensure that the iconography is accurate (see under Thimphu, page 73). Modern paintings are also available at certain tourist outlets in the capital.

Bhutanese hand-woven cotton, silk and woollen fabrics are for sale at the National Handicraft Emporium and other outlets. Cotton and silk are sold in loom lengths, three of which are used to make a traditional *gho* or *kira*. Woollen fabrics, best purchased at Zung-ne in the Chu-me valley of Bumthang, are sold in lengths known as *yathra*, which are used to make sweaters, blankets and scarves. Machine-manufactured cottons, brocades and silks in traditional designs are imported from India and sold for lower prices than hand-made textiles. Bhutanese raw silk and the blue and red checked cotton are particularly wellknown. Some intricately woven hand-made silk textiles are very highly priced, and find their way into museum collections overseas.

Intricately carved covers for loose-leaf Tibetan books are available. In Eastern Bhutan wood-carvers make large wooden bowls with lids, fashioned sometimes from the gnarl of a single giant avocado tree. Smaller *tsampa* containers with lids and wooden drinking cups inlaid with silver or pewter are among the best buys. Cut wooden moulds for dough-offerings (*zan-par*) may also be of interest, as are square woodblocks used for printing prayer flags. Wooden cabinets, tables and altar shrines carved and brightly painted with traditional motifs are also for sale in the larger towns. Most can be exported in sections for assembly.

Jewellery

Traditional Bhutanese jewellery is similar to Tibetan jewellery, and includes amulet boxes, necklaces, brooches, rings, earrings and hair-ornaments, inset with red coral, blue turquoise or yellow amber stones. Men often prize small ornate cases used for carrying betel nut (*paan* or *doma*). There are a few good outlets in Thimphu but much of the jewellery on sale in the markets is of poor quality or else manufactured in Nepal – particularly the finely worked filigree silver and white metal pieces.

Philately
Attractive and highly prized national stamps are sold at the GPO, Thimphu, and the Philatelic Bureau, Phuntsoling, in sets or presentation albums. There are stamps depicting Buddhist deities, mandalas and historical figures, local flora, fauna and village life, as well as novelty stamps depicting three-dimensional mushrooms and Walt Disney characters, and others that can be played like vinyl records. For further information, contact www.bhutanpost.com.bt.

Photography
The only print film widely available in Bhutan is Konika ASA 100. Kodak and Fuji print film can sometimes be found, but it is best to bring you own supply. If you are taking slides you will have to bring all your own film, and if you are using digital equipment, you will have to bring your own replacement smart cards or memory sticks. Video cartridges for Camcorders are sold at the Sony Shop in Thimphu. Generally speaking, it is prudent to over-compensate by bringing more film than you think you will need.

The larger electrical stores in Thimphu, Paro and Phuntsoling carry an assortment of modern Indian-made electrical goods, including cameras, DVD equipment and televisions.

Prayer flags
Multicoloured sets of prayer flags printed with mantras and protective animals, and fashioned of varying sizes are sold in all the traditional markets. Cheaper and smaller versions of these are also printed on paper for dispersal on mountain passes.

Statues
The best statues for sale in Bhutan are the *cire perdue* images of gilded brass and copper manufactured in Patan in Nepal. These are preferred by locals to the cheaper and less refined yellow brass images that are imported from India. Indigenous metal and clay sculptures are also highly esteemed, but they cannot be exported from the country.

Trekking equipment
Most trekkers will bring their own equipment or rely on equipment supplied by local Bhutanese tour operators. There are no outlets for specialist trekking equipment in Thimphu, selling good-quality tents, boots, sleeping bags, down jackets or trousers.

Sport and activities

Archery
The most popular sport in Bhutan and the one which brings more Bhutanese competitors to the Olympic Games than any other is archery. Archery grounds are found in all the district towns and county villages (*gewok*) of Bhutan, most with long-range wooden targets placed 140 m away from the point of fire. Archers use both the traditional bamboo long bow and the modern carbonite high-velocity crossbow. Weekend competitions take place throughout the country, and they are known for their partisan rivalry. Team-mates and cheer-girls urge on their own side, while loudly and lewdly insulting their opponents. Tournaments are also organised biannually by the **Bhutan National Archery Federation**.

Mountain biking and motor-cycling
Mountain biking can be arduous over long distances because there are many steep passes to cross, but pleasant in the upper Thimphu and Paro valleys. For information on both long and short itineraries, contact the **Bhutan Mountain Biking Club**

(www.bhutanmtb.com). Motor-cycling is exhilarating and sometimes dangerous on the winding mountain roads. Contact **Himalaya Roadrunners** (www.ridehigh.com), who organise motor-cycling tours in Bhutan.

Mountaineering

Bhutan's snow mountains were surveyed in 1964-65 by Michael Ward and Frederic Jackson, who climbed a number of peaks under 6,000 m. Although Bhutan has no 8,000-m peaks, there are 21 above 7,000 m, including the world's highest unclimbed peak, Mount Gangkar Punsum (7,541 m). Mountaineering was only permitted between 1983 and 1994, during which time the Japanese climbed Mount Kulha Gangri (7,239 m) in 1985 and Doug Scott's team climbed Mount Jichu Drakye (6,989 m) in 1988. The sacred Mount Jomolhari was previously climbed from Tibet in 1937 and from the Bhutanese side in 1970. Climbers regard the snow and weather conditions of the Bhutan Himalaya to be among the most treacherous of all. In 1994 the government decided to ban mountaineering above 6,000 m, taking into account both the risks to climbers and the potential desecration of sacred mountain peaks. Trekkers may still climb peaks below 6,000 m without seeking special permission.

Photography

Recommended films: for colour prints, **Fuji HR100** or equivalent, and **Fuji HR1600** for interiors; for colour slides, **Kodak chrome 3 ASA 25** and 64, and **Kodak Tungsten ASA 160** for interiors; for black and white, **Kodak T-max ASA 100** and **Kodak Tri-X** for interiors.

Outdoor photography is free of charge, and there is some spectacular scenery, but be careful not to film members of the royal family or sensitive military installations. Internal photography is not generally permitted within temples, monasteries or *dzongs*, but you may freely film the outside of such buildings. The early mornings and late afternoons usually offer the best conditions for filming, and at other times try under-exposure by half a stop.

An ultra-violet filter or polariser can help reduce the exposure problem caused by high-altitude solar glare. A good wide-angle lens will give the best results when you are filming mountain panoramas; and when filming people or the colourful pageantry of the *tsechu* festivals it will be best to use a non-intrusive telephoto lens, without flash. If you do find yourself taking close-ups, remember to ask permission first, and offer to send copies by post when you return home. If you travel to Bhutan during the rainy season, make sure to protect film against humidity, and at all times try to protect your equipment from dust by using a lens hood and a good camera bag.

There are special rules for commercial filming projects in Bhutan. For details, contact the Department of Tourism.

River rafting and kayaking

There are a few rivers in Bhutan where the Department of Tourism is encouraging rafting and kayaking, ranging in degree of difficulty from Grade 3 to Grade 5. Certain stretches of white water have been designated for rafting or kayaking on the Paro-chu, the Pho-chu and Mo-chu tributaries of the Puna Tsang-chu, which converge at Punakha, as well as on the Dang-chu around Wangdu Podrang, the Mangde-chu in Trongsar, the Chamkhar-chu and Tang-chu in Bumthang, and the Kuri-chu in Lhuntse. For details and costing, contact **Lotus Adventures** in Thimphu (T975-2-322191, equbhu@druknet.bt).

Western sports

Modern **spectator sports** like football, tennis, and basketball have a certain degree of local popularity during the summer and autumn months in particular, but there will be few opportunities for casual visitors to participate. There is a covered swimming pool in Thimphu, and the country also has four **golf** courses, including those in Thimphu, Ha,

Dewathang, and even Jomolhari Base Camp. Golfing trips are organised by the **Bhutan Youth Golf Association** (www.golfbhutan.com). **Fishing** is possible under licence in certain lakes, but generally frowned upon in Buddhist countries such as Bhutan, where the population gain merit by releasing captured fish into the rivers.

Wildlife safari and botany

The **Royal Manas National Park** in southern Bhutan, which is the best area of the country for wildlife observation, has been closed recently on account of the Assamese insurgency movements. The **Black Mountains National Park** in Central Bhutan currently offers the best prospects for bird-watching, and for bears, tigers, wild boar, leopards and red pandas. Other wildlife sanctuaries in Eastern Bhutan include those of Bomdeling (in Tashi Yangtse), Sakteng (in Tashigang), Thrumshing La (in Mongar) and Khaling (in Samdrub Jongkhar). In the west of the country there is the **Jigme Dorji National Park** (in Gasa, Punakha, Thimphu and Paro), and the **Torsa Strict Nature Reserve** (in Ha). The **Phibsoo Wildlife Sanctuary** (in Sarpang) is the country's largest area of natural sal forest, and Sakteng is an important reserve for rhododendrons. For further details of wildlife sanctuaries in Bhutan, see page 258.

Trekking

The main recreational pursuit that attracts travellers to Bhutan is trekking. Northern Bhutan and even some sub-tropical parts of the south offer great scope for trekking since forests and high-altitude pastures make up most of the country, and some of these remote areas are even now only accessible on foot or horseback. There are no roads, and villages are few and far between. Trekking conditions are very different from those in Nepal, where the travel agencies have had many years' experience at organising treks and where the routes have often been over-trekked. With Bhutan's small, scattered population you might trek for hours, and sometimes days, without seeing a single house, and only passing the odd person with pack animals along the track. Somewhat like trekking in Tibet, Bhutan still offers the prospect of an original, fresh experience off the beaten track – some of the trails are old, disused trade routes dating from the period when the Tibet–Bhutan border could easily be crossed, or before the construction of the lateral highway. The trails are more precipitous than in Nepal, and physically exacting because you will constantly be climbing or descending steep inclines. Most treks start around 2,400 m and generally ascend to 4,000 m quite rapidly. As on the Kawa Karpo pilgrimage circuit in south-east Tibet, there is very little open space for camping, and you will frequently have to trek seven to nine hours per day to reach a suitable clearing. The trails are not always well mapped or well defined, so it is easy to lose one's way. High-altitude rescue is non-existent. It is therefore essential to trek with a reliable local guide.

Campsites and pack animals

There are no tea-houses or lodges where trekkers can stay overnight, with welcoming thermoses of hot water. In the countryside the Bhutanese are fully occupied tending animals and working in the fields and they do not have time, or the need, to take in guests – the traces of fire camps in rocky shelters provide ample proof of this. Because of the inaccessibility of most of the countryside, people are reluctant to sell any food since a shop could be three days' walk away. In remote areas, barter is a standard mode of exchange; salt or edible oil are more likely to see eggs materialise than a bank-note. It is therefore essential to have tents and provisions.

You are advised to bring your own sleeping bag and trekking gear (see below for a check-list), and you will have to carry a small backpack with your water bottle, camera and other essential items. Tour operators provide full camping support for the duration

Trekking seasons in Bhutan

	Jan	Feb	Mar	Apr	May
Druk Path	✗	✗	✓✓	✓✓	✓✓
Jomolhari Trek I	✗	✗	✓✓	✓✓	✓✓
Laya/Gasa	✗	✗	✗	✓✓	✓✓
Gasa Hot Springs	✓✓	✓✓	✓✓	✓✓	✓✓
Dagala Thousand Lakes	✗	✗	✓✓	✓✓	✓✓
Snowman	✗	✗	✓✓	✓	✓✓
Samtengang	✓✓	✓✓	✓✓	✓✓	✓✓
Gangteng	✓✓	✓✓	✓✓	✓✓	✓✓
Bumthang Cultural	✗	✗	✓✓	✓✓	✓✓
Dur Hot Spring	✗	✗	✓✓	✓✓	✓

✓✓ A good season for trekking.
✓   A moderate season – there are chances of rain during the trek in these months.
✗   The months when trekking is closed due to snow.

of the trek: two-person tents with foam mats, dining and toilet tents, and three hot meals daily. Lunch is usually pre-cooked in the morning, stored in hot-cases and served during a brief halt in the middle of the day. In addition to your local trekking guide and cook, you will have campsite assistants or waiters, and muleteers or yak-men responsible for the pack animals. All the equipment will be transported by pack animals, not by porters –the economy is not dependent on tourism and so the Bhutanese do not hire themselves as porters. Since the trekking months coincide with the busy agricultural season, the owners of pack animals have to be contacted in advance, and then flattered and cajoled before they agree to participate. Also, in the course of a trek, the pack animals will be changed when crossing district frontiers.

The fast mountain streams are crossed by ingenious log or liana and split bamboo bridges, while wider rivers may have more substantial wooden ones – often protected by prayer flags. In the 15th century Tangtong Gyelpo (see box, page 104) built a series of iron chain bridges. The chains were often made in Bhutan, using a small quantity of arsenic to reduce the melting point of iron, and transported great distances. Over 50 such bridges were erected throughout the Himalayan region. Some of them had nine lengths of chain suspended to form the frame of a bridge which would then be tied with wire and have matting placed underfoot.

Ecological issues

The government and the Department of Tourism in particular are responsible for implementing an ecologically oriented trekking programme, ensuring that trekkers and their crews do not litter the still pristine environment. Many treks also take place in the national parks, such as the Jigme Dorje Wangchuk Sanctuary (7,813 sq km), which occupies the north-western belt of the country. Here conservation of flora and fauna is the responsibility of the Royal Society for the Protection of Nature. All trekkers and visitors are advised to follow the Himalayan Code of Practice (see page 35). Support crews should carry all necessary fuel for cooking, but in practice you will find that local yak-men and muleteers still gather wood for camp-fires. Latrines should be dug whenever a camp is set up and refilled whenever the camp is broken up. Used toilet paper that cannot be buried should be burnt, and other garbage should be

Jun	Jul	Aug	Sep	Oct	Nov	Dec
✓✓	✓	✓	✓✓	✓✓	✓✓	✕
✓✓	✓	✓	✓✓	✓✓	✓✓	✕
✓✓	✓	✓	✓✓	✓✓	✕	✕
✓	✓	✓	✓	✓✓	✓✓	✓✓
✓✓	✓	✓	✓✓	✓✓	✕	✕
✓✓	✓✓	✓✓	✓	✕	✕	✕
✓✓	✓	✓	✓	✓✓	✓✓	✓✓
✓✓	✓	✓	✓✓	✓✓	✓✓	✓✓
✓✓	✓	✓	✓✓	✓✓	✓✓	✕
✓	✓	✓	✓✓	✓✓	✓✓	✕

carried along to the end of the trek. Try to be mindful of the need for conservation of the local environment, even if the crew sometimes set a bad example themselves!

Trekking season

The climate is much wetter in Bhutan than it is in Tibet and even in Nepal. Therefore the trekking season is much shorter and for some high-altitude treks choosing a period between snow and rain can be difficult. The best months are March-April and October-November. However if you wish to see alpine flowers at their best you will have to travel during the wet season (July-August) when trails are muddy and leeches abound, particularly below 2,000 m. High passes are snow-bound in the winter months, from late November until early March. While trekking in autumn, the optimum time of year, the temperature will fluctuate from the high 20s to -10°C. Spring is the best time if you want to see the dazzling variety of rhododendrons. The table on page 48 shows the optimum period for each of the best known treks in Bhutan.

Trekking in Bhutan is logistically complicated because it is still a wild country. However, tour operators here know the problems well; they will help you with the choice of trek and the season, taking into account your own preferences and physical fitness.

Trekking equipment

Since tour operators will guarantee to provide full camping and trekking support, you will not have to bring your own tents, ground mats or food (unless you need specialist equipment). Nonetheless there are certain items that you will have to carry with you from home. Careful preparation is required for trekking in Bhutan. You don't want to carry anything more than what is essential. Various trekking items can be purchased or hired cheaply in Kathmandu, Bangkok and other gateway cities, but there are no specialist shops in Thimphu. You should carry your luggage in a zip-fastening, preferably waterproof, duffel bag or hold-all, which will be carried on the back of a pack animal, and keep your immediate necessities in a small knapsack, or shoulder bag (camera bag). Trekking gear should be kept down to about 15 kg, which is an ideal weight for pack animals.

⁝ Choosing a trek

	Start point	End point	Duration
Druk Path	Paro-Dopshare	Thimphu-Motithang	6 days
Jomolhari Trek I	Paro-Drukgyel	Thimphu-Dodina	10 days
Laya/Gasa	Paro-Drukgyel	Punakha-Tashithang	15 days
Gasa Hot Springs	Punakha-Tashithang	Punakha-Tashithang	5 days
Dagala Thousand Lakes	Thimphu-Chudzom	Thimphu-Simtokha	6 days
Snowman	Paro-Drukgyel	Trongsa-Sephu/ Nikachu	24 days
Samtengang	Punakha-Punakha Dzong	Wangdu-Chudzomsa	4 days
Gangteng	Gangtey-Phobjikha	Wangdu-Tikke Zampa	3 days
Bumthang Cultural	Bumthang-Toktu Zampa	Bumthang-Mesithang	3 days
Dur Hot Spring	Bumthang-Toktu Zampa	Bumthang-Toktu Zampa	8 days

Bedding You will need to bring your own sleeping bag, suitable for all weather conditions (at least three-season quality and preferably four-season quality). A cotton or silk inset sheet sleeping bag and hot water bottle will be useful if above 4,000 m.

Clothing The weather will be warm to hot during the day and can be cool to freezing at night, and is often dusty and windy depending on the location and season. The low-lying valleys can be quite hot and you may sweat profusely while ascending the many ridges and passes. At higher elevations (4,500-5,500 m), the dry atmosphere stops perspiration and trekking can become easier, despite the thinner air and slow progress. Because the temperatures in Bhutan are subject to extreme fluctuations you need to think in terms of 'layered clothing' that you can peel off and put on with ease.

The following items of clothing are essential, particularly if you will be trekking above 4,000 m: long thermal underwear (silk, cotton or wool), several short-sleeved sweat-shirts or T-shirts (polypropylene or cotton), two or three cotton shirts with pockets, swimming costume (for hot springs and outdoor bathing), hiking shorts with pockets (for men only), long trekking trousers (possibly one heavy, one light-weight), long skirts or *chubas* (essential for women), waterproof and windproof trousers, lightweight wool sweaters (at least two, one to be worn over the other), fleece jacket, down or fibre-filled jacket, poncho or waterproof jacket, scarf or cravat, handkerchiefs, sun-hat, sun glasses, wool hat or balaclava, gloves, several pairs of hiking socks (wool or polypropylene), comfortable walking shoes or boots (waterproof boots required for trekking in snow, be sure to wear them in first), light sandals or canvas shoes, and gaiters (to keep boots and socks mud-free and leech-free). In general, Gore-tex is recommended for both walking boots and trekking clothes.

Toiletries You will have to carry soap, shampoo, shaving cream, toothpaste, a bar of washing soap for laundry, dental floss, wet wipes, sunscreen, lip-salve, insect repellent, contact lens cleaning fluid, face cream, disinfectant, tampons and toilet paper. A small first-aid kit will also be useful, and you should keep plasters or elastoplast for blisters in your knapsack for immediate use.

Minimum extra days	Rating	Maximum elevation/Place
4 days	Moderate	4,210m/Phume La
4 days	Moderate	4,890m/Nyile La
4 days	Strenuous	5,005m/Sinche La
6 days	Mild	2,430m
4 days	Moderate	4,500m/ Labatamba-Panka
7 days	Strenuous	5,140m/Rinchen Zoe La
6 days	Moderate	1,500m
6 days	Mild	3,440m/Tsele La
7 days	Mild	3,360m/Phepe La
7 days	Moderate	4,700m/Juli La

Other useful items In addition to the duffel bag and knap-sack already mentioned, you will need stuff-bags or plastic garbage bags to protect your luggage from the rain, a folding umbrella, a strong torch or head-lamp with extra alkaline batteries, an adjustable hiking pole, a screw-top water bottle with water purification tabs and rehydration powders, a waterproof pouch or belt for money and passport, a Swiss-army knife with bottle opener/corkscrew attachments, as well as a can opener, scissors, sewing kit, cigarette lighter and trowel (for burning used toilet paper and burying excrement), and pocket-size screwdriver.

Dietary supplements Although organised treks will have a Bhutanese cook to prepare main meals, you may prefer to carry some supplements to vary the diet. Some people like to carry freeze-dried meals, and instant soups are particularly welcome at higher elevations. You can bring your own tea, coffee or energising drink, as well as high-energy muesli bars, chocolate, beef jerky, fresh cheese, pâté, meusli and so forth.

Choosing a trek

Currently there are 13 designated trekking routes in Bhutan being promoted by the Department of Tourism. The table on above shows the number of days, the overall trekking distance, the maximum elevation and degree of difficulty for 10 of the better known treks. For a detailed outline of each of the treks, readers can usually refer to the description of the districts in which they respectively begin. For example, the Druk Path and Jomolhari treks are described under Paro district, the Samtengang trek under Punakha, the Gangteng trek under Wangdu Podrang, and the Bumthang Cultural and Dur Hot Springs treks under Bumthang, The exceptions are the few longer treks which pass through several districts in the Tibet–Bhutan border area. Among them, the Rodang La trek is described under Bumthang and Lhuntse, the Laya/Gasa trek under Thimphu and Gasa, and the Snowman trek under Paro, Gasa and Wangdu Podrang. There are a number of tour operators leading treks in Bhutan. These are listed under Thimphu, and a few recommended operators are listed on page 15.

Referring to the table above, the treks have been rated as Strenuous, Moderate and Mild. The factor used for determining each class is the duration of the trek. Other factors such as the vegetation, altitude, the several uphill and downhill hikes each day have not been considered as they are similar on most of the treks. On an average day you will be walking for six to seven hours and the number of days spent hiking is represented in the Duration column. The number of extra days needed apart from the actual trek days for sightseeing, acclimatising and driving before or after the trek is represented in the Minimum Extra Days column.

Health

Local populations in Bhutan are exposed to a range of health risks not encountered in the West. Despite the fact that most of the area lies geographically within the Temperate Zone, the climate is occasionally tropical in, for example, the Himalayan foothills bordering the Duars. Insects can be a great nuisance in these areas and some are carriers of serious diseases such as malaria, dengue fever, filariasis and various worm infections. The central hills and rain forests also abound with leeches during the monsoon months. Much of the country is economically underdeveloped, so infectious diseases still predominate in a way that has not been usual in the West for some decades. There is an obvious difference in health risks for travellers who stay in relatively comfortable hotels in Paro or Thimphu as opposed to those who venture into remote rural areas, whether driving or trekking on foot. If you are apprehensive, make local enquiries about health risks and take the general advice of western families who have lived in the area.

The health care in the region is varied. There are some well-qualified doctors and many of them do speak English, but the quality and range of medical care diminishes very rapidly as you move away from the main urban centres. There are traditions of medicine wholly different from the western model, and you may be confronted with unusual modes of treatment such as herbal medicine, moxabustion and acupuncture. At least you can be sure that local practitioners have a lot of experience treating the particular diseases of their region. If you are in one of the neighbouring gateway cities, it may be worthwhile asking your embassy or consulate to provide a list of recommended doctors. Providing embassies with information of your whereabouts can be also useful if a friend/relative gets ill at home and there is a desperate search for you around the globe. You can also ask them about locally recommended medical dos and don'ts. If you do get ill and you have the opportunity, check with your medical insurer whether the medical centre or hospital to which you have been referred is of a suitable standard.

Before you go

Ideally, you should see your GP or travel clinic at least six weeks before your departure for general advice on travel risks, malaria and vaccinations. Take out medical insurance and make sure it covers all eventualities, especially evacuation to your home country by a medically equipped plane if necessary. Get a dental check (especially if you are going to be away for more than a month), obtain a spare glasses prescription, a spare oral contraceptive prescription (or enough pills to last), know your own blood group, and if you suffer a long-term condition such as diabetes or epilepsy, arrange for a check up with your doctor and make sure that you have a Medic Alert bracelet/necklace with this information on it. Consult your doctor before departure and ensure that you bring adequate supplies of any necessary prescribed drug. Start your anti-malarial medication, if required (see below). If you are visiting

doctor and that you prepare for the physical demands of your trip by undertaking some exercise each day (walking, swimming or jogging).

Recommended vaccinations
No vaccinations are required for Bhutan, although the following are recommended.

Polio	yes, if none in last 10 years.
Tetanus	yes, if you haven't had one in the last 10 years (after five doses you have had enough for life).
Diptheria	yes, if none in last 10 years.
Typhoid	yes, if nil in last three years.
Hepatitis A	yes, as the disease can be caught easily from food/water.
Rabies	yes, if you are trekking off the beaten track.
Japanese Encephalitis	may need to be considered, depending on the duration of your trip and proximity to farming.

There is no requirement for immunisation against yellow fever unless you are travelling from an infected area (parts of Central Africa or Latin America).

What to take

If you are visiting very remote areas, it becomes more important to ensure that you have all the necessary first-aid items, especially for trekking trips. You may want to bring a supply of antacid tablets, antiseptic ointment, band aid and corn plasters, disinfectant wipes, disposable gloves, fungicidal powder for feet, iron supplements, rehydration salts, tablets for travel sickness, vitamins and water-sterilising tablets. For longer trips, a clean needle pack, clean dental pack and water filtration devices are common-sense measures. For other useful items, see page 49.

Anti-malarial medication The malaria risk in Bhutan is in the southern belt of five districts: Tsirang, Samtse, Samdrub Jongkhar, Sarpang, and Zhemgang. Specialist advice is required as to which type to take. General principles are that all except Malarone should be continued for four weeks after leaving the malarial area. Malarone needs to be continued for only seven days afterwards (if a tablet is missed or vomited seek specialist advice). The start times for the anti-malarials vary in that if you have never taken Lariam (Mefloquine) before it is advised to start it at least two to three weeks before the entry to a malarial zone (this is to help identify serious side-effects early). Chloroquine and Paludrine are often started a week before trip to establish a pattern, but Doxycycline and Malarone can be started only one to two days before entry to the malarial area.

It is risky to buy medicinal tablets abroad because the doses may differ and there may be a trade in false drugs.

Ciproxin (Ciprofloxacin) A useful antibiotic for some forms of traveller's diarrhoea.

Immodium A great standby for those diarrhoeas that occur at awkward times (ie before a long coach/train journey or on a trek). It helps stop the flow of diarrhoea and in my view is of more benefit than harm. (It was believed that letting the bacteria or viruses flow out had to be more beneficial. However, with Immodium they still come out, just in a more solid form.)

MedicAlert These simple bracelets, or an equivalent, should be carried or worn by anyone with a significant medical condition.

Mosquito repellents Remember that DEET (Di-ethyltoluamide) is the gold standard. Apply the repellent every four to six hours but more often if you are sweating heavily. If a non-DEET product is used check who tested it. Validated products (tested at the

include Mosiguard, Non-DEET Jungle Formula and non-DEET Autan. If you want to use citronella remember that it must be applied very frequently (ie hourly) to be effective. If you are a popular target for insect bites or develop lumps quite soon after being bitten, carry an Aspivenin kit. This syringe suction device is available from many chemists and draws out some of the allergic materials and provides quick relief.

Painkillers Paracetamol or a suitable painkiller can have multiple uses for symptoms but remember that more than eight paracetamol a day can lead to liver failure. Paracetamol is readily available in Bhutan.

Pepto-Bismol Used a lot by Americans for diarrhoea. It certainly relieves symptoms, but like Immodium it is not a cure for the underlying disease. Be aware that it turns the stool black as well as making it more solid.

Sterile needles Bhutan's larger hospitals and medical centres do not seem to have any shortage of sterile, single-use needles but, to be safe, you should bring your own supply; the standard 'green' size are the most versatile.

Sun screen The Australians have a great campaign, which has reduced skin cancer. It is called Slip, Slap, Slop. Slip on a shirt, Slap on a hat, Slop on sun screen.

On the road

When trekking in Bhutan, remember that the Himalayas are very high, very cold, very remote and potentially very dangerous. Do not travel there alone, when you are ill or if you are poorly equipped. Telephone communication can be non-existent in some areas, making mountain rescue extremely difficult.

Altitude sickness

Symptoms Altitude sickness at higher elevations is the commonest ailment travellers face in Bhutan. Acute mountain sickness can strike from about 3,000 m upwards and in general is more likely to affect those who ascend rapidly (for example by plane) and those who over-exert themselves. Teenagers are particularly prone. On reaching heights above 3,000 m, heart pounding and shortness of breath, especially on exertion, are almost universal and a normal response to the lack of oxygen in the air. Acute mountain sickness takes a few hours or days to come on and presents with headache, lassitude, dizziness, loss of appetite, nausea and vomiting. Insomnia is common and often associated with a suffocating feeling when lying down in bed. You may notice that your breathing tends to wax and wane at night and your face is puffy in the mornings – this is all part of the syndrome.

Cures If the symptoms are mild, the treatment is rest, painkillers (preferably not aspirin-based) for the headaches and anti-sickness pills for vomiting. Oxygen may help at very high altitudes but is only likely to be available in Bhutan on the most organized trekking tours. Should the symptoms be severe and prolonged it is best to descend to a lower altitude immediately and reascend, if necessary, slowly and in stages. The symptoms disappear very quickly with even a few 100 m of descent.

There is a further, albeit rare, hazard due to rapid ascent to high altitude – a kind of complicated mountain sickness presenting as acute pulmonary oedema or acute cerebral oedema. Both conditions are more common the higher you go. Pulmonary oedema comes on quite rapidly with breathlessness, noisy breathing, cough, blueness of the lips and frothing at the mouth. Cerebral oedema usually presents with confusion, going on to unconsciousness. Anybody developing these serious conditions must be brought down to low altitude as soon as possible and taken to hospital.

Other problems experienced at high altitude are hypothermia (see page 56), sunburn (see page 57), excessively dry air causing coughs, skin cracking, sore eyes (it may be wise to leave your contact lenses out) and sore nostrils or nose bleeds. You are advised to carry throat lozenges and an expectorant for dry coughs, as well as an effective lip-salve with a high SPF.

Prevention The best way of preventing acute mountain sickness is a relatively slow ascent. When trekking to high altitude, some time spent walking at medium altitude, getting fit and getting adapted, is beneficial. On arrival at places over 3,000 m, a few hours' rest and the avoidance of alcohol, cigarettes and heavy food will go a long way towards preventing acute mountain sickness. You are advised to drink plenty of fluids throughout your stay. You should have a daily intake of 4 litres at high altitude and keep your water bottle full and handy at all times. It is important to pace yourself when trekking; move slowly and in a relaxed manner to minimise discomfort. Do not ascend to high altitude if you are pregnant, if you have a history of heart, lung or blood disease, or if you are suffering from a bad cold or chest infection. Never ascend to high altitude in the 24 hours following scuba diving.

Avian flu and SARS
There is the possibility that avian flu or SARS might rear its head in Bhutan. Check the news reports and, if there is a problem in an area you are to visit, seek expert advice.

Dengue fever
Unfortunately there is no vaccine against this, and the mosquitoes that carry it bite during the day. You will feel like a mule has kicked you for two to three days, you will then get better for a few days and then feel that the mule has kicked you again. It should all be over in seven to 10 days. Heed all the anti-mosquito measures that you can.

Diarrhoea and intestinal upset
Although the dry and sunny atmosphere and low population density in Bhutan mean that bacteria are not as plentiful and as virulent as at lower altitudes in Nepal, India and China, you will be lucky not to experience diarrhoea or intestinal upset at some point during your stay. One study showed that up to 70% of all travellers may suffer during their trip.

Symptoms Diarrhoea can refer either to loose stools or an increased frequency; both of these can be a nuisance. It should be short lasting, but persistence beyond two weeks, with blood or pain, requires specialist medical attention.

Cures Ciproxin (Ciprofloaxcin) is a useful antibiotic for bacterial traveller's diarrhoea. It can be obtained by private prescription in the UK. You need to take one 500 mg tablet when the diarrhoea starts and if you do not feel better in 24 hours, the diarrhoea is likely to have a non-bacterial cause and may be viral (in which case there is little you can do apart from keep yourself hydrated and wait for it to settle on its own). The key treatment with all diarrhoeas is rehydration. Try to keep hydrated by taking the right mixture of salt and water. This is available as Oral Rehydration Salts (ORS) in ready-made sachets or can be made up by adding a teaspoon of sugar and a half teaspoon of salt to a litre of clean water. Drink at least one large cup of this drink for each loose stool. You can also use, flat carbonated drinks as an alternative. Immodium and Pepto-Bismol provide symptomatic relief.

Prevention The standard advice is to be careful with water and ice for drinking. Ask yourself where the water came from. Tap water may be unsafe, especially after heavy rain. If you have any doubts then boil it or filter and treat it. There are many filter/treatment devices now available on the market. Food can also transmit disease. Be wary of salads (what were they washed in, who handled them), re-heated foods or food that has been left out in the sun having been cooked earlier in the day. There is a simple adage that says wash it, peel it, boil it or forget it. Also be wary of unpasteurised dairy products, which can transmit a range of diseases from brucellosis (fevers and constipation), to listeria (meningitis) and tuberculosis of the gut (obstruction, constipation, fevers and weight loss).

Hepatitis

Symptoms Hepatitis means inflammation of the liver. Viral causes of the disease can be acquired anywhere in the world. The most obvious symptom is a yellowing of your skin or the whites of your eyes. However, prior to this all that you may notice is itching and tiredness.

Cures Early on, depending on the type of hepatitis, a vaccine or immunoglobulin may reduce the duration of the illness.

Prevention Pre-travel hepatitis A vaccine is the best bet. Hepatitis B (for which there is a vaccine) is spread through blood and unprotected sexual intercourse, both of which can be avoided. Unfortunately there is no vaccine for hepatitis C or the increasing alphabetical list of other hepatitis viruses.

Hypothermia

Remember that, especially in the mountains, there can be a large and sudden drop in temperature between sun and shade and between night and day, so dress accordingly. Loose-fitting cotton clothes are the best for hot weather. To avoid hypothermia, which is when your core temperature falls below 35°C, several layers of suitable clothing, including warm jackets and woollens, are essential, especially after dark at high altitude. If you feel cold, move about rather than standing still.

Leptospirosis

Various forms of leptospirosis occur throughout the world, transmitted by a bacterium which is excreted in rodent urine. Fresh water and moist soil harbour the organisms, which enter the body through cuts and scratches. Leptospirosis is most common in rural areas, in proximity to farming and animal-raising activities during warmer months. Urban disease may occur in areas of rodent infestation. If you suffer from any form of prolonged fever consult a doctor.

Malaria

Malaria is not prevalent in the mid-mountain belt of Bhutan, but you should take advice from a travel clinic if you are visiting Southern Bhutan, or travelling there via India, Nepal, Thailand or Bangladesh where you may be subject to some risk. Anti-malarial medication is recommended for low-lying sub-tropical areas of the south and east during the rainy season. Insect repellent is essential.

Symptoms Malaria can cause death within 24 hours. It can start as something resembling an attack of flu. You may feel tired, lethargic, headachy, feverish; or more seriously, develop fits, followed by coma and then death. Have a low index of suspicion because it is very easy to write off vague symptoms, which may actually be malaria. If you have a temperature, go to a doctor as soon as you can and ask for a malaria test. On your return home if you suffer any of these symptoms, get tested as soon as possible. Even if any previous test had proved negative, the test could save your life.

Cures Treatment is with drugs and could be oral or into a vein depending on the seriousness of the infection. Always remember ABCD: Awareness (of whether the disease is present in the area you are travelling in), Bite avoidance, Chemoprohylaxis and Diagnosis.

Prevention This is best summarized by the B and C of the ABCD: bite avoidance and chemoprophylaxis. Wear clothes that cover arms and legs and use effective insect repellents in areas with known risks of insect-spread disease. Use a mosquito net dipped in permethrin as both a physical and chemical barrier at night in the same areas. Guard against the contraction of malaria with the correct anti-malarials (see above). Some would prefer to take test kits for malaria with them and have standby treatment available. However, the field tests of the blood kits have had poor results: when you have malaria you are usually too ill to be able to do the tests correctly enough to make the right diagnosis. Standby treatment

(treatment that you carry and take yourself for malaria) should still ideally be supervised by a doctor since the drugs themselves can be toxic if taken incorrectly. Note that the Royal Homeopathic Hospital in the UK does not advocate homeopathic options for malaria prevention or treatment.

Rabies

Although it is less endemic than in other countries in the region, such as India, rabies is present in Bhutan. Recently, the Thimphu Valley, in particular, has been experiencing increased incidence of rabies because of the growing number of stray dogs. Avoid dogs that are behaving strangely. If you are bitten by a domestic or wild animal, do not leave things to chance: scrub the wound with soap and water and/or disinfectant, try to at least determine the animal's ownership, where possible, and seek medical assistance at once. The course of treatment depends on whether you have already been satisfactorily vaccinated against rabies. If you have (this is worthwhile if you are spending lengths of time in developing countries) then some further doses of vaccine are all that is required. If not already vaccinated then anti-rabies serum (immunoglobulin) may be required in addition. It is important to finish the course of treatment.

Respiratory problems

Apart from altitude sickness, the major irritant to health in northern Bhutan is the dryess of the atmosphere, which can cause respiratory problems. These are common, perhaps made worse by temperature and climatic changes and the proximity of Bhutan to the densely populated Indian plains. You are advised to carry throat lozenges and an expectorant for dry coughs.

Sexual health

The range of visible and invisible diseases is awesome. Unprotected sex can spread HIV, hepatitis B and C, gonorrhoea (green discharge), chlamydia (nothing to see but may cause painful urination and later female infertility), painful recurrent herpes, syphilis and warts, just to name a few. You can cut down the risk by using condoms, a femidom or avoiding sex altogether.

Skin rashes

Prickly heat is a very common, intensely itchy rash that can be avoided by frequent washing and by wearing loose clothing. It is cured by allowing skin to dry off (through use of powder and spending two nights in an air-conditioned hotel!). Rashes can also be caused by bed bugs and lice, which are commonly found in the bedding in truck stops.

Sun protection

Symptoms The burning power of the sun is phenomenal, especially at high altitudes. White Britons are notorious for becoming red because they like to stay out longer than everyone else and do not use adequate sun protection. This can lead to sunburn, which is painful and followed by flaking of skin. Aloe vera gel is a good pain reliever for sunburn. Long-term sun damage leads to a loss of elasticity of skin and the development of pre-cancerous lesions. Years later a mild or a very malignant form of cancer may develop. The milder basal cell carcinoma, if detected early, can be treated by cutting it out or freezing it. The much nastier malignant melanoma may have already spread to bone and brain at the time that it is first noticed. Glare from the sun can also cause conjunctivitis so wear sunglasses, especially near the snowline.

Prevention Sun screen. SPF stands for Sun Protection Factor. It is measured by determining how long a given person takes to 'burn' with and without the sun screen product on. So, if it takes 10 times longer to burn with the sunscreen product applied, then that product has an SPF of 10. If it only takes twice as long then the SPF is 2. The higher the SPF the greater the protection. However, do not use higher factors just in order to stay out in the sun longer. 'Flash frying' (desperate bursts of excessive exposure), as it is called, is known to increase the risks of skin cancer. As well as wearing sun screen, always a sun hat and a shirt.

Ticks

Ticks usually attach themselves to the lower parts of the body, and are often noticed after walking in areas where cattle have grazed. They take a while to attach themselves strongly, but swell up as they start to suck blood. The important thing is to remove them gently, so that they do not leave their head parts in your skin because this can cause a nasty allergic reaction some days later. Do not use petrol, vaseline, lighted cigarettes etc to remove the tick, but, with a pair of tweezers remove it gently by gripping it at the attached (head) end and rock it out in very much the same way that a tooth is extracted.

Water

There are a number of ways of purifying water. Dirty water should first be strained through a filter bag and then boiled or treated. Bringing water to a rolling boil at sea level is sufficient to make the water safe for drinking, but at higher altitudes you have to boil the water for a few minutes longer to ensure all microbes are killed. There are sterilising methods that can be used and there are proprietary preparations containing chlorine (eg Puritabs) or iodine (eg Pota Aqua) compounds. Chlorine compounds generally do not kill protozoa (eg giardia). There are a number of water filters now on the market available in personal and expedition size. They work either on mechanical or chemical principles, or may do both. Make sure you take the spare parts or spare chemicals with you.

Further information

Websites

Foreign and Commonwealth Office (FCO) (UK), www.fco.gov.uk This is a key travel advice site, with useful information on the country, people, climate, and lists the UK embassies/consulates. The site also promotes the concept of 'Know Before You Go' and encourages travel insurance and travel health advice. It has links to the Department of Health travel advice site, see below.

Department of Health Travel Advice (UK), www.doh.gov.uk/traveladvice This excellent site is also available as a free booklet, the T6, from post offices. It lists the vaccine advice requirements for each country.

Medic Alert (UK), www.medicalalert. co.uk This is the website of the foundation that produces bracelets and necklaces for those with existing medical problems. Once you have ordered your bracelet/necklace you write your key medical details on paper inside it, so that if you collapse, a medical person can identify you as someone with epilepsy or allergy to peanuts etc.

Blood Care Foundation (UK), www.bloodcare.org.uk The Blood Care Foundation is a Kent-based charity "dedicated to the provision of screened blood and resuscitation fluids in countries where these are not readily available". They will dispatch certified non-infected blood of the right type to your hospital/clinic. The blood is flown in from various centres around the world.

The Health Protection Agency, www.hpa.org.uk This site has up-to-date malaria advice guidelines for travel around the world. It gives specific advice about the right drugs for each location. It also has useful information for those who are pregnant, suffering from epilepsy or planning to travel with children.

World Health Organisation, www.who.int The WHO site has links to the WHO Blue Book on travel advice. This lists the diseases in different regions of the world. It describes vaccination schedules and makes clear which countries have Yellow Fever Vaccination certificate requirements and malarial risk.

Fit for Travel (UK), www.fitfortravel.scot
.nhs.uk This site from Scotland provides a
quick A-Z of vaccine and travel health advice
requirements for each country.
British Travel Health Association (UK),
www.btha.org This is the official website of
an organisation of travel health professionals.
Travel Screening Services (UK),
www.travelscreening.co.uk This is the
author's website. A private clinic dedicated
to integrated travel health. The clinic gives
vaccine, travel health advice, email and SMS
text vaccine reminders, and screens returned
travellers for tropical diseases.

Books

The Travellers Good Health Guide, Dr Ted
Lankester, ISBN 0-85969-827-0.
*Expedition Medicine (The Royal Geographic
Society)*, David Warrell and Sarah Anderson
(eds) ISBN 1-86197-040-4.
International Travel and Health, World Health
Organisation Geneva ISBN 92-4-158026 7.
The World's Most Dangerous Places, Robert
Young Pelton, Coskun Aral and Wink Dulles
ISBN 1-566952-140-9.

Keeping in touch

Communications

Internet

The national internet service provider Druknet (**www.druknet.bt**) has been
functioning since 1999, and you will have to register with Druknet to log on. There are
internet cafés in Thimphu and other towns, such as Paro, Phuntsoling, Jakar and
Tashigang, but they are not yet as universal as they have become in India and SE Asia
in recent years. Hotels and restaurants will often offer internet facilities. As elsewhere,
this has become the most inexpensive form of communication, and the rates are very
competitive, averaging Nu 3-5 per hour.

If you intend to take an address book, do leave a duplicate at home in case of
loss or water damage, or, better still, open a free email account and mail the
information to yourself before leaving home.

Post

The **Bhutan Postal Service**, introduced as recently as 1962, covers most of the
country. Some Bhutanese postage stamps have become collectors' items (see page
45). There is a regular mail service and an EMS express mail service, which is quite
effective. If you use the ordinary service, you should allow at least two weeks for
delivery to Australia and Europe and longer for the Americas. The EMS service is
cheaper than couriers such as DHL. Postage stamps for letters and postcards are
widely available in the Bhutan Post offices in larger towns, and also in the main
tourist hotels of Thimphu and Paro. Some hotels also provide post box facilities.
Larger packages should preferably be mailed from Thimphu – the shop where you
make your purchases will be able to assist, but hold on to all receipts. Air mail and sea
mail options are both possible.

Stamps for postcards cost Nu 3 to neighbouring countries of the subcontinent
and Nu 20 to all other countries. Stamps for letters posted to destinations within the
subcontinent cost Nu 4 and Nu 20 for all other destinations (max. 20 g). Parcels
(maximum 30 kg) sent by surface mail begin at Nu 266 to the UK and Nu 398 to the
USA for a 1 kg parcel; and Nu 266 to UK or Nu 398 to USA for a 1 kg airmail parcel. EMS
rates to the UK and the USA are Nu 900 for a 500g letter, and Nu 1,000 for a 500g
packet, and to India Nu 350 and Nu 250 respectively.

‎ Telephone codes

→ **IDD**: 975
→ **International access code**: 00
→ **Area codes**: Thimphu (02); Punakha (02); Bumthang (03); Trongsar (03); Mongar (04); Lhuntse (04); Tashigang (04); Tashi Yangtse (04); Phuntsoling (05); Sarpang (06); Samdrub Jongkhar (07); Paro (08).
→ **Directory enquiries**: T140
→ **International enquiries**: T116

For professional courier services you could also contact **DHL** in Thimphu (T975-2-324729, dhl@druknet.bt). For collecting mail, there is a post restante facility in the Thimphu GPO, but it may be better to use the post box of your hotel or tour operator.

Telephone and fax services

The **Bhutan Telephone Service** was inaugurated in 1963, and Thimphu's satellite earth station was opened in 1990. Most of the country is now internally connected, so that both domestic DDD (or STD) and international IDD (or ISD) calls can easily be made from public call offices or hotels. Their connections are excellent and the fax services are also very reliable. DDD calls cost Nu 2-8 per minute, and a 10% discount is offered on IDD calls made between 1800-0900. Bhutan now has a local mobile network (B-Mobile), with coverage between Thimphu, Paro, Chukha and Phuntsoling, but no international roaming facility, so your cell phone will not work here. For details contact **Bhutan Telecom**, T2-320194, F2-320193. However, satellite calls can be made through Bhutan Telecom using Indian-made Thuria phones. These are particularly useful when trekking in the more remote areas.

Media

The Saturday newspaper *Kuensal* publishes in English, Dzongkha and Nepali, and there is also an online version at **www.kuenselonline.com**, with local and international news updates, editorials, government announcements and a readers' forum. Annual subscription is also possible: US$66 Europe, US$76 North America, US$ 15 Indian subcontinent. Indian publications, both newspapers and magazines, arrive some three days late, and some international newspapers and magazines can also be found in Thimphu bookstores.

There are local television and radio services in Bhutan, operated by the **Bhutan Broadcasting Service** (BBS). Radio broadcasts (1600-2000) can be heard Monday-Saturday on 60 MHz and FM 96 in English, Dzongkha, Sharchokpa and Nepali. Sunday broadcasts are longer, 1000-1600. The radio reception for **BBC World Service** and **VOA** is also good.

BBS television broadcasts nightly a digest of local news, documentaries, and some dubbed or subtitled imports (2000-2100). Cable television is also available. The main cable company is **Sigma Cable Service**, PO Box 810, Thimphu, T322809, which offers its paying subscribers 45 channels, including the international rolling news channels CNN and BBC World, as well as the Star TV and Zee TV packages, National Geographic and Discovery channels, and assorted Indian and HBO movie channels. The smaller cable companies, **K.C. Cable** and **Tandrin Cable**, also operate in Thimphu and Bumthang respectively. Sigma also plans to introduce a cable internet service.

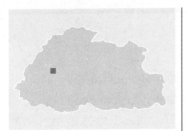

☃ Footprint features

Introduction

Bhutan's capital, Thimphu, meaning 'Uplands of Thim', is a growing city, but the population is still estimated to be no more than 50,000. The name Thimphu derives from Dechenphuk hermitage in the upper reaches of the Wang-chu valley, where the local protector deity Genyen Jagpa Melen is said to have manifested to welcome the seventh hierarch of Ralung on his visit from Tibet to Bhutan in 1333, and then 'vanished' (*thim*) into a rock.

The city has excellent handicraft outlets including the **National Institute of Traditional Arts and Crafts** and the weekend **Changlingmethang Market**, but there are also major sites of national importance: the 13th-century **Changangkha monastery**, the seat of government at **Tashi Chodzong** (built 1772, and refurbished 1962-69) and the **Memorial Chorten** (1974), dedicated to the late third king of Bhutan, all lie within the city. Beyond the city, the 14th-century Dechenphuk hermitage, 13th-century Tango monastery and the Cheri Dorjeden retreat, dating from 1620, are all accessible on hiking trails (see the Western Bhutan chapter for details).

★ Don't miss...

❶ **Changlingmethang Market** Fresh produce, indigenous artefacts and a rare chance to practise your bargaining skills, page 68.

❷ **National Textile Museum** The displays highlight the weaving techniques, fabrics and patterns associated with different parts of the country, page 69.

❸ **Memorial Chorten** This modern three-storey stupa is dedicated to the late third king of Bhutan, Jigme Dorji Wangchuk, page 70.

❹ **Changangkha Lhakang** The central image of the 13th-century monastery is a large, 11-faced, thousand-armed Mahakarunika, page 71.

❺ **Handicrafts** Among the city's best outlets are the National Institute of Traditional Arts and Crafts and the National Handicrafts Emporium, pages 73 and 81.

Background

→ *Altitude: 2,350 m. Phone code: (975) 2. Colour map 0, grid 00.*

Until the mid 1950s Thimphu was only a small agricultural community. Nearby were two important fortresses (*dzong*), hilltop monasteries and temples, a royal palace of recent construction at Dechen Choling, and a number of outlying hamlets: Mutigthang (Bh. Motithang), Changangkha and Kawangjangsa to the west; Chang Zamtog, Zamar Zingkhar, Yangchenphuk and Lungtenphuk to the south; and Zilunkha, Langjuphakha, Hejo and Tagbab to the north. These old names remain, the hamlets having been absorbed into the modern urban development of Thimphu.

In 1952-3, following the Chinese occupation of neighbouring Tibet and the accession of Bhutan's third king Jigmi Dorje Wangchuk, a decision was taken to move the capital here from the more remote central regions of the country. Tashi Chodzong in Thimphu had long been established as the summer residence of the official monastic order of Bhutan, and there were early temples and monasteries at Tango, Dechenphuk and Changangkha that had been associated with the original historic foundation of the Drukpa Kagyu school in Bhutan by Phagom Zhikpo and his sons in the 13th century.

Since the late 1960s Thimphu has experienced unprecedented urban development. Only a few families have maintained the traditional agricultural pursuits of the valley. Now the growing population largely comprises civil servants and shopkeepers. Hotels, restaurants, shops, government offices, foreign aid offices, embassies, entertainment and leisure facilities, and the local transport infrastructure have all been established here since the coronation of the present king in 1974. ▸▸ *For Sleeping, Eating and other listings, see pages 75-85.*

Orientation and sights

By Bhutanese standards Thimphu is busy and lively, though to an outsider it may still appear as an uncrowded haven, and it is certainly Asia's smallest capital city. It would be hard to lose one's way walking around! The distance from Thimphu to Paro Airport is 55 km and to Phuntsoling on the Indian border, 179 km. ▸▸ *For Transport, see page 82.*

Riverside roads

The major roads through the city run from south to north, following the alignment of the valley. **Dechen lam,** the only main road on the east bank of the Wang-chu, runs from the Simtokha intersection south of town to the Dechen Choling Palace complex in the far north of the valley, passing the bus station, schools, hand-made paper factories, a few secluded hotels – Pinewood, Riverview and Jambayang among them – and the **National Assembly Building** at Langjopakha. Bridges link this road with Chogyal lam on the west bank or city side of the river at a southern intersection (known as **Lungten Zampa**) near the bus station, and also at a northern intersection below the National Assembly Building. Further upstream other bridges span the Wang-chu on **Drukar lam,** leading to Tashi Chodzong, and on **Demchog lam,** leading via the Dzongkha Development Computer Centre and the Woodcraft Centre to the Indian Embassy. Both of these roads branch off Dechen lam.

Heading north from Lungten Zampa bridge on Chogyal lam, you will pass in succession the Thimphu Archery Field, the **Changlingmethang Stadium,** the District Government HQ, the Yigya Dungyur Chapel, **Zangdok Pelri Temple,** the **weekend market,** the Veterinary Hospital and the **Royal Academy of Performing Arts,** before

Samardzingka

Located on the high ground to the east of the Wang-chu, Samardzingka appears to
have at one time been a branch monastery of the Nenying tradition which was later
absorbed by the Drukpa Kagyu following the 17th-century unification of Bhutan by
Zhabdrung Ngawang Namgyel (see page 239).

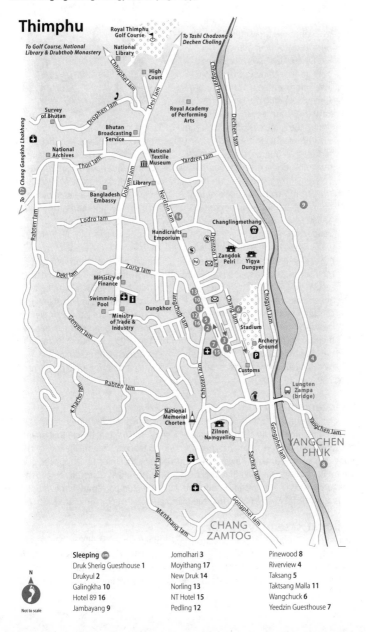

Thimphu

Sleeping
Druk Sherig Guesthouse **1**
Drukyul **2**
Galingkha **10**
Hotel 89 **16**
Jambayang **9**

Jomolhari **3**
Moyithang **17**
New Druk **14**
Norling **13**
NT Hotel **15**
Pedling **12**

Pinewood **8**
Riverview **4**
Taksang **5**
Taktsang Malla **11**
Wangchuck **6**
Yeedzin Guesthouse **7**

N
Not to scale

Dzongs

Traditionally in the Tibetan world, the *dzong* is an administrative fortress or castle, often situated on a strategic hilltop location, like the medieval fortresses of Gyantse, Zhigatse and Gongkar. In Bhutan, this model was adopted during the 17th century by Zhabdrung Ngawang Namgyel (pictured), founder of the Bhutanese state, who combined both administrative and monastic institutions within his fortresses, somewhat along the lines of the Potala Palace in Lhasa, which was constructed during the same period by Dalai Lama V. Although there were earlier fortresses in Bhutan, the Zhabdrung built most of the great *dzongs* that can be seen at the present day on strategic sites, from which the countryside of his new kingdom could be controlled and hostile invasions from Tibet warded off.

Over the centuries that followed, the *dzongs* of Bhutan consolidated themselves as centres of spiritual and secular power. Rival provincial governors of the 18th and 19th centuries would battle for their control, knowing that this would enhance their authority and prestige within the country as a whole. The *dzongs* have also functioned as focal points for the country's artistic and intellectual heritage, and their construction, ornamentation and maintenance have absorbed much of the nation's wealth. Many of them have been damaged by armed assailants, by fires and earthquakes, and subsequently rebuilt.

The high external walls which taper inwards are made of compressed earth and stone, and then whitewashed. The wooden windows and balconies, all built without nails, are richly ornamented, and the roofs are either shingled or made of corrugated iron. While each of the *dzongs* in Bhutan has its own distinctive features, the model suggests that there will be a central

Lungten Zampa

This concrete bridge at the southern end of town, which carries motor vehicles and pedestrians into the city centre, has a long history. The original bridge that spanned the Wang-chu here was the place where the Tibetan teacher Phagom Zhikpo (b. 1184), progenitor of the Drukpa Kagyu school in Bhutan, first met his prophesied wife Sonam Paldron and realised that their descendants would successfully establish the lineage. It was in a grotto under the Lungten Zampa ('bridge of prophetic declaration'), still visible today, that the marriage was first consummated.

National Assembly Building

The newest of Thimphu's traditionally designed buildings, located alongside the east bank of the Wang-chu, slightly to the north of town, dates from the early 1990s. It was originally constructed as a SAARC convention centre, and since 1993 it has housed the biannual National Assembly. Alongside it is the formal Royal Banquet Hall.

tower (*utse*) containing a series of temples (*lhakhang*), flanked by two wings, one of which would be occupied by the monastic community (*rabde*) and the other by the lay administration (*zhungde*). Each of the two wings would have its own flagstoned courtyard (*dochal*), with the surrounding rooms (private bedrooms, offices, study-rooms etc) forming a quadrangle. The interior walls of both temples and offices are often painted with murals depicting Buddhist motifs, narratives, historical figures and meditational deities.

Seven of the main *dzongs* in Bhutan have large monastic communities, including Tashi Chodzong in Thimphu and Dechen Dzong in Punakha, where the official Drukpa Kagyu order under the authority of the Je Khenpo is based according to the season. However, the original military function of the *dzong* is still very much in evidence. Some of them have watch-towers (*ta-dzong*), secret supply tunnels that could enable the community within to withstand a long siege, and moats with only a cantilever bridge offering access. The main entrance is angled so as to facilitate the defenders, and even nowadays it will be guarded by the

Bhutanese Police who register all-comers and enforce the formal dress code required for admission.

Local communities congregate within the main courtyard of their *dzong* to attend the major Buddhist festivals, including *tsechu* and *drubchen* ceremonies, as well as seasonal agricultural feasts. These events provide an opportunity for villagers to wear their finest clothes and indulge in merrymaking after the ceremonies. Among Buddhist festivals, the *tsechu* is held on or around the 10th day of the lunar month, in different parts of the kingdom, throughout the year, to commemorate the deeds of Guru Padmakara (Pema Jungne), the great 8th-century master from Oddiyana. In the non-religious festivals archery contests often feature prominently. The archers aim at targets at a distance of about 150 m and every village has its own range.

The term *dzong* has acquired another contemporary usage in neighbouring Tibet, where it denotes a 'county' level of political administration. By the same token, in Bhutan, the related term *dzongkhag* denotes the 20 districts into which the administration of the country is divided.

Zangdok Pelri Temple

This privately owned temple in Zangdok Pelri style was constructed in the 1980s by Akhu Trokmi, alongside a natural well and at a place where a warlord had once been mortally wounded, as an act of atonement for his own former act of manslaughter. The ground floor contains central 4-m images of the trio Shantaraksita, Padmakara and King Trisong Desten (Khenlobchosum), flanked by 13 3-m statues of the aspects of Padmakara described in the cycle of teachings known as *Spontaneously Accomplished Wishes* (*Sampa Lhundrub*). The murals depict the Lords of the Three Enlightened Families and the Twenty-five Disciples of Padmakara. Upstairs on the second floor the central image depicts 11-headed thousand-armed Mahakarunika, flanked by the eight standing bodhisattvas. There are four projecting chapels, one in each of the four directions, dedicated to four different aspects of Tara. On the third floor the central image depicts Amitabha, flanked by the bodhisattvas Avalokiteshvara and Vajrapani. The murals on this level depict aspects of the wrathful female deity Krodhakali (Troma Nagmo), according to the revelations of Dudjom Lingpa. The founder of the temple, Akhu Trokmi, is also known as the composer of Bhutan's national anthem. The temple is nowadays under the guidance of Chatrel Rinpoche, a senior Nyingma teacher from Katok in Eastern Tibet, who resides mostly at Yanglesho in Nepal and Darjiling. Each month on the 10th lunar day, ceremonies are performed according to Jigme Lingpa's 18th- century revelation, *Assembly of the Awareness Holders* (*Rigdzin Dupa*), and on the 25th day according to Dudjom Lingpa's 19th-century revelation, *Krodhakali*.

Adjacent to this temple there is an older **Mani Wheel Chapel** (Yigya Dungjur Lhakhang), with a rotating wheel containing 100 million imprints of the Hundred Syllable Mantra of the peaceful meditational deity Vajrasattva.

Changlingmethang Stadium

The Changlingmethang Stadium on Chogyal lam was constructed on a site where the first king of Bhutan, Ugyen Wangchuk, won a decisive battle in 1885, ensuring the future authority of the monarchy. The complex includes a football ground, archery ground, billiard hall, and courts for tennis, squash and basketball.

Changlingmethang market

This is an enclosed area of platform stalls that are occupied from Friday afternoon to Sunday evening. There are vendors selling fresh fruit and vegetables, grains, pulses, spices and homemade cheese balls (*datse*), which are used to make a fiery cooking sauce. One section often frequented by visitors at the north end of the complex sells indigenous artefacts: Buddhist ritual implements, prayer flags, offering scarves, wooden bowls, textiles, rattan work and so forth. This is one of the few places in Bhutan where bargaining occurs.

Royal Academy of Performing Arts

ⓘ *Chubar-chu area, between Chogyal lam and Desi lam, T322569, Mon-Fri 0845-1630.*
This is a training school and base for the Royal Dance Troupe. Here the secular tradition of folk dance and song is primarily maintained, although there are elements of sacred masked dancing that are taught as well. The troupe has a busy schedule throughout the year, but short one-hour performances can usually be pre-arranged.

Central and southern Thimphu

Nordzin lam and around

Further west, running parallel to Chogyal lam, is **Nordzin lam**, the commercial thoroughfare of the city. This road is intersected by three roundabouts at its southern, central and northern points. The southern roundabout (the **Dzogchen lam** intersection) is located near an ornate petrol station constructed in a unique Bhutanese design. From here the traffic moves north through a one-way system. On the left you will pass Sigma Cable TV, Dabzang Bar, the Food Corporation of Bhutan, Druk Bookstore, Hotel Holiday Home, Sony, Bata Shoes, NT Hotel, Hotel Grand, several electronics outlets general stores, and an internet bar. On the right, you will pass in succession a lane leading to the Taxi Stand, Khandu Store, the turn-off into Odzin lam (see below), a large construction site which conceals the Clock Tower from view, the Royal Insurance Company of Bhutan and a sports shop.

The second roundabout (at the **Chorten lam/Gaton lam** intersection) is an important commercial hub. Here are Cyber Café, Bhutan Post, Druk Computers and Kunjang Home Appliances, as well as Druk Jewellery, the Pedling, Galingkha and Taktsang Malla hotels and popular restaurants such as Arts Café, Plums Café, Swiss Bakery and Blue Poppy.

Continuing northwards and uphill from this second roundabout on Nordzin lam, the traffic moves in both directions. On the left you will pass in succession general stores, music shops and pharmacies, the Norling Hotel (with photocopy facilities

⦙ The Four Harmonious Brethren (Thunpa Punzhi)

This well-known motif, frequently depicted on the outer walls of monasteries, temples, palaces and ordinary buildings throughout Bhutan and Tibet, symbolizes the theme of co-operation, between individuals, races and nations, based on Buddhist principles. The parable recounts how a peacock, monkey, rabbit and elephant all joined forces to pluck excellent fruit from the highest trees in their forest. The seed of the fruit tree was planted by the peacock, watered by the rabbit, fertilised by the monkey and protected by the elephant. Later when the tree was fully grown, the elephant alone could not reach the branches that were heavy with fruit – but the monkey climbed on the elephant's back, supporting the rabbit who in turn helped the peacock to reach the fruit. So it is that through co-operation based on mutual respect all things are possible.

downstairs), the Riksum Institute of Information Technology, Dragon Shopping Complex, more general stores, Kesang Wangmo Restaurant and Bar, Hotel Sunrise, Dekyiling Hotel, Dekhang Handicrafts, Karma Bar, Dochula Store, Takin Travel, Rinchen Zangmo Handicrafts, Royal Bhutan Securities, Druk Liquor Store, Zhide Restaurant & Bar, Megah Books, and (after the Pende lam intersection), the Duty Free Shop, the **National Textile Museum**, Government Bookstore, and the National Library Bookstore. Close by is the **Thimphu (JWD) Public Library** ① *T322814, Mon-Fri 1230-1730, Sat 0900-1300,* which has a small collection of English-language publications for loan and reference only. Opposite on the right you will pass Kalzang Kurto Handicrafts and the Druk Shopping Complex (which includes Tandin Hotel), before the road opens out into a square. This area is also interspersed with a number of small restaurants and bars.

The main premises on the square are Ethometho Handicrafts, Pekhang Bookstore, Ethometho Tours, Luger Cinema and Centrepoint Complex. Then, after the Dremton lam intersection on the right, you will pass Zhechen Publications, Kuenphen Colour Laboratory, Lekzang Restaurant and Bar, the Bank of Bhutan, the National Handicrafts Emporium and the New Druk Hotel, which is due to open in 2005. Uphill from here, there is an area of green belt on the right.

The final roundabout (at the **Dobum lam/Desi lam** intersection) marks the northern end of Nordzin lam, where the Department of Urban Development is located (formerly the old Bhutan Hotel). Close by is the Bhutan Chamber of Commerce and Industry.

National Textile Museum
① *Located between the second and third roundabouts on the west side of Nordzin lam. T321516, Tue-Fri 0900-1700, Sat 1300-1600, Sun 1000-1500, Nu 150 (Nu 25 for SAARC nationals).*
While Nordzin lam and the adjacent streets are a haven for shopping, entertainment and commercial activities, this building stands out. The museum was founded in 2001 and houses a series of changing exhibitions designed to highlight the different weaving techniques, fabrics and patterns associated with different parts of the country. Prominence is given to the weaving tradition of Lhuntse in Eastern Bhutan. There is a shop selling diversely priced items, ranging from Nu 1,600 to Nu 25,000.

Gaton lam, Odzin lam and Chang lam
Gaton lam runs downhill from the second roundabout to connect with both Odzin lam and Chang lam. On the left are Lotus Adventures, Midpoint Restaurant, Tasty

Restaurant, Benez Restaurant & Bar, Bhutan Kitchen and Sakteng Health Club. On the opposite side is a barber shop, Lhari General Store, and Dragon Treks & Tours.

There are two short parallel streets, located between Nordzin lam and Chogyal lam (the riverside road). Among them, **Odzin lam** is a one-way street approachable from Gaton lam and the second roundabout. The west side of the street has a branch of Citibank and the main downtown bus stop, but the main landmark is the Clock Tower. On the east side a number of buildings are passed in succession: Dondrub Information Technology, Zamlha Enterprises, New Complex liquor store, Atsara Cyber Café, two art galleries, Druktrin Handicrafts, DHL, various travel agencies, including Lhomon, Bhutan Travel Service, Yudruk and Lama Tours, the Druk Hotel, DSB Bookstore, a grocery store, internet bar, Jomolhari Hotel and Druk Sherig Guesthouse.

Chang lam runs parallel and to the east of Odzin lam, with which it is connected by a series of lanes. This is the centre of Thimphu's nightlife. On the left you will pass Changlingmethang Sports Stadium, followed by a car park and taxi park. On the right are the Millennium Hotel, DG Furniture, Bhutan Handicrafts (which has a training school for young artists upstairs), Dzomsa Café and Nightclub, the Wangchuk Hotel, an electrical store and supermarket, Galing Printing and Desktop Publishing, the Om Bar, Headquarters Bar & Discotheque, the Red Panda Bar, a telephone outlet, the District Revenue and Customs Office, All Stars Nightclub, SNS Restaurant, Thinley Photocopy and the Shangrila Beauty Salon.

Drenton lam and Samten lam

The crescent formed by **Drenton lam** and **Samten lam** connects Nordzin lam with the Weekend Market. Along here are the Police Station, Bhutan Post and Philatelic Bureau, Bhutan National Bank and the offices of the United Nations Development Programme.

Towards the Memorial Chorten

Roads branch westwards from each of the three roundabouts on Nordzin lam towards the **Memorial Chorten**. Among them, **Dzogchen lam**, starting from the petrol station, offers the shortest and most direct approach. The small temple of **Zilnon Namgyeling**, which lies south of the petrol station, is dedicated to the charismatic form of Guru Padmakara, known as Nangsi Zilnon. **Chorten lam** starts from the second roundabout, after Plums Café, and here you will pass on the left Hotel 89, Lhanam Hotel and the IBF Hospital. Opposite on the right there are the offices of the BBDF and a turn-off into **Jangchub lam**, which leads to the Swimming Pool Complex on Dobum lam. En route you will pass the Yidzin Guesthouse on the left and, further on, the Dolma Lhakhang, the Thai Embassy and finally the Thai Pavilion on the right.

Dobum lam runs from the third roundabout on Nordzin lam to the Memorial Chorten. The east side of the street houses private homes and government offices, including the Ministry of Finance, the Ministry of Trade and Industry and the Department of Tourism. On the west side Thori lam, Lodro lam and Rabten lam all branch uphill towards the affluent suburbs of Mutigthang. On this side of the street you pass the Liaison Office of Denmark, NTTA, the Embassy of Bangladesh, Changangkha High School, the Midnight Bar, the Army Welfare Project, the Swimming Pool Complex, Jichudrake Bakery, the Department of Employment and Kunga Rabten Junior School.

Memorial Chorten

In downtown Thimphu, the most significant building of interest is the Memorial Chorten, constructed in 1974 by Dung-se Rinpoche Trinle Norbu, to commemorate the late third king, Jigme Dorji Wangchuk, at the behest of the Royal Grandmother Ashi Phuntsok Chodron. This stupa is a fine modern example of the multiple chapel type (*tashigomang*), containing within its three storeys enormous three-dimensional mandalas of meditational deities. There are vestibules in each of the four cardinal directions, their ceilings respectively depicting the mandalas of Vajrasattva (east), Ratnasambhava (south), Hayagriva (west) and Vajrakila (north). On the ground level, there is a large east-facing image of Shakyamuni Buddha.

Within the three successive storeys of the building are intricately sculpted three-dimensional clusters of deities, representing three of the most important 'treasure-cycles' (*terma*) of the Nyingma school of Tibetan Buddhism. On the **ground floor** they depict the cycle of *Vajrakila: Dagger of Razor-sharp Meteorite* (*Phurpa Namchak Putri*), which was revealed during the 19th century by Dudjom Lingpa. On the **middle floor** they depict the cycle of the *Eight Wrathful Meditational Deities: Gathering of the Sugatas* (*Kabgye Deshek Dupa*), revealed during the 12th century by Nyangrel Nyima Ozer. On the **top floor** the images depict the cycle of the *Gathering of the Guru's Intention* (*Lama Gongdu*), revealed during the 14th century by Sangye Lingpa. This is one of the most magnificent of all contemporary Tibetan or Bhutanese style monuments, and it is constantly circumambulated by local citizens and itinerant pilgrims, who hold it and the memory of the revered third king with great devotion.

Southern suburbs

A southern ring road, called **Gongphel lam**, links the Memorial Chorten with the southern bridge across the Wang-chu, passing through the suburbs of **Chang Zamtog**. This road offers access to the General Hospital, the Education Department, Chang Zamtog High School, Save the Children, the Fire Brigade and the offices of the national newspaper *Kuensel*.

West Thimphu

The western approach roads known as Ganden lam, Thori lam and Rabten lam all wind uphill to reach the city's most fashionable residential area: Mutigthang (Bh Motithang). Among them, **Ganden lam** runs from Zilunkha suburbs, past Drubthob Monastery, directly to the Youth Centre (formerly the old Mutigthang Hotel), and to the woodland **zoo** that lies behind it. **Thori lam** branches off Dobum lam just after the Department of Urban Development. Continuing uphill on the left from here, you will pass the Bangladesh Embassy, the Visual Institute of Technology, DHL, a lane leading to **Changangkha Lhakhang** and the Druk Incense Factory, while on the right you will pass the National Archives, a lane (leading to the Royal Audit Authority), the Department of Legal Affairs, Jigme Namgyel Junior High School, Mutigthang High School, the New Mutigthang Hotel and the Kunga Choling State Guesthouse. **Rabten lam** leads uphill from the Memorial Chorten, passing on the right Helvetas Offices and Rinchen Kunphen Primary School, and on the left the Forestry Department and Changangkha Lhakhang.

Changangkha Lhakhang

According to the instructions of Phajo Drukgom Zhikpo, the Changangkha Lhakhang was built on a promontory overlooking the entire Thimphu valley in the 13th century, by Phajo's son Nyima, whose descendants inherited the custodianship of the temple. Nyima's grandson Lama Sonam Gyeltsen invited Jamyang Kunga Sangye (r. 1314-47), the seventh hierarch of Ralung monastery in Tibet, who gave empowerments there and expanded the building. Some extant murals at Changangkha reputedly date from that early period. Refurbishments were subsequently undertaken in the 16th century by Ngawang Chogyel (1465-1540), the 14th hierarch of Ralung in the course of his third visit to Bhutan. Later in the 17th century the senior lama of Changangkha Lhakhang, Kunga Pekar, had a daughter Damcho Tendzin (1606-60) who married a cousin of Zhabdrung Ngawang Namgyel and gave birth to Tendzin Rabgye, the fourth and most illustrious of all the regents of Bhutan.

The central image of the temple is a large 11-faced thousand-armed Mahakarunika. The murals include an authentic depiction, facing the entrance, of Tsangpa Gya-re (1161-1211), the founder of the Drukpa Kagyu school in Tibet.

There are many charming Bhutanese houses in the Changangkha area, each with its distinctive flower garden. Among them is the residence of the late contemporary Nyingma lama Nyoshul Khenpo Jamyang Dorje of Katok in Eastern Tibet, whose published works are available at the National Library Bookshop.

Thimphu Zoo

Located in woodlands behind the Youth Centre is a small fenced zoo where takins can be seen feeding in the early morning. Other wild animals were released from captivity on Buddhist principles, following a royal decree.

Telecom Tower

The Bhutan Telecom Tower is located in Sangyegang, a branch road of Ganden lam, which is something of a lovers' lane at night, in close proximity to the zoo. There are fine urban panoramas from the hillside below the tower.

Wangditse Gonpa

One hour's walking distance uphill from the Telecom Tower is Wangditse Gonpa, founded in 1750 during the tenure of the eighth regent Druk Rabgye (r. 1707-19). The main temple, which was recently renovated, contains images of the protector deities Jnananatha, Shridevi and Tseringma.

North Thimphu

Heading north on **Nordzin lam** from the third roundabout, on the left you will pass the Hathi General Store and a lane leading to the offices of the Bhutan Broadcasting Services. The road curves slightly to the northeast at this point as you pass Bumthang Bar & Restaurant, Orgyan Pema Store and Drolam Bar, before crossing the bridge that spans the Chubar-chu. Now the road forks, left on to Chophel lam and right on to Desi lam, with the Thimphu Royal Golf Course between them.

If at this point you turn left on to **Chophel lam**, you will soon reach the Drophen lam intersection, leading to Bhutan Telecom and Druknet offices, and the Survey of Bhutan. Then, opposite the golf course, **Pendzo lam** branches off on the left, leading towards the **National Library**, Sangye Traditional Arts & Crafts, the **Folk Heritage Museum**, the **National Institute for Traditional Arts & Crafts**, the Sangye Zangmo Restaurant and the **Hospital of Traditional Medicine**, with its compounding factory. This whole area is known as Kawajangsa.

Continuing northwards on Chophel lam, you will pass the Golf Course Restaurant on the right, and two roads that give access to the central government buildings of Tashi Chodzong on the right, before the road converges with Ganden lam (see above). The combined road, now known as **Jalu lam**, leads north out of town in the direction of **Dechen Phodrang**, the oldest fortress of the Thimphu valley, which is occupied by the Central Monastic School, and to the cremation ground at Hejong.

If at the Chubar-chu bridge fork, you turn right on to **Desi lam**, you will pass the elegant High Court with its shingled roof, and follow the eastern side of the golf course round to the government buildings at the entrance to **Tashi Chodzong**, where the road converges with the riverside Chogyal lam (see above). An extension of these roads continues north, following the river upstream to Hejong, the Indian Embassy and **Dechen Choling Palace**.

National Library of Bhutan (Pendzokhang)

ⓘ *T322885, Mon-Fri 0930-1300, 1400-1700.*

The National Library, under the guidance of Minyak Tulku, is located on Pendzo lam, west of the golf course. It was founded in 1967 to facilitate the collection and preservation of classical printed books and manuscripts. On the ground floor there is a chapel dedicated to Guru Padmakara, Pema Lingpa and Zhabdrung Ngawang Namgyel. Many Tibetan texts are stored here and at the library's branch at Kunga Rabten Palace in Trongsar. There is an active conservation department, with temperature-controlled rooms in which rare manuscripts and woodblocks can be protected from the summer humidity, and a new computerised cataloguing system. There is a journals section, containing back issues of *Kuensal*, the national newspaper, in three languages, and assorted reports commissioned by the government and by NGOs; and a small English-language section, with books on Bhutan, Tibetan Buddhism and related subjects.

Folk Heritage Museum (Pelkhye Tonkhyim)

ⓘ *Pendzo lam, T327133, Tue-Fri 1000-1630, Sat 1030-1300, Sun 1130-1530, Nu 150 (Nu 25 for SAARC nationals).*

The museum is a three-storied Bhutanese farmhouse of typical construction (see page 262), containing traditional agricultural and domestic implements.

National Institute for Traditional Arts & Crafts

ⓘ *T322302, F327072, izc@druknet.bt, Mon-Sat 0900-1700.*

The National Institute for Traditional Arts & Crafts (Tashi Gepheling) on Pendzo lam, offers a six-year course in all 13 traditional subjects (see page 263) to gifted students. The main emphasis is on *tangkha* painting, but sculpture, woodwork, embroidery and all the other skills are also studied. Works of art produced by the students are for sale.

National Institute for Traditional Medicine

ⓘ *T324647, Mon-Fri 0900-1500.*

The National Institute for Traditional Medicine (Sorig Menkhang), located on Serzhong lam, and under the direction of Drungtso Pema Dorje, was founded in 1988 to produce indigenous medical products to meet the local demand for traditional medications. The extensive pharmacoepia of traditional medicine is very similar to that of classical Tibetan medicine, with compounds being prepared from herbs, gemstones, minerals and animal products. Ingredients are collected from remote border areas on fieldwork expeditions. Medical theory is based on the imbalance of the three humours (wind, bile and phlegm) and diagnoses are made through pulse palpation and urinalysis. For a detailed explanation of this system with full illustration, see Parfianovitch, Dorje and Meyer, *Tibetan Medical Paintings* (Serindia, 1992). Medical compounding facilities here have been upgraded with funding provided by the European Union.

Drubthob Gonpa

Drubthob Monastery is accessible from Ganden lam in Zilunkha. The monastery was originally founded by a later emanation of the accomplished spiritual master (*drubthob*) Tangtong Gyelpo and is said to offer geomantic protection to the large *dzongs* located further north from fire, which has always been a serious hazard in Bhutanese wooden structures. The present building dates only from the 1980s. Nowadays there is a small nunnery housed here.

Dechen Phodrang

Approached on Tenzin lam, an extension of Ganden lam, Dechen Phodrang is the central monastic school for the Drukpa Kagyu order in Bhutan. Nestling against a ridge to the south of the Samten-chu side-valley, this building was the first fortress constructed in Bhutan by Gyelwa Lhanangpa in 1216. At that time it was known as Dongon Dzong (blue stone fortress). Later the fortress was absorbed by the Drukpa Kagyu descendants of Phajo Drukgom Zhikpo, and in 1641 it was taken over as a seat of government by Zhabdrung Ngawang Namgyel, the founder of the Bhutanese state, and renamed Tashi Chodzong (fortress of the auspicious dharma). It then functioned as the summer residence of the official monastic order, while Pungthang Dewachenpo Dzong in Punakha became the winter residence. Following the Zhabdrung's established model, the *dzong* initially housed both the secular bureaucracy and the monastic community, but, for lack of space, the bureaucrats were moved to a newly constructed lower *dzong* (see below), which was founded by the 13th regent of Bhutan, Chogyel Sherab Wangchuk (r. 1744-63). When the original fortress was damaged by fire in 1771, it was abandoned as a seat of government, and adopted instead as a residence by the local governor. Further refurbishment was undertaken, following another fire in 1895.

The state monastic school has been based here since 1971. There are some 450 student monks, undertaking an eight-year study programme in the traditional subjects (Vinaya, Abhidharma, Pramana, Prajnaparamita, Madhyamaka), as well as in more advanced tantric studies. On the ground floor the main hall has a central image of Shakyamuni Buddha, and a Guru Lhakhang, dedicated to Padmakara, where the restoration of some original murals is being funded by UNESCO. On the upper levels there is a chapel dedicated to Zhabdrung Ngawang Namgyel and a protector chapel.

Tashi Chodzong

Tashi Chodzong is the seat of the Bhutanese central government, located on the west bank of the Wang-chu. A fortress known as the lower *dzong* was originally founded on this site by the 13th regent of Bhutan, Chogyel Sherab Wangchuk (r. 1744-63), when it was realised that the original Tashi Chodzong (now known as Dechen Phodrang) would be too small to accommodate the combined monastic and secular administration. Later in 1772, when the upper *dzong* had been badly damaged by fire, the seat of government and the monastic body were moved in their entirety to the lower fortress, which was further expanded by the regent Zhidar (1768-73) and Je Khenpo Yonten Thaye (1771-75). From that time on only the lower fortress has been known by the name Tashi Chodzong. Further restorations were carried out in 1870 (following the fire of 1866) and in 1902 (following the earthquake of 1897 when the central tower was damaged). The Lhakhang Sarpa (new temple) was added in 1907, the year in which the Bhutanese monarchy was first established.

In 1962, following the third king Jigme Dorji Wangchuk's decision to move the national capital to Thimphu, the reconstruction of Tashi Chodzong was undertaken over a five-year period, using traditional building techniques, without architectural plans and without nails. Only the central tower and the surrounding temples were left intact. The outer walls, fashioned of trimmed granite, are 2 m thick in places, and two storeys in height, with even higher watchtowers at the four corners. The completed building was consecrated in June, 1969.

Approaching from Chogyael or Desi lam, at first Tashi Chodzong is not clearly visible because it has been constructed in a depression, hidden from view. At the northern end of the golf course there are three short avenues, lined with rose bushes and Bhutanese-style lamp posts, and then suddenly the grand building comes into view at close range. Its elegance and symmetry are remarkable, the simplicity of the walls contrasting with the intricacy of the woodwork and roofs. In front of the *dzong* you will also notice smaller outbuildings where several government departments are based. On the west side there is a detached tower, known as **Nekhang**, containing an image of Shakyamuni Buddha flanked by the local protector deities Genyen Jagpa Melan and Dorje Daktsen. The residential quarters of the royal bodyguards are to the rear. There are two gates: one leading into the southern administrative courtyard and the other into the northern monastic courtyard. Between them is the central five-storey tower (*utse*). Half of the building is therefore an active monastery to which non-Buddhists are not allowed access when the monks are in residence during the summer months.

The **southern courtyard** is entered by the eastern gate, where ornate relief sculptures depict the Four Guardian Kings, flanked by the gatekeepers Acala and Hayagriva, and the yogin Drukpa Kun-le, accompanied by his pet dog. A mural to the right illustrates the motif of the Four Harmonious Brethren (see box, page 69). A wide staircase now leads into the administrative courtyard, paved with even rectangular slabs, which is surrounded by the offices of the ministries of home affairs and finance, and by the Royal Chamber and the Secretariat for Religious Affairs. The distinctive Bhutanese architectural style, with its ornately carved wooden columns and ceilings, is seen here at its best advantage.

A large central tower, housing various temples, separates this southern courtyard from the **northern courtyard** of the state monastic body (*dratsang*), where the sacred masked dances of the Thimphu *tsechu* are performed each year (For late 2004 and 2005 dates, see page 41, and for a detailed description, see page 273). A large appliqué *tangkha* (Sangye Khorsum Thondrol), depicting Shakyamuni flanked by his foremost students Sariputra and Maudgalyayana, is displayed outdoors on this occasion.

At the centre of this courtyard is the **Lhakhang Sarpa** (new temple), containing an impressive image of Padmakara (dated 1907) in the charismatic form Khamsum Zilnon. On the north wing is the **Monastic Assembly Hall**, with its portico depicting elaborate cosmological diagrams and the Wheel of Rebirth. Its lower storey functions as the summer headquarters of the state monastic body, and it contains a large image of Buddha Shakyamuni, the head of which is visible from the viewing chamber above. This viewing chamber contains the king's gilded throne, and it is decorated with marvellous murals depicting scenes from the life of the Buddha, and a ceiling panel depicting Shakyamuni flanked by the Sixteen Elders. Formerly the National Assembly convened in this room twice a year, before a new building was constructed across the river. Sometimes tailors proficient in elaborate appliqué and embroidery can also be seen at work here. Outside the entrance to the northern courtyard, a traditional cantilever bridge with a shingled roof leads across the Wang-chu to the National Assembly Building.

Festivals Each year during the seventh month of the lunar calendar, a *drubchen* ceremony and *tsechu* festival are held back-to-back. In 2004 these events are scheduled for 18-25 September and in 2005 for 8-15 September.

Dechen Choling Palace

Four kilometres north of Tashi Chodzong is **Dechen Choling Palace**, where the King of Bhutan resides. The palace was constructed in the early 1950s following the third king's decision to relocate the capital to Thimphu. Government goldsmiths and silversmiths may be observed at work here. The private temples and monastic complex of the late Royal Grandmother, Ashi Phuntsog Chodron, are located on a ridge to the west of the palace. In the remote **Dechen Choling Lhakhang** there are images of Guru Padmakara, Sri Heruka and Yumka Dechen Gyelmo – the three root deities of the *Longchen Nyingtig* tradition – a statue depicting the late Bomtha Ponlob Khenpo, along with a reliquary stupa containing his brain relics. The murals here depict the Hundred Peaceful and Wrathful Deities, according to the Karma Lingpa tradition.

🛌 Sleeping

As yet there are no international five-star hotels in Thimphu, but this is set to change as the Singapore-based Aman Hotel chain expand their Bhutanese base within the next two years.

Central Thimphu *p68, map p65*

AL New Druk Hotel, Nordzin lam, is now under construction adjacent to the Handicrafts Emporium. A 58-room deluxe hotel in a prime location – doubles at Nu 5,000, and singles at Nu 3,375, with international standard multi-cuisine restaurant, bowling alley and private swimming pool.

A Druk Hotel, Odzin lam, T322966/322977, F322677, drukhotel@druknet.bt. A 53-room centrally located hotel that is currently considered by many to be the best in town, with a lively atmosphere – deluxe doubles at Nu 3,200, standard doubles at Nu 2,500, deluxe singles at Nu 3,000, standard singles at Nu 2,000 and suites at Nu 5,500. Sales tax 10% and service charge 5%. Discounts are available in low season. All rooms have attached bathroom (24-hr hot running water), cable TV and heating. The hotel has a multi-cuisine restaurant, particularly known for its Indian food (capacity 50-100), with glitzy bar, discotheque, business centre, hair salon and health club (gym, steam bath, sauna).

A Jomolhari Hotel, Odzin lam, T325506/ 322747, F324412, jumolhari@hotmail.com. A comfortable 27-room, centrally located hotel. All rooms are carpeted, with cable TV, heating, telephone and attached bathroom (24-hr hot water supply) – deluxe doubles at Nu 3,000, standard doubles at Nu 2,200, deluxe singles at Nu 2,600, standard singles at Nu 1,800 and suites at Nu 5,500. Sales tax 10%. The multi-cuisine restaurant is good but slow in service.

A Pedling Hotel, Jangchub lam, T325714, F323592, peddling@druknet.bt, adjacent to the Swiss Bakery, has 39 fine carpeted rooms with cable TV, telephone and attached bathroom (24-hr hot running water), under the ownership of Gangteng Monastery and under the careful management of Mr Karma Khorko – deluxe doubles at Nu 2,500, standard doubles at Nu 1,700, deluxe singles

at Nu 2,000, standard singles at Nu 1,450 and suites at Nu 3,500. Sales tax 10%. Business centre with internet access, and a good restaurant and bar, specialising in Indian, Tibetan, Chinese, Continental and Bhutanese cuisine. Also efficient laundry service, car rental service, in-house tour information service and foreign exchange facility.

B Druk Sherig Guesthouse, Odzin lam, T322598, F322714, travelbt@druknet.bt, popular with WWF expatriate workers and Buddhist pilgrims, has 12 rooms – doubles at Nu 1,200, singles at Nu 950. The top-floor restaurant has a capacity of 25, but apart from breakfast other meals have to be pre-arranged.

B Galingkha Hotel, Chorten lam, T328126, F322677. A well-located 10-room hotel, opposite the Swiss Bakery – with doubles at Nu 1,500 and singles at Nu 1,000. The rooms have good downtown views, with an informal bar and in-house restaurant (seating capacity 30), specialising in Indian and Bhutanese cuisine.

B Taktsang Malla Hotel, Chorten lam, T322102, F323284. A 16-room hotel, located behind the Galingkha, with 16 rooms – doubles at Nu 1,200 and singles at Nu 1,000. No in-house restaurant.

B Wangchuk Hotel, 17 Chang lam, T323532, F326232, htlwchuk@druknet.bt, overlooking the stadium and close to Thimphu's nightlife, has 20 carpeted wood-panelled rooms with fine Bhutanese décor, cable TV, telephone, heating and attached bathroom (24-hr hot running water) – standard doubles at Nu 1,050 and singles at Nu 850. The hotel has a small restaurant (capacity 40), which is popular with expatriate workers, a gift shop on the first floor, a fax and email service, as well as foreign exchange facilities. Visa credit cards are accepted here.

C Yeedzin Guesthouse, Jangchub lam, T322932, F324995, yeedzin@druknet.bt, is one of the most attractive in town, a pleasant family-run hotel, under the management of Ashi Chime Wangmo, quiet but very close to the town centre, with 19 rooms – doubles at Nu 800, singles at Nu 550 and suites with kitchen facilities at Nu 900-1,000 (available to long-term guests). All rooms have telephones and attached bathrooms (24-hr hot water supply). The multi-cuisine restaurant, which is popular with locals and expatriates, has a capacity of 25. There is also a fax and laundry service.

D **Hotel 89**, Chorten lam, T322931, has 20 small rooms, and it the most popular of all hotels for Indian tourists – standard room rate Nu 550. Most establishments in this category will generally be frequented by Indian visitors, except in the busy festival season when international tour groups sometimes have no alternative accommodation.

D **Norling Hotel**, Nordzin lam, T322997, has 13 small rooms, which have recently been refurbished – doubles at Nu 495, singles at Nu 385.

D **NT Hotel**, Nordzin lam, T324414, F325051, nte@druknet.bt, formerly known as the Kelwang Hotel, has 8 simple rooms – range Nu 300-500. The downstairs restaurant has a capacity of 40.

D **Tandin Hotel**, Nordzin lam, T323380, located inside the Druk Shopping Complex near the
Luger Cinema, has 21 small rooms – doubles at Nu 450 and singles at Nu 350 – and a very good Indian restaurant.

D **Yoedzar Hotel**, Odzin lam, T324007, F325927, has 22 basic rooms – doubles at Nu 550, singles at Nu 450 – and an excellent tandoori restaurant.

E **Taksengkhyungdruk Hotel**, Nordzin lam, T321509, has 20 rooms, all with attached bathroom and cable TV – doubles at Nu 300 and singles at Nu 200.

Other hotels in this category include **Metok Pema Hotel**, with 21 rooms, **Hotel AV**, Nordzin lam, with 15 rooms, **Millennium Hotel**, Chang lam, T332360, **Sunshine Hotel**, Nordzin lam, T323306, **Hotel Holiday Home**, Nordzin lam, and **Hotel Grand**, Nordzin lam, which has 8 rooms.

West Thimphu *p71*

A **New Mutigthang Hotel**, Thori lam, T322435/323890, F323392. A small and intimate 15-room hotel owned by Bhutan Tourism Corporation Limited, located in the affluent western suburbs, high above the town – doubles at Nu 1,290 and singles at Nu 1,020. The rooms are wood-panelled with attached bathrooms (24-hr hot running water).

B **Rabten Apartments**, Thori lam, T323587, rabten@druknet.bt, has 7 apartments available for long-term rental – Nu 16,000 per month. There is a good Bhutanese restaurant, but tables have to be reserved in advance.

East of the river *p64*

A **Riverview Hotel**, T325029, F323496. A modern 51-room hotel. Each room has a balcony with a town view, telephone and attached bathroom with 24-hr hot water supply – deluxe doubles at Nu 2,400, standard doubles at Nu 1,800, deluxe singles at Nu 2,000, standard singles at Nu 1,500, suites at Nu 4,000 and deluxe suites at Nu 6,000. Discounts are available in low season. The hotel has its own restaurant (capacity 98), bar, handicraft and gift shop, business centre with internet facilities, a conference room and a Saturday night discotheque. Credit cards are accepted. Taxis can be ordered for short rides into town.

B **Jambayang Resort**, T322349, F323669, jambayangs@druknet.bt. Located above the Riverview Hotel, with outstanding views of Thimphu, this 16-room hotel has superior wood-panelled rooms (attached bath) in the main building – doubles at Nu 1,200 and singles at Nu 900 – and an annex with 4 apartments (kitchen etc) where expatriate workers sometimes stay – monthly rental Nu 15,000. All rooms have telephone, cable TV, and bathrooms with 24-hr hot running water. Excellent restaurant, serving local, continental and Chinese dishes, popular with local residents and expatriates alike. The business centre offers email and photocopy facilities.

B **Pinewood Hotel**, T325924, F325507, pinewood@druknet.bt. A remote hill-top hotel with 9 rooms (attached bath), located above the Yangchenphu High School – deluxe doubles at Nu 1,800, standard doubles at Nu 1,500, singles at Nu 1,200 and suites at Nu 3,500. It has an in-house Thai restaurant (capacity 25-30), but reservations have to be made in advance. The hotel is isolated, and in recent years has had to dispute access with the neighbouring school.

Thimphu City Sleeping

🍴 Eating

All major hotel restaurants offer Indian, Chinese, Continental and local Bhutanese dishes, including the fiery *emadatse* (cheese with hot peppers). Among them, the **Jambayang Restaurant** is highly recommended, but for Indian food in particular the best and most authentic are **Tandin Hotel**, **Jomolhari Hotel**, **Hotel 89** and **Yoedzar Hotel**. Other hotels offering a good range of multi-cuisine menus include **Wangchuk Hotel** and **Pedling Hotel**. Only the **Pinewood Hotel** has Thai cuisine on the menu. Most hotels generally provide a buffet service (Nu 250-350). Á la carte menus are extensive but many listed items are not actually available! Outside the cold winter season chicken is often the only meat that can be served. In general hotel restaurants are all at the top end of the range (**$$$**). However, the **Druk Hotel** does offer an Indian-style business lunch for Nu 75.

Most non-hotel restaurants serve Indian and Bhutanese cuisine, with some Tibetan dishes (*momo*, *thukpa*) and westernised Chinese cuisine (chowmien etc). They can conveniently be divided between mid-range and budget establishments as follows:

$$ Arts Café, Jangchub lam. Located next to the Pedling Hotel, in the former Bhutan Arts & Crafts shop, offering superior Continental and Asian cuisine. An increasingly popular venue, now favoured by UNDP staff, especially on Fri evenings. Open daily 0900-2200.

$$ Bhutan Kitchen, Gaton lam, T331919, F331918. Located above the Sakteng Health Club, with a capacity of 100, this upmarket restaurant is professionally managed and suitable for deluxe tourists, with a multi-cuisine menu, and varied drinks menu, including arak, the local beverage. The décor is one of specially designed traditional stone and wood work, featuring a display of Bhutanese kitchen objects and ingredients for Bhutanese dishes.

$$ Blue Poppy, Jangchub lam, T322003. Located next door to the Pedling Hotel, with a standard multi-cuisine menu. Open daily 0900-2200.

$$ Golf Course Restaurant, Chophel lam, T327231. This is the equivalent of Thimphu Royal Golf Course's 19th hole, with restaurant and bar, popular among the sporting fraternity. Open Tue-Sun 0830-1900.

$$ Lhanam Restaurant, Chorten lam, T321556, is a popular lunchtime venue for office workers. Nepalese dishes and *momos* are the specialities on offer. Open daily 0900-2100.

$$ Midpoint Restaurant, Gaton lam, T321269. Centrally located with indoor and outdoor dining tables. The house speciality is South Indian cuisine, particularly masala dosa.

$$ Mila Hotel, Nordzin lam, T322175. Located within the Dragon Shopping Complex, this Bhutanese restaurant has live traditional music in the evenings. Audience participation is encouraged.

$$ Plums Café, Chorten lam, T324307, is a smart upmarket restaurant, possibly the best in town outside the hotels, with crisp tablecloths. It is a popular meeting place for local residents and visitors alike. The cuisine is Bhutanese and Chinese, offering both buffet and á la carte options. Open Mon-Sat 1100-2130.

$$ Rabten Restaurant, Thori lam, T323587, has some of the best Bhutanese delicacies in town – made to order only.

$$ Seasons Restaurant, Namsay Shopping Centre, offering salads, sandwiches, pizza and soups.

$$ SNS Restaurant, Chang lam, T326117. Located close to the centre of Thimphu's nightlife, offering Japanese snacks and *momos*.

$$ Swiss Bakery, Chorten lam, T322259. A long -established meeting place for expatriates, this coffee shop also serves omelettes, pasta, hamburgers, freshly made sandwiches, and a selection of pastries and cakes. Open Wed-Mon 0800-1900.

$ Benez Restaurant, Gaton lam, T325180. A small 6-table restaurant, serving Chinese, Indian and Continental fare (chicken sizzlers etc). Very good value for money, open all hours but very popular in the evenings.

$ Bumthang Restaurant & Bar, Nordzin lam. A quiet watering hole, conveniently situated near the Bhutan Broadcasting Services.

$ **Central Café**, Nordzin lam, T326557. Located on the second floor of the Centrepoint Complex, this is a popular lunchtime venue for local office workers.

$ **Chedzom Restaurant & Bar**, Nordzin lam. Located near the Library Bookshop, offering simple Tibetan cuisine.

$ **Dekyiling Hotel**, Nordzin lam, opposite Bank of Bhutan, offers inexpensive Nepalese cuisine.

$ **Dungkar Nado Rinchen Restaurant and Bar**, Nordzin lam, next to the Government Bookstore, offers standard Bhutanese fare.

$ **Jichudrake Bakery**, Dobum lam, T322980. Situated south of the swimming pool complex, for authentic Viennese-style pastries and pies. Take-away service only. Open daily 0700-1200, 1330-1930.

$ **Kesang Wangmo Restaurant and Bar**, Nordzin lam, opposite Bank of Bhutan, offers lunchtime menu for Bhutanese office workers.

$ **Lekzang Restaurant and Bar**, Nordzin lam, near Bank of Bhutan, is a very popular spot for office workers on account of its location, with Bhutanese, Tibetan and Indian dishes on the menu.

$ **Lham Tsering Restaurant and Bar**, Nordzin lam, next to the Textile Museum, has standard Bhutanese and Tibetan dishes on offer.

$ **Sangye Zangmo Restaurant**, Pendzo lam, T323587, located near the Institutes of Arts & Crafts and Traditional Medicine, offers Tibetan and Bhutanese dishes. Popular with staff and students alike.

$ **Sonam Chodzom Restaurant & Bar**, Nordzin lam. Located near the Library Bookstore, offering simple Bhutanese cuisine.

$ **Tasty Restaurant**, Gaton lam, T323329. Located near Midpoint Restaurant, good for Tibetan-style snacks.

$ **Zhide Restaurant**, Nordzin lam, T325196, next to the Druk Liquor Store, offers good quality and reasonably priced Bhutanese cuisine.

Thimphu City Bars & clubs

🍸 Bars and clubs

Thimphu is very quiet by western standards, although some local bars stay open quite late and there are many parties held in private houses. The local people devote much time to picnics, parties and board games, especially playing cards and *karom*. At weekends, some visitors and expatriates enjoy mingling with affluent locals at Thimphu's nightclubs. All bars close on Tue, the national abstinence day.

Benez Bar, Chang lam, T325180, is an intimate and popular bar, often crowded with few seats available.

Druk Hotel Bar, with modern décor, strobe lights and karaoke, serves overpriced cocktails.

Headquarters Bar, Chang lam, formerly known as Jojo's One Stop Shop, is the largest bar in town, with pool and snooker tables, and an in-house disco. Bar open 1100-1400 daily except Tue.

Om Bar, T326344, located near the Headquarters Bar. Spacious and draughty, but popular meeting place for locals and expatriates, particularly when the nearby discotheques open on Fri evenings.

Other less salubrious establishments include **Dabzang Bar**, Nordzin lam, next door to Sigma Cable TV; **Drolam Bar**, Nordzin lam, next to Chubar Bridge; **Karma Bar**, Nordzin lam, upstairs, next to Tenpa General Store; **Kesang Wangmo Bar**, Nordzin lam, opposite Bank of Bhutan; **Lekzang Bar**, Nordzin lam; **Midnight Bar**, Dobum lam, next to Army Welfare Project; **Red Panda Bar**, Chang lam; **Tsering Bar**, Nordzin lam, next to Duty Free Shop.

Outside the hotels, there are three popular discotheques in town: **All Stars Nightclub**, Chang lam, has an admission charge of Nu 300. Open Wed, Fri-Sat 2100-0200.

Dzomsa Café and Nightclub, T324869, Chang lam. Open late Wed and Sat.

Headquarters Bar & Discotheque, Chang lam. Open 2200-0200 on Wed, Fri and Sat.

🔴 *For an explanation of sleeping and eating price codes used in this guide, see inside the*
⚫ *front cover. Other relevant information is found in Essentials, see pages 39-40.*

⊕ Entertainment

Traditional folk dances and songs are performed on request at the **Royal Academy of Performing Arts**. There are also live traditional music nights, similar to the Tibetan *nangmating*, held at the **Mila Hotel** on Nordzin lam. The performers include professional singers and comedians. Audience participation encouraged. Admission: Nu 50, song request Nu 100. Other musical

performances are sometimes at **Tashi Nencha Music Studio**, T322804, near the Zangdok Pelri Temple.

The **Luger Cinema** is located in the square on Nordzin lam. Most movies shown here are of the Bollywood variety, and the hall is often crowded. There are also a profusion of video parlours throughout the downtown area.

⊙ Shopping

Nordzin lam and adjacent streets have rows of neat, traditionally painted shops – some of them are grocers, others are general stores (*tsongkhang*), selling assorted products and toiletries of Indian origin, while yet others are outlets for traditional Bhutanese handicrafts. Most accept only Bhutanese or Indian currency. Usually open 0800-2000, Mon-Sun. Closed Tue and Wed. There is an interesting market at Changlingmethang on Sat and Sun.

Books, maps, cards and newspapers

Megah Bookshop, T321063, on Nordzin lam, next to the Pende lam intersection, sells books published in Tibetan, Dzongkha and English, as well as magazines, prayer-flags and newly made Buddhist ritual implements.

DSB Bookstore, T323123, located on a lane behind the Druk Hotel, is good for Indian publications.

Druk Bookstore, located on the southern part of Nordzin lam, next to the Food Corporation of Bhutan, stocks Tibetan and Dzongkha textbooks and Buddhist statues imported from Patan in Nepal.

Government Bookstore and **National Library Bookstore**, located in the northern section of Nordzin lam, both stock Tibetan and Dzongkha language publications in traditional loose-leaf and modern bound formats, and a few in-house English language publications on Bhutanese cultural themes.

Pekhang, T323094, adjacent to the Luger

Cinema, is small, but stocks an excellent selection of books and maps, including imported magazines.

For cards with traditional Bhutanese motifs, try **Ethometho Handicrafts** on Nordzin lam, or **Druktrin Handicrafts**, behind the Wangchuk Hotel.

Electrical goods

If you need to purchase electrical equipment (including adaptors etc), or have to make emergency repairs, the best shops are **Sony Service Centre** on Nordzin lam (southern section), **Kunjang Home Appliances** on Chorten lam, and the small electrical store behind the Druk Hotel.

General stores

Mostly located on Nordzin lam, they include: Khandu Tsongkhang, Tenpa Tsongkhang and Singye General Store (**southern section**), Yangdzom Tsongkhang, Pema's Store, Kunga Tsongkhang, Gyeltsen Tsongkhang, Tsering Chodon Tsongkhang, Dochula Tsongkhang, Sonam Pelkhang, Sonam Rinchen Store, Norling Tsongkhang and Sharchokpa Store (**northern section**), as well as Hathi Tsongkhang and Oryan Pema Tsongkhang (**Pendzo lam/ Chubar Bridge area**). In Gaton lam, Choden Tsongkhang and Lhari General Store are well stocked.

Handicrafts

A few of the shops in Thimphu now accept American Express cards. Otherwise, payment can always be made in Bhutanese currency or US dollars.

Warning Do not bargain since prices are generally comparable. An exception might be made in the case of certain outstanding pieces which are highly priced. It is not permitted to buy antiques, and for any purchase, one should always ask for and keep the receipt.

Handicrafts Emporium, Nordzin lam, T322810, has an extensive range of artefacts including sculptures, textiles, masks, bamboo and wood work, jewellery, *tangkha* paintings and books, all at fixed government prices. Open daily 0900-1300 and 1400-1700. Credit cards accepted.

Druktrin Rural Handicrafts Centre, located behind the Wangchuk Hotel, T324500, F326232, druktrin@druknet.bt, also has a good general selection of indigenous handicrafts, including wooden bowls from Eastern Bhutan, as does the Weekend Market at Changlingmethang.

Other general outlets for arts and crafts include: **Namgyay Handicrafts** on Gaton lam, **Bhutan Handicrafts**, T324469, on Chang lam, **Kalzang Kurto Handicrafts**, on Nordzin lam, next to the Druk Shopping Complex, and **Rinchen Zangmo Handicrafts**, opposite the Bank of Bhutan, on Nordzin lam.

More specifically, for newly made painted **scrolls** (*tangkha*), try the shop affiliated to the **National Institute for Arts & Crafts** or the nearby **Sangye Traditional Arts & Crafts**, on Pendzo lam, T327419.

Hand-woven **textiles** are sold in all the handicraft shops at prices ranging from US$10 to USD$5,000, but for an excellent range of traditional old and new textiles, try **Druktrin Rural Handicrafts Centre**. The small shop inside the **Yeedzin Guesthouse** also has an interesting selection of exquisite hand-woven textiles. The entire weaving process can be observed at the **Gagyel Lhundrub Weaving Centre**, T327534, in Chang Zamtog, which also has its own shop. For Bhutanese machine-woven textiles, which are much cheaper, check **Sephu Gyeltshen**, Shop 35, on Nordzin lam, and its outlet in the Druk Shopping Complex, and other small shops opposite the Bank of Bhutan.

For **watercolours** with Bhutanese themes, visit the **Yudruk Gallery**, T321905, and the **Art Shop Gallery**, T325664, both located on Odzin lam, near the Druk Hotel.

For **woodwork** (including small foldaway tables) and **masks**, as well as painted scrolls, try **Choki Handicrafts**, on Pendzo lam, T324728. Amex accepted.

Ethnic jewellery is available at **Norling Handicrafts**, T323577, and **Tsering Dolkar**, T323324, which are located in the Dragon Shopping Complex on Nordzin lam, opposite the cinema; or **Kelzang Handicrafts**, T321353, in the Druk Shopping Complex, and **Druk Jewellery** on Chorten lam.

Greeting cards, envelopes and calendars made from traditional **hand-made paper** can be purchased at the **Jungshi Handmade Paper Factory**, and **Mangala Paper House**, T322898, both located on Dechen lam, near the Riverview Hotel.

For imported cire perdue Buddhist **statues** from Nepal, try the **Druk Bookstore**, on the southern section of Nordzin lam; and for locally produced **incense**, try the **Druk Incense Unit**, on Thori lam.

Health club, beautician and hairdresser
Sakteng Health Club, below Bhutan Kitchen, on Gaton lam.
Shangrila Beauty Salon, on Chang lam. There is also a healthclub and hairdresser in the **Druk Hotel**. Simpler facilities are available on the west side of Nordzin lam (southern section) and on Gaton lam.

Imported goods
Some shops in the Dragon Shopping Complex and Druk Shopping Complex on Nordzin lam sell toiletries and clothes imported from Thailand and Bangladesh. For foreign alcohol, cigarettes, French wine, chocolates and other items, the **Duty Free Shop** (T322167) on Nordzin lam has a surprising selection. However duty-free discounts are only available to diplomats, government officials and certain NGO employees. A second shop has been opened in the Bhutan Post building on Drenton lam. Payment in dollars only (0900-1600, closed Sat afternoon and Sun).

Music

There are many small general stores on Nordzin lam selling cassettes and CDs. Specialist outlets include the **Norling Music Shop**, next to Norling Pharmacy, and the **Music Palace**, opposite the Luger Cinema.

Photography

Print films and batteries are available at photo shops situated in the basement of the Druk Shopping Complex, as well as at **Kuenphen Colour Laboratory** near the Drenton lam intersection, at **Photofield** and **Sunrise**. There are processing facilities for prints, but not of a high standard.

Stamps

Postage stamps are available at **Bhutan Post**, T322381, on Drenton lam, and albums for stamp collectors at the **Philatelic Bureau**, T322296, in the same building. Stamps and postcards are also sold at a small counter inside the Tandin Hotel.

▲ Activities and tours

For a complete list of tour companies and travel agents, see Essentials, p16.

Archery

Archery is practised widely, but with such style that it requires some training. Archery equipment, including fibreglass and carbonite bows is sold at **Yangphel Archery Shop**, T323323, on Chorten lam.

Football

Football matches are regularly held at the **Changlingmethang Stadium**, and archery contests at weekend morning fixtures at the range to the south of the stadium.

Golf

Royal Thimphu Golf Club, T325429, located between Chophel lam and Desi lam, has a 9-hole course, open daily, admission US$25 per day, club hire US$15, popular with Japanese and Indian visitors in particular.

Swimming

Swimming Pool Complex, T322064, on Dobum lam, also has a gymnasium and basketball court. Open Mon-Fri 1600-2000, and weekends 1300-1800. Admission: Nu 70 (per hour).

Tennis and squash

There are 2 tennis courts, with facilities for squash and basketball, at the northern end of **Changlingmethang Stadium**.

Trekking and climbing

Trekking can be pre-arranged by most of the international and Bhutanese tour operators listed above (p16). Trekking equipment is not generally available, but to supplement your gear you could try **DD Tsongkhang**, T325797, opposite the Luger Cinema on Nordzin lam. Rock climbing activities are organised by the **Thimphu Vertical Club**, T322966, verticalbhutan@hotmail.com.

☺ Transport

Thimphu is a very easy city for walking around, and if you are on a pre-arranged tour, you will have your own transportation provided. However it is possible to get around town by public bus or taxi.

Bus

Local The terminus is on Chang lam, and the fare range is Nu 1-7. There are currently 9 routes around Thimphu: **1 East–West Route** (7 buses daily in summer, commencing 0730, ending 1830, and 3 or 4 in winter, commencing 0830, ending 1615). **2 Cross Service Terminus–Hejhong via Chubar-chu** (7 or 8 buses daily in summer, commencing 0730, ending 1830, and 3 or 4 in winter, commencing 0830, ending 1615). **3 Terminus–Babesa** (6 buses daily in summer, commencing 0700, ending 1830, and 4 in winter, commencing 0730, ending 1700). **4 Terminus–Dechen Choling** (5 or 6 buses daily in summer, commencing 0730 and ending 1730, and 4 buses in winter, commencing 0830, ending 1700).

5 Terminus–Mutigthang via Chubar-chu (4-6 buses daily in summer, commencing 0730 and ending 1700, and 4 buses in winter, commencing 0830 and ending 1630). **6 Terminus–Mutigthang via Kuensel Office** (4-6 buses in summer, commencing 0730, ending 1700, and 4 in winter, commencing 0830, ending 1630). **7 Cross Service Terminus–Hejhong via Kuensel Office** (7 or 8 buses in summer, commencing 0715 and ending 1800, and 3 or 4 in winter, commencing 0815 and ending 1615). **8 Terminus–Babesa** (6 buses daily in summer, commencing 0730 and ending 1845, and 4 in winter, commencing 0745 and ending 1715).

9 Terminus–Dechen Choling (6 buses daily in summer, commencing 0800 and ending 1800, and 4 in wnter, commencing 0830 and ending 1700). **NB** Services are modified on Sat. A limited serviced or no service at all operates on Sun and national holidays.

Long distance Long-distance travel by public bus is uncomfortable, irregular and slow on Bhutan's winding roads. Expatriate workers in Bhutan may sometimes have to make use of this service, but most visitors will have pre-arranged transport provided by the tourism department. The long-distance bus station is adjacent to the Lungten Zampa bridge. The government long-distance coach company, **Bhutan Post Express**, links **Thimphu** with the following destinations: **Phuntsoling** (179 km), **Trongsar** (199 km), **Mongar** (460 km) and **Gelekphuk** (258 km). There are also 21 other independent bus companies. For schedules and fares, see box on the next page.

Taxi
Taxis can easily be hired for the 55 km, 2-hour drive to Paro Airport (Nu 400) or the 179 km, 6-hour drive to Phuntsoling on the Indian border (Nu 1,000). Taxis are easily flagged down in the street or found at the taxi stand on the corner of Chang lam. The fares have to be negotiated in advance, even when the meter is running. Approximate city trip: Nu 30-50.

● Directory

Airline offices
Druk Air, Central Space Control, PO Box 209, Thimphu, T322215, F322775, drukairthimphu@druknet.bt, have recently been appointed as the general sales agents for Thai International in Bhutan.

Banks
Bank of Bhutan, T322266, Nordzin lam, open Mon-Fri 0900-1300, Sat 0900-1100. **Bhutan National Bank**, T322767, Drenton lam, open Mon-Fri 0900-1500, Sat 0900-1100 (now the only bank in the country with an ATM machine). Other banks here include **Citibank**, representing the Bank of Bhutan, Odzin lam, open 1400-1800, daily except Tue. **American Express** have an outlet at Chundu Travels (T322592).

Embassies
Bangladesh Embassy, T322539, F322629, on Thori lam, **Indian Embassy**, T322162, F323195, located in the Jhongzina district of north Thimphu, **Thai Embassy**, T323978, F323807, on Jangchub lam.

Hospitals and medical services
General Hospital, also known JDW National Referral Hospital, T322496, on Gongphel lam. India Bhutan Friendship Hospital, T322485, on Chorten lam. Institute of Traditional Medicine, Serzhong lam, T322153. Veterinary Hospital, on Chophel lam. **Emergency ambulance calls**: T112. Pharmacies (see map) can be found on Odzin lam and on Nordzin lam.

Internet
Outside the major hotels, which all provide internet access, try **Atsara Cyber Café**,

Long-distance buses from Thimphu

Company	Destination	Days	Time	Fare
Bhutan Post Express	Phuntsoling	Daily	0700	Nu 156
	Trongsar	Sun-Fri	0730	Nu 99
	Mongar	Tue, Thu, Sun	0730	Nu 306
	Gelekphuk	Tue, Thu, Sat	0700	Nu 174
Sherab Travels	Paro	Daily	1430	Nu 36
	Wangdu	Daily	0800, 0830, 1400	Nu 33
	Punakha	Daily	0830	Nu 38
	Dramphu	Mon, Wed, Fri	0730	Nu 111
	Tashigang	Tue	0700	Nu 455
KW Express	Tarkar	Wed, Fri, Sun	0700	Nu 123
C Norbu Travels	Samtse	Tue, Thu, Sat	0730	Nu 145
Bumthang Singye Travels	Jakar	Tue, Sat	0700	Nu 165
Phunsum Travels	Jakar	Tue, Sat	0700	Nu 165
DP Express Rinchen	Ha	Tue, Thu, Sat	1000	Nu 57
Wangyal Transport	Phunsoling	Daily	0900	Nu 84
Jampal Transport	Lhuntse	Thu	0700	Nu 370
Dophu Travels	Phuntsoling	Daily	0730	Nu 84
	Tashigang	Wed	0700	Nu 455
Lamzang Travel	Chukha	Daily	1400	Nu 48

T325276, in Centre Complex, on Odzin lam, near Druk Hotel. **Info Tech Solutions**, T326474, on Chang lam; **Internet Bar**, T326936, below Plums Café; **MG Cyberpoint**, T324664, inside the Dragon Shopping Complex on the west side of Nordzin lam. Charge: Nu 3 per minute.

Post
Postal facilities, including **EMS express** delivery, are available at Bhutan Post, T322381, on Drenton lam. Open Mon-Fri 0830-1230, 1330-1630, Sat 0900-1230. **DHL**, T324729, have an office at the intersection of Thori lam and Rabten lam, on the way to the New Mutigithang Hotel.

Company	Destination	Days	Time	Fare
KCD Travel	Phuntsoling	Mon, Wed, Fri, Sun	1200	Nu 115
Chopel Phuntsong Dokhal Travels	Tashi Yangste	Mon	0730	Nu 420
Dramzop Travels	Phuntsoling	Daily	1200	Nu 115
Samphel Transport	Tashi Yangtse	Daily	0700	Nu 420
Blue Hills Travel	Phuntsoling	Mon	1000	Nu 115
	Punakha	Daily	1400	Nu 36
Dawa Transport	Paro	Daily	1400	Nu 27
	Tarkar	Mon, Wed, Fri	0700	Nu 154
Tharlam Travels	Ha	Tue, Thu, Sat	0930	Nu 57
	Punakha	Daily	0800	Nu 57
	Kabesa	Daily	0800	Nu 57
PD Travel	Phuntsoling	Tue, Wed, Fri	1230	Nu 115
	Gelekphuk	Tue, Wed, Fri	0700	Nu 173
Kunga Travel	Dramphu	Tue, Thu, Sat	0730	Nu 82
	Phuntsoling	Daily	1130	Nu 156
Kurto Chusa Express	Lhuntse	Mon	0700	Nu 436
Leksol Travel	Paro	Daily	0900	Nu 27
	Phuntsoling	Daily	0800, 1100	Nu 84, Nu 115
	Gelekphuk	Daily	0700	Nu 128

Thimphu City Directory

Telephone

All the major hotels and even some of the smaller hotels now have fax and IDD telephone services. Calls can also be made from STD/IDD shops, such as the one on Chang lam, or the branch at Rinsin Store on Dobum lam, next to the Lodro lam intersection. **B-Mobile** operate a local network in major towns.

Tourist offices

Department of Tourism, Dobum lam, PO Box 126, T323251, F323695.

Useful information

Local directory enquiries: T140.
International directory enquiries: T116;
Police: T113; Fire department: T110.

Thimphu City

⁚ Footprint features

Introduction

The whole of Bhutan is divided into 20 administrative districts (*dzongkhag*), of which 10 are located west of the Black Mountains. This important region, known as Western Bhutan, is the most accessible part of the country and is the cultural stronghold of the Drukpa Kagyu school, from which Zhabdrung Ngawang Namgyel secured the entire country under his allegiance during the 17th century. Bhutan's national language, Dzongkha, is the lingua franca of Western Bhutan.

Five of the western districts occupy the central hills and northern mountains: Thimphu, Paro, Ha, Punakha and Wangdu. Another of them, Gasa, is isolated in the northern nomadic borderland, while the other four, Samtse, Chukha, Tsirang and Tarkarna, all lie further south, in sub-tropical terrain, in close proximity to the Bengal Duars of India. Three major river systems demarcate this region. The Amo-chu, rises in Dromo county in Tibet, and flows through Ha and Chukha districts to enter India at the Buxa Duar. The Wang-chu with its Ha-chu and Paro-chu tributaries rises in Bhutan south of the Great Himalayan range, and flows into India at the Bura Duar. Further east, the Punatsang-chu with its Dang-chu tributary enters India at the Bhulka Duar.

Each administrative district comprises several counties or subdivisions (*gewog*), each of which is described in turn, highlighting places of historical and touristic importance in close proximity to the main motor roads, as well as the lesser jeep tracks, trekking routes and more remote sites.

★ Don't miss...

1. **Cheri Dorjeden** A hilltop hermitage of the Drukpa Kagyu school, where Zhabdrung Ngawang Namgyel founded the Central Monastic Body of Bhutan in the 17th century, page 95.
2. **Kyerchu Lhakhang** A seventh-century geomantic temple founded by Tibet's unifying king, Songtsen Gampo, on the left foot of the supine ogress, page 112.
3. **Nyizergang Stupa** A towering 31 m stupa (built 1999) that protrudes through the wooded hills overlooking the Mo-chu in Punakha district. Its images and murals illustrate the best of recent Bhutanese art, page 140.
4. **Wangdu Phodrang** A fortress founded by Zhabdrung Ngawang Namgyel in 1638 on the basis of a prediction received in a dream to guard the approach road into the Black Mountains of Central Bhutan, page 150.

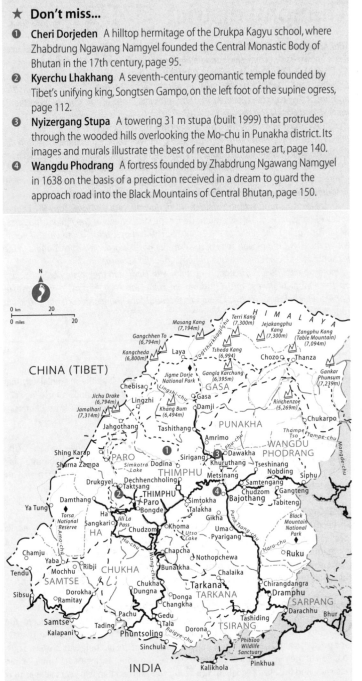

Thimphu district ཐིམ་ཕུ → Area: 1,935 sq km.

Thimphu district is formed by the upper reaches of the south-flowing Wang-chu river (here known as the Thim-chu), and its feeder streams, as well as by the source of the Mo-chu. At the heart of the district is Bhutan's capital city, and so the communication infrastructure here is better than in other parts of the country. The district administrative capital is located in Thimphu city, north of the Changlingmethang market, and beside the river.

Summers are warm here, and the winters dry and cold (average rainfall: 500-1,000 mm). About 56% of the district is forested, mostly with conifer and pine, including the northern parts that fall within the Jigme Dorje National Park. Grazing pastures account for some 17% of the land, and cropland for less than 2%. The main crops are apples, chillies, potatoes, maize and assorted green vegetables. Cash crops (apples and potatoes) are largely exported via Phuntsoling to India and Bangladesh.

There are 10 counties in the district: Naro, Kawang and Chang occupy the central valley of the Wang-chu, Mewang and Genye the side valleys of two major tributaries, while Tobisa and Babisa lie to the east of Dochu La pass, and So and Lingzhi nestle within the Great Himalayan zone of the extreme north, bordering Tibet. Dagala in the far south is a fascinating lakeland plateau, ideal for yak grazing.

Motorable roads link the nation's capital with Dodina in the north, Dochu La pass on the lateral highway, and Chudzom en route for Paro Airport in the west, or Phuntsoling in the south. Away from this thoroughfare, there are fascinating trekking routes in all directions. ▸▸ *For Sleeping, Eating and other listings, see page 102.*

Chang county

Chang includes the southern parts of Thimphu city, as well as the main highway that leads south-west towards **Chudzom** from where the roads to Paro and Phuntsoling split, and north-east to **Dochu La** pass (3,050 m) on the road to Punakha and Central Bhutan.

Thadranang Gonpa

Above the Yangchenphu High School and the Pinewood Hotel, on the east bank of the Wang-chu, there is a difficult two-hour hike that leads steeply uphill through pine forest towards the Lungtenphug military camp and Thadranang Gonpa (3,270 m). This monastery was constructed in 1731 by Tsuklak Gyatso of the Drukpa Kagyu school.

Simtokha Dzong

Six kilometres downstream from the city, Simtokha Dzong (2,250 m) is strategically located at the junction of the Paro, Punakha and Thimphu roads. Built in 1629 for geomantic reasons on a site where an ogress (*sinmo*) had possessed the rocks (*do*), this fortress was the first to be constructed in Bhutan by Zhabdrung Ngawang Namgyel. The site had formerly been the residence of one Lama Pangka Shongpa.

Background The fortress itself is said to have been modelled on Gyantse Castle in Tibet and the project was funded by Bhutanese and Tibetan followers of the Zhabdrung, working under the supervision of his cousin Mipham Tsewang Tendzin (see pages 94 and 240). During its initial construction, the building was besieged by a coalition of the Five Groups of Lamas (see page 240), but the ringleader Lama Palden was slain and the attack repelled. The *dzong* was consecrated two years later in 1631 by the Zhabdrung's tutor Lhawang Lodro, and given the name Sangak Zabdon Phodrang (palace of the profundity of secret mantras).

However, in 1634 when the forces of Tsangpa Tenkyong Wangpo invaded Bhutan from Zhigatse, they captured the fortress with the aid of the coalition, and took hostages. Then, somewhat surprisingly, all the invaders appear to have died due to a gunpowder explosion when the roof collapsed. In 1671 the building was restored by the third regent of the new Bhutanese state, Mingyur Tenpa; and there have been many refurbishments undertaken in the centuries that followed. In 1961 King Jigme Dorji Wangchuk turned the fortress into a national teacher training centre for the Dzongkha language, and more recently the buildings adjacent to the *dzong* have functioned as the **Simtokha Institute for Language and Cultural Studies,** a coeducational school under the guidance of Lopon Lungten (T3323495). There are currently 170 monks based at Simtokha.

The site The fortress is surrounded by a high wall, 60 m square, and entered via a cantilever bridge at the southern gate. The central tower has four large *mani* wheels flanking its entrance, and the circumambulatory walkway around it has a full set of small *mani* wheels, aligned alongside fine bas relief slate carvings which depict the Eighty-four Accomplished Masters of Ancient India and the Drukpa Kagyu lineage-holders.

The **antechamber** has fine murals depicting Shambhala, the Four Guardian Kings, the Wheel of Rebirth (see box, page 268) and the motif known as Domtsen Dampa. The paintings were restored in 1983 in memory of a Japanese Buddhist who passed away in Bhutan.

Within the **inner sanctum** there are large, impressive metal-cast images depicting Shakyamuni Buddha in the earth-touching gesture, flanked by his foremost students Shariputra and Maudgalyayana, and the eight standing bodhisattvas. Immediately in front are smaller statues depicting (L-R): Guru Padmakara, Tsangpa Gyare and Zhabdrung Ngawang Namgyel, and the walls have stacks containing the manuscript volumes of the *Kangyur*. The exquisite murals here are among the finest in Bhutan, depicting the Sixteen Elders. The **West Chapel** contains images of (L-R): Four-armed Avalokiteshvara, Mahakarunika and Tara, with background murals representing Avalokiteshvara, Green and White Tara, and historical personages (the Three Religious Kings of Tibet, the early translators and Zhabdrung Ngawang Namgyel, among them). The **East Chapel** is dedicated to the protector deities of the Drukpa Kagyu tradition, including Chamdrel. **Upstairs** in the tower, there is the private apartment of Zhabdrung Ngawang Namgyel and his subsequent incarnations. A side-chapel off the courtyard functions as a small assembly hall.

Talakha Gonpa

Accessible from **Chamgang** village, to the south of Simtokha on a rough but muddy side-road, Talakha Gonpa (3,050 m) was constructed during the tenure of the 34th Je Khenpo of Bhutan, Shedrub Ozer (1861-65). A vigorous climb leads uphill from the monastery to **Talakha Peak** (4,280 m), which offers wonderful views of the ranges to the north of Thimphu. Previously it was possible to walk to the monastery from Simtokha, but the trail has recently been fenced off to protect a number of apple orchards.

Royal Botanical Garden

From the terminus of the number three and number eight buses at **Babesa**, a motorable road leads up to the Royal Botanical Garden at Serbithang. The garden was opened in 1999, and has become a favourite picnic spot for locals. There is a shop selling seedlings and herbal medicines.

Ganchen Nyizergang Lhakhang

Another trail from Babesa leads uphill for about 1½ km to reach the temple of Gangchen Nyizergang. This is a branch of the ancient Gendun Choling monastery in

Shar, which has Nyingmapa antecedents. The lineage is said to have converged with the Drukpa school during the 18th century during the lifetime of Drogon Trinle, since when it has functioned as a residence of the successive Nyizer Tulkus, one of whom, Trinle Lhundrub, served as the 67th Je Khenpo of Bhutan. In 2001, the temple here was refurbished by Lopon Jigme Trinle.

Dochu La Highway

The lateral highway runs east from Simtokha to cross Dochu La pass (3,050 m) en route for Punakha and Wangdu Phodrang. The road climbs rapidly, passing after 15 km the village of **Yusupang**, where there is a forestry research station. A short, two-hour trail leads downhill from here into the valley and climbs steeply to reach **Tashigang** nunnery. Built in 1768 by the 12th Je Khenpo Kunga Gyatso, the Tashigang complex has several meditation hermitages, surrounding the main temple. Both monks and nuns are in residence here nowadays.

Above Yusupang, the highway winds uphill through pine forest and apple orchards to reach the police checkpoint at the village of **Lhongtso** (Bh. Hongtso, 2,890 m), where the local settlements are inhabited by many Bhutanese nationals of recent Tibetan origin. All foreign travellers heading east from here require special documents that are issued by the Department of Tourism or other host agencies. Above the road is **Thegchen Chokhor Gonpa**, a small monastery that was founded by the 14th hierarch of Ralung, Ngawang Chogyel (1465-1540), during one of his visits to Bhutan.

Passing through the checkpoint, the highway continues to climb, until it reaches the magnificent prayer-flag bedecked **Dochu La** pass (3,050 m). From mid-October to February there are spectacular mountain views of the Himalayan snow peaks to the north. Locals believe that a demoness frequenting the pass was subdued by Ngawang Chogyel's relative Drukpa Kun-le when he visited Bhutan in the 16th century, at which time it was given the name Dokyong La (Dochu La is the local pronunciation). The demoness was then obliged to take an oath of allegiance to protect Buddhism thereafter. **Lungchudzekha Gonpa** is accessible on a three- to four-hour trek from the pass. The distance from Thimphu to Dochu La is 23 km.

Tobisa and Barbisa counties

Tobisa occupies the eastern slopes of Dochu La, as the highway heads downhill through thick forest of rhododendron, cypress and daphne. The road passes a large white landmark stupa, where a milestone shows that the distance to Tashigang in Eastern Bhutan is 530 km. It then zigzags through Lampari and Lumitsawa to the village of **Trinlegang** (1,860 m), which is now known nowadays for its expertise in volleyball. Here there is a famous hermitage that was founded in the early 16th century by Ngawang Chogyel of Ralung. The village houses have their entrances painted with the traditional phallus motif to distract the unwelcome ingress of demonic or malign forces

Now the vegetation becomes more tropical – orange groves, cactuses and bamboo thickets are passed – and the buzzing of cicadas fills the air, as the road continues downhill through the Tobe Rongchu valley to **Mandrelgang**, a site that features prominently in the Tibetan opera *Drowa Zangmo*. Along the roadside are rocks painted with sacred mantras. On the opposite side of the Tobe Rongchu valley, you can see the road that leads to **Taleda College**, a 17th-century foundation, now affiliated to Nalanda University in India. Higher still on the same ridge is **Talo Gonpa**.

Barbisa occupies the lower reaches of the Tobe Rong-chu valley, where the river flows into the Mo-chu. The highway continues winding downhill from Mandrelgang to the road-junction at **Metsinang**, 42 km from Thimphu. For a description of Metsinang and the Mo-chu valley, see page 139.

Kawang county

Kawang includes the northern and western suburbs of Thimphu city, and a vast area to the north. There are several sites of interest, most of them accessible only on trekking routes off the motor road.

Pangri Zampa

Heading north from town on Dechen lam, you will pass the forestry institute at Tagbab and Dechen Choling Palace (see page 75), before reaching the village of **Karbisa**. Alongside, in a cypress meadow, are the picturesque five-storey temples of Druk Podrangding at Pangri Zampa, which were founded by the 14th hierarch of Ralung, Ngawang Chogyel in the course of his fifth visit from Tibet, during the early 16th century. His son Ngawang Drakpa (r. 1506-30) also resided here and gave empowerments, and his grandson, Zhabdrung Ngawang Namgyel, is said to have been guided here in a visionary dream by a raven emanation of the protector deity Jnananatha when he fled Tibet for Bhutan in 1616.

Hiking trail to Punakha From Pangri Zampa there is an old trekking route (40 km) which leads into the Punakha district to the east. The trail climbs through beautiful rhododendron forests via Kabjisa to **Sinchu La** pass (3,400 m), and thence downhill via Tonshinkha to **Sirigang** (1,350 m), from where there is a motorable road into Punakha.

Dechenphuk

Across the river from Pangri Zampa, near Dechen Choling Palace, there is a turn-off leading 2 km through a rough side-valley, where, above a flight of stone steps, the hermitage of **Dechenphuk** (2,660 m) is located. The original buildings were constructed here by Dampa, one of the illustrious sons of Phajo Drukgom Zhikpo (d. 1251), and maintained by his descendants. In particular Dampa's grandson Loden Gyelpo invited the seventh hierarch of Ralung Jamyang Kunga Senge (r. 1314-47) to visit Bhutan. On reaching Dechenphuk, the lama was received by the local deity Genyen Jagpa Melen, who manifested before him in a human form and then dissolved (*thim*) into a rock – an event which later gave its name to the entire district – Thimphu. Transformed into the Buddhist protector deity Sogdag Shenpa Marpo, the deity pledged to guard the Drukpa Kagyu school thereafter. Jamyang Kunga Senge established an active meditation hermitage alongside the rock.

Later hierarchs of Ralung, including Ngawang Drakpa and Ngagi Wangchuk (1517-54) reaffirmed the oath of allegiance that the local protector had made. Significantly, this was also one of the first acts that Zhabdrung Ngawang Namgyel performed when he first reached Bhutan in 1616, and even now the site is revered as the sacred abode of the Drukpa Kagyu protectors. The white-walled shingle-roofed monastery has original murals that are being restored under the auspices of UNESCO. The taller red building, which is more impressive, is a protector chapel dedicated to Genyen Jagpa Melen, and it contains assorted weaponry, typical of protector chapels.

Tango Gonpa

Driving north-west from Karbisa through the Wang-chu valley, the motor road crosses to the east bank at **Begana** and then, 12 km from town, a motorable trail forks eastwards to the car park in the gorge of the Tango Rongchu, below Tango Gonpa. Two hiking trails lead uphill to the monastery, the shorter and more precipitous route taking about 40 minutes and the longer trail over one hour.

Background It was here in the early 13th century that Phajo Drukgom Zhigpo entered into a long retreat focusing on the horse-necked meditational deity

Hayagriva. After 10 months, he heard the neighing of a horse, and beheld a vision of Hayagriva, predicting that his family line would subsequently benefit the Drukpa Kagyu school. Therefore he built a temple alongside his cave hermitage and named it Tango ('horse-head'). It was here in 1251 that Phajo passed away. The complex was inherited by his son Dampa, from whom the nobility of Paro claim their descent.

Later, Ngawang Tendzin, the son of Drukpa Kun-le and Pelzang Butri, was recognised as the reincarnation of Phajo's son Gaton, and he restored Tango Gonpa, which had become dilapidated. A wonderful extant mural of Drukpa Kun-le playing a lute may date from that period. His son, Tsewang Tendzin (1574-1643), was revered in turn as the incarnation of Phajo. It was he who offered all the estates to his cousin Zhabdrung Ngawang Namgyel, following the flight from Tibet to Bhutan. The Zhabdrung entered into meditation in a nearby cave hermitage and successfully performed the wrathful rites of *abhicara* against the King of Tsang who had tried to defeat him. A sandalwood image of Avalokiteshvara carved by the Zhabdrung himself was installed in the main temple. Later, in 1618 the Zhabdrung survived a minor earthquake at Tango, and when his father Mipham Tenpei Nyima passed away in Tibet the following year he had the remains brought here for cremation.

Tsewang Tendzin's son was Tri Rinpoche Tendzin Rabgye (1638-94), the fourth regent of the new Bhutanese state. During his lifetime, Tango was restored in 1688 and reconsecrated the following year — an event said to have been attended by Rup Narayan, the nephew of King Prata Narayan of Kuch Bihar. Since that time Tango has been the main seat of the Tri Rinpoche incarnations. During the incumbency of Tri Rinpoche Mipham Wangpo (1709-38), the complex was expanded by the eighth regent Druk Rabgye (r. 1707-19). Later incarnations, including Jigme Senge (1742-89) and Ngawang Jampal Gyatso (1790-1820), also safeguarded the temple, and Zhabdrung Jigme Chogyel (1862-1904) commissioned the golden roof. Currently, Tri Rinpoche VII Tendzin Gyatso is in residence here.

The site Outside the impressive three-storey building, the encircling rows of *mani* wheels are set within niches containing finely executed bas relief slates which illustrate the Eighty-four Accomplished Masters of ancient India. To the left of the courtyard there is the abode of the *nagini* consort of the local protector Genyen Dontsab. The covered gallery that runs along the outer temple walls within the courtyard has exquisite murals depicting the Drukpa Kagyu lineage, starting from Vajradhara, Tilopa, Naropa, Marpa, Milarepa and Gampopa, and continuing from Tsangpa Gyare through the hierarchs of Ralung to Zhabdrung Ngawang Namgyel and his successors.

Entering the temple, on the **ground floor** there are two chapels. The **larger** of the two has images on the left wall depicting (L-R): Vajrasattva with consort, Tara, Amitayus, Tilopa, Hayagriva, and Sonam Peldron, the consort of Phajo Drukgom Zhikpo. The inner wall has images depicting (L-R): Phajo Drukgom Zhikpo, Shakyamuni (flanked by his foremost students Shariputra and Maudgalyayana), Mahakarunika, Manjughosa and Guru Padmakara. Then, arrayed along the right wall are (L-R): Four-armed Avalokiteshvara, Je Khenpo Ngawang Trinle, Vajrapani, Nyima (son of Phajo Drukgom Zhikpo) and local protector deities. In the centre of the hall is a shrine dedicated to the protector Genyen Dontsab. Fine murals provide a backdrop for these images, those of the left wall depicting (L-R): Phajo Drukgom Zhikpo, Shakyamuni flanked by the Sixteen Elders, and Zhabdrung Ngawang Namgyel; those of the inner wall depicting (L-R): Shakyamuni and aspects of Avalokiteshvara; and those of the right wall depicting (L-R): various bodhisattvas, Drukpa Kun-le, the Three Deities of Longevity, and Four-armed Avalokiteshvara.

The **smaller chapel** on the ground floor has a flagstone floor. It contains images of Shakyamuni Buddha, flanked by Shariputra, Maudgalyayana and the Eight Bodhisattvas, with miniatures depicting the Thousand Buddhas of the Auspicious Aeon. Images of the side-walls include Simhanada (left), Jananatha and Tri Rinpoche

Tendzin Rabgye (right). Other sacred objects preserved here include a stone footprint of Guru Padmakara, an imprint of the hoof of Zhabdrung's mother's horse, and the throne of Tri Rinpoche. The volumes of the *Tangyur* are stacked along the side-walls.

On the **second floor** the central image depicts Four-armed Avalokiteshvara, and there are murals of the Thousand Buddhas of the Auspicious Aeon. Adjacent to this chapel is the private residence of the Je Khenpos. In recent times it has been occupied by the 61st Je Khenpo Samten Gyatso (r. 1946-55) and the 65th incumbent Yeshe Senge (r. 1965-68), among others. On the **third floor** the images depict (L-R): Zhabdrung Ngawang Namgyel, Amitayus and Tri Rinpoche Tendzin Rabgye, alongside an Enlightenment Stupa. The small room next door is the private residence of Tri Rinpoche Tendzin Rabgye. It has a central image of Guru Padmakara, and realistic statues of the progenitors of the Drukpa lineage, as well as an original 17th- century Hayagriva. The murals here depict the more recent incarnations of Tri Rinpoche, including Mipham Wangpo.

The **cave hermitage** at Tango contains images of (L-R): Khandro Sonam Peldron (above), Phajo Drukgom Zhikpo (below), Amitayus, Hayagriva, Guru Padmakara, Mipham Tenpei Nyima – the father of Zhabdrung Ngawang Namgyel, who was cremated here (above) – and Tsangpa Gyare, progenitor of the Drukpa Kagyu lineage in Tibet (below). The murals within the cave depict Shakyamuni Buddha flanked by the Sixteen Elders. Nowadays there are 170 monks at Tango.

A steeper climb from the car park below Tango Gonpa leads to **Dro-le Gonpa** (3,400 m), where a former Je Khenpo of Bhutan remains in meditative retreat. The ascent to the hermitage will take over two hours, but you will be rewarded with outstanding views of the Thimphu valley.

Dodina

Rejoining the motor road below the car park, you can drive as far north as Dodina (2,600 m) on the banks of the Wang-chu, where the road comes to an abrupt end, some 20 km north of Pangri Zampa. A footbridge spans the river here, leading to the ruined 13th- century hermitage of Phajo Drukgom Zhikpo and his consort Sonam Peldron. Several children of Phajo were born at this hermitage, and there is a legend that Phajo threw his seven baby sons into the river, and the four that miraculously survived were prophesied to uphold the Drukpa lineage, the other three being wretched demons in human guise. An old weather-beaten stupa stands alongside the ruins as a testament to these events.

Cheri Dorjeden

Climbing steeply from Dodina, above the Cheri-chu gorge, you will follow the trail that leads to Cheri Dorjeden Gonpa, a name that evokes the grandeur of Chakpori (Iron Hill) in Lhasa, with which it is cognate – Cheri being a local Dzongkha pronunciation.

Background As the number of affiliated monks increased at Tango, Zhabdrung Ngawang Namgyel resolved to build a new monastery, where his Lhomon tradition of the Drukpa Kagyu would flourish and where his father's mortal remains could be interred in a reliquary stupa. With funds and labour donated by his relative Tsewang Tendzin, he founded the three-storey monastery in 1620. The silver reliquary stupa containing the remains of his father Tenpei Nyima was constructed by Newar craftsmen the following year, following the arrival of his tutor Lhawang Lodro (1550-1634) from Tibet. The establishment of the Central Monastic Body (Dratsang) of Bhutan dates from that period.

Zhabdrung himself entered a strict three-year retreat at Cheri, commencing in 1623, through which he consolidated the spiritual prowess required for his subsequent political unification of the country. By 1627 the community of monks had rapidly expanded to over 100, and Pekar Jungne was appointed as the first Je Khenpo of Bhutan. The Zhabdrung also received the full-fledged monastic ordination here from his mentor Lhawang Lodro in 1633. This burgeoning population soon necessitated a move to Punakha Dzong, which became the official winter residence of the monastic community in 1637. Dongon Dzong (see page 74) was established as the official summer residence in 1641, after which time Cheri Gonpa has functioned more as a retreat hermitage.

The first and third regents of the new Bhutanese state, Tendzin Drugye and Mingyur Tenpa, both passed away here in retreat, in 1656 and 1680 respectively, as did the fourth Je Khenpo Damcho Pekar in 1708. Even today this hilltop bastion is revered as the national hermitage of Bhutan.

The site Climbing steeply from the suspension bridge at Dodina, you will first pass a meditation grotto associated with Phajo Drukgom Zhikpo and his consort. The imprint of the hooves of his yak, named Nyima Senge, can also been seen on the rocks. Further uphill is the reliquary stupa of the renowned 20th-century *yogin* Lopon Sonam Zangpo, and an as yet unopened *terma*-repository, embedded in the rocks.

The first building one reaches in the complex is the **Dungten Lhakhang**, containing the silver reliquary stupa of the Zhabdrung's father Tenpei Nyima. Alongside the stupa are images of Guru Padmakara, the Zhabdrung himself, and various protector deities, headed by Jnananatha.

Above, and beside a storeroom, is the **main chapel**, dedicated to the Three Deities of Longevity. Here, the main images depict (L-R): White Tara, Amitayus, Vaishravana, Vijaya and Green Tara, and other precious relics include the walking stick, sword and dagger of the Zhabdrung, as well as a yak bell that was once in his possession. The **antechamber** has fine murals depicting Guru Padmakara, flanked by his consorts Mandarava and Yeshe Tsogyel (on the left), Padmakara, Amitabha and Four-armed Avalokiteshvara (to the rear), and Phagmodrupa Dorje Gyelpo with his lineages (on the right).

The **Dudul Lhakhang**, built around the cave where Zhabdrung performed his three-year retreat, contains a revered teaching throne and central images including (L-R): a photograph of Zhabdrung Jigme Dorje (1905-31), Amitayus, Phajo Drukgom Zhikpo, Jowo Shakyamuni, King Songtsen Gampo of Tibet, Shakyamuni, Tenpei Nyima and the first Je Khenpo Pekar Jungne (below) with Manjughosa and Milarepa (above).

The inner sanctum of the Gonkhang has images depicting the foremost protector deities, Jnananatha and Shridevi, and an antechamber with statues of the Four Guardian Kings and a manuscript version of the *Kangyur*. Nowadays there are only nine monks in residence at Cheri, which still maintains the air of a tranquil hermitage. Sacred masked dances are performed in the courtyard on the 13th and 14th days of the ninth lunar month.

Naro county

Naro county lies to the north of Kawang, and is accessible only on a difficult four-day trekking route that follows the Wang-chu upstream from Dodina to its source in Lingzhi county, and thence into the upper reaches of the Mo-chu around Lingzhi Dzong. There are no hotels or guesthouses en route, and so it will be necessary to camp.

Dodina to Lingzhi Dzong trek
Day 1 Dodina–Dolam Kencho A old rock-strewn logging trail follows the river upstream from Dodina to a small tributary from where it falls and then climbs through bamboo forest to reach a pass (3,120 m). Descending to another stream (3,060 m) it then climbs sharply to a higher ridge (3,340 m) before falling slightly to the meadow campsite (3,320 m) at Dolam Kencho (8 km, three to four hours' trekking).

Day 2 Dolam Kencho–Barshong Taking a side trail that leads uphill through rhododendron forest you cross a second ridge at 3,340 m, before plunging sharply over streams and smaller ridges, on the east bank of the Wang-chu. Clearings soon appear, with colourful names: Dom Shisa (the place where a bear died) and Ta Gumei Thang (the meadow where one waits for horses). From here the trail follows the riverside larch forest and climbs steeply through rhododendron and birch forest to the ruins of Barshong Dzong (3,710 m), where there is a meadow camp (15 km, five to six hours' trekking).

Day 3 Barshong–Shodu Descending to the river bank (3,580 m), the trail now criss-crosses the river on log bridges six times, climbing slowly across the feeder streams and forest marshland that define the gorge. Eventually it reaches a steep stone staircase leading up to a cliff where there are meditation grottoes, once frequented by the Zhabdrung, before crossing the river once more to reach the campsite (4,080 m) at Shodu (16 km, five to six hours' trekking).

Day 4 Shodu–Lingzhi Dzong The trail descends a sand-covered slope to rejoin the river, crossing again to the east bank by a log bridge, and follows the river westwards towards its source. Bypassing a stupa (4,150 m), it crosses the Jaradinthang-chu tributary on a log bridge (4,340 m), and several feeder streams, climbing northwards to reach the shores of Khedo-tso Lake (4,720 m). The ascent leads to a second smaller lake, where herds of blue sheep can be observed grazing, before climbing higher on a narrow trail to reach the watershed **Yele La** pass (4,930 m). Mount Jomolhari and other peaks of the Great Himalayan range now come into view. The trail then zigzags steeply to enter the valley of the Mo-chu, where the ground is marshy and waterlogged. Reaching the west bank, it cuts north-eastwards through the Mo-chu gorge to emerge at the nomadic settlement of Lingzhi Dzong (4,010 m, 22 km, eight to nine hours' trekking). On the ascent of Yele La, the trail crosses over from Naro county into Lingzhi county.

Lingzhi county

Lingzhi is an isolated nomadic area in the upper reaches of the Mo-chu valley. There are no motorable roads at all, and arduous trekking access is possible from Paro via Nyile La (4,870 m), from Thimphu via Yele La (4,930 m) or from Laya via Sinche La (5,005 m). The ancient trade route offering access from Lingzhi to Khangmar county in Western Tibet via Wake La in the north is presently closed, but this route was the one preferred by both Phajo Drukgom Zhikpo and Zhabdrung Ngawang Namgyel when they first travelled to Bhutan. Subsequently this cross-border trail was followed by several invading armies from Zhigatse and Lhasa.

The subsistence economy of Lingzhi is largely nomadic, but highland barley and wheat do grow, and there is a market for local medicinal herbs, including caterpillar fungus, which are used in traditional medicine. The main building here is the diminutive **Yulgyel Dzong** (4,220 m), which overlooks the village. This was one of the Zhabdrung's few non-monastic fortresses, built to monitor the nearby Tibetan frontier. It was originally constructed by the third regent of the new Bhutanese state, Mingyur Tenpa (r. 1667-80), and rebuilt in the 1950s following its destruction by an earthquake in 1897. The most important monastery in Lingzhi is **Geu Gonpa**, located on a cliff-top in the north of the valley, which was originally founded by Chikarwa, a student of Gotsangpa of the Upper Drukpa lineage.

An interesting day excursion from Lingzhi will take you to **Chokham-tso** lake (4,340 m), where blue sheep and musk deer can sometimes be seen grazing, near the base camp of Mount Jichu Drakye (6,974 m).

There are ancient trade routes from Lingzhi that have become modern trekking routes, extending through the Jigme Dorje National Park, to Laya in the east and to Paro via Jagothang in the west.

Lingzhi to Laya trek

The eastern trek to Laya takes five days: Once again there are no hotels, guesthouses or restaurants en route.

Day 1 Lingzhi–Chebisa A pleasant trail from Lingzhi leads along the ridge of the river valley, which is known for its aromatic medicinal herbs, and down into a side-valley where Goyak settlement (3,890 m) is located. This is a typical cluster of stone houses, surrounded by fields of highland barley. Climbing another ridge, the trail soon enters Chebisa valley and reaches the campsite (3,880 m) opposite a village of the same name (10 km, five to six hours' trekking).

Day 2 Chebisa–Shomuthang Leaving all settlements and villages behind, the trail again climbs through high-altitude pastures, frequented by the blue sheep and grazing yaks. Crossing Gobu La pass (4,440 m), it descends to ford a stream (4,190 m), and then climbs a further ridge (4,230 m) to reach the forested valley of the Jolethang-chu, where Shakshepasa helipad is located. From here, the trail winds uphill to the yak pastures of Jachim (4,260 m), before dropping down to the meadow camp at Shomuthang (4,220 ms), alongside a tributary of the Mo-chu (17 km, seven hours' trekking).

Day 3 Shomuthang–Robluthang Criss-crossing the river, with the peak of Mount Gang Bum (6,840 m) in the distance to the south-east, the trail gradually ascends Jari La pass (4,747 m). There are fine views of the snow peak of Mount Gangchentak (6,840 m) to the north, and more distant views of Mount Tserim Gang and Mount Jomolhari. The switchback trail now zigzags downhill to meet a stream. Rhododendrons grow thickly in these parts, as the trail meanders down to cross a small bridge over the Jolethang-chu, and reach the meadow clearing at Tseri Jathang, a summertime sanctuary for the takin, the national animal of Bhutan. Climbing again, it then bypasses a small lake to reach the rock-strewn meadow camp (4,160 m) at Robluthang (18 km, six to seven hours' trekking).

Day 4 Robluthang–Limithang This is one of the most difficult days on the route, as the trail zigzags up the hillside through burnt-out forest and marshy terrain, to reach a glacial valley. Fording a stream (4,470 m), and climbing through pastures potholed with marmot burrows, **Sinche La** pass (5,005 m) comes into view. This is the highest point on the trek, and as it is crossed, the snow massif of Mount Gangchentak can be seen to the north. A long winding descent though boulder- and moraine-strewn valleys follows, as the trail crosses the Gang-chu twice, and climbs through rhododendron and cedar forest to a meadow campsite at Limithang (4,140 m), alongside the Zamdo nangi-chu. Limithang (lit. Lebnathang – 'the place where the Zhabdrung arrived') was the first destination of Zhabdrung Ngawang Namgyel when he fled from Tibet across the nearby Wake La pass in 1616. Mount Gangchentak dominates the skyline to the north (19 km, six to seven hours' trekking).

Day 5 Limithang–Laya Limithang is in the Laya region of Gasa district, and here women still wear the distinctive Laya dress (black tunics with colourful striped skirts and conical bamboo hats). The trail criss-crosses the winding course of the Zamdo nangi-chu, passing through an uninhabited forest on the long descent. The undergrowth is thick and somewhat claustrophobic. At one point it leads underneath a waterfall. Soon the trail forks, one branch leading down to a military campsite by the riverbank and the other climbing slightly to reach the western side of Laya village. There is a platform campsite (3,840 m) above the eastern side of the village, nestling below the snow peak of Mt Tsenda Gang (7,100 m) (10 km, four to five hours' trekking).

Lingzhi to Jagothang trek

To reach the upper Paro valley from Lingzhi you will have to trek initially to **Jagothang**. This is an 18-km hike that will take about seven hours to complete. The trail leaves the Mo-chu valley, heading west, and zigzags through a series of switchbacks, climbing out of the yak pastures formed by the Jaje-chu, through rhododendron and birch forest. Crossing a promontory (4,360 m), the trail continues to climb in a southerly direction, following the contours of the hillside, before descending slightly to reach an idyllic meadow in the valley floor (4,450 m), with a stream running through it. A steep ascent along scree-covered slopes now leads uphill to the windswept **Nyile La** pass (4,870 m), which offers magnificent panoramas of Mounts Jomolhari, Jichu Drakye and Tserim Gang (6,789 m). Then it descends through scree and moraine to the scrubland where blue sheep can sometimes be seen grazing. As the glacial valley is left behind, the twin snow peaks of Mount Jomolhari come into view and the trail falls towards the source of the Paro-chu at Jagothang (4,080 m). The campsite is located near the base of Mount Jomolhari, below a ruined fortress (Jago Dzong), which was once a stronghold of Phajo Drukgom Zhikpo.

Day hikes can be undertaken in the Jagothang area, offering close ridge-top views of Mount Jomolhari or Mount Jichu Drakye, or a visit to the alpine lake Tsophu.

So county

So occupies the mountainous area around the source of the Paro-chu and its feeder rivers. From Jagothang there are then two divergent trekking routes to Sharna Zampa in Paro, a northern trail that takes two days and a southerly route that can be done in three days. The Tourism Department of Bhutan nowadays markets these routes in reverse as the Jomolhari Treks I and II.

Northern Jagothang to Paro trek

→ *This is the more direct approach which follows a route close to the Tibetan frontier.*

Day 1 Jagothang–Thangthangka Descending from Jagothang, the trail traverses the semi-nomadic, semi-pastoral terrain of Dangochang and crosses a plateau to reach the small settlement at Takethang, before coming down into the village of So. Yak herding is commonplace in this region. The early morning views of Mount Jomolhari are impressive, as the descent continues, past a landmark stupa and a whitewashed Mani Stone Wall (3,790 m) to reach an Indo-Bhutanese military outpost and the picturesque meadow campsite (3,630 m) at Thangthangka (19 km, five to six hours' trekking).

Day 2 Thangthangka–Sharna Zampa Descending a ridge that overlooks a bend in the river, the trail undulates downwards through birch and fir forest to cross the Paro-chu, where it converges with the old trade route across **Tremo-La** pass into Tibet, just before the clearing at Shing Karap (3,130 m). Then, descending steadily through conifer forest, ferns and wild rhododendron country, it follows the muddy riverbank of the Paro-chu, out of the Jigme Dorji National Park, to the meadow campsite (2,850 m) at Sharna Zampa (22 km, seven to eight hours' trekking). Across the river from here there is a helipad and an archery field.

→ *This is one day longer than the previous route.*

Day 1 Jagothang–Dumdzo The trail crosses the Paro-chu outside Jagothang and zigzags uphill to reach Tsophu lake (4,380 m). Continue climbing past a second lake and then through a hidden valley to **Bonte La** pass (4,890 m), before winding downhill across yak trails to reach the bridge over the Dumdzo-chu, and the campsite (3,800 m) on the south bank of this river (16 km, six to seven hours' trekking).

Day 2 Dumdzo–Thombu Zhong Crossing a ridge and a stream, the trail climbs through a side-valley and turns south to ascend Takhung La pass (4,520 m), and reach the campsite shelter (4,180 m) of the yak herder huts in the defile of Thombu Zhong (11 km, four to five hours' trekking).

Day 3 Thombu Zhong–Sharna Zampa Crossing Thombu La (4,380 m), the trail descends steeply through a series of switchbacks to reach the helipad at Gunitsawa (2,730 m). The campsite at Sharna Zampa (2,850 m) is upstream from here (13 km, four to five hours' trekking). The route from Sharna Zampa into the central Paro valley is described below (page 118).

Mewang county

Mewang lies in the extreme west of Thimphu district, along the valley of the Bemangrong-chu which flows into the Wang-chu below Khasadrachu.

Thimphu–Chudzom highway

The western branch of the lateral highway from Thimphu runs close to the river in the valley floor, passing a biodegradable sewage treatment plant, rice fields, apple orchards and the conifer forests of **Namseling**, where the valley widens. There is also an older road from Thimphu that climbs above the river and bifurcates — an overpass leading uphill to Dochu La pass (see page 92), and an underpass continuing into Simtokha Dzong (see page 90). From Simtokha Dzong the old road falls to Babesa, passing two roadside statues that depict Dhritarashtra and Vaishravana, the Guardian Kings of the east and north, before rejoining the highway above Namseling.

Further downstream at **Khasadrapchu** there are small roadside shops and restaurants. Across the river is the old Thimphu hydroelectric power station. Here, a side-road follows the Bamangrong-chu upstream from its confluence with the Wang-chu, into a rarely visited part of the country. The trail passes a leprosy clinic and a marble factory at **Bijimenang** before reaching the trailhead at **Tsaluma**. Near Tsaluma there is a meditation cave associated with Guru Padmakara. The main attraction in this area is **Jemalangtso Lake**, which is also accessible on trekking routes from Thimphu and Paro.

From Khasadrapchu the highway continues to follow the Wang-chu downstream. Across the river on the west bank, **Kharbi** village, where most of the inhabitants are engaged in traditional metal crafts, is accessible by bridge. Then, just 2 km before Chudzom (29 km from Thimphu), a rough jeep trail branches off the highway, heading south-east through the Genyitsang-chu side-valley for Bama and Genyekha. The Dagala lakes are accessible from here on a trekking route. The overall distance on the highway from Thimphu to Chudzom, where the Paro and Phuntsoling roads diverge, is 31 km.

Thimphu to Jemalangtso trek

Starting from Kyebitso meadow behind the Youth Centre in the western suburb of Mutigthang, a steep 5-km uphill hike will bring you through the forest to **Phajoding** (3,640 m). The extensive monastery here is named after the 13th-century Drukpa Kagyu

master Phajo Drugom Zhikpo, who frequented this site. In all there are 10 temples and
15 residential buildings, most of them constructed in 1748 by the ninth Je Khenpo
Shakya Rinchen (1744-55), whose lifelike image is venerated within the **Khangzang
Lhakhang**. The **Ogmin Lhakhang**, built in 1789 by the 16th Je Khenpo Sherab Senge
(1784-91), is also a grand building. The largest temple at Phajoding is the **Jampa
Lhakhang**, dedicated to Maitreya, where the state monastic school is based.

The ridge above (4,100 m) Phajoding gives access to the cliff-hanging hermitage of
Thujedrak, where Phajo received visionary teachings from Avalokiteshvara, and
brought forth a spring of sacred water (*drub-chu*) in a place where there had previously
been barren rock. The original name of the site, Bumo Drakar, was consequently
changed to Thujedrak (Rock of the Great Compassionate One). From here a two-day trek
route leads to the lakes of **Jemalangtso** in Mewang county

Day 1 Phajoding–Simkotra Lake From the campsite above Phajoding (3,750 m)
the trail climbs again to Thujedrak hermitage (3,950 m), and then heads directly for
Phume La pass (4,080 m). There are fine views of the Thimphu valley below, and of
Mount Gangkar Punsum to the north-east, as the trail continues to climb, passing a
rarely used sky-burial site and a small lake (4,110 m) en route for **Labana La** pass
(4,210 m). A long descent then leads to a small campsite (4,110 m) overlooking
Simkotra Lake (10 km, three to four hours' trekking).

Day 2 Simkotra Lake–Jemalangtso Lake The trail climbs to a ridge (4,150 m)
and then descends to the shore of Janyetso (3,950 m), before undulating over a
series of ridges to reach the campsite (3,870 m) at the lower end of picturesque
Jemalangtso Lake (11 km, 4 hours' trekking). The route from Paro to Jemalangtso is
described below (page 118).

Genye and Dagala counties

These occupy the southernmost parts of Thimphu district. There are a few places of
historic importance in the Dagala region, among them the Senge Gyeltsenphuk Cave
where Phajo Drukgom Zhikpo meditated and met one of his consorts, the mother of
his son Dampa.

Dagala Thousand Lakes trek

There is a leisurely four-day trek through Genye and Dagala counties, starting from
the trailhead at Khoma village, where there is a Basic Health Unit, about 8 km from
the highway in the Genyitsang-chu valley. The initial campsite at Genye Zampa
Bridge (2,800 m), below Genyekha village, is less than 2 km from Khoma.

Day 1 Genye Zampa–Gur Crossing the suspension bridge at Genye Zampa, the
trail follows the east bank of the river, heading south-east to traverse the
Dolungu-chu tributary by a small log bridge. Following an old trade route into Dagana,
it then climbs through oak forest, past an observation post (3,220 m) and a higher
ridge (3,350 m) from where a narrow pathway winds down to the campsite (3,290 m)
in the yak pasture at **Gur** (5 km, four hours' trekking).

Day 2 Gur–Labatama The trail continues climbing the ridge, through spruce and
pine forest, to cross a number of side-valleys and streams en route for **Pangalabtsa La**
pass (4,250 m). On the descent from the pass there are fine panoramas of the
extensive rolling pastures of the Dagala range, as the trail enters the wide Lamatama
valley to reach the campsite (4,300 m) at **Utso Lake** (12 km, five hours' trekking).

Day 3 Labatama–Panka Taking a higher trail, as the pack animals follow a lower route, you climb along the western shore of Dajatso Lake, into a saddle and on to a higher lake (4,350 m), before dropping into the Docha-chu valley and crossing a series of ridges to reach the campsite (4,000 m) at **Panka** (8 km, six to seven hours' trekking).

Day 4 Panka–Talakha Gonpa Heading northwards on fairly level ground, the trail climbs gradually to cross **Tale La** pass (4,180 m) before descending through bamboo groves to Talakha Gonpa (3,080 m), which has already been described (see page 91) (8 km, six to seven hours' trekking). Four-wheel drive vehicles can traverse the muddy 6-km drive from Talakha to **Chamgang**, from where it is but a short drive into Thimphu.

Sleeping and eating

Dochu La Highway *p92*
Simple refreshments are available on the west side of the checkpost at **Tendzin Restaurant & Bar**, and at **Lhongtso Bar**. On the east side, there are the **Rinchen Restaurant** and **Tsering Phuntsok Restaurant**, along with a number of small roadside stalls selling apples on the right, while the **Gakye Restaurant** is opposite on the left.

Dochu La Cafeteria, located on the hillside above the pass, Dokyong Trokhang, T329011, 325278, offers breakfast (Nu 120) and a set lunch menu (Nu 230). A new extension to the restaurant, with a seating capacity of 40, is heated by Bumthang-style *burkhari* wood stoves during the winter months. The gift shop, which stocks paintings, textiles and other items of interest to tourists, is overpriced. More interesting is the powerful telescope in the restaurant, which was donated by the Kyoto University Alpine Club, following their successful ascent of Mt Gyelpo Matsen

(7,158 m) in 1985. An elongated photograph fastened above the windows illustrates the snow peaks that can be seen from the ridge above the restaurant, using this telescope. From west to east they include: Gangbum (6,526 m), Gangchentak (6,840 m), Gyelpo Matsen, Tsenda Gang (7,100 m), Teri Gang (7,300 m), Kangphu Gang (7,170 m), Dzongophu Gang (7,100 m) and Gangkar Punsum (7,541 m).

Tobisa and Barbisa counties *p92*
At **Trinlegang**, there is the small **Sangye Bar & Restaurant**. There are a number of small shops and roadside restaurants in **Mandrelgang**.
Dechen Hill Resort, T322204, located on an unpaved side-road above the highway, near Mandrelgang within a rhododendron grove, has 18 rooms with private toilets—doubles at Nu 1,400 and singles at Nu 1,050. Hot-stone baths are available. There are a number of small shops and roadside restaurants in Mandrelgang.

Paro district རྤ་རོ → *Area: 1,285 sq km.*

Named after the Paro-chu, a tributary of the Wang-chu (Raidak), which rises below the snowpeak of Mount Jomolhari on the Tibetan frontier, Paro district is one of the most beautiful valleys in Bhutan. Tranquil and unpolluted, its upper reaches are carpeted by thick blue pine forest and its elegant farmhouses, with their shingled roofs, exude a quiet and understated air of prosperity. From the arid confluence of the Paro and Thimphu rivers at Chudzom, the valley gradually opens out, reaching its widest extent at Paro Airport. Further north, the valley bifurcates, the Dopshari side-valley running north and the main valley running north-west.

In Paro town, an impressive cantilever bridge marks the traditional approach to Rinpung Dzong, an imposing fortress constructed in 1645 to defend Bhutan from

Tibetan invasion forces. Further north, in the mid-reaches of the valley, lies the seventh century geomantic temple of Kyerchu, founded by Tibet's unifying king Songtsen Gampo, and the vertiginous cliff-hanging hermitages of Taktsang. At the head of the Paro Valley, close to Bhutan's premier Amanrila Resort Hotel, are the ruins of Drugyel Dzong, built in 1649 to commemorate the Bhutanese victory over Tibeto-Mongol forces. The revered Himalayan snow peak of Mt Jomohari (7,314 m) loom above on the border.

Summers are warm here, and the winters quite cold (average rainfall: 500-1,000 mm). About 59% of the district is forested, mostly with blue pine, including the northern parts which, like those of neighbouring Thimphu, fall within the Jigme Dorje National Park. Grazing pastures account for only 6.4% of the land, and crops for 5.7%. The Paro valley is therefore one of the more fertile parts of the country. The main crops are apples, wheat, potatoes and vegetables. Cash crops (apples and potatoes), like those of Thimphu, are mostly exported.

There are 10 counties in the district: Doga and Shapa occupy the lower reaches of the Paro-chu, above the confluence at Chudzom; Wangchang, Humrel and Lamgong occupy the mid-reaches of the river, including the town of Paro, the airport and the most important historic sites in the valley; Tsento corresponds to the upper reaches of the Paro-chu, in the Great Himalayan zone; Dopshari and Doteng are formed by the side-valley of the Do-chu; while Lungnyi and Naja offer access to Ha in the west.

Paro is one of the busiest and more developed parts of Bhutan – the country's only airport is located here, as are the first international standard five-star hotels. The administrative capital of the district is located in Paro town. Motorable roads link Paro with Drugyel Dzong in the north-west (16 km), Ha in the west (62 km), and Chudzom in the south (24 km). The distance from Paro via Chudzom to Thimphu is 55 km, and to Phuntsoling on the Indian border 165 km. There are fascinating short hikes and treks throughout the valley. ▶▶ *For Sleeping, Eating and other listings, see pages 119-123.*

Chudzom county

The river confluence at Chudzom is marked by three geomantic stupas, constructed in the diverse Newar, Tibetan and Bhutanese styles. The gorge where the Paro-chu and Wang-chu converge is surprisingly arid, but it is the hub of an important road network. From here you can drive 31 km to Thimphu (see page 61), 148 km on the east bank of the Wang-chu to Phuntsoling on the Indian border, 79 km to Ha on the west bank of the Wang-chu, or 24 km to Paro, following the course of the Paro-chu upstream. There is a vehicle checkpoint at Chudzom, a few roadside vendors, and a small Indian coffee shop run by Dantak (the Indian road construction company).

Wangsingha Nunnery

Above the road and accessible on a motorable lane is **Wangsingha nunnery**, which was revived by the late Khandro Lhamo, consort of Dilgo Khyentse Rinpoche, during the 1990s, and has 35 nuns, now under the supervision of Lama Ngodrub. The main temple contains a central image of Guru Padmakara, flanked by Shakyamuni Buddha and Vajrasattva. The murals are of high quality. Adjacent to the door they depict the Twelve Deeds of Shakyamuni (left) and the Fifty-eight Wrathful Deities of the *Magical Net Tantra* (right). On the left, behind a teaching throne that was once used by Dilgo Khyenste Rinpoche, are murals depicting the lineage of the Zhabdrung Rinpoches (near side), and Nyangrel Nyima Ozer surrounded by the great treasure finders (far side). On the wall facing the door the murals depict Guru Padmakara with his eight manifestations and eight Indian teachers, and the Forty-two Peaceful Deities of the *Magical Net Tantra*.

⦂ The life of Tangtong Gyelpo

The mighty lord among accomplished masters, Tangtong Gyelpo, was the combined emanation of Avalokiteshvara and the glorious Hayagriva, who came forth [miraculously], as if Guru Padmakara had [once again] taken birth from the womb. He incarnated at Olpa Lhartse in Western Tibet in 1385. Adhering to more than five hundred tutors he pursued study and reflection without limit. Although he was a naturally arisen, mighty lord among accomplished masters, by virtue of necessity, he received the Northern Treasures in their entirety from Kunpang Donyo Gyeltsen and the

Shangpa doctrines from Lama Dorje Zhonu, and manifestly attained accomplishments in both of these traditions. Through the disciplined conduct [of an adherent of the secret mantras] he journeyed to all parts of the Southern Continent, and its subcontinents and, in particular, to such places as the Lotus Light Palace on Camaradvipa, where he received teachings from the precious Guru Padmakara and numberless accomplished masters, and the dakinis and protectors of the sacred Buddhist teachings paid homage to him.

Tangtong Gyelpo built many temples at geomantic focal points, which repelled invading armies from Tibet. He bound all the venomous gods and demons under oaths of allegiance. From Chimphu hermitage at Samye he extracted five texts inscribed on paper scrolls, including the *Attainment of Longevity: Giver of the Glory of Immortality*. From Drampagyang he brought forth the *Attainment of Mind: Utterly Secret and Unsurpassed*, from Drubtso Pemaling, the *Jewel Hoard of Esoteric Instruction*, from Taktsang at Paro in Bhutan, a ten span long paper scroll which combined the profound,

---

Doga and Shapa counties

Doga extends from the confluence of the Paro-chu and Wang-chu at Chudzom as far as Isuna village on the main road leading to the airport, and Shapa lies further upstream, between Doga and Paro town.

Tachogang Lhakhang

About 4 km on this road from Chudzom, and accessible on the east bank of the Paro-chu is Tachogang Lhakhang. This celebrated temple was constructed by the great bridge-builder, engineer and revealer of concealed texts, Tangtong Gyelpo (see above), circa 1420, to commemorate his visionary experience of the emanational horse Balaha. The soil around the temple is rich in iron, which Tangtong Gyelpo mined for the construction of his suspension bridges. One of them actually spanned the Paro-chu below the temple, but it was destroyed by floods in 1969. Only a small section of iron chain now remains on display here. The temple, though originally affiliated with the Chakzampa branch of the Nyingma tradition,

essential points of all the sutras and tantras, from the Palace of Secret Mantras in Tsari, the cycle of *Profound Doctrines which are Mind Treasures*, and from Zilchen Phuk in Tsari, the *Illuminating Lamp of his own Prophetic Declarations*, and the *Means for the Attainment of the Protector Deity Ksetrapala*. He discovered many other profound treasures as well, and, in exchange, he concealed many treasure-troves at those sites.

Tangtong Gyelpo subdued an evil, extremist king, who resided at Kamata in India, and barbarian tribes on the borders of Tibet, and he introduced them to the Buddhist teachings. The array of his miraculous abilities was immeasurable. He produced uncountable images, books, and stupas, respectively representing the buddha-body, speech and mind, which surpassed the range of the intellect. He built fifty-eight iron suspension bridges and established one hundred and eighteen coracle ferry-crossings. These and other inconceivable deeds are universally renowned. Above and beyond that, on these occasions, in order to encourage virtuous conduct, he choreographed the lives of the past bodhisattvas, religious kings, and other great teachers in dramatic performances. This operatic tradition, which today is known as A-che Lhamo, originated as an aspect of Tangtong Gyelpo's perfectly wonderful enlightened activity, so meaningful to behold.

Finally, when the master reached his one hundred and twenty-fifth year (1509), he passed away bodily, in the way of a sky farer. At that time his spiritual son Nyima Zangpo sang a lament, at which he returned and conferred his extensive testament. Then, he passed away at Pal Riwoche near Zhigatse.

Until the present day, many worthy persons have been blessed by the body of his deathless pristine cognition. The host of his disciples was infinite, and, in particular, owing to the auspicious circumstance of this great accomplished master's attainment of the state of a deathless awareness holder, who could control the duration of his own life, there were many holders of his lineage who attained the accomplishment of longevity.

Adapted from Dudjom Rinpoche's *The Nyingma School of Tibetan Buddhism* (Trans. G. Dorje & M. Kapstein)

appears to have been destroyed during the 17th century on account of its sympathy for the coalition of the Five Groups of Lamas (see page 240). It was restored by the local governor Awu Tsewang, at the instigation of Tendzin Rabgye.

Drak Karpo and around

From Tachogang, the road passes through an uninhabited stretch for 3 km until reaching the bridge at Isuna, where it crosses to the east bank of the Paro-chu. A hiking trail leads above the small settlement here to the remote meditation cave of **Drak Karpo**, once frequented by Guru Padmakara. Upstream on the east bank, after 11 km, are the suburbs of Bongde. On the way the road bypasses the settlement of Mende, across the river, and the military camp at Shap Bera; while, above the road, is **Samtenling Gonpa**, one of the eight monasteries founded in Bhutan by Longchen Rabjampa (see page 236).

Bongde

At the Bongde intersection, where a branch road heads west for Jili La pass (3,810 m) and the valley of Ha, there are some finely decorated Bhutanese country houses, and small temples, including **Bongde Lhakhang** and **Changchi Lhakhang**. **Pelri Gonpa**, a former Nenyingpa monastery is on a knoll across the river to the east. From here it is only a short, 5-km drive into Paro town. The approach road passes high above **Khangku Lhakhang** and Paro Airport, offering excellent views of the magnificent Paro valley.

Paro and around

Wangchang and Humrel counties are at the heart of the Paro valley, including within it the airport, the town and Rinpung Dzong. The very names Wangchang and Humrel hark back to the early consolidation of Drukpa Kagyu power in Western Bhutan.

Orientation

The town of Paro (2,280 m), situated at the confluence of the Paro-chu and Do-chu valleys, some distance north of the airport, has been under construction since 1985. The new airport terminal building was opened only in 2000. Most foreign visitors to Bhutan arrive here by air from India, Nepal or Thailand. Thimphu is at least 90-minute drive away.

Driving north from Paro Airport, the main road crosses to the west bank of the river, while a branch road winds its way past the National Teacher Training Centre (TTC) and uphill to the Bhutan Resort and the five-star Uma Resort Hotel, which overlook the valley. A Japanese-built riverside embankment protects the town and the airport from flooding. Heading into town on the main road, you will pass an old footbridge on the right, the Codex Corporation Offices on the left, followed by the Ministries of Agriculture and Renewable Natural Resources. Here a motor bridge carries traffic out of town, to the east bank, heading uphill in the direction of **Rinpung Dzong** and the **National Museum**.

Continuing on the main road, you will pass on the right a stupa complex and the Palace of **Orgyan Pelrithang** beyond it. Opposite are a telephone booth, the Lha Restaurant, Druk Air Offices and the Paro Archery Ground, fronted by a row of traditional stupas at **Druk Choding**. A road now branches off to the left, leading uphill to **Gangtey Palace**, the police and fire brigade stations, Paro Hospital and a cluster of hotels (Samten Choling, Dechen Resort, Pemaling Villa, Bhutan Mandala Resort, Olathang Hotel and Pelri Cottages). The highway to Thimphu veers south from that road.

Continuing north along the main road, you enter the downtown area. The main street here is lined by traditional, ornately decorated houses, many of which have shop fronts that provide basic supplies to the local populace – cooking utensils, groceries and so forth. On the left you will pass the vegetable market, Sertri General Store, Sangye Pem General Shop, Sham Bahadur Suba Shop, Chodron Restaurant, Rinpung Restaurant, Wangdu Yangkyab Store, a shopping complex with a rural products market upstairs and the weekend open-air market behind, Kumari Vishnu General Store, Tsering General Shop, Karma General Store and Sarasvati Vishnu General Store. Opposite on the right are the entrance to the palace, and the Central Furniture Store.

Lanes now branch off the main road on both sides. Then, on the left you will pass Chokyid Hotel, Denka General Shop, TT Automobiles, Sonam Tashi General Shop and Sherab Wangchuk General Shop. Opposite on the right there is a large taxi stand, in front of a crescent. Turning into the crescent you will pass in succession Zamling Hotel, Tashi Import & Export Company, Rinpung Internet Bar & Phone Booth, a lane (leading to Chorten Lhakhang), Coffee Corner, Peljorling Hotel & Garden Café, Bhutan Food Corporation, Chungdu Imports, Rinpung General Store, Tsewang Rigdzin Restaurant & Bar, Athe General Store, Dago Tsering General Store and Jatrongmi General Store. At this point the crescent rejoins the main road.

Continuing along the main road, opposite the taxi stand, you will pass on the left Mindruk Tsering General Store, M &T Rinpung General Store, Phul Kumari Butchers, Ngodrup Tsering General Shop, Krishna Gurung General Shop, Yegyel Bar & Restaurant, Norbu Dolma Restaurant, Tsenkyak Dorje General Store and Paro Butcher Shop. Now another lane intersects on the left (leading to Jichu General Shop and Bhagi Ram Cobblers), after which you will pass Norbu Zangpo General Shop, Ngawang Zangmo General Shop, Chime Dolma General Shop, Dawa Chodron Phone Booth & Video Shop, Pema Phone Booth, Yangdzom Bar & Restaurant, Gyeltsen Tailors, Karma Dolma Photo Studio, Phurbu Lhamo General Shop and Chokyi General Shop. Opposite on the right are Tsenkyak Handicrafts, Kordala Tailors, Dechen General Shop, Vishnu Bhakta General Shop, a phone booth, Sangye Bidha General Shop, Dechen Zangmo General Shop, KK Shop, Pema Dorje General Shop and Lotay Handicrafts.

After another lane on the left (leading to Druk Jewellery), you will pass Penpa Restaurant, a shopping complex (containing Pelwang Photo Studio, Oasis Beauty Salon, and Nyinda Store), Menjong Handicrafts (with a restaurant upstairs), Palden Wangmo General Store, Sumchok Dolma General Store, Lotay General Store and Kalzang Furniture. Opposite on the right are Lekye General Store, a parking area, the Bank of Bhutan (with Sonam Trophel Restaurant upstairs), the Paro Canteen & General Store, the Lhachen Jakhyung Bar & Restaurant, Namgyel's Corner and the Pema Dorji Pharmacy.

Now on the left a lane leads off to Langa General Shop, Bhankul Thakur Barber Shop and Tsering Zangmo General Store. Continuing on the main road, you will pass Tamdin Tsewang Electronics, NB Chetri Electronics, a liquor wholesaler, Jachung Milk

Paro Valley

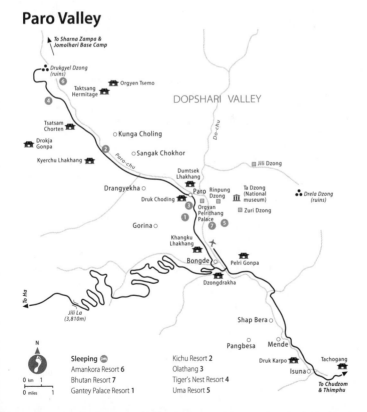

To Sharna Zampa &
Jomolhari Base Camp

Drukgyel Dzong
(ruins)

Taktsang
Hermitage

Orgyen Tsemo

DOPSHARI VALLEY

Tsatsam
Chorten

Kunga Choling

Drokja
Gonpa

Sangak Chokhor

Kyerchu Lhakhang

Paro-chu

Do-chu

Jili Dzong

Dumtsek
Lhakhang

Drangyekha

Paro
Rinpung
Dzong

Ta Dzong
(National
museum)

Drela Dzong
(ruins)

Druk Choding

Orgyan
Pelrithang
Palace

Zuri Dzong

Gorina

Khangku
Lhakhang

Bongde

Pelri Gonpa

Dzongdrakha

To Ha

Jili La
(3,810m)

Shap Bera

Pangbesa

Mende

Druk Karpo

Tachogang

Isuna

To Chudzom
& Thimphu

N

Sleeping
Amankora Resort **6**
Bhutan Resort **7**
Gantey Palace Resort **1**

0 km 1
0 miles 1

Kichu Resort **2**
Olathang **3**
Tiger's Nest Resort **4**
Uma Resort **5**

⁝ The function of Buddhist iconography

It is important to remember that, with the probable exception of images representing historical lineage-holders, Buddhist images are not regarded as representing concrete or inherently existing beings in the Judeo- Christian or even in the Hindu sense. Rather, the deities are revered as pure expressions of buddha-mind, which are to be visualised in the course of meditation in their pure light forms: a coalescence of pure appearance and emptiness. Through such meditations, blessings are obtained from the teachers of the past; spiritual accomplishments are matured through the meditational deities, enlightened activities are engaged in through the agency of the *dakinis*, and spiritual development is safe-guarded by the protector deities. These therefore are the four main classes of image to be observed in Tibetan and Bhutanese shrines. Among them, the images representing the spiritual teachers of the past are exemplified by Buddha Shakyamuni, Padmakara, Tsangpa Gyare and Zhabdrung Ngawang Namgyel; those representing the meditational deities by Vajrakumara, Cakrasamvara and Kalacakra; those representing *dakinis* or female agents of enlightened activity by Vajravarahi; and the protector deities by Mahakala, Panjaranatha, Shridevi and so forth.

& Bakery, Vishnumaya Rai General Store, Yangdzom Restaurant & Bar (with Sangye Khandro Restaurant & Bar upstairs), Karma Dorje Restaurant and Paro Post Office. Opposite on the right are Pema Electrical & Hardware, Chodron General Shop, RICB Insurance, PM Electronics, Himalayan General Shop, Peldzom Enterprises, Lakshmi Maya General Shop, Tsering General Shop and Kunphen Pharmacy. After the post office a square opens out on the left, with the offices of Bharat Petroleum. Opposite it on the right is the Royal Bhutan Police Office.

Beyond the square, on the left you will pass Gangkar Phunsum Restaurant, Paro Bus Station, Dawa Restaurant and Samten Auto Repairs, opposite a bridge that leads across the river to Dumtsek Lhakhang, the National Museum, and the Dopchari valley. Further north on the main street, the area to the left is open country, while on the right you will pass Tashi Commercial Corporation (with the Millennium Complex Disco upstairs), Norbuling Garage, Sangye Auto Repairs and Dawa Bus Station. Uphill from here the paved road leads out of town to Khyerchu Lhakhang and Drukgyel Dzong.

Druk Choding and around

In the old marketplace, the temple of **Druk Choding**, also known informally as Tsongdu Naktsang, which lies near the Archery Ground, was constructed in 1529 by Ngawang Chogyel, the 14th hierarch of Ralung in Tibet, on a site where his host Drungdrung Gyelchog, the great-great-grandson of Phajo Drukgom Zhikpo, had summoned the local deities to protect the Drukpa order. Drungdrung is said to have crushed a large riverside rock known as Humral Drak through his occult prowess because one obstructive demon lurking within it had refused to take the oath of allegiance. The rock is located on the cliff below Rinpung Dzong. Within the upper storey of the temple are murals dating from the time of Ngawang Chogyel.

Opposite Druk Choding is the entrance to the palace of **Orgyan Pelrithang**, concealed within woodland and separated from the road by a perimeter wall. Constructed by Tsering Peljor, the governor of Paro, around 1930, the elegant

Paro City

To Kyerchu Lhakhang & Drugyel Dzong

Dawa Transport

To Dumstek Lhakhang & National Museum

Bank of Bhutan

Dawa Chodron Phone Booth

STD

To Chorten Lhakhang

Taxi Stand

Hospital & Fire Brigade

Weekend

Vegetable
Druk Choding
Archery Ground
Palace Gardens
Orgyan Pelrithang Palace
Stupa Complex

To Rinpung Dzong & Museum

To Border

Not to scale

Sleeping
Bhutan Resort 1
Bhutan Mandala Resort 2
Dechen Resort 3
Gangtey Palace 4
Olathang 5
Peljorling 6
Pelri Cottages 7
Pemaling Villa 8
Rinpung 13
Samten Choling 9
Uma Resort 10
Welcome 11
Zamling 12

Eating
Chodron 1

Dawa 2
Gangkar Phunsum 3
Garden Café 4
Jachung Mille & Bakery 5
Lachen Jakhyung Bar & Restaurant 6
Lha 14
Norbu Dolma 7
Paro Canteen 8
Penpa 9
Sangye Khandro Restaurant & Bar 10
Sonam Trophel 11
Tsewang Rigdzin Restaurant & Bar 12
Yegyel Bar & Restaurant 13

building is modelled on the three-storey celestial palace of Guru Padmakara, known as Zangdok Pelri, and it now functions as a royal residence. Outside the palace wall on the main road there is a cluster of six square stupas, which commemorate the life of Ugyen Wangchuk, the first king of Bhutan.

Chorten Lhakhang, located near the river and behind the crescent on the main street, is seldom visited, but it does contain a chapel in its upper storey. South of that building, close to the Olathang Hotel turn-off, is **Gantey Resort**, the splendid former residence of the governors of Paro, now also converted into a hotel.

Rinpung Dzong

The imposing fortress of Rinpung Dzong, with its high, tapering white walls, dominates the skyline and the life of Paro. There are spectacular panoramas of the building from various ridges overlooking the Paro valley, and the best view is probably from the west bank of the Paro-chu, just south of the Nyamei Zampa. There is an elegant suspension bridge of traditional design with a covered walkway, which replaced an original destroyed by floods in 1969. The name Rinpung is a contraction of Rinchen Pung ('Mound of Gemstones').

Background. A five-storey castle, known as **Humrel Dzong**, was constructed on this site by Drungdrung Gyelchog during the 16th century, above the large rock where he had subdued the ocal deities and bound them under an oath of allegiance to the Drukpa school. t functioned as the residence of his son Namka Gyeltsen and his descendants, the lords of Humrel, until 1644 when it was offered to Zhabdrung Ngawang Namgyel, the founder of the new Bhutanese state, shortly after he had successfully repelled the invading forces of Zhigatse. The Zhabdrung demolished the old building and laid the foundations for a new, more imposing fortress, which was completed and consecrated the following year (1645). The new *dzong*

Western Bhutan Paro district

had a shingled bridge with guardhouses at either end on its south wing, and dungeons on the other three walls, the narrow window slits of which are still clearly visible. Langon Tendzin Drukdra was appointed as the first governor of Paro at that time and he took up residence in the *dzong*.

Throughout the 17th and 18th centuries Rinpung Dzong served as a bastion against invasions from the north. It survived an earthquake in 1897, but was destroyed by fire in 1907 when all the treasures except the enormous **Tongdrol Tangkha** (30 m x 45 m) were destroyed. This *tangka*, which was commissioned by the 13th regent Sherab Wangchuk (r. 1744-63), depicts Guru Padmakara flanked by his two foremost consorts and surrounded by his eight manifestations. On the last day of the Paro *tsechu* festival, it is unfurled for a few hours and sacred masked dances are performed in front of it.

Rinpung Dzong was rebuilt immediately after the fire, following the original design, by the then governor of Paro, Dawa Peljor. It is now regarded as one of the finest examples of Bhutanese architecture – with fine, intricate woodwork, large beams slotted into each other and held together without nails. Nowadays it functions as the administrative headquarters of Paro district, and houses a state-sponsored Drukpa Kagyu monastic community of some 200 monks.

The site The fortress is constructed on a steep hillside and entered from the north – not from the bridge at the southern approach. The north gate where visitors have to register is approached from the car park, alongside the wall where the aforementioned Tongdrol Tangkha is displayed. **Zuri Dzong** lies to the south-east, and **Ta Dzong** (now the National Museum) to the north-east. In the vestibule of the gate are the well-known motifs Sogpo Taktri (Tiger-leading Mongol) and Atsara Langtri (Elephant-leading Ascetic), which reflect the unique position of Tibetan and Bhutanese Buddhism, forming a bridge between the Mongolian and Indian worlds.

The **northern courtyard**, which is surrounded by administrative offices, is some 6 m higher than the lower monastic courtyard to the south. In all the *dzong* has 13 temples, including six within the central tower. The only temple in the administrative courtyard is the **Mitrukpa Lhakhang**, containing a central image of Aksobhya Buddha flanked by 12 aspects of Tara. A fine *tangkha* of Aksobhya hangs on the south-east wall.

The courtyard leads into the six-storey **central tower** (*utse*), entering it on the third level. Within the tower there is a temple on each floor. Some of the chapels are poorly lit and draughty. The highest temple at the roof of the tower is the **Utse Lhakhang**, dedicated to Hayagriva and Amitayus. On the fifth floor the **Kagyu Lhakhang** contains an image of Vajradhara, flanked by Tilopa, Naropa and the main holders of the Drukpa Kagyu lineage. On the fourth floor the **Guru Lhakhang** has a central image of Guru Padmakara flanked by his foremost consorts Mandarava and Yeshe Tsogyel, Amitayus and Avalokiteshvara. The murals here depict (L-R): the motif of the Four Harmonious Brethren, Zangdok Pelri Paradise, Shakyamuni, Zhabdrung Ngawang Namgyel, the Sixteen Elders, Vajrakumara, the Eight Manifestations of Padmakara, Padmavajravikrama, the Fifty-eight Wrathful Deities (twice) and the Forty-two Peaceful Deities. On the third floor there is a **Gonkhang** dedicated to Jnananatha, and another **protector chapel** on the floor below. The first-floor chapel, known as **Rabmang Zheldzomkhang**, contains a set of the eight stupas, symbolic of the deeds of Shakyamuni Buddha.

A wooden staircase leads down into the lower courtyard of the monastic community, where 200 monks reside. On the west (left) wing is the **Dukhang**, where the monks of Rinpung Dzong will assemble. Its vestibule has murals depicting scenes from the life of Milarepa. Inside are large images depicting the Buddhas of the Three Times, with the volumes of the *Kangyur* stacked to the sides. An inner recess functions as a *torma*-making room. The murals are quite extraordinary here, with 10 exquisite panels depicting the Seven Generations of Past Buddhas individually along with those of the Medicine Buddha Bhaisajyaguru, and Maitreya. Each of these central figures is surrounded by a thousand identical miniature figures.

On the other side of the courtyard (east), there are two temples, the **Lhakhang Sarpa** and the **Kunra Lhakhang.** The vestibule giving access to the latter has finely executed murals representing the world according to the view of the *Kalacakra Tantra*, and that of the *Abhidharmakosa*. Inside, the central image is that of Maitreya, flanked by smaller figures including Zhabdrung Ngawang Namgyel on the left. The extraordinary murals depict (L-R): on the **left wall**: the Eight Manifestations of Padmakara, Shakyamuni with the Sixteen Elders, Zhabdrung Ngawang Namgyel with his lineage, and Shakyamuni; on the **inner wall**: the Three Deities of Longevity, Zhabdrung surmounted by Vajrasattva and Green and White Tara; on the **right wall**: the Eight Medicine Buddhas, Manjughosa with Nagarjuna and Vajrabhairava, Marpa with Milarepa, and Avalokiteshvara with Thangtong Gyelpo and Gotsangpa; and Yamari, and on the **facing wall**: the Thirty-five Confession Buddhas, with the Accomplished Masters of Ancient India and the Drukpa Kagyu lineage, Zhabdrung Ngawang Namgyel with four retainers, Mahottara Heruka with the Eight Deities of the Transmitted Precepts, surmounted by Samantabhadra and consort, Guru Padmakara, Avalokiteshvara, Amitabha and King Trisong Detsen, further Drukpa Kagyu lineage holders, and the gatekeepers Vajrapani and Hayagriva together.

National Museum

① *T271257, Tue-Sat 0900-1600, Sun 1100-1600, Nu 100.*

The National Museum of Bhutan is located inside Ta Dzong, which is the largest of the original watchtowers, constructed around 1656 by Tendzin Drukdra, the governor of Paro who later served as the second regent of the new Bhutanese state. Ugyen Wangchuk, the first king of Bhutan, was emprisoned here in 1872 while embroiled in the conflict that eventually led to the establishment of the monarchy in 1907. The round watchtower was refurbished in 1965 by King Jigme Dorji Wangchuk, and since 1968 it has housed the National Museum of Bhutan. The museum is managed by Semo Chime, daughet of the late Dilgo Khyentse Rinpoche, on behalf of the National Commission for Cultural Affairs. The building commands an excellent view of Paro Dzong and the valley.

The site At the entrance there is a collection of iron chains, which are all remnants gathered from various iron suspension bridges built by Thangtong Gyelpo during the 15th century. The exhibits are arranged on six floors of the building in galleries that are entered in a clockwise sequence. No cameras are allowed inside. The **first floor gallery** houses traditional textiles, costumes, equestrian gear and manuscripts. The **second floor gallery** exhibits a large collection of painted scrolls, along with appliqué and embroidered *tangkhas*, *torma*-offering cakes and thread-cross spirit-catching devices for rites of exorcism. An alcove on this level contains a series of images and carved slates, set within decorative niches, along with ritual implements. A central staircase leads up to the **third floor gallery** where Bhutan's exotic philatelic collection is on display, alongside a chapel in the form of a life-sustaining tree (Tsokshing Lhakhang). The branches of the tree point towards icons representing Shakyamuni Buddha, and the diverse Buddhist traditions (L-R): Atisha (Kadampa lineage), Sakya Pandita (Sakya lineage), Tsongkhapa (Gelukpa lineage), Gampopa (Kagyupa lineage), Guru Padmakara (Nyingma lineage) and Vajradhara (Kagyu lineage). Descending to the **first basement**, there is a gallery exhibiting silverwork, jewellery, looms, armour and weaponry, some of which was captured from Tibetan invading forces (see page 241). On the same level there is a circular gallery exhibiting household artefacts. Descending to the **second basement** there is an exhibition of Bhutanese taxidermy

> ⁞ Carry a torch (erratic electricity supply) and allow at least one hour to visit all floors.

(takins, blue sheep, bears, musk deer etc) and butterflies, as well as rattan work from Khyeng. The **third basement** has large monastic cauldrons and the dungeons, as well as the exit.

Dumtsek Lhakhang

Dumtsek Lhakhang was constructed by the great bridge-builder Thangtong Gyelpo in 1433 at a geomantic power place, on the head of a demoness overlooking the confluence of the Paro-chu and the Do-chu rivers. The temple is in the form of a stupa, similar to the great stupa of Gyantse in Tibet, which dates from the same period. The approach road to the National Museum conveniently passes in front of the temple, but special permission is required for access. The building was restored in 1841 by the 25th Je Khenpo Sherab Gyeltsen (1836-39) and is a unique repository of the Buddhist iconography of the Drukpa Kagyu school.

The site   The three storeys, connected by a steep ladder, contain precious images and paintings, which are arranged, like those of Gyantse in neighbouring Tibet, in the form of a hierarchical mandala. On the ground floor the temple is surrounded by an outer and an inner circumambulatory walkway. The **ground floor** has a central image of Vajrasattva, flanked by the other four meditational buddhas, aspects of Avalokiteshvara, Vajrapani and historical figures such as Guru Padmakara and Thangtong Gyelpo. On the **second floor**, the protector chapel (*gonkhang*) is dedicated to Jnananatha and his retainers, and there are murals depicting the Hundred Peaceful and Wrathful Deities. On the **third floor** there are murals depicting the deities of the Unsurpassed Yogatantras – Cakrasamvara, Hevajra, Kalacakra, Guhyasamaja, Vajrabhairava, Hayagriva, Vajravarahi and Mahamaya – as well as the Drukpa Kagyu lineage holders of ancient India and Tibet, including the progenitor Tsangpa Gyare (see page 238). **NB** A torch will be essential here.

Across the road from Dumtsek Lhakhang is the diminutive **Pana Lhakhang**, which may date from the royal dynastic period of King Songtsen Gampo (see page 228).

Lamgong county

Lamgong county, north of Paro town, is the focal point for spiritual activity in the valley, since both Kyerchu Lhakhang and Taktsang hermitage are located here.

Kyerchu Lhakhang

Following the main road upstream from Paro, through an avenue of willow trees, after 2 km you will reach the geomantic temple of Kyerchu Lhakhang (Bh. Kichu). Across the river and the rice fields from here, you can see the smaller temples at Sangak Chokhor and Kunga Choling.

Background   Situated to the left side of the road amid masses of prayer flags, Kyerchu Lhakhang is revered as one of the four further-taming geomantic temples (*yangdul lhakhang*) built by the Tibetan king **Songtsen Gampo** during the seventh century on the body of the supine ogress (Sinmo Kangyel). Geomantically speaking, the ogress represented the rigours and hostility of the Tibetan landscape, which was to be tamed and civilised by the construction of Buddhist temples at selected power points on its surface. A full description of the network of Songtsen Gampo's 12 main geomantic temples is given below (see page 228). Kyerchu specifically is said to have been constructed on 'the left foot of the supine ogress'.

During the second phase of Buddhist propagation in Tibet and Bhutan, which followed the collapse of the Yarlung dynasty (see page 234), the temple was adopted by the Lhapa Kagyu during the 13th century and thereafter by the Drukpa Kagyu.

Nonetheless, it appears to have become overgrown until Pema Lingpa famously rediscovered it during the 16th century (see page 237). Several discoverers of concealed texts (*terton*) are said to have unearthed their teachings within the Jowo Lhakhang at Kyerchu. Among them were the Bonpo Garton Trogyel, and the Buddhists Gya Phurbugon and Letro Lingpa, the latter being a student of Pema Lingpa. The gilded roof was added in 1830, and in 1839, the site was fully restored by the 25th Je Khenpo Sherab Gyeltsen, who, together with the governor of Paro, commissioned a large central image of 11-faced Mahakarunika. More recently, in 1968, the late Queen Mother of Bhutan had a second temple constructed alongside the original in the same style, but dedicated to Mahottara Heruka, Guru Padmakara and the eight main meditational deities of the Nyingma school.

The site The entire complex of buildings is situated within a decorative courtyard, with three stupas. The walls by the entrance gate have murals depicting the Four Guarding Kings and the protector Genyen Dorje Dradul. The original seventh-century Jowo Lhakhang lies directly in front, with the new Guru Lhakhang to the right.

Entering the **Jowo Lhakhang**, there are six images of Mahakarunika, flanking the doorway to the inner sanctum, arrayed in two groups of three. Between them is the main altar, and slightly to the left, the teaching throne of the late Dillgo Khyentse Rinpoche (1910-91). Entering the **inner sanctum**, the central image depicts Jowo Shakyamuni, surmounted by an elegant garuda aureole. This revered image is said to depict the Buddha at the age of eight, and it is flanked by the eight standing bodhisattvas, and by statues of Zhabdrung (left) and Guru Padmakara (right). Immediately in front are smaller images of Guru Padmakara, with his foremost consorts Mandarava and Yeshe Tsogyel. The murals of this ancient temple depict the 12 deeds and past lives of Shaykamuni Buddha, the Sixteen Elders, a vertical band depicting Guru Padmakara, Zhabdrung Ngawang Namgyel, Je Khenpo XXV, and the protectors Tsheringma and Genyen Dorje Dradul. An inner chamber, accessed from the rear of the throne, contains the revered place where Dilgo Khyentse Rinpoche passed away in 1991. The simple room has a statue of Guru Padmakara and there are also a number of murals depicting the Forty-two Peaceful Deities and Zangdokpelri.

The **Guru Lhakhang** contains images of (L-R): Mahottara Heruka, Guru Padmakara in the charismatic form Nangsi Zilnon, Avalokiteshvara in the form Dungal Rangdrol, Kurukulla and a gilded Guru Padmakara. In front is a lifelike statue of the late Dilgo Khyentse Rinpoche, with the long, elegant fingernails that he characteristically had, a statue of the bearded Zhabdrung Ngawang Namgyel, and the reliquary stupa containing the mortal remains of Dilgo Khyentse. A sofa used by the late Queen Mother is located alongside the reliquary stupa, and the teaching throne is beside the entrance. Murals in this temple depict the Deities of the Eight Transmitted Precepts.

Tsatsam Chorten

Following the river upstream from Kyerchu, after 3 km, the complex of Tsatsam Chorten looms to the left of the road, below Dronja Gonpa. This is where the late Dilgo Khyentse Rinpoche was cremated, and it is where his successor currently resides. There are three main temples and two residential buildings here. The **Serdung Lhakhang**, adjacent to the site of the funeral pyre, houses a large golden reliquary stupa containing the ashes of Dilgo Khyentse Rinpoche. The **Phurba Lhakhang** contains (L-R): an image resembling Dilgo Khyenste, a smaller golden reliquary stupa, and an image of the meditational deity Vajrakila with nine faces and 18 arms, according to the tradition of Nyak Jnanakumara, which was fashioned by Khyentse Rinpoche himself. The **Gyelyum Lhakhang**, commissioned by the late Queen Mother, contains images of (L-R): Guru Padmakara with his consorts

♣ The 12 aspects of Padmakara, the Precious Guru

The 'lotus-born' guru Padmakara (Tib. Pema Jungne), who is revered throughout the Himalayan world as the Second Buddha, introduced the most advanced meditative practices of Mahayoga and Atiyoga from Oddiyana and India into Tibet and Bhutan during the eighth century. He is regarded as the progenitor of most Nyingma lineages, and the practices associated with him have the means to transfer a profound blessing through the lineage. According to various biographies, Padmakara is one of the 12 distinct names which he received in the course of his long teaching career in Oddiyana, India, Nepal, Tibet and Bhutan. The cave hermitages frequented by him throughout this region, where he left impressions of his feet, head and ritual implements in solid rock as a blessing for posterity, are too numerous to mention. Padmakara is additionally known by the epithet Guru Rinpoche, the 'precious spiritual teacher'.

Each of the different aspects of the Precious Guru has its own distinct iconography, and meditative practices. The relationship of the 12 aspects to the 12 months of the lunar calendar may be summarised as follows:

On the 10th day of the first lunar month, the Precious Guru renounced his kingdom in Oddiyana, to practice meditation in the great charnel ground of Sitavana, near Bodh Gaya. As he attained liberation, gathering a host of *dakinis* around him, he became known as **Shantaraksita**.

On the 10th day of the second lunar month, the Precious Guru received monastic ordination, and mastered both the sutras and the tantras. At this juncture, he received the two names **Shakyasimha** and **Matiman Vararuci** (Loden Chokse).

On the 10th day of the third lunar month, the Precious Guru was burnt at the stake by the King of Zahor, but he transformed the pyre into Rewalsar Lake, at which time he received the name 'deathless' **Padmakara** (Pema Jungne).

On the 10th day of the fourth lunar month, the Precious Guru was again burnt at the stake in Oddiyana, and once again turned the pyre into water, receiving the name **Padmavajra**.

On the 10th day of the fifth lunar month, the Precious Guru wrathfully subdued a community of eternalists in Southern India, establishing the triumph of Buddhism, at which time he received the name **Simhanada** (Senge Dradrok).

Mandarava and Yeshe Tsogyel, and Vajrakila with three faces and six arms. The **Khyentse Labrang**, where the young reincarnation of Dilgo Khyentse Rinpoche studies under the guidance of Khenpo Yeshe Gyatso, is nearby, alongside a private study room and chapel.

Taktsang hermitage

Taktsang hermitage (Tiger's Lair) is located on the face of a sheer 1,000-m cliff above the Paro valley, and to the right side of the road, some 5 km north of Kyerchu. It is an impressive sight but far from inaccessible.

Background During the eighth century, Guru Padmakara, the great Buddhist master of Oddiyana, travelled the length and breadth of the Himalayan regions, establishing Buddhism from Zahor in the north-west through Central Tibet, Nepal and Bhutan, as far as Kham and Amdo in Eastern Tibet. The sacred sites associated with the precious guru include some of the most dramatic and remote power places in the region. Taktsang is one of 13 awesome tiger lairs frequented by this master,

On the 10th day of the sixth lunar month, the Precious Guru was born miraculously from a lotus on the Dhanakosa Lake in Oddiyana, receiving the name **Saroruhavajra** (Tsokye Dorjechang).

On the 10th day of the seventh lunar month, the Precious Guru reversed the flow of the Ganges at Tamradvipa, converting a group of eternalists to Buddhism, and then he received the name **Garundavikrama** (Khadingtsel).

On the 10th day of the eighth lunar month, the Precious Guru transmuted poison offered him by some eternalists and assumed the radiant form of **Suryarashmi** (Nyima Ozer).

On the 10th day of the ninth lunar month, the Precious Guru assumed the form of Vajrakumara to overwhelm negative forces at Yanglesho in Nepal, and attained the Great Seal (*mahamudra*) through the meditational deity Shri Heruka, at which time he received the name **Vajra Kapalamala** (Dorje Totreng).

On the 10th day of the 10th lunar month, the Precious Guru established the highest Buddhist teachings in Tibet and paved the way for the construction of Samye Monastery, at which time he received the name **Padmasambhava**.

On the 10th day of the 11th lunar month, the Precious Guru manifested his wrathful tiger-riding form at Taktsang in Paro, and made prophetic declarations concerning the future revelation of his concealed teachings (*terma*). At this juncture he received the name **Dorje Drolod**.

On the 10th day of the 12th lunar month, the Precious Guru was enthroned as crown prince of Oddiyana, receiving the name **Padmaraja** (Pema Gyelpo).

These diverse events in the career of Padmakara are commemorated in the 10th-day feast-offering ceremonies (*tsechu*), which are held each month, some of them in conjunction with sacred masked dances. Among the 12 aspects, primacy is given to a frequently depicted iconographic cluster, with Padmakara at the centre, flanked by his two foremost consorts, Mandarava and Yeshe Tsogyel, and surrounded by his Eight Manifestations (*Tsengye*). The eight manifestations, already included in the above list, are: Saroruhavajra, Padmaraja, Shakyasimha, Matiman Vararuci, Padmasambhava, Suryarashmi, Simhanada and Dorje Drolo.

who, according to legend, is said to have flown there from **Khenpajong** in north-east Bhutan on the back of a tigress, in order to subdue negative spiritual forces, hostile to Buddhism, through his tiger-riding emanation, known as Dorje Drolod. In 853, one of Padmasambhava's Tibetan students known as Langchen Pelgyi Senge meditated in the main cave at Taktsang, which later came to be known as Taktsang Pelphuk, after his own name. A recently restored stupa at the entrance to this cave contains his mortal remains.

Subsequently many great spiritual masters of Tibet passed periods here in profound meditation – notably 11th- and 12th- century figures such as Milarepa, Phadampa Sangye and Machik Labdron, and 14th to 15th century figures, such as Tangtong Gyelpo, who discovered a long scroll of hidden texts in the cave in 1433. Sonam Gyeltsen of Nyarong (1466-1540) soon established the pre-eminence of the Katok lineage at Taktsang and in 1508 he founded the monastery of **Orgyan Tsemo**, on the ridge above the hermitage. Branches were quickly established throughout the Paro valley at Langmalung, Khandro Chidu, Tentong Choding, Dolpo Shaladrak and Jigon Gongma.

Later, when Zhabdrung Ngawang Namgyel formed the new Bhutanese state, he visited Taktsang in the company of his mentor Rigdzin Nyingpo, and took possession of the site, offering it to Jinpa Gyeltsen, a brother of the fourth regent Tendzin Rabgye. The Zhabdrung performed elaborate Vajrakila rituals at Taktsang, and experienced numerous visions. Since that time the state monastic community has held an annual prayer festival here, during the fifth lunar month. A new two-storey temple was constructed by the fourth regent in 1692, and later refurbished by the 34th, Je Khenpo Shedrub Ozer (1861-65). More recent renovations were undertaken in the 1950s and 1980s, but disaster struck the main building at Taktsang on 19 April 1998, when a criminal act reduced two of the three temples to ruins, creating a shock-wave inside and outside the country. The government quickly implemented a restoration plan, and the temples have now been authentically restored.

The site   The approach road to Taktsang crosses a bridge over the Paro-chu and follows the Sekar-chu tributary upstream through pine forest for 3 km, where the motorable trail comes to an end at a parking area above Tsatsam Gonpa (2,600 m). From here, horses can be arranged on request, but pilgrims prefer to hike uphill. On the ascent, the trail climbs steeply through oak and pine forest, zigzagging to reach an exposed ridge, where the Taktsang Cafeteria (2,940 m) is located. This hike takes about one hour. Here you may rest and admire the magnificent panoramic views of the hermitage. The cafeteria, under the management of the Olathang Hotel, serves refreshments and meals, and it has a small handicraft shop. The trail ascends steeply from the ridge, wider than before, with railings and safety netting for protection, climbing to a high observation post (3,140 m), where there is a white stupa, almost opposite the hermitage, but separated from it by a 900-m chasm. If you have obtained a special permit, you may continue past the policed checkpoint, down the flight of cliff-hanging steps on the narrow trail to the hermitage. A waterfall plunges down the chasm here, and alongside it there is a retreat hermitage associated with Guru Padmakara, and a shrine dedicated to the water spirits marking the place where he brought forth a spring of water through his spiritual prowess. There is also a small cave on this site where the previous Je Khenpo Gendun Rinchen was born.

Among the temples that are now restored following the fire, the first complex, the **Drubkhang**, comprises three chapels one above the other. The **uppermost chapel** has images of Guru Padmakara in his tiger-tiding aspect Dorje Drolod, Vajrakila and others, as well as a stupa known as the Dedrub Chorten (stupa of faith), which replaces the former reliquary of Langchen Pelgyi Senge. Formerly, before the fire, it had a large image of Padmakara and murals depicting him surrounded by his eight manifestations, as well as murals of the *Lama Gongdu* and *Vajrakila* cycles.

Below it in a **second chapel** are new images of Vajrakila and Guru Padmakara. Formerly it contained a revered 'speaking' image of Padmakara, smaller images of Tendzin Rabgye and Langchen Pelgyi Senge, and a variety of fine murals, depicting Shakyamuni Buddha, Zhabdrung Ngawang Namgyel, Amitayus, the great religious kings of Tibet and the three cycles of deities known collectively as *Kagong Phursum*.

Underneath that is the **cave of meditative attainment** (*druphuk*) where Guru Padmakara stayed in retreat for three months. It contains a wrathful image of Dorje Drolod riding the tigress, while adjacent murals depict the meditational deity Vajrakila. His seat is still visible here, and outside the entrance is the Nyindadrak, a rock with imprints of the sun, moon and the precious guru's thumb.

Within the complex of the adjacent **secret recess** (*sangphuk*), there are large 2-3-m high newly sculpted images of Guru Padmakara with his eight manifestations including Dorje Drolod, as well as the *Vajrakila* and *Gongdu* cycles of meditational deities. There is a *torma*-shaped impression made by the Precious Guru in the rock above. Next to the secret recess, there is an empty chapel, followed by a small doorway that leads to a deep, 6-m crevice overlooking the valley. This is said to have been the actual tiger's lair back in the eighth century.

To the right of this complex, there are another three small temples: the lowest is empty, the middle one contains images of the Three Deities of Longevity, and the uppermost one contains an image of the local protector Senge Samdrub.

Orgyen Tsemo

From the aforementioned observation post overlooking Taktsang hermitage, another trail leads upwards to the summit. Here there are three further temples. Among them, **Orgyen Tsemo** with its amazing frescoes of Guru Padmakara and his followers, was a branch of Katok, built in 1508 by Sonam Gyeltsen of Nyarong (1466-1540) and restored as recently as 1958. **Ozergang** was constructed in 1646, and **Zangdok Pelri** in 1853. All the sites at Taktsang are visited by pilgrims from Bhutan and the Tibetan Buddhist world, although non-Buddhists are currently only allowed to within 100 m of the hermitage complex.

Tsento county

Tsento county occupies the entire northern region of Paro district, from Drukgyel Dzong, where the motor road comes to an end, as far as Sharna Zampa, and the Jomolhari trekking routes to Thimphu.

Drukgyel Dzong

Continuing north from Tsatsam Chorten, the road passes through Drukgyel village, 11 km from town, where the British Council–funded Drukgyel High School is said by some to be the best school in Bhutan. After a further 3 km, the paved road comes to an abrupt end, near the Amankora Resort, at Drukgyel Dzong.

This castle ('fortress of the victorious Drukpas') was built in 1649 to commemorate the Bhutanese victory over the Tibeto-Mongol forces of Lhasa under Depa Norbu, who surrendered at this very place in the Paro valley. The location was also ideal for protecting Paro from further invasions. In later centuries, the impressive five-storey structure became a focal point for cross-border trade with Phagri in Dromo county of Tibet, across Tremo La pass, but it was ruined by fire in 1951. Later, in 1985, a shingled roof was added to protect what remained of the building from further damage.

Situated on a hill, Drukgyel Dzong stands against the snow peak of Mount Jomolhari (7,313 m), protected by three towers, and it can be approached only from one direction, giving the impression that it shuts off the Paro valley. Its position ensured that no one could travel on the Paro-Tibet road without being seen. The battlements, the massive sloping ramparts, and subterranean siege tunnels can still be seen by visitors today.

Drukgyel Dzong to Sharna Zampa trek

From Drukgyel Dzong there is an 18-km hike to **Gunyitsawa** where there is a small helipad, near **Sharna Zampa** bridge. Only the first 5 km can be travelled by jeep on a rough trail. The Himalayan snow peak of Mount Jomolhari (7,314 m) can be seen on the approach on clear days. The trail climbs gradually through the upper reaches of the Paro valley, passing farmland and small villages at Chang Zampa, Mitshi Zampa and Sangatung, to reach an area of apple orchards and pine forest. Trekking permits are endorsed at the Gunyitsawa military check-post. Then the trail leads slightly uphill, heading towards the meadow campsite (2,870 m) at Sharna Bridge (17 km, 5 hours' trekking).

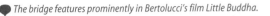 *The bridge features prominently in Bertolucci's film Little Buddha.*

Sharna Zampa to Jagothang trek

There are two demanding trekking routes from Sharna Zampa to Jagothang in the northern reaches of Thimphu district. Both routes offer excellent views of the mountains, glaciers, gorges and waterfalls, and there are opportunities to see yaks in their pasture, and alpine flowers, rhododendrons and orchids according to the season. The best months are late April, May and October. Nowadays the Department of Tourism refers to these routes as Jomolhari Treks I and II. They have already been described in reverse (see page 99).

Dopshari and Doteng counties

These counties occupy the side-valley of the Do-chu, which flows into the Paro-chu below Dumtsek Lhakhang. A Japanese-built dirt road, used primarily by agricutural workers, has recently made the mid-reaches of this quiet valley more accessible.

Druk Path trek

Although most people drive from Paro to Thimphu, there is an easy three-day trek that starts in the Dopshari valley and crosses the watershed pass (3,490 m) to reach Jemalangtso Lake and **Phajoding** (3,058 m), an 18th-century temple complex in Thimphu district. This trail offers the not-so-energetic a wonderful, relaxed insight into Bhutanese life. There are some fine ridge views of the mountains and pleasant walks through lush forest. In April-May the rhododendrons are in bloom and are a spectacular sight.

Day 1 National Museum–Jili Dzong A gravel road leads from the National Museum into Dopshari county, climbing gradually at first, past Kunga Lhakhang (2,640 m), and through pine forest to Damchena where it terminates. A hiking trail then winds gently uphill before descending to the meadow campsite below **Jili Dzong** (3,480 m). This isolated fortress was a former residence of the 14th hierarch of Ralung, Ngawang Chogyel (1465-1540). The temple here contains a 4-m-tall statue of Shakyamuni Buddha, and it has recently been refurbished (10 km, four to five hours' trekking).

Day 2 Jili Dzong–Jangchulakha The trail follows a ridge through rhododendron and alpine forest, and undulates to reach a meadow clearing, from where Mount Jomolhari is visible. Continuing through the forest, the trail descends to the yak grazing pastures (3,780 m) around Jangchulakha (10 km, four hours' trekking).

Day 3 Jangchulakha–Jemalangtso Lake One trail follows the high ridge, from where there are good Himalayan panoramas, while the easier route winds downhill through Tsokham to the valley floor of the Bemangrong-chu, where they join up again before crossing the river. Then climbing through a boulder-strewn terrain where dwarf rhododendrons grow, the trail crosses a ridge to reach the lakeside (3,870 m) at Jemalangtso (11 km, 4 hours' trekking). The three-day trek from Jemalangtso through Phajoding to Thimphu has already been described in reverse (see page 100).

Lungnyi county

Lungnyi county is the area to the west of Paro town, bordering on neighbouring Ha district, and extending from the Bongde intersection to Jili La pass (3,810 m) on a well-paved road surface. The distance from Paro to Jili La via Bongde is 41 km.

Dzongdrakha Gonpa

Following the winding road from Bongde, there are good views of Dzongdrakha Gonpa. This was originally a Kadampa hermitage, associated with Rinchen Samten Pelzang (b. 1262) of Nenying, who encouraged Gonpo Dorje of Lato to unearth sacred buddha relics concealed within a rock here. The **Karmo Gulshe Stupa** was built to contain these relics, and subsequently the cliff-hanging monastery of Dzongdrakha was established.

Jili La

The road continues to wind upwards through dense spruce and larch forest, where the hues change from gold to red to orange, according to the season. **Changnangkha Lhakhang**, an ancient residence of Phajo's son Dampa, lies to the north of the road. Sacred dances commemorating the struggle between Phajo and the Lhanangpa order are performed there each year. Higher still, perched on a cliff face to the north of the road is **Jili Gonpa**, a nunnery with seven temples and several residential buildings with over 100 nuns. Glimpses of Mount Jomolhari appear through the forest, and about 17 km before the pass there are distant views of Jili Dzong in the far east of the Paro valley (see page 118), and of Taktsang in the north-east. Higher still, towards Jili La (Bh. Cheli La) pass, the snow peaks of Jomolhari and Jichu Drakye are both visible, as a broad mountain panorama opens out amid the yak pastures. The descent into Ha district is described below (page 123).

Trekking from Jili La

There is a very pleasant trek, following the road across Jili La into Ha, and returning via Kale La and Sage La passes, which are both important burial areas. Towards the end, the trail descends into deciduous forest and re-enters the Paro valley. Although comparatively short (under seven days), the variation in altitude and vegetation plus the rich flora and fauna and stunning views make it an exceptionally good trek in October-November and April.

Naja county

Naja county to the south-west lies in the mid-reaches of the Ha-chu river, between the Doga area below Chudzom and Ha proper. The main road from the Chudzom intersection into Ha is 79 km. Passing first through Doga county, it winds its way out of the Wang-chu valley to bypass Dobji Dzong, and Mendegang, after which it enters a side-valley, passing through Rangshingang, where there are roadside restaurants, and Bitekha. The terrain then becomes forested again, as the road follows the course of the Ha-chu, passing below Jabcha Gonpa, Jabpa Nagu and Jabpa Lingzhi, before entering Ha district, only 9 km from the town.

⊜ Sleeping

Paro and around *p106, map p109*
Central Paro
D **Peljorling Hotel**, T8-271365, located in the crescent behind the taxi stand, has 5 rooms and an in-house restaurant – doubles at Nu 750 (Nu 550 for Indians and Nu 350 for Bhutanese), and singles at Nu 650 (Nu 450 for Indians and Nu 250 for Bhutanese).

D **Welcome Hotel**, T8-271845, located near the square, has doubles at Nu 450 and singles at Nu 300.
D **Zamling Hotel**, T8-271302, located in the crescent behind the taxi stand, has 5 simple rooms with attached bathroom – doubles at Nu 400 and singles at Nu 250.
E **Rinpung Hotel**, T8-271709, in the crescent, is a noisy establishment, with doubles at Nu 350 and singles at Nu 200.

E **Yangdzom Hotel**, T8-271366, is of a similar standard.

South Paro

AL Uma Resort Hotel, T8-271597, F8-271513, info.paro@uma.como.bz, www.comohotels.co.uk. A new 5-star international standard hotel, founded by Como Hotels' Christina Ong, on the site of the former Druk Hotel near the airport, opened in 2004, on 15 hectares of land, and provides an all-inclusive package. There are 20 rooms in the main building – including 9 rooms at Nu 28,250. In additon there are 9 villas set within the hotel grounds. Each villa has its own spa with massage table, dressing area, hot-stone bath, and pantry with butler access. The exterior of the main building resembles a *dzong*, with intricate painted wood carvings, and an understated elegance aimed at providing "a discreet luxury experience that is close to nature". To this end, the hotel promises holistic therapies, yoga, meditation, hydrotherapy, steam room, gymnasium, exercise rooms, juice bar and indoor swimming pool. The in-house restaurant has an international menu with an emphasis on high-quality indigenous and regional cuisine.

A Bhutan Resort, T8-271609, F8-271728, lama@druknet.bt. A quiet and comfortable hotel, located below the Uma Resort Hotel and affiliated to Gangri Travel, with 10 cottages, each containg 2 double rooms, with attached bathrooms, telephones, cable TV, and fine views of the Paro valley. The outdoor pavilion-style restaurant is near the main building – doubles at Nu 2,000 and singles at Nu 1,800.

A Pegyel Hotel, T/F8-271472, located 9 km south of town in the riverside village of Shaba, has 15 rooms – doubles at Nu 1,800 and singles at Nu 1,500. The hotel has a new swimming pool with a hot-stone bath facilty, and it is the only one that supplies its own water from a well.

West Paro

A Olathang Hotel, T8-271453/271304, F8-271454, ohotel@druknet.bt. A spacious hotel, built for the coronation in 1974, with 60 rooms (27 in the main building and the remainder in 22 outlying cottages), owned by Bhutan Tourism Corporation Limited, and located in the western suburbs, above the town – doubles at Nu 2,000 (main building) or Nu 2,500 (cottages), singles at Nu 1,625 (main building) or Nu 2,125 (cottages), and suites at Nu 2,750 (single), Nu 3,125 (double) or Nu 6,250 (deluxe). The rooms have attached bathrooms (24-hr hot running water), electric heaters, cable TV and IDD telephones. The hotel has a restaurant in the main building with a room service menu, currency exchange facility, conference room and laundry service.

A Pemaling Villa, T8-271473, near the Olathang Hotel, has 8 comfortable rooms – doubles at Nu 2,500 and singles at Nu 1,112, but it only opens during the Paro *tsechu* season, and closes in the rainy season. The restaurant here features Thai cuisine.

B Bhutan Mandala Resort, T8-271997, located below the Olathang Hotel, with 12 rooms – doubles at Nu 1,500 and singles at Nu 1,000. There is an in-house restaurant with fine mountain panoramas, and an internet bar.

B Dechen Resort, T/F8-271392, dchncot@druknet.bt, has 15 rooms, in a quite location below Paro Hospital – doubles at Nu 1,700 and singles at Nu 1,300. The rooms have attached bathroom, cable TV and telephone. Frequented by expatriates, this establishment has one of the best Indian restaurants in Bhutan.

B Gantey Palace, T8-271301, F8-271452, located in the former 19th-century residence of the governor of Paro, close to town, has 23 comfortable rooms – doubles at Nu 1,500 (Nu 900 for Indians, Nu 750 for Bhutanese), and singles at Nu 1,300 (Nu 780 for Indians, Nu 650 for Bhutanese). There are also 3 suites at Nu 1,900-2,200 (Nu 1,140-1,260 for Indians and Nu 950-1,050 for Bhutanese). The in-house restaurant has a dining capacity of 50, with bar serving traditional Bhutanese wine, and a hot-stone bath.

B Pelri Cottages, T/F8-271683, located above the Olathang Hotel, has 14 rooms – rate Nu 2,000 during the Paro Tsechu season and 50% doscount in off-season. There is a newly built dining facility.

B Samten Choling Hotel, T8-271449, F8-271826, has 14 rooms (including 3 outside the main building) – doubles at Nu

1,400 and singles at Nu 1,200. There is an in-house multi-cuisine restaurant with room service, bar, traditional hot-stone bath, foreign exchange facility, laundry service and cultural programme. Visa cards accepted.

North Paro

AL Amankora Resort, local reservations, T2-331333, international bookings, T0065-6887-3337, www.amanresorts.com, at Balakha village near Drukgyel Dzong, the first of 6 international 5-star deluxe hotels owned in Bhutan by Singapore-based Aman Resorts, built at a cost of US$20 million, and opened in 2004, with 24 suites in 6 blocks of 4 (2 up and 2 down). The rooms have natural earth walls, gently sloping roofs and wooden-panelled interiors, with king-size beds, burkhari wood-burning stoves and large terrazzo-clad baths. Communal facilities include the library, multi-cuisine restaurant, and the spa, which is surrounded by scented pine forest and offers treatments using local herbs and body scrubs given with yak-hair mittens! The hotel offers a 7-day all-inclusive package – double occupancy from Nu 48,000 per day and single occupancy from Nu 40,000 per day, which is the most extravagant in the country, even if it does include one spa wellness treatment per person per day. Evenings at Amankora include informative lectures on the regional history, religion, flora and fauna.
A Kichu Resort, T8-271646, F8-271466, intkichu@druknet.bt. A modern, 52-room hotel, affiliated to International Treks and Tours, with a number of well spread-out buildings on the bank of the Paro-chu, near Kyerchu Lhakhang – standard doubles at Nu 2,000, deluxe doubles at Nu 2,500, standard singles at Nu 1,875, and deluxe singles at Nu 2,000, deluxe suites at Nu 5,000. The main building has a restaurant, bar, gift shop and conference hall.
B Tigers Nest Resort, T8-271310, F8-271640, located opposite the Taktsang hermitage on the left side of the motor road, with 15 rooms – doubles at Nu 1,500 and singles at Nu 1,300. There are fine views of Taktsang from here, and the restaurant has a dining capacity of 50. Hot-stone baths are also available.

⊘ Eating

Paro *p106, map p109*

All major **hotel restaurants** offer multi-cuisine options. The best are considered to be the **Amankora Resort**, the **Uma Resort** and the **Dechen Resort**. Hotels in the AL and A categories generally have restaurants at the top end of the range ($$$). The cheaper hotels, **Zamling**, **Yangdzom** and **Rinpung** among them, offer wholesome Nepalese-style *dhal bhat* and some Bhutanese dishes.

The choice is more limited outside the hotels. Most restaurants serve either Indian, Bhutanese or Tibetan cuisine.
$$ Airport Restaurant, managed by the Olathang Hotel group, caters for individual travellers and tour groups.
$$ Garden Café, next to Peljorling Hotel, T8-271365, offers snacks and Indian-style cuisine.
$$ Sangye Khandro Restaurant & Bar, T8-271821, located above the Yangdzom Hotel, set lunches for individuals and groups at Nu 230.
$$ Sonam Trophel Restaurant, T8-271287, located above the Bank of Bhutan, offers Bhutanese and Tibetan cuisine (*momo*, *thupka*, etc).
$ Chodron Restaurant, in the crescent, offers simple Tibetan-style dishes.
$ Jachung Milk & Bakery, on the west side of the main road, sells freshly made bread and pastries.

Other restaurants in this category include: **Tsewang Rigdzin Restaurant & Bar**, in the crescent, and on the west side: **Yegyel Bar & Restaurant**, **Norbu Dolma Restaurant**, **Penpa Restaurant**, **Paro Canteen & General Store**, **Lhachen Jakhyung Bar & Restaurant**, **Karma Dorje Restaurant**, **Gangkar Phunsum Restaurant** and **Dawa Restaurant**.

Near the airport, the **Lha Restaurant** offers snacks and Nepalese-style meals.

⊕ Entertainment

Paro *p106, map p109*

Traditional cultural performances and informative lecture programmes are held in some of the hotels in Paro, notably the **Amankora Resort**, **Uma Resort** and the **Samten Choling**.

Outside the hotels, the focal point for Paro's night life is the **Millennium Club Discotheque**, at the north end of town. Open Sat 2000.

✪ Festivals

Paro *p106, map p109*
An important 5-day *tsechu* festival is held at Rinpung Dzong during the 1st month of the lunar calendar. This is scheduled for 21-25 Mar in 2005.

⊙ Shopping

Paro *p106, map p109*
The main street in Paro has many small shops, with windows at the front and doors to the rear. As in Thimphu, some of them are general stores (*tsongkhang*), selling assorted products of Indian origin, as well as music CDs and videos. The weekend market is located behind Druk Choding.

Beautician and hairdresser
Oasis Beauty Salon, inside a shopping complex on the west side of the main street, is the most fashionable in town. Simpler facilities are available at Bhankul Thakur Barber Shop.

Electrical goods
Electrical equipment of Indian origin (including adaptors etc) can be found towards the north end of town, at Tamdin Tsewang Electronics, Chetri Electronics, Pema Electrical & Hardware and PM Electronics.

Handicrafts
The official government shop for painted scrolls, textiles, masks, bamboo, woodwork and jewellery is the Handicrafts Emporium, T8-271211, 0900-1800. Private outlets include: Tsenkyak Handicrafts, T8-271633, and Menjong Handicrafts which are both centrally located, Druk Jewellery, located on a lane to the west of main street, and Lotay Handicrafts further north. For brocade, painted scrolls, textiles and ready-to-wear Bhuatese clothing, try Gyeltsen Tailors, which usually has a good selection.

Photography
Print films, processing and batteries are available at Karma Dolma Photo Studio, and Pelwang Photo Studio, but you are advised to always carry extra batteries and films as you may not find what you require, and if you do, you will have to pay much more than you would at home. Repair shops are generally not up to standard.

Stamps
Postage stamps are available at Bhutan Post, located on the square.

▲ Activities and tours

Paro *p106, map p109*
Paro has a famous **archery** ground, located near the Druk Choding temple. Contests frequently take place at the weekends.

⊖ Transport

Paro *p106, map p109*
Air
Airline offices Druk Air HQ, T975-8-271856, F975-8-271861, www.drukair.com.bt, issue and reconfirm flight tickets to Kathmandu, Delhi, Kolkata, Bangkok, Dhaka and Yangon.

Road
Taxis can be hired at the airport or at the downtown taxi stand for the 55-km drive to **Thimphu** (Nu 400) or the 165-km, 6-hour drive to **Phuntsoling** on the Indian border (Nu 1,000).

There are 4 private **bus** companies, operating out of Paro. For schedules and fares, see box, page 123.

❶ Directory

Paro *p106*
Ambulance T112. **Banks** Bank of Bhutan, located in the downtown area. Open Mon-Fri 0900-1300, Sat 0900-1100. At present there are no ATM machines.
Hospitals Paro Hospital, is in the west of town, near the Gangtey Palace Hotel.
Internet Outside the major hotels which offer internet access, try Rinpung Internet Bar & Phone Booth, which is located in the crescent. Charge: Nu 3 per minute.

☃ Long-distance buses from Paro

Company	Destination	Days	Time	Price
Dawa Transport	Drukgyel	Daily	0700, 1630	Nu 10
	Thimphu	Daily	0900	Nu 27
	Ha	Mon, Wed, Fri	1400	Nu 53
	Phuntsoling	Mon, Wed, Thu, Fri, Sat	0900	Nu 111
KCD Travels	Phuntsoling	Tue, Thu, Sun	0830	Nu 81
Sherab Travel	Thimphu	Daily	1030	Nu 36
Leksol Travel	Thimphu	Daily	1000	Nu 27

Pharmacies The best pharmacies in town are **Pema Dorji Pharmacy** and **Kunphen Pharmacy**, on the main street. **Postal facilities**, including EMS express delivery, are available at **Bhutan Post**. Open Mon-Fri 0830-1230, 1330-1630, Sat 0900-1230. **Telecommunications** All the major hotels and even some of the smaller hotels now have fax and IDD telephone services. Calls can also be made from STD/IDD shops, such as **Dawa Chodron Phone Booth &**

Video Shop, and **Pema Phone Booth**, opposite the taxi stand. **Tour companies and travel agents** Some of the hotels in Paro are affiliated with Thimphu-based travel agents, but there are no agencies itself in Paro. **Useful information** Local directory enquiries:T140. **International directory enquiries:** T116. **Police:** T113. **Fire department:** T110.

Ha district ཧཱ་བདེ / ཧ → *Area: 1,707 sq km.*

Named after the Had (or Lhade) River, locally pronounced as 'Ha', which converges with the Paro and Thimphu tributaries of the Wang-chu (Raidak) at Chudzom, Ha district extends from the Great Himalayan range in the north to the Amo-chu river and its tributaries in the south-west. The Amo-chu flows into Bhutan from Tibet's Dromo county, but six of its tributaries rise in Ha. The district is not as prosperous as Paro or Thimphu.

Summers are cool, and the winters very cold with frequent snowfall (average rainfall: 750-2,000 mm). As much as 78% of the district is still forested, mostly with conifers but also with broadleaf trees. However, grazing pastures are richer in Ha, with over 7% of the land given over to yak and cattle rearing. Yak meat from Ha, available in the winter months, is regarded as the best in the country. However, less than 2% of the land in Ha is cultivated. There is no rice growing in Ha, and the cash crops – cardamom, apples, potatoes and oranges – are all cultivated in the Amo-chu valley to the south-west.

There are five counties in the district: Katsho, where the capital is located, Sama and Usu in the lower Ha valley, Dri (Bji) in the upper Ha valley, and Sangbe in the Amo-chu valley.

Motorable roads link Ha with Paro via Jili La in the west, with Damthang in the north, and Chudzom in the south (for Thimphu and Phuntsoling). The distance from Ha to Paro is 68 km and to Chudzom 79 km. ➤➤ *For Sleeping, Eating and other lisitngs, see page 126.*

Katsho county

Katsho county is at the heart of the district. On the 26-km descent from Jili La pass (see page 119), the road winds its way through charred conifer forest. There are distant panoramas of the Ha-chu valley below, and the Amo-chu valley far to the west. Heading down into the valley floor, the road then forks, right for the main part of town (2,670 m) and the road to Damthang (14 km), and left for the historic sites of the valley and the road to Chudzom.

Ha town
Turning right for the town, the road passes through a forestry department checkpoint. To the right there is a large encampment occupied by the Indian Army (IMTRAT) and an Indian military hospital. Opposite on the left are a basketball court, a golf course with sand bunkers, Karma General Store, Tsewang Chodzom General Store & Bar, Tsewang Norbu General Store & Bar, Samten Restaurant & Bar, Samten General Store, Gelek General Store, Tsengyel General Store and Chokyi General Store. Now the countryside opens out on both sides of the road for 150 m, leading towards the town gateway.

Passing through the town gateway, there are army camps on both sides. Then on the right you will pass the police station, Karpola General Store & Bar and Ha High School. Opposite on the left you will pass Gita General Store, Dorjemo Store & Bar, Sonam General Store & Bar, Lhab Tsering General Store, Tsering Phuntsok General Store & Bar, Chokyi Hair Salon, Thinley Electronics and Dorje General Store. A lane now leads to a footbridge spanning the Ha-chu. Continuing beyond the lane, on the left are Phurba Tsering General Store, the Rural Sanitary Mart, Drukgyel Photo Studio, Yeshe Namgyel General Store, Dago General Store, Sonam Restaurant, Rinchen Dorje Restaurant & Bar, Dargye Restaurant & Bar (with phone booth), Wangchuk General Store, Tamdin General Store and Bhutan Post. On the right at this point there is a large parking area, and the Tsentsen General Store.

After another lane on the left, you will pass KCD Bus Company, Thinley Dorje General Store, Dorje General Store, Kyichu Restaurant and Dramdzob Transport Company with Kuensal Newspaper Shop and Lekyi Restaurant & Bar opposite on the right. The road now crosses a bridge over one of the feeder streams. Then, on the left are: the Food Corporation of Bhutan, Dawa Budha Hotel & Bar, Ram Bahadur Tailors, Karma General Store, the vegetable market, Sonam Chodron General Store, Sambo Restaurant & Bar, the archery ground and a large parking lot. Opposite on the right are the Bank of Bhutan, Gelek General Store & Bar, Dzong Canteen, the entrance to the district government offices, Gangla Restaurant & Bar, Dorjemo Bar, Phurba General Store, Kinley Restaurant & Bar, Phuntsok Dorje General Store, Pachu Tsering General Store, Chuncho Dorje General Store, Rikyi General Store, Wangchuk General Store & Bar, Sonam Tendzin Restaurant & Bar and the upper market. At this point the road curves sharply to cross the river, leading to Ha Primary School and out of town in the direction of Damthang.

Wangchuk Dzong and Lhakhang Karpo
Heading left from the Jili La intersection (see page 119), the road crosses to the west bank of the Ha-chu, where the historic sites of the valley are located, in an army cantonment zone. **Wangchuk Dzong** lies slightly uphill on the left. The present building, small in structure, dates from 1915. Below the parade ground and opposite

Lhakpa General Store, is the **Lhakhang Karpo** (White Temple), the most important site in the valley, which along with the adjacent Lhakhang Nakpo (Black Temple) is said to have been built by a pigeon emanation of King Songtsen Gampo during the seventh century. Another legend recounts how local nomads from the Mount Khyungdu area on the Tibetan border to the north of Ha, suddenly came here to build the two temples in a single day, giving the valley its name Ha (sudden).

In front of Lhakhang Karpo is a large courtyard, with an observation pavilion, where *tsechu* dances are performed from the eighth to the 10th days of the eighth lunar month, following the Thimphu Tsechu. The temple is entered through a side door, where the vestibule has murals depicting the motifs of the Four Harmonious Brethren and the Old Man of Longevity. There is an altar in the centre of the hall with the volumes of the *Kangyur* stacked on the wall behind it. The main images are situated to the right and they depict the Three Deities of Longevity, flanked by the Eight Bodhisattvas and Mahakarunika. The head of the central image of Amitayus is oversized, apparently because it was brought there separately and soldered to the body. Smaller images here depict Four-armed Avalokiteshvara, and, near the door, the protector deities of the Drukpa Kagyu tradition. To the left of the entrance are murals depicting (L-R): the Eight Manifestations of Guru Padmakara, Guru Padmakara with Shantaraksita and King Trisong Desten, Vajrasattva, and after the teaching throne, which has a window above it, Mahakarunika and the Sixteen Elders. Currently there are 30 Drukpa Kagyu monks in residence, under the guidance of Lame Neten.

Dri county

Dri (Bji) county occupies the entire north of Ha district, including the headwaters of the Ha-chu which rise below the sacred Mount Khyungdu and three tributaries of the Amo-chu, including the Langmarpo-chu. The only motorable access into this region is by the paved road from Ha to **Damthang** (14 km). The road bypasses **Katsho** village (leading to Katsho Gonpa), **Yangthang Gonpa** and a few hamlets, some of them located in sheltered side-valleys to the east of the river, like Chubarnang and Talung. At Damthang itself the Bhutanese army has a border patrol encampment, but its presence here does not seem to deter cross-border smuggling with Tibet, which has become one of the main pursuits of the inhabitants of Ha. Further north towards the Great Himalayan zone, **Gyamdu Gonpa** is an important site. Originally a Barawa monastery, it was absorbed by the Drukpa Kagyu during the 17th century.

Sama and Usu counties

Sama and Usu counties are accessed on the main road that leads from Chudzom and Naja along the course of the Ha valley into central Ha. The distance from Chudzom to Ha along this road is 79 km. After **Jabpa Lingzhi** and **Shari**, the riverside road into Ha passes through thick forest, eventually emerging at **Jyemnkana** village, where there is a primary school, and **Pugekha**. From here it bypasses Karnak and Beltsang villages, to reach the forestry department checkpoint on the outskirts of town.

Sangbe county

Sangbe county in the extreme southeast of the district follows the course of the Amo-chu valley. There are no motorable roads here, but the area around Sangbe Dzong is a significant cardamom-growing region. The population is fairly isolated and, for climatic reasons, engaged for the most part in pastoral farming. Formerly, there was an active trade through the Amo-chu valley, which links Bhutan with the Dromo (Chumbi) valley of western Tibet.

◉ ❼ Sleeping and eating

Ha is relatively undeveloped. There are no hotels in the district, and most visitors will either visit on a day excursion from Paro or Thimphu, or stay over at trekking campsites.

Ha town *p124*
There are a number of small, simple roadside restaurants and bars in the town, all serving only local Bhutanese or Indian cuisine, including to the south of town; **Samten Restaurant & Bar**; in the centre of town, near Bhutan Post, **Sonam Restaurant**, **Rinchen Dorje Restaurant & Bar**, and **Dargye Restaurant & Bar** (with phone booth); and in the north of town **Lekyi Restaurant & Bar**, **Sambo Restaurant & Bar**, **Dzong Canteen**, **Dorjemo Bar**, **Kinley Restaurant & Bar** and **Sonam Tendzin Restaurant & Bar**.

◉ Shopping

Ha town *p124*
The main street has several small general stores which have been listed above. Many of them cater to the Indian Army, which is based here in numbers. There are 2 open-air markets: the vegetable market opposite the Bank of Bhutan, and the upper market at the north end of town.
Chokyi Hair Salon, opposite Ha High School: is the best hairdresser and beautician in town.
Drukgyel Photo Studio, opposite Ha High school: print films and batteries.
Bhutan Post, located near KCD Bus Company: postage stamps are available.
Thinley Electronics, opposite Ha High School: electrical equipment of Indian origin.

▲ Activities and tours

Ha town *p124*
Ha has a small **archery** ground, located opposite the district government offices. Contests are held occasionally at weekends.

◉ Transport

Ha town *p124*
Taxis are hard to find. There are 3 private **bus** companies, operating out of Ha. KCD Bus Company have a service to **Thimphu** on Thu and Sun (d. 0730) at Nu 57, and a service to **Paro** on the same days at Nu 53 (large bus) or Nu 78 (minibus). **Dramzop Travel** run to **Thimphu** on Tue, Thu and Sat at Nu 57. Dawa Transport run outbound from Ha to **Paro** on Tue, Thu and Sat (d. 1630) at Nu 53, and inbound from Paro to Ha on Mon, Wed and Fri (d. 1400), also at Nu 53.

❶ Directory

Ha town *p124*
Banks Bank of Bhutan, located in the downtown area. Open Mon-Fri 0900-1300, Sat 0900-1100. At present it has no ATM machine. **Hospitals and medical services** Ha Basic Health Unit & Dispensary is in the south of town. Indian Military Hospital is also in the south, opposite the golf course. **Post** Bhutan Post, Open 0830-1230, 1330-1630, Sat 0900-1230. **Telecommunications** STD domestic calls can be made from **Dargye Restaurant & Bar**, opposite the parking area and from some of the general stores.

 For an explanation of sleeping and eating price codes used in this guide, see inside the front cover. Other relevant information is found in Essentials, see pages 39-40.

Samtse district ﾉﾉﾉﾉﾉ → *Area: 1,582 sq km.*

Samtse county in the extreme south-west of the country is an important agricultural and industrial area, inhabited larely by Lhotsampa people of Nepali origin. There are two major river systems: the Di-chu (Jaldhaka), which rises in the north-west, close to the Tibetan border, and flows through the western counties; and the Amo-chu, which rises in Tibet and flows through the eastern counties.

Summers are hot and humid, and the winters dry and cool (average rainfall: 1,500-4,000 mm). Some 80% of the district is richly forested, with bamboo, siris and panisaj growing alongside birch, oak and chestnut. There is hardly any grazing pasture here, but a remarkably high concentration of livestock. Almost 16% of the land is cultivated. Maize, rice, wheat, millet, ginger, cardamom and betel nut all grow in Samtse, and it is an important area for fruit plantations: bananas, oranges, mangos and jackfruit. The cash crops, cardamom and oranges, are easily exported to neighbouring India.

There are 16 counties in the district: Bangra, Tendru, Biru and Sipsu are all in the Di-chu valley; Lahirini, Dumto, Demchukha, Dorokha and Tading are all in the Amo-chu valley; Mayona is isolated in the north-east; while the others – Charghare, Gumauni, Nainitai, Chengmari, Samtse and Pagli – all border West Bengal in the south.

Despite its industrial and agricultural importance, Samtse district is remarkably isolated. There is no motor road connecting it directly with the rest of the country. Visitors to Samtse have to travel from Phuntsoling through Indian territory to reach the county capital, 74 km away – some two and a half hours' driving distance! The only motorable road within the district links the town of Samtse with Sipsue and Tendruk, 54 kilometres to the northwest. ▶▶ *For Sleeping, eating and other listings, see page 128.*

Samtse county

Samtse county is at the heart of this district, which has been part of Bhutan since 1668 when the forces of Zhabdrung Ngawang Namgyel pushed westwards as far as Kalimpong, Sikkim, and Dromo county in Tibet. **Kalimpong** remained in Bhutanese control until 1865 when it was wrested by the British, but the links between Samtse and Kalimpong have continued into more recent times in both trade and education. For many years the Bhutanese elite would send their children to schools in Kalimpong. This is one reason for the government's decision to base the National Institute of Education in Samtse town. The other main attraction here is the large new stupa, constructed by Khenpo Karpo, a senior student of the late Dudjom Rinpoche, head of the Nyingma school of Tibetan Buddhism.

Samtse town

Entering Bhutan from India at the Bhutan Gate, the road swings eastwards into town, passing the cinema and insurance company on the left, and a petrol station on the right. At the parking lot turn left for the Tashi Hotel, Hindu temple, the New Stupa, Bhutan Post & Telecom, Samtse School and the National Institute of Education, or turn left into the downtown area.

The commercial heart of the town is located in a circus, constructed around the weekend open-air market. Starting from the parking lot, you will pass Thakuri Vegetable Shop, Bijay Hair Salon, Asha General Shop, Norbu Hotel & Bar, Dophu Travels, Lhakon Beer, Karma Shop, Yangkhyil Automobiles, Pema General Store, Food Corporation of Bhutan, Yangdzom General, Mahabir Stores, Satya Narayan Stores, Karma Shop, Chega Bar, Pasang Wangmo Bar, Chetri Bar, Kinley Store, Tsering

Yangdzom Bar, Pundak Store, Ashoda General Store, Norbu Lhamo Bar, Arun Restaurant & Bar, Kiba Shop, Bakhu Restaurant, Archana General Store, Dressco Tailors, Goyal Grocery, Sonam Wangmo Textiles, Pavitri Pharmacy, Yamuna Hardware, Binod Store, SKD Kerosene, SKO Telephone Booth, Desang Store, Norbu Lhamo Electronics, Pela Restaurant, Tendzin Restaurant and Hotel Tashi.

Other counties

Pagli county, which borders West Bengal in the south, has the Penden Crement Factory, based at the town of **Gomtu**. Here, too, and further east at **Tading** there are a number of other industries, including the Druk Fruit Processing Plant and the Bhutan Army Distillery.

Further west, a motor road connects Samtse with the towns of Chengmari, Gumauni and Sibsu (30 km), which all have a large Lhotsampa (Nepalese) population. The road continues to follow the Di-chu upstream from Sibsu for 24 km to the trailhead at **Tendruk**, an important area for livestock rearing. In the north-east of the district, the remote village of **Dorokha**, located in the Amo valley, is home to the Lhopu (Doya) people.

⬤ ❶ Sleeping and eating

Samtse town p127
The only hotel in Samtse is **Tashi Hotel**, located opposite the parking lot. There are several small restaurants and bars, all serving Nepalese or local Bhutanese cuisine. They include on the south side of the circus: **Norbu Hotel & Bar**; on the west side of the circus: **Chega Bar, Pasang Wangmo Bar** and **Chetri Bar**; on the north side of the circus: **Tsering Yangdzom Bar, Norbu Lhamo Bar, Arun Restaurant & Bar** and **Bakhu Restaurant**; and on the east side: **Pela Restaurant** and **Tendzin Restaurant**.

◔ Shopping

Samtse town p127
The main street has several small general stores which have been listed above. Many of them cater to the Indian Army. The open-air vegetable and meat market is open at weekends.

Try **Norbu Lhamo Electronics**, next to Pela Restaurant, for electrical goods.
Bijay Hair Salon, near the parking lot, is a

health club, beautician and hairdresser. Postage stamps are available at **Bhutan Post**, located uphill, near the new stupa.

⬤ Transport

Samtse town p127
Dophu Travels operate a **bus** service via India to **Phuntsoling**, departing daily at 1000 and 1400.

❶ Directory

Samtse town p127
Hospitals and medical
services **Samtse Hospital** is in the east of town. Medical supplies can also be obtained from **Pavitri Pharmacy** in the downtown area.**Telecommunications**
STD domestic calls can be made from SKO Communications in the downtown area. Postal and telephone facilities are available at **Bhutan Post & Telecom**, located below Samtse School. Open Mon-Fri 0830-1230, 1330-1630, Sat 0900-1230.

Chukha district ཆུ་ཁ → *Area: 1,802 sq. km.*

Chukha district provides Bhutan with its main land access to India in the south. The Wang-chu flows south-eastwards through Chukha from the confluence of its three main headwaters at Chudzom, and enters West Bengal through the Duars. The river is swollen within the district by four tributaries: Jachorong-chu, Sibjalum-chu, Gadu-chu and Piplang-chu. Further west, the Dung-chu, Ne-chu and Padzeka-chu all flow into India near the large border town of Phuntsoling.

Summers are very hot, and the winters are cold, particularly in the north (average rainfall: 750-4,000 mm). Nearly 85% of the land is forested with broadleaf and conifers. Grazing pasture amounts to less than 2%, but dairy products still contribute significantly to the economy. About 9% of the land is cultivated, the main cash crops being oranges, potatoes, cardamom and betel nut, which are sold in the markets of Phuntsoling. Corn, wheat, barley, chilies, ginger and vegetables are grown for subsistence. The district has a relatively high concentration of industrial development. There are two large hydroelectric plants at Chukha and Tala, while a third is scheduled to open soon.

There are 11 counties in the district: Chapcha, Dragcho (Bjagcho), Bongo, Tala and Getanang are all in the Wang-chu valley to the east, while Dungna, Metab, Gele and Phuntsoling are all in the valley of the Dung-chu, further west. Logchinang and Bhalujora are formed by the valleys of the Ne-chu and Padzeka-chu respectively.

The main motorable road links Phuntsoling on the Indian border with Paro (165 km) and Thimphu (179 km). It was the first paved road to be constructed in Bhutan in 1962. Phuntsoling is also linked to other southern border towns through India: 74 km to Samtse, 121 km to Kalikhola, 195 km to Gelekphuk and 356 km to Samdrub Jongkhar.

▸▸ For Sleeping, Eating and other listings, see pages 133-135.

Chapcha and Dragcho counties

Heading south from the Chudzom intersection (see page 103), the main road to India follows the east bank of the Wang-chu through a narrow gorge, passing below **Dobji Dzong**, and through the village of Hebji Damchu, before zigzagging uphill to a ridge where there are sheer cliffs on both sides. This ridge leads up to **Chapcha La** pass (2,900 m), from where the entire Wang-chu gorge is visible, snaking its way southwards to the Bengal plains. Crossing Chapcha La, it reaches the prosperous potato farming village of **Chapcha** (2,450 m) after 23 km. Here, surmounted by **Chapcha Dzong**, there is an important road maintenance camp. At **Ringthangka Lhakhang** in Chapcha there is an extant teaching throne, which Zhabdrung Ngawang Namgyel used when he visited the area in 1620.

Now the road switchbacks downhill to rejoin the river valley, adjacent to the Tachok Zampa bridge, before climbing through forest to reach the attractive settlement of **Bunarkha** (2,270 m). Further south at **Tsimakothi Dzong**, where the main monastic body of Chukha is based, *tsechu* dances are performed annually, during the second lunar month (March/April). In 2005 this event is scheduled for 18-20 March.

The road then passes **Tsimazham** village, below the *dzong*, and the turn-off for **Tsimalakha**, where the offices of the Chukha Hydroelectric Project are based. It then descends to the dam site, where there is an immigration checkpoint, before crossing the Thegchen Zampa bridge to reach the west bank of the Wang-chu. With a capacity of 336 MW per hour, the hydroelectic power of Chukha is exported to India. From an observation point overlooking the transmission station, alongside the ruins of **Chukha Dzong**, a branch road leads some 8 km to the intake end of an even larger hydroelectric bore tunnel which emerges further south at Tala. This project has a planned capacity of 1,020 MW, and together with the Chukha project, it will soon be the country's most important source of revenue.

Chukha Dzong was formerly the capital of this entire southern region before the recent dam construction and the flooding of the Chukha gorge necessitated the shifting of the capital further south to Phuntsoling.

After **Wangkha** village, the road leaves the misty and humid Wang-chu gorge, which is sparsely populated, and climbs a ridge, alongside the Takti-chu falls, where leeches abound during the monsoon season.

Bongo, Tala and Gele counties

Entering Bongo county, the main road descends into the valley of the Gedu-chu, passing through the small settlements of Asinabari and Chasilakha, before crossing the river. It then climbs to the large village of **Gedu** (2,200 m), 28 km from Chukha, where the local plywood factory was closed in 1996 for environmental reasons. Some of their facilities have been taken over by the Tala Hydroelectric Project. At Gedu, a side road branches south-east for Mirching and **Tala** itself, where the new dam is located. The main road descends to **Jumja** village, where there is a dairy farm, before veering sharply to the north-west through Gele county. At **Kamji** village, where the main attraction is the small **Kunga Choling Lhakhang**, it finally turns south-westwards, through dairy-farming country around Suntalakha, and through tropical jungle, as it descends into Phuntsoling.

Phuntsoling town and county

The road continues its abrupt descent through a series of switchback turns at **Sorchen**, where landslides are commonplace during the rainy season. Below this danger point, there is an industrial complex and a military camp before the immigration checkpoint at **Rinchending** comes into view. The distance from Gedu to Rinchending is 41 km. Here departures for all those leaving Bhutan are recorded and all passports are stamped.

Just below Rinchending is the low-lying town of **Kharbandi**, where the Royal Technical Institute and Bhutan Ploytechnic Institute are based. Below the former, there is a winter residence of the late Royal Grandmother, and **Kharbandi Gonpa** (400 m), a small monastery constructed in 1967, which offers fine views over the foothills and the Bengal plains. The main temple contains images of Shakyamuni Buddha, Guru Padmakara and Zhabdrung Ngawang Namgyel, as well as paintings depicting the deeds of Shakyamuni Buddha. The complex is encircled by the eight stupas, which symbolise the major events in the life of the Buddha.

Below Kharbandi the road winds steeply through teak jungle and out of the foothills to **Phuntsoling** (Bh. Phuentsholing), a large town, situated on the Indian border, where the hills meet the plains. Phuntsoling is a typical frontier town, situated on the south bank of the Dhoti-chu, a tributary of the Amo-chu, where Bhutanese, Nepalese, Bengali and Indian cultures meet head on. A traditionally painted gateway welcomes visitors to the Bhutanese frontier post. Commercially it is an important town with small-scale industries (dairy, soft drinks, matches). All imported goods to the capital Thimphu transit through Phuntsoling, so each morning trucks (and buses) roar through the streets. The town is not particularly attractive, but has an interesting mix of population and a definite tropical air.

The distance from Chudzom to Phuntsoling is 147 km and from Rinchending 5 km.

Orientation

Descending into town on **Zhung lam**, you will pass on the right the Indian Embassy Liaison Office and a football ground, with a park and archery ground on the left. Behind the park on **Tashi lam** is the Bhutanese immigration office and **Samdrub lam** lane leading to the Royal Insurance Corporation of Bhutan, the Bank of Bhutan, the Bhutan National Bank, the Post Office and Phuntsoling Hospital.

Continuing to the main traffic circle, turn left on Sang lam, which is a side road into India, proceed straight ahead on Zhung lam for Bhutan Gate on the actual border, or turn right for the taxi stand. Beyond the taxi stand, by the banks of the Dhoti-chu are a carpet factory, Norgyay Cinema, the new bus station, the crocodile-breeding centre (a tank of gharial and marsh mugger crocodiles) and an industrial zone with a polythene processing factory and a Pepsi Cola bottling plant.

If you head directly for the **Bhutan Gate** on **Zhung lam**, on the left you will pass the old bus station (where there are clean pay-for-use toilets), the Druk Hotel, a petrol station, and the Bhutanese customs and police offices. Opposite on the right you will pass in succession Kashi Stores, Ashok Restaurant, Hotel Moonlight, Hotel Blue Dragon, Kesang Dekar Pan Shop, Druk Dejo Store, Hello Bhutan Bookstall, DT Communications, two STD phone booths, Phajoding Internet Café, Rabten Agencies and Wangchuk Legal Services. At this point you can turn right into Gaton lam or continue straight ahead to the gate, passing Kunga Hotel, Kunley Drukpa Restaurant, Druk X-Ray Clinic and C. Wang Pathology. Beyond the gate is the bustling Indian border town of **Jaigaon**. ↠ *For information on the border crossing procedures, see page 30.*

> ‡ Since 2001 foreign nationals have been allowed to enter the town from India for one night, without paying the high tourist rates required for the rest of Bhutan.

Western Bhutan Chukha district

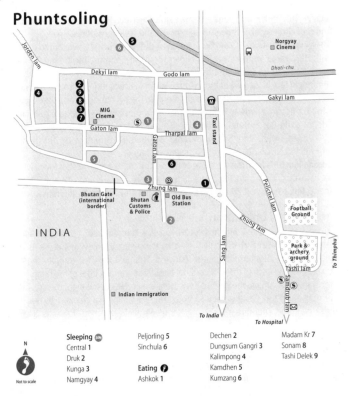

Phuntsoling

Jorden lam
Dekyi lam
Godo lam
Norgyay Cinema
Dhoti-chu
Gakyi lam
MIG Cinema
Gaton lam
Tharpai lam
Taxi stand
Gaton lam
Peljrchel lam
Zhung lam
Bhutan Gate (international border)
Bhutan Customs & Police
Old Bus Station
Football Ground
INDIA
Zhung lam
Sang lam
Park & archery ground
Tashi lam
Samdrub lam
Indian immigration
To Thimphu
To India
To Hospital

N
Not to scale

Sleeping	Peljorling 5	Dechen 2	Madam Kr 7
Central 1	Sinchula 6	Dungsum Gangri 3	Sonam 8
Druk 2		Kalimpong 4	Tashi Delek 9
Kunga 3	Eating	Kamdhen 5	
Namgyay 4	Ashkok 1	Kumzang 6	

If you turn right on to Gaton lam, opposite the Kunga Hotel, you will pass Agarwal Company, Rabden Pharmacy and Gonphel Pharmacy. A turn-off on the right leads into **Tharpa lam**, which surrounds a large park containing the **Zangdokpelri Lhakhang**. On the south side of the park there is a row of shops (Kelwang Electronics, Tsering Tsenga Store, Kanchen Hall, Phuntsog Store and four Indian shops). On the east side of the park, there are five India-owned stores and several Bhutanese businesses, including Kunga Yonten Pan Shop, Norzang Store, Bhutan Sales Corporation, Druk Store and Tashi Rabten Store. On the north side of the park, are the Namgyay Hotel, Bhutan Enterprises, Thinley Wangmo Hardware, Deki Corporation and TTC Supermarket, as well as eight Indian businesses.

Gaton lam runs west from the park to the edge of town. Heading west on this street, you will pass on the right the Central Hotel, the Bank of Bhutan, Hans Stationery, a phone booth and MIG Cinema Centre (with a lane of small restaurants behind). Opposite on the left are Tselha Cable TV, a pedestrian lane, a number of electronics stores and Druk Carpet Industry. A turn-off on the left now leads via Hotel Peljorling back to the Bhutan Gate. Further west on Gaton lam, you will pass on the right Hotel Dechen, Rignam Hotel, a turn-off for Hotel Suriya, Hotel Himalaya, Hotel KC, Chime Transport and Kalimpong Restaurant, while on the left are Rigya Hotel, Bhutan Photo Studio, Loyal Photo Studio and Tsomo Hotel. At the western extremity of Gaton lam you will find the Beauty Art Salon, Bhutan Bar and a photocopy shop with STD facilities.

West of Tharpa lam, there are **two parallel streets**, which both give access to the taxi stand and the vegetable market at their north end. On the first of these you will find Bhutan Fast Food, and Dorji Bar, while the second has a number of small tailors, grocery and electrical stores, Rangzen Hotel, Quick Bar, Bhutan Hotel, Dolma Restaurant and Om Hotel. On a third parallel street, known as **Godo lam**, you will find the Sangye Bar, Druk Handicrafts, Pemba Lama Bar, Hotel Penjore, Hotel Sharma, and a number of clothing and shoe shops, grocers and jewellery stores.

Dekyi lam runs from the old bus station at the west end of Godo lam to the edge of town. Here there are pharmacies, clinics, Tendzin Chophel Bar, Gechu Shopping Complex, Dekyi Hotel and Shot Bar.

Phunsum lam is located at the extreme north of town, running from the southern traffic circle, along the Dhoti-chu embankment, to the new bus station. Heading north from the traffic circle, you will pass on the left a number of small bars and shops, including Panda Bar & Hotel, as well as Kunten Tsidon Hotel, Hotel Step In, Laxmi Hotel, Kenken Hotel, and Sangyay Dema Restaurant. Opposite on the right are Eastern Hill Hotel, Yeshey Hotel and Gegyay Restaurant.

Jorden lam runs from the west end of Gaton lam to the north-west of town, where it meets with Dekyi lam and Phunsum lam. Here are Hotel Nyima, Dophu Transport Company, Rana Transport Company, Paradise Hotel and Tsering Restaurant & Bar.

Zangdokpelri Lhakhang

The main site of interest within the town is the **Zangdokpelri** temple, which was constructed in 1982 and modelled on the three-storey celestial palace of Guru Padmakara. It is situated within the park on Tharpa lam. The complex has four entrances – one in each of the four cardinal directions – and in front of the temple there is a rectangular pond. On the ground floor there are images of the eight manifestations of Guru Padmakara. On the second floor are Mahakarunika flanked by the Eight Bodhisattvas and Zhabdrung Ngawang Namgyel; while the third floor has a central image of Amitabha. Immediately behind the temple are two *mani* wheel chapels.

Doya

The Doya tribal homeland is located in the extreme south-west enclave of Phuntsoling county at Taba-Dramten and Loto-Kuchu, across the Amo-chu. Like the

Toktop people of Toktokha south of Paro, they are considered to be among the **133**
indigenous Monpa inhabitants of Bhutan (see page 259).

● Sleeping

Chapcha and Dragcho counties *p129*
Damchu Hotel, 4 km south of Hebji Dzong, has rooms and a small restaurant.
Dekyi Hotel & Bar, at Chukha, is a roadside stop, catering to truck drivers.
Karma Hotel, T8-478221, at Tsimazham, has simple accommodation (Nu 150), and a more basic menu.

Phuntsoling *p130, map p131*
B **Druk Hotel**, T5-252426. F5-252929, h-druk@druknet.bt, on Zhung lam, has 32 rooms with telephone and television – doubles at Nu 2,000 and singles at Nu 1,500, with bar and restaurant serving good Indian cuisine.
C **Central Hotel**, T5-252172, F5-252173, on Gaton lam, has 23 rooms and largely Indian clientele – doubles at Nu 785 and singles at Nu 550.
C **Namgyay Hotel**, T5-252374, F5-253946, on Tharpa lam, has 16 rooms with telephone and television – doubles at Nu 750 and singles at Nu 550.
C **Peljorling Hotel**, T5-252833, F5-252915, on Zhung lam, has 23 simpler rooms and a busy restaurant – doubles at Nu 850 and singles at Nu 550.
D **Kunga Hotel**, T5-252293, on the corner of Gaton lam and Zhung lam, has 15 rooms with television – doubles at Nu 390 and singles at Nu 280. The clients are mostly Bhutanese and Indian.
D **Sinchula Hotel**, T5-252589, F5-252155, on Phunsum lam, has 15 basic rooms, with rooftop terrace – doubles at Nu 550 and singles at Nu 390.
E **Bhutan Hotel**, T5-252576, popular with Bhutanese visitors, has 23 rooms – doubles at Nu 200 and singles at Nu 100.
Other hotels in this budget category (some of which may not accept foreign guests) include: On **Zhung lam** are Moonlight, Blue Dragon and Park View. Nearby on **Gaton lam** are the Tsomo Hotel, Rigya Hotel, Punjab Grand Hotel, Dechen Hotel and Suriya Hotel. On **Godo lam** are the Penjore Hotel and Sharma Hotel. Among the parallel streets is the **Om Hotel**

while on **Dekyi lam** the Dekyi Hotel and Himalaya Hotel can be found. There are a number of places on **Jorden lam** including the Saluja Hotel, Rignam Hotel, Paradise Hotel, KC Hotel, Holiday Inn and Nyima Hotel. Finally, on **Phunsum lam** are the Eastern Hill Hotel, Yeshey Hotel, Laxmi Hotel, Step In Hotel, Kunten Tsidon Hotel and CD Hotel.

Jaigaon *p131*
If you are obliged to stay overnight in Jaigaon, on the Indian side of the border, the most convenient option is the **Hotel Kasturi** (03566-63036), next door to the immigration checkpoint, which has doubles at Rd 450 and singles at Rs 250.

● Eating

Bongo, Tala and Gele counties *p130*
Lhamu Restaurant & Bar, T5-272332, is the best of several roadside restaurants in Gedu.

Chapcha and Dragcho counties *p129*
Bunarkha Cafeteria, T8-478216, at Bunarkha village, founded by Bhutan Tourism Corporation Ltd, an impressive menu, and clean bathroom facilities.

Phuntsoling *p130, map p131*
The best restaurants, all of them serving Indian and Nepalese cuisine, are found in the Druk, Namgyay, Peljorling, Kunga and Sinchula hotels. Indian and Bhutanese dishes are also available outside the hotels at the following simple restaurants (all N category): on **Zhung lam**: Ashok Restaurant; on **Tharpa lam**: Kunzang Restaurant; behind MIG Cinema on **Gaton lam**: Madan Kr Restaurant, Dungsum Gangri Restaurant, Sonam Restaurant, Tashi Delek Restaurant and Dechen Restaurant,also Bhutan Fast Food; on **Godo lam**: Kamdhen (KC's) Restaurant; on **Phunsum lam**: Panda Hotel & Bar, Sangyay Dema Restaurant and Gegye Restaurant; and on **Jorden lam**: Kalimpong Restaurant and Tsering Restaurant & Bar.
For bread and cakes, try **Druk Bakery**, in Tashi Commercial Corporation, on Zhung

Western Bhutan Chukha district

lam. Interestingly, the town has at least 19 small shops catering to the national addiction, *paan*!

☺ Entertainment

Phuntsoling *p130, map p131*
Bars
Many of the hotels have bars, the most popular being **Peljorling Hotel** and **Bhutan Hotel**. Other street bars include: at the far end of **Zhung lam**: Bhutan Bar; on **Dekyi lam**: Shot Bar and Tendzin Chophel Bar; on **Godo lam**: Sangyay Bar, Pemba Lama Bar, Pasang Bar, Yeshe Dorjee Bar and Pema Bar; on the **parallel streets**: M&B Bar, Phida Bar, Quick Bar; on **Phunsum lam**: Rinzin Bar, Doko Bar, Lepa Dorjee Bar, Rinchen Bar and Tashi Yangdzom Bar.

Cinemas
Bollywood movies are shown daily at **MIG Cinema** on Gaton lam and at **Norgyay Cinema**, behind the new bus station.

Nightclubs
For night life the only real option is **My Place Discotheque**, in the basement of Gechu Shopping Complex, on the corner of Dekyi lam and Gaton lam.

○ Shopping

Phuntsoling *p130, map p131*
The downtown area has many small privately owned general stores (*tsongkhang*), selling assorted products of Indian origin. The open-air vegetable market is located behind Zangdokpelri Lhakhang. The biggest department stores are **Tashi Commercial Corporation**, with two outlets – one near Bhutan Gate and the other on the corner of Gaton lam and Tharpa lam; and the **Gechu Shopping Complex**.

Handicrafts
There are not many good outlets in Phuntsoling for local products. The best is Druk Handicrafts, next to the vegetable market. The **Bhutan Trade Centre**, on Dekyi lam may be worth a visit. For jewellery, try **MB Goldsmith** and **Ganesh Jewellery** which are both on Godo lam. For hand-woven carpets, try **Druk Carpet Industry**, on Gaton

lam, or the factory on Gakyi lam, near the new bus station.

Books and stationers
For magazines and newspapers, try **Hello Bhutan Bookstall** on Zhung lam. For notebooks, diaries etc, try **Hans Stationary** on Gaton lam.

Electrical goods
Electrical equipment of is sold at a number of outlets on Gaton lam: **Kaya Electronics**, **Bhutan Electronics**, **Pelri Yangkyil Electronics** and **KCD Electronics**, as well as at **Tendzin Electronics** on Jorden lam, **Kelwang Electronics** on Tharpai lam and **Wangdi Electricals** on Phunsum lam.

Beautician and hairdresser
Beauty Art Salon, at the far end of Zhung lam, is the most fashionable, but other less expensive and simpler alternatives are found on Godo lam: **Dechen Hair Cutting Salon**, **New Hair Cutting** and **Raj Hair Cutting Salon** among them.

Photography
Print films, processing and batteries are available on Gaton lam at **Bhutan Photo Studio**, **Loyal Photo Studio** and **Sunder Photo Studio**. These studios also offer a swift passport photo service.

Stamps
Postage stamps are available at **Bhutan Post**, Samdrub lam.

▲ Activities and tours

Phuntsoling *p130, map p131*
The **archery** ground is on Tashi lam, to the east of town. The **soccer** field is opposite. There is a **snooker** and **pool** club, behind Norgyay Cinema.

◎ Transport

Phuntsoling *p130, map p131*
Taxis can be hired at the downtown taxi stand for the 179-km 6-hour drive to **Thimphu** (approximately Nu 1,000). Most visitors arriving at or leaving from Phuntsoling will have transportation arranged by their tour operators or host organisations.

⁝ Long-distance buses from Phuntsoling

Company	Destination	Days	Time	Fare
Bhutan Post Express	Thimphu	Daily	0700	Nu 156 (deluxe)
	Siliguri	daily	0630	Nu 55
	Kolkata	Mon, Wed, Thu, Fri, Sun	1500	Nu 300
Dawa Transport	Paro	Tue-Sun	0900	Nu 111
KCD Travels	Paro	Mon, Wed, Fri	0830	Nu 81
Leksol Travel	Thimphu	Daily	0800, 1100	Nu 84, Nu 115

NB The Bhutan Post Express services to Gelekphuk and Samdrub Jongkhar are both currently suspended.

There are 9 **bus** companies, operating the busy route between Phuntsoling and **Thimphu**. The most expensive are **Bhutan Post Express** and **Kunga Travel**, which offer a daily deluxe service at Nu 156. **Dramzop Travel** and **Leksol Travel** also have a standard service at Nu 115, while **Rinchen Wangyal Transport**, **Dophu Travels** and **Leksol Travel** offer budget travel at Nu 84. For schedule information on buses from Phuntsoling, see above.

Transport to India
Bhutan Post Express have daily bus services to **Siliguri** (150 km) and an overnight service to Kolkata (see box, page 135). There are also bus connections with **Darjiling**, **Kalimpong** (179 km), **Gangtok**, and **Bagdogra Airport**, as well as **Kakarbhitta** on the Indo-Nepal border – all 3-4 hours' driving distance.

❶ Directory

Phuntsoling *p130*
Banks Bank of Bhutan and Bhutan National Bank, both located in Samdrub lam, offer foreign exchange facilities. Open Mon-Fri 0900-1300, Sat 0900-1100. The former also has another branch on Gaton lam.
Hospitals and medical
services Phuntsoling Hospital is in the south-east part of town, off Sambdrub lam. There are also private clinics – **C Wang Clinic** and **KD Ultrasound/ X-Ray Clinic** are both located on Dekyi lam; while **Rapten Medical** and **Gonphel Medical** are opposite the Kunga Hotel. The **Druk X-Ray Clinic** and **C Wang Pathology** are located next door to the Bhutan Gate on the border. There is also a dental clinic on the pedestrian lane behind Gaton lam. **Internet** Phajoding Internet Bar, which is located opposite the Druk Hotel on Zhung lam, charges Nu 3 per minute.
Post including EMS express delivery, are available at **Bhutan Post**. Open Mon-Fri 0830-1230, 1330-1630, Sat 0900-1230.
Telecommunications IDD calls can be made from the major hotels and from the many STD/IDD phone shops, on Zhung lam, Godo lam and Phunsum lam. **Useful information** Local directory enquiries:T140. International directory enquiries: T116. Police: T113. Fire department: T110.

Punakha district སྤུ་ན་ཁ → Area: 974 sq km.

Punakha district lies to the east of Dochu La pass, and is approached on the central highway from Thimphu to Bumthang. Pungtang Dechen Dzong, strategically located on the Punatsang-chu at the confluence of its Pho-chu and Mo-chu tributaries, functioned as a capital of Bhutan until 1964, and it is still the winter residence of the State Monastic Body.

Summers are hot in Punakha, and the winters are cool (average rainfall: 500-1,500 mm). Some 85% of the district is forested, with a mix of conifer and broadleaf trees, particuarly in the northern valleys, which fall within the Jigme Dorje National Park. Grazing pastures are scant (less than 2%) but well used. Only 4% of the land is cultivated here, mostly along the river valleys where rice is the main crop. Wheat, maize, barley and potatoes are also grown, along with apples, grapes and oranges.

There are 10 counties in the district: Kabjisa, Gonshari and Guma in the Mo-chu valley; Chubu, between the two rivers; Towang, Drimednang (Bjimenang) and Shenganang in the Pho-chu valley; and Talo, Dzoma and Lingmukha, all of which are south of the confluence.

The paved motor road from Thimphu enters the district north of the Metsinang intersection, and follows the west bank of the Punatsang-chu upstream through Kuruthang to the confluence. From here unpaved motorable roads follow the Mo-chu upstream to Tashithang on the Gasa border, and the Phochu upstream as far as Dawakha. There are two other motorable tracks, one leading west to Talo Gonpa and the other east into the Shengrong-chu valley as far as Jachikha. The distance from Thimphu to Kuruthang is 67 km and to Pungthang Dechen Dzong 71 km. ▶ For Sleeping, Eating and other listings, see pages 141-143.

Punatsang-chu valley

The lateral highway descends from the Dochu La pass through Mandrelgang (see page 92) from where it follows the contours of a side valley down through Lobesa and the checkpoint at **Metsinang**, which marks the end of Thimphu district. Metsinang ('the place that was burnt by fire') is at a very low elevation and there are productive papaya plantations. Three roads intersect here: west to Simtokha (54 km), east to Tashigang (490 km) and north to Punakha Dzong (12 km).

Chime Lhakhang

Heading north from the intersection, at **Sopsokha** near Metsinang, there is a narrow trail which leads across muddy paddy fields and through Pana village to Chime Lhakhang. This temple was founded circa 1499 by Ngawang Chogyel, the 14nth hierarch of Ralung, on a site where his close relative, the yogin Drukpa Kun-le, had not long before built a stupa commemorating an aged student's attainment of the fruitional rainbow-light body (*Jalu phowa chenpo*). Legend tells how Drukpa Kun-le met the old man named Tendzin at Lobesa and taught him to recite mantras with such profanity that he was locked away by his embarrased relatives. Continuing with the practice in this enforced retreat, the old man's physical body vanished into rainbow light after a month! Owing to its associations with Drukpa Kun-le, many infertile Bhutanese couples go there on pilgrimage even now, believing that the blessing of this sacred place will enable them to conceive a son and heir.

The site The temple is in a wonderful hilltop setting, with excellent views of the Punatsang-chu below. A large prayer wheel marks the start of the circumambulatory pathway, and the entire building is encircled by small *mani* wheels in their respective niches, and some fine slate carvings depicting the meditational deity Vairocana with consort, and so forth. Entering the courtyard, there is a tree where the local protector is said to reside. Inside the temple, on the wall adjacent to the door, there is a shrine dedicated to Amitayus, a mural depicting the familial and teaching lineages of Drukpa Kun-le, and a larger mural depicting the *Lama Gongdu* cycle of deities. The side-walls depict Guru Padmakara with his eight manifestations (left) and several aspects of Amitayus (right). The altar has images of (L-R): Mahakarunika, Guru Padmakara, Shakyamuni and the Lords of the Three Families, with the volumes of the Lhasa edition of the *Kangyur* stacked up in the far corner. In the centre of the hall are statues of Drukpa Kun-le and Ngawang Chogyel, alongside Drukpa Kun-le's original stupa. Precious relics here include Drukpa Kun-le's bow and arrow, and his wooden phallus with which the caretaker monks bless visiting pilgrims.

Olokha

Winding through Sopsokha village, the road to Punakha descends to cross the Thaberong-chu river, and as it climbs a ridge leading into the Punatsang-chu valley there is a turn-off on the left at **Olokha**, leading to **Talo Gonpa** and **Taleda College** (see page 92). Branching uphill from this trail there is an access road for the upmarket and well-located Zangdok Pelri and Meri Punsum hotels. The distance from Metsinang to Olakha is 5 km, and from Olakha to Talo Gonpa 17 km.

Khuruthang

Crossing from Olokha into the Punatsang-chu valley, the road begins to follow the riverbank upsteam, heading towards the confluence of its two main tributaries. After 2 km, a turn-off leads into **Khuruthang** (1,300 m), the new district capital of Punakha, founded in 1999. This new town is laid out in a grid, with three long streets bisected by shorter transverse roads.

Heading along **East Street**, you will find Gadenling Restaurant, Dechen General Shop and a stupa, followed by the first side street on the left, which leads to the Diamond Hotel, Welcome Hotel and Druk Communications. Continuing along East Street you will pass Kunzang General Store, Metok Shop and a large open space (for future development). After the second side street, you will pass the bus stop and taxi stand on the right and opposite on the left, Bhutan Post, a telephone booth and the Royal Bhutan Insurance Company. A third side street now branches off to the left, leading to Friends Bar & Restaurant, Pasang Lhamo Hotel and DDS Restaurant & Bar. Just before the fourth and final side street, which leads to the Namgyal Lhamo Restaurant, you will find Pradhan Musical Instruments.

Central Street is less developed. Along here you will find Lam Jamyang General Store, Relax Hotel, Zomlha Hotel and Damchen Lodge. Then on **West Street** there is a pharmacy, Dandi Dolma General Store, the Bank of Bhutan and Kunga Hotel. If you stay on the riverside road without entering the town, you will pass on the right the vegetable market, Damchen Resort, the Football Field and the Junior High School.

Pungthang Dechen Dzong

Four kilometres north of Khuruthang, the road reaches the confluence of the Mo-chu (Mother) and Pho-chu (Father) tributaries. On the approach there are magnificent panoramas of the imposing Pungthang Dechen Dzong, which strategically occupies the land between the two rivers, somewhat reminiscent of Chamdo on the Mekong in Eastern Tibet. On the opposite bank of the Mo-chu are Punakha Junior High School, followed by the police station, an army camp and a small post office.

Background This region has been a bastion of the Drukpa Kagyu school since the 13th century, when Phajo Drukgom Zhikpo's son Wangchuk was appointed as an overseer of the valley (at that time known as Thed). But later, when Zhabdrung Ngawang Namgyel reached Bhutan, his entry into Punakha from Gasa was opposed by masters of the Barawa tradition. The Zhabdrung took over the Barawa temple of Gon Tsepuk Lhakhang, and had a vision of Guru Padmakara advising him to consolidate Drukpa power in the region by building a *dzong* between the two rivers, at a place which he himself had frequented during the eighth century, and which resembled the trunk of a reclining elephant. At that time there was a small temple on this site, which had been built by Panchen Ngagi Rinchen in 1328. Henceforth the temple would be known as the Dzongchung ('small fortress').

The foundations of the new fortress were laid in 1637 and the massive walls were then constructed on the model of Ralung by the artisan Balingpa. On its completion, sacred relics were installed, including the self-produced image of Kharsapani, which the Zhabdrung had brought from Ralung in Tibet. The State Monastic Body soon moved here from Cheri Gonpa in Thimphu, under the guidance of the monastic preceptor Pekar Jungne. When in 1639 the third Tibetan invasion of Bhutan was repelled with Ladakhi assistance (see page 241), the captured armour of the vanquished Tibetans was installed in a victory chapel within the *dzong*. At that time, Punakha became the Zhabdrung's main residence, and it was here that he eventually passed away in 1651.

Despite being ravaged over the centuries that followed by fires, an earthquake and severe floods, Pungthang Dechen Dzong continued to function as the capital of Bhutan until 1955. Reconstruction work was undertaken after the fires of 1750 and 1798, and during the intervening tenure of the 13th regent Sherab Wangchuk. A series of catastrophes during the 19th century – the fires of 1802, 1831 and 1849, and the earthquake of 1897 – failed to destroy the building. Nor did the floods of 1960 and 1994, or the recent fire of 1986. The litany of disasters ensured that the *dzong* would undergo continuous repairs. In fact, the most recent phase of restoration, undertaken by the present king, is still on-going. Even now the Pungthang Dechen Dzong functions as the winter residence of the State Monastic Body, and the winter headquarters of the Je Khenpo (Head Monastic Preceptor of Bhutan). Apart from its courtyard, it is open to foreign visitors only in summer when the monks reside at Thimphu.

The site The walls of the massive fortress are 180 m in length and 72 m wide. The entrance is approached via a motorable cantilever bridge that spans the Mo-chu. The remains of an 18th- century cantilever footbridge can be seen alongside it. Opposite the entrance to the circular **Dzongchung**, which contains a sacred image of Shakyamuni Buddha, a flight of retractable wooden steps leads up to the thick wooden gate. All visitors are registered on arrival.

In the **vestibule** there are murals depicting the Four Guardian Kings, the Wheel of Rebirth and a diagram of geometric poetry (*kunzang khorlo*). The **corridor** beyond it has murals on the left depicting the symbols of long-life (*mi tsering*) and more geometric poetry, while on the right are the motifs of the Four Harmonious Brethren (*thunpa punzhi*) and the Ascetic leading an Elephant (*atsara langtri*). The *dzong* has three successive courtyards (*dochal*): the northern one nearest the entrance has administrative functions, the middle one containing the six-storey tower (*utse*) is the monastic residence, and the southern courtyard houses the reliquary temples of Pema Lingpa and Zhabdrung Ngawang Namgyel, as well as the large assembly hall. Altogether there are 21 halls and chapels, however most of them still out of bounds to visitors.

The **first courtyard** has a stupa at its centre, backed by a large shady tree. The stupa was rebuilt in 1981. On the left a staircase leads up to the gallery where the private apartment of the Je Khenpo is located. Downstairs on the left is the **Wangchuk Lhakhang**, dedicated to the protector deity Maheshvara, and containing peripheral murals of Jambhala, Orgyan Norlha, Avalokiteshvara and various protectors. Opposite on the right are the monastic finance offices, and the administrative offices of Punakha district. At the far end of the courtyard, to the left of the stairs, there are two small shrines, one containing a water stone (*chudo*) from the Mo-chu and the other a *nagini* protector. A corridor leads directly from the Wangchuk Lhakhang into the third courtyard.

The **second courtyard** contains the **six-storey tower** with its golden spire, which was donated in 1676 by the third regent Migyur Tenpa. Its uppermost chapel contains the most sacred image in Bhutan, that of Kharsapani, which emerged naturally from the vertebra of Tsangpa Gyare, following his cremation (see page 239). Another chapel contains a set of eight sandalwood stupas, known as Ngulbum Chorten, and a gold manuscript of the *Kangyur*, which were commissioned by the second and third regents. Yet another chapel is the **Yulgyel Gonkhang**, which was built to hold the armour captured from the Tibetan invaders of 1639. A recently constructed **Yeshe Gonpo Lhakhang**, dedicated to the protector deity Jnananatha, occupies most of the courtyard nowadays, replacing the damaged original which Zhabdrung Ngawang Namgyel had constructed in 1643. There is currently no access to the hall, but visitors can enter a viewing gallery upstairs, alongside a small **Gonkhang.** The monastic residential buildings are to the right. It was in this courtyard that King Ugyen Wangchuk was crowned king of Bhutan in 1907.

The **third courtyard** is entered from the corridor on the left. There is a small shrine dedicated to *nagini* protectors adjacent to the exit. On the right side of the courtyard is the venerated **Marchen Lhakhang**, containing the embalmed human remains of the Zhabdrung (d 1651) in a reliquary stupa. The gilded spire was donated by the third regent. Security guards block the entrance to this chapel – only the king and the Je Khenpo may enter, along with the two caretaker attendants, known as Marchen Zimpon. At the southern end of the courtyard is the massive new **assembly hall** (Dukhang Sarpa), which replaces the incinerated Kungarawa hall built by the second regent Tendzin Drukdra in the 1660s. This hall, which is still under renovation, has 64 gilded pillars – the four innermost ones decorated with red gold; and its impressive entrance gate has 11 lion capitals. The central images here depict (L-R): Guru Padmakara, Shakyamuni Buddha and Zhabdrung Ngawang Namgyel, flanked by the eight standing bodhisattvas. In the upper gallery there are miniatures of the Thousand Buddhas and five ornate ceiling-painted mandalas. Above this assembly hall, in the **Neten Lhakhang**, there are images of the Sixteen Elders, which were reputedly made by the Zhabdrung's own hand. The murals here depict the Seven Generations of Past Buddhas, the Thirty-five Confession Buddhas and the lineage of Zhabdrung Ngawang Namgyel. The **vestibule** has statues of the Four Guardian Kings, and murals of Zangdok Pelri and Sukhavati paradises.

Mo-chu valley

The paved road from Pungthang Dechen Dzong follows the west bank of the Mo-chu upstream. After 6 km a side-road leads down to a parking area in front of the suspension footbridge that carries pilgrims and villagers across the river to the great Nyizergang Stupa at Hapaisa in Chubu county. This is also a starting point for river-rafting on the Mo-chu. The trail crosses the bridge and then climbs sharply through farmland and forest, passing a small protector temple en route, before reaching the monument.

This towering 31-m stupa is one of the largest in Bhutan. Set majestically on a hilltop promontory across the river, it is now a major landmark. The construction, which took eight years to complete, was commissioned by the four queens and built by Lama Nyingkhu, a student of the late Dudjom Rinpoche (head of the Nyingma school of Tibetan Buddhism), who resides in Thimphu. The consecration took place at the end of 1999, marking the millennium, and its contents are clearly inspired by the iconography of the Memorial Chorten in Thimphu (see page 70). There is a royal residence used by the queens to the left of the entrance, behind two large *mani* wheels. To the rear of the complex there are residential buildings and on the slopes above there is a geomantic jewel-shaped rock, where the local protector of the site is said to reside.

Entering the stupa, on the **ground floor** there is a three-dimensional mandala depicting the assembly of the meditational deity Vajrakila in the form *Namchak Putri*. The surrounding murals depict the 16 protectors of Vajrakila. On the teaching throne there is a large portrait of the present king. On the **second floor** the central image is Trailokyavijaya (conqueror of the three world systems of desire, form and formlessness), which also gives the stupa its formal Bhutanese name, Khamsum Yul-le Namgyel Chorten. He is surrounded by four female *dakinis*: Kurukulla, Simhavaktra, Kalakrodheshvari and Vajravarahi. Above there is a second tier of images: a brass Guru Padmakara flanked by two brass buddhas from Thailand. Side images here depict Zhabdrung Ngawang Namgyel and Dudjom Lingpa; and there are murals illustrating the meditational deities of the eight transmitted precepts (Kabgye). On the **third floor** the central image is Ushnisavijaya in the form Vajrakila, surrounded by the aspects of the other four enlightened families (Phurba Rignga). The finely executed murals depict the cycle of the *Lama Gongdu*.

On each of these floors, the murals are interspersed with the relevant historical treasure-finders and lineage-holders, such as Dudjom Lingpa (ground floor), Nyangrel Nyima Ozer (second floor) and Sangye Lingpa (third floor). On the **fourth floor** in the open-air chapel of the *harmika*, there is an old 'speaking' image of Shakyamuni Buddha, which was brought here from Pungthang Dechen Dzong.

Sirigang and Tashithang

The paved motor road continues to follow the west bank of the Mo-chu upstream on a very scenic route, passing paddy fields, sandbanks, small villages and forests. **Sirigang** (1,350 m) in Kabjisa county is the trailhead for a 40-km trek to Pangri Zampa in Thimphu, crossing **Sinchu La pass** (3,400 m) en route. This trek has already been described in reverse (see page 93). The motorable road soon reaches **Tashithang** (1,840 m) at which point it enters Gasa district (see page 143). The distance from Pungthang Dechen Dzong to Tashithang is 18 km, the last five of which are currently unpaved.

Gon Tsepuk

One of the most revered cave hermitages lies in Gonshari county to the east of the Mo-chu at Gon Tsepuk, a location where Guru Padmakara practised the means for attainment of Amitayus (Boundless Life). In later centuries this area came under the influence of the Barawa tradition until the Zhabdrung took over the temple in 1636. It is said that the Barawa had tried to stop this by hurling lightning bolts at the Zhabdrung, but they could only ignite a nearby cypress tree, the traces of which can still be seen today.

Pho-chu valley

There are fewer sites of interest in the Pho-chu valley, which is motorable as far as **Dawakha** in Towang county. River-rafting on the Pho-chu has become quite popular in recent years; and it is possible to trek as far as the hot springs at **Tsachuphu**.

Samtengang winter trek

From Punakha there is a four-day trek through Shenganang and Lingmukha counties, which can be undertaken even in the cold season on account of its low elevation.

Day 1 Pungthang Dechen Dzong–Lingmukha Crossing a footbridge over the Pho-chu at Khuruthang, the trail climbs gradually though chir pine forest and paddy fields, before bifurcating – east for Shenanang and south for Lingmukha. In the Shengarong-chu valley, the main monastery is **Neba Gonpa**, south of Jazhikha, where a motorable side road from Punakha comes to an end. Heading south from the fork the trail soon reaches **Lingmukha**, where there is a small temple founded by the Nyingmapa treasure-finder Dorje Lingpa (1346-1405). This temple was maintained by the master's son Choying Gyatso, from whom many local families later claimed descent (12 km, four hours' trekking).

Day 2 Lingmukha–Chungsakha Passing through rhododendron and oak forest, the trail bypasses a temple founded by Drukpa Kun-le, en route for the campsite at Chungsakha (14 km, five hours' trekking).

Day 3 Chungsakha–Samtengang Descending into the Pe-chu valley (1,420 m), the trail crosses into Wangdu Phodrang district, and climbs through the farming village of Sha to reach the campsite at Samtengang (13 km, five hours' trekking). Lutsagang in Sha is famous for the sojourn of Drukpa Kun-le here in the 16th century. It is said that the master slew a bull for consumption at a local festival here and then resurrected it! The main Drukpa monastery in Phangyul is Sharpa Phuntsoling, which was founded by Kunga Peljor, the 13th hierarch of Ralung in the 15th century. However, the Sakya tradition also had a strong presence here at one time.

Day 4 Samtengang–Chudzomsa On the final day of this easy trek, the trail descends steeply along a grassy incline to reach the main road at Chudzomsa (15 km, five to six hours' trekking). From here, it is a 20-minute drive into Bajothang.

◓ Sleeping

Punatsang-chu valley *p136*
B **YT Hotel**, T2-481331, F2-481527, hotelyt@druknet.bt, located in Lobesa, is a family-run hotel with 13 rooms – doubles at Nu 950 and singles at Nu 850. There are a number of small roadside stalls, and snacks are available at the Pasang Restaurant & Samol Bar.

Khuruthang *p137*
Singapore-based Aman Resorts are currently building a new 5-star luxury hotel near Pungthang Dechen Dzong.
A **Zangdok Pelri Hotel**, T2-584125. F2-584203,

above Olakha, is by far the best hotel in the district with 45 rooms, all with televisions – doubles at Nu 1,440, singles at Nu 1,200 and suites at Nu 4,000-5,000. There is a plush multi-cuisine restaurant, offering breakfast at Nu 120, lunch and dinner at Nu 260, a well-situated bar, business centre and an outdoor swimming pool. The sunrise mountain panoramas from Laptsakha (above the hotel on the Talo Road) are most impressive.
B **Damchen Lodge**, T2-584353, on Central Street in Khuruthang, has 21 rooms – doubles at Nu 1,300 and singles at Nu 1,100, but no bathtubs.

B Damchen Resort, T2-584354, F2-584203, located by the riverside, has 5 chalet-style rooms – doubles at Nu 1,300 and singles at Nu 1,100, with Blue River Club disco at weekends, outdoor and indoor dining facilities. The complex is spacious, with a water feature, backed by a somewhat grotesque image of laughing Milarepa.

B Meri Phunsum Hotel, T2-584236, F2-584237, mpuensum@druknet.bt, slightly below the Zangdok Pelri Hotel, overlooking the Punatsang-chu valley, has 17 good-sized rooms – doubles at Nu 1,000, singles at Nu 800, and deluxe rooms at Nu 1,200. During the off-season the hotel offers a 20% discount. The hotel has a small business centre, multi-cuisine restaurant and bar.

D Kunga Hotel, T5-584128, on West Street in Khuruthang, has 7 rooms – 4 with private bathrooms at Nu 550 and 3 without at Nu 300.

D Welcome Hotel, T5-584106, on Central Street in Khuruthang, has 8 simple rooms – doubles at Nu 400 and singles at Nu 300.

E Guesthouses in this budget category (some of which may not accept foreign guests) include: **Diamond Hotel, Relax Hotel, Zomlha Hotel** and **Pasang Lhamo Hotel**.

🍴 Eating

Khuruthang p137
The **Zangdok Pelri** and **Meri Phunsum** hotels both offer expensive multi-cuisine. In Khuruthang, the restaurant of the **Welcome Hotel** has a varied menu. Other simple options for Bhutanese and Nepalese cuisine (all $ category) include: **Friends Bar & Restaurant, Gadenling Restaurant, DDS Restaurant & Bar** and **Namgyal Lhamo Restaurant**.

🎭 Entertainment

Khuruthang p137
Not much happens in Khuruthang. The **Blue River Club** at the **Damchen Resort** offers some weekend distraction.

🎉 Festivals

Punatsang-chu valley p136
The **Punakha Serda** and **Dromcho** are

annual festivals, held at **Pungthang Dechen Dzong** during in the first month of the lunar year. Serda originated following the defeat of the invading Tibetan forces, who had come to seize the aforementioned Kharsapani image in 1639, and who were deceived by the Zhabdrung into thinking that he had cast the image into the Mo-chu. To commemorate this event, a group of laymen dressed in medieval military garb and a group of monks form a noisy procession down on the riverbank where the Je Khenpo throws some oranges into the river, re-enacting the Zhabdrung's ruse. This event is followed by the Dromcho, commemorating the seasonal migration of the State Monastic Body from Punakha to Thimphu during the spring. The event is an occasion for the display of the celebrated Punakha Thongdrol, a giant appliqué scroll, said to "liberate onlookers who behold it" (*thongdrol*). The original *thongdrol* of Punakha was destroyed in an earler fire, and since 1993 it has been replaced by an even larger scroll that measures 28 m by 23 m. Fifty-one artists laboured for 2 whole years to make the *thongdrol*, at the cost of US$70,000. Tentative dates for 2005 are 12-17 Feb.

🛍 Shopping

Khuruthang p137
There are a few basic shops and general stores (*tsongkhang*), selling groceries and other daily necessities. The vegetable market is located by the riverside.
Postage stamps are available at **Bhutan Post**, located on East Street.

🚌 Transport

Khuruthang p137
Nearly all visitors to Punakha will have pre-arranged transportation. It is not easy to find a taxi here. If you have to travel by bus, **Sherab Travels** and **Blue Hills Travels** both offer a daily service to and from **Thimphu** for Nu 36-38.

🏢 Directory

Khuruthang p137
Banks Bank of Bhutan, West Street. Open Mon-Fri 0900-1300, Sat 0900-1100.

Hospitals and medical
services Punakha Hospital is located near Pungthang Dechen Dzong. In town there is a small pharmacy. **Internet** Facilities are only available in the major hotels. **Postal facilities**, including EMS express delivery, are available at Bhutan Post. Open Mon-Fri 0830-1230, 1330-1630, Sat 0900-1230.

Telecommunications IDD calls can be made from the major hotels and from the STD/IDD phone booth, next to Bhutan Post, on East Street.

Gasa district དགའ་ས → *Area: 4,409 sq km.*

Gasa is the largest of all the districts in Bhutan, but it is also the most isolated and the most sparsely populated. The northern frontier of Gasa is separated from Khangmar county of Tibet by the formidable Himalayan snow range, which stretches from Mount Gyelpo Matsen (7,158 m) to Mount Zongaphugang (7,060 m) and Mount Kulha Kangri (7,554 m). Local traders still gain access to Khangmar via the frontier passes of Yak La and Phiru La. Bhutan's highest mountain, Gangkar Punsum (7,540 metres) is also located in this district, making the northern reaches attractive to trekking expeditions. The elevations here range from 1,500-7,500 m! Nearly all the headwaters of the Mo-chu and Pho-chu, which converge at Pungthang Dechen Dzong, rise in the Great Himalayan range of Gasa district.

The summers are cool, and the terrain is mostly covered by snow in winter. Snow also falls during the spring and autumn. About 36% of the land is covered by snow peaks and glaciers, and 33% by conifer and scrub forest. There is hardly any agriculture, but the pastures (over 5%) are heavily grazed by yaks. Local people subsist on the sale of animal products, which are transported by horse caravans to the markets in Punakha.

There are only four counties in the district: Gonkha-me, Gonkha-to and Laya are all in the Mo-chu valley, while the vast Lunanang area occupies the source of the Pho-chu and its feeder rivers.

The only motorable road in Gasa runs from Tashithang in Punakha to Damji in Gonkha-me, 16 km distant. All other trails in the district are traditional trade routes and modern trekking routes.

Gonkha county

The newly constructed but unpaved motor road to Damji passes through sub-tropical terrain where takins and monkeys can sometimes be seen along the riverbanks. Gonkha was one of the first parts of Bhutan to have come under the influence of Zhabdrung Ngawang Namgyel in 1616 on account of its early associations with Phajo Drukgom Zhikpo, from whose son Wangchuk the local officials claimed descent. The lama gave many long-life empowerments here. Until 2003 when the road was opened it was necessary to hike uphill from Tashithang, and many trekkers heading for Gasa and Laya still prefer that option. **Damji** (2,430 m), the main settlement in lower Gonkha, is a large agricultural village surrounded by rice terraces. There is a useful campsite by the banks of the Mo-chu below Damji.

Damji to Laya trek

From Damji there is a three-day trek via Gasa and Koina to Laya in the Himalayan zone in the extreme north of the district. Bhutanese tour operators market the first part of this route as the Gasa Hot Springs Trek. The best season is between spring

Western Bhutan Gasa district

and autumn. The monsoon is to be avoided owing to the overwhelming number of leeches between Punakha and Gasa.

Day 1 Damji–Gasa Hot Springs Leaving Damji the trail cross the Lepena-chu by a suspension bridge that spans the deep ravine (2,300 m) and continues through the small hamlet of **Gayza** (2,500 m) before undulating along ridges above the main course of the Mo-chu. It then descends through oak and pine forest, passing an observation point from which Tashi Tongmon Dzong and the hot springs are visible in the distance; and continues downhill to cross the Mo-chu by a cable suspension bridge (2,360 m). On the far bank, the trail turns northwards to reach a fork about one hour above the hot springs at Gasa (2,770 m). There are ideal camping areas and a small hotel at the hot springs (Gasa *tsa-chu*, temperature 40°C), with several small medicinal pools and a shower facility (18 km, five to six hours' trekking).

Day 2 Gasa Hot Springs–Koina Climbing from the hot springs, after two hours you will reach a police checkpoint at the entrance to **Gasa**, where trekking permits are inspected. Gasa was once a thriving market town where yak caravans would congregate. The officials of Gasa, including Tendzin Drukgyel, the first regent of the Bhutanese state, were instrumental in inviting the Zhabdrung from Tibet in 1616. Today, with Tibetan cross-border trade being severely curtailed, its role has been considerably diminished. In this small district capital there are a number of small shops and basic amenities, and the local government is based at the renovated **Tashi Tongmon Dzong**, which has an unusual round wall at the front. This fortress was originally constructed in 1646 by Zhabdrung Ngawang Namgyel to defend the nearby frontier from Tibetan invasions. A stone pathway leads uphill to the *dzong*, clinic and school.

The trail to Koina continues past teahouses and a sports ground to reach a ridge with four landmark stupas (2,810 m) on the outskirts of the village. Then it follows the contour of a side-valley, before descending to the valley floor and crossing a stream. A long ascent through bamboo forest ensues, as Gasa Dzong comes into view across the valley. After crossing **Bari La** pass (3,900 m), which is a good resting place, the muddy trail descends through forested side-valleys to cross the Koina-chu, an important tributary of the Mo-chu. At **Koina** (3,050 m) there is a marshy campsite, situated in a forest clearing near the riverbank. Unfortunately, there is no alternative site with clean running water (14 km, six to seven hours' trekking).

Day 3 Koina–Laya Climbing through the side-valley of the Koina-chu, the trail emerges above the deep Mo-chu gorge. It winds up and down several ridges, and in certain sections it falls close to the riverbank. There are outstanding views of the crashing river, its feeder tributaries and waterfalls. In the afternoon, you ford a feeder river known as the Bahiyung-chu (3,290 m) and climb on a muddy trail over a ridge to reach a wooden bridge over the Tokserkagi-chu. Here, on the outskirts of Laya (3,840 m), there is a military checkpoint, where trekking permits are inspected (19 km, six to seven hours' trekking). Above the eastern side of the village there is a platform campsite, nestling below the snow peak of Tsenda Gang (7,100 m).

Laya county

Situated at the foot of distant Mount Gyelpo Matsen (Bh. Masang Gang, 7,165 m), Laya or Layak has the distinction of being the second highest village in Bhutan. The village is in the valley of the Mo-chu Gango-chu, a principal source of the Mo-chu. The inhabitants of Laya (Bh. Layaps) still worship divinities which may be related to the pre-Buddhist Bon religion, and guard their villages of painted wooden houses with wooden images. Most are semi-nomadic – they grow wheat, barley, mustard and turnips, but in summertime their pastures are among the best in the country for yak breeding. Here you will see yak herders dressed in a very distinctive costume, and dwelling in black yak-tweed tents (*ba*), as they go about their daily business. The women too are more reminiscent of nomadic Tibetan peoples with their long hair, conical bamboo hats, striped skirts and black jackets with silver beading. You will see herdsmen in blackened yak-hair tents or stone dwellings, with tall prayer flags and exorcist thread crosses. The villagers are well-disposed to strangers, and they will probably have distinctive local items of dress and jewellery for sale, along with imported Nepalese jewellery. Cultural ring dances are frequently performed, and not simply staged for the benefit of visitors. There is a small local monastery and a sacred stupa containing stone footprints of Zhabdrung Ngawang Namgyel, the 17th-century founder of the Bhutanese state, and his horse's hooves. The village also has a small general store, a hospital and an archery field. In the higher reaches there are large flocks of blue sheep and takins, which are rare elsewhere in the Himalayas. Bears are relatively common, and the guides make a lot of noise so as not to take them by surprise and thereby avoid danger.

Jomolhari trek

The Laya trek can be combined with the Jomolhari trek, which makes a strenuous two-week journey, crossing several 4,000-m passes into Paro. The section from Laya to Paro takes nine days, with overnight stops at Limithang, Robluthang, Shomuthang, Chebisa, Lingzhi, Jangothang, Thangtangka and Sharna Zampa. This route has already been described in reverse (see page 98). If you are continuing to trek from Laya, yaks will replace horses as pack animals.

Lunanang county

Even more isolated than Laya, Lunanang is a vast region around the source of the Pho-chu and its Tang-chu tributary, with formidable Himalayan barriers to the north that mostly lie within the Jigme Dorje National Park. There is a six-day trek from Laya to Thanza, the county capital, on an old trade route, which the Bhutanese travel services nowadays market as part of the extensive 25-day Snowman Trek. This starts from Paro, combining the Jomolhari trek with a hike into the Nikar-chu valley near Trongsar (see page 146), and can tax even experienced trekkers as it crosses eight high passes (356 km altogether). The trek can be reduced to 18 days by starting in Punakha rather than Paro. Uncertain weather conditions add to the difficulty of this trek. Best season: August-September.

Laya to Thanza trek

Day 1 Laya–Rodophu The trail initially follows the Mo-chu down to its confluence with the Rodo-chu, and after about one hour it starts to climb gradually and soon reaches a promontory where there are fine vistas of both the Mo-chu and Rodo-chu. Then, heading up the Rodo-chu valley, it pases through mixed conifer, maple and rhododendron forest, to emerge in full view of the Tsenda Gang glacier (7,100 m) at Rodophu (4,160 m). The campsite is accessed by a wooden bridge spanning the river here (19 km, six to seven hours' trekking).

Day 2 Rodophu–Narethang Following the Rodo-chu upstream over undulating terrain covered in dwarf rhododendrons and arid scrubland, the trail reaches an open valley (4,600 m) and ascends gradually to cross Tsomo La (4,780 m), from where Mount Jomolhari can be seen in the distance. Now level, the trail crosses a small, exposed plateau frequented by yak caravans, to reach the campsite at

Narethang (4,600 m) which is situated beneath Mount Gangla Karchung (6,395 m) (17 km, five to six hours' trekking).

Day 3 Narethang–Tarina The trail ascends slowly to cross Gangla Karchung La pass (5,120 m), which offers mountain panoramas of Gangbum (6,526 m), Tsenda Gang (7,100 m), Teri Gang (7,300 m) and Jejekangphu Gang (7,300 m).

On the moraine-strewn descent, the trail reaches a spectacular vertical cliff that overlooks two glacial lakes emerging from the base of Mount Teri Gang. One of them was responsible for the flooding of the Pho-chu, which devastated Punakha Dzong in 1960. A precipitous descent follows through rhododendron bushes to reach the valley floor and the campsite at Tarina (4,020 m) in the Tang-chu basin (18 km, five to six hours' trekking).

Day 4 Tarina–Woche Following the Tang-chu downstream through conifer forest and bypassing high waterfalls, the trail then climbs steadily for two hours into a side-valley where Woche village (3,940 m) in Lunanang is located (17 km, six to seven hours' trekking).

Day 5 Woche–Lhedi Below the campsite the trail continues uphill through the Woche valley and across the Woche-chu, before climbing through lakeland terrain to Keche La pass (4,580 m).

The snow peaks of Jejekangphu Gang, where the Woche-chu rises, are now visible. Then, descending into the Pho-chu valley, the trail passes through the agricultural village of Thega (4,040 m), where turnips, radishes, potatoes and buckwheat grow. In the afternoon you continue following the windswept trail down into Lhedi (3,700 m), alongside the river. The village has no shops but there is a small basic health unit, a wireless station and a primary school (17 km, five to six hours' trekking).

Day 6 Lhedi–Thanza Following the main source of the Pho-chu upstream, the trail heads north-east for Chozo (4,090 m), another small subsistence farming village which has its own *dzong*. There is evidence of damage caused by floods in the area, necessitating several short detours. In the distance there are fine views of Zongophu Gang (7,100 m) in the Eastern Himalayas, as the trail rises through yak grazing pastures and then leaves the riverbank, climbing through a bluff to reach the villages of Thanza (4,090 m) or Toncha (17 km, seven to eight hours' trekking). **Thanza** is the main settlement in Lunanang, and the village still retains its old character. There are a number of glacial lakes nearby, the largest being **Raksatreng Tso**, which can be visited on a four- to five-hour hike. The bursting waters of this lake were responsible for two major flash floods downstream in Punakha, in 1969 and 1996.

Thanza to Sephu trek

Another seven-day trek leads south from Thanza in Lunanang to Sephu and Nikarchu Bridge on the Wangdu–Trongsar highway (see page 154). This is the final section of the arduous Snowman trek. The views of Mount Gangkar Punsum (7,239 m) are superb, and you pass lakes, glacial rivers, moraines, beautiful forests teaming with Himalayan birds, and flower-filled alpine meadows.

Day 1 Thanza–Danji The short trail to Danji climbs from Toncha to a ridge-top boulder, from where there are fine views across Lunanang. Then heading south-east through a side-valley on an easy track the trail soon reaches the meadow camp at Danji (4,300 m), which is a natural habitat of the blue sheep. Here the trail bifurcates: east for Gangkar Phunsum based camp and Bumthang, or south for Trongsar (8 km, three to four hours' trekking).

Day 2 Danji–Tshochena Climbing through a rock-strewn valley, the trail undulates to reach Jaze La pass (5,150 m), and then descends through a typical alpine terrain of lakes and snow peaks to Tshochena (4,970 m), where there is a lakeshore camp (12 km, five to six hours' trekking).

Day 3 Tshochena–Jichu Dramo After following the lakeshore, the trail then crosses a ridge (5,100 m), from which snow peaks are visible in all directions. The Pho-chu is visible below, winding its way towards Punakha. Undulating over a number of smallish hills, the trail then bypasses a glacial lake on the ascent of Loju La pass (4,940 m). From here a saddle leads into a hanging glacial valley and on to Jichu Dramo (4,880 m), where there is a meadow campsite (14 km, four to five hours' trekking).

Day 4 Jichu Dramo–Chukarpo Now the trail begins its long ascent of the Rinchenzo La pass (5,220 metres), which forms a watershed between the Pho-chu and Mangde-chu systems. Here on the highest point of the trek, there are outstanding panoramas of the Eastern Himalayan peaks, particularly the western side of Gangkar Phunsum, and the valley of the Thampe-chu, a major tributary of the Mangde-chu, is visible to the south. At this point the trail crosses the district border into Wangdu Phodrang district (see page 148). The descent into the upper reaches of the Thampe-chu valley leads through marshy lakeland terrain, precipitous moraine and fertile pastures. On reaching the river, the trail fords across to the west bank, and enters a forested zone, where the campsite at Chukarpo (4,600 m) is located (18 km, five to six hours' trekking).

Day 5 Chukarpo–Thampe Tso Descending for two hours, the trail reaches the takin-grazing pastures at Galapang-chu (4,010 m), before climbing sharply through juniper and conifer forest for about one hour to Thampe Tso (4,230 m), a stunningly beautiful turquoise lake with a campsite at its southern shore (18 km, five to six hours' trekking).

Day 6 Thampe Tso–Maurothang Climbing through blue sheep country, the trail crosses Thampe La Pass (4,580 m), and descends to the shores of Om Tso (4,230 m), a lake where the great treasure-finder Pema Lingpa discovered a number of *terma*. Then passing a waterfall and a second small lake, it descends precipitously into the upper reaches of the Nikar-chu, where it crosses the river by a wooden bridge and continues on to the campsite at Maurothang (4,000 m), situated in a forest clearing by the riverside (14 km, five hours' trekking). Here the yaks are replaced with horses as pack animals.

Day 7 Maurothang–Sephu On the final day of the trek, the trail continues downhill, crossing to the east bank of the Nikar-chu, and passing through bamboo thickets, broadleaf forest and cultivated fields. Above the village of Sephu (2,500 m), it emerges on to a grassy knoll, and merges with a tractor road that converges with the highway alongside Nikarchu Bridge (18 km, five to six hours' trekking). From here you can drive east to Trongsar (see page 162) or west to Wangdu Phodrang (see below).

Wangdu Phodrang district

དབང་འདུས → *Area: 4,038 sq km.*

Wangdu Phodrang is the one of the largest districts, bordering Punakha in the west, Gasa in the north, Tarkarna, Tsirang and Sarpang in the south, with Trongsar and Bumthang in the east. It is therefore an important crossroads for east–west and north–south traffic. In the east of the district the Black Mountains form the main watershed between Western and Central Bhutan. North-east of the watershed are the headwaters of the Mangde-chu and its feeder rivers, the Thampe-chu and Nyakha-chu, while to the west are the mid-reaches of the Punatsang-chu (Sankosh), along with those of its tributaries: the Dang-chu, Kiwang-chu, Hangta-chu and Hetsho-chu.

Summer temperatures are hot in Wangdu Phodrang, but the winters are cool and much of the north will be snowbound (average rainfall: 1,000 mm). Some 74% of the land is forested, with a mix of conifer and broadleaf trees. A large part of the district falls within the Black Mountains Forest Reserve and the Jigme Dorje National Park. Phobjika valley is a well-known winter nesting place for the black-necked crane, and it will soon have the district's only five-star hotel. Rich grazing pastures (3.5%) are found in the higher valleys and ridges, and in Phobjika. Only 2% of the land is cultivated, with rice yielding two crops per year in the Dang-chu valley. Potatoes and dairy products are the main cash crops, but there are very few citrus fruits growing here.

There are 15 counties in the district: Nahi, Gasetsho Gongma, Ogma and Daga are all to the west of the Punatsang-chu, while Rupisa and Athang lie to its east. Further north, Kazhi is in the upper reaches of the Yak-chu which itself flows into the Pho-chu in the north of Punakaha. Thetsho, Phangyu, Drena (Bjena), Nyisho and Dangchu all occupy the valley of the Dang-chu and its feeder rivers. Gangteng and Phobji are in the Phobjika valley, while Sephu is in the upper reaches of the Mangde-chu.

Two major highways intersect at the Wangdu Bridge over the Punatsang-chu: with roads leading west to Thimphu and Punakha, south to Tarkarna and Tsirang, and east to Bumthang. The administrative capital, also known as Wangdu Phodrang (Bh. Wangduephodrang), overlooks this strategic junction. The distance from Wangdu Phodrang to Thimphu is 75 km, to Punakha 21 km, to Trongsar 129 km, and to Dramphu 108 km. ▸▸ For Sleeping, Eating and other listings, see pages 155-156.

Thetsho county

Heading south from the **Metsinang** intersection on the main lateral highway (see page 136), the road passes the National Resources Training Institute at Lobesa, and enters Wangdu Phodrang district, following the Punatsang-chu down past the Dragon's Nest Hotel to its confluence with the Dang-chu at Wangdu Bridge. Wangdu Phodrang Dzong is now visible on the hilltop across the river, and below it on the far bank is the new town of **Bajothang**, which is destined to become the future district capital.

Internal travel documents are all registered at an immigration checkpoint alongside the bridge. Most foreign visitors will head east here, and there are still restrictions in place on southbound traffic into Tsirang, four hours distant (see page 156). Crossing the river by the modern Swiss-built bridge, you will notice downstream the towers of the original cantilever bridge, dated 1685, which was destroyed by floods in 1968. High up on the west bank, and visible as the road climbs into town, is the isolated village of **Rinchengang**, where the skills of

Drukpa Kun-le, the Divine Madman

The 'mad' yogin Drukpa Kunlek (1455-1529) was a contemporary of Pema Lingpa, and elder relative of the regent of Ralung, Ngawang Chogyel. He is revered as an eccentric culture hero, whose unconventional life and sexual exploits are explicitly recorded in biographical form. After completing his formal studies at Ralung, he became a realised master of tantric practice and the Great Seal (*mahamudra*), and roamed as an itinerant master, dispensing his compassionate shock-therapy to all who required his assistance, in all walks of life.

On reaching Paro in 1490, he slew an old lady who was on the point of death and insisted that the locals keep her corpse locked in a store-room for seven days, during which time the body was transformed into rainbow light (a sign of peerless spiritual accomplishment). Another of his skills was in guiding to liberation the minds of many deceased persons and animals in the after-death state (*bardo*). At Tobesa he seduced the beautiful wife of a devout householder in order to propagate his teachings. For the miraculous events surrounding the foundation of Chime Lhakhang, see page 136.

Another tale recounts how, at Kurje Lhakhang in Bumthang, he cavorted with local girls in order to enrage and quell a local chieftain who subsequently sponsored the building of Monsib Lhakhang. In Western Bhutan he subdued proud male and female demons with his male organ and its representation on the head of a walking stick, symbolising the indestructible nature of his buddha-mind. Then, at Sha Lutsogang in Wangdu, Drukpa Kun-le devoured a goat's head and the body of a bull, and at the snap of his finger, he resurrected them as a single creature–the takin, national animal of Bhutan!

traditional stone masonry are preserved. It is said that many of Bhutan's fortresses and temples have been built by artisans from Rinchengang.

Wangdu Phodrang orientation

Heading into town, the road passes the vegetable market on the left and a turn-off that leads downhill to the high school, an agricultural research station, and the new development at Bajothang. It then rounds a sharp bend, passing the entrance to the army training camp. Opposite, there are a number of small, privately owned shops: Lal Bahadur, Sangye Ngodrub, Namgyay, Tsering Lhamo, Sonam Rabjung, Karma General Store, Senge General Store, Tinley Wangmo, Mani Gyeltsen and Dorje General Store. Then, as the road descends towards the town centre, you will pass on the right: Jamyang Enterprises, Tashi Wangdi Pharmacy, Dawa Zangmo Store, Lhamo Shop, Pasang Shop, Pema Tsewang Pharmacy, Senge Store, Gyeltsen Lhamo, Chodron General, Wangchuk Bar, Dema Restaurant, Dondrub Photo Studio, Lekim General Store, Sonam Topgyay Store, Kunga Dem Store, the Post Office, Darlami Store, Gyatso Store and Dawa Sangye Restaurant & Bar. Opposite on the left are Pema Shop, Dorje General Store, Sonam Wangchuk Tailor, Tendzin Wangdu General Store and Sangye Zangmo, followed by the bus station and taxi stand.

At the downtown traffic circle, where driving licences are inspected, you can turn left for Trongsar or right for the *dzong* and the government buildings. The town is kept scrupulously clean by the district administrator, and many of the buildings and shops have elegant slate roofs. Locally produced bamboo handicrafts are also highly prized. On the former road, you will pass opposite the petrol pump, Lhundrub

Store, Thalpa Lhamo, a newspaper kiosk, Sangye Dorje, Zangmo Store, Druk Hair Salon, an electrical repair store and Pema Hotel & Bar. After the petrol pump on the left you will pass TCC Supermarket, Pema Khandro Phone Booth, Wangdu Junior High School, a shoe shop, Food Corporation of Bhutan, Jamyang Dorje Store and the District Hospital.

Turning right at the traffic circle, you will pass on the left the Black-necked Crane Restaurant, Tashi Topgyel Lodge and the Bank of Bhutan, while opposite on the right are Sangye Restaurant, Pemba General Store, New Kunga Restaurant and the Orchard Hotel. Now the road bifurcates – left for the police station and right for the High Court, the telephone exchange, the archery ground and the *dzong*.

Wangdu Phodrang Dzong

The strategically located Wangdu Phodrang Dzong (1,240 m) was built by Zhabdrung Ngawang Namgyel in 1638, following a dream which he had at Chime Lhakhang (see page 136). It is said that the protector deity Mahakala appeared, exhorting him to build a fortress on a rocky spur where ravens fly off in all four directions. The Zhabdrung quickly realised that a fortress constructed on this hilltop site would control the surrounding country — hence the name Wangdu Phodrang ('palace gathering all within its power'). But this is actually a shorthand version of the formal name: Druk Khamsum Wangdu Chokyi Phodrang ('palace of Drukpa Buddhism Gathering All the Three World Systems within its Power'). The construction of the new *dzong* was entrusted to Lopon Nyama Ku-ke who was appointed as its first governor. The prophecy turned out to be accurate in that it was from this stronghold and nearby Chotse Dzong that Migyur Tenpa brought the whole of Central and Eastern Bhutan within the fold of the new Bhutanese state between 1647 and 1655. The shingle-roofed fortress stands impressively on a rocky outcrop, overlooking the confluence of the Dang-chu and Punatsang-chu below, and the layout of the building actually follows the contour of the hill. Repairs have been made here, as elsewhere, following a fire in 1837 and the earthquake of 1897.

The fortress has a single entrance on its northern side. To the right of the entrance is the house of the district administrator Pema Dorje and to the left a *nagini* shrine and a small park. Vistors are required to register at the entrance. Unless special permission has been obtained in advance, the complex is only open to foreign visitors during the annual *tsechu* ceremonies. Within the **vestibule** are murals depicting the Four Guardian Kings and a set of large *mani* wheels (two on the left and one on the right).

Within the oblong-shaped **administrative courtyard**, a gallery runs along the side-walls. The offices here function as the administrative headquarters for the whole district. A large, shady tree fills the centre of the courtyard and behind it is the central tower (*utse*), from the window of which a large appliqué Tongdrol *tangkha* depicting Guru Padmakara with his Eight Manifestations is displayed during the *tsechu* ceremonies. In the right-hand corner is the monastic kitchen, which caters for the 170 monks who are resident here. A two-tier gallery runs along both sides of the building, giving direct access from the administrative courtyard to the rear sections of the building.

A bridge spans a narrow ravine, leading by a flight of stairs up to the **Gonkhang**, which is dedicated to Mahakala and Shridevi, and encircled by a row of prayer wheels. There are four other surrounding chapels. Then, passing through the southern **monastic courtyard**, you will reach the entrance to the main assembly hall. Here there are large impressive images of the Buddhas of the Three Times, flanked by Guru Padmakara and Zhabdrung Ngawang Namgyel. A verandah on the west wall overlooks the Punatsang-chu gorge directly below. The murals of the assembly hall depict the Sixteen Elders and the Thirty-five Confession Buddhas.

Dang-chu valley

The lateral highway runs from Wangdu Phodrang through the Dang-chu gorge to cross the Black Mountains. A signpost at the edge of town shows the distances as follows: Nabding (40 km), Gangteng Gonpa (57 km), Pele La (60 km), and Trongsar (129 km). The terrain is lightly forested and there are villages located high above on both sides of the valley. Down below close to the river a prison is clearly visible. As the road leaves Rupisa county for Drena (Bjena), it gradually winds down to the level of the river itself. Slate quarried in this area is highly prized by the stone masons of Wangdu Phodrang.

Eight kilometres from town, the road reaches **Chudzomsa** and the Kichu Resort, where the Pe-chu flows into the Dang-chu. There is a trailhead here for the easy four-day Samtengang winter trek. The trail passes through **Samtengang** in Nyitso county, and the **Pe-chu** valley in Phangyul county, before crossing the district border to **Lingmukha** in Punakha. This route has already been described in reverse (see page 141). A cable lift upstream from Chudzomsa carries supplies and timber across **Tashi La** pass (2,800 m) to and from the isolated interior of Drena, particularly to Nachen and Kotokha. Tourists are generally discouraged from using the cable for safety reasons, but trekkers will sometimes resort to it in an emergency (see page 154).

Four kilometres further upstream the road crosses to the south bank via **Tikke Bridge**, and begins to climb more steeply through Dangchu county into the thicker forests of the Black Mountains. There are fewer settlements in this narrow part of the gorge, the main one being **Naobding** (2,640 m), which is situated in a clearing 28 km uphill from the bridge. The smaller hamlet of **Dungdung Nyelsa**, is surrounded by rhododendron forest, 7 km above Nobding. There is a fork here – the new motor road on the right, which opened in 2001, now carries all traffic to Gangteng and Pele La, while the old road to the left, which is subject to frequent landslides, is mostly disused. Continuing steeply uphill on the new road, for 5 km, you will reach the **Lawa La** intersection, where a gravel road branches southwards for Gangteng Monastery. A signpost here indicates the distances: Gangteng (6 km), Phobjika (13 km), Pele La (3 km) and Trongsar (72 km).

Gangteng and Phobjika: counties of the Black Mountains

Taking the gravel side-road you drive through oak and rhododendron forests to cross a pass (3,360 m) leading into the wide glacial valley of Phobjika (3,000 m). This is an important wildlife conservation zone within the Black Mountains National Park (see page 258), a natural habitat for wild boar, black bears, leopards, barking deer and foxes. Here, too, nesting black-necked cranes from Central Asia can be observed in autumn. The valley is remarkably spacious, unusual in Bhutan but reminiscent of many in neighbouring Tibet. The road winds its way down to a junction, where you may turn left for Gangteng Gonpa or right, following the Nike-chu through to Tabting and Damcho Lhakhang.

Gangteng Sangak Choling

Heading down to Gangteng, the road passes Kunzang Choling hermitage, where an active meditation retreat programme has been running since 1990. Gangteng Sangak Choling, which overlooks the valley, is the largest Nyingma monastery to the west of the Black Mountains. The complex was founded in 1613 by Pema Trinle, a grandson and reincarnation of the influential treasure-finder Pema Lingpa (see box, page 176). The incarnate line descended from Pema Trinle represents the body aspect of Pema Lingpa, when contrasted with his speech and mind emanations, who have their main residence in Bumthang (see below, page 166). The community here comprises both celibate monks and married mantrins (*ngakpa*). The latter, who are generally known as *gomchen* in Bhutan, have families inhabiting the large village that surrounds the monastery. Since 1682 when the second incumbent Tendzin Lekpei Dondrub completed his construction of the winter residence at Phuntsok Rabtenling, Gangteng monastery has functioned primarily as a summer resdence for followers of the Pema Lingpa tradition. For a summary of the full lineage see box, page 180. The present incumbent, Rigdzin Kunzang Pema Namgyel (b. 1955), is the ninth incarnation.

Gangteng monastery has three storeys and a rooftop spire, containing altogether 14 chapels and halls within it. The main **assembly hall** has eight large pillars, and its precious iconography reflects the spiritual revelations (*terma*) of Pema Lingpa. However the woodwork has been badly damaged by woodworm and the structure is currently being restored.

On the **ground floor**, there is a central image of Guru Padmakara, flanked by 1,000 similar miniatures, and murals depicting the Thousand Buddhas. The reliquary stupa behind the central image contains the mortal remains of Peling Kutrul II Tendzin Lekpei Dondrub, the founder of the monastery. Behind it there is an inner sanctum, containing images of the Seven Generations of Past Buddhas, flanked by the gatekeepers Hayagriva and Acala.

On the **second floor** there is a small Gonkhang alongside the main hall. In the hall the central image again depicts Guru Padmakara, with a small Zhiwarepa in front and murals of the Sixteen Elders behind. The wall to the left has murals depicting Pema Lingpa, with Shakyamuni Buddha and the Lords of the Three Enlightened Families, while those to the right depict Guru Padmakara with his eight manifestations, in front of which are statues of Vajradhara and a representative image (*kutsab*) of Guru Padmakara that was unearthed as *terma*.

On the **third floor**, the **Guru Lhakhang** contains images of Guru Padmakara flanked by his eight manifestations, alongside a manuscript edition of the *Kangyur*, while the murals to the left depict Peling Thuk-se VIII Kunzang Zilnon (a 19th-century lineage holder) and the Thirty-five Confession Buddhas. Opposite on the right wall are murals representing Pema Lingpa surrounded by his lineage, and Sungtrul VIII Kunzang Dechen Dorje (1843-91).

The **main hall** on this level also has fascinating murals which emphasise the visionary teachings of Pema Lingpa: on the left they include Zangdok Pelri paradise, Amitayus with the assembled deities of the *Tsetri Dorje Trengwa*, and Guru Padmakara surrounded by visionary aspects derived from the *Kunzang Gongdu*. Opposite on the right they include Sukhavati paradise, followed by Guru Padmakara with his eight manifestations. The inner wall has images derived from the *Drakpo Themed* cycle, with Padmakara at the centre, while the murals depict Shantaraksita, Padmakara and King Trisong Desten, surrounded by other members of the royal family of the Yarlung dynasty, along with the eight main disciples of Padmakara who received the Eight Transmiited Precepts (Kabgye) from him at Chimphu in Tibet. Resting on the teaching throne at the centre of the hall is a stone footprint of Pema Lingpa.

The monastery has under its custodianship a number of precious artefacts, including two *vajras* which were used by the treasure-finders Konchok Lingpa and Dorje Lingpa, and a ritual dagger (*kila*) which had been retrieved as treasure by Pema Lingpa along with the *Lama Norbu Gyatso* cycle of teachings.

Alongside the monastery is a **college** for Buddhist studies (shedra), which was founded in 1986.

Phobjika Reserve

The Black Mountains are largely inhabited by nomadic yak-herders and shepherds, interspersed with a few small settlements where potatoes are farmed. The higher

⚇ The yak and the dri

No creature exemplifies the uniqueness of the Tibetan plateau and the Himalayan kingdom of Bhutan like the yak. Hardy, stubborn, frisky, and apparently clumsy though deceptively agile on precipitous rugged terrain, this 'grunting ox' (*Bos grunniens*) comes in many shapes and sizes: the male of the species is known as the yak, and the female as the dri. These animals have been domesticated and tended by nomads for thousands of years, giving rise also to the hybrid dzo (a cross between a bull and a dri), which has become an ideal ploughing animal in high-altitude farming villages.

Since antiquity, the yak has been used as a pack animal and is rarely ridden in the manner of a horse. Prior to the construction of motorable roads, yak caravans were the principal means for the transportation of freight, and they still are in many remote parts of the country. Through slow, they are untiringly capable of carrying loads of over 50 kg across 5,000-m passes, and they withstand temperatures of -30°C. For the nomads who rear the yak, this creature is the source of their wealth and livelihood. The flesh provides meat (*tsak-sha*), which may be cooked or freeze dried; the milk of the dri provides butter (*mar*) and cheese (*chura*). The hide is used for high-calved traditional boots and clothing. The soft inner hair (*ku-lu*) is used for the production of high-quality sweaters. The coarse outer hair (*tsid-pa*) is spun by the nomads themselves and used for making their black yak wool tent dwellings (*ba*).

pastures above the valley are ideal for yaks, which subsist on high-altitude dwarf bamboo and other grasses. The Phobjika valley is snow-bound in winter, when the community from Gangteng moves to lower elevations. On the road down to Tabiting village, where there are shops and a small school, you will pass the **Crane Observation & Education Centre**, run by the Royal Society for the Protection of Nature (open Mon-Fri). Telescopes are available here for viewing the 250-odd black-necked cranes which migrate here from Central Asia in late October and can be seen circling above the fields from November to March. It is also possible to view the roosting places of the cranes on the valley floor, close to the river, from specially designed wooden hideouts.

For those wishing to avoid the motor road, there is an easy three-day trek from Tabiting village in Phobjika to Tikke Bridge in the Dang-chu gorge (see page 151). En route you will pass through small villages and splendid forests of giant junipers, daphne bushes, rhododendrons and magnolia. The rhododendron season (April) is highly recommended, since you can then see hundreds in bloom.

Day 1 Tabiting–Gogona Starting from the warden's office at the entrance to the Black Mountains National Park in Tabiting (2,830 m), the trail climbs through fields, pine forest and meadows of dwarf bamboo to **Kelwag** and then zigzags more steeply through mixed forest of juniper, bamboo, rhododendron and magnolia, on the approach to Tsela La pass (3,440 m). The descent leads through the bamboo and mixed forest of the Kangha-chu valley to **Tserina** (3,120 m), where the trail forks: a lower branch leading to the large campsite at **Dzomdu Gyakha** and an upper one to the isolated nomadic area of Gogona (3,100 m), where there is a dairy research station, and a small campsite at Dangchu village (3,040 m). The main place of interest here is **Gogona Lhakhang**, a small community of *gomchen*, affiliated to Gangteng Gonpa, with images of Amitabha, Avalokiteshvara and Guru Padmakara.

The local people of Gogona speak a distinctly nomadic dialect, known in Bhutan as Bjop-kha (Tib. Drokpei ke); and Dangchu is an important centre for weaving (15 km, six to seven hours' trekking).

Day 2 Gogona–Khotokha Climbing through a large meadow and forest of mixed conifers, azaleas and rhododendrons, the trail ascends the thickly forested Shobju La (3,410 m). From the pass, the descent leads through a broad valley on a rocky tractor trail that is used by the lumber industry, passing through Dolando and Gangri Chi above the village of Khotokha (2,790 m). The main sites here are Rinchenling Gonpa and Do-le Gonpa, which are both Drukpa Kagyu monasteries (16 km, six to seven hours' trekking).

Day 3 Khotokha–Tikke Bridge Crossing the Padza-chu, the trail climbs northwards to reach a cluster of four stupas at Chorten Karpo. From here to the ridge (2,880 m) near Tashi La pass the ascent is more gentle and forested. It is possible to cut the trek short at this point by descending from Tashi La pass on the cable lift. Locals who use this service are charged Nu 60 and foreign visitors Nu 250. Otherwise continue downhill into the Dang-chu gorge – an area of diverse vegetation, beloved by birdwatchers. At Tikke Bridge, the trail rejoins the highway.

Sephu county: across the Black Mountains

From the main road at the Lawa La intersection (see above, page 151), it is a short, 3-km ascent through rhododendron and magnolia forest to the watershed at **Pele La** pass (3,420 metres). The dwarf bamboo that grows in this area is ideal for gazing yaks. On the way up, in clear weather there are fine views of Mounts Jomolhari and Jichu Drakye to the northwest. On the far side of the pass, the road descends into Sephu county, bypassing the nomadic settlement of **Gangchudar**, as conifer forest gives way to broadleaf trees. **Rukubji** is the largest agricultural settlement on this road. From here the road descends to cross the Nikhar-chu over the iron suspension bridge at **Sephu** village. There is a post office here and a number of small roadside stalls, selling snacks and dumplings, as well as rattanware mats and baskets.

Sephu is the trailhead for the long and difficult trek to Lunanang and Laya in Gasa district. This route has already been described in reverse (see page 145). Beyond Sephu, the road leads out of Wangdu and into the Trongsar district of Central Bhutan, as it descends into the valley of the Mangde-chu.

Counties of the Punatsang-chu valley

If you follow the road that leads southwards from the immigration checkpoint at the Wangdu Bridge (see page 148), remaining on the west bank of the Punatsang-chu, you will pass through the Gasetso, Daga and Athang areas, heading into Tsirang. In this region there are a few small Drukpa Kagyu temples of note, including those of Khotang Jangsa, Wagang, and Lutruk Gonpa, which were all founded by Ngagi Wangchuk of Ralung during the 16th century. Later in 1627 Zhabdrung Ngawang Namgyel toured the region, consolidating his power as far as south as Jarok Gang. **NB** Although the road is relatively new, casual visitors are generally discouraged from taking this route into southern Bhutan.

Sleeping

Wangdu Phodrang *p148*

Uma Resorts are building a 5-star Wangdu Phodrang Lodge, north of town, overlooking the Punatsang-chu. This hotel will have 10 rooms, with in-house restaurant, spa and yoga facilities.

A **Dragon Nest Resort**, T2-481366, F2-481274, dorji@druknet.bt, located by the Punatsang-chu riverside below Wangdu Phodrang, has 17 carpeted rooms overlooking the river, with attached bathrooms and some with televisions – doubles at Nu 1,700 and singles at Nu 1,400. There is also an in-house internet bar next to the restaurant.

C **Orchard Hotel**, T2-481297, centrally located, has 3 superior rooms with private bathrooms in the main building – doubles at Nu 700 and singles at Nu 600; as well as 6 simpler rooms in an annexe with shared facilities at Nu 500. A tented restaurant is set up during the *tsechu* period.

D **Tashi Topgyel Lodge**, next to the Bank of Bhutan, is centrally located and family run, with 4 simple rooms – doubles at Nu 400 and singles at Nu 300 (shared WC and shower facilities). There is a small restaurant and bar.

Dang-chu valley *p151*

A **Kichu Resort**, T2-481359, F2-481360, located at Rabunang near Chudzomsa, 8 km to the east in the Dang-chu gorge, offers the best accommodation in the district, with 22 fine chalet-style rooms with their own verandahs and 24-hr hot water supply – doubles at Nu 2,000 and singles at Nu 1,800. There is a good vegetarian restaurant, a well-stocked bar, and a volleyball court. **NB** Insect repellent will be a useful asset here during the summer months.

Gangteng and Phobjika *p151*

Aman Resorts are building a 5-star international-standard hotel in the Phobjika valley. Pending its completion, only simple accommodation is available.

C **Phuntsocholing Guesthouse**, a traditional Bhutanese family lodge located near Tabiting, with doubles at Nu 800 and singles at Nu 600. No private bathroom, but friendly service with evening cultural performances.

C **Thekchen Phodrang Guesthouse**, located opposite Gangteng Gonpa, has 8 chilly concrete rooms, all with private bathroom – Nu 800 double and Nu 600 single. There is a communal dining room/lounge area.

Eating

Wangdu Phodrang *p148*

Apart from the hotels, the **Black-necked Crane Restaurant** offers Nepali-style meals. **Kunga Hotel**, T2-481256, is good for Bhutanese and Tibetan-style dishes. **Dema Restaurant** has a laid-back atmosphere.

Dang-chu valley *p151*

Gaden Tashiding Restaurant, located above Nobding, is the best roadside inn on this stretch. There are also simple teahouses at Dungdung Nyelsa.

Festivals

Wangdu Phodrang Dzong *p150*

The annual three-day *tsechu* ceremonies are held here during the 7th month of the lunar calendar.

Shopping

Wangdu Phodrang *p148*

There are a many privately owned general stores (*tsongkhang*), selling groceries and other daily necessities. The open market is located below the town on the road to Bajothang.

Postage stamps are available at **Bhutan Post**, near the traffic circle, behind Sigey Store.

Gangteng and Phobjika *p151*

Norsang Carpet Factory, located behind Phuntsocholing Guesthouse, is a small cottage industry, founded in 1992. Carpets, mostly about 1m by 2m, are on display and for sale: Nu 3,000-3,500. Some basic groceries can also be picked up at the local shops in Tabiting.

Transport

Wangdu Phodrang *p148*

Nearly all visitors to Wangdu Phodrang will have pre-arranged transportation, and many just pass through en route for Trongsar or Thimphu, having seen the *dzong*. **Bus** services running from Thimphu to Trongsar, Jakar and Tashigang all stop here. For details, see under Thimphu (p82).

Directory

Wangdu Phodrang *p148*
Banks Bank of Bhutan, next to the Traffic Circle. Open Mon-Fri 0900-1300, Sat 0900-1100. **Hospitals and medical services** Wangdu Phodrang Hospital is located on the east side of town. Indian-produced medicines can also be purchased at Pema Tsewang Pharmacy. **Internet** Facilities are only available in the major hotels. **Post**, including EMS express delivery, are available at Bhutan Post, Open Mon-Fri 0830-1230, 1330-1630, Sat 0900-1230. **Telecommunications** IDD calls can be made from the major hotels and from the Pema Khandro STD/IDD phone booth.

Tsirang district རྩི་རང་

→ *Area: 639 sq km.*

Tsirang is the second smallest district in Bhutan, bounded by Wangdu Phodrang to the north, Tarkarna to the west and Sarpang to the south. Tsirang lies to the east of the Punatsang-chu river, and it includes the headwaters of its tributaries, the Buri-chum Choche-chu and Kali Khola.

Summers in Tsirang are very hot and humid, and the winters are cool and dry (average rainfall: 1,000-3,000 mm). About 76% of the land is forested, mostly with bamboo, oak, chir pine, panisaj and lemon grass. Grazing pastures are sparse but the proportion of cultivated land is high (22%). Oranges are the main crop, supplemented by cardamom and other citrus fruits. Much of the population is of Lhotsampa origin.

There are 12 counties in the district: Patale, Drangra, Tsokhana, Chanautre, Gairigang and Beteni all in the Punatsang-chu valley; Gozeling, Kikhorthang and Dunglegang all in the central Choche-chu valley; Phuntenchu and Semjong are in the Biru-chu valley; and Lamedranga is in the Kali Khola basin.

The administrative capital of Tsirang is located at Dramphu on the southern highway, 99 km from Wangdu Bridge (see page 148), and 60 km north of Sarpang on the Indian border. There are other motorable side-roads through to Lamedranga and Dunglegang, as well as into Tarkarna district. ▸▸ For Transport listings, see page 158.

Patale, Drangra and Gozeling counties

Heading south from Wangdu Bridge on the west bank of the Punatsang-chu, the road soon passes into Tsirang district and crosses to the east bank at Mithuntror. Temperatures rise in the searing heat of the gorge, as the road passes through the small settlements of Sunkoshtra and Kawalpani. Further south at Chanchey Doban, the road leave the gorge and forks – south-west for Tarkarna and south-east for Dramphu. Taking the latter, you will soon arrive in the district capital after 12 km.

Dramphu

Dramphu in Kikhorthang is a growing town, located on a high ridge above the Choche-chu valley, straddling the southern highway. Entering the town from the north, on the left side of the highway you will pass the police station, Sharma Shop, Hotel KDPD, Salami General Store, Thingu Shop, Kunzang Hotel & Bar, Tashedelek Hotel & Bar, Hotel 2000, Dargo General Store, Sangay Store and other small shops leading towards the post office, Dramphu General Hospital and Tsirang Dzong. Opposite on the right side of the highway are: the weekend market, Sonam General Store, Tawang General Store, Sangye Hotel & Bar and several other small shops before the bus stand. Beyond the bus stand, are further small shops, the Bank of Bhutan and Bhutan Telecom. South of the *dzong* and Bhutan Telecom, there is an important police checkpoint, which monitors all traffic heading south into Sarpang and the border area (see page 196).

The **dzong** at Tsirang is small and only contains images of Shakyamuni Buddha, flanked by Zhabdrung Ngawang Namgyel and Guru Padmakara.

Lamedranga county

The southern highway from Dramphu cuts south-eastwards, crossing the Kalikhola river to enter Sarpang county, and in doing so it passes through the villages of Toribari, Noonpani and Jogidara, which are inhabited predominantly by Lhotsampa peoples of Nepali origin.

Tarkarna district སྦུག་དགར

→ *Area: 1,389 sq km.*

Tarkarna district (Bh. Dagana) lies to the south of Thimphu and Wangdu Phodrang, with Chukha to the west, Tsirang to the east and Sarpang to the south. The valley of the Punatsang-chu river lies to the east of the district, and much of the terrain is occupied by its feeder rivers, the Tarkar-chu and the Sami-chu.

As in neighbouring Tsirang, the summers are hot and the winters cool (average rainfall: 750-2,000 mm). As much as 82% of the land is still forested, mostly with broadleaf species, and there is little pasture. About 13% of the land is cultivated with orange groves and cardamom, as well as millet, rice and wheat.

There are 11 counties in the district: Lajab, Tsangkha, Drugegang, Tashding and Suntale all occupy the west bank of the Punatsang-chu; Khilpisa, Gozhing, Kalidzingkha and Tsezang are all in the Tarkar-chu valley; while Emeri and Dorona are in the Sami-chu valley.

Very few visitors travel into Tarkarna. The motor road, often destroyed by monsoon rains, has ensured its isolation. The administrative capital is located at Tarkar Dzong in Tsezang, where the headwaters of the Tarkar-chu converge. Access is from Chanchey Daban on the southern highway, where a bridge leads traffic across to the west bank of the Punatsang-chu to Tashiding. Here it leaves the river, following the valley of the Tarkar-chu upstream to the capital. The distance from Wangdu Bridge to Tarkar Dzong is 164 km.

Tarkarna

The district capital Tarkarna is a small town, built alongside the winding road that commands a view over the confluence of the Langang-chu and Dora-chu tributaries of the Tarkar-chu. Entering the town from the south, you will pass a row of shops on the left, facing the steep gorge. These include: Gyeltsen General Store and Namgyel Store. A lane then leads downhill on the right to the local high school. Continuing along the main street, you will find, on the left: Pasang Norbu Store, Tsering Lhamo Bar & Store, Sonam Wangchuk Bar & Shop, among others. Opposite on the right are the post office and Dawana Bar. A stupa with three entrances (Chorten Gosum) marks the approach to the older part of the town. Tarkar Dzong is situated at a bend in the road. Below it is Tarkar Lhakhang, and after the bend you will find the police station, Bhutan Telecom and Tarkar Guesthouse.

Tarkar Dzong

The fortress known as Tarkar Tashi Yangtse Dzong was built in 1655 by Nyerpa Druk Namgyel who had been despatched with an army into the Tarkar-chu valley by Zhabdrung Ngawang Namgyel in 1649 to subdue "criminal unrest". Tenpa Trnle was appointed as its first governor. The position of Tarkar governor (*ponlop*) carried high rank and powerful status during the 18th and 19th centuries. The central tower of the *dzong* has fine images and murals on its middle and upper floors. On the middle floor, the Lama Lhakhang contains images of Zhabdrung Jikme Drakpa (right) and Tsangpa Gyare (left), with murals depicting the eight manifestations of Guru Padmakara. On the top floor, there is a Gonkhang, containing images of Chamdrel, flanked by Jnananatha and Chengye Lhamo, and murals illustrating the Lords of the Three Enlightened Families.

⊖ Transport

Dramphu *p156*
Public bus services from Thimphu to Dramphu are operated by **Sherab Travels** on Mon, Wed and Fri at 0730 (Nu 111), and by **Kunga Travel** on Tue, Thu and Sat at 0730 (Nu 82).

Tarkarna *p157*
Public bus services from Thimphu to Tarkarna are operated by **KW Express** on Wed, Fri and Sun at 0700 (Nu 123), and by **Dawa Transport** on Mon, Wed and Fri at 0730 (Nu 154).

Footprint features

Introduction

Crossing the Black Mountains into Central Bhutan, the terrain changes dramatically. The landscape is more spacious and the valleys of the Mangde-chu and its Bumthang-chu tributary, which comprise this region, are broader. Archaeological evidence and historical sources both suggest that Bumthang, the cultural heart and former capital of Bhutan, had been inhabited in Neolithic times; and the earliest contacts with Buddhism appear to have been made here as well. The area was brought within the fold of the Bhutanese state in 1647, after the consolidation of the western regions. Even today the central parts of the country are known for the rich diversity of their Buddhist traditions.

An extended itinerary of about 10 days will enable you to explore the heritage of Central Bhutan, but be prepared for long drives and a less developed infrastructure. The lateral highway was built only in the 1970s, and from June to September there are frequent delays caused by landslides. At present accommodation will be in rustic lodges rather than large hotels, although the Aman and Como chains will soon be opening top-end hotels at Phobjika and Jakar. Central Bhutan includes the four districts of Trongsar, Zhemgang, Sarpang and Bumthang.

★ Don't miss...

1. **Kunga Rabten** The former winter palace of the second king of Bhutan was constructed in the 1920s. It now houses part of the National Library, page 165.

2. **Kurje Lhakhang** A complex of three grand temples and royal funerary platforms. The oldest temple, founded in 1652, houses the sacred eighth-century body imprint of Guru Padmakara, page 178.

3. **Bumthang Cultural Trek** An easy three-day hike from Thangbi Lhakhang in Chokhor to Ugyen Choling in Tang. Explore the museum of Ugyen Choling at the end of the trek, page 183.

4. **Kunzang Drak** Climb steeply to the ridge-top hermitage, founded in 1488 by Pema Lingpa, above his own birthplace, page 186.

5. **Shertang La Pass** Enjoy magnificent views of Mt Gangkar Punsum, before descending into the Ura valley, page 190.

Trongsar district གྲོང་གསར

→ *Area: 1,807 sq km.*

Trongsar lies at the geographical centre of Bhutan, bordering Wangdu Phodrang in the west, Bumthang in the east, and Sarpang and Zhemgang in the south. The Mangde-chu rises below Mount Gangkar Punsum, and is itself an important tributary of the Drangme-chu (Manas), the major river system east of the Black Mountains. In its upper reaches the Mangde-chu flows through Trongsar and it is fed by four main tributaries: Sinmo-chu and Khechi-chu in the north, Ne-chu in the west and Nabji-chu in the south.

Summers are pleasantly warm in Trongsar, but the winters are cold (average rainfall: 1,500-3,000 mm). Nearly 88% of the land is still forested, two-thirds with broadleaf trees and the remainder with conifers. Much of western Trongsar falls within the Black Mountains Nature Reserve, and it is a natural habitat for wildlife. Less than 4% of the land is suitable for grazing, and 6% is cultivated. The main crops are maize, potatoes, rice, wheat and buckwheat, as well as citrus fruits, shiitake mushrooms and cardamom. The nearest large market is at Gelekphuk in Sarpang, 244 km to the south.

There are five counties in the district: Nubi in the upper reaches of the Mangde-chu, where the capital is located, Tansibji on the approach to Pele La pass, Drakteng (Bjakteng) and Langti on the road to Zhemgang, and Korphu in the south-west.

The lateral highway from Wangdu Phodrang runs via Pele La pass to the administrative capital at Trongsar, where it then bifurcates: a branch road leading southwards to Zhemgang, and the main road continuing east into Bumthang. The distance from Trongsar to Wangdu Phodrang is 129 km, to Jakar in Bumthang 68 km, and to Zhemgang 107 km. ▸▸ *For Sleeping, Eating and other listings, see pages 165-166.*

Tangsibji county

The lateral highway between Wangdu Phodrang and Trongsar was paved as late as 1985. After the descent from Pele La pass to Sephu (see page 154), the road enters the district of Trongsar, following the Nikhar-chu downstream through a long, narrow gorge for about 10 km. The forest of rhododendron, oak, dwarf bamboo and mixed conifers gradually gives way to cultivated farmland. Two kilometres below the village of Chendebji, visible across the river, the road reaches **Chendebji Chorten** (2,430 m). According to a well-known legend the great 16th-century yogin Drukpa Kun-le refused to visit this area east of Pele La, because he had received no prophecy prompting him to go there. The local spirits therefore remained dissident and hostile. To remedy this and suppress the local malevolent forces, a magnificent white-domed stupa was constructed here in Nepalese style during the early 18th century by Lama Shida. Alongside this geomantic landmark is a smaller stupa in Bhutanese style, which dates from 1982, and a long wall of *mani* stones, decorated with fine bas relief slate images of the Thirty-five Confession Buddhas. From here to Trongsar the distance is 42 km.

On leaving the gorge, the road passes cultivated farmland and climbs above the village of **Tangsibji**, before turning north through Chuserwa, into the wide Mangde-chu valley. The magnificent structure of Chotse Dzong soon comes into view across the river from **Tashiling**, overhanging a precipitous ridge.

Nubi county

There is no direct access to Trongsar Dzong from Tashiling. Instead the road enters Nubi county and winds for 14 km, northwest via Tsamkhar to cross the Mangde-chu at

Drizam (Bjizam) by a Bailey bridge. A trekking route leads upstream from here via Brangzhing and Bemji, to connect with the Dur-Gangkar Punsum trail (see page 182). Crossing the bridge by the motor road, you climb abruptly south-east, along the edge of a sheer precipice, into town (2,370 m). About 2 km before reaching town, you will pass the New Yangkhyil Resort, which offers fine views of Chotse Dzong.

Trongsar town orientation

The town of Trongsar (lit. 'new town') has been developing since 1982. Many of the shops here are owned by Bhutanese of recent Tibetan origin. On the approach to town a side road branches off on the left, winding uphill to the district hospital, Sherabling Tourist Lodge, Trongsar High School and Kunga Choling, a branch of Gangteng Monastery founded by the present Gangteng Tulku.

Continuing into town, you will pass the vegetable market and the Trupang Palace on the left. Jigme Dorji Wangchuk, the third king of Bhutan, was born here in 1928 and it now functions as a royel guesthouse. Beyond the palace are the Food Corporation of Bhutan, the Bank of Bhutan and Sonam Chodron General Store. Opposite on the right are the bus stop, the car park, Kinley General Store, Letro General Store and Nado General Store. Now the road forks — right for Bhutan Post and **Chotse Dzong** (see below), and left for the downtown area. Heading downtown towards the traffic circle, you will pass on the right the office of the Road Safety and Transport Authority (RSTA), Trongsa Hotel, Sonam Topgyel Hotel, Karma Leto Store, Norling Hotel, Rabden General Store, Dolma General Store, Namgyey Dolma General Store and Shambhala Hotel. Opposite on the left are the offices of the Chotse Dzong Renovation Project.

At the traffic circle, the southern and eastern highways diverge. If you turn left on the **Bumthang road**, you will pass on the right side a telephone booth, the immigration checkpost, Kunga Hotel and Lhasa Hotel; and on the left side Sangye Wangmo Store, the Tashidelek Restaurant & Bar and the Watchtower (Ta Dzong). From here the road winds uphill to Phunzhi Guesthouse on its way out of town.

Returning to the traffic circle, if you turn right on to the **Zhemgang road**, you will pass on the right side after the Shambhala Hotel, Tselha Store, Kinley Wangmo Store & Bar, Karma General Store, Wangchuk General Store, Nyida Karsum Hotel and Tashi Tsering Store. Opposite are Namgyel Lhamo Store, Lingtsang Store and petrol station.

Chokhor Rabtentse Dzong (Chotse Dzong)

Chotse Dzong is the largest and most impressively situated *dzong* in Bhutan, perched high on a cliff above the deep Mangde-chu gorge and dominated by a double-winged watchtower ('Ta Dzong'), from which all approaches could be monitored with ease. Here Bhutanese architecture is seen at its best. The huge, many-levelled fortress with its intricate wood carvings has a maze of courtyards and covered passages, which follow the contour of the hillside.

Background The original building on this commanding ridge was the hermitage of **Mon Drubde Lhakhang**, which had been constructed in 1543 by Ngagi Wangchuk, the great-grandfather of Zhabdrung Ngawang Namgyel, in the course of his visit from Tibet. According to legend, Ngagi Wangchuk entered into meditation while seated on the ridge at Yuli and perceived a subtle luminosity at the place where the Gonkhang now stands. He saw this as an auspicious omen for the building of a new hermitage and on inspecting the site more closely he saw imprints resembling the footprints of the protectress Shridevi's horse. So he and his followers built the Mon Drubde Lhakhang.

Later in 1647, following the consolidation of Western Bhutan within the new Drukpa state, Zhabdrung Ngawang Namgyel encouraged Mingyur Tenpa, who was then the senior lama at nearby Chungseng Dargyegang monastery, to build a new fortress on the site of this temple. The massive structure was given the name Chokhor Rabtentse Dzong, and Mingyur Tenpa was appointed as its first governor

(Chotse *ponlob*). It was from here that he successfully launched his military campaigns in Central and Eastern Bhutan.

The original fortress was subsequently enlarged by Mingyur Tenpa in 1652 and the Jamkhang, dedicated to Maitreya, was added in 1771. During the 19th century, Chotse Dzong was the seat of the most powerful governor of the country, commanding the whole of the central and eastern region. It was from this position of power that Ugyen Wangchuk emerged as the first hereditary king of Bhutan in 1907. Following an earthquake in 1897, the fortress was repaired by the then governor Jigme Namgyal, father of the first king. The second king Jigme Wangchuk also ruled the country from here, and subsequent crown princes have continued to hold the honoured title of Tsongsar Governor. Although no longer an active royal residence, Chotse Dzong is still revered as a former residence of Bhutan's royal family, for which reason foreign visitors require a special permit to enter. Current renovations are being undertaken by the Dzong Renovation Project, based in the town.

The site Nowadays Chotse Dzong contains 23 temples, and houses the district bureaucracy as well as a monastic community of 200 monks, who move in summer to Kurje Monastery in Bumthang. There are entrance gates in each of the four cardinal directions. Above the main eastern gate there is an exquisite painting of the gatekeeper Acala.

The **northern courtyard** is occupied by district government offices, and this is also where sacred masked dances are performed during the *tsechu* ceremonies of the 11th lunar month. At its centre there is the Dungkhor Lhakhang, containing an enormous prayer wheel, and in the north-west corner is the building added by Mingyur Tenpa in 1652 (currently undergoing renovation).

The **central tower** (*utse*) has a vestibule with murals depicting the Zangdok Pelri paradise, Pungthang Dechen Dzong, Svayambhunath in Nepal and the cosmology of the *Abhidharmakosa*. Most of the temples are contained within the tower, and they are dedicated to meditational deities such as Maitreya, Yamantaka, Hevajra and Kalacakra. There is also a large **assembly hall**, containing an image of Shakyamuni Buddha, and narrative murals illustrating the royal court of the first king who designed the hall. Another room contains a large xylographic collection, where texts are still printed in the traditional manner.

In the **southern monastic courtyard**, the **Chorten Lhakhang** occupies the site of Ngagi Wangchuk's original 16th-century hermitage. It contains an image of Aksobhya (Mitrukpa), which is the most revered in the *dzong*, so that the chapel is also known as the Mitrukpa Lhakhang. The murals here depict the Sixteen Elders, and Ngagi Wangchuk himself, whose reliquary stupa is enshrined in the inner sanctum.

Ta Dzong

The watchtower east of Chotse Dzong is shaped like a tower with two protruding wings. It contains a recently renovated temple dedicated to Gesar, the legendary epic warrior king, and another named after the governor Jigme Namgyal, father of the first king of Bhutan.

Yotong La

The lateral highway from Trongsar to Bumthang zigzags eastwards, bypassing the Phunzhi Guesthouse after 7 km and it climbs through forest terrain to reach the trailhead for **Dorji Gonpa**, visible in the valley below. Thirteen kilometres from Trongsar, Dorji Gonpa is currently being absorbed by the Simtokha Institute (see page 91), which plans to move here from Thimphu. Now the road traverses **Yotong La** pass (3,551 m), which marks the border between Trongsar and Bumthang districts. On the ascent there are fine panoramas to the west, overlooking Chotse Dzong. For a description of this road into Bumthang, see page 166.

Drakteng and Langthi counties

If you take the southern road from the traffic circle at Trongsar, you will follow the gorge of the Mangde-chu downstream through Drakteng (Bjakteng) and Langthi counties. For the first stretch of 15 km, this road runs parallel to the Wangdu Phodrang highway, across the river, before turning south-east, at **Takse Gonpa**. The valley is wide at this point and the terraced slopes have rice paddies. Soon you will reach Kunga Rabten Palace, 23 km from town.

Kunga Rabten Phodrang

The palace of Kunga Rabten, which is nowadays affiliated to the National Library of Bhutan, is accessible from the motor road. Formerly it was the winter residence of the second king, Jigme Wangchuk, and his junior consort. Constructed in the 1920s by Droka Mingyur, it has been well preserved on account of its royal connections.

Entering the palace, a gallery runs around the courtyard on all four sides. To the left of the central tower there is a royal apartment and an outhouse where the royal bodyguards would stay. The **central tower** (*utse*), which has finely decorated woodwork, is a three-storey building. The ground floor and the second floor, which were once used respectively as a granary and a military garrison, are now empty. On the third floor, there are three adjoining rooms. The main entrance leads into the central room, known as the **Sangye Lhakhang**, which contains images of Shakyamuni Buddha and the Twenty-one Aspects of Tara. The room to the left was the **private residence** of King Jigme Wangchuk, while the room to the right is the **Kangyur Lhakhang**, now housing part of the National Library of Bhutan.

Near the palace there is an active nunnery under the supervision of Lama Tsultrim Gyatso, a well-known teacher from Nangchen in Eastern Tibet. Down the valley from here is **Wangdu Choling Palace**, a residence of the second king's brother, which is still used periodically by the royal family.

Towards Zhemgang

After Kunga Rabten, the road descends once again to the level of the Mangde-chu, passing a series of farming villages where the Wachi-chu and Thripa-chu flow into the gorge. South of Jangbi and Bateng, the gorge begins to narrow, and the road plunges down to 1,400 m, passing through a wild uninhabited region, on its way into Zhemgang.

◉ Sleeping

Trongsar town *p163*
Aman Resorts announced that they will be opening a 5-star hotel in Trongsar, but its construction is some way off.
A **New Yangkhyil Resort**, T3-521126, located 2 km from town on the road to Drizam Bridge, is a friendly and well-run Tibetan hotel, with 19 standard rooms – doubles at Nu 2,200 and singles at Nu 1,800, and 1 deluxe room at Nu 2,500 (plus sales tax 10%). The hotel has a good bar and restaurant (capacity 40-50), with fine views of Chotse Dzong, and internet, laundry and conference facilities.
C **Norling Hotel**, T3-521171, F3-521178, is centrally located with 10 rooms – doubles at Nu 1,050 and singles at Nu 850, and 1 suite

at Nu 2,600. Some of the rooms are chalet-style, with private bathrooms. There is a good restaurant here.
C **Phunzhi Guesthouse**, T3-521197, F3-521197, located 7 km from town, at Jorpang on the Bumthang road, has 22 chalet-style rooms overlooking the valley in a tranquil setting, under the proprietorship of Dasho Dargye Tsering – doubles at Nu 1,000 and singles at Nu 800. There is a steep footpath from here to the watchtower and the town.
C **Sherabling Tourist Lodge**, T3-521116, F3-521107, located on a quiet side-road overlooking the *dzong* and managed by Bhutan Tourism Corporation Ltd, has 12

double rooms at Nu 1,105, 1 single at Nu 845 and 1 suite at Nu 2,600. Some of the rooms are chalet-style, with private bathrooms.

D **Kunga Hotel**, T3-521139, located next to the police checkpost, is a small hotel under Tibetan management, with simple rooms (no attached bathroom).

D **Ugencholing Hotel**, T3-521400, located on the main street, has 8 rooms – doubles at Nu 350 and singles at Nu 250.

E **Nyidakarsum Lodge**, T3-521126, is a Tibetan-run hotel, with 6 simple rooms (3 with attached bathroom), and a Tibetan restaurant downstairs.

E **Shambhala Hotel**, T3-521135, also under Tibetan management, has 8 simple rooms (no attached bathroom).

🍴 Eating

Trongsar town *p163*

The **Norling** hotel has reasonably good Bhutanese and Nepali cuisine. The smaller hotels all have good Tibetan restaurants (average price Nu 60-180). Among non-hotel restaurants, the **Tashidelek**, located below the watchtower, is recommended.

❋ Festivals

Trongsar town *p163*

Accommodation can be hard to find during the **tsechu festival**, which is held annually at Chotse Dzong during the **11th lunar month**. In 2004 this event will take place on 20-22 Dec, and in 2006 on 8-10 Jan.

◯ Shopping

Trongsar town *p163*

There are a few small general stores (*tsongkhang*), selling groceries and sundry items. Postage **stamps** are available at **Bhutan Post**, located on the road to the *dzong*.

⊖ Transport

Trongsar town *p163*

Nearly all visitors to Trongsar will have pre-arranged transportation, and many just pass through en route for **Bumthang**, **Zhemgang** or **Wangdu Phodrang**, stopping only to see Chotse Dzong. Public **bus** services running from **Thimphu** to Trongsar are operated by **Bhutan Post Express**, departing Thimphu daily except Sat at 0730 and in the opposite direction, daily except Sun at 0730 (Nu 99).

❶ Directory

Trongsar town *p163*

Banks Bank of Bhutan, opposite the bus stop Mon-Fri 0900-1300, Sat 0900-1100. **Internet** Facilities are only available in the larger lodges and hotels. **Hospitals and medical services** Trongsar Hospital is located in the extreme north of the town, on the way to Kunga Choling. **Post** including EMS express delivery, are available at Bhutan Post, Mon-Fri 0830-1230, 1330-1630, Sat 0900-1230. **Telephone** IDD calls can be made from hotels and from the phone booth alongside the traffic circle.

Bumthang district བུམ་ཐང་

→ *Area: 2,714 sq km.*

Bumthang is justifiably regarded as the cultural heart of Bhutan. Here there is a rich diversity of languages and traditions reflecting elements of Bhutanese society that predate the Zhabdrung's 17th-century unification of the country. The district shares an international boundary with the Lhodrak county of Tibet in the north, Wangdu Phodrang and Trongsar lie to the west, Lhuntse to the east, and Zhemgang to the south. Bhutan's highest mountain, Gangkar Punsum (7,540 m) straddles the border between Bumthang and Wangdu Phodrang.

Four rivers flow through wide glacial valleys to converge at the 'vase-shaped' bulge of central Bumthang. Among them, the Chamkhar-chu (the main river) rises in the far north, around Lhadem and flows south through the Chokhor valley to enter Zhemgang district (see page 193). The Kanggang-chu rises in the west, near Yotong La pass, and flows through Chu-me valley, converging with the Chamkhar-chu at Kereline, south of Jakar. The Tang-chu rises in the north-east near Lhuntse, and flows through the Tang valley before emptying into the Chamkhar-chu. Lastly, the Lirgang-chu rises in the south-east and flows through Ura valley, merging with the Chamkhar-chu further downstream. All these valleys are wide and gently sloping, offering a sense of spaciousness, almost unequalled elsewhere in the country.

Summers are short and cool in Bumthang and the winters are quite cold (average rainfall: 1,000-1,500 mm). The nights can be chilly, even in summertime, and there are strong afternoon winds. Nearly 67% of the land is covered with mixed conifer forest, 8% is pastureland suitable for the grazing of yaks, cattle and sheep; and only 2% is cultivated. The main crops are buckwheat, barley, wheat, rye, potatoes and apples, but dairy products are also marketed. Lumbering and hand-made woollen textiles are important for the local economy. Most exports are sent to India through Gelekphuk (see page 197).

There are four counties in the district: Chume in the south-west, Chokhor in the north-west, Tang in the north-east and Ura in the south-east. The administrative capital is at Jakar in the Chokhor valley. The lateral highway from Trongsar runs via Yotong La pass to Jakar, from where it cuts south-east through Ura into Mongar district. There are also motorable side-roads heading part of the way through the Chokhor and Tang valleys. The distance from Jakar to Trongsar is 68 km, and to Mongar in Eastern Bhutan 193 km. The northern border with Tibet on Monla Karchung La pass is currently closed.

Most of the interesting temples and beautiful monasteries are only accessible to trekkers, hiking away from the motor roads. Bumthang is also a fantastic area for day walks. The villages have beautifully painted wooden house façades, and the fields look best in autumn when the buckwheat turns deep orange.

Bumthang is the stronghold of the Nyingmapa school in Bhutan, chiefly on account of the activities of three important Nyingmapa lamas of the 14th and 15th century: Longchen Rabjampa, Dorje Lingpa and Pema Lingpa, the last of whom was actually born in Bumthang. The construction of the motor road and the implementation of development projects through Swiss, Austrian and Indian government aid have brought a new prosperity to this once isolated rural area.

The four valleys of Bumthang give the visitor an opportunity to explore the remote countryside of Central Bhutan where life has remained virtually unchanged for centuries. You can watch people producing baskets, weaving on traditional looms or making hand-made paper from daphne bark; and there are opportunities for cultural trekking. ▸▸ *For Sleeping, Eating and other listings, see pages 191-193.*

Chu-me valley

After crossing **Yotong La** pass on the 28-km drive eastwards from Trongsar (see page 162), the road descends gradually into the upper reaches of the Khangang-chu to enter the long Chu-me valley (2,700 m) at the landmark **Chochik Lhakhang**. Chu-me is sanctified by the temples of Buli, Tharpaling and Trekar. The first village on the descent is **Getsa**. Around here the land is fertile, yielding crops of wheat, barley, potatoes and the local staple, buckwheat.

Buli Lhakhang

The small temple of Buli Lhakhang is visible within a cluster of village houses to the left of the road at Getsa, and it is possible to drive almost as far as the entrance. This is an important shrine, built by Tukse Choying, son of the great treasure-finder Dorje Lingpa (1346-1405). The temple has three storeys. The **ground floor** contains the Jokhang, with its image of Maitreya wearing the bodhisattva crown. On the **second floor** there are images of the Buddhas of the Three Times, with murals to the left depicting the Twenty-one Aspects of Tara and the Lords of the Three Enlightened Families, and those to the right depicting Guru Padmakara with his eight manifestations, the Hundred Peaceful and Wrathful Deities, and the lineage of Dorje Lingpa. There are some fine *tangkas* hanging in the centre of this hall. Upstairs on the **third storey**, there are images of the Three Deities of Longevity, with a small protector chapel dedicated to Jnananatha on the left. The murals of the left wall depict the lineage of Zhabdrung Ngawang Namgyel, and the Thirty-five Confession Buddhas, while those of the right wall depict Shakyamuni Buddha and the Three Deities of Longevity.

Samtenling

The fields beyond the village are frequented by black-necked cranes during the winter months. Higher up the valley to the east, on a forested hillock, are the ruins of **Samtenling**, one of the monasteries founded by Longchen Rabjampa during his 10 years' exile in Bumthang.

Tharpaling Jangchub Choling

At kilometre-marker 775, there is another turn-off on the north side of the road that leads 9 km through the village houses of Getsa, to a clearing below the hermitage of Tharpaling. This is revered as the most important of all the eight monasteries founded

Bumthang Valleys

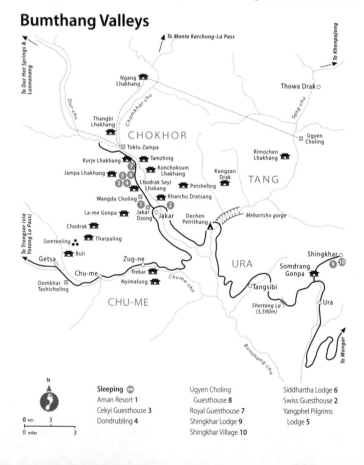

To Monla Karchung-La Pass

To Dur Hot Springs & Lunnanang

To Khenpajong

Ngang Lhakhang

Thowa Drak

Dur-chu

Chamkhar-chu

Tang-chu

Thangbi Lhakhang

CHOKHOR

Toktu Zampa

Ugyen Choling

Kurje Lhakhang

Tamzhing

Konchoksum Lhakhang

Rimochen Lhakhang

Jampa Lhakhang

Lhodrak Seyi Lhakhang

Kungzan Drak

TANG

Petsheling

Wangdu Choling

Kharchu Dratsang

La-me Gonpa

Jakar Dzong

Jakar

Dechen Pelrithang

Mebartsho gorge

Chodrak

Samtenling

Tharpaling

Buli

Shingkhar

Getsa

Zug-ne

URA

Somdrang Gonpa

To Trongsar (via Yotong La Pass)

Chu-me

Trekar

Chume-chu

Domkhar Tashicholing

Nyimalung

Tangsibi

Ura

CHU-ME

Shertang La (3,590m)

Bumthang-chu

To Mongar

N

0 km   3
0 miles   3

Sleeping
Aman Resort **1**
Cekyi Guesthouse **3**
Dondrubling **4**

Ugyen Choling
  Guesthouse **8**
Royal Guesthouse **7**
Shingkhar Lodge **9**
Shingkhar Village **10**

Siddhartha Lodge **6**
Swiss Guesthouse **2**
Yangphel Pilgrims
  Lodge **5**

in Bhutan by Longchen Rabjampa during his enforced period of exile (see page 236); and literary sources specifically date its establishment to 1352.

A steep climb leads sharply uphill and above the tree-line to the isolated monastery (3,700 m), which abuts a cliff to the rear. Outside the main assembly hall there is a row of eight stupas, commemorating the major deeds in the life of Shakyamuni Buddha, which were consecrated on 7 November 2001. The complex nowadays houses more than 100 monks, and the **assembly hall** (*dukhang*) has two storeys. The **lower hall** contains images of Shantarakista, Guru Padmakara and King Trisong Detsen, flanked by Longchen Rabjampa (left) and Jigme Lingpa (right). The interesting murals to the rear depict the Twelve Teachers of the Great Perfection, who preceded Shakyamuni Buddha. On the left wall are a number of photographs depicting contemporary and recent lineage-holders. The **upper hall**, which was renovated by the first king of Bhutan, has a central image of the primordial Buddha, Samantabhadra in union with consort, flanked by Guru Padmakara (left) and Longchen Rabjampa (right). The murals of the left wall depict Longchen Rabjampa, surrounded by the lineage-holders of his *Nyingthig* teachings; and those of the right wall have a series of decorative motifs.

The **monastic college**, situated slightly above the assembly hall, was founded in 1985 and currently has 18 students. Behind the altar and facing the teaching throne in the hall there are a number of small images including those depicting Guru Padmakara and Ju Mipham Gyatso, with books stacked to the left and right. The murals are particularly exquisite – those of the inner wall illustrating the Sixteen Elders, those of the left wall illustrating Shantaraksita, Guru Padmakara and King Trisong Detsen; and Longchen Rabjampa with Pema Lingpa (left) and Jigme Lingpa (right); while those of the right wall depict Manjughosa flanked by the eight masters of classical Indian Buddhism, who are collectively known as the Six Ornaments and Two Supreme Ones.

Chodrak hermitage

Above Tharpaling are the white-walled buildings of Chodrak (3,800 m), an active hermitage of the Drukpa Kagyu school, which was founded originally in 1234 by Lorepa (1187-1250), alongside a celebrated Guru Padmakara cave. The site is said to have then been possessed by malign forces, and consequently abandoned until the Punakha master Ngawang Trinle exorcised it and repaired the buildings during the 18th century.

The **meditation grotto of Guru Padmakara** (Guru Druphuk) at Chodrak contains a self-originated stupa, a sacred spring (*drubchu*), and fragments of a robe. Alongside it is the **meditation grotto of Lorepa** (Lorepa Druphuk), containing miniatures of the Sixteen Elders. There are also two temples in the complex: The **Lorepa Lhakhang** contains images of Mahakarunika and Guru Padmakara, flanked by smaller representations of the Kagyu lineage-holders. On the altar there is a stone footprint of Guru Padmakara, and a stone imbued with the hairs of a hundred thousand *dakinis*.

The **Thukje Lhakhang** contains a large Mahakarunika, sourrounded by a thousand smaller Mahakarunika statues. The murals depict three forms of Vajrasattva, surrounded by a thousand miniature representations of Vajrasattva. Outside in the vestibule, the murals depict the Six Ornaments and Two Supreme Ones (left) and the Progenitors of the Eight Great Lineages of Attainment (Drubpa Shingta Chenpo Gye).

High above the cliffs at Chodrak, towards the hilltop ridge, there is a stone teaching throne which Longchen Rabjampa once used, and a small, shallow cave where he meditated. The isolated hermitage of the 20th-century Nyingma master Nyoshul Khen Rinpoche can also be seen here. From the ridge there is a three-hour trekking route to La-me Gonpa and Jakar in the Chamkhar-chu valley (see page 173).

Domkhar Tashicholing

Continuing down the Chu-me valley from Getsa, after 2 km the road crosses the bridge at **Domkhar**, where the Kekthamjam-chu flows into the Kanggang-chu. A side-road on

⁝ The life of Dorje Lingpa

Dorje Lingpa (see icon, page 236) was the third of the five treasure-finders who were revered as emanation of King Trisong Detsen, and as an actual embodiment of the great translator Vairocana. He was born in 1346 at Dranang Entsa in Southern Tibet. His father was Khuton Sonam Gyeltsen, who hailed from a line of *mantrins* who were holders of indestructible reality, and his mother was named Karmogyen. They gave him the name Orgyen Zangpo. The signs and wonders associated with his awakening to the genuine enlightened family were inconceivable. In his seventh year he received the vows of a novice from Trapa Shakya at Pangshong Lharika. Under that teacher, and others as well, he completed the study of sutra and mantra teachings, of both the ancient and new traditions.

In his 13th year he had seven visions of the precious Guru Padmakara. Then, following an inventory, which had been discovered in the earlier treasures of Guru Chowang, he found his first treasure-trove behind the sacred image of Tara at Tradruk Temple. It included the *Means for the Attainment of the Three Root Deities*, minor means for attainment, inventories and their supplements, wrathful mantras, and instructions on alchemy, there being 108 of each, along with their specific prophecies. In his 15th year Dorje Lingpa opened the way to the treasures of Okar Rock in the lower valley of Jing. The precious Guru Padmakara actually arrived inside that most spacious cave of attainment, constructed a mandala and gave him empowerment. Preceding each separate scroll of yellow paper, he gave him the transmission and sacraments consecrated as treasures.

Moreover, Dorje Lingpa also discovered an image of the precious

Guru Padmakara, four volumes that had belonged to King Trisong Detsen, a hundred paper scrolls, four vases containing the water of life, amulets containing sacramental substances, and so forth. Among the treasures, he discovered such teachings as the *Biographical Injunction of Guru Padmakara in Eight Chapters*, the *Vast Expanse of the View: a Father-Tantra of the Great Perfection*, the *Sun which Illumines the Expanse: A Mother-Tantra*, the *Further Innermost Spirituality of the Dakinis: Conjunction of Sun and Moon*), the *Ten Father-Tantra Cycles of the Innermost Spirituality*, the *Four Cycles of the Gathering*, and the *Eight Appendices*.

Then, gradually, beginning with his discovery of the *Ten Cycles of Experiential Guidance* and other texts at Mutik Shelgi Bamgong, and up to the time when Yeshe Tshogyel actually manifested at the Longevity Cave in Jampa Lhakhang and gave him the water of life, spiritual elixir which had been produced at Yanglesho, the life-supporting turquoise ornaments of King Trisong Detsen and of Yeshe Tshogyel herself, a wish-fulfilling gem, teachings, and many wrathful mantras, Dorje Lingpa discovered 43 great treasure-troves at different treasure-sites (108 altogether if one counts their subdivisions). When he discovered treasures at Chimphu near Samye, he encountered Guru Padmakara [in visions] 13 times. At Chuwori, he emanated two bodies and, having publicly extracted treasure from two places at once, he left behind impressions of his feet embedded in the rock, one cubit deep.

In the cave of Metsornyen at Zabulung, Dorje Lingpa received donations from the protector deities Nyenchen Thangla and Gangkar Sha-me. He assembled the many great gods and demons of the Land of Snows and undertook the great attainment of the Eight Transmitted Precepts (*Kabgye Drubchen*). To all of them he gave empowerment. He travelled emanationally to the eight great charnel grounds, where he met the eight awareness-holders, who had been the teachers of Guru Padmakara; and he received their *Instructions of the Eight Confidences*. When he discovered such treasures, the precious Guru Padmakara, Yeshe Tshogyel, Vairocana, and others actually appeared and bestowed empowerments and instructions upon him.

By displaying a wonderful array of miraculous abilities he loosened all fetters of doubt and secured others in irreversible faith. He also left behind many impressions of his body, hands, and feet in rocks. At Zabulung, Kharchu, and Zhoto Tidro, respectively, he found 108 rites for empowerment, consecration, fulfilment of commitments and repentance, burnt offerings, and subjugation. Such are examples of his extensive service on behalf of the happiness of Tibet.

Among Dorje Lingpa's discoveries, which were profound, vast, and limitless, the foremost were his revelations pertaining to Guru Padmakara, the Great Perfection, and Mahakarunika, the Great Compassionate One. He found wonderful images such as that of Vajrasattva, which he discovered at Phungpo Riwoche, and the 11-faced Mahakarunika and the sandalwood image of Tara, which he discovered in the Vase Pillar of the Jokhang in Lhasa. He also discovered sacramental objects and spiritual elixir, treasures of wealth, including the wish-fulfilling gem, and Bon works including the *Golden Surgical Needle of the Great Perfection* and the *Greater, Medium and Lesser Aural Lineages of Tavihricha*. In addition, he profusely discovered texts on medical science and astrology, and his enlightened activity was extensive.

The family lineage descended from his son Choyingpa, an emanation of Nubchen Sangye Yeshe, has existed up to the present day in the region of Mon. It is also said that Dorje Lingpa offered the *Cycle of Yamantaka* (*Shed-kor*) and the cycle of the *Jambhalas of the Five Families* (*Dzam-lha Rig-nga*) to the lord among conquerors, Karmapa Rolpei Dorje. He established his principal seat at Lingmukha in Bhutan. Also, he took charge of the monasteries of Lhodrak, Paro, Uke in Ze, and others, and so widely benefitted living beings.

When he had completed his service to the teaching and to living creatures, in his 60th year (1405) he delivered his testament, the *Great Prophetic Declaration*, and, accompanied by wondrous omens, he passed away at Draklong. His corpse remained for three years without decay, during which time it sometimes continued to benefit beings by speaking and reciting four-line dedications of merit. When Dorje Lingpa's remains were finally offered on the funeral pyre many divine images and relics appeared. With a roar of the flames his right foot flew from the crematorium to his spiritual son Tashi Jungne, and his left to Thokme Gyagarwa, as their shares of the remains. From them the sacred relics multiplied many-fold, and it appears that they lasted until later times.

The lineage of Dorje Lingpa's descendants persisted until later with its seat at Orgyen Choling in Bumthang. The river of his profound doctrine has continued as a distant lineage until the present day without decline.

Adapted from Dudjom Rinpoche's *The Nyingma School of Tibetan Buddhism* (Trans. G. Dorje & M. Kapstein).

the right follows the former uphill for 500 m to **Domkhar Tashicholing**. This was the summer palace of Bhutan's second king, built in 1937 as an exact replica of Kunga Rabten Phodrang in Trongsar (see page 165). The building is no longer in use as a royal residence, and was offered to the late Karmapa XVI in 1968. More recently the site was rebought by the government who built a new Drukpa Kagyu college to its rear.

About 4 km above **Domkhar Tashicholing**, the side-road reaches **Chorten Nyingpo Lhakhang**, which was founded in 1587 by Tenpei Nyima of Ralung. The stone teaching throne which he used at that time is still visible here. The nearby hydroelectric power station was built with Indian aid in 1989.

Chu-me

Continuing east from the Domkhar Bridge on the main road, you will soon reach Chu-me, the largest settlement in the valley, where there are shops, a junior high school and the Sonam Kunphen High School. This is prime sheep-herding country, and woollen textiles are important for the local economy. The Wool Development Project, east of the village, is seeking to raise the quality of local wool with Australian aid.

Zug-ne

From Chu-me the road continues on to **Zug-ne**, 24 km below Yotong La pass, towards the lower end of the valley. The village of Zug-ne (2,750 m) is famous for its small geomantic temple, **Zug-ne Lhakhang**, which has a central image of Vairocana Buddha, and is reckoned to date from the seventh century. The murals here were renovated as recently as 1978.

Zug-ne is also famous for its weaving cottage industries. At the Thokme Yeshe Textile Factory and Gonpo Tashi Textile Factory in the east of Zug-ne, you can see weavers using back-strap and pedal looms to make lengths of hand-woven woollen cloth in various geometric patterns. This fabric is the speciality of the Bumthang area, and the lengths, known as *yatra*, can be used for making blankets, woollen jackets, cushions or bed covers. Nearby the factories there is a second small hydroelectric project on the Khanggang-chu.

Trekar Lhakhang

Only 2 km east of Zug-ne, the road winds around a bend in the river and on the far bank the village and temple of Trekar come into view on a hilltop promontory. Trekar Lhakhang (locally pronounced Prakhar) means 'white monkey' temple - a reference to the simian creatures who, as legend would have it, hastened the construction of the original temple. The temple was founded in the late 16th century by Tenpei Nyima, the grandson of Pema Lingpa and son of Dawa Gyeltsen (b. 1499), whose incarnation lineages played an important role in the Buddhist tradition of Bumthang and the Lhodrak region of Tibet to the north. Dawa Gyeltsen's embalmed remains are contained here in a reliquary stupa.

The three-storey temple has on its **ground floor** a chapel dedicated to Shakyamuni Buddha. On the **middle floor** the main images depict Guru Padmakara with his eight manifestations, and on the **top floor** is the central reliquary stupa of Dawa Gyeltsen.

Nyimalung Gonpa

From Trekar, a short uphill drive on a narrow road (or a 30-minute walk) will bring you through the forest to Nyimalung, where the Nyingma monastery of Tubten Dongak Shedrub Dargye Choling has over 100 monks in residence, 21 of them in a monastic college. Founded by Dorling Khyentrul in 1935, the monastery maintains a high reputation for its monastic discipline and artistic heritage.

The temple has two storeys, but it is now being expanded. On the **ground floor**, the central images depict (L-R): Longchen Rabjampa, Four-armed Avalokiteshvara, Shakyamuni Buddha, Guru Padmakara and Pema Lingpa. Above the door is a mural depicting Bhaisajyaguru, the buddha of medicine; with the Hundred Peaceful and Wrathful Deities according to Karma Lingpa's tradition on the left and Pema Ledreltsel, Longchen Rabjampa and Jigme Lingpa on the right. On the wall adjacent to the large floor mandala, the murals depict Mahakarunika, Dorling Khyentrul, the founder of the monastery, and the early lineage-holders of the Nyingmapa oral teachings, foremost among them being Nyak Jnanakumara, Nubchen Sangye Yeshe and Zur Shakya Jungne. The far wall has murals depicting Guru Padmakara with his eight manifestations and the Sukhavati paradise.

The **upper floor** has images of (L-R): Vajrakila, Guru Padmakara and his tiger-riding aspect Dorje Drolo, with the volumes of the *Kangyur* on the left, those of the *Rinchen Terdzo* and the *Collected Works* of Dilgo Khyentse Rinpoche on the right. The murals to the left of the door depict Shakyamuni surrounded by the Sixteen Elders, while those to the right depict the Twelve Teachers of the Great Perfection, Vajrakila, Sriheruka and Bhaisajyaguru. The teaching throne bears a large portrait of the late Dilgo Khyentse Rinpoche; and the murals beyond it depict Avalokiteshvara and the lineage-holders of the Pema Lingpa tradition. The wall facing the door has murals illustrating the Twenty-five Disciples of Padmakara and the Eight Awareness Holders of Ancient India.

Towards Kiki La Pass

Rejoining the main road, you continue the descent through the Chu-me valley, passing the orchards and forest around **Mangar**, before finally leaving the Khanggang-chu basin, as the road veers eastwards to climb **Kiki La pass** (2,860 m). On the far side of the pass the road soon descends into the Chokhor valley of central Bumthang. The distance from Zug-ne to the district capital at Jakar is 16 km.

Jakar

From **Kiki La** pass, the entire breadth of the Chokhor valley is visible on a clear day – from the prominent buildings of Jakar Dzong and Kurje Lhakhang in the lower reaches to the distant snow peaks on the Tibet border. The 9-km descent from the pass to Jakar follows the west bank of the Chamkhar-chu upstream into town.

The administrative capital of Bumthang is **Jakar** (2,800 m) – also written as Chamkhar – where an important bridge spans the Chamkhar-chu, carrying traffic in different directions. The town, which occupies the plain below Jakar Dzong, is currently undergoing rapid urbanization, by Bhutanese standards, and there are many small shops, mostly owned by Bhutanese nationals of Tibetan origin.

Orientation

Entering the town from Trongsar via Kiki La, you will pass the BTCL Mifam Lodge on the right and a turn-off leading uphill to the River Lodge on the left. Continuing into town, you will pass the petrol station and football field on the right, followed by Himalayan Pizza and the Bus Station. A lane opposite the bus station leads to Jakar Telecentre, and another on the right leads to KD General Store, Dechen Lhamo FCB Store, Hotel Home, Tsewang Dorje Hotel, a phone booth, a watch and radio repair shop, and eventually back to the football ground.

Staying on the main road, you will now reach the Town Gate. Beyond the gate, you will pass on the left Bumthang Telephone Booth, Tashi General Store & Restaurant and Norbu Store, while on the right are Yangchen Hotel, NC Restaurant & Bar, Tsewang Lhamo General Store, Kunga Bar & Store, Tendzin General Store, Damo Store and Bhutanese Traditional Crafts. Now you will reach the main traffic circle in the downtown area. Turn left for **Jakar Dzong** (see page 174) and **Kurje Lhakhang** (see page 178); or turn right for **Tamzhing Lhakhang** and the road to Mongar.

If you turn left at the traffic circle, on the left you will pass the District Credit Office, and Phuntsog General Store, with the Udee Shopping Complex opposite on the right. The road then crosses a bridge over the Chamkhar-chu, before passing traditional village houses, Yewang Hotel & Bar and Udee Furniture Store & Woodcarving Factory on the left, and Thubten Bar, a petrol station, the Agricultural Corporation, Vegetable Dye Products, Kaila Guesthouse and Special Bar on the right. Now the road forks alongside a *mani* wheel chapel, a footpath crossing the river to the west and the main motorable road heading north-west. Continuing on the motor road you will pass on the right side a beehive project, Jakar Junior High School (where a turn-off heads west to Jakar Village Lodge, **Jakar Dzong** and **La-me Gonpa**), and the archery ground (where another side-road branches north-east to the new, unfinished Aman Hotel). The road continues on past Mountain Lodge, Bumthang Hospital, Se Lhakhang, **Wangdu Choling Palace**, **Jampa Lhakhang** and **Kurje Lhakhang**, where it becomes a trekking route. The distance from the traffic circle to Kurje Lhakhang is 7 km.

If you turn right at the traffic circle, on the left side after Udee Shopping Complex you will pass an internet café, a Mani Dungkhor Chapel, a lane leading to **Jakar Lhakhang** (see below), Doro Store, Bumthang Traditional Gift Shop, Kunzang Store, Sonam Zangmo Hotel & Bar, Peep-in Restaurant & Bar, Pema Chodon Bar, Tsering Shop, Karma Shop, Dechen Shop & Bar, Gonpo Tendzin Auto Spare-parts, Paldron Shoe Repairs, Gyurmin Bar and Kunga Paljor Bar. Opposite on the right are Bhutan Handicrafts, a phone booth, Bhutan Post, Thubten Store, Pema Store, Namgyey Import Showroom, Tsultrim General Store, Bank of Bhutan, Bhutan Royal Insurance Corporation, Jintha Bar & Store, and after a lane, Tsering Bar, Tamdrin Store, Pema Yangchen Pharmacy, Pema Yangdzom General, Yeshe Lhamo Store, Pema Dorje Bar, Tendzin Store, Bumthang Wine Store, Karchung General Store, a row of private houses, the national sheep-breeding centre, Yeshe Lhamo Shop, Bumthang Singye Express Bus Company and a lane leading to the vegetable market.

At this point the road passes a stupa, marking the place where the severed head of a vanquished Tibetan general was buried, and crosses a major bridge over the Chamkhar-chu. Here, it forks – south-east for Gonkhar Guesthouse and Mongar (193 km) and north for Ozer Lham Shop and **Tamzhing Lhakhang**, at the trailhead. The distance from the bridge to Tamzhing is 5 km. At Ozer Lham Shop, a side-road leads uphill to TD Automobile Workshop, the Cheese Factory, Swiss Guesthouse, a dairy farm, Kharchu Dratsang and Petsheling Gonpa.

Jakar Lhakhang

The small Nyingma temple in town, was founded in 1445 by descendants of Dorje Lingpa, and it contains a central statue of Guru Padmakara, and a fine stupa with an inset image of Usinsavijaya.

West side of the Chokhor valley

Jakar Dzong

Background According to legend, when Ngagi Wangchuk of Ralung visited Bumthang in 1543 he founded a temple on a ridge to the west of the river at a place where a 'white bird' (*jakar*) alighted. The building was completed in 1549 and named Jakar Dzong ('fortress of the white bird'). Mipham Chogyel, grandfather of Zhabdrung Ngawang Namgyel, also visited in 1567 and consolidated the somewhat tenuous influence of the Drukpa Kagyu school in Bumthang. Later following the Zhabdrung's unification of Western Bhutan, Mingyur Tenpa, the then governor of Chotse Dzong, was assigned the task of bringing the Central and Eastern regions within the Drukpa fold. Guided by Lama Nam-se, an illegitimate relative of the Zhabdrung, the Drukpa forces captured the palace of the Chokhor governor at Yurwazhing. In 1647 Jakar

Dzong was rebuilt by Mingyur Tenpa, and given the formal name Jakar Yul-le Namgyel
Dzong, commemorating the victories of his Drukpa forces. Later refurbishments were
undertaken in 1683 by Tendzin Rabgye, and in 1905, following the 1897 earthquake.

The site Jakar Dzong is one of the largest in Bhutan, with impressive fortress walls
and an elegant structure, but the interior is simple and unelaborate. The entrance on
the east side leads into a small administrative courtyard, with the central tower set
back against the west wall. The tower has three storeys, the **ground floor** containing
the **Jampei Lhakhang**, dedicated to Maitreya, seated within a bare-walled chapel. On
the **middle floor** there is the **Yidam Lhakhang**, containing a statue of the Zhabdrung's
father Tenpei Nyima, and murals depicting Guru Padmakara with his eight
manifestations. On the top floor, there is a Gonkhang, dedicated to Jnananatha, wall
murals on the left depicting the Kagyu lineage-holders and those on the right
depicting the assembly of the Zhabdrung's incarnations (Zhabdrung Phunsumtsok).
The monastic courtyard, which is a seasonal summer base for the monastic
community of Chotse Dzong (see page 163), contains an **assembly hall** with an image
of the meditational deity Vajrakila at the centre.

La-me Gonpa

Four kilometres beyond Jakar Dzong, the motor road comes to an end at La-me Gonpa,
a palatial monastery founded by Sonam Drukgyel, a former governor of Trongsar and
great-grandfather of King Ugyen Wangchuk in the early 19th century. The building was
later restored by the first king and continued to function as a royal residence for some
time. Nowadays the Integrated Forest Development Project is based here. Much of the
original wooden structure has rotted and is now being replaced.

There is a three-hour trek from La-me Gonpa, across the ridge to Chodrak
hermitage in the Chu-me valley (see page 169).

Wangdu Choling Phodrang

From the archery ground north of Jakar Junior High School, a lane winds uphill to
Wangdu Choling – an elegant palace, which was founded by the governor of Trongsar,
Jigme Namgyel, in 1857. The upper floor of the palace still contains his private chapel.
The first king of Bhutan, Ugyen Wangchuk, was born here, and following his coronation,
he and his son both adopted Wangdu Choling as their main summer residence. In the
winter months the entire court would move to Kunga Rabten (see page 165) in Trongsar
district. In 1952 Wangdu Choling ceased to function as the foremost royal residence,
when the third king moved his capital to Punakha and Thimphu.

Lhodrak Se Lhakhang

Driving north from the archery ground, just after Bumthang Hospital, which was built
with Swiss aid in 1988-89, on the right side of the road you will reach the entrance to
Lhodrak Se Lhakhang. Founded in 1963 as a monastic school for
exiled monks from Se in Lhodrak (Southern Tibet), the temple
houses 25 student monks. Behind the teaching throne, the
central image depicts Marpa Lotsawa, the great translator from
Lhodrak, who was the progenitor of the Kagyu lineages in Tibet.
Flanking him are images of Shakyamuni Buddha and the Sixteen

*The building is not open
to the public, and its
pleasant gardens will soon
house the new 5-star
Aman Hotel.*

Elders, and a small library. The murals here depict aspects of Avalokiteshvara (left of
the door), Mahakarunika (left wall), Amitayus (right corner) and Guru Padmakara with
his eight manifestations (right of the door). To the right of the teaching throne there is
a photograph of Sekhar Gutok, the famous nine-storey tower built by Marpa's student
Milarepa in Lhodrak.

Just above Lhodrak Se Lhakhang on the road, there is the Lekyi Guesthouse, and
the new Dondrubling Hotel.

The life of Pema Lingpa

Pema Lingpa, who was hailed as the fourth of the five treasure-finders who were emanations of King Trisong Detsen, was also the last of the five pure incarnations of the royal princess Pemasel. His birth, at Bumthang in 1450 was attended by many omens. His father was named Dondrub Zangpo of the Nyo clan, and his mother Trongma Peldzom. Since, in his immediately previous life, he had been the all-knowing master Longchen Rabjampa, he awoke to the genuine enlightened family during his childhood. He learned several scripts, crafts, and so forth, without having been taught.

In particular, on Wednesday, 31 July, 1476, at Yige Drukma, Pema Lingpa actually beheld the visage of Guru Padmakara, who blessed him and placed in his hands an inventory of 108 great treasure-troves. Accordingly, in his 27th year, he brought forth the first of all his profound treasures: the *Luminous Expanse of the Great Perfection* from Lake Mebar, where the Tang River meanders

in the form of a knot near Naring Drak. Surrounded by a multitude of people he entered the lake without hesitation, holding a burning lamp in his hand. Then, when he re-emerged, the lamp in his hand was still burning, and he carried under his arm a great treasure-chest, about the size of a clay pot. Everyone was amazed and became established in the faith of conviction. Consequently, Pema Lingpa's indisputable reputation covered the land like the sun and moon.

In the same way, he discovered the *Great Perfection: the Gathering of Samantabhadra's Intention* at Samye Chimphu. Then, from their respective treasure-sites, he brought forth the cycle of the *Small Son, which is the Non-dual Tantra of the Great Perfection*, the *Guru: an Ocean of Gems*: the *Great Compassionate One: the Lamp Which Dispels Darkness*, the *Eight Transmitted Precepts: the Mirror of Mind*, Vajrakila: the *Utterly Secret Vital Razor*, the cycle of the *Attainment of Nectar Elixir*, *Vajrapani as Subduer of the Arrogant and as Slight Rage*, the *Greater, Medium, and Lesser teachings of the Wrathful Guru*, the *Guidance on Longevity: Garland of Indestructible Reality*, the Attainment of Longevity: Integrating Gems with the Path, the *Black Trilogy*, and many others. Likewise, the profusion of sacramental objects, and of images, books and stupas, and representative images of Guru Padmakara which he discovered surpasses the imagination.

In particular, in a ravine this treasure-finder unearthed Kyerchu Lhakhang in Paro, which had become

Jampa Lhakhang
Continuing along the motor road, after 1 km you will reach the Yangphel Pilgrims' Lodge and Siddhartha Lodge, where a turn-off on the left leads directly to Jampa Lhakhang.

Background This is revered as the most ancient of all the temples in Bumthang, founded in the seventh century by the Tibetan king Songtsen Gampo, like Kyerchu in the Paro valley, as a geomantic temple – this time on the 'left knee of the ogress'. It is

overgrown, and which can now be visited by everyone at the present day. Among the riches Pema Lingpa discovered as treasures were the life-supporting turquoise gems of the religious king Trisong Detsen, called "Blazing Light", the "Blazing Light of a Thousand Mountains", and the "Red House Snow Peak", the seamless robes of Princess Pemasel, a clairvoyant mirror, and many other especially sublime riches of the royal dynasty.

Although an inventory of 108 treasure-troves had come into Pema Lingpa's hands, he could not discover more than half of them. Later, when the treasure-finder was approaching death, his son Thukse Dawa Gyeltsen, asked for permission to find the others, but the master said, "It will be hard for you to find the treasure-teachings. But if you purely guard your commitments and pray to me, you may possibly find some minor ones." Accordingly, Thukse Dawa Gyeltsen is known to have brought forth some treasure-troves, too.

Concerning the host of disciples who were his spiritual sons, there is a prophetic declaration among his treasures:

Ten thousand will be associated by (the force of) past deeds.

One thousand and two will be associated by aspiration.

Those associated through the profound essential point will be 11.

Seven will be mandala-holders.

And three will be spiritual sons, dear to his heart.

In conformity with this prophecy, an inconceivable number of disciples appeared during his lifetime. Among them, the foremost were the six emanational treasure-finders: the six great accomplished masters: the six great sons who had manifested the signs of accomplishment: Tsultrim Peljor, the great preceptor of Jonang Phuntsoling, Nangso Gyelwa Dondrub, and Trulku Chokden Gonpo, who were the three spiritual sons whose intention was the same as that of the treasure-finder himself, and his four physical sons, who were emanations of the Lords of the Three Families. Of these, Thukse Dawa Gyeltsen who was the emanation of Avalokiteshvara had inconceivable expressive powers of blessing. He realised the intention of his father and as a result his enlightened activity became extensive.

The transmission of Pema Lingpa's profound teachings was gradually passed down and propagated by Trulku Natsok Rangdrol and Umdze Dondrub Pelbar, who were renowned as the two incomparable masters of his lineage, as well as by his own successive speech emanations (Sungtrul) and those of his spiritual son (Thukse), who occupied the main seat at Lhalung in Lhodrak. Up to the present day the lineage has been spread throughout the regions of Bhutan, Central Tibet, Tsang and Dokham. The entire stream of its empowerments, transmissions, and guidance continues without decline.

Adapted from Dudjom Rinpoche's The Nyingma School of Tibetan Buddhism (Trans. G. Dorje & M. Kapstein).

said that when Guru Padmakara taught Buddhism to King Sendhaka during the eighth century, he did so from the temple roof. The original temple contains a large image of Maitreya, flanked by the eight standing bodhisattvas, four on each side. The chain-mail gate protecting the central image was added by Pema Lingpa in the 15th century. Subsequent repairs were undertaken during the 19th and early 20th centuries, and four chapels were added to form a courtyard. Among these, the Dukhor Lhakhang was built by King Ugyen Wangchuk, the Guru Lhakhang by Tsondru

Gyeltsen, the administrator of Jakar Dzong, the Chorten Lhakhang by Princess Ashi Wangmo and the Sangye Lhakhang by King Jigme Wangchuk.

The site Entering the courtyard, you will notice the large prayer wheels by the gate, and a covered altar in the middle, where butter lamps are offered. The **Sangye Lhakhang** is on the left side of the courtyard and above the gate. It contains images of the Seven Generations of Past Buddhas, flanked by the bodhisattvas Manjughosa and Avalokiteshvara, and the gatekeepers Hayagriva and Vajrapani. The murals depict Vaishravana, Guru Padmakara with his eight manifestations, Mahakarunika, the Eight Buddhas of Medicine with Bhaisajyaguru at the centre, and the lineage-holders of the Pema Lingpa tradition.

The **Guru Lhakhang** is situated immediately to the left of the main temple. The main images here depict (L-R): Amitayus, Guru Padmakara and Four-armed Avalokiteshvara. The murals of the left wall depict Mahakarunika and the Sukhavati paradise, and those of the right depict aspects of Tara. The protector deity Gonpo Lekden can be seen alongside the window.

Facing the main gate is the original seventh-century geomantic temple, **Jampa Lhakhang**. There are three steps leading into the chapel, indicative of the Buddhas of the Three Times. Inside the central image depicts the future Buddha Maitreya, with Shakyamuni, buddha of the present on the left, and Dipamkara, buddha of the past on the right. Flanking them are the Eight Bodhisattvas, and in the far right corner Zhabdrung Ngawang Namgyel. In front of Maitreya is a *terma*-site (*terkha*), where Dorje Lingpa discovered certain concealed teachings. As at the Jokhang in Lhasa, an image of Guru Padmakara is set within an alcove, facing the central image. The Precious Guru is said to have meditated here and left an impression of his foot in stone.

To the right of the main temple, you will next enter the **Dukhor Lhakhang**, dedicated to the meditational deity Kalacakra ('wheel of time'), and his extensive entourage. The murals here illustrate the Forty-two Peaceful Deities (adjacent to the door) and Fifty-eight Wrathful Deities (right), according to Pema Lingpa's tradition. An icon depicting this charismatic master can be seen in the corner, between the two assemblies.

The final chapel, known as the **Chorten Lhakhang**, is located to the right of the courtyard. It contains the reliquary stupa of Pontsen Khenpo, a master of the Karma Kagyu tradition and spiritual mentor of the first and second kings, who passed away in 1940. Alongside the stupa there is an image of a previous Karmapa, and murals depicting Shakyamuni Buddha surrounded by the Sixteen Elders (left) and the lineage-holders of the Karma Kagyu tradition (right).

Behind the complex there are two stupas, dedicated to members of the royal family.

Chamkhar Lhakhang

Continuing north on the road from Yangphel Pilgrims' Lodge you will soon reach Chamkhar Lhakhang, on the right sided of the road. The original nine-storey 'iron castle' (*chamkhar*) here was the palace of the eighth-century King Sedarkha (see page 230), who invited Guru Padmakara to Bumthang. Sometime during the 14th century, Dorje Lingpa replaced it with a more modest building, known as Dechen Phodrang, and the local chieftain, Chamkhar Lama, is said to be descended from him. The present building, containing a central image of Guru Padmakara, was constructed in the early 20th century and houses the ritual dance masks used at the Jampa Lhakhang *drubchen*. Chamkhar Lama by tradition still presides over this festival. Just north of Chamkhar Lhakhang is the Royal Guesthouse, which is used for hosting official visits.

Kurje Lhakhang

Driving north from Chamkhar Lhakhang, the paved motor road passes through the old town gateway, and comes to an end alongside the impressive buildings of Kurje Lhakhang (2,640 m). The distance from Jakar town to Kurje Lhakhang is only 7 km. To the north-east a footbridge spans the Chamkhar-chu and it is interesting to walk across to explore the east side of the valley on foot. An old stepping stone ford (*dozam*) lies downstream from the bridge. Legend holds that it was once a proper bridge that was destroyed by demonic forces. On the far bank you can easily walk the 5 km to Jakar and visit the sites on the east side of the valley (see page 173).

Kurje Lhakhang is named after the sacred power place where Guru Padmakara left the imprint of his body in solid rock. This he did to subdue the malevolent force of the local deity Shelging Karpo who had bewitched his host King Sedarkha. Through the magical emanational display of his eight manifestations and those of his consort, the king's daughter, the Precious Guru coxed the demon out of his mountain lair in the form of a snowlion, and then assumed the form of a Garuda, which seized the demon and bound him under an oath of allegiance to Buddhism.

The complex of buildings at Kurje Lhakhang is surrounded by a perimeter comprising 108 stupas. Entering the courtyard from the east, the long monastic residential building is on the left, between two large stupas – one in Bhutanese style and the other in Tibetan style. These and a cairn of stones (*tho*) mark the site of the funerary chortens of the first three kings of Bhutan. The community of resident monks moves here from Chotse Dzong in Trongsar during the summer months; and it is here that they hold their annual *tsechu* ceremonies. Within the courtyard there is a tall cypress tree, descended from one that sprang up there when Guru Padmakara thrust his staff into the ground.

There are three temples within the complex. **Guru Lhakhang**, the nearest on the right, is the oldest, dating from 1652 when it was founded by Mingyur Tenpa. **Sampa Lhundrub Lhakhang**, in the centre, was constructed by the first king Ugyen Wangchuk in 1900. **Ngedon Shedrub Gatseling**, on the left, was founded in 1984 by the late Queen Mother, Asjhi Kesang Wangchuk, on the advice of her teacher, the late Dilgo Khyentse Rinpoche.

Guru Lhakhang Entering the **lower floor** of the building on the west side, the pilgrim detours through a narrow passageway in the rock, which is regarded as a gauge of negative past actions. Beyond this tunnel is the chapel dedicated to the Buddhas of the Three Times, whose images are within its inner sanctum. In the main hall, there is an image of Peling Sungtrul VIII Tenpei Nyima (1843-1891) and smaller images of the Guardian Kings of the Four Directions. The murals here depict Mahakarunika and four other aspects of Avalokiteshvara (left of door), Jambhala and other wealth-protecting deities (right of door), and various aspects of Tara (facing door). On the **upper floor**, there is an image of the local protector Shelging Karpo with a small altar alongside the door. The inner sanctum on the left contains images of Guru Padmakara flanked by his eight manifestations, with two smaller representations of the central figure at either end, each of them flanked by the two consorts Mandarava and Yeshe Tsogyel. Hidden behind the inner sanctum is the meditation cave containing the imprint of the Precious Guru's body, which gives the complex its name. In the main hall there are one thousand miniature images of Guru Padmakara (between the door and the window), murals depicting aspects of Tara (right of the window) and behind a glass case facing the door, the Sixteen Elders and Twenty-five Disciples of Guru Padmakara, each within an individual grotto. In the far corner, near the window, are brass images of the Lords of the Three Enlightened Families. The ceiling-painted mandalas are derived from the *Lama Gongdu* cycle of teachings; and near the roof there is a carving depicting the Precious Guru's Garuda emanation seizing the demon Shelging Karpo, who had manifested as a snowlion.

Sampa Lhundrub Lhakhang The temple in the centre of the complex, which was built in 1900, is entered through a door on the east side. The **vestibule** has fine murals depicting the Four Guardian Kings, the foremost Nyingma protectors Vajrasadhu and

Incarnate lineages stemming from Pema Lingpa

The influence on Bhutanese spiritual and cultural life of the great treasure-finder Pema Lingpa (1450-1521), from whom the royal family of Bhutan claim descent, is indeed remarkable. The 21 volumes of his *Collected Works* include many teachings and practices pertaining to Mahayoga, Anuyoga and Atiyoga, which are still maintained at the present day. His contributions to painting, sculpture, drama and architecture are also well documented. The rich Nyingmapa heritage at Gangteng and other locations east of the Black Mountains, as well as at Lhalung in the neighbouring Lhodrak county of Tibet, are testament to his great achievements.

When Pema Lingpa passed away in 1521, his teachings were passed on to future generations through a family lineage, and through the successive incarnations of his body (*kutrul*) and speech (*sungtrul*), and the mind aspect embodied in his son Dawa Gyeltsen (*tukse*).

Among them, the lineage of **body incarnations**, who maintain the seat of Gangteng Sangak Choling, and (since 1682) the winter residence of Phuntsok Rabtenling, are:

Pema Trinle (1564-1642)
Tendzin Lekpei Dondrub (1645-1726)
Kunzang Pema Namgyel (d. ca. 1750)
Tendzin Sizhi Namgyel (ca. 1761-1796)
Orgyan Gelek Namgyel (d. ca. 1842)
Orgyan Tenpei Nyima (ca. 1873-1900)
Orgyan Tenpei Nyingje (1862-1904)
Orgyan Trinle Dorje
Rigdzin Kunzang Pema Namgyel (b. 1955)

The lineage of **speech incarnations**, whose traditional seats included Tamzhing Lhundrub Choling in Bumthang and Layak Guru Lhakhang in Lhodrak, and who now reside at Drametse Tekchok Namdrol Orgyan Choling in Mongar, are:

Sungtrul II Tendzin Drakpa (1536-1597)
Sungtrul III Tsultrim Dorje (1598-1669)
Sungtrul IV Ngawang Kunzang Dorje (1680-1723)
Sungtrul V Kunzang Tsewang (1725-1762)
Sungtrul VI Kunzang Tenpei Gyeltsen (1763-1817)
Sungtrul VII Kunzang Ngawang Chokyi Lodro (1819-1842)
Sungtrul VIII Kunzang Tenpei Nyima (1843-1891)
Sungtrul IX Tendzin Chokyi Gyeltsen (1894-1925)
Sungtrul X Tubten Chokyi Dorje (1930-1955)
Sungtrul XI Kunzang Rinchen Pema Namgyel (b. 1968)

The lineage of **mind incarnations**, stemming from Pema Lingpa's son Dawa Gyeltsen, had their traditional seat at Lhalung (since 1672), and share the residence of Tamzhing Lhakhang in Bumthang with the Sungtrul line. They comprise:

Tukse I Dawa Gyeltsen (b. 1499)
Tukse II Nyida Gyeltsen
Tukse III Nyida Longyang
Tukse IV Tendzin Gyurme Dorje (b. 1641-ca. 1702)
Tukse V Gyurme Chokdrub Pelbar (ca. 1708-1750)
Tukse VI Tendzin Chokyi Nyima (ca. 1752-1775)
Tukse VII Kunzang Lungrik Chokyi Gocha (ca. 1780-1825)
Tukse VIII Kunzang Zilnon Zhepatsel
Tukse IX Tubten Pelbar (1906-1939)
Tukse X Tekchok Tenpei Gyeltsen (b. 1951)

Ekajati, and various local protectors of Bumthang including Yakdu Nakpo, Kyebu Lungtsen and Shelging Karpo. The **hall** has an **inner sanctum** on the right containing a 10-m-high image of Guru Padmakara in the charismatic form Nangsi Zilnon, flanked by his 13 aspects as they are described in the text known as *Sampa Lhundrub* ('Spontaneously Granted Wishes'). In front is a row of smaller images depicting (L-R): Zhabdrung Ngawang Namgyel, Vijaya, Vajrasattva, Shakyamuni Buddha and Padmakara flanked by the consorts Mandarava and Yeshe Tsogyel. In the **main hall** a smaller Nangsi Zilnon image, commissioned in the 1960s by a government minister, faces the door; and the teaching throne is on the left. The murals here depict Shakyamuni Buddha with his students, Shariputra and Maudgalyayana (left wall), Zangdok Pelri paradise (right wall), Dorje Lingpa (right wall) and Zhabdrung Ngawang Namgyel (left wall), all surrounded by the Thirty-five Confession Buddhas.

Ngedon Shedrub Gatseling This new three-storey temple, which was consecrated in 1990, is still under construction. The entrance vestibule has fine murals depicting the Four Guardian Kings, with the Wheel of Rebirth on the right, and scenes from the life of Shakyamuni Buddha on the left. Inside on the **ground floor** are images of Shakyamuni Buddha, flanked by Shariputra and Maudgalyayana, while the side-walls have bas relief images of the Sixteen Elders in their respective grottoes.

Zangdok Pelri Lhakhang South of the complex at Kunje Lhakhang, there is a newly built temple in Zangdok Pelri style – its three storeys dedicated respectively to Guru Padmakara, Avalokiteshvara and Amitabha, who represent the three Buddha bodies.

Toktu Zampa

The paved road comes to an end at Kurje Lhakhang, but it is possible to drive a further 3 km north-west on an unpaved surface to **Toktu Zampa**, following the Dur-chu upstream from its confluence with the Chamkhar-chu at Kurje. The bridge at Toktu Zampa is an important trailhead for two treks, one following the Yoleng-chu upstream and across the watershed into Trongsar and towards Mount Gangkar Punsum Base Camp (see page 162), and the other following the Chamkhar-chu north-east, across the watershed into the Tang valley (see page 186).

Dewathang Lhakhang

On the road between Kurje Lhakhang and Toktu Zampa, there is a small temple, known as Dewathang Lhakhang, which was founded in 1954 by Polu Khenpo Thubten Kunga Gyeltsen with the support of Dasho Phuntsog Wangdu. A large prayer wheel abuts the south wall of the building.

The site The **entrance vestibule** has images of the Four Guardian Kings, and murals depicting local protector deities, as well as the full assembly of deities according to Longsel Nyingpo's revelation entitled *Mahakarunika Dugngal Rangdrol* (right), and the refuge tree of the Karma Kagyu lineage (left).

On the **ground floor** the central image is a full-size gilded copper Guru Padmakara in the form Nangsi Zilnon, flanked by two stupas designed to subdue spirits of attachment (left) and to commemorate the victory of Shakyamuni over the sufferings of the world (right). On either side of these stupas are gilded clay images of the 12 main aspects of Guru Padmakara that are described in Chogyur Dechen Lingpa's 19th-century revelation, *Thukdrub Barched Kunsel*. Also in front are small statues of Thangtong Gyelpo (left) and Zhabdrung Ngawang Namgyel (right). The murals to the rear depict the Twelve Masters of the Great Perfection, and Longchen Rabjampa with his spiritual sons. In front of the main altar there is the reliquary stupa of Pelpung Beru Khyentse (1896-1945), bearing his photograph, and a copy of the *Prajnaparamita Sutra* (the long version in 16 volumes). Photographs are also on display of the present Dalai Lama and Sakya Gongma. The murals on the right wall depict Longchen Rabjampa surrounded by the *Nyingthig* lineage-holders of both the Central Tibetan and Kham traditions, along with the temple's sponsor, and on the left side Zhabdrung Ngawang Namgyel, with his series of incarnations.

Thangbi Lhakhang

If you leave the road at Toktu Zampa and follow a narrow pathway over a stream and alongside fields of buckwheat, after 20 minutes you will reach Thangbi Lhakhang, noticeable through the trees with its distinctive yellow roof. On the way you will pass a roadside rock bearing an impression of Guru Padmakara's head.

Background Thangbi was founded in 1470 by the influential Zhamar IV (1453-1524) of the Karma Kagyu school, during his visit to Bhutan. However, the founder was forced to return to Tibet following a dispute with his contemporary Pema Lingpa, who took over the temple. Nowadays there are 20 married *mantrins* (*gomchen*) in residence here. Even so, the iconography at Thangbi continues to reflect the temple's eclectic origins.

The site Entering the **main hall** through a chain-mail curtain, which is said to have been made by the hand of Pema Lingpa, you will find recent images depicting the Buddhas of the Three Times, flanked by the eight bodhisattvas. The central Shakyamuni image is also flanked by Shariputra and Maudgalyayana. To the left are smaller, exquisitely crafted clay images of Pema Lingpa and a previous Karmapa, with Zhamar IV to the right. The hall has no murals, and is painted in red ochre.

Upstairs, there are two chapels. In the vestibule of the larger one, the **Jampa Lhakhang,** are murals depicting the aspects of Guru Padmakara described in the *Thugdrub Barched Kunsel* on the left, and Zangdok Pelri paradise, Kampa Pakshi and Tara on the right. Within the hall the central image depicts Maitreya, flanked by small statues of the Kagyu lineage-holders. The murals here depict Shakyamuni Buddha with the Sixteen Elders (left), Guru Padmakara with the Nyingma lineage-holders, and Vajradhara with the Kagyu lineage-holders. Below Guru Padmakara is the terton Jatson Nyingpo, flanked by Guru Drakpo and Sengdongma, according to the revelation known as *Konchog Chidu*. Above Guru Padmakara are the lineage-holders of the *Nyingtig* tradition, starting with Samantabhadra, Vajrasattva, Prahevajra, Vimalamitra and Longchen Rabjampa. To the left of the door there is a mural of Vajrayogini with Zhamar IV to the right.

The smaller **Kangyur Lhakhang** has statues of the various Karmapas, with a xylograph edition of the *Kangyur* stacked along the sides, and assorted sacred dance masks, Jowo Rinpoche (upstairs), as well as a large shrine room dedicated to the protector deities. Opposite this chapel, is the entrance to the **Gonkhang**, dedicated to the aspect of the protector Mahakala known as Bernakchen.

Dur Hot Springs trek

A four-day trek of average difficulty (best in spring and autumn) leads through the Yoleng-chu valley to the Dur Hot Springs.

Day 1 Toktu Zampa–Gorsum Drive from Toktu Zampa on a rough track as far as Dur Zampa (5 km), where the Dur-chu and Yoleng-chu converge. Then hike along the west bank of the trout-filled Yoleng-chu, climbing very gradually to reach Gorsum (3,120 m), where an overnight camp will be set up (18 km, six to seven hours' trekking).

Day 2 Gorsum–Lungsum The muddy trail crosses to the east bank today, passing through a thick forest of cypress, juniper, spruce, hemlock and maple, and climbing gradually to the campsite at Lungsum (3,160 m; 12 km, five hours' trekking).

Day 3 Lungsum–Tsochenchen Remaining on the east bank, the trail continues to rise through forested terrain, to reach a campsite at Tsochenchen (3,780 m) above the tree-line, and near the river's source (17 km, six to seven hours' trekking).

Day 4 Tsochenchen–Dur Hot Springs Today the trail traverses the shore of a small lake and climbs to cross the watershed Juli La pass (4,700 m), which offers good mountain panoramas on a clear day. It then descends past another lake before crossing Goktong La pass (4,640 m), and zigzagging through forest to the campsite at Dur Hot Springs (3,590 m). Musk deer, herds of blue sheep and Himalayan bear may be seen en route (18 km, six to seven hours' trekking).

Extensions After resting at the hot springs, it is possible to return on the same trail to Toktu Zampa in only three days. Alternatively, there are onward routes into Trongsar district, heading either north-west for Gangkar Punsum Base Camp or south-west for the Mangde-chu gorge

Toktu Zampa to Ugyen Choling trek

This is a relatively easy three-day trek, best in spring and autumn, crossing into the Tang valley. This is marketed by the travel services as the Bumthang Cultural trek.

Day 1 Toktu Zampa–Ngang Lhakhang Taking the aforementioned trail to Thangbi Lhakhang, you continue following the Chamkhar-chu upstream on the east bank, through pleasant meadows and pine forest on a gradual ascent. Bypassing a riverside *mani* stone wall, the trail then crosses the river by a suspension bridge, and climbs steeply to the settlement at Ngang Lhakhang ('swan lake', 2,800 m) where you camp overnight (12 km, four to five hours' trekking).

The temple at **Ngang Lhakhang** was built during the 15th century by Namka Samdrub on a site where Guru Padmakara had once meditated. The buildings here are somewhat run-down, but the images and murals have undergone restoration, as recently as 1971. The lower chapel is dedicated to Guru Padmakara, flanked by his foremost consorts Mandarava and Yeshe Tsogyel, while the upper chapel includes a Gonkhang dedicated to Jnananatha.

Day 2 Ngang Lhakhang–Tahung The trail crosses a meadow and then forks right on a narrow track through rocks and muddy fields. After crossing a stream, it rock-hops back and forth and begins to climb gradually through bamboo and birch forest and rhododendrons, to reach Phephela pass (3,360 m), which is the highest point on this trek. Descending through forested terrain from the pass, the trail fords streams and clearings of open pasture, before crossing a wooden bridge near the village of Tahung (2,790 m) where there is a fine meadow camp (16 km, six to seven hours' trekking).

Day 3 Tahung–Gamling Descending from the meadow to the sheep development centre at Wobthang, the trail now becomes a tractor route, and enters the valley of the Tang-chu, following the east bank downstream to a bridge, where it forks. Here you may cross the bridge, heading through Tang village for the campsite at Mesithang on the west bank, or remain on the east bank and camp at Gamling village, if you wish to visit **Ugyen Choling** (see page 188) or trek to **Lhuntse** (see page 207). The distance from Tahung to Mesithang is 16 km (five to six hours' trekking) and to Gamling only 10 km (two to three hours' trekking). From the trailhead at Mesithang it is a 15-km drive on a dirt road to the paved lateral highway, and from Gamling it will be necessary to trek as far as the trailhead at Kizam (one hour).

There are old trade routes following the Chamkar-chu upstream through Sodrusam and Lhedeng to **Monla Karchung La** pass on the Tibet frontier. This was a frequently followed route to Tibet in medieval and even recent times. In the 15th century Pema Lingpa followed this route into Lhodrak and Southern Tibet, where his tradition was established north of the border, and hierarchs of Ralung, such as Ngagi Wangchuk and Tenpei Nyima, ancestors of the Zhabdrung, travelled the same trail in reverse.

East side of the Chokhor valley

If you drive east out of Jakar town, after crossing the motor bridge over the Chamkhar-chu, you can turn right for Mongar (193 km) or follow the east bank of the river upstream. If you take the latter road and turn off at Ozer Lham Shop, the road that winds uphill to the Swiss Guesthouse also leads to Kharchu Dratsang.

Kharchu Dratsang

This is a large monastery, founded by the Bhutanese-born Namkhei Nyingpo Rinpoche, whose ancestral monastery is at Kharchu, across the border in Southern Tibet. Since its foundation in the 1970s the monastery has grown in size and stature – it now houses 300 monks, who are engaged in Buddhist meditation practice, daily rituals and study.

The site There are two main buildings here, in addition to the uphill hermitage, where Namkhei Nyingpo Rinpoche spends much time in retreat. Among them, the **assembly hall** (*dukhang*) is one of the largest in the country, with images of (L-R): Guru Padmakara with his eight manifestations, Padmapani, Shakyamuni Buddha, Guru Drakpo, and Rikdzin Godemchen, the founder of the *Jangter* tradition, surrounded by nine other accomplished masters. The murals here depict the Mahayoga teachings of the Nyingma school—the tantra class embodied in the extraordinary wrathful figure of Mahottara Heruka, whose innermost pair of hands hold Samantabhadra and consort (the primordial Buddha) and whose outer hands hold at their finger-tips the Hundred Peaceful and Wrathful Deities. The murals of the so-called sadhana class depict the eight great meditational deities of the Nyingma school, with their Indian lineage-holders above, and their Tibetan recipients below. The first in the line is Shri Heruka, the meditational deity of the eighth-century Namkhei Nyingpo, student of Guru Padmakara, from whom the founder of the monastery acquires his name.

The smaller **Guru Lhakhang** has a central image of Guru Padmakara in the form Nangsi Zilnon, and a small Gonkhang to the left. The murals are in narrative style, illustrating the life of the Precious Guru, as recounted in Sangye Lingpa's 14th-century revelation, the *Katang Sertreng*. Some scenes, including the rape of Yeshe Tsogyel, are graphically depicted.

Petsheling Gonpa

Petsheling monastery, under the guidance of Petsheling Tulku, is located about three hours' hiking distance above the Swiss Guesthouse on a steep incline. It offers fine panoramic views of the central Bumthang valley. There is a four-hour trek from here across the ridge to Kunzang Drak hermitage in the Tang valley (see page 186).

Konchoksum Lhakhang

Continuing upstream from Ozer Lham Shop, where you can buy Swiss cheese, honey and alcoholic fruit drinks, the road passes the diminutive Konchoksum Lhakhang on the right. The temple also goes by the names Tselung Lhakhang and Chokhor Lhakhang. Here, there is a celebrated bell with an eighth-century inscription, linking it to the royal family of Tibet.

The main image at Konchoksum Lhakhang depicts Vairocana Buddha – itself indicative of the temple's antiquity – flanked on the left by Longchen Rabjampa and Four-armed Avalokiteshvara, and on the right by Guru Padmakara and Pema Lingpa. The murals illustrate the Pema Lingpa lineage (rear), the Twenty-five Disciples of Guru Padmakara (left) and the Thirty-five Confession Buddhas (right). Tibetan sources suggest that the temple was associated in its earliest phase with King Trisong Detsen, who fashioned the Vairocana image, and with Guru Padmakara, as well as the Bon teacher Draktsel who was active here in 1039. Later, in the 15th century, Pema Lingpa unearthed certain teachings here, in the form of treasures (*terma*) from a subterranean lake, which he subsequently sealed with a stone.

Tamzhing Lhundrub Choling

The paved road on the east bank of the Chamkhar-chu ends at Tamzhing monastery, a short distanced beyond Konchoksum Lhakhang. Founded in 1501 by Pema Lingpa, Tamzhing is the principal residence in Bhutan of the Peling Sungtrul line of incarnations, and it is also a secondary residence of the Peling Thukse line of incarnations, who have their main seat at Lhalung in the Lhodrak region of Southern Tibet. Tamzhing, therefore, along with Gangteng monastery, is a vital centre for the spiritual practices and liturgies of Pema Lingpa's tradition. Restoration work was undertaken in the late 19th century by Peling Sungtrul VIII Kunzang Ngedon Tenpei Nyima; but original murals do survive, especially those of the ground floor vestibule, which are among the oldest extant paintings in Bhutan. In style these are reminiscent of Tibetan murals of the 15th and 16th centuries, which have the central figure flanked by vertically stacked peripheral figures. Since 1959 many monks from Lhalung have crossed the border to settle at Tamzhing, where they continue to maintain their unique heritage. Currently there are 60 monks resident in the monastic quarters of the outer courtyard. The inner courtyard has a small Mani Wheel Chapel on the left, dated 1914.

The main temple has two storeys, with a circumambulatory pathway (*khorlam*) around the courtyard and the inner sanctum, and a gallery immediately above it. In the **vestibule**, the original 16th-century murals depict, on the left side of the door, the Wheel of Rebirth, protectors including Shridevi and Shenpa Marnak, Pema Lingpa, Karmapa VII Chodrak Gyatso, Yeshe Tsogyel, Guru Padmakara, Manjushrimitra, Prahevajra, Vajradhara and the Buddhas of the Five Enlightened Families. On the right side they include the foremost Nyingma protectors, Rahula, Ekajati and Mahakala, followed by Vaishravana, Vajrakila, Prajnaparamita, Vajrapani, Avalokiteshvara, Manjughosa, the Hundred Peaceful and Wrathful Deities, Samantabhadra, Hayagriva, Guru Drakpo and Amitayus.

On the **circumambulatory pathway**, there are faded murals which cannot easily be dated. Those of the outer wall depict Bhasajyaguru, flanked by the Sixteen Elders, while those of the inner walls include depictions of the *Nyingtig* lineage holders and of Pema Lingpa (right) and Ratna Lingpa (left). Near the mural of Pema Lingpa there is a heavy suit of chain-mail armour, weighting about 25 kg, which is said to have been made by Pema Lingpa's own hand. Visiting pilgrims carry this suit around the walkway on their shoulders as an act of merit.

Within the **assembly hall** are the three teaching thrones used by the incumbent Peling Sungtrul, Thukse and Kutrul incarnations (who respectively represent Pema Lingpa's buddha speech, mind and body). Behind them, the **inner sanctum** contains a large central image of Guru Padmakara, his eyes raised upwards in the gaze of the Buddha-body of Reality (*dharmakaya*). To the left are Dipamkara and Shakyamuni, with Maitreya and Four-armed Avalokiteshvara to the right. Flanking these are images representing the eight manifestations of Guru Padmakara. The murals of the inner sanctum, which were last restored in the late 20th century, depict the lineage-holders of the Pema Lingpa tradition, ending with Peling Sungtrul VIII, on the left, and the iconography of Pema Lingpa's revelation, *Lama Norbu Gyatso*, on the right. According to local tradition, the images of Guru Padmakara, the Buddhas of the Three Timestra and Four-armed Avalokiteshvara were all fashioned by Pema Lingpa himself, as were all the murals of the ground floor.

The **upper floor** has a remarkably low ceiling, suitable for those of short stature like Pema Lingpa. The **gallery**, which overlooks the assembly hall below, has murals depicting the Thousand Buddhas of the aeon and the Twenty-one Aspects of Tara. On the west wing there is a small **Gonkhang**, its entrance guarded by the gatekeepers Vajrapani and Hayagriva. Formerly this was Pema Lingpa's private residence, and it contains alongside the protectors of his lineage, a likeness of himself. Adjacent to it is a **Kangyur Lhakhang**, containing the texts of the Buddhist canon. The main chapel, located immediately above the inner sanctum, is the **Tsepak Lhakhang**, dedicated to Amitayus. The murals here depict the Forty-two Peaceful Deities (left) and the Fifty-eight Wrathful Deities (right), along with several pre-eminent 19th-century lineage-holders, such as Jamyang Khyentse Wangpo. Outside, in the **circumambulatory pathway** around this chapel, there are other murals depicting Guru Padmakara with Amitabha and Avalokiteshvara; and also his 13 aspects, which are described in the *Sampa Lhundrub* revelation. These are followed by the Eighty-four Accomplished Masters of Ancient India. The murals of the upper floor were left unpainted, in pale white and red, according to Pema Lingpa's own injunction.

Padmasambhava Lhakhang
About 100 m above the road at Tamzhing, there is a small temple, known as Padmasambhava Lhakhang. This shrine was founded in 1490 by Pema Lingpa, at the site of a sacred cave hermitage that had been associated with Guru Padmakara's visit to Bumthang. The temple was expanded and restored during the 19th and 20th centuries.

Tang valley

If you turn south-east, after crossing the bridge over the Chamkhar-chu at Jakar, you will follow the highway downstream, past a sheep-breeding farm at Dechen Pelrithang (2,800 m), to reach the entrance of the Tang valley after 9 km. Just before the highway starts to climb through a series of switchback bends en route for Ura and Mongar, there is an unpaved turn-off on the left, about 1 km after the sheep-breeding farm, which leads into the narrow gorge of the Tang valley. The land here is more suited to sheep farming and has been left fairly undeveloped.

Mebartsho Gorge
Driving into the gorge on the unpaved road, after 2 km you will reach a parking lot, from where you can walk along a footpath, down to the river, which is spanned by a wooden bridge. Mebartsho ('burning lake') is revered in the annals of Bhutan as the place where, in 1475, Pema Lingpa publicly and spectacularly plunged into the river with a burning lamp in his hand to retrieve sacramental treasures from its murky depths and re-emerged holding the sacred objects, with the lamp still burning! To commemorate this event, pilgrims still come here to place small lighted lamps on the river. There are prayer flags strewn across the gorge below the bridge, marking this site. A large boulder overlooking the bridge has painted carvings that depict Pema Lingpa with his two sons, but there is no temple. The nunnery of **Tang Thekchok Choling**, under the guidance of Gangteng Tulku, is located nearby.

Kunzang Drak Gonpa
Continuing upstream on the unpaved motor road, after 7 km you will reach **Drangchel**, the birthplace of Pema Lingpa. Perched on a high cliff above the road you will notice

the monastic hermitage of Kunzang Drak, which Pema Lingpa founded in 1488. The site was deemed sacred on account of its associations with Guru Padmakara and his student Namkhei Nyingpo; and it is named after the primordial Buddha Samantabhadra (Tib. Kuntuzangpo), whose form the young Pema Lingpa perceived in the rocks above his home, in the course of an early visionary experience. There are three footpaths leading steeply uphill to the hermitage, the shortest taking just over one hour and the longest close to three hours.

On the ascent, you will first pass the residence of Gangteng III Kunzang Pema Namgyel (d. 1750), which is now being rebuilt. There are distant views from here of **Chogyam Lhakhang**, where Guru Chowang discovered *Vajrakila* texts, and of the remote hermitage at Thowa Drak (see page 189). Then, on the left side of the trail there is a rock with an impression of Pema Lingpa's buttocks, overlooking the valley where he encountered Guru Padmakara in a vision. To the right of the trail there is a smaller rock with the impression of Guru Padmakara's *vajra* and head, and slightly above it a cave associated with his consort Yeshe Tsogyel.

Continuing sharply uphill through a tunnel and across a wooden bridge, the trail reaches the **Gonkhang**, which contains images of Gonpo Lekden and Gonpo Maning. Formerly this was a residence of Pema Lingpa and his sons. Then it turns sharply south-west towards the main temple, following a precipitous ridge, where there are five cliffs, indicative of the Five Buddhas of the Enlightened Families.

The **main temple** has a wooden gallery with prayer wheels. The view from here over the sheer cliff face is memorable. Inside the temple there are images of (L-R): Pema Lingpa, Namkhei Nyingpo (here shown with a moustache) and Guru Padmakara — the last of these reputedly fashioned by Pema Lingpa in person. Just below the main temple is the **Wangkhang**, containing an image of Mahakarunika that was also made by Pema Lingpa; and above it is the **Ozerphuk**, an enclosed cave formerly associated with Pema Lingpa's son Dawa Gyeltsen, where life-giving water (*tsepame drubchu*) pours from the rocks down a bamboo tube. Pilgrims believe that this water will help cure epilepsy and stroke. Behind this cave is a yellow sulphurous rock, associated with the wealth-granting deity Jambhala. To the south of the main temple is Pema Lingpa's own meditation cave, containing the master's wooden teaching throne, a lifelike statue (*ngadrama*) of him, and his gilded stone footprint. Lower down from this cave is a stone teaching throne, which was once used by Guru Padmakara and later rediscovered by Pema Lingpa.

Climbing slightly north from the main temple, you will reach the **Khandroma Lakhang**, containing a gilded copper image of Pema Lingpa, along with images of Guru Padmakara and his eight Indian teachers, and a copy of the *Prajnaparamita Sutra* (long version in 16 volumes). It also contains a heavy rock, which pilgrims try to lift in order to purify their negative past actions. Outside there is a wooden post, imbued with the life-force of one hundred thousand *dakinis*; and a stupa built by Peling Tukse Dawa Gyeltsen. A steep climb from here leads up to a humid cave containing the sacred spring of Rahula (*drangsong-chu*).

Nowadays there are 25 young novice monks in residence at Kunzang Drak, under the guidance of Gangteng Tulku and Khenpo Orgyan from Byelakuppe in South India.

Rimochen Lhakhang

Continuing up the Tang valley on the unpaved motor road, after 3 km from Drangchel you will pass through the village of **Jamzhong**, where there is a long wall of sacred stone carvings and a large new prayer wheel. Tang Junior High School is located 2 km upstream from here; and after just 1 further km, you will reach Rimochen.

The temple of Rimochen is located below an enormous rock, which has tawny bands, reminiscent of a tiger's stripes. Lower down by the roadside, there is another large rock containing a body-imprint of Guru Padmakara and his consorts. The temple is said to be named after the latter 'rock markings' (*rimochen*). A flight of steps leads past a large prayer wheel and up to the cave hermitage, its entrance guarded by statues of the Four Guardian Kings. The actual temple is to the right of the cave. It was founded in the late 14th century by Dorje Lingpa, following an earlier prophesy of Longchen Rabjampa, and later restored by one of his descendants, the governor of Trongsar, Tsokye Dorje.

Entering the temple, the images are arrayed on the left side, with Guru Padmakara at the centre, flanked by his eight manifestations. A teaching throne is positioned below the window, facing the images and the altar. The murals here depict Guru Padmakara with his eight manifestations and Zangdok Pelri paradise (near right corner), Milarepa and Gampopa (far right corner), and Zhabdrung Ngawang Namgyel surrounded by his Drukpa lineage-holders (facing). On the far bank of the Tang-chu river, opposite Rimochen Lhakhang, you will notice a number of interesting rock cavities.

Kizam

Just 3 km north of Rimochen, the motor road comes to an end at **Kizam**, where a bridge spans the Tang-chu. There is a trekking route from here via Gamling to Tahung and Ngang Lhakhang in Chokhor (see page 183). The distance from Jakar to this trailhead is 31 km.

Ugyen Choling

From the Kizam Bridge, where there are small shops, it is a 45-minute hike uphill through small villages, light forest and farmland, to a sacred spring (*drubchu*), and from there to the hilltop ridge where Ugyen Choling is located. In the 14th century the great Nyingma master Longchen Rabjampa established a meditation hermitage higher up the hillside, and in the century that followed the great treasure-finder Dorje Lingpa discovered several texts in this locale. His descendants continued to live here through to the 19th century, including the illustrious governor of Trongsar, Tsokye Dorje, who rebuilt the complex before ceding power to the father of Bhutan's first king. Most of the building was damaged by the 1987 earthquake, and the whole structure was subsequently renovated by Ugyen Dorje, the administrator of Jakar.

Until recently Ugyen Choling functioned as a private residence, and it is still privately owned by a member of the royal family, Ashi Kunzang Wangmo, and her Swiss husband. Nowadays it has been turned into a research institute and museum, offering a fascinating insight into the aristocratic life of the Lama Chojes of Bhutan. The complex includes a two-storey temple (*tsuklakhang*) with four chapels, a four-storey central tower (*utse*), a two-storey residence (*shagkor*), and a guesthouse situated in the west gate field (*nubgothang*).

Entering the temple, the **Dolma Lhakhang** on the ground floor contains images of the Twenty-one Aspects of Tara. Climbing the stairs to a landing, where there are images of the Four Guardian Kings, you continue up to the entrance of the **Jokhang** on the upper floor (also known as the Dorje Lingpa Lhakhang). This chapel has a central image of Jowo Shakyamuni, at the age of 12, modelled on the renowned image of the Jokhang in Lhasa, and flanked on the left by Dorje Lingpa's father and Guru Padmakara, and on the right by Dorje Lingpa and his son, Chokten Gonpo. A teaching throne is positioned below the window, with photographs of the previous Pelpung Beru Khyentse and the late Khenpo Jikpun of Larungar in Eastern Tibet. The murals adjacent to the door depict the *Rigdzin Dupa*, according to Jigme Lingpa's revelation, while those on the opposite wall depict the Peaceful and Wrathful Deities according to Dorje Lingpa's revelation, and the Zangdok Pelri paradise. Between these murals is an ornate doorway leading into the **Gonkhang**, dedicated to Jnananatha, which is closed to the public. The last temple on the upper floor is the **Dorsem Lhakhang**, dedicated to Vajrasattva.

Within the **central tower**, the ground floor is used as a granary, the next as a kitchen and storeroom for provisions and artefacts used in trading with Tibet, the

third as the family living quarters and armoury, and the fourth as a library and printing 189
room, alongside a chapel dedicated to Amitayus. The items on display in this living
museum are well captioned and informative.

Chogyam Lhakhang

Below Ugyen Choling there is a small temple, known as Chogyam Lhakhang, which was
built by Lama Chogyam, known locally as Tang Rinpoche, a student of Khenpo Jikpun
from Larungar in Eastern Tibet. The site appears to have been associated originally with
Guru Chowang, who discovered *Vajrakila* texts here in the 13th century. Lama Chogyam
passed away in 1999 and his son owns a shop near the bridge at Kizam.

Thowa Drak Gonpa

In the upper reaches of the Tang valley, about four hours' hiking distance from Ugyen
Choling, there is the hermitage of Thowa Drak (3,400 m), which has ancient
associations with Guru Padmakara. It was here that the Precious Guru left his wooden
Garuda contraption, having used it to expel the evil king, Khyikhyi Rato from the
'hidden land' of neighbouring Khenpajong, which lies to the east of Lhedam in
Bumthang and in Lhuntse district. Even now Thowa Drak is revered as an entrance to
this hidden land, which was consecrated by Guru Padmakara. There are many
grottoes and caverns dotted over the hillside. In 1238 a Drukpa Kagyu presence was
established here by Lorepa, and subsequently, in the 15th century, the Nyingma cave
hermitage was founded by Dorje Lingpa. The hermitage was regenerated in the 18th
century by the followers of Jigme Lingpa and his Bhutanese student Jigme Kundrol,
who maintain the popular *Longchen Nyingthig* tradition.

Trekking route to Lhuntse

There is a moderately difficult four-day trek from Ugyen Choling to Lhuntse via Rodang
La pass on an ancient trade route, which could be extended by combining it with the
Bumthang Cultural trek (see page 183) and the Lhuntse to Tashi Yangtse trek (see
page 207). The best season for this route is late autumn.

Day 1 Ugyen Choling–Phokpe Climbing from Ugyen Choling on a muddy cattle trail,
the path becomes firmer around 3,000 m, and continues to climb through meadow
clearings and forest. Phokpe Gonpa is visible on the opposite side of the valley, as the
trail enters a side-valley on the approach to Rodong La pass. Camp overnight at **Phokpe**
(3,680 m) on nomadic pastureland (17 km, five to six hours' trekking).

Day 2 Phokpe–Peme Following a rhododendron-covered ridge uphill from the
campsite, you will reach a stone staircase that leads up to **Rodong La pass** (4,160
m), and cross the pass about two hours from camp. There follows a difficult
vertiginous descent over rough terrain and stepping stones. In places the trail
follows the contour of the cliff face and is supported by wooden buttresses. Then,
descending along a ridge, through conifer and broadleaf forest, the trail reaches a
meadow clearing at **Peme** (3,000 m). Camp here alongside a ruined royal granary
(20 km, seven to eight hours' trekking).

Day 3 Peme–Khyinyel Lhakhang The muddy trail descends into the
Noyargong-chu valley, passing though areas of dwarf bamboo and tropical ferns to
reach the haunted meadow of **Sang Sangbe** (2,300 m). Yamalung Gonpa is then
visible to the south, as the trail continues downhill through small villages and rice
fields, before crossing the Noyargong-chu suspension bridge (1,660 m). The
inhabitants of this region speak a Kurto dialect, related more to the language of
Bumthang than to Dzongkha. From the bridge, the trail climbs through terraced rice
fields at **Bu-le**, and follows a number of agricultural side-valleys, passing through

small settlements, including Kulepang (1,930 m) and **Gonda** (2,040 m), before reaching **Khyinyel Lhakhang** (2,010 m). Khyinyel Lhakhang ('sleeping dog temple') is considered by some sources as one of King Songtsen Gampo's extensive network of 108 geomantic temples. The images of the temple depict Shakyamuni Buddha flanked by a previous Karmapa on the left and Zhabdrung Ngawang Namgyel on the right, along with Milarepa and Guru Padmakara. Camp alongside the monastery (21 km, seven to eight hours' trekking).

Day 4 Khyinyel Lhakhang–Tangmachu On the final day of the trek, the trail undulates through Gorsam, where there is a clinic and a small school, and enters the Kuri-chu valley at **Umling Mani** (2,180 m), a major landmark on this route. From here it follows the Kuri-chu upstream, and cuts through a side-valley to reach Gumbar Gang (2,120 m), before crossing two lower passes: Dzerim La (1,940 m) and Tage La (1,760 m) on its descent to join the unpaved motor road at Tangmachu High School. In the saddle between these two passes there is the village of **Menjabi**, where the traditional Bhutanese farmhouses are large and sturdy. Camp at Tangmachu or drive down into Lhuntse, 21 km distant (18 km, six to seven hours' trekking). For the extension of this trek from Tangmachu to Tashi Yangtse, see page 208.

Ura valley

From the bridge at Jakar, the road to Ura and Mongar follows the east bank of the Chamkhar-chu downstream, passing the entrance to the Tang valley after 9 km, and a bridge over the Tang-chu, after which it climbs in a series of switchback bends through open countryside to reach the small agricultural settlement of **Tangsibi**, 24 km from Jakar. Ura is the highest of Bumthang's four valleys, and the approach to Shertang La pass (3,590 m) offers a splendid view of Bhutan's highest peak, Mount Gangkar Punsum (7,541 m). From here there is a long descent into Ura village, nestling below the road and above the Lirgang-chu. The distance from Jakar to Ura is 48 km.

Somdrang Gonpa
On the descent into the Ura valley, before reaching the village, there is a turn-off on the left that leads along an unpaved road to Somdrang Gonpa. Pema Lingpa's ancestors settled here in 1288, and one of Pema Lingpa's hand-made iron chains can be seen hanging on the window of the ground floor.

Shingkhar Gonpa
The village of Shingkhar (3,400 m) is accessible from Somdrang on a one-hour hike across a ridge, or on a rough 9-km drive from the main road. Shingkar Gonpa was founded by Longchen Rabjampa circa 1350.

Ura village
Continuing along the paved road into Ura, you will pass on the right a lane leading through to **Gaden Lhakhang**. Then, the next turning on the right leads into the large village of Ura (3,100 m). Ura consists of closely built shingled houses with cobblestone streets, where the community subsists on the basis of pastoral farming and the potato crop. Electricity is provided here by a local hydroelectric plant. As one might expect in this prime sheep-breeding region, the women of Ura wear distinctive clothing, which includes a type of sheepskin shawl. Dominating the village, the **Ura Lhakhang** was built in 1986. It contains a large image of Guru Padmakara in the form Nangsi Zilnon, which fills all storeys of the building, and is flanked by beautiful murals depicting the eight manifestations.

● Sleeping

Jakar and the Chokhor valley *p173*
The new 5-star **Aman Hotel** is expected to open in 2005, and the Como Hotel chain will also be opening a 5-star **Uma Resort**, complete with 10 guest rooms, dining, spa and yoga facilities. All the hotels or lodges in Bumthang are heated by *burkhari* wood stoves (unless stated otherwise). All of them have family-run dining rooms.
B Dondrubling Resort, T/F3-631419, a new hotel due to open in 2005, located near Bumthang Hospital, with 24 rooms (all with attached bathrooms) – doubles at Nu 1,500 and singles at Nu 1,250.
B Mifam Lodge, T3-631107, F3-631138, located on the south side of the valley, with excellent views, has 10 good rooms (with modern attached bathrooms), operated by BTCL, with doubles at Nu 1,100 and singles at Nu 950. There is a good in-house restaurant.
B Mountain Lodge, T3-631255, F3-631275, well located on the west side of the valley, overlooking Wangdu Choling Palace, and managed by Ethometho Travel Agency, has 23 wood-panelled rooms (with attached bathroom) – doubles at Nu 1,150 and singles at Nu 950.
B Swiss Guesthouse, T3-6311145, F3-631278, located in an apple orchard in a quiet setting on the east side of the valley above the Swiss Farm at Karsunphe, has 22 rooms, including 9 in a new building (with private bathrooms) and 13 in the old building (with shared bathrooms) – superior at Nu 1,500 and economy at Nu 450-650. Elegant dining rooms and pristine tap water distinguish this hotel from others in the valley.
C Gongkhar Lodge, T3-631288, F3-631345, located on the east side of the valley in view of Jakar Dzong , has 10 excellent rooms – doubles at Nu 1,050 and singles at Nu 850. There is a good in-house restaurant.
C Jakar Village Lodge, T3-631242, F3-631377, gaseyivl@druknet.bt, situated below Jakar Dzong, has 16 chalet-style rooms – doubles at Nu 1,050 and singles at Nu 850. There is a good Bhutanese restaurant here.
C Lekyi Lodge, T/F3-631434, located near Bumthang Hospital, has 21 rooms, with electric heaters (10 with attached bathroom and 11 without) – doubles at Nu 900 and singles at Nu 850 – and a pleasantly decorated dining room.
C River Lodge, T3-631287, south of town, is a converted farmhouse – doubles at Nu 950 and singles at Nu 800.
C Siddartha Lodge, T3-631774, F3-631775, near Jampa Lhakang, 10 rooms – doubles at Nu 1,000 and singles at Nu 800.
C Udee Guesthouse, T3-631139, located in town, has 7 simple rooms – doubles at Nu 1,050 and singles at Nu 850.
C Yangphel Lodge, T3-631176, F3-631191, located near Jampa Lhakhang, has 10 traditional rooms – doubles at Nu 1,000 and singles at Nu 850. Offers a hot-stone bath.
D Kaila Lodge, T3-631219, F3-631247, located in town, has 12 simple rooms arranged around a courtyard – doubles at Nu 750 and singles at Nu 600. There is a good restaurant, managed by a former cook of the Swiss Guesthouse.
D Tamzhing Guesthouse, near Tamzhing monastery, has 8 rooms, and a delightfully peaceful atmosphere.
D Tsering Guesthouse, T/F3-631244, located in town, has 8 simple rooms – doubles at Nu 800 and singles at Nu 700.

Tang valley *p186*
D Ugyen Choling Guesthouse, within the grounds of Ugyen Choling, T3-631221, ucholing@hotmail.com, managed by the Ugyen Choling Trust, has 6 rooms – doubles at Nu 800 and singles at Nu 300.

Ura valley *p190*
D Shingkhar Lodge, in Shingkhar village, under the management of Masangang Tours and Treks, has 6 rooms (Nu 700).
D Shingkhar Village Guesthouse, located in Shingkhar village, has 6 simple rooms (Nu 700) and provides meals.
D Zambala Hotel, T3-635003, by the roadside, has 10 rooms and a communal dining room.

● Eating

Jakar and the Chokhor valley *p173*
The **Swiss Guesthouse** offers fondue (Nu 560 for a party of 4), and other Swiss

specialities. **Himalayan Pizza**, T3-631437, offers Italian spaghetti and pizzas. All the hotels and lodges have good Bhutanese cuisine on the menu. There are also many small, inexpensive roadside restaurants in the downtown area, serving Tibetan and Bhutanese dishes. Among them are **Hotel Home**, **Tsewang Dorje Hotel**, **Tashi General Store & Restaurant**, **Yangchen Hotel**, **NC Restaurant & Bar** and **Sonam Zangmo Hotel & Bar**.

❶ Bars and clubs

Jakar and the Chokhor valley *p173*
There are many small bars in town to the east of the traffic circle. They include **Gyurmin Bar**, **Kunga Paljor Bar**, **Jintha Bar & Store**, **Tsering Bar**, **Pema Dorje Bar**, **Sonam Zangmo Hotel & Bar**, **Peep-in Restaurant & Bar**, **Pema Chodon Bar** and **Dechen Shop & Bar**. Nightlife here is minimal, but **Thinley Guesthouse** (Dekiling) does have a weekend discotheque – open 2000 till late, entrance fee Nu 100 (single), Nu 150 (couple).

❶ Shopping

Chu-me *p167*
Both **Thokme Yeshe** and **Gonpo Tashi** textile factories at Zug-ne have roadside shops where hand-woven woollen cloth and garments can be purchased.

Jakar and the Chokhor valley *p173*
There are several general stores (*tsongkhang*) in Jakar, selling **groceries** and items of both Indian and Chinese origin.

Bumthang **crafts** are also on sale in town, at **Bumthang Traditional Gift Shop**, and **Bhutanese Traditional Crafts**, near the Town Gate. Woollen products (a local speciality) can be purchased at the **National Sheep-breeding Centre**. Woodcarvings, including intricately carved tables, are available at **Udee Furniture and Woodcarving Factory**.

Swiss **cheese** and locally brewed Red Panda beer and other brands can be purchased from **Ozer Lham Shop**, T3-631193, a retail outlet for the Swiss Farm, on the east side of the valley. Locally produced alcoholic **drinks** can also be

purchased at the **Bhutan Wine Shop**.

Postage **stamps** are available at Bhutan Post, located east of the traffic circle.

❀ Festivals

The Bumthang area is famous for its *tsechu* and *drubchen* festivals. As many as 20 such events are held within the district in the course of the lunar year.

Chu-me valley *p167*
Tsechu festivals
Buli Gompa Held during the **2nd month of the lunar calendar.**
Trekar Lhakhang Held in the courtyard of an adjacent building, commencing on the 18th of the **8th lunar month**. In 2004 this is scheduled for 29-31 Oct and in 2005 for 18-20 Oct.
Nyimalung Gonpa Held in the **5th lunar month**. This is scheduled for for 15-17 Jun in 2005. A large *thongdrol* appliqué depicting Padmakara with his 8 manifestations is housed at Nyimalung and displayed publicly at both the Trekar and Nyimalung festivals.

Jakar and the Chokhor valley *p173*
Drubchen festival
In 2004, the *drubchen* ceremonies at **Jampa Lhakhang** will take place on 28 Oct-1 Nov, and in 2005 on 17-21 Oct.

Tsechu festivals
A *tsechu* ceremony is held at **Kurje Lhakhang** annually by the monks of Chotse Dzong who take up temporary residence at Kurje during the summer months. In 2005 this will take place on 17 Jun.

Other events
The sacred masked dances of the **Mani Cham** are performed annually at **Thangbi Lhakhang**. In 2004, this event is scheduled for 27-29 Sep, and in 2005 for 17-19 Sep.

A 3-day ceremony of sacred masked dances, known as **Ngang Lhakhang Shey,** is held at **Ngang Lhakhang** annually in Dec.

The annual offering ceremony at Tamzhing monastery, known as **Tamzhing Phala Chopa**, will be held in 2004 on 22-24 Sep, and in 2005 on 12-14 Sep.

An annual 3-day *tsechu* festival is held at **Ugyen Choling** in the **8th month** of the lunar calendar.

Ura valley *p190*
There are several small village festivals held in Ura. In the village itself, the 5-day **Ura Yakcho** is held during the **3rd lunar month**, which in 2005 is 19-23 April.

In Shingnyer village, the 1-day **Metokchopa** offering festival is held during the **10th month** of the lunar calendar.

Tsechu festivals
Gaden Lhakhang An annual 1-day festival during the **1st month** of the lunar calendar.
Tangsibi A 3-day festival held during the **1st month** of the lunar calendar.
Somdrang Gonpa An annual 3-day festival is held in the **9th month** of the lunar calendar.
Shingkar Gonpa An annual 5-day festival is held in the **8th month** of the lunar calendar.

⊖ Transport

Two public **buses** operated by **Bumthang Singye Express** and **Phunsum Travels** run from **Thimphu** via Trongsar to Jakar, both departing Thimphu at 0700 on Tue and Sat (Nu 165). The return leg from Bumthang to **Thimphu** is operated on Thu and Sun. Tickets are sold at **Bumthang Singye Express** office in Jakar, 1 day prior to the journey. Most visitors to Bumthang will have pre-arranged transportation. For vehicle repairs, contact **TD Automobile Workshop** (T3-631106), near the Swiss Guesthouse, or **Gonpo Tendzin Auto Spare-parts**, in Jakar.

⊙ Directory

Jakar and the Chokhor valley *p173*
Banks Bank of Bhutan, T3-631123, east of the post office, Mon-Fri 0900-1300, Sat 0900-1100. **Internet** Facilities are available in the lodges, at the internet café next to Jakar Lhakhang, T3-631250, and at the **Jakar Telecentre**, Mon-Fri 0900-1300, Sat 0900-1300, Nu 3-5 per min. **Hospitals and medical services** Bumthang Hospital is located on the west side of the valley, north of Jakar Dzong. Indian-manufactured medications can be purchased at **Pema Yangchen Pharmacy**. **Post** including EMS express delivery, are available at **Bhutan Post**, Mon-Fri 0830-1230, 1330-1630, Sat 0900-1230. **Telecommunications** IDD calls can be made from tourist lodges and from the phone booth near the traffic circle.

Zhemgang district གཞལ་སྒང་

→ *Area: 2,116 sq km.*
Zhemgang is a region of deep gorges formed by the Mangde-chu and Chamkhar-chu, which converge here before flowing into the Drangme-chu (Manas) in the extreme south of the district, close to the Indian border. Trongsar and Sarpang lie to the west, with Bumthang to the north, and Mongar and Sambrub Jongkhar to the east.

The great variation in local climate is due to the marked difference in elevation between the northern hills, which are within the temperate zone, and the southern foothills, which are sub-tropical and exposed to the full brunt of the subcontinental monsoon (average rainfall: 1,000-5,000 mm). Nearly 87% of the land is covered with pristine broadleaf forest, falling partly within the Black Mountains Nature Reserve, and the Royal Manas National Park. There is little pastureland here, but nearly 11% is given over to rice, maize, millet, buckwheat and potato cultivation. Oranges, cardamom and rattan are the main cash crops. Most of Zhemgang is considered a botanical paradise, in that it contains many unique plants, including carnivorous plants and exceedingly rare species of orchid. Descending from 1,900 m in the north to 200 m in the south, the land is covered by tropical forests, yielding most of Bhutan's bamboo and rattan produce, as well as bananas, mangos, edible roots and so forth.

There are seven counties in the district: Trong, Nangkhor, Phangkhar and Ngangla fall within the valley of the Mangde-chu; Shingkhar and Bardo in the gorge of the Chamkhar-chu; and remote Droka (Bjoka), isolated from Eastern Bhutan by the Drangme-chu which forms its south-east border. The administrative capital is located at Zhemgang, some 107 km south of Trongsar on a wind-exposed ridge above the Mangde-chu gorge. From here to Gelekphuk on the Indian border the distance is 137 km. ➤➤ *For Sleeping, Eating and other listings see page 195.*

Zhemgang town

Entering Zhemgang district from Trongsar, the southern highway soon leaves the Mangde-chu, climbing high above the gorge to reach Zhemgang Dzong and the new district capital.

Orientation
A turn-off on the right leads uphill to the District Guesthouse, and just after a quaint petrol station, the road forks. If you turn right here, you will pass the police station, Yangdzom Hotel & Bar, Tashi Namgyel General Store, the Bank of Bhutan, Galay Store, a lane leading to the Basic Health Unit, Sonam General Store, Kunga Restaurant cum Bar, Kichenla Store and Chokyi Store, before driving through a residential area to the primary and high schools.

If you turn left at the intersection, you will pass Kesang Norbu General Store, Chemo Chaki General Store, Kunzang Zhemgang Hotel, Karma Gelek Transport, Sonam Lhaden Hotel & Bar, Yeshe Lhamo General Store and a small Zangdok Pelri–style temple alongside a stupa. Here, at a police checkpoint, the road forks again – right for the post office and **Zhemgang Dzong** (see below), and left for Gelekphuk in Sarpang district. Bhutan Telecom and Kelzang Cable TV Network are located on the Gelekphuk road.

Zhemgang Dzong
Background Zhemgang Dzong is a small but impressive building. Before Zhabdrung Ngawang Namgyel unified Bhutan in the 17th century the whole of Zhemgang and neighbouring Mongar belonged to the ancient region of **Khyeng**, where the inhabitants speak Khyeng-ka, a distinctive dialect of Bumthang-ka. Khyeng itself was a loose federation of independent principalities, ruled by local chieftains (*dung*). Some, like the chieftains of Buli, Nyakhar and Tunglabi, were more influential than others, but only Nyakhar resisted the victorious Drukpa forces in 1647. Following the principalities' absorption within the new state, the Zhabdrung decided to construct Zhemgang Dzong in order to maintain his authority over the entire Khyeng region. Previously there had been a small temple on this wind-swept hilltop site, founded by the celebrated Lama Shang, founder of the Shangpa Kagyu school, in 1163. The name Zhemgang is said to be a derivative of his own name. The whole of Khyeng was administered from the new *dzong* until 1963 when the region was divided into three separate districts: Zhamgang, Mongar and Sarpang. The most recent restoration of the *dzong* was undertaken at that time.

The site Entering the courtyard, the **central tower** (*utse*) has three storeys: the ground floor is a store room, the middle floor is the official residence and the third floor has a chapel containing a gold image of Lama Shang, backing on to a protector chapel, which contains images of Jnananatha and the Four Guardian Kings, with murals of Guru Padmakara and his eight manifestations on the left, and the Thirty-five Confession Buddhas on the right.

The oldest artefact of interest here is the pillar at **Nabji** village near Zhemgang, commemorating an eighth-century treaty between King Sendhaka and King Nawoche (see page 230).

Trong and Nangkhor counties

Tingtingbi and Gongphu

South of town, the road to Gelekphuk winds its way downhill through a series of switchbacks to cross the Mangde-chu at **Tingtibi**. From here it climbs sharply through Bertigang to cross the watershed pass at **Tomala**, on the border of Sarpang district (see page 196). A motorable branch road continues to follow the west bank of the Mangde-chu downstream from Tingtingbi to **Gongphu**, another of the ancient Khyeng principalities, where there are hot springs.

Buli

The Burgong-chu valley in Nangkhor is an isolated area, accessible on a trekking trail from Zurphe on the Tingtingbi-Gongphu road. The most important site here is **Buli Gonpa**, which was founded by Pema Lingpa following his visit to the valley in 1478. The seat of the once influential chieftain of Buli is located further up the valley and across the river.

Phangkhar and Ngangla counties

There is a rough, motorable track leading south from Gongphu. These low-lying parts of the Mangde-chu valley fall within the **Royal Manas National Park** – a region of extraordinary biodiversity (see also page 259). Mangoes, bananas, bamboo shoots, edible roots and yams all grow naturally here, but access has unfortunately been restricted in recent years on account of the Assamese insurgency movement (see page 247). In the most southerly enclave of **Panbang**, where the Mangde-chu and Drangme-chu have their confluence near the Indian border, there is a cottage industry producing the round, decorative picnic baskets (*bangchung*), which are in great demand throughout the country.

Shingkhar and Bardo counties

The valley of the Chamkhar-chu, which flows through this area from Bumthang to converge with the Mangde-chu south of Gongphu, has long had close associations with the clan chieftains (*dung*) of Bumthang who own land here and move their herds south into Khyeng during the winter months.

⊜ Sleeping

Zhemgang town *p194*
C **District Guesthouse**, T3-741218, is located at the northern end of town – doubles at Nu 900 and singles at Nu 850.
D **Kunzang Zhemgang Hotel**, T3-741105, is located near the *dzong* – doubles at Nu 500 and singles at Nu 400.

⊕ Eating

Zhemgang town *p194*
For Bhutanese and Tibetan cuisine, try Kunga Restaurant & Bar, near the bank, Yangdzom Hotel & Bar, near the police station, or Sonam Lhaden Hotel & Bar, near the police checkpoint.

○ Shopping

Zhemgang town p194
There are a few small general stores
(tsongkhang), selling groceries and sundry
items. Postage **stamps** are available at
Bhutan Post, located near the dzong.

⊖ Transport

Zhemgang town p194
Zhemgang is on the main road between
Trongsar and Gelekphuk, and **buses** will
stop here. **Karma Gayley Travel** have daily
departures from **Thimphu** at 0700, as do
Bhutan Post Express on Tue, Thu and Sat;
and **PD Travel** on Tue, Wed and Fri.

However, most visitors to Zhemgang will
have their own transportation.

● Directory

Zhemgang town p194
Banks Bank of Bhutan, next door to Galay
General Store, Mon-Fri 0900-1300, Sat
0900-1100. **Hospitals and medical
services** Zhemgang Basic Health Unit is
located behind the Bank of Bhutan.
Post including EMS express delivery, are
available at Bhutan Post. Open Mon-Fri
0830-1230, 1330-1630, Sat 0900-1230.
Telecommunications IDD calls can be
made from Bhutan Telecom.

Sarpang district ག་སར་སྤང་

→ Area: 2,288 sq km.

Sarpang district shares a long southern border with India, and provides export outlets
for the cash crops of Tarkarna, Tsirang, Trongsar and Bumthang at the large frontier
towns of Sarpang and Gelekphuk. Several rivers rising in the northern hills of the
district flow through the Duars into Assam.

The summers are hot and humid in Sarpang, and the winters cool and dry. The
monsoon is severe (average rainfall: 1,500-5,000 mm). More than 83% of the land is
covered with teak and other types of broadleaf forest, and the Phibsoo National Park
in the south-west borders the Buxa Tiger Reserve in India. Despite the shortage of
true pastureland in Sarpang, livestock farming is well developed, but crop raising is
more important – about 12% of the land is used for rice, maize and mustard
cultivation. The highest yield of rice is found around Gelekphuk. Cash crops include
cardamom, sugar cane, ginger and various fruits — guavas, pineapples, oranges,
lemons, bananas and mangoes.

There are 14 counties in the district, of which only Doban, Surey and Serzhong lack
a land border with India. Kalikhola, Deorali and Nichula all fall within the valley of the
Punatsang-chu (Manas) in the south-west, just before it flows out of Bhutan. Senge
falls within the Phibsoo National Park, Hile is in the Sarpang-chu valley, Leopani and
Bhur in the Bhur Khola valley, Gelekphuk in the Moa Khola valley, Danabari and Lalai
in the Takjal Khola valley, and Taklai in the south-east, within the valleys of the
Kanamakra Khola and the Kakutang Khola. Most of these rivers and counties have
Nepali names, indicative of the largely Lhotsampa population.

There are two main roads. One runs from Dramphu in Tsirang to Sarpang (60 km)
and the other from Zhemgang to Gelekphuk (137 km). The administrative capital is
located at Sarpang, and a lateral road now runs here from Gelekphuk, 33 km to the
east. The distance from Gelekphuk to Phuntsoling, via India, is 195 km, and to
Samdrub Jongkhar 241 km. ▸▸ For Sleeping, Eating and other listings, see pages 197-198.

Surey, Serzhong and Gelekphuk counties

The road from Zhemgang crosses into Sarpang district at Tomala, and descends through the upper reaches of the Moa Khola river system, passing through a small settlement at Serathang to reach the large frontier town of Gelekphuk.

Gelekphuk town

Heading into town from Zhemgang, a branch road leads west to Sarpang (33 km), and another due south to the Bhutan Gate on the border. The downtown area lies to the east of the border road, along three parallel streets. **North Street** gives access to the Bank of Bhutan, Bhutan National Bank, the Revenue and Customs Office, the post office, Bhutan Telecom, the bus station and the Royal Bhutan Police. **Central Street** is a commercial area, where you will find the Lakshmi Hotel, Kamakhya Hotel, the cinema, Central Book Store and the large

Currently the Indian border at Gelekphuk is not open for foreign travellers or tourists as an official crossing point.

Sunday Market, with photo studios, general stores, clothing stores and Tashi Commercial Corporation along its northern side. **South Street**, nearest to the border, is relatively undeveloped. Two north–south running- streets intersect to form a grid. Among them **West Street** has a number of hotels, including Pyagyel Hotel, Pema Hotel, Sonam Hotel, Druk Hotel, Kuku Hotel, U Me Hotel and Dragon Hotel, as well as Karma Gelek Transport. On **East Street** you will find Pema Restaurant, Tsering Cable TV Network, Tashi Paykheel Hotel, S. Lhamo Bakery, Druk Hair Salon, Gurung Pharmacy, Prasad Hotel, Tinley Buddha Bar and various grocery stores.

There is nothing for the casual visitor in Gelekphuk, although this may change when the problem of Assamese insurgency is resolved and the national parks are reopened.

Taklai county

Part of the **Royal Manas National Park** (see page 195) falls within Taklai county. A motorable trail leads east from Gelekphuk for 25 km to Kanamakra, at the entrance to the park. The valley of the Kanamakra Khola has a number of jungle lodges, but they are closed just now, pending resolution of the Assamese insurgency problem. For a description of the Royal Manas National Park see page 259.

West of Sarpang town

The main road from Sarpang on the Indian border runs through the valley of the Kali Khola to Dramphu in Tsirang county (see page 156). The **Phibsoo National Park** (see page 259) is located in Senge county, to the east of the Punatsang-chu valley. The border town of **Kalikhola** is located west of the Punatsang-chu, and it is an important trading centre, despite the fact that it is not yet connected with the interior by motor road beyond Deorali. When this road is eventually extended into Takarna, it will provide easier access for cross-border trade.

● Sleeping

Gelekphuk town *p197*
D **Tashi Paykheel Hotel**, T6-251143, is located on East Street – doubles at Nu 500 and singles at Nu 300.
E **Dragon Hotel**, T6-251252, is located on

West Street – doubles at Nu 200 and singles at Nu 150.
E **Druk Hotel**, T6-251202, is located on West Street – doubles at Nu 300 and singles at Nu 250.

🍴 Eating

Gelekphuk town *p197*

For Bhutanese and Tibetan cuisine, try **Pema Restaurant**, on the corner of North and East streets, and **S Lhamo Bakery** on East Street. Many of the small hotels on West Street are also restaurants, among them **Sonam Hotel** and **Pema Hotel**. For alcoholic beverages, try **Tinley Buddha Bar** and the **Bhutan Wine Shop**, both on East Street.

🛍 Shopping

Gelekphuk town *p197*

There are many general stores (*tsongkhang*) on Central and East streets, selling groceries and assorted Indian imports. The biggest supermarket is **Tashi Commercial Corporation** at the far end of Central Street. Postage **stamps** are available at **Bhutan Post**, located on North Street.

🚌 Transport

Gelekphuk town *p197*

Buses run from **Thimphu** via Wangdu Phodrang and Trongsar to Gelekphuk. There are 3 services: **Karma Gayley Travel** have daily departures (Nu 128); **Bhutan Post Express** runs on Tue, Thu and Sat (Nu 174); and **PD Travel** on Tue, Wed and Fri (Nu 173). **Bhutan Post Express** also have a service from **Trongsar** to Gelekphuk on Tue, Thu and Sat, and a daily service from **Phuntsoling** via India to Gelekphuk. Buses run from Gelekphuk to **Trongsar** on Sun, Mon and Thu at 0700, and daily to **Phuntsoling** at 0800.

🗂 Directory

Gelekphuk town *p197*

Banks Bank of Bhutan and **Bhutan National Bank** are both located on North Street, Mon-Fri 0900-1300, Sat 0900-1100. **Hospitals and medical services** Try Gurung Pharmacy on East Street. **Post** including EMS express delivery, are available at **Bhutan Post**, on North Street, Mon-Fri 0830-1230, 1330-1630, Sat 0900-1230. **Telecommunications** IDD calls can be made from **Bhutan Telecom** on North Street, and from some of the hotels.

Eastern Bhutan

Introduction

The densely populated region of Eastern Bhutan is separated from Central Bhutan by a high mountain barrier range that extends from the Tibet border in the north almost to the Assamese plains in the south. The Himalayas are lower in this region, and two major rivers cut their way from Tibet into Bhutan, the Kuri-chu from Lhodrak and the Tawang-chu from Tsona (via Arunachal Pradesh). Together with the Kulong-chu that rises in Tashi Yangtse district, they form the mighty Drangme-chu (Nepali: Manas), and their combined waters flow south-west to converge with the Mangde-chu (the main river of Central Bhutan), just north of the Indian border.

There is less forest cover here, probably on account of the age-old practice of slash-and-burn agriculture (*tseri*), and the cultivated land is much more abundant. Spring and autumn are the best months for travel in this region, and in winter the climate is warmer than in the western or central parts of the country.

Some of the most magical sites in Eastern Bhutan are located near the Tibetan border: these include the hidden land of Khenpajong and Guru Padmakara's hermitage at Monka Nering Senge Dzong, while the important Chorten Kora in Tashi Yangtse guards the entrance to Bomdeling. An extended itinerary of about five or six days will provide sufficient access to the main cultural centres of Eastern Bhutan, but the infrastructure is even less developed than in the Central region, the roads more gruelling, many side-valleys are steep and inaccessible, and the accommodation is considerably more spartan. Eastern Bhutan includes the six districts of Mongar, Lhuntse, Tashigang, Tashi Yangtse, Pema Gatshel and Samdrub Jongkhar.

★ Don't miss...

① **Dungkhar** Ancestral home of Bhutan's royal family and famous for high-quality, hand woven brocade dresses (*kushutura*), page 209.

② **Monka Nering Senge Dzong** An isolated hermitage near the Tibetan border, founded by Guru Padmakara and his Tibetan consort Yeshe Tsogyel during the eighth century to cultivate the teachings of Vajrakila, page 210.

③ **Tashigang** Experience the bustling street café culture in the largest mid-mountain town east of Thimphu, page 212.

④ **Sakteng Wildlife Sanctuary** An enclave bordering Arunachal Pradesh, where diverse species of rhododendrons grow and where the abominable snowman is said to lurk, page 214.

⑤ **Pema Gatshel** Said to resemble a lotus flower surrounded by forested hills, where the village houses are raised on stilts and roofed with bamboo matting, page 222.

Background

Since ancient times the trade routes between Tibet and Assam have followed the river valleys through Eastern Bhutan, and this must account in part for the high population density. Most people speak Tsangla and other Sharchokpa languages, which belong to the East Bodish group and are completely unlike Dzongkha, while the inhabitants of Kurto (northern Lhuntse) speak a language related to that of Bumthang. There are also a plethora of tiny ethnic minorities speaking diverse Monpa and Tibeto-Burman dialects. Until the 17th century the region had more affinity with Tawang and the Tsona area of Southern Tibet, and lacked political cohesion. There were many small states ruled by hereditary chieftains, based on a clan system. Mingyur Tenpa, the third regent of Bhutan, was responsible for bringing the whole of Eastern Bhutan under the sway of the newly established Drukpa state. The fortresses (*dzong*) of Lhuntse, Tashi Yangtse, Zhongar and Tashigang were all built by him between 1647 and 1655. However, the Nyingmapa affiliations of Eastern Bhutan are deep-rooted. Teachers of the Pema Lingpa tradition and more recently of the Dudjom Tersar tradition are greatly revered throughout the region.

Mongar district མོན་འདྲ

→ *Area: 1,947 sq km.*

Mongar is the gateway to Eastern Bhutan, bordered by Lhunste in the north, Zhemgang in the west, Tashi Yangtse and Tashigang in the east, and Pema Gathsel in the south. The Drangme-chu forms the eastern boundary, and the Kuri-chu flows south from Lhuntse, swollen by its tributaries – the Shongleri-chu, Yunari-chu and Gongola-chu – which all rise within the district, before converging with the Drangme-chu in the south-west.

The climate is temperate in the north and sub-tropical in the low-lying southern parts, with characteristically hot summers and cold winters (average rainfall: 1,000-2,000 mm). Nearly 89% of the land is covered in broadleaf and mixed conifer forest – more so than in other parts of Eastern Bhutan – but nearly 4% of the land is used for grazing and 10% is cultivated. The main crops are rice, maize, potatoes, wheat and oranges, along with other sub-tropical fruits such as mangoes and bananas. Industries that have developed here include essential oils, distilled from lemon grass, and alcohol production.

There are 11 counties in the district: Saleng, Tsamang Tsakaling and Mongar all in the Kuri-chu river system; Ngatshang, Drametse and Chekhar in the valley of the Sheri-chu (a tributary of the Drangme-chu); Silambi and Gongdu in the Gubaregong-chu valley (another tributary of the Drangme-chu); and Thangrong and Kengkhar on the west bank of the Drangme-chu.

The lateral highway from Jakar to Tashigang passes through Mongar, and a branch road leads north into Lhuntse, following the Kuri-chu upstream. The administrative capital is located at Mongar town, 193 km from Jakar, 76 km from Lhuntse, and 92 km from Tashigang.» For Sleeping, Eating and other listings, see pages 206-207.

Saleng county

After leaving Ura valley in Bumthang (see page 190), the lateral highway passes the entrance to **Thrumshing La National Park**, where there is a small hydroelectric plant, and crosses the Liri Zam Bridge over the Lirgang-chu. It then undulates through spectacular terrain, over Wangthang La, down across the Gezam-chu, and climbs again through conifer and rhododendron forest to reach **Thrumshing La** (3,750 m). The distance from Ura to the pass is 36 km. On a clear day Mount Gangkar Punsum is visible to the north-east, but most days are misty and the pass can be snowbound in winter.

The descent from the pass leads into Mongar district, passing through conifer forest to emerge at the pastoral settlement of **Sengor** (3,000 m) after 20 km. The road maintenance department responsible for clearing landslides and snow from the pass is based here. The inhabitants speak Bumthang-ka, in contrast to those further down in the Kuri-chu valley, who speak Khyeng-ka or Tsangla.

From Sengor, the road plunges down into the misty Shongjeri-chu gorge, winding through an endless series of precarious switchback turns, as the vegetation changes from alpine forest to semi-tropical bamboo. In places the track is dug out of the precipitous cliffs, over which waterfalls cascade. The dramatic 22-km descent to the encampment of **Namling** takes three hours, somewhat disconcertingly passing many stupas which were erected in memory of deceased road workers! From here another near vertical descent follows a ridge for 17 km, down to **Tridangbi**, where the Shongjeri-chu is at last visible in the gorge below. Now it winds through fields of maize and rice terraces to reach the tropical fruit plantations of the valley floor, and follows the north bank of the river downstream to the village of **Lingmithang** (650 m). The houses around here have roofs made of bamboo matting, and the staple crop is maize. There are few amenities in the village: a post office, dairy and pig farms, and a lumbar yard.

On the descent to Limithang, the ruins of **Zhongar Dzong** protrude through a forested mound to the south of the river. A temple had been established here by Mipham Tenpei Nyima, the father of Zhabdrung Ngawang Namgyel during the 16th century. Then, following the advance of the Drukpa forces into the Zhongar area and the submission of the rival chieftains of Ngatshang and Chitshang, Mingyur Tenpa founded Zhongar Dzong on the same strategic hilltop. This massive building was destroyed by fire in 1899, and it was never rebuilt.

From Limithang, the road soon enters the Kuri-chu valley, following the west bank of this river upstream to **Kuri Zampa** (570 m), a prayer-flag strewn Bailey bridge that carries all traffic across into Eastern Bhutan. Near the bridge there is a landmark stupa, containing relics from the destroyed Zhongar Dzong. The Essential Oils Development Project has a factory distilling lemon grass and other herbs here, mostly for export to Germany. The distance from Tridangbi to Kuri Zampa is 29 km and from Sengor 62 km.

Silambi and Gongdu counties

The south-western parts of Mongar district, where the Kuri-chu and Drangme-chu rivers have their confluence, is isolated and as yet unconnected by motorable roads. It is a region where the Khyeng-ka dialect predominates.

Mongar county

Entering Mongar county on the east bank of the river, two roads diverge: south to the new town at **Gyalpozhing** (4 km) and north to the district capital at **Mongar** (25 km). Just south of Gyalpozhing there is a 60MW hydroelectric project that provides power to Mongar. There is a long-term plan to develop Gyalpozhing and construct a 64-km extension road that will follow the east bank of the Kuri-chu down to its confluence with the Drangme-chu in Khengkhar, and thence through Pema Gatshel district to the Indian border.

Heading north for Mongar on the paved highway, the road forks again at the **Gangola** intersection, 13 km from the bridge. Turn left here for **Lhuntse** (see page 207) or right for Mongar. Continuing east for Mongar, the road climbs above the Kuri-chu valley for 12 km, through fields of maize, to reach the exposed hilltop town.

Mongar town

Mongar (1,600 metres) is a small, sleepy town built across the open hillside, and was completely replanned in 1997. Entering the town from Kuri Zampa, a turn-off on the left leads to the football ground, the well-equipped general hospital, the vegetable market, the Pilgrims' Dharamsala and the bus station. If you continue directly into town, you will pass on the left: the Newlee Hotel, Kunga Rinchen Shop, Druk Kunden Guesthouse, Samling Hotel, Zhongar Telephone Booth, O.G. General Store, Rigzin Dorje General Store, Bank of Bhutan, Sangyey General Shop, Kunzang Wangdi General Store, Lazangmo Store, Palden Singye Store, Kunzang Palden Store, Kalzang Photo Studio, Yeshe Chodon General Store, Tashiling Hotel, Sonam Hotel, Lodge & Bar and Nazangla Store. Opposite on the right are: a stupa, the parking lot and the new Bank of Bhutan building.

Now side-roads branch off the main street on both sides – the one on the left leading to the bus station and the one on the right to the police station, the post office and **Mongar Dzong**. Continuing eastwards along the main street, on the left you will pass Singye Shop, Tashipekhil PCO and Dena Restaurant. Then the two roads converge again, and head out of town in the direction of Tashigang, passing an agricultural centre and primary school on the left and a turn-off on the right that leads to Zhongar Lodge and Mongar High School.

Mongar Dzong

The central tower of Mongar Dzong was constructed in the late 19th century, following the destruction of Zhongar Dzong by fire (see above, page 203). The tower was expanded into a *dzong* in 1930, and the present building dates from a period of reconstruction in 1953. As elsewhere, Mongar Dzong combines both administrative and monastic functions – there are about 60 monks in residence. The central tower has three storeys. The chapel on the **ground floor** has murals depicting the assembled deities of Sangye Lingpa's *Lama Gongdu*. The middle floor contains the **Lama Lhakhang**, dedicated to the lineage-holders of the Kagyu school. The large mural to the left depicts Vajradhara and the one to the right Amitayus. On the top floor the **Neten Lhakhang** has murals depicting the Twelve Deeds of Shakyamuni Buddha (left) and the Sixteen Elders (right).

Ngatshang and Chakhar counties

From Mongar you can take a three-day side trip to **Lhuntse Dzong** (see page 207), or drive straight to **Tashigang**. The road from Mongar to Tashigang is relatively easy. A 17- km drive leads gently uphill, past Kilikhar Shedra and through a beautiful orchid and rhododendron forest to **Kori La** pass (2,450 m). It then zigzags down through broadleaf forest to Guru Lhakhang in the former kingdom of **Ngatshang** (1,890 m), and on through fields of maize to **Yadi** (1,480 m), 21 km below the pass. There are very basic roadside restaurant and guesthouse facilities in Yadi. A narrow, unpaved track branches off the highway below Yadi, heading 10 km for **Shershong**. This is the trailhead for the two-day pilgrimage to **Agya Ne**, a sacred power place associated with Guru Padmakara, where there are 100 miraculous letters 'A' (symbolic of the uncreated emptiness underlying all phenomena) engraved in the rocks.

After Yadi, another branch road cuts south-east for Chekhar village, where there is a small hydroelectric plant. The highway then twists and turns through a series of dramatic loops to emerge at **Sherichu** (600 m) where the Sheri-chu flows into the Drangme-chu, and a steel bridge carries traffic in the direction of Tashigang. The distance from Mongar to the bridge is 93 km.

Drametse county

Crossing the bridge over the Drangme-chu, the road follows the hilly pastures on the north bank of this river upstream for 12 km to **Thugdari**, a small village located at the turn-off for Drametse Gonpa, and then continues through **Yayung** to enter Tashigang district (see page 211).

Drametse Gonpa

The largest monastery in Eastern Bhutan is accessible 19 km along a difficult muddy trail, on a hilltop location from which distant Kanglung College can be seen, far to the south. Locally grown potatoes are exported to India. On the approach to the monastery, which is surrounded by a small village, you will pass the post office and Sangye Wangmo Store to the left of the road. After the monastery there are two other stores: Karchung General and the Food Corporation of Bhutan, with a basic health unit and Dramitse High School slightly further on.

Background The monastery was founded in the mid-16th century by Choden Zangmo, a great-granddaughter of the treasure-finder Pema Lingpa. By all accounts, she travelled from Tibet in her youth to practise Buddhism at Petsheling Gonpa in Bumthang under the guidance of Pema Lingpa but constantly found herself being harassed by unwanted suitors on account of her great beauty. Seeking to escape to a peaceful place, without hostility, she asked Pema Lingpa for assistance and he gave her a white conch shell, admonishing her to stay in the sacred place where it would resonate well since that locale would be conducive to Buddhist practice. So Choden Zangmo moved east from Tamzhing, and, as she went, the conch failed to register a pure sound at the hermitage of Agya Ne and at Sershong. However, when she reached the hilltop of Drametse ('heights without hostility'), the shell resonated purely, and so she knew that she should establish a monastery there in that safe location.

Choden Zangmo passed away at Drametse, having entrusted the succession of the monastery which she had founded to her son Tokden Karpo (also known as Yeshe Gyelpo). Sacred relics were retrieved from her funeral pyre and these are preserved at the monastery even now in a reliquary stupa. During her lifetime, Choden Zangmo's brother Kunga Gyeltsen visited Drametse and had a visionary experience of the Zangdok Pelri paradise, on the basis of which he choreographed the popular sacred dance that is now known as the 'drum dance of Drametse' (*drametse ngacham*).

The familial line of spiritual succession at Drametse (known as Drametse Choje) passed through Tokden Karpo to Lama Daza. His son happened to be the governor of Trongsar Tendzin Chogyel. Subsequently many illustrious figures were born at Drametse. They included three successive Zhabdrung Rinpoches – Jigme Drakpa (1791-1830), Jigme Norbu (1831-1861) and Jigme Chogyel (1862-1904) – as well as two of the Tango Tulku incarnations, two of the Gangteng Tulku incarnations, one of the Nyizergang Tulku incarnations, and three district governors. This prestigious heritage is reflected in the far-reaching influence that Drametse has had throughout Eastern Bhutan.

Restoration work was undertaken at Drametse in the late 17th century, following the unification of the Drukpa state, and later in the early 20th century. Since 1992 the monastery has been placed by royal decree under the guidance of Sungtrul XI Kunzang Rinchen Pema Namgyel. Further refurbishments followed, and a gilded spire was added in 1998. More recently, in 2001 an enormous, newly commissioned *thongdrol* appliqué (about 11 m by 9 m), depicting Pema Lingpa, was unveiled and consecrated here. Currently there are about 60 *mantrins* (*gomchen*) and a few monks in residence.

The site The courtyard has impressive flagstones, and the outer vestibule of the three-storey central tower (*utse*) has recently restored murals. Inside, on the ground floor, the **Guru Lhakhang** contains the sacred reliquary stupa of Choden Zangmo. On the middle floor there is a library and the **Tamdrin Lhakhang**, containing images of Hayagriva and the Five Long-Living Sisters (Tsering Chenga), who are the protectors associated with the Everest range. Situated on the top floor, the **Lama Lhakhang** has an image of Shakyamuni Buddha flanked by Zhabdrung Jigme Norbu and Gangteng VII Ugyen Tenpei Nyingje. There are no murals of note in any of these chapels.

Tsakaling county

From the Gangola intersection west of Mongar town (see page 202), the branch road to Lhuntse winds through **Chali** and **Tormazhang**, before descending to the east bank of the Kuri-chu upstream, and continuing through the settlement of **Rewan** to enter Lhuntse district.

⬤ Sleeping

Mongar town *p203*
B **Zhongar Lodge**, T4-641107, the government guesthouse located behind the *dzong*, has 7 rooms in the old building (3 with private WC), and 3 rooms in the new building (2 with wc) – doubles at Nu 1,200 and singles at Nu 1,000. Reservations are made only through the district administration, and priority is given to official guests.
C **Druk Kunden Guesthouse**, T4-641121, located at the west end of town, near the football ground, has 5 rooms – 1 with attached bathroom at Nu 800 and 4 without at Nu 500.
D **Samling Hotel**, T4-641265, F4-641265, adjacent to Druk Kunden Guesthouse, has 8 rooms – those with attached bathroom at Nu 350 and those without at Nu 250.
E **Pilgrims' Dharamsala**, near Dena Restaurant, provides the most basic shared accommodation for pilgrims.
E **Sonam Hotel, Lodge & Bar**, opposite the bus station, has 10 simple rooms at Nu 150.
E **Tashiling Hotel**, T4-641207, opposite the bus station, has 5 simple rooms at Nu 150, catering largely to long-distance public bus passengers who stop overnight in Mongar.

⦿ Eating

Mongar town *p203*
The best restaurant in town, serving Bhutanese and Tibetan cuisine, is **Newlee Hotel**, T4-641240, west of the Druk Kunden Guesthouse. This is the focal point for Mongar's social life. The top 3 hotels also serve wholesome local cuisine. Simpler fare is available at **Dena Restaurant**, east of the bus station.

⦿ Shopping

Mongar town *p203*
There are a few small general stores (*tsongkhang*), selling groceries and sundry items. Postage **stamps** are available at **Bhutan Post**, located on the way to Mongar Dzong.

⦿ Festivals

Drametse county *p205*
The 3-day **Drametse tsechu** is held annually during the 9th month of the lunar calendar at Drametse Gonpa. In 2004 this event is scheduled for 18-21 Nov, and in 2005 for 7-10 Dec.

⊖ Transport

Mongar town *p203*
Mongar is an important hub on the road network linking Jakar, Tashigang and Lhuntse. Many long-distance **buses**, including the Thimphu – Tashigang service, will stop overnight here. **Bhutan Post Express** have a service from **Thimphu** to Mongar on Tue, Thu and Sun, departing at 0730 (Nu 306). The return service operates on the same weekdays at 0600. DDTKT have a service from Mongar to **Tashigang** on Mon, Wed and Fri at 06.30, and **Jamphel Transport** have a daily service to **Lhuntse**, departing at 0700.

ⓘ Directory

Mongar town *p203*
Banks Bank of Bhutan, T4-641123, now relocated to a new street behind the parking area. Open Mon-Fri 0900-1300, Sat 0900-1100. **Hospitals and medical services** Mongar General Hospital, T4-641112, is located uphill from the football ground. **Post** Bhutan Post, open 0830-1230, 1330-1630, Sat 0900-1230. **Telecommunications** IDD calls can be made from **Zhongar Telephone Booth**, near the Samling Hotel.

Lhuntse district ལྷུན་རྩེ → *Area: 2,888 sq km.*

Lhuntse, with easy geographical access to Lhodrak in Tibet, was once an important hub for cross-border trade, but in recent years it has been relatively isolated. The district is bordered by Bumthang in the west, Mongar in the south and Tashi Yangtse in the east. The Kuri-chu flows from Lhodrak in Tibet directly through Lhuntse, and it is joined by feeder rivers rising within the district: the Yarigang-chu, Badzraguru-chu and Kyiling-chu, which flow through the 'hidden land' of Khenpalung, the Khoma-chu which flows from the sacred power place of Senge Dzong to converge with the Kuri-chu near Lhuntse Dzong, and the Nayargang-chu and Wobrag-chu which once gave traders and kings trekking access to Bumthang.

Summers are warm in Lhuntse and the winters are cold (average rainfall: 1,000-1,500 mm). More than 75% of the land is covered by mixed conifer and broadleaf forest, which has not been exploited due to lack of infrastructure. Some 3% of the land is suitable for grazing cattle and yaks, and only 4% is cultivated, along the Kuri-chu valley. The main crops here are chillies, potatoes, lemon grass (used for essential oils) and soya beans. Despite the poor infrastructure, Lhunste is quite densely populated. The inhabitants speak a dialect of Bumthang-ka. The weaving industry is particularly important, and in mountain villages women will spend most of their days at the loom. Many of the best and most expensive hand-made textiles are produced here. The steep terrain is ideally suited for trekking and exploration on foot.

There are eight counties: Kurto (the old name for Lhuntse) in the north-west, Gangzur, where the capital is located, Khoma in the north-east, Menjabi, Minje and Tsenkhar all in the Kuri-chu valley, with Mestho and Jare to the south-west.

A branch road extends northwards from Gangola on the lateral highway into Lhuntse, following the Kuri-chu upstream. The administrative capital is located at Lhuntse Dzong, 76 km from Mongar. ⏩ *For Sleeping, Eating and other Listings see page 210-211.*

Tsenkhar and Jare counties

From **Rewan** (see page 206) the paved road enters Lhuntse district near a large Tibetan-style stupa, which is encircled by 108 miniature stupas. The first settlement is at **Autsho** (920 m), 26 km from the Gangola intersection. Most villages, like **Domkhar**, are located high above the road on the upper slopes of the valley. In places the cliff walls rise precipitously above the road. Heading north, the road then winds uphill to **Gorgan**, overlooking the confluence of the Noyurgang-chu, which flows in from the west.

Minje, Menjabi and Mestho counties

Soon the valley starts to open out, as the road passes below the small hamlets of Yoma, Budur and Kupinyaisa, and then descends through the village of **Minje** to cross the Kuri-chu at a suspension bridge in **Tangmachu** (1,150 m). Tangmachu, 26 km from Autsho, is a cluster of agricultural settlements, with terraces of rice, maize and millet. A 10-km dirt road heads south-west to Tangmachu High School, from where it is possible to trek via **Menjabi** to Ugyen Choling in Bumthang over four days (see page 188).

Tangmachu to Tashi Yangtse trek
Another four-day trek of considerable logistical difficulty leads from Tangmachu via the Dong La pass into Tashi Yangtse.

Day 1 Tangmachu–Minje Climbing east from the suspension bridge at Tangmachu, the trail passes through the small farming hamlet of Chusa, and then rises more steeply through grassy slopes where fragrant herbs abound. Camp overnight at Darchupang Lhakhang (1,830 m), above the village of Minje (16 km, four to five hours' trekking).

Day 2 Minje–Pemi Leaving the settlements behind, the narrow trail proceeds uphill through dense forest to emerge at a meadow clearing and then down once again below the tree-line to Pemi (2,450 m), which is a seasonal nomadic pasture (20 km, six to seven hours' trekking).

Day 3 Pemi–Taupang The overgrown trail undulates through variegated forest across several ridges on its ascent of **Dong La** pass (3,900 m), which marks the division between Lhuntse and Tashi Yangtse districts. The descent through conifer forest negotiates a slippery and rocky trail before climbing again through Lisipang meadow and finally falling through Yesupang meadow to reach the north bank of the Dongdi-chu. Fording the river, the trail worsens as it twists through thick riverside jungle to the campsite at Taupang (2,450 m) (21 km, seven to eight hours' trekking).

Day 4 Taupang–Tashi Yangtse Continuing along the south bank of the Dongdi-chu, the forest trail is humid and muddy. After two hours, it climbs out of the forest to emerge at the small agricultural settlement of Shakshing. From here it follows higher and firmer ground as far as Tonshing village, after which it once again plunges down into the riverside mire. Just before reaching Tashi Yangtse, a cantilever-style footbridge leads across to the north bank, and it is but a short distance over the Kulong-chu to the trailhead (24 km, eight to nine hours' trekking).

Gangzur county

Heading north on the west bank of the Kuri-chu from Tangmachu, the paved road passes through **Murmu** and **Sumpa** hydrology station, and soon, at the confluence of the Khoma-chu, it turns north-east, following the bend of the river, and Lhuntse Dzong appears in the foreground. A footbridge crosses the river here, giving trekking access to Khoma (see page 210). Continuing on the main road, the gorge narrows, as the road climbs into **Gangzur town**. The distance from Tangmachu to Gangzur is 13 km.

is a small town, nestling below the magnificently situated **Lhuntse Dzong** at the head of the valley. Entering the town, the road winds past the District Hospital on the right, and the police station on the left. Opposite the police station are Rinchen Palden Store, Karmala Store, Kunzang Lhamo General Store and Tendzin General Store. The road then bends again, passing on the left Wangda General Store, Lhuntse Liquor Store, Yeshela General Store, Shangrila Restaurant & Bar and a lane that leads to the post office and the Bank of Bhutan. The *dzong* is located at the next bend, and higher still is the District Guesthouse.

Lhundrub Rinchentse Phodrang (Lhuntse) Dzong

This hilltop *dzong* is spectacularly situated on a rocky hilltop known as Linglingthang, with sheer cliffs on all sides. Formerly a monastery had been founded here in 1543 by Kunga Wangpo, a son of Pema Lingpa; and only nine years later in 1552 Ngagi Wangchuk of Ralung established a small residential building. Later in 1654, the Drukpa forces under Mingyur Tenpa entered Lhuntse to intervene in a local internecine feud, and crushed the resistance offered by the chieftains of Kyiling and Phagdung. The residence was subsequently expanded into a large fortress, which Mingyur Tenpa named Lhundrub Rinchentse (contracted to Lhuntse). The whole of Kurto was thereafter administered from Lhuntse Dzong, under the governorship of Lama Druk Phuntsog and his successors. Recent restoration work was undertaken here in the 1960s and 1970s.

A flagstone path leads uphill to the entrance from the parking area. The ground within the fortress is uneven – the administrative courtyard being at a lower level than the central tower and the monastic courtyard. The central tower (*utse*) has three storeys. On the ground floor there is a **Guru Lhakhang**, containing images of Guru Padmakara and his eight manifestations. The murals here depict the Twenty-one Aspects of Tara. On the middle floor the **Gonkhang** is dedicated to the aspect of Mahakala known as Jnananatha, flanked by the Four Guardian Kings. The murals here are faint and hard to identify. On the top floor the **Tsepame Lhakhang** has a central image of Shakyamuni Buddha, flanked by Zhabdrung Ngawang Namgyel on the left and Guru Padmakara on the right. The murals depict the Sixteen Elders (left) and the incarnations of Zhabdrung Rinpoche (Zhabdrung Phunsum Tsokpa, right). In the monastic courtyard, which presently houses more than 100 monks, the main building is on the right. On the **ground floor** it has a chapel dedicated to Mahakarunika, and upstairs an **assembly hall**, containing images of the Buddhas of the Three Times. Opposite on the left side, another building contains the **Mitrukpa Lhakhang**, dedicated to Aksobhya.

Kurto county

A new, 37-km motor road is currently under construction from Lhuntse Dzong to Dungkhar in the far north, where the Badzaguru-chu flows into Kuri-chu. So far it is possible to drive part of the way along this road, as far as Zhamling, and it will still take almost a full day's trek to reach Dungkhar.

Dungkhar

Dungkhar is the ancestral home of the Bhutanese royal family. Since the 16th century, families from Bumthang had settled here on the lucrative Tibetan trade route, among them Kunga Wangpo, a son of Pema Lingpa, from whom the royal family claim descent. This was where Jigme Namgyal, the father of the first king, was born in 1825, and his family protector chapel can still be seen above the village. The area had earlier associations with Guru Padmakara, whose meditation hermitage is situated across the river at **Tergang**, above the confluence of the Badzaguru-chu valley. Pema Lingpa also built a small temple below the village at Goshopang meadow. Nowadays the Dungkhar area is famous for its high-quality hand-woven brocade dresses (*kushutura*), which command high prices in the markets of Thimphu.

The river valleys of the Yangrigong-chu and Badraguru-chu in the north-east of the district (out of bounds for foreigners) comprise much of the sacred 'hidden land' of **Khenpalung.** Renowned for its fragrant artemisia herbs, this region was consecrated by Guru Padmakara as a sacred land conducive to Buddhist meditation, following his eviction of the malign king Khyikhyi Rato (see page 232).

North of Dungkhar, the old trade route follows the Kuri-chu upstream through **Thunbi** on the east bank and **Takpang** on the west bank, heading towards the northern border at **Ngortong Zampa**, a bridge that offers easy access to the Lhodrak region of Tibet. This border crossing is currently closed.

Khoma county

The remote valley of the Khoma-chu is accessible on a trekking route from a footbridge that spans the Kuri-chu south of Lhuntse Dzong. The trail follows the Khoma-chu upstream, reaching **Khoma** village on the north bank after two hours. High across the river from here on the south bank is the village of **Gonpo Karpo**, which like Dungkhar is also well known for its high-quality brocade weaving. A trail follows the Khoma-chu further upstream through **Tshikang** and **Rangmoteng** in its upper reaches, on the approach to Senge Dzong. The trek from the bridge to Senge Dzong takes three days, and special permission is required.

Further north-east, beyond the source of the Khoma-chu, **Phode La** pass (4,965 m) marks the sealed border between Tibet and Bhutan.

Monka Nering Senge Dzong

This is the one of the five foremost meditation sites in the Tibetan Buddhist world associated with Guru Padmakara. The sacred power places associated with his buddha body, speech, mind and attributes are all located inside Tibet, but the fifth, indicative of his buddha activities, is located here at Senge Dzong. This, therefore, is one of the great focal points for pilgrimage for all followers of the Nyingmapa tradition; and its remote location in north-eastern Bhutan means that it is currently the most inaccessible of them all. The hermitage at Senge Dzong was founded by Yeshe Tsogyel, foremost Tibetan consort of Guru Padmakara, and it was where she experientially cultivated the teachings on the meditational deity Vajrakila, who embodies enlightened activity. Many treasure doctrines were also concealed at Senge Dzong during that time.

◉ Sleeping

Gangzur town *p208*
D **District Guesthouse**, T4-545109, located behind the *dzong*, provides the only accommodation in town, with 6 simple rooms. Special permission from the district administration is required if wish to stay here.

◐ Eating

Gangzur town *p208*
Shangrila Restaurant & Bar, T4-545123, situated below the lane leading to the post office, offers basic Tibetan cuisine – steamed

dumplings and noodles, in its ground-floor restaurant.

◯ Shopping

Gangzur town *p208*
There are a few general stores in town. Postage **stamps** are available at **Bhutan Post**, located on a lane below Lhuntse Dzong.

◉ Festivals

Gangzur county *p208*
A 3-day annual *tsechu* ceremony is held at

Lhuntse Dzong during the 10th month of the lunar calendar. In 2004 this is scheduled for 20-22 Dec and in 2006 for 8-10 Jan.

local service between **Mongar** and Lhuntse operated by **Jampal Transport** runs daily in both directions.

⊖ Transport

Gangzur town *p208*
Gangzur is accessible only by motor road from **Mongar**, 76 km to the south. **Buses** leave from **Thimphu** for Lhuntse on Mon and Thu at 0700, operated respectively by **Kurto Chusa Express** (Nu 436) and **Jampal Transport** (Nu 370). The return services from Lhuntse to **Thimphu** are reversed, **Kurto Chusa Express** departing on Thu mornings and **Jampal Transport** on Mon mornings. A

❶ Directory

Gangzur town *p208*
Banks Bank of Bhutan, near the post office, Mon-Fri 0900-1300, Sat 0900-1100.
Hospitals and medical services Lhuntse District Hospital is located at the southern end of town.
Post Postal facilities are available at Bhutan Post, Mon-Fri 0830-1230, 1330-1630, Sat 0900-1230.

Tashigang district

→ *Area: 2,283 sq km.*
Tashigang (Bh. Trashigang) is bordered by Mongar and Pema Gatsel in the west, Tashi Yangtse in the north, Samdrub Jongkhar in the south, the Tsona county of Tibet in the north-east and the Indian state of Arunachal Pradesh in the south-east. The Drangme-chu (also known as the Tawang-chu) flows from Tibet through Tashi Yangtse to converge with the Gamri-chu rising near Sakteng in the east, and their combined waters flow south-west from Tashigang along the Mongar border towards the Indian frontier. In the south-east of the district, the Nyero Ama-chu and the Jamo-chu rise in the central hills of Tashigang and flow into Samdrub Jongkhar.

The climate is warm in summer and cool in winter (average rainfall: 1,000-2,000 mm). About 79% of the terrain is covered with mixed conifer and broadleaf forest. Only 5% of the land is used for grazing, but 14% is cultivated. The main crops are maize, rice, wheat, millet, chillies, garlic, apples and oranges. Tashigang is a district densely populated by Tsangla speakers, and it is an important hub for commercial traffic between Mongar, Lhuntse and Tashi Yangtse and the lucrative Indian markets of Assam. There are no major industries here, but Sherabtse College in Kanglung is the only degree-standard college in the country.

There are 16 counties in the district: Yangnyer on the roads to Mongar and Tashi Yangtse; Samkhar where the capital is located; Shongphu, Bartsham, Bidung, Redri, Phongme and Sakteng in the Gamri-chu valley; Kanglung, Udzorong, Khaling and Lumang on the road to Samdrub Jongkhar; Nanong in the south-west; and Thrimshing, Kangpara and Merak in the remote south-east.

The administrative capital is located at Tashigang, 92 km, from Mongar, 53 km from Tashi Yangtse, and 180 km from Samdrub Jongkhar. ⏵ *For Sleeping, Eating and other listings, see pages 216-217.*

Yangnyer and Samkhar counties

The lateral highway from Mongar to Tashigang crosses the district border after **Yayung**. The road in this stretch is subject to landslides during the rainy season. Tashigang Dzong comes into view, across the river to the south-east, as the road descends to the intersection at Chakzam bridge (710 m). The distance from Yadi to the bridge is 45 km. An immigration checkpoint is located on the north side of the bridge. Once travel permits have been inspected, you may take the west bank road to Tashi Yangtse (see page 217), or cross the Drangme-chu for Tashigang. Another dirt road leads north-west from the bridge towards the hilltop villages of Gangthung and Yangnyer.

Crossing the Drangme-chu, the highway initially follows the river downstream on the east bank, as far as **Chenari**, where there are intensive fruit plantations. Here, it begins to turn and climb through a series of switchback bends to another key intersection. Turn right for Samdrub Jongkhar and Pema Gatshel (see page 221), or left for Tashigang. Taking the latter road, you follow the Drangme-chu upstream into the forested enclave of **Tashigang.** The *dzong* occupies a high spur above the confluence of the Kulong-chu and Gamri-chu, upstream from Chakzam Bridge. The distance from Chakzam to Tashigang is only 9 km.

Tashigang

Tashigang (1,150 m), nestling in the forested slopes and valley floor of the Mithidang-chu, is the largest and busiest town in Eastern Bhutan, and it is second only to Thimphu in the mid-mountain belt of the country. The town, traditionally known as Wengkhar, has an attractive ambience, with its painted houses amid flowering bougainvilleas, its tiny shops, the 'square' and its cafés, which hum with activity at the end of the day. Tropical fruits and crops thrive around here. Apples are pressed for cider and brandy production, and the local *endi* silk is spun from silkworms bred on castor oil plants.

Orientation

Entering the town on the main road, you will pass Sherab Dorje General Store and Kilengang Wangmo Store on the right, with Deepak Hair Salon and a shoe repair stall on the left. A large stupa now appears on the right, followed by the Bank of Bhutan, and a bridge that carries traffic into the commercial heart of the town. A side-road veers sharply uphill on the left, before the bridge, leading to the *dzong*. Along here you will find on the right Tendzin Restaurant & Bar, Jangchub Bar, Drubthob Sherab Store, Drubthob Restaurant, Cheki Restaurant & Bar, T. Chodzom Store, Gyeltsen Bar, T. Phuntsog Store, Sonam Wangdi Store, Phuntsog Wangdu Store, Ugyen Wangchuk Store and the Food Corporation of Bhutan. Opposite on the left are: Tendzin General Store, Wangdi Shop, Fremo Store, Gaden Restaurant, Chodron Tsering Store and Dekyi Yangdzom General Store. **Tashigang Dzong** is located at the top end of this road.

Returning downhill and crossing the bridge, you will pass on the right Sonam Yangdzom Restaurant, K.C.S. Store, a public call office and the Karmapa Restaurant, after which the road opens out into a square, with a large prayer wheel at its centre. This is the focal point of town life – many businesses and offices are located around the square. Starting from the Karmapa Restaurant on the corner, these include: Sonam Restaurant, Bhutan National Bank, Sangye Hotel, Karma Chodron Bar, Seldron Restaurant, Druk Deothjung Hotel, Pema Bakery, Army Welfare Project, Revenue & Customs Offices, Phunsum Restaurant, Tsering Dorje Store, Kota Store, RICB and Sangye Bumo Store. After the square, a side-road on the left branches uphill for the bus station. Along here you will find Bhutan Post, Karma Restaurant, Tsering Sonam Watch Repairs and the vegetable market.

Continuing along the main street, on the right you will pass Ugyen Hotel & Bar, a public call office, T. Yangkhyil Store, an electronics store, Tashi Yangdzom Shop, Karchung Drukpa Store, Wangdi Store and Kunphen Pharmacy. Opposite on the left you will pass Bhutan Hair Salon, another public call office, and an unpaved side-road that leads out of town to Rangjung. After the next bend, you will find the Bhutan Post and Tashigang High School on the right, with the Royal Guesthouse, District Hospital and Kelling Lodge accessible on the left.

Tashigang Dzong

The impregnable Tashigang Dzong, which stands on a spur overlooking the Gamri-chu river 400 m below, was built at Wengkhar in 1659 by Pekar Chophel and Damcho Rabgye, at the behest of Mingyur Tenpa, following the submission of the feuding petty states that held sway in the Gamri valley prior to the arrival of the Drukpa forces. In earlier centuries there had been a castle on this hilltop promontory, founded by the chieftain Serdung in the 12th century. Then, following the submission of the chieftain Tsewang to the Drukpa forces under Lama Nam-se, all 10 counties of Tashigang were brought within the fold of the new Bhutanese state, and administered from this newly constructed *dzong*. Not long after its construction, the *dzong* was expanded by Tendzin Rabgye, the fourth regent, in the 1680s. Damage caused by fire was repaired at the start of the 20th century, and the most recent restoration work was undertaken in 1950.

Unusually, at Tashigang Dzong there is a single courtyard, shared by the administrative and monastic bodies. Part of an old Tangtong Gyelpo iron-chain bridge can be seen hanging on a wall. Among the most important temples are the **Lama Lhakhang**, dedicated to the eight great Indian teachers of Guru Padmakara, the **Guru Lhakhang**, dedicated to Guru Padmakara and his eight manifestations, and the **Tsokzhing Lhakhang**, dedicated to the great lineage-holders of the Kagyu and Nyingma traditions. Within the central tower, the **Tsechu Lhakhang** contains ritual masks and appliqué *tangkhas* that are in use during the *tsechu* festival, and the **Gonkhang** has a central image of the protector Mahakala in the form Jnananatha.

East along the Gamri-chu valley

A paved motor road from Tashigang follows the Gamri-chu upstream on its south bank, as far as Rangjung in Shongphu county. From here it continues as an unpaved dirt road through **Radi** and Phongme. Eventually the road will be extended as far as **Sakteng** in the extreme east. **Ngawang Travels** operates a daily open-air truck service from Tashigang, also offering some access to Bartsham and Bidung on the north bank.

From Tashigang the road winds its way down to the south bank of the Gamri-chu to a bridge (820 m), where it forks – a rough side-road heading across the river to **Bartsham Gonpa** (19 km), and the paved road continuing on the south bank to Rangjung (17 km). Taking the latter, you will pass through **Lungten Zampa**, a footbridge leading across the river to Bidung, before climbing through agricultural land to Rangjung village.

Rangjung

Rangjung (1,120 m) is a surprisingly large township, with an important monastery. Entering the town from Tashigang, you reach a junction, with Rangjung High School on the left and a hydroelectric power plant on the right. Head left into town or right on the unpaved road to Phongme (see below).

On the way into town, you will pass on the left Wangdi General Store, Yeshe General Store, Jampal Lhamo Restaurant & Shop, Thinley General Shop, Yudron Bar & Restaurant, Thubten General Store and Jigme General Store. Opposite on the right are Yeshe Zangmo General Store, Ugyen Wangchuk Store, the Food Corporation of Bhutan, T. Dorje Store, Dakpa Restaurant, Karma Store and Pema Dura Shop. Now you will reach the large, elaborate stupa at the town centre, which has its mantras inscribed in *Ranjana* (medieval Sanskrit) script. Beyond the stupa, on the left you will pass Bhutan Post, Jadur Wangdi General Store, Rigdzin Chophel Bar and Yeshe Jigme General Store, while on the right are Ngawang Dorje Mani Liquor Store, Jadur Wangdi Bar, Kunzang Tsedrub General Store and Karma General Store. At the far end of the street, the road forks, uphill on the left to Rangjung Osel Choling and right for the primary school.

Rangjung Osel Choling was built in 1989 by Garab Rinpoche, a son of Dungse Rinpoche Tinley Norbu and grandson of the late Dudjom Rinpoche. The monastery maintains the tradition of the Dudjom Tersar lineage, which has great popularity throughout the border areas of Eastern Bhutan, including Sakteng and Merak. The main temple is a single-storey building, with central images of Guru Padmakara, flanked by Shantaraksita and King Trisong Detsen. The murals, which are of high quality, depict the eight great Indian teachers of Guru Padmakara. Currently there are 105 young monks in residence.

Rangjung to Phongme

From Rangjung, the road, now unpaved, climbs steadily for 8 km to **Radi**, a small roadside settlement which has a post office, a primary school and a single store, but no restaurant. Downhill from here, accessible on a footpath, is the village of **Tsangkhar**, where the inhabitants have established a cottage industry for raw silk garments. After Radi, the road becomes rougher as it continues climbing through the tree-line, passing the nunnery at **Thekchok Kunzang Chorten**, and coming to an end at the village of Phongme (1,840 m). Here there is a small general store and a hilltop temple, **Phongme Lhakhang**, which contains a central image of Mahakarunika in the ground-floor chapel, and images of Shakyamuni, Guru Padmakara and Zhabdrung Ngawang Namgyel upstairs. The distance from Rangjung to Phongme is 18 km.

Sakteng county

From Phongme there is a three-day trekking route through the upper reaches of the Gamri-chu to Sakteng (special permission required). Sakteng is a high-altitude valley, inhabited by yak and sheep pastoralists who wear a distinctive costume, made of yak-hair and sheepskin. The tight-fitting yak-hair caps worn by the men are particularly distinctive. The people of Sakteng, who speak a Drokpa dialect, similar to Tibetan, are particularly devoted to the late Dudjom Rinpoche and his cycle of *terma* teachings.

East of Sakteng, the frontier passes of **Nyingzang La** and **Ngonkha La** lead directly to **Tawang** (disputed territory, now in Arunachal Pradesh).

Merak and Kangpara counties

South of Sakteng, the nomadic enclave of Merak is even more isolated. Here, the Nyera Ama-chu and Jomo-chu rise on the southern slopes of Mount Jomo Gangkhar and flow south into Samdrub Jongkhar. The inhabitants of Merak are similar to those of Sakteng in their language, dress, lifestyle and spiritual affiliations. Kangpara is located in the valley of the Nyera Ama-chu, downstream from Merak, and also relatively isolated.

Kanglung county

The 180-km southern highway from Tashigang to Samdrub Jongkhar was built in 1963-1965, and it is now a paved road. The entire journey takes about six hours, following ridges rather than valleys most of the way. Starting from the intersection 3 km south of Tashigang (see page 211), the road cuts south, passing through **Pam**, a small village that gives access to nearby **Rangzhikhar Gonpa**. From here the road climbs gently to the village of Rongthung, and then along a ridge to **Kanglung** (1,870 m).

 The thickly forested Sakteng Wildlife Sanctuary (page 259) is proclaimed as the world's only protected reserve for the abominable snowman (Tib/ Bh. migu, Nep. yeti)!

Sherabtse College

Kanglung is the location of **Sherabtse College**, the only degree-standard institution in Bhutan, which was founded by a Darjiling-based Jesuit, the late Father William Mackey in 1964. Father Mac, as he was known throughout the Eastern Himalayan world, was a highly respected individual with eclectic interests in Tibetan and Bhutanese Buddhism. Originally conceived as a junior high school, Kanglung has been functioning as a university campus since 1978 – the local **Zangdok Pelri Lhakhang** dates from that same year, and the site is extensive, housing over 300 students. A strict ban on alcohol and tobacco is enforced at Kanglung. For an amusing and highly readable insight into student life here, see *Beyond the Sky and the Earth*, which recounts the experiences of a Canadian expatriate teacher, Jamie Zeppa. The distance from Tashigang to Kanglung is 22 km.

South from Kanglung

From Kanglung the road continues to climb through maize and potato fields, to **Yonphu Gonpa**, in the vicinity of which there is a military encampment and a disused military airstrip. West from here at **Udzarong**, where the Wengli Bridge spans the Drangme-chu, there is an important battlefield, where in the 17th century the Drukpa forces commanded by Lama Nam-se accepted the surrender of the various independent chieftains of Tashigang. Above Yonphu Gonpa the road crosses **Yonphu La** pass (2,190 m), and follows a series of ridges with picturesque views of the surrounding villages, through to Khaling. The distance from Kanglung to Khaling is 32 km.

Khaling

Khaling (2,100 m) is a broad valley, near the source of the Jeri-chu, and a one-time centre of fierce resistance to the Drukpa assimilation of Eastern Bhutan. Below the main street, where there are small general stores and simple roadside restaurants, there is the National School for the Disabled, where, among other activities, blind people are trained in a Dzongkha version of Braille. About 3 km after Khaling the road reaches the National Handloom Development Project, which is managed by the National Women' Association of Bhutan. Here the village weavers of Khaling make lengths of hand-spun cotton cloth in diverse designs, working to order. Some pieces are available for sale on site but most will be sold in the markets of Thimphu.

Lumang county and further south

After Khaling, the road climbs into uninhabited terrain, where wild rhododendrons grow, and soon reaches its highest point (2,430 m) before descending to **Wamrong** in Lumang county. At this point an unpaved side-road branches off, heading south-east for Thrimshing.

Wamrong (2,130 m) is an important stopping point for public buses running between Tashigang and Samdrub Jongkhar. The distance from Khaling to Wamrong is 27 km. At the southern end of town, there is an immigration checkpost where all travel documents will be inspected. The road then descends through the Norewegian-funded Riserbu Hospital, and follows the ridges downhill for 20 km to **Tselingkhor**, where it forks: left for Pema Gatshel (29 km) and right for Samdrub Jongkhar (73 km).

⊜ Sleeping

Tashigang *p212*

C **Kelling Lodge**, T4-521145, F4-521300, located above the District Hospital at some distance from the town centre, offers the best accommodation, but this is a government guesthouse and special permission must be sought by those wishing to stay here. It has 10 rooms – doubles at Nu 1,200 and singles at Nu 1,000.

D **Druk Deothjung Hotel**, T4-521214, F4-521269, located in the town square, has 13 rooms (attached toilets flushed with geysers), doubles at Nu 1,000 and singles at Nu 800.

E **Sangye Hotel**, T4-521226, also in the square, has 9 very basic rooms – at Nu 150 – catering mostly for domestic travellers.

E **Ugyen Hotel**, T4-521140, opposite the lane that leads to the bus station, has 15 simple rooms – doubles at Nu 150 and singles at Nu 100.

Rangjung *p213*

Rangjung Lodge, T4-561146, adjacent to the monastery, has six good and well maintained rooms.

❼ Eating

Tashigang *p212*

The best restaurants in Tashigang are all outside the hotels, but the fare consists of simple Bhutanese and Tibetan dishes (price range Nu 30-40). Among the best of these are in and around the town square: **Karmapa Restaurant**, on the corner; **Phunsum Restaurant**, T4-521137, once a popular haunt of Canadian expatriates; **Sonam Yangdzom Restaurant**, near the bridge; and **Seldron Restaurant**, T4-521140, near the Bhutan National Bank. On the approach road to the *dzong* there are 3 others: **Tendzin Restaurant & Bar**, **Drubthob Hotel** and **Gaden Hotel**. **Pema Bakery**, T4-521196, next door to Druk Doethjung Hotel, sells bread rolls and cakes.

Kanglung *p214*

Outside the gates of Sherabtse College, **Phala's Restaurant**, T4-535117, is a favourite with the college students, and there is also an Indian snack bar.

South from Kanglung *p215*

Wamrong has several small restaurants, including the **Yeshe Dorje Restaurant**, T4-571119, catering to itinerant travellers.

⊙ Entertainment

Tashigang *p212*

The town has many small bars with open-air seating. Some restaurants, including the **Phunsum**, **Tendzin** and **Karmapa** also have lively bars. Others include **Jangchub Bar** and **Gyeltsen Bar**, on the road to the *dzong*, and **Karma Chodron Bar**, located on the square.

⊛ Festivals

Tashigang *p212*

The 3-day *tsechu* festival is held at **Tashigang Dzong** during the 9th month of the lunar calendar. In 2004 this will correspond to 19-22 Nov, and in 2005 to 8-11 Dec.

⊙ Shopping

Tashigang *p212*

There are many general stores (*tsongkhang*) in the downtown area, selling groceries, electronic goods, stationery and sundry items. Some books and newspapers can also be purchased at **Kunphen Pharmacy**. Postage **stamps** are available at **Bhutan Post**, next to the bus station, and at another outlet near Tashigang High School.

⊝ Transport

Tashigang *p212*

Tashigang is connected by public **bus** service with Thimphu and other district capitals of Eastern Bhutan. **Sherab Travels** and **Dophu Travels** have departures from **Thimphu** for Tashigang on Tue and Wed respectively at 0700 (minibus: Nu 455), returning to Thimphu on Thu and Sat, respectively at 0600. **Phunsum Travels** have a larger bus, which makes the same journey to Thimphu on Mon. **Bhutan Post Express** operates a daily service from Tashigang to **Samdrub Jongkhar**, departing at 0730.

DTDK Transport operates a local service between Tashigang and **Mongar** on Mon, Wed and Fri, departing Mongar at 0700 and departing Tashigang at 1300. **Ngawang Travels** operate a public truck service to **Tashi Yangtse** on Wed and Sat, departing at 0800 and returning in the afternoon. They also have a daily truck service to **Radi**, outbound at 0730 and inbound at 1400; and a more limited service to **Phongme** on Wed, Fri and Sun at the same times. **Ngawang Travels** also operates a public bus service between Tashigang and **Womrong**, on Tue, Thu, Sat and Sun, departing Tashigang at 0700, and returning In the afternoon.

⊙ Directory

Tashigang *p212*
Banks Bank of Bhutan, T4-521294, located between the stupa and the bridge, Mon-Fri 0900-1300, Sat 0900-1100. **Bhutan National Bank**, T4-521129, on the square, has the same opening hours. **Hospitals and medical services** Tashigang District Hospital is located near Kelling Lodge on the outskirts of town. Indian-made medications can be purchased at **Kunphen Pharmacy**, near the Royal Guest House. **Post** Bhutan Post, Mon-Fri 0830-1230, 1330-1630, Sat 0900-1230. **Telecommunications** IDD and STD calls can be made from the public call offices on the main street.

Tashi Yangtse district
བཀྲ་ཤིས་གཡང་རྩེ → *Area: 1,438 sq km.*

Tashi Yangtse, in the north-east of Bhutan, is bordered by Tibet in the north and east, by Lhuntse in the west, and by Mongar and Tashigang in the south. The Kulong-chu flows south from its source just below the Tibetan border, through Tashi Yangtse to converge with the Tawang-chu at Doksum, forming the Drangme-chu, which in turn converges with the Gamri-chu at Chakzam. On its southerly course, the waters of the Kulong-chu are swollen by smaller feeder rivers: the Rongmala-chu and Wobmunang-chu in the north-east, and the Dongdi-chu in the west. In the extreme north-east of the district Me La pass leads into the Tsona county of Tibet.

The climate is variable here. At lower elevations the summers can be hot, while the winters are cold, particularly above 3,000 m (average rainfall: 1,000-1,500 mm). About 77% of the land is covered with mixed conifer and broadleaf forest, only 3% is used for grazing, and a meagre 8% is cultivated. The main crops are maize, millet, rice, potatoes, beans, chillies, walnuts and oranges. Dairy produce and lemon grass distillation also contribute to the local economy. Tashi Yangtse lies on the old trade routes with Tsona in Southern Tibet, and Tawang, now in the Indian state of Arunachal Pradesh.

There are eight counties in the district: Jamkhar, Tongmijangsa and Ramjar in the lower reaches of the Kulong-chu; Khamdang, Yangtse and Bumdeling in the middle and upper reaches; and Totsho and Yalang in the Tawang-chu valley to the east. The administrative capital is located at Tashi Yangtse Dzong, 53 km from Tashigang. The road network within the district is largely undeveloped, so hiking footpaths are still widely used. ▸▸ *For Sleeping, Eating and other listings, see pages 221.*

Jamkhar and Ramjar counties

The road to Tashi Yangtse diverges from the Mongar–Tashigang road at **Chakzam** Bridge (see page 212) and follows a sparsely forested ridge above the west bank of the Drangme-chu, reaching Gom Kora in about 30 minutes.

Stupas

The stupa (Tib. *chorten*) is a receptacle of offerings, symbolising the buddha-mind and emptiness (*shunyata*) – which is the 'actual reality' (*dharmata*) of all phenomenal appearances. When Shakyamuni Buddha passed away, poignantly offering his disciples a final instruction on the impermanence of conditioned phenomena, the funerary relics were interred in eight stupas, symbolic of that underlying reality, and distributed among the princes of the eight kingdoms which were his devotees: Kushinagara, Magadha, Vaishali, Kapilavastu, Calakalpa, Ramagrama, Visnudvipa and Papa. Later, the practice of erecting such stupas as repositories of offerings at crossroads and geomantic sites became popular in ancient India, particularly among some of the Mahasanghika schools. Emperor Ashoka then is credited with the multiplication of the original buddha-relics, which he reputedly inserted within 84,000 stupas constructed throughout the far-flung reaches of his Mauryan Empire and adjacent kingdoms. Some of these are said to survive at the present day, at Patan in Nepal and elsewhere.

The original stupas appear to have had a central axis, with a square base, and a hemispherical dome forming a bulbous container where the relics would be interred. Books and sacred artefacts would also be inserted. The stupas of Sanchi and Sarnath in Northern India are fine examples. As a ubiquitous Buddhism monument, the stupa has taken on a diversity of forms throughout the Buddhist world, in South-east Asia, China, Japan and Inner Asia. The Nepalese-style of stupa construction, seen at Svayambhu and Bodhnath, is similar to the classical Indian model, with a large dome, surmounted by a *harmika* tower,13-stepped spire and finial. The four sides of the *harmika* are painted with the all-seeing eyes of the buddhas, and the number one (in Sanskrit), which symbolises the uniqueness of

Gom Kora

Gom Kora lies to the right (east) of the road, 13 km from Chakzam. The temple, which was built by Mingyur Tenpa in the 17th century, has two storeys. The ground floor is a simple store-room, while the chapel upstairs contains a central image of Bhaisajyaguru, the buddha of medicine, flanked on the left by Mahakarunika and on the right by Guru Padmakara. The murals, which may well be original, depict the eight meditational deities of the Nyingma tradition (Kabgye Lhatsok). Sacred relics, like the hoof of the precious Guru's horse and a dragon's egg, are kept on the altar. The temple is situated above a large black rock with a meditation cave (*gompuk*) underneath. When in the eighth century Guru Padmakara meditated in the cave, he was startled by the appearance of a demonic cobra rising from the river, which caused him to leave an impression of his hat in the cave roof. Undeterred, he manifested as a Garuda and persuaded the malign being to leave his meditation undisturbed, sealing this agreement with the impressions of his thumb, which can still be seen embedded in the solid rock. Since then pilgrims have revered this site as a sacred power place, and they have continued to circumambulate (*korwa*) the meditation cave. The name Gom Kora is a contraction, meaning the 'place where the meditation cave is circumambulated'. The pathway around the cave includes a narrow, twisting passageway through which pilgrims crawl and wriggle to test their negative past actions.

buddhahood. Later stupas of Tibetan design have five characteristic parts: a square or rectangular base, a bulbous dome, an oblong *harmika*, a tiered conical spire, and a bindu-shaped finial, respectively symbolising the five elements: earth, water, fire, air and space. Examples of both types can be seen in Bhutan: the Nepalese style at Chendebji in Trongsar district, and Chorten Kora in Tashi Yangtse, and the Tibetan type at the Memorial Chorten in Thimphu.

Sometimes a series of eight stupas will be constructed in a straight alignment. Each of the eight will have its own distinctive design. Together they form a set, indicative of the eight principal deeds of Shakyamuni Buddha: his birth, victory over cyclic existence, enlightenment, teaching, descent from Tusita, resolution of schism, performance of miracles, and final nirvana. Such sets can be seen in Paro, Thimphu and elsewhere in Bhutan.

In areas of southern and south-east Tibet, as well as in Bhutan, there is also a rustic style of stupa construction, taking the form of a simplified rectangular structure, surmounted by a red potentilla architrave, *harmika* tower and spire. Other stupas function as gateways (such as the Bhutanese-built Chorten Kangnyi at Mount Kailash and the Dago Kani in Lhasa). Some even contain multiple chapels within them (*tashigomang*) – such as the Kumbum at Gyantse in western Tibet and the Memorial Chorten in Thimphu.

The original functionality of the stupa was never forgotten, and the custom of cremating important lamas in a temporary funerary stupa (*purdung*), or of interring their embalmed bodies within a reliquary stupa (*dungten*) or 'golden reliquary stupa' (*serdung*) is still widely practised. Examples in Bhutan include the reliquary stupa of Zhabdrung Ngawang Namgyel at Punakha and the reliquary stupa of the late Nyoshul Khen Rinpoche in Thimphu.

Khamdang county

Just 2 km after Gom Kora the road passes through **Doksum,** where the Kulong-chu and Tawang-chu converge to form the Drangme-chu. An old trade route cuts north-east, offering access on foot to Yalang, Jangputse, Khyinyel and other villages in the Tawang-chu valley, near the Indian border. These villages are all within Totsho and Yalang counties. Doksum also provides trekking access to **Tongmijangsa** in the west.

Doksum and around

Doksum (860 m) is a one-street town with several stores serving the surrounding village communities. The women of Doksum are known for their weaving skills. Entering the town from the main road, you will pass on the right Tsering Chodron Restaurant, Ugyen Dorje Store and Yeshe Tsering Store, while on the left are the Phurba Hotel, Shentimo Store, Sonam Zangmo Shop, Kerosene Oil Store, Ugyen Dorje General Store, Dorje Wangdi Store, Kunzang Zangmo Shop, Tendzin Store, Sonam Dorje Shop, the post office and the basic health unit. About 100 m behind the village there are the remnants of a disused iron-chain bridge, attributed to Tangtong Gyelpo. At Doksum the road crosses to the east bank of the Kulong-chu and climbs high above the river, following its course upstream through the rice fields. After 6 km, a paved side-road branches right, leading uphill to **Rangthang Aung** (2,100 m), a small village with a junior high school. Above the village are the ruins of **Tsenkharla Dzong**, reputedly built by the exiled Tibetan Prince Tsangma during the ninth century (see page 233).

Yangtse county

The agricultural settlements of the Kulong-chu valley are soon left behind as the road continues northwards through a narrow, verdant gorge towards **Dongtir**. Here, the original fortress of Tashi Yangtse overlooks the confluence of the Dongdi-chu with the Kulong-chu, commanding an ancient trade route between Tashigang and Lhuntse. There is a difficult four-day trekking route from Dongtir to Tangmachu in Lhuntse (see page 189). The distance from Doksum to Tashi Yangtse along the road is 28 km.

Tashi Yangtse Dzong

The old Tashi Yangtse Dzong (1,850 m) was founded in 1656 following the Drukpa conquest of the area, on the site of an earlier residence of Pema Lingpa, and renovated as recently as 1976. The building still has the appearance of a large country house rather than a fortress, and it is approached across the river by way of an old drawbridge covered with bamboo mats.

Tashi Yangtse town

Just 3 km north of the old *dzong* the gorge widens, and the great white stupa of Chorten Kora comes into view, with the new Tashi Yangtse Dzong and the small district capital in the background. Entering the small town from the south, you will pass **Chorten Kora** on the right by the riverside, followed by a small shop and a Bhutanese-style stupa. After the bus station and Tendzin Gyatso Store on the left, the road comes to an abrupt end at the offices of the Bumdeling Wild Life Sanctuary. A winding, paved side-road leads uphill from here on the far bank of the river. Along here you will pass Sonam Chodron Lodge, Shop & Bar on the left. The road then forks at the Bhutanese stupa. Turn right for Pema Gyeltsen General Store, a lane leading down to Chorten Kora, Kunzang Lhamo General Store, a liquor store, Sangye Norbu Store and the District Hospital; or turn left and head uphill to the post office, Yangtse High School, the Forest Ranger's Office, the police station, the new **Tashi Yangtse Dzong** and the District Guesthouse.

Chorten Kora

The enormous stupa of Chorten Kora with its distinctive white-washed dome is located at a geomantic focal point, marking the entrance to Bumdeling. According to legend, Guru Padmakara subdued the malign and negative forces of Bumdeling and made a prophetic declaration to the effect that a large stupa should be constructed at this gateway in the future. Accordingly, in 1740, a local lama named Ngawang Lodro travelled to Nepal and carved a small replica of the Jarung Khashor Stupa at Boudnath inside a radish. This model was used to construct a smaller stupa, which the local inhabitants could then venerate, without having to make the arduous journey to Nepal. The stupa was consecrated in 1782 by the 13th Je Khenpo Yonten Thaye, and renovated by the second king of Bhutan in the 1940s. Next to the stupa is a temple dedicated to Guru Padmakara. The new *dzong* above Chorten Kora was constructed only in 1997.

Bumdeling county

A three-hour trek from Chorten Kora through the Kulung-chu valley leads to Bumdeling, a winter breeding ground for the black-necked crane, and somewhat smaller than the Phobjika sanctuary (see page 152). There are small monasteries, like Rigsum Gonpa, and riverside settlements at Torphel and Todrang, below the confluence of the Rongmala-chu. In the extreme north-east of the district the Me La pass leads through the **Rongmala-chu valley** into the Tsona region of Southern Tibet (presently closed).

Sleeping

Tashi Yangtse town *p220*
Camping is still the best option here.
D District Guesthouse, T4-781148, located behind the police station, has the best accommodation – doubles at Nu 500 and singles at Nu 300.
E Sonam Chodron Lodge, T4-781152, has 6 very basic rooms – doubles at Nu 200 and singles at Nu 150.

Eating

Tashi Yangtse town *p220*
The only restaurant in town is at the **Sonam Chodron Lodge**, serving simple Bhutanese and Tibetan dishes.

Festivals

Gom Kora *p217*
The *tsechu* festival at Gom Kora is held each year during the 1st month of the lunar calendar. In 2005 this event is scheduled for 18-20 Mar. A large painted *thongdrol* scroll is displayed in public at that time. The precious old *thongdrol* and its new replacement are stored in the temple. During the festival the main activities are centred on the grotto, which pilgrims constantly circumambulate, day and night.

Tashi Yangtse town *p220*
Two important festivals are held at Chorten Kora during the 1st month of the lunar calendar. The first is an occasion for people across the border in Tawang to perform circumambulation (*kora*) of the stupa (*chorten*) in memory of a small girl from Tawang who entered the stupa during its construction, never to reappear. The second, which takes place two weeks later, is important for the inhabitants of Eastern Bhutan. In 2005 these events are scheduled for 23 Feb and 10 Mar.

Shopping

Tashi Yangtse town *p220*
Tashi Yangtse has a branch of the **National Institute for Arts & Crafts**, T4-781141, F4-781149, which since its inception in 1997 has offered a 6-year intensive vocational course in all the 13 traditional arts and crafts (see page 263). The institute has a small shop, but many other stores in town also sell traditional crafts. Large wooden bowls made from avocado tree gnarls and smaller drinking bowls made of maple tree gnarl are highly prized (Nu 700-Nu 8,000 or more).

Transport

Tashi Yangtse town *p220*
Tashi Yangtse is connected by public **bus** with Thimphu and Tashigang. **Chophel Phuntsog Dokhal Travels** operate a service from **Thimphu** on Mon at 0730 (Nu 420), returning to Thimphu on Thu at 0730. **Samphel Transport** have a similar service, inbound from Thimphu to Tashi Yangtse on Fri at 0700 and outbound on Mon at 0700. **Ngawang Travels** operate a public truck service between Tashi Yangtse and **Tashigang** on Wed and Sat, departing from Tashigang at 0800 and returning in the afternoon.

Pema Gatshel district
པད་དགའ་ཚལ → *Area: 518 sq km.*

Pema Gatshel is the smallest district in Bhutan, bordered by Mongar in the north and west, Tashigang in the east, and Samdrub Jongkhar in the south. The Drangme-chu forms a natural boundary with Mongar, and the only major rivers within the district are the Uri-chu, which rises south of Pema Gatshel Dzong, and the Jeri-chu. Both rivers empty into the Drangme-chu in the north.

Summers can be hot in Pema Gatshel, and the winters are cool and dry (average rainfall: 1,500-3,000 mm). About 54% of the terrain is covered with broadleaf forest, there are no grazing pastures and no land over 3,000 m, but agriculture is practised intensively – as much as 45% of the land is cultivated. The main crops are maize, millet, buckwheat, potatoes, green vegetables and oranges. The few dairy farms here are all located on land where traditional slash-and-burn methods have long been used. Apart from agriculture, the main industry in Pema Gatshel is gypsum mining.

There are seven counties in the district: Zobe and Shumar on the motor road, Yurung, Chimung and Dungmin on the south bank of the Drangme-chu, with Chongshing and Khar further south. The administrative capital is located at Pema Gatshel Dzong, 130 km from Tashigang and 102 km from Samdrub Jongkhar. ▶ For Sleeping, Eating and other listings, see page 223.

Zobe and Shumar counties

From the turn-off at **Tshelingkhor** (see page 215), a paved side-road winds westwards to Pema Gatshel Dzong, the district capital, located in the hills above the upper reaches of the Uri-chu. Many of the village houses in this region are raised on stilts and roofed with bamboo matting — an architectural feature found throughout north-east India and South-east Asia, areas exposed to the full brunt of the monsoon. Prior to 1981 Pema Gatshel was known by the traditional name Khedung, and affiliated to Mongar district. When the late Dudjom Rinpoche, Jigdrel Yeshe Dorje, a native of Pemako in Southern Tibet first visited Khedung, he found that the terrain reminded him of a lotus flower surrounded by forested hills, dotted with small villages, and so he renamed the area Pema Gatshel ('delightful lotus groves'). The Royal Government of Bhutan officially recognised this change, in view of the respect in which Dudjom Rinpoche's name and tradition are held throughout Eastern Bhutan. The distance from Tselingkhor to the district capital is 29 km.

Pema Gatshel town

Entering the town, you will notice Kheri Gonpa above the road on the right. Winding downhill to a junction, turn right for Nangkhor High School and the gypsum mine, or left into the commercial part of town. Heading into town along the main street, you will pass on the left a kerosene oil store, Sonam Norbu General Store, the Food Corporation of Bhutan, a roadside prayer wheel, Chogyel Norbu Hotel & Bar and Shawala General Store. Opposite on the right are Tsewang General Store, Tsegyel Bar, Thinley Wangdi Shop, Sangye Wangmo Shop, Dechen Wangdi General Store, Leki Wangmo Store, Kunzang General Store, Kunzang Bar, Kelzang Jigme General Store, a public call office and Tashi Phuntsog General Store.

Beyond this point a series of lanes extend on the left, the first leading to the District Guesthouse and the animal husbandry office, the second to Pema Gatshel Dzong, and the third to the junior high school and the fourth to the post office, Bank of Bhutan and a military camp. The road then winds back and forth, passing the agricultural bureau on the right and the district hospital on the left.

Pema Gatshel Dzong

Built in 1981, the *dzong* is unusual in that it has no central tower, and a single courtyard that is shared equally by the lay administration and the monastic body. The **main building** has three storeys – the ground floor for political administration, and the **middle floor** with a chapel containing images of Shantaraksita, Guru Padmakara and King Trisong Detsen, flanked by the eight manifestations of Guru Padmakara, and the Twenty-one aspects of Tara; on the **top floor**, there is a chapel containing one thousand miniature images of Tara. This building presently has no murals of note. To the rear there is a two-storey **assembly hall** and monastic college (*dratsang*). On the ground floor it houses a central image of Guru Padmakara flanked by Avalokiteshvara on the left and Amitayus on the right, with murals on the side walls depicting the Sukhavati and Zangdok Pelri paradises. Upstairs, there is the residence of the incumbent Lama Neten.

Yongla Gonpa

Located 12 km above the town, Yongla Gonpa is the seat of Khedrub Jigme Kundrol, a Bhutanese student of Rigdzin Jigme Lingpa, whose *Longchen Nyingtig* revelations spread throughout Eastern Bhutan during the late 18th and 19th centuries. The monastery was built here, according to a prophetic declaration of Jigme Lingpa, because it resembled a ritual dagger, emblematic of the meditational deity Vajrakila. Even nowadays, Yongla Gonpa is revered as the main centre of activity for the *Longchen Nyingtig* lineage in Bhutan.

Dungsam Wildlife Reserve

Most of the outlying areas of the district are occupied by the **Dungsam Wildlife Reserve** (180 sq km), which is named after an ancient kingdom once established in this region, south-east of the Drangme-chu. The reserve has no motorable access.

⊜ 𝟎 Sleeping and eating

Pema Gatshel *p222*
D **District Guesthouse**, located near the animal husbandry office, is the best option – doubles at Nu 500 and singles at Nu 300.
E **Chogyel Norbu Hotel & Bar**, on the main street, has very basic accommodation at Nu 150. Bhutanese-style meals are available here. Drinks are also available across the street at the Kunzang Bar.

❁ Festivals

Pema Gatshel *p222*
The annual *tsechu* festival is held at the *dzong*
in the 9th month of the lunar calendar, which in 2004 will correspond to 18-21 Nov, and in 2005 to 7-10 Dec.

O Shopping

Pema Gatshel *p222*
There is a weaving school here, managed by the **National Women's Association of Bhutan**, ensuring that traditional techniques and designs are passed on to younger generations. The products of the school are available for sale. Postage **stamps** are available at **Bhutan Post**, next to the Bank of Bhutan.

⊖ Transport

Pema Gatshel *p222*
There are presently no public **bus** services giving access to Pema Gatshel. Visitors will have pre-arranged their own transportation.

❶ Directory

Pema Gatshel *p222*
Banks Bank of Bhutan, located next to the post office, Mon-Fri 0900-1300, Sat 0900-1100. **Hospitals and medical services** Pema Gatshel District Hospital, is located at Barcheri, on the outskirts of town. **Post** Bhutan Post, Open 0830-1230, 1330-1630, Sat 0900-1230.
Telecommunications IDD and STD calls can be made from the public call office on the main street.

Samdrub Jongkhar district
བསམ་འགྲུབ་རྗོང་མཁ་

→ Area: 2,308 sq km.

Samdrub Jongkhar, in the extreme south-east of Bhutan, borders on India to the east and south, and on the north it shares a border with Zhemgang, Pema Gatshel and Tashigang districts. The main rivers all flow south through the Assamese Duars into the Brahmaputra. They include the Deu-chu, west of Dewathang, the Nyera Ama-chu to the east of Dewathang, the Nonori-chu, which flows through Samrang, and the Jomo-chu (Dhanasiri), which rises in Tashigang and flows into India through Draipham.

Summers are hot and humid in Samdrub Jongkhar, and the winters are cool and dry (average rainfall: 1,000-5,000 mm). About 77% of the land is covered with broadleaf forest, there are no grazing pastures and no land over 3,000 m, and 18% is cultivated. The main crops are oranges, cardamom, potatoes and ginger. Much of the population is centred in the border areas, and is predominantly Lhotsampa, and Hindu rather than Buddhist by tradition. There are important cultural differences and modes of subsistence, such as fish-farming, that are frowned upon by the Bhutanese majority.

There are 11 counties in the district: Onrong on the main motor road, Gomdar, Martshala and Bakuli in the valley of the Nyera Ama-chu, Dechenling and Norbugang to the west, Dalim and Samrang to the east, and Lauri, Serthi and Hastinapur in the Jomo-chu valley in the far east. The administrative capital is located at Samdrub Jongkhar, 180 km from Tashigang, and 101 km from Guwahati in Assam. ⟩⟩ For Sleeping, Eating and other listings, see page 226.

Orong county

From the intersection at **Tshelingkhor** (see page 215), the southern highway follows a ridge down into Orong county, between the Deu-chu and the Nyera Ama-chu valleys. Reaching the settlement of **Narphung**, it crosses a penultimate pass at Narphung La (1,700 m), and traverses yet another ridge, before ascending the final pass (1,920 m) that leads down via Morong (1,600 m) to the plains. The town of **Dewathang**, 55 km from the Pema Gatshel turn-off, is at the point where the road runs down to the plains.

Dewathang
Dewathang (870 m) has a number of government institutions, including a technical training college, a military encampment, a road maintenance department and a Buddhist Studies College. The town has a military past – it was here that battles were fought between the British Indian Army and Bhutan during the Duar War of 1864-65. The British forces were initially defeated, but they returned to destroy the old fort. The war ended with the Treaty of Sinchula, according to which the Bhutanese agreed to a permanent annexation of the Dewathang area and Kalimpong by British India. Later in 1949, when independent India renewed its strategic alliance with Bhutan, the Dewathang enclave was returned to Bhutanese sovereignty.

Dewathang to Bhangtar
From Dewathang a branch road cuts eastwards for **Bakuli** in the Nyera Ama-chu valley, and follows the west bank of that river downstream to **Bhangtar** on the Assamese border. The distance from Dewathang to Bhangtar is 49 km, but the road is closed to cross-border international traffic.

Samdrub Jongkhar town

The main road from Dewathang winds to the south-west and suddenly the full extent of the Duars and the Assamese plains come into view. Passing through jungle terrain, the road skirts Chodron Chemical Industries, an important manufacturer of carbides, ferro-silicon and cement, and comes to a halt at an immigration checkpoint on the north side of Samdrub Jongkhar town. During the Assamese insurgency troubles of recent years, foreigners have not been granted access to Assam on this road, but the hope is that recent successes by the Bhutanese army in expelling the infiltrators to Indian custody could encourage the authorities to reopen this important route to Guwahati in Assam. If cross-border restrictions are lifted, it will be possible to proceed through the Bhutan Gate at the south of the town, and cross over to the Indian frontier town of Darranga. Guwahati Airport in Assam is a good four hours' drive away, via Kumarikata and Charali.

Six hours' drive from Tashigang and 18 km from Dewathang, Samdrub Jongkhar is the tropical gateway to Assam, with a mixed Lhotsampa, Indian and Drukpa population. Nowadays it is an important market town, serving the mountain districts of Mongar, Tashigang, Lhuntse and Tashi Yangtse in Eastern Bhutan, and providing an international export outlet for their produce.

Orientation

Heading into town from the checkpoint, the road passes the new Samdrub Jongkhar Dzong on the right, and then forks – left for the junior high school and the General Hospital, and right for the downtown area. Continuing into town, you will pass on the left the revenue and customs office, the telecommunications office, an army general store and the bus station. Opposite on the left is the Bank of Bhutan. Another police checkpoint has to be negotiated at this point before crossing a bridge that leads to the main traffic circle. Here you can proceed straight ahead for the Bhutan Gate on the border, or turn left into the main street.

Turning into the **main street**, you will pass on the left the Yang Hotel, Kota Ama Pan Shop and Tashi Yangdzom Yarn Shop, after which a branch road intersects. Opposite on the right are Sharma Store, Tashi Commercial Corporation, Choudmal Agarwal Store, Eastern Shopping Complex, Vijay Store and a small police station. After the turn-off on the left, you will pass a public call office, the Shambhala Hotel, a second public call office, Nobooz Bookstore and Mothi & Co. Ltd.

At this point the main street opens out into a large square with parking facilities. On the right side of the square are Sangye Shop, Sharma Pan Shop, Wangdi Restaurant, Wangdi Pan Shop, the cinema hall, Dawa Footwear, Cosmolight Studio, Zambala Hotel, National Printing Press, D. Tshomo Groceries, Gupta Tailoring, Pelzang Shop and Gupta Studio. On the left side of the square are the Peace Hotel, Anand Store and the Jabdrub Hotel. On the far side of the square are Govind Store, Drukyul Store, Satnarayan Cloth Store, Tiptop Hair Salon, Sunder Tailoring, Choudari Cloth Shop, Hanuman Store, Wangmo Cloth Shop, Durga Store, Galing Footwear, Dechen Store, Chudu Store, Chodron Store, Punjab Hotel and Bhutan Studio.

If you turn north on to the aforementioned branch road, along here in the Lower Market you will find: Go Go Hair Salon, Kelzang Hotel, Hifi Lodge, Laya Dorje Vegetables, Peljorling Hotel, Wangchuk Hotel & Bar, Dondrub Hotel, Tsopema Hotel, Kunga Hotel, Tsewang Gyeltsen Fish Shop, Unique Hotel, Karma Hotel, Choden Bar, Seldron Vegetables and Yeshe General Store.

Jomo-chu valley

In the far east of the district, the Jomo-chu (Dhanasiri) valley is not accessible by road beyond the border town of Draipham. **Bhutan Post Express** operates a canter truck service through Indian territory, on the 190-km detour via Kumarikata and Charali that links Draipham with Samdrub Jongkhar.

Sleeping

Samdrub Jongkhar *p225*
C **Hifi Lodge**, T7-251455, has 18 rooms – doubles at Nu 1,100 and singles at NU 800.
D **Chodron Hotel**, T7-251335, is a small establishment, with 1 superior double (attached bath) at Nu 750, and one superior single (attached bath) at Nu 600. There are also 6 ordinary rooms – 3 doubles at Nu 400 and 3 singles at Nu 350. The restaurant can seat 16 persons but closes by 2100.
D **Peljorling Hotel**, T7-251094/ 251308, F7-251318, in the square, has 13 rooms – doubles at Nu 800 and singles at Nu 700 – with a bar downstairs and the Chopstix Restaurant upstairs.
E **Shambhala Hotel**, T7-251222, is a simple Indian-style hotel with 19 rooms – doubles at Nu 400 and singles at Nu 300, good Indian restaurant.
E **Unique Hotel**, T7-251270, has 15 simpler rooms, 9 doubles with attached bathroom at Nu 200 and 6 without – doubles at Nu 200 and singles at Nu 150. The dining room has a capacity of 12.

Eating

Samdrub Jongkhar *p225*
The best restaurants are in the **Peljorling**, **Hifi** and **Shambhala** hotels. In the lower market area there are other options for outside dining. Bhutanese cuisine is available at **Wangchuk Hotel & Bar**, **Dondrub Hotel**, **Tsopema Hotel** and **Kunga Hotel**. Indian cuisine can be found at **Peace Hotel** and **Punjab Hotel**, on the square.

Shopping

Samdrub Jongkhar *p225*
There are many general stores (*tsongkhang*) in the downtown area, selling groceries,
books, cloth and ready-to-wear clothes. The biggest supermarket is **Tashi Commercial Corporation**. Newspapers and books are on sale at **Nobooz Bookstore**. Postage stamps are available at **Bhutan Post**, near the *dzong*.

Transport

Samdrub Jongkhar *p225*
Many public **bus** services to Samdrub Jongkhar were suspended at the height of the Assamese troubles, but they are now being resumed. **Bhutan Post Express** have a monopoly on all the routes in this sector. They run daily buses from **Phuntsoling** (356 km), departing 0530 and 0600, **Mongar** on Tue, Thu and Sat at 0700, and **Tashigang**, daily at 0730. The return service from Samdrub Jongkhar to Phuntsoling runs daily at 0600 and 0630, to Tashigang daily at 0730 and to Mongar on Mon, Wed and Fri at 0630. The same company also runs local services within the district: to **Dewathang** on Sun (at 0700 and 1400), to **Bhangtar** on Wed (at 0730), to **Draipham** on Fri (0700) and to **Nganglam** on Sun (0700). The last 3 of these routes are by canter truck on a rough surface.

Directory

Samdrub Jongkhar *p225*
Banks Bank of Bhutan, T4-521294, located just north of the bridge, Mon-Fri 0900-1300, Sat 0900-1100. **Hospitals and medical services** Samdrub Jongkhar General Hospital is located at the north end of town. **Post** Bhutan Post, 0830-1230, 1330-1630, Sat 0900-1230.
Telecommunications IDD and STD calls can be made from the public call offices on the main street.

Background

Footprint features

History

Archaeology

Despite the paucity of archaeological research, stone axe heads found in Bhutan suggest that the mid-mountain belt was inhabited by humans around 2000 BC, somewhat later than the comparable Neolithic implements unearthed at Guro near Chamdo in Eastern Tibet. There are also a number of free-standing megaliths, which the historian Michael Aris in his authoritative work, *Bhutan*, suggests were either sacred power-markers, since many of them are located near or even within Buddhist temples of later construction, or boundary markers, such as the well-known megalith between **Tang** and **Ura** valleys in Bumthang.

Monpa

Bhutanese sources themselves refer to the earliest known inhabitants as Monpa, a word cognate with the Tibetan *mun-pa*, meaning 'darkness' or 'barbarity'. In the Tibetan language Bhutan is invariably called Lho-mon ('Southern Mon'). Within present-day Tibet the Monpa form an identifiable ethnic group, inhabiting the frontier counties of Metok, Nyangtri and Tsona, which border the Indian state of Arunachal Pradesh, to the east of Bhutan. These peoples, numbering 8,496 according to the 2001 Chinese National Census, still practise the slash-and-burn method of agriculture. The Bhutanese similarly refer to the forest-dwelling tribal inhabitants of **Khyeng, Mandelung** and **Zhongsar** in south-central Bhutan as Monpa, and regard them as the residual population of the central hills who were forced south into the thick jungle by new waves of migration from Tibet. It is important to note that although these diverse Monpa groups may not all be linguistically homogenous, there are at least close links between the dialects spoken by the Monpa of Tawang (presently in Arunachal Pradesh) and those of Bumthang, Khyeng, Mangdelung and Kurto in Central Bhutan. The actual numbers of Monpa in Bhutan are uncertain – there are related tribal groups found at **Toktokha** in southern Paro and at **Taba-Dramten** in southern Chukha, as well as in the vicinity of Jalpaiguri, in neighbouring West Bengal.

Sharchokpa

The indigenous inhabitants of Eastern Bhutan during that period seem to have been those whose descendants even now occupy much of Central and Eastern Bhutan, and who speak the Tibeto-Burman language known as Tsangla (see page 259). Contemporary linguists regard **Tsangla** as one of the diverse languages or dialects spoken by the Lopa aboriginal peoples. Within neighbouring Tibet there are about 2,980 Lopas (2001 Chinese National Census), inhabiting border areas of Nang, Menling, Metok and Dzayul counties. They and the related Lhopa of Arunachal Pradesh, such as the Adi and Mishmi, were traditionally hunter-gatherers and bamboo weavers. Nowadays in Bhutan the Tsangla-speakers are known as **Sharchokpa** (locally pronounced 'Sharchop') or 'Easterners'. The royal succession of Prince Tsangma of Tibet among the Sharchokpas is discussed on page 233.

King Songtsen Gampo's geomantic temples

When Tibet was first unified by the martial kings Namri Songtsen and Songtsen Gampo during the seventh century, Bhutan appears to have come firmly within the Tibetan sphere of influence. People of Tibetan descent, formerly known in Bhutan as the Ngalong (ie the 'earliest to rise up within the fold of Tibetan Buddhism'), appear to have settled there gradually, from this time onwards. **Lhasa** was established as the capital of this empire, and the original Potala Palace was constructed as the foremost royal residence. In the course of forging his empire King Songtsen Gampo (r. 629-650)

Taming the ogress: the geomantic temples of Tibet and Bhutan

When the Tang princess Wencheng arrived in Tibet, she introduced Chinese divination texts including the so-called Portang scrolls. According to the ancient Chinese model of government, spheres of influence were based on six concentric zones, namely: an imperial centre, a royal domain zone, a princes' domain, a pacification zone, a zone of allied barbarians, and a zone of cultureless savagery. The Tibetan geomantic temples were laid out according to four such zones, corresponding to the imperial centre, the royal domain zone, the pacification zone, and that of the allied barbarians. Just as China was conceived of as a supine turtle, so the Tibetan terrain was seen as a supine ogress or demoness (Sinmo Kangyel), and geomantic temples were to be constructed at focal points on her body: the **Jokhang** temple at the heart, the four 'district controlling' temples (*runon lhakhang*) on her shoulders and hips,

the four 'border taming' temples (*tadul lhakhang*) on her elbows and knees, and the four 'further taming' temples (*yangdul lhakhang*) on her hands and feet.

According to literary sources such as the Mani Kabum, Buton, Longdol Lama and Drukchen IV Pema Karpo, the four 'district controlling' temples are: **Tradruk** (left shoulder), **Katsel** (right shoulder), **Yeru Tsangdram** (right hip) and **Rulak Drompagyang** (left hip). These same authors list the four 'border taming' temples as: **Khomting** (left elbow), **Buchu** (right elbow), **Jang Traduntse** (near Saga, right knee); and **Mon Bumthang** (left knee); while the four further taming temples are listed as: **Jang Tsangpa Lungnon** (left hand), **Den Langtang Dronma** (right hand), **Mangyul Jamtrin** (right foot) and **Paro Kyerchu** (left foot). These are the central temples among the 108 reputedly built in this period throughout Tibet and Bhutan.

encountered the prevailing Buddhist civilisations of neighbouring India, Khotan and China, and quickly immersed himself in spiritual pursuits, reputedly under the influence of his foreign queens: Bhrikuti, the daughter of Amshuvarman, king of Nepal; and Wencheng, daughter of Tang Taizong, emperor of China. These queens are revered for having brought to Lhasa as their dowry two renowned images of the historical Buddha – one in the form of Jowo Mikyo Dorje, which Bhrikuti introduced from Nepal and one in the form of Jowo Shakyamuni, which was transported from China. Although there were probably earlier Buddhist contacts with Tibet during the reign of King Lhatotori Nyentsen (374-493) and even with Bhutan, it was Songtsen Gampo who first made concerted efforts to establish Buddhism within his domain. Early literary sources, such as the *Mani Kabum* (parts of which have been dated 12th century), and Sonam Gyeltsen's *Clear Mirror of Royal Geneology* (1368), are among the historical works that chronicle Songtsen Gampo's achievements.

The king constructed a series of geomantic temples at important power places across the length and breadth of the land, and these are revered as the earliest shrines of Tibetan Buddhism. In an ingenious adaptation of ancient Chinese geomancy, the king conceived of the physical terrain of his country in the form of a reclining ogress, lying on her back (*Sinpo Kangyel*). The **Jokhang** chapel of the Trulnang Temple in Lhasa was constructed on her heart, and, to stabilise the realm, 12 other major temples were built around it, at far-flung locations on her limbs (see box, page 229). Two of these surrounding temples are in Bhutan: **Kyerchu Lhakhang** in

Paro (see page 112) and **Jampa Lhakhang** in Bumthang (see page 176), which were built respectively on the ogress' left foot and left knee. Some sources suggest that other temples in Ha, Bumthang and Lhuntse may also date from this early period.

Among his other achievements, the king sent his most able minister, Tonmi Sambhota, to India where the Uchen (capital letter) script was developed from an Indian prototype to represent the Tibetan language. This is still the script used for printing classical and modern texts in Tibet and Bhutan at the present day. According to some sources, in later years, the king abdicated in favour first of his son and later in favour of his grandson; he passed his final years in spiritual retreat. His tomb is the celebrated **Banso Marpo** in the Chongye valley of Southern Tibet (although other traditions claim him to have been interred in the Jokhang).

The years immediately following Songtsen Gampo's unification of Tibet and the Himalayan regions saw engagement in wide-ranging military campaigns. From 665-692 the Yarlung kings controlled the Central Asian oases and cities, and this Tibetan influence is reflected in the manuscripts and paintings preserved in the **Dunhuang** caves, which have been dated 650-747. Conflict with Tang China began in 670, and by 680 the Tibetan army had advanced as far south,east as the **Nan-chao** Kingdom (modern Dali in Yunnan province). King Tride Tsukten (r. 704-755) constructed a number of Buddhist shrines, including the temple of Drakmar Keru, and extended his imperial influence westwards into Brusha (the Burushaski region of Gilgit) by 737. Throughout this period Bhutan was regarded as lying within the southern fold of the Tibetan empire.

King Sedarkha and the first visit of Padmakara to Bhutan

In the early eighth century the population of **Bumthang** in Central Bhutan came under the sway of King Sedarkha (also known as Sindharaja). This figure, whose original name was Prince Kunjom, appears to have fled to Bhutan from India. According to legend, he was the middle of seven sons of King Singala of Kapilavastu, who received the name Sindharaja after being exiled by his father and siblings to the land of Sindha. He in turn was ousted from his Indian domains by one King Nawoche and forced to flee into exile. Arriving in Bumthang he built a nine-storey 'iron castle' (**Chamkhar**) in the Chokhor valley, and firmly established his authority there (see page 178). However, one of his sons, Prince Takla Mebar, was slain by Nawoche, in consequence of which the king became anguished in bereavement, so that his protector deities could no longer be propitiated in the correct manner. The enraged protectors seized the king's vital spirit, bringing dire calamities upon his kingdom. The royal ministers then decided to invite the great master Guru Padmakara (Pema Jungne) from the **Yanglesho** cave hermitage in Nepal to cure the king through his spiritual prowess.

Guru Padmakara (also known by other names including Padmasambhava and Guru Rinpoche) reached Bumthang in 746, and immediately subdued the venomous spirits that had possessed the king. En route for Chamkhar, he stabbed his ritual dagger into a boulder at **Trumzur Mon** in south-central Bhutan, demarcating the boundary between the disputed kingdoms, and left his footprint in the **Orgyan Drak** rock, both of which are still visible today. Padmakara entered into meditative retreat with his new consort, Bumden Tsomo, at **Drakmar Dorje Tsekpa** in Bumthang, and performed many miracles: he thrust his staff into the ground, giving rise to a sandalwood tree that can still be seen there; he brought forth water of spiritual attainment from the rock-side and he left an impression of his body in solid rock, which can still be seen inside **Kurje Lhakhang** today (see page 178). The malevolent spirit Shelging Karpo, who had caused the king's malaise, then manifested and was bound under an oath of allegiance to Buddhism. Proceeding to Chamkhar, the great master restored the king to his senses and granted him certain esoteric instructions on the meditational deity Hayagriva. Before leaving Bumthang, Guru Padmakara

The establishment of Buddhism

Padmakara's labour in crushing the obstructive demonic forces on Mount Hepori paved the way for the establishment of Buddhist monasticism in Tibet. King Trisong Detsen, at Shantaraksita's suggestion, ensured that the complex was to be modelled on the plan of **Odantapuri Monastery** (at modern Bihar Shariff), where the buildings themselves represented the Buddhist cosmological order (with Mount Sumeru in the centre, surrounded by four continents and eight subcontinents, sun and moon, all within a perimeter wall known as the Cakravala). This construction would therefore come to symbolise the establishment of a new Buddhist world order on the plateau. Humans were engaged in this unprecedented building project by day, and spirits by night. Hence the monastery's full name: **Glorious Inconceivable Temple of Unchanging Spontaneous Presence** (Pel Samye Migyur Lhundrub Tsuklakhang).

King Trisong Detsen then established an integrated programme for the translation of the Buddhist classics into Tibetan, bringing together teams of Indian scholars (*pandita*) and Tibetan translators (*lotsawa*). He and a celebrated group of 24 subjects received instruction on the highest tantras from Padmakara in particular, but also from Vimalamitra, Buddhaguhya and others, and through their meditations they attained the supreme realisations and accomplishments of Buddhist practice. In addition, Shantaraksita was requested to preside over the ordination of Tibet's first seven trial monks, namely: Ba Trizhi (Srighosa), Ba Selnang (Jnanendra), Pagor Vairocana (Vairocanaraksita), Ngenlam Gyelwa Choyang, Khonlui Wangpo Sungwa (Nagendraraksita), Ma Rinchen Chok and Lasum Gyelwei Jangchub.

In 792 a debate was held between Kamalashila, an Indian proponent of the graduated path to buddhahood, which emphasises the performance of virtuous deeds, and Hoshang Mo-ho-yen, a Chinese proponent of the instantaneous path to buddhahood, with its emphasis on meditation and inaction. Kamalashila emerged as the victor, but it is clear from Nubchen's treatise, Samten Migdron, that both views were integrated within the overall path to buddhahood. It was in these ways that the king established the future of Buddhism in his empire.

established a solemn pact between King Sedarkha and his southern neighbour, the Indian king Nawoche, exhorting them to confirm their oath by touching a stone obelisk, which can still be seen at **Nabi Lhakhang** today (see page 195). He then returned to India, after predicting that the county's future prosperity would be assured if the king were to adopt Buddhist principles. The king duly obliged with the result that he himself was able to revisit the land of his birth.

King Trisong Detsen's establishment of Buddhism

In 730, Tride Tsukten's Tibetan consort Nanamza gave birth to a son – Trisong Detsen, perhaps the greatest of all the Tibetan kings, in whose reign Buddhism was formally established as the state religion. Trisong Detsen (r. 755-797) initially sent his armies against Tang China, eventually occupying the imperial capital Xi'an in 763. The Zhol pillar was erected at Lhasa to commemorate this event. Increasingly, the king sought to promote Buddhism, and he invited the Indian preceptor Shantaraksita to found the country's first monastery at **Samye** (see box, page 231).

Owing to obstacles instigated by hostile non-Buddhist forces, the king accepted Shantaraksita's advice and invited Guru Padmakara, the foremost exponent of the tantras and the Dzogchen meditative tradition in India to participate in the establishing of Buddhism. Padmakara bound the hostile demons of Tibet under an oath of allegiance to Buddhism, enabling the monastery's construction to be completed and the first monks to be ordained.

The king then instituted a methodical translation programme for the rendering of Sanskrit and Chinese Buddhist texts in Tibetan. Intelligent children were sent to India to be trained as translators, and their prolific work ranks among the greatest literary endeavours of all time. Meanwhile, Padmakara, Vimalamitra and other accomplished masters of the Indian tantra traditions imparted their meditative instructions and lineages to the custodianship of their Tibetan disciples in remote but spectacularly located mountain caves. In particular, at tiger dens throughout the Tibetan plateau and adjacent Himalayan regions, the Precious Guru manifested in the awesome tiger-riding form of Dorje Drolod, in order to make predictions concerning the future rediscovery of his concealed teachings and to impart teachings on the meditational deity Vajrakila. Two of these 'tiger den' caves happen to be in present-day Bhutan – at **Monka Nering Senge Dzong**, the foremost site associated with buddha-activity in Lhuntse district (see page 210), and at the cliff-hanging hermitage of **Taktsang** in Paro (see page 114). In this way his Tibetan and Monpa followers were brought to spiritual maturity and attained profound understanding of the nature of mind and the nature of phenomenal reality.

Denma Tsemang and the second visit of Padmakara to Bhutan

While Padmakara was residing in Tibet, during the lifetime of King Trisong Detsen, he fulfilled an earlier promise made to King Sedarkha by returning to Bumthang in the company of his student Denma Tsemang. At **Dorje Tsekpa** he imparted teachings on the Great Perfection to these two and to other fortunate individuals. Then, in the upper reaches of **Murulung**, he manifested in a wrathful fiery form to subdue the demon Gache Zhonu, leaving his footprints in stone at the place nowadays called **Zhabjetang**. Other bodily imprints were left at **Shukpei Drak** and on a rock across the river from Dorje Tsekpa. Further teachings on the Great Perfection were given at **Rimochen** in the Tang valley (see page 187), before he eventually returned to Tibet. More generally, Bhutanese legends recount that Padmakara transformed the carnivorous and long-haired Monpa inhabitants of Bhutan into pan-eating, short-haired devotees of Buddhism!

Khyikha Rato and the third visit of Padmakara to Bhutan

According to the local tradition of Central and Eastern Bhutan, Queen Margyen, consort of King Trisong Detsen, had an illegitimate son of bestial descent named Khyikha Rato ('dog-mouth, goat-skull'). This unseemly offspring was regarded by the king as an ill-omen, and so he along with all his retainers, was sent into exile, initially to Lhodrak and thence to the isolated valley of **Khenpalung** in north-eastern Bhutan. The prince built a grand wooden palace at **Yarelung**, while his artisans and Bon priests took up residence at **Jekarlung**. His ministers and subjects built their homes within the ravine and on the mountainsides. Then, when Trisong Detsen had passed away and the royal succession had fallen eventually to his youngest son Mutik Tsenpo (r. 804–813), Khyikha Rato sought revenge by sending an Indian army against Samye Monastery. The invasion was thwarted through the prescience and magical prowess of Guru Padmakara, who was then residing at the Yarlung Sheldrak cave with the young king. Then, to prevent future hostile acts, Padmakara proceeded to Khenpalung, where, according to legend, he tricked Khyikha Rato into a wooden Garuda contraption, which flew off to **Kyana** in Bumthang. He sealed Khenpalung as a hidden land (*beyul*), which would be reopened in the future for the timely benefit of posterity, and continued on to Chamkar in Bumthang where he revisited King Sedarkha. Some sources have conflated Khyikha Rato with Prince Murub Tsepo, a middle son of Trisong Detsen who was slain in the course of a military campaign against the Batahor tribes of the Qilian Range in Amdo. Descendents of the followers of Khyikha Rato are said to have settled at **Kyitsum** and **Gyelkhar** in Bumthang.

The reign of King Tri Relpachen

King Trisong Detsen's successors all acted as lavish patrons of Buddhism, sometimes at the expense of the older Bon tradition, and the status of Tibet's ancient aristocratic families was diminished. This trend reached its zenith during the reign of Tri Relpachen (r. 813-841), who had each monk supported by seven households. Among his many achievements, the most important one politically is the peace treaty agreed with China in 823, which clearly defined the Sino-Tibetan border at Chorten Karpo in the Sang-chu valley of Amdo. Obelisks were erected there and in Lhasa to commemorate this momentous event, the one in Lhasa surviving intact until today. The strong Buddhist sympathies of the king attracted an inevitable backlash on the past of disgruntled Bon and aristocratic groups. This resulted in his assassination at the hands of his elder brother, the apostate Langdarma Udumtsen, in 841; and with this act, the period of the great religious kings came to an abrupt end.

Persecution of Buddhism

When Langdarma came to power following the assassination of his brother, the Bonpo soon found themselves once more in the ascendancy. Old scores against the Buddhists were settled and a widespread persecution ensued. The monasteries and temples were desecrated or closed down and Buddhist practice was driven underground. Only practitioners of the tantras survived in Central Tibet, whether in their remote mountain retreats or by living their lives incognito in small village communities. The monastic tradition could only survive in the remote north-east of Amdo, where at **Dentik** and **Achung Namdzong**, three far-sighted monks transmitted the Vinaya lineage to Lachen Gongpa Rabsel, ensuring that the lineage of monastic ordination would continue unbroken into the future.

The flight of Prince Tsangma to Eastern Bhutan

Langdarma had another brother named Prince Tsangma who in 841 was forced into exile on account of his Buddhist sympathies. Some Tibetan sources suggest that he fled to **Kharchu** in Lhodrak, while other works and indigenous Bhutanese accounts say that he travelled first to **Namtong Karpo** in Dromo, and thence into Bhutan, passing through **Paro**, **Thimphu** and **Zhongar** before crossing the Kuri-chu to reach Eastern Bhutan. Many clan chieftains of the Sharchokpa in Eastern Bhutan, including those of Jowo, Je, Jar, Tungde and Wangma, claimed their descent from the Tibetan royal line of Prince Tsangma, even after the Drukpa unification of Bhutan in the 17th century. A series of fortresses were built by this royal lineage, extending through Bumthang and as far east as **Pelkhar** in modern Arunachal Pradesh, north towards Tsona in Tibet, and south towards the Assamese kingdom of Kamata.

The disintegration of the Tibetan Empire

Langdarma's severe persecution of Buddhism was itself brought to an abrupt end in 846, when he was assassinated by the Buddhist master Lhalung Pelgyi Dorje, a black-hatted and black-clothed figure, who shot the apostate king with an arrow and fled in disguise, reversing his clothes to reveal their white lining! This act is commemorated in the famous black hat dance (*shanak*) that is frequently performed on ceremonial occasions. Lhalung Pelgyi Dorje eventually reached the safety of Achung Namdzong in Amdo where he remained in penance for the rest of his life.

The succession to the throne was then disputed by Langdarma's two sons, Tride Yumten, the son of his senior consort, and Namde Osung, the son of his junior consort. Osung gained control of Lhasa while Yumten moved to Yarlung, and this event heralded the demise of the royal dynasty. The disintegration of the empire's political cohesion is considered to have begun around 869.

Siblings of Lhalung Pelgyi Dorje and the Dung of Bumthang

Lhalung Pelgyi Dorje's assassination of the king also endangered the lives of his six brothers. Three of them fled via Lhodrak to **Kurelung** and **Zhongar Molwalung** in Bhutan, where they established their estates. The other three fled from Phari in Tibet to Paro and thence to Bumthang, where they constructed their fortresses respectively in **Tang**, **Chokhor** and the nomadic borderlands to the north. Other aristocratic families of both matrilineal and patrilineal descent can still be found around **Bumthang**, **Khyeng** and **Kurto** in Central Bhutan. The latter include the so-called Dung families who also claim to have a divine or princely origin in ancient Tibet. As the centralising power of the Tibetan empire disintegrated, Tibetan potentates sought sanctuary in Bhutan, which was then known as Lhomon (Southern Mon). Many small valleys of Central Bhutan fell under the sway of these noble lords, who maintained their own localised spheres of influence.

The later diffusion of Buddhism in Tibet

While anarchy prevailed in much of Central Tibet, the Buddhist heritage of Padmakara and Shantaraksita continued to flourish from 900 to 1100 in the Tsong-chu valley, in the remote north-eastern parts of Amdo. Around 953 or 978 Lu-me and his fellow monks successfully restored the monastic ordination in Central Tibet, having received it from Lachen Gongpa Rabsel in Amdo. They then embarked upon an extensive temple-building programme in the Kyi-chu and Brahmaputra valleys, which laid the basis for the later diffusion of Buddhism. Meanwhile, further west in Guge, descendants of the royal family had effectively established a troglodyte kingdom along the canyons of the upper Sutlej and Karnalii rivers, where they revived their traditional royal sponsorship of Buddhism. Among the most important of these kings were Yeshe-o (947-1024) who was a fifth-generation descendant of Langdarma, and his nephew Jangchub-o (984-1078). They were both patrons of Rinchen Zangpo (958-1055), the great translator of the later diffusion, and Atisha (982-1054), the renowned Bengali Buddhist master. It was Atisha who reinforced the ethical discipline of the gradual path to enlightenment and its compassionate ideals, rather than the practices of the tantras, which apparently had been dangerously misapplied by some corrupt practitioners.

During this period, translators once again began travelling to India to study Sanskrit and receive teachings in the various aspects of the Indian Buddhist tradition. The texts that they found were naturally those in vogue in 11th-century India, in contrast to those previously introduced during the eighth century by Guru Padmakara and his followers. Consequently a distinction evolved between the 'old translations' of the early period and the 'new translations' of the later period. Among this new wave of translators were Rinchen Zangpo and Ngok Lotsawa who represented the Kadampa tradition (associated with Atisha), Drokmi Lotsawa (992-1074) who represented the Sakyapa tradition (of Gayadhara and Virupa), and Marpa Lotsawa (1012-1097) who represented the Kagyupa tradition (of Tilopa and Naropa). By contrast, lineage-holders who maintained the earlier teachings of Padmakara during the 11th and 12fth centuries, such as Zurpoche Shakya Jungne and Rongzom Chokyi Zangpo, became known as the Nyingmapa.

The foundation of large temples and monasteries soon followed: Toling in 996, Zhalu in 1040, Reting in 1054, Sakya in 1073, Ukpalung in the late 11th century, Katok in 1159, and the Kagyu monasteries of Daklha Gampo, Kampo Nenang, Karma Gon, Tsurphu, Densatil, Drigung, Taklung and Ralung – all in the 12th century.

The later diffusion of Buddhism in Bhutan

Following the disintegration of the Tibetan empire in the ninth century, waves of settlers arrived from Tibet to occupy Southern Mon. Between the 11th and 15th centuries, the pre-Buddhist Bon tradition was active in Bhutan, and the major Tibetan schools of Buddhism, notably the Nyingma, Sakya and Kagyu, established monasteries and temples throughout the Bhutanese valleys, as cultural and economic ties with Tibet continued to have paramount importance. The teachings of these schools were handed down to future generations, either in an unbroken line of oral transmission (*kama*) or in a series of concealed teachings and revelations (*terma*), some of which were rediscovered in later centuries.

The Bon tradition in Bhutan

The original, unreformed Bon tradition gradually transformed itself through contacts with Tibetan Buddhism, adopting Buddhist liturgies, iconography and systems of meditation. In Bhutan during the 11th century, some concealed teachings pertaining to both Bon and Buddhism were rediscovered in the **Paro** valley by the 'treasure-finders' Dr Kutsa and Garton Trogyel, and elsewhere by Bonpo Draktsel, Khungpo Palgye and Rashak Chobar. The celebrated Nyingmapa treasure-finder Dorje Lingpa is also said to have discovered certain Bon texts in **Bumthang**, There are no extant traces of former Bon monasteries in **Trongsar** and **Shar**, but some elements probably do survive within the folklore and divinatory traditions in remote countryside areas.

Kadampa activity in Bhutan

During the lifetime of King Relpachen, the Dromo and Paro regions were bequeathed to the faithful minister Go Trizhing, whose son established a temple at **Nenying** in Khangmar county, only 15 km south-west of Gyantse. Following the disintegration of the Tibetan empire, and the subsequent arrival of Atisha in Tibet (1042), the temple complex at Nenying was reconstituted as a Kadampa monastery by Jampel Sangwa of Samye. In particular, the lineage-holder Rinchen Samten Pelzang (b. 1262) encouraged Gonpo Dorje of Lato to unearth the Buddha relics concealed in a rock at **Dzongdraka** in the upper Paro valley. The **Karmo Gulshe Stupa** was built to contain these relics, and the cliff-hanging monastery of Dzongdraka was founded (see page 119). Rinchen Samten Pelzang himself visited the region, and he encouraged his student Jamyang Rinchen Gyeltsen (fl. 14th century) to establish a series of related monasteries at Taraka, **Samar Dzingka**, Nazhing Rama, Puduk and Kyabtra. He was a teacher of both Remdawa and Tsongkhapa, the founder of the Gelukpa school. Another of his students, Jamyang Rinchen Drupa, who also studied under the Gelukpa masters Khedrubje and Gyeltsabje, consolidated the Nenying tradition in Western Bhutan during the early 15th century.

Other Kadampa monasteries were founded in the northern nomadic region of Lingzhi (**Drok Gonpa**) and Gasa (**Tagon**) during the 14th century, and a student of Dalai Lama I Gendun Drupa, named Lobzang Tenpei Dronme, even established a foothold in **Shar**. Both the Gelukpa lineage (known in Bhutan as Geden Shingtapa) and the older Nenying tradition continued to flourish until they were eventually eclipsed by Zhabdrung Ngawang Namgyel's unification of Bhutan in the 17th century.

Sakyapa activity in Bhutan

Hierarchs of the Sakyapa school ruled most of Tibet under Mongol patronage from 1235 to 1349. During that period, Pawo Takzham travelled from Sakya to establish a monastery at **Lhading** (Bh. Hadi), north of Paro. Other related monasteries, including **Pagar Gonpa** and **Pangye Gonpa**, were subsequently established near Wangdu and in Shar by Kyangdu Panchen Drapa. The influential Ngorpa lineage, stemming from Ngorchen Kunga Zangpo (1382-1444) also penetrated Bhutan, where in the late 15th century Trinle Rabyang founded **Chizhing** (Bh. Pchishing) in Wangyul, among others.

Although these Sakya monasteries were permitted to coexist with the ruling Drukpa hierarchy after the unification of Bhutan in 1642, they were all soon absorbed within the fold of the dominant Drukpa Kagyu school.

Nyingmapa activity in Bhutan

The first indigenous treasure-finder (*terton*) of the Nyingma tradition in Bhutan appears to have been Sarben Chokme, a native of Paro who discovered certain concealed teachings at **Taktsang** during the 11th century. Several other treasure-finders also visited Bhutan from Tibet during this medieval period. Among them, the most important were Guru Chowang (1212-1270), Ugpa Lingpa (13th century), Sherab Mebar (1267-1326) and Dorje Lingpa (1346-1405). Guru Chowang, a native of Lhodrak to the north of Bhutan, discovered texts hidden in **Bumthang**, and descendants of his son Pema Wangchen are still found in the **Kurto** region of Lhuntse. Ugpa Lingpa was a descendant of the renowned Zur family of Shang in Western Tibet, who founded the monastery of **Nyizergang** in Shar. Sherab Mebar, a master of some notoriety, discovered texts in Paro and founded a temple at **Tangsabji** in Ura. Dorje Lingpa was more influential and particularly active in Paro and Bumthang. A hagiographical account of his life has already been given (see page 170). Descendants of his son Choying Gyatso maintained temples at **Lingmukha**, **Jakar** and **Chamkhar**, while his students and reincarnations were also important lineage-holders.

Longchen Rabjampa (1308-1363) from Dranang in Tibet is revered as the great redactor and doxographer of the Nyingma teachings par excellence. Above all he promoted the practice of the Great Perfection (Dzogpa Chenpo), which he had received through an oral transmission and through his own revealed teachings. Towards the end of his life he was exiled to Bhutan by the then king of Tibet, Tai Situ Jangchub Gyeltsen (r. 1350-1371), who had mistakenly regarded him as an ally of his opponent Drigung Gompa Kunrin. Although eventually reconciled with the king, while sojourning in Bhutan he founded eight monasteries throughout the country. These included **Tharpaling** in Chume (see page 168), **Orgyenling** in Tang, **Dechenling** in Ura, **Drechakling** in Ngenlung, **Pemaling** in Khotang, **Samtenling** in Paro, and two monasteries known as **Kunzangling**, (one in Kurto and the other in Menlok). One of his Bhutanese students, Datong Tulku Paljor Gyeltsen, also founded temples east of Paro. Later, in 18th-century Tibet, the teachings of Longchen Rabjampa were revived by Jigme Lingpa (1730-1798) whose own student Jigme Kundrol taught extensively in Central and Eastern Bhutan. **Thowa Drak** in Bumthang (see page 189) and **Yongla Gonpa** (see page 223) in Dungsam were both founded by him.

Tangtong Gyelpo (1385-1464), a native of Olpa Lhartse in Western Tibet, is renowned not only as a great Buddhist teacher and revealer of concealed texts, but as a master bridge builder, engineer, and choreographer of Tibetan opera and folk dances. For a hagiographical account of his life, see page 104. In 1433 he visited Western Bhutan, where he discovered hidden texts at **Taktsang** in Paro and built a number of iron-chain bridges, at **Chukha**, **Bardrong** near Wangdu, and in **Shar**. He also founded **Tachokgang** monastery at Chukha and its various branches, including **Dumtsek Lhakhang** in Paro, **Purdo Gonpa** and **Dolteng Silma**.

Dorje Lingpa

Then, he returned to Tibet, taking with him sufficient iron for the construction of the Chuwori suspension bridge that formerly spanned the Brahmaputra. Later, on a second visit to Bhutan, he visited the **Bumthang** area on pilgrimage.

Of the six major Nyingmapa monasteries in Tibet the only one which established an offshoot in Bhutan was **Katok**, which had been founded in 1159 by Katokpa Dampa Deshek (1122-1192). Sonam Gyeltsen of Nyarong (1466-1540), who had been educated at Katok, travelled to southern Tibet in the company of his teacher Zhakla Yeshebum to explore the hidden land of Sikkim. Then in 1508 he founded the monastery of **Orgyan Tsemo** (see page 115), above Taktsang in Paro, and established the so-called Lhomon Katokpa lineage. Sonam Gyeltsen appears to have been on good terms with his illustrious contemporary, Pema Lingpa (see below). In the Paro valleys branch monasteries of Katok were soon founded at **Langmalung, Khandro Chidu, Tentong Choding, Dolpo Shaladrak** and **Jigon Gongma**. Two generations later, further branches of the lineage were established in the Bumthang area by Tendzin Drakpa, at **Chidzong** in Lutsori, as well as at **Baling** and **Thegchengang** in Khotang. In this way, the teaching traditions of Katok were extensively propagated in Bhutan.

Pema Lingpa (1450-1521) is undoubtedly the most influential of all Nyingmapa masters in Bhutanese history. This prolific discoverer of concealed teachings, revered as an incarnation of Longchen Rabjampa, was a native of Chokhor in Bumthang who travelled widely throughout Tibet and Bhutan. For a hagiographical account of his life, see page 176. A skilled metalworker and choreographer of sacred masked dances, Pema Lingpa founded many temples, including **Tamzhing Lhakhang** and **Kunzang Drak** in Bumthang, and he also unearthed Songtsen Gampo's geomantic temple at **Kyerchu** in Paro, which had become overgrown by jungle. Pema Lingpa's familial and incarnate lineages have continued down to the present day in Central and Eastern Bhutan and the neighbouring Lhodrak region of Southern Tibet. The incarnate lines of his buddha body, speech and mind are even now unbroken, and their incumbents are among the most influential of all Buddhist masters in present-day Bhutan. Among them are the successive incarnations of his speech, starting with Sungtrul Tendzin Drakpa (1536-1597) and the successive incarnations of his spiritual son Tukse Dawa Gyeltsen (b. 1499), who maintained their residences jointly at **Lhalung** in Tibet and **Tamzhing** in Bumthang, and the successive incarnations of his body, starting with Pema Trinle (1564-1642) whose principal residence is **Gangteng Sangak Choling** in Phobjika (see page 151). Furthermore, Dalai Lama VI of Tibet and Ugyen Wangchuk, the first king of Bhutan, both claimed descent from Pema Lingpa. The extensive texts revealed by Pema Lingpa fill 21 volumes.

Kagyupa activity in Bhutan

Among all the diverse traditions of Tibetan Buddhism, the one which exerted the most influence on Bhutanese spiritual and secular life has been the Kagyu school, which is based on the teachings introduced to Tibet from India by Marpa Lotsawa (1012-1097). Among Marpa's foremost students, Milarepa (1040-1123) is said to have composed a series of six spiritual songs following a three-month meditation retreat at **Taktsang** in Paro, and Ngok Choku Dorje (1036-1102) founded the monastery of **Langmoling** in the upper Tang valley, which was later absorbed by the Drukpa Kagyu. Milarepa's foremost student Gampopa Dakpo Lharje (1079-1153) is the progenitor of the four major branches of the Kagyu tradition, including the order established by Karmapa Dusumkhyenpa (1110-1193), which established only a slender presence in Bhutan at **Thangkhabe** (Bh. Thangbi) in Chokhor.

Far more significant in the Bhutanese context is the branch established by Phagmodrupa Dorje Gyelpo (1110-1170), which itself gave rise to eight subsects – two of which were destined to play significant roles in Bhutanese history. Among them, the Drigung tradition, established at Drigung Til monastery in Central Tibet by Jigten Gonpo (1143-1217), once vied with the Sakyapas for the patronage of Mongol princes.

One of Jigten Gonpo's students named Gyelwa Lhanangpa (1164-1224), who held ancestral estates in Western Bhutan, established a branch monastery at **Chelkha** in the northern Paro valley, and the fortress of **Dongon Dzong** in Thimphu (now the seat of the Bhutanese government). Extant accounts of Lhanangpa's life are mostly dominated by his rivalry with the Drukpa Kagyu lama, Phajo Drukgom Zhikpo (1184-1251). Both men were seeking an identical sphere of influence in Western Bhutan. All Lhanangpa's estates and institutions were later absorbed by the Drukpa Kagyu following the Zhabdrung's political unification in 1641.

Tibetan origins of the Drukpa Kagyu school

Phagmodrupa Dorje Gyelpo had another follower, named Lingrepa Pema Dorje. His disciple, Tsangpa Gya-re Yeshe Dorje (1161-1211), founded the monastery of **Druk Jangchub Choling** in Central Tibet in 1189. This institution, though small, gave its name to the influential Drukpa Kagyu order, and later to the country of Bhutan, which since 1641 has been known as Druk-yul (land of the Drukpa Kagyupas). Another somewhat larger monastery was established by Tsangpa Gayre at **Ralung** in modern Gyantse county and it quickly became the main seat of this tradition, extending its influence throughout the Tibetan plateau. The hierarchs of Ralung came to be regarded at the heads of the Drukpa Kagyu school, and from the 15th century onwards these were identified with the successive reincarnations of Tsangpa Gya-re himself (see box, page 239). A geographical distinction also evolved between the Lower Drukpa, stemming from Lorepa Wangchuk Tsondru (1187-1250), the Upper Drukpa, stemming from Gotsangpa Gonpo Dorje (1189-1258), who was especially active in far-west Tibet around Mount Kailash, and the Middle Drukpa, stemming from Sangye Bonre Darma Senge (1177-1237), who was a nephew of Tsangpa Gya-re.

Early Drukpa Kagyu activity in Bhutan

In Bhutan, Lorepa himself founded **Chodrak** monastery in Bumthang (now a Nyingmapa nunnery), and Chilkarwa of the Upper Drukpa school founded **Chikarkha** monastery in Paro. Barawa Gyeltsen Pelzang (1310-1391), revered as an incarnation of the Upper Drukpa master Yangonpa, also visited Bhutan on two occasions, establishing the monastery of **Drangyekha** in Paro. However, the dominant influence was that of the Middle Drukpa. This was largely due to the seminal role played in Western Bhutan by Phajo Drukgom Zhikpo (1184-1251) and his five sons, whose descendants are found throughout Western Bhutan. Phajo was despatched to Bhutan by his teacher Sangye Bonre Darma Senge in 1224. He established his main seat at **Tango** in the upper Thimphu valley, and passed away there (see page 93).

Among his sons, Dampa built the protector shrine of **Dechenphuk** in Thimphu and **Changangkha** in Paro, and his family maintained excellent relations with the mother monastery at Ralung. Another son, Nyima, founded Changangkha Chakhang in Thimphu, also in the 13th century. The seventh hierarch of Ralung, Jamyang Kunga Sangye (r. 1314-1347) was invited to Bhutan in 1333, and he refurbished Changangkha. His son Lodro Sangye (r. 1345-1390) built the temple at **Zabsal**. In 1461 the 13th hierarch of Ralung, Drukchen II Choje Kunga Peljor (1426-1476), visited Paro on the first of his four trips to Bhutan, which took him as far east as Bumthang. He built a number of temples and monasteries in Paro (including **Do Chorten**, **Drela Gongkar Dzong**, **Gongkar Dechending** and **Lateng Gonpa**), and **Sharpa Phuntsoling** in Wangdu.

The 14th hierarch Ngawang Chogyel (1465-1540) visited Bhutan on six occasions, starting from 1497. His travels took him through Paro, where he founded **Samten Tsemo** and **Druk Choding** (still standing in Paro marketplace), and Thimphu, where he renovated Changangkha temple, and built **Druk Podrangding** at Pangri Zampa. Some extant murals at Changangkha may date from that period. Further east, he founded the renowned **Chime Lhakhang** near Punakha, among others. A younger relative of Ngawang Chogyel, Drukpa Kun-le (1455-1529), sometimes known as the

⁝ Incarnations of Tsangpa Gya-re at Ralung Monastery

Drukchen I	Tsangpa Gya-re (1161-1211)
Drukchen II	Choje Kunga Peljor (1426-1476)
Drukchen III	Jamyang Chodrak (1477-1523)
Drukchen IV	Pema Karpo (1527-1592)
Drukchen V	Paksam Wangpo (1593-1641)
Drukchen VI	Mipam Wangpo (1641-1717)
Drukchen VII	Trin-le Shingta (1718-1766)
Drukchen VIII	Kunzik Chokyi Nangwa (1767-1822)
Drukchen IX	Jigme Migyur Wangyel (1823-1883)
Drukchen X	Mipam Chokyi Wangpo (1884-1930)
Drukchen XI	Tendzin Khyenrab Gelek Wangpo (1931-1960)
Drukchen XII	Jigme Pema Wangchen (b. 1963)

'divine madman', lived as a peripatetic and unconventional yogin, and is revered throughout Bhutan as a seminal culture hero, integrating inner spiritual realisations with bizarre and sometimes profane external conduct (see box, page 149). He founded **Montsip Lhakhang** in Bumthang, and built **Karbi Chorten** in Punakha in order to subdue malign forces. Ngawang Drakpa (r. 1506-1530), the 16th hierarch of Ralung and son of Ngawang Chogyel, visited Dechenphuk and Pangri Zampa in Thimphu, and continuing east towards Wangdu, he built **Chungseng Dargyegang** and **Khotang Gonsar**. His younger brother Ngagi Wangchuk travelled from Ralung to Bhutan in 1540, and he was particularly active in Trongsar and Bumthang. His temple of **Mon Drubde** is located within Chotse Dzong at Trongsar, the temple of **Jakar** within Jakar Dzong, and the temple of **Linglingtang** near Lhunste Dzong.

Conflicting interests of the Ralung hierarchs and the reincarnations of Tsangpa Gya-re

The officially recognised reincarnation of Tsangpa Gya-re, Drukchen II Kunga Peljor, visited Bhutan from 1461, as we have seen. However the subsequent incarnations, Drukchen III Jamyang Chodrak (1477-1523) and Drukchen IV Pema Karpo (1527-1592), were born outside the ruling family of Ralung hierarchs and this was destined to become a cause of future conflict. Pema Karpo was in fact the most illustrious and prolific of all scholars within the Drukpa Kagyu school. His collected writings, amounting to some 300 texts printed in 14 volumes, cover all the classical sciences including Buddhist philosophy, astrology, divination and history, and they are widely recognised as authoritative and prestigious sources throughout the Drukpa Kagyu tradition, even in Bhutan, which he appears not to have visited. His contemporary, Mipham Chogyel (r. 1543-1606), who was the 17th hierarch of the ruling house of Ralung and the son of Ngagi Wangchuk, did visit both Western and Central Bhutan from 1567. The monasteries he founded there included **Thekchentse Lhakhang** near Lhuntse Dzong. His son Mipham Tenpei Nyima (1567-1619) built **Chorten Nyingba** in Chume around 1586, and carried the Drukpa Kagyu teachings into south-eastern Bhutan, where he founded **Yongla Gonpa** in Pema Gatshel and **Zhongar Dzong**. More significantly, he was the father of Zhabdrung Ngawang Namgyel (1594-1651), founder of the unified Bhutanese state.

The flight of Zhabdrung Ngawang Namgyel

After Pema Karpo passed away in 1592, Ngawang Namgyel was enthroned as the 18th hierarch of Ralung in 1606, and in his early years he focused on his studies, particularly

⦚ Incarnations of Zhabdrung Ngawang Namgyel

The successive mind and speech emanations of Zhabdrung Ngawang Namgyel (1594-1651) were frequently rivals. Although none of them had the authority of the first, from the mid-18th century the mind incarnation did succeed in bringing a semblance of unity that survived until the foundation of the Bhutanese monarchy n 1907. The lineage of mind incarnations (*tuktrul*) is as follows:

Zhabdrung I	Ngawang Namgyel (1594-1651)
Zhabdrung II	Jigme Drakpa (1724-1761)
Zhabdrung III	Chokyi Gyeltsen (1762-1788)
Zhabdrung IV	Jigme Drakpa (1791-1830)
Zhabdrung V	Jigme Norbu (1831-1861)
Zhabdrung VI	Jigme Chogyel (1862-1904)
Zhabdrung VII	Jigme Dorje (1905-1931)

the works of Pema Karpo, and on painting and sculpture, both of which he mastered. However, efforts to have him also recognised as the rightful reincarnation of Pema Karpo were thwarted by the Tsangpa rulers of Tibet who were based at Zhigatse, and who instead recognised the claim of a rival candidate, Drukchen V Pagsam Wangpo (1593-1641). Despite attempts at reconciliation, Ngawang Namgyel was forced into exile from Ralung in 1616, carrying with him a precious image of Kharsapani, which had been naturally fashioned from the first vertebra of Tsangpa Gya-re. Encouraged by Tendzin Drugye, a senior chant-leader at Ralung who was of Bhutanese birth, he fled south to **Laya** and thence to **Pangri Zampa** in the upper Thimphu valley and **Druk Choding** in Paro, seeking sanctuary in his ancestral domains. From this point on the line of the Drukchen incarnations at Ralung diverged from that of the Zhabdrungs in Bhutan.

Consolidation of the Drukpa state and the three Tsangpa invasions

In 1617 the Tsangpa ruler of Tibet, Phuntsok Namgyel, sent an army to confront the Zhabdrung at **Paro**, but his forces were repelled and General Lagu-ne was slain. The Zhabdrung now returned to **Tango** where he forged an alliance with Tsewang Tendzin, a grandson of Drukpa Kun-le. In 1620 he constructed a silver reliquary stupa at Cheri to hold the ashes of his deceased father, which were smuggled out of Tibet, and he instituted the monastic body there at the newly founded **Cheri Gonpa** (see page 95). He simultaneously entered into diplomatic relations with King Prata Narayana of neighbouring Kuch Bihar to the south. Then, following a prolonged retreat, in 1626 he resolved to formally establish a unified system of government for the country, combining both spiritual and temporal authority. Although Bhutan had throughout this period been a significant region for Tibetan Buddhist missionary activity, the country still lacked political cohesion. In the western parts of his newly formed kingdom, the Zhabdrung began to construct a series of fortified castles (*dzong*) on the Tibetan model. In 1629 **Sinmo Dokha Dzong** (Bh. Simtokha) was constructed to the south of the Thimphu valley. The plan was opposed by the so-called Five Groups of Lamas (Bh. Lam Khag Nga), representatives of other Buddhist schools who felt their position in Bhutan was being undermined by the Zhabdrung's increasing authority. However, this makeshift alliance of the Lhanangpa, Nenyingpa, Barawa, Chakzampa and Geden Shingtapa schools was repelled and the building completed. Here, in 1631, a son, Ngawang Jampal Dorje, was born to the Zhabdrung and his second consort Gokar Dolma.

Two years later the Zhabdrung assumed the full monastic vows at Cheri Gonpa, and as his charismatic influence continued to grow, the Five Groups of Lamas allied themselves with the new Tsangpa ruler of Tibet, Karma Tenkyong Wangpo, in 1634. They jointly launched a series of multiple attacks, which once again failed, although the fortress at Simtokha was damaged. Senior figures of the Jonang and Sakya schools in Tibet successfully mediated in order to secure the release of the captured Tibetan forces. The Zhabdrung then constructed other fortresses, further to the east: **Dechen Podrang Dzong** in Punakha was founded in 1637 to accommodate the monastic community of Cheri Gonpa, who moved here from Thimphu; and in 1638 the **Khamsum Wangdu Chokyi Podrang Dzong** was built further south, on a ridge overlooking the confluence of the Punatsang-chu and the Dang-chu.

A new alliance was forged between the Five Groups of Lamas and the Tsangpa ruler in 1639 when the third Tibetan invasion laid siege to the two new fortresses. But this army was repelled when Gyelpo Tendzin, brother of the king of distant Ladakh, took command of the Zhabdrung's forces. Finally, in 1640 Karmapa X and other senior Tibetan incarnate lamas mediated to resolve the disputed Ralung succession. Accordingly, the Tsangpa rulers of Tibet recognised Drukchen V Paksam Wangpo as the Drukchen and the Zhabdrung as the supreme authority of Southern Mon (Bhutan), in exchange for a 'rice-tribute'. The power of the Five Groups was effectively eclipsed. In 1641 Dongon Dzong in Thimphu was absorbed by the Drukpa Kagyu school, and eventually renamed **Tashi Chodzong**. The Zhabdrung instated the tradition whereby the monastic community would move there in the summer months from Punakha.

Conflict with the Dewar Zhung in Tibet

In 1642 the administration of the Tsangpa rulers of Tibet was brought to an abrupt end when the Mongol armies of Gushi Qan decisively intervened on behalf of Dalai Lama V, who re-established the Tibetan capital in Lhasa for the first time since the empire of the early kings. The new regent of Tibet, Sonam Chopel, and King Gushi Qan refused to accept the reconciliation agreed shortly before the death of the last Tsangpa ruler, and accused the Bhutanese of assisting the Garpa revolt against the new regime. In 1644 a Tibeto-Mongol army was despatched to Paro from Dromo, but it appears to have quickly succumbed to the heat and humidity. The army's captured weaponry was removed to Punakha Dzong, to be put on permanent display in the **Yulgyel Gonkhang**. To strengthen security in the west, the **Rinpung Dzong** was founded in Paro that same year. In 1646 the hierarch of Sakya and Panchen IV Chokyi Gyeltsen of Tashilhunpo mediated to secure the release of the captured officers, and the former agreement forged with the Tsangpa ruler was re-established. Further fortresses were built in the northern borderland as military outposts, including **Tashi Tongmon Dzong** in Gasa and **Yulgyel Dzong** in Lingzhi.

In 1649 the Tibeto-Mongol forces launched yet another assault on Bhutan, laying siege to the *dzongs* at Punakha, Thimphu and Paro. However, they were poorly commanded and repelled within three months. Much of the armour and weaponry left behind is on display in the **National Museum** in Paro. To commemorate this ignominious retreat and his personal triumph, the Zhabdrung built **Drugyel Dzong** in the upper Paro valley that same year, and he instated the *dromcho* new-year festival at Punakha Dzong. In these ways he consolidated the whole of Western Bhutan under his rule.

The Zhabdrung's final years

Between 1649 and 1651 the Zhabdrung's general, Nyerpa Druk Namgyel, conducted a military campaign in **Tarkarna** (Bh. Dagana) on the southern borders of the country, and established the new Drukpa rule in these parts, in recognition of which **Tarkar Tashi Yangtse Dzong** was built.

However, the Zhabdrung himself grew more intent on his spiritual pursuits, keen as he was to build a memorial stupa containing terracotta relics on behalf of all those who had died in past military actions. In 1651 he withdrew from the world and entered into solitary retreat, during which he passed away, probably in 1656. In the interests of national security, his death was kept secret for half a century, until 1705. Around the same time, the death of Dalai Lama V in Lhasa was also kept secret for reasons of political expediency.

Theocractic control

Having unified Western Bhutan, the Zhabdrung introduced a code of spiritual and temporal law (*katrim*) based very much on the systems that had evolved inside Tibet from King Songtsen Gampo's seventh-century code of justice. This code was transmitted orally until 1729 when it was committed to writing in 16 folios by the 10th Je Khenpo Tendzin Chogyel. The articles concerned kingship, monastic and civil duties, crime and punishment, inheritance, commerce, land ownership, barter, corvee labour, and social prohibitions. Following the Sakyapa model, whereby spiritual and temporal power were combined (rather than the Phagmodrupa and Tsangpa model, which clearly defined a separation of such powers), the Zhabdrung envisaged the future Bhutanese state as being embodied in his own blood line, with spiritual matters being delegated to an abbatial succession known as the **Je Khenpo** and temporal matters being assigned to an appointed regent, known as the **Desi**. In fact the Zhabdrung's son Jampel Dorje (1631-1681) had no male heirs and played no significant role in Bhutanese life. The unifying role as head of state therefore passed to the six successive reincarnations of the Zhabdrung's buddha mind (**Zhabdrung Tuktrul**) from 1724 through to the founding of the Bhutanese monarchy in 1907.

Seventy Je Khenpos have headed the Drukpa Kagyu order in Bhutan since the first was appointed by the Zhabdrung in 1633, down to the present incumbent, Tulku Jigme Chodrak. Under them were four senior masters (*lopon*) responsible for supervising tantric practice, rituals, linguistic and dialectical studies. At the same time, a succession of 55 Desis have held executive power in Bhutan until the theocratic system was replaced by the monarchy in 1907. Many of them were in fact political monks. Under them were the governors (*ponlop*) of the three original provinces, Paro, Tarkar (Dagana) and Trongsar, as well as three chieftains (*dzongpon*) of Punakha, Thimphu and Wangdu fortresses, which developed as centres of local administration and bastions of Buddhist learning. Other senior officials included the head-chamberlain (*gongzim*), and two ministers responsible for protocol and justice. Lower-ranking officials known as *drungpon* would liaise between the fortresses and the populace, while everyday village affairs were in the hands of the appointed headmen (Bh. *gup*). This dual system and its legal code based on Buddhist principles endured until 1907 despite the inherent threat of decentralisation frequently posed by powerful provincial governors and local officials during the hiatus following the death of the Zhabdrung and the accession to power of his recognised incarnation.

Expansion into Central and Eastern Bhutan

Throughout the years when the Zhabdrung was consolidating his authority in Western Bhutan, the Central and Eastern regions, where different languages were spoken, remained under the sway of as many as 21 local chieftains, some of them descendants of the Dung families of Bumthang, and others claiming descent from Prince Tsangma. Following the appointment of Migyur Tenpa as governor of Trongsar, a concerted military campaign ensued, with the assistance of one Lama Nam-se, which between 1647 and 1655 saw the entire Central and Eastern regions forcefully integrated within the new Bhutanese state. All the local chieftains from the Dung of **Chokhor** in Bumthang and Lhabudar of Ragsa in **Kurto**, and as far east as **Khaling**, **Merak** and **Sakteng** succumbed, as did the Dung of Nyakhar in **Khyeng**.

Adherents of the Nyingmapa order, who were mostly followers of the teachings of Pema Lingpa, were permitted to maintain their traditions, but the few establishments representative of other Buddhist schools in the region were absorbed by the Drukpa Kagyu. Six fortresses were built to enforce new legislation concerning barter, taxation and corvee labour in these Central and Eastern areas – **Jakar Dzong**, **Lhuntse Dzong**, **Zhongar Dzong**, **Tashi Yangtse Dzong**, **Zhemgang Dzong** and **Tashigang Dzong** – all of them under the authority of the governor of Trongsar. More specifically, the four areas of Mangde were placed directly under under Trongsar, the four valleys of Bumthang under Jakar Dzong, the four valleys of Kurto under Lhuntse Dzong, the five areas of Yangtse under Tashi Yangtse Dzong, the seven areas of Zhongar under Zhongar Dzong, the 10 areas of Tashigang under Tashigang Dzong, the three areas of Khyeng under Zhemgang Dzong, and the three valleys of Dungsum under Pema Gatshel Dzong.

Regents of the 17th century

During the long period when the Zhabdrung's death was concealed, there were four regents who handled all affairs of state. All of them had been among his closest associates and it was in their interest to consolidate the power of the newly formed state. Tendzin Drugye (r. 1651-1656), the first regent and Bhutanese by birth, had accompanied the Zhabdrung on his initial flight to Bhutan in 1616. He is credited with the establishment of the **National Code of Conduc**t (*Driklam Namzhak*), which created a distinctive sense of Bhutanese national identity. During his tenure the Central and Eastern regions were firmly brought within the fold of the emerging state. His successor, Langon Tendzin Drukdra (r. 1656-1668), was the Zhabdrung's half-brother, and he served as the first governor of Paro before assuming the role of regent. He successfully repelled another Tibeto-Mongol invasion in 1657, as his foes succumbed to the summer humidity and epidemics. He encouraged the study of classical sciences, including arts and crafts, and constructed a number of important buildings, including **Drugyel Dzong** and **Ta Dzong** in Paro and the **Kungarawa Hall** of Punakha Dzong.

The third regent, Migyur Tenpa (r. 1668-1680), originally served as the governor of Trongsar, during the period of expansion into Central and Eastern Bhutan. He completed unfinished work on a series of eight sandalwood stupas (**Ngulbum Chorten**) at Punakha Dzong, and a gilded manuscript version of the *Kangyur*. In 1671 he also completed the renovation of **Simtokha Dzong**. Then in 1668 the Drukpa forces took control of **Kalimpong** and even penetrated Sikkim and Dromo before being turned back by the Tibetans. Two further invasions were launched from Tibet, that same year and in 1675, but the fighting was as inconclusive as before. Kalimpong subsequently remained in Bhutanese control until 1865, when it was wrested by the British. Bhutanese influence in **Ladakh**, **Lahaul** and the **Ngari** region of far-west Tibet increased at this time too, with the result that several hermitages and monasteries, including Drirapuk and Dzutrulpuk at sacred **Mount Kailash**, came under their direct control, as did certain shrines at **Svayambhunath** in Nepal. Mingyur Tenpa was eventually deposed in 1680 by the chieftain of Punakha Dzong, Gendun Chopel.

The fourth regent, Tendzin Rabgye (r. 1680-1695), had been groomed by the Zhabdrung as a crown prince (*gyelse*) in his youth, and he was probably the only regent to have had a high spiritual standing. He expanded the monastic community at **Punakha** and introduced many of the formal sacred dances that are still performed at *tsechu* ceremonies in the fortresses of Bhutan today (see page 265). He refurbished many fortresses in the Central and Eastern regions, and built a new one, the **Damsang Dzong**, in Ha. At the same time he exhibited an eclectic spirit, extending the hand of friendship to Nyingmapa and Sakyapa adherents, while building new temples at **Taktsang** in Paro, **Tango** in Thimphu and **Tachogang**, the seat of Tangtong Gyelpo. Throughout the tenure of these first four regents consistent efforts were made to conceal the death of the Zhabdrung.

When the Zhabdrung's death was publicly announced in 1705 by Kunga Gyeltsen, the reincarnation of the Zhabdrung's son, Jampel Dorje, a prolonged power struggle ensued, as self-interested regents and governors strived to have the authority of succession invested in their own preferred candidates for the Zhabdrung's reincarnation. The body incarnation (*kutrul*) of the Zhabdrung was born in Sikkim and never brought to Bhutan. The speech incarnation (*sungtrul*) was born in Daganang, and had some influence on Bhutanese affairs, particularly during the incumbency of Sungtrul I Chokle Namgyel (1708-1736). The mind incarnation (*tuktrul*), Jigme Drakpa (1724-1761), was born at Dranang in Southern Tibet. In consequence of the bitter internecine rivalry between the various factions, the then ruler of Tibet, Pholha-ne Miwang Sonam Tobgye, was asked to intervene militarily by one of the factions. The conflict was only resolved in 1734 following the mediation of Pholha-ne and Manchu imperial arbitration in Beijing, when the country was reunified under the authority of the mind incarnation Jigme Drakpa. This resulted in a theoretical loss of sovereignty, as an annual tribute had to be paid to Lhasa by the Bhutanese legation there. At the same time, as Michael Aris has noted, the very presence of this legation later guaranteed Bhutan's independence. Later mind incarnations of the Zhabdrung never exercised the authority that the first had enjoyed. The longest-serving regent, Sherab Wangchuk (r. 1744-1763), offered some stability, but bloody rivalry continued through the decades that followed his death. According to Lopon Pema Tsewang's *History of Bhutan*, nearly half of all the 55 regents who held executive power in Bhutan until the establishment of the monarchy in 1907 were assassinated.

Early contacts with British India

From earliest times until the mid-18th century, the inhabitants of Bhutan had remained firmly within the Tibetan cultural orbit, notwithstanding the aforementioned conflicts. Two Portuguese Jesuit priests, Estevao Cacella and Joas Cabral, did travel from India through Bhutan in 1627 en route for Tibet, and they made contact with the Zhabdrung at **Cheri**, but the intractable and virtually impenetrable terrain of Southern Bhutan ensured that contact with the Indian subcontinent was minimal. Only the Maharaja of neighbouring **Kuch Bihar** had entered into some form of diplomatic relations with the Zhabdrung. However, in 1765 the 15th regent, Druk Tendzin, began interfering in the royal succession to the throne of Kuch Bihar, and claimants to the throne requested for military assistance from British East India Company. The Indian troops sent by Warren Hastings drove out the Bhutanese, and in 1773 they took possession of Kuch Bihar and the southern borderlands of Bhutan. The Bhutanese were thus forced to look southwards. A peace treaty brokered by Panchen Lama VI Palden Yeshe of Zhigatse in Tibet was then signed at Kolkata in 1774, returning the captured territory in return for lumbering rights in southern Bhutan. That same year, Warren Hastings sent a mission to Thimphu, headed by George Bogle, who was also ordered to plant potatoes there, while waiting for permission to continue on to Zhigatse. Further missions were sent in 1776-77 under Alexander Hamilton and in 1783 under Samuel Turner. During this period, trade developed with the East India Company and relations appear to have been positive on both sides.

The Duar Wars

During the minor years of Zhabdrung Jigme Drakpa II (1791-1830), the governor of Trongsar, Tsaphukpa Dorje, further weakened the country through his machinations and internecine revolts. The British acquired neighbouring Assam during the Burmese war of 1825-26, and with it they took over seasonal occupancy of the **Assamese Duars**, the rugged territory where the Himalayan rivers meet the plains, north of the Brahmaputra, which was regarded as an important tract for tea plantations. Between 1836 and 1841, the British forcibly annexed these Assamese Duars and created the present-day boundary, agreeing to pay a small annual subsidy of 10,000 rupees as long as the Bhutanese remained peaceful. However, Bhutanese raiders continued to make forays across the border, and in the aftermath of the Indian mutiny of 1857, they launched attacks on both the neighbouring **Bengal Duars** and the kingdom of Kuch Bihar. A British mission forced its way into Western Bhutan in 1864 under Ashley Eden, but this did not please the Bhutanese, who humiliated the envoy and demanded the unconditional return of all the Duars. The Duar War of 1864-65 which followed ended with the **Treaty of Sinchula**, according to which the Bhutanese agreed to a permanent annexation of the Duars and Kalimpong area by British India and to the imposition of a free-trade agreement. In exchange, the Bhutanese received a modest monetary compensation.

The rise of the Bhutanese monarchy

By 1865, the fabric of the dual theocratic system had been worn down in consequence of this period of turmoil, leaving Central and Eastern Bhutan in the power of the provincial governor of **Trongsar**, Jigme Namgyel (1825-1881). His son, Ugyen Wangchuk (1862-1926), who inherited the governorship on his father's death, consolidated his control by seizing Simtokha Dzong and defeating troops who were loyal to the chieftains of Punakha and Tashi Chodzong fortresses. Then, in 1885 he inflicted a crushing defeat on the governor of Paro at Thimphu, and with his enhanced power, he soon forged a renewed sense of national unity. The post of regent was now largely a ceremonial one, the real power resting in the hands of the governor. Ugyen Wangchuk purposefully entered into an increasing co-operation with the British, acting as an intermediary between them and the Tibetans in 1904 at the time of the Younghusband expedition into Tibet, in return for which he received a knighthood in 1906. The award was presented by John Claude White in the course of his second expedition to Bhutan. The history of the Bhutanese monarchy is recounted in Michael Aris' *The Raven Crown*.

King Urgyen Wangchuk

Assured of British imperial support, Ugyen Wangchuk was successfully elected as the hereditary monarch of Bhutan (Druk Gyelpo) in 1907, following the death of the 55th regent, Choktrul Yeshe Ngodrub. The sixth Zhabdrung Jigme Dorje (1905-1931) had just been born, and so with all power in his hands, the new king abolished the incarnating theocracy, which was the legacy of the first Zhabdrung. Secular rule was henceforth vested in his family, who were descendants of the great treasure-finder Pema Lingpa, while the religious role of the Je Khenpo as head of the Drukpa Kagyu order continued. In 1910, in return for increasing its annual subsidy for the Duars to 100,000 rupees per annum, Bhutan signed the **Treaty of Punakha** and agreed to accept British guidance in its external affairs. Bhutan, however, did not receive help in building roads, expanding communications and developing the economy as did Sikkim, which was then a British protectorate. The pace of development was therefore much slower.

King Jigme Wangchuk

Following the death of Ugyen Wangchuk in 1926, the first king was succeeded by his son Jigme Wangchuk (1905-1952). During his reign Bhutanese isolation continued, despite the impact of World War II on neighbouring India and China. He established his summer palace at **Wangdu Choling** in Bumthang (a residence constructed by his grandfather in 1857), and his winter palace at **Kunga Rabten** in Trongsar district. During the reign of this second king, a few western-style schools were established with British aid, and Bhutanese students were encouraged to study in India. Under a 1949 treaty between Bhutan and newly independent India, Bhutan entered a non-binding agreement to 'be guided by the advice' of India in its foreign affairs, and in return received a small tract of land around **Dewathang** in the Assamese Duars.

King Jigme Dorji Wangchuk

The third king, Jigme Dorji Wangchuk (1928-1972), had been educated in Britain and in India. Following his coronation in 1952, he soon founded a new National Assembly (Tshogdu), and formulated a new legal and judicial system, with a modern army and police force. In terms of social policy, he abolished serfdom, but still remained devoted to Buddhism and the national culture. In 1958 the king invited Pandit Nehru and his daughter Indira Gandhi on a private visit to Bhutan. The next year, following the abortive Tibetan uprising against Chinese rule in Lhasa, he changed political direction, and purposefully began the process that would take Bhutan out of its self-imposed isolationist phase, in order to safeguard the county's independence. In this way, the third king embarked on a process of modernisation and economic development. A five-year development plan was launched in 1961, with India financing the construction of the **Chukha hydroelectric project**. Then in 1962, Bhutan officially joined the Colombo Plan, in return for which technical and scientific training was provided. Despite opposition from conservative forces to the pace of change, the king initiated a road-building programme, which gradually made the country more accessible to the outside world. In 1969 the country joined the Universal Postal Union, and perhaps his greatest achievement, in 1971, shortly before his death, he successfully applied for UN membership. The affection with which the third king is viewed in Bhutan is shown in the grandeur of his **Memorial Chorten**, subsequently erected in Thimphu (see page 70).

King Jigme Senge Wangchuk

The fourth and present king of Bhutan, Jigme Senge Wangchuk (b. 1955), ascended the throne in 1974, while still a teenager. The coronation was attended by the international media, and a number of hotels were built to accommodate the visitors. Influenced by his father, his policy has been to promote socio-economic development with a view to achieving economic self-reliance, while conserving the natural environment and the Buddhist heritage of Bhutan. In social policy, he abolished the age-old practice of corvee labour, and restructured the political administration of the country on more democratic principles (see page 247). In 1979 he privately married four daughters of Yab Ugyen Dorje, who was a nephew of the sixth Zhabdrung Jigme Dorje. The formal Royal Wedding Ceremony was not actually held until 1988. The crown prince, Jigme Gesar Namgyel Wangchuk, was born in 1980. Through the continuing efforts of the fourth king, Bhutan has become a member of many international organisations, including the Nonaligned Movement, the South Asian Association for Regional Cooperation, the Asian Development Bank, the World Bank and the International Monetary Fund. In addition, Bhutan now has diplomatic relations with India, Bangladesh, Nepal, Maldives, Kuwait, Switzerland, Norway, the European Union, Japan, Sri Lanka and Thailand.

Nepalese migration

Prior to the 20th century, the inhospitable terrain of Southern Bhutan remained uninhabited until small numbers of ethnic Nepalis began moving into the foothills. This modest migration continued throughout the first half of the 20th century, as Nepali forest labourers were brought in, later settling as tenant farmers and eventually acquiring Bhutanese nationality in 1958. The term Lhotsampa ('inhabitants of the southern borderlands') refers almost exclusively to this ethnic Nepalese community, which occupies the five southern districts of the country, where they outnumber the indigenous Bhutanese. The Nepali language was given official status and the alien Hindu customs and traditions of the migrants were accorded respect. Civil servants of Nepali origin were and continue to be posted throughout the country.

However, with the recent opening up of the country and the endeavour to develop its infrastructure, large numbers of economic migrants followed in the wake of those early settlers, the majority of them also ethnic Nepali. Following the 1988 census, those latecomers who had no residential rights prior to 1958 were declared illegal immigrants, and pressurised into leaving the country, as efforts were made to strengthen the Bhutanese sense of national identity. Nepali-speaking civil servants had to adopt traditional Bhutanese dress, and the teaching of their language was downgraded in schools. These policies no doubt reflected the sense of insecurity that the Bhutanese feel when they observe the demographic situation in neighbouring Sikkim, where Nepalis are now the dominant community, with Lepchas and Bhotias (Tibetans) in a minority. Between 1988 and 1993 more than 80,000 of these illegal migrants fled from Bhutan to south-eastern Nepal, where they were registered by UNHCR in the Jhapa encampments. The population of the camps has since risen to about 100,000 as the Bhutanese and Nepalese governments try to resolve the problem through bilateral negotiation. A Nepali and Bhutanese ministerial joint committee (MJC) was established in order to categorise the refugees. However, the problem even now appears to be intractable. For example, of the 12,183 refugees at the Khudunabari camp in eastern Nepal, only 293 were recognised as bona fide Bhutanese who had been wrongly evicted. More than 70% were classified as voluntary migrants and almost 25% as non-Bhutanese nationals. For further insight into this problem, readers are referred to Michael Hutt's *Unbecoming Citizens: Culture, Nationhood and the Flight of Refugees from Bhutan* (OUP, 2003). Even so, the Lhotsampa are still estimated to comprise about 30% of the total national population of Bhutan.

Assamese insurgency movements

Militant separatists have been active in north-east India for many years. The United Liberation Front of Assam (ULFA), founded in 1979, and the Bodo Liberation Tiger Force (BLTF), which represents the Mechi tribal community, have drifted into the neighbouring jungles of south-eastern Bhutan, from where they periodically launch terrorist assaults across the border. These problems have continued despite the Indian army's strong and visible presence in the Assamese Duars and the king of Bhutan's resolve to confront the militants from his side. The districts of Samdrub Jongkhar and Pema Gatshel still have restricted access on account of this problem. However, there are indications that these difficulties may soon be resolved. In the winter months of 2003-04, the Bhutanese army effectively expelled over 1,000 insurgents from their forest sanctuary into Assam, where they were detained by the Indian army. This action subsequently incurred the wrath of ULFA leaders in Guwahati who say they will now target Bhutanese interests.

Modern Bhutan

Government

Central government His Majesty King Jigme Senge Wangchuk is the **head of state**, presiding over the exceutive, legislature, judiciary and the armed forces. Executive decisions are made by the **cabinet** (*lhengye zhungtsog*), which comprises the ministers (Bh. *lyonpo*) of Home Affairs, Finance, Foreign Affairs, Agriculture, Health, Trade and Industry, Construction, Education, Energy, and Communications. Ministers since 1998 have been elected by the National Assembly, and chairmanship of the cabinet changes annually on a rotational basis. There has been no prime minister since the assassination of Jigme Palden Dorje in 1964. The **Royal Advisory Council**

⁞ Modern Bhutan: statistics

→ **Official name** Druk-Yul

→ **Capital** Thimphu

→ **National flag** Saffron and orange red, divided diagonally, with a white dragon in the centre

→ **Other national symbols** *Bird*: raven; *Animal*: takin; *Flower*: blue poppy; *Tree*: cypress; *Day*:17 December; *Anthem*: Druk Tsendhen (The Thunder Dragon Kingdom)

→ **Official language** Dzongkha

→ **Key statistics** *Population*: 2004 (estimate) 740,000; Urban 21%; Agricultural 66%; Drukpas 67%; Nepalese origin 30%; others 3%. *Population density*: 12.76 per sq km. *Birth rate*: 2.5%. *Death rate*: 0.9%. *Life expectancy*: 67 years. *Literacy*: 57%, M 54%, F 40%. *GDP*: 656 USD. *Land use*: forested 72%, permanent pasture and agriculture 8%, snow/glacier 7.5%, scrub forest 8.1, other 4.5%. *Growth rate*: 3.1%. *Religion*: Buddhist 70%, Hindu 28%, other 2%.

(*kalyon*), a permanently standing body established in 1965, reports to the king and liaises between the cabinet and National Assembly, ensuring that approved legislation is actually implemented. The chaiman of this council is appointed by the king, and its eight other members include two representatives of the official monastic order and six lay citizens. The cabinet also liaises with a number of **autonomous agencies,** including the Council for Ecclesiastical Affairs (*dratsang lhentsog*), the Royal Civil Service Commission (founded 1992), the Planning Commission, the National Environment Commission (founded 1989), the National Employment Board, the Royal Monetary Authority, the National Technical Training Authority, the Royal Institute of Management (based at Simtokha), the Office of Legal Affairs, the Centre for Bhutan Studies, the Dzongkha Development Commission, and the National Commission for Cultural Affairs (founded 1985). Among them, the **Council for Ecclesiastical Affairs** (*dratsang lhentsog*) has nine members, presided over by the Je Khenpo, the elected head of the Drukpa Kagyu order. Since 1968, the official monastic communities (*rabde*), which have their seats in the district *dzongs*, have been subsidised by the government, and their vast land holdings have been gradually purchased by the government for redistribution among the peasantry. The **National Commission for Cultural Affairs** (*soldzin lhentsog*) administers the National Museum in Paro, and the National Library, the Royal Academy of Performing Arts and the Textile Museum, which are all based in Thimphu.

Legislative decisions are made by the **National Assembly** (*tsogdu*), which was created in 1953 and given enhanced powers in 1998. The National Assembly, under the guidance of its elected speaker, has 150 members who are elected for a three-year term. They include 105 district representatives (Bh. *chimi*) who are elected by village headmen, 10 monastic representatives elected by the official Drukpa Kagyu order, and 35 high-ranking officials who are nominated by the king or the government. The National Assembly convenes biannually at the new Assembly Hall near Tashi Chodzong in Thimphu, but the speaker has the authority to convene special meetings if necessary. The Royal Audit Authority is an autonomous agency that reports to the National Assembly.

The judiciary is presided over by the **High Court** (*trimkhang gongma*), comprising eight senior judges under the chief justice. Final appeals may also be made to the king himself. The legal code (*trimzhung chenmo*), though based on the medieval Buddhist laws of the Zhabdrung (which themselves had Tibetan antecedents), was

established in 1957 and revised in 2001. All new laws have to be passed by the
National Assembly. Bhutan's first written constitution is currently being drafted.

District government The modern reorganisation of Bhutan's system of regional and local government has resulted in a more decentralised, multi-tiered administration. District government was thoroughly reorganised in the latter half of the 20th century. In place of the old provincial governorships, there are now four **zonal administrators** (*dzongde chichab*), presiding over the four zones (*dzongde*) into which the country has been divided. Each zone comprises five districts (*dzongkhag*), presided over by their own **district commissioners** (*dzongdag*). These officials are appointed by the king and responsible to the Ministry of Home Affairs. Within each district there is also a district progressive council (DYT), which makes recommendations to the National Assembly through its elected representatives (*chimi*), and a district court (*dzongkhag trimkhang*), under its own magistrate. The larger and more populous districts are divided into smaller subdistricts (*dungkhag*), presided over by a **subdistrct officer** (*dungpa*). Subdistrict courts (*dungtrim*) also have their own magistrates.

Local government Within each of Bhutan's 20 districts, there are a number of counties or blocks (*gewok*), each comprising a number of villages or hamlets. The **headman** (*gup/ mandal*) is elected by the local community for a three-year term, and he also has the authority to resolve legal disputes within his jurisdiction. **Block Progressive Councils** (GYT) meet to discuss local issues, reporting to their corresponding District Progressive Councils. These headmen also have an important role in electing their representatives to the National Assembly.

Economy

In 2003, the per capita income was estimated at US$1,300, and the annual growth rate at 7.7%. The annual inflation rate stands at around 3%. Although these figures tend to place Bhutan among the least developed nations, the country is unlike others within that category, in that there is no famine in this land of subsistence farming, little malnutrition, good housing, and a favourable ratio of population to cultivated land, with approximately 98% of the land being owned by the peasants who work it.

Infrastructure In 1961, the third king initiated a continuing series of five-year plans, which at the outset focused on road construction and basic administrative infrastructures. The result is that motorable roads, airline services and modern satellite communication systems that now link Bhutan with the outside world, propelling the country rapidly away from its long-sought isolation. In 1999 the Bhutanese Broadcasting Service (BBS) opnend its first television station, and Druknet became the country's first internet service provider.

Industrial development Subsequent five-year plans have focused on the economic exploitation of Bhutan's considerable natural resources, including forestry, agriculture, mining and electricity. Bhutan has no oil or natural gas. Government policy favours sustainable rather than uncontrolled free-market development, and has always adopted a cautious approach to multinational investment. The ninth and latest in the series of five-year plans (2001) seeks to control urban growth though planning measures that will encourage the rural majority to remain in the countryside and not migrate to the new district towns in excessive numbers. To this end, some commercial enterprises and educational institutes have been moved into the countryside.

Hydroelectric power The government sees the key to future national prosperity in the exploitation of the country's fast-flowing rivers. A series of hydroelectric projects has been initiated with Indian engineering assistance. There are currently four major plants: at Chukha and Tala on the Wang-chu, at Mongar on the Kuri-chu, and below Wangdu Phodrang on the Baso-chu. The oldest of these is the Chukha project, which currently produces 336 MW (78% exported to India). The Tala project is expected to have a massive capacity of 1,020 MW, and it is generally estimated that the country has the potential to generate 30,000 MW, most of which would be exported to neighbouring India. Currently, the export of hydroelectric power accounts for 40% of government revenue, and this will undoubtedly increase in the years ahead. At the same time, efforts are being made to supply remote rural communities with their own localised hydroelectric schemes or solar-energy sources.

Agricultural production   Some 85% of the population are engaged in subsistence farming, but only 7.8% of the land is arable. The most important areas of cultivation are in the Duars and the river valleys of Central Bhutan. The main crops are maize (output 40,000 tonnes) and rice (output 43,000 tonnes), cultivated on the valley floors and, wherever possible, on the terraced and irrigated slopes up to 2,400 m. Between 2,400 m and 2,900 m, millet (7,000 tonnes), wheat (5,000 tonnes), buckwheat and barley (4,000 tonnes) are also grown. Hot pepper (output 7,000 tonnes) is the favoured vegetable in kitchen gardens all over the country. Apples (5,000 tonnes) and potatoes (33,000 tonnes) are particularly important cash crops for the mid-mountain belt, while at altitudes between 300 m and 1,300 m, oranges (62,000 tonnes) and sugar cane (12,000 tonnes) are abundant.

The export of agricultural products, including preserves, jams, marmalade, canned fruit, apples, cardamom and mushrooms is also important for the economy. There are more than 100 types of edible mushroom growing in the mid-mountain belt, including the *masutake* that is exported to Japan and South-east Asia. Nonetheless, most farming continues at subsistence level, and in recent years even rice has had to be imported.

Pastoral farming is also a significant factor. Cattle, pigs, horses, sheep and goats are reared, and in high nomadic areas over 3,500 m, yaks are the main form of livestock. A small dairy farm was started at Bumthang in Central Bhutan with Swiss aid and it produces excellent cheese.

Forestry production   The extensive forests, which cover 72% of the land, are scientifically managed, but nonetheless damaged by shifting cultivation in the east, by the widespread use of oak for firewood, and also by ageing and blight. The Bhutanese government is very conservation oriented and is assisted in this task by various international organisations. The export of raw timber is prohibited, but locally produced furniture and block-boards, made from sissoo and pine, are exported to India and Bangladesh. The annual production of veneer woods and plywood is 3 million tonnes. Essential oils produced from lemon grass in Eastern Bhutan are exported to Germany, for use in perfumes and deodorants. Turpentine from the resin of the chir pine is exported to India.

Hand-made traditional artefacts are also important in this sector: engraved woodblocks for printing loose-leaf Buddhist texts are made from birch, strong lightweight paper from the daphne laurel, wooden bowls from the maple and avocado, baskets from bamboo, roof shingles from the blue pine, rope from hemp, and herbal medicines from a variety of Himalayan plants (see page 256). Altogether, the rural sector of the economy, comprising agriculture, livestock and forestry, accounts for almost 35% of GDP.

Mining   Conservation issues are paramount in this sector of the economy. Most of the small-scale mines and quarries that are managed by the Department of Mines are found in the southern border areas. Dolomite (output 50,000 tonnes) and limestone

Coal (30,000 tonnes) is also mined in the south-east.

Other industries   In the southern parts of the country there are factories producing cement (output 36 million tonnes), calcium carbide and ferrosilicon, as well as high-density polythene pipe. Local distillery products amount to 47,000 tonnes. Most of this trade is with India and Bangladesh. Bhutanese postage stamps are also a significant source of foreign exchange, and it is possible to purchase them by mail order. For information, contact the Chief Controller of Stamps, Philatelic Bureau, GPO, Thimphu, Bhutan, F00975-223108.

Imports   The main imports, 60% of which are obtained from India and the remainder through trade with Japan, the EU, USA and so forth, are petroleum, fuel, machinery, fabrics, vehicles and grain. The curtailment of trade with Tibet in 1959 encouraged economic dependence on India. Even now trade with Tibet is minimal, and restricted to specific trade fairs in Lhodrak and Southern Tibet, at which Bhutanese delegations participate, and local cross-border smuggling. In these ways, grain and sugar are carried on yak trains into Tibet and watches, thermos flasks, crockery and shoes from China are imported. There is some hope that the current thaw in Sino-Indian relations will eventually have a positive impact on trading relations with Tibet.

Foreign aid   Almost half of the annual national budget of Bhutan (US$211 million in 2003) is provided by foreign aid. While much of this funding is provided by India for hydroelectric development, the United Nations Development Programme, which has had offices in Thimphu since 1979, also contributes in this area, as well as towards improved infrastructure, and various health and educational projects. Other UN organisations based in Bhutan include UNESCO, UNICEF, FAO, WHO and IFAD. Several countries, including Japan, Canada, Dermark, Holland, Switzerland, Austria and New Zealand, also have their own organisations that provide funding for designated development and conservation-oriented projects. For a list of such organisations, see page 25. The World Wildlife Fund is also active in Bhutan.

Social policy

Health   Development plans introduced during the 1980s and 1990s have given more primacy to issues of health and education, as well as to cultural and environmental conservation. Althought health standards are poor from a western perspective, health care is now free for all citizens. The infant mortality rate is estimated at 105 per thousand, and the child immunisation rate is almost 100%, even in remote rural areas. The life expectancy rate is estimated at 54 years. Throughout the remote rural areas of Bhutan, there are basic health units (BHU) staffed by nurses and midwives who can reach more than 78% of the population. Each of the 20 district towns also has its own hospital, and there are larger referral hospitals in Thimphu, Paro and Tashigang.

Education   Education was traditionally provided by Buddhist monasteries, which were bastions of learning. Prior to 1951, Bhutanese monks and laymen would often go to study classical subjects, medicine and the arts, inside Tibet, regardless of the political relations between the two countries. This educative role is still maintained by the Buddhist colleges (*shedra*), which are affiliated to the larger monastic communities in the *dzongs* of Bhutan. Secular western-style education has been introduced only since 1961. Prior to that, wealthy Bhutanese would send their children to expensive public schools in neighbouring Darjiling, Kalimpong and even overseas. **Primary education** is provided over a seven-year curriculum, which in some areas begins as late as age eight or nine. In all state-funded schools, the medium of instruction is now English, although Dzongkha is taught as a second language, and other regional languages are also encouraged in Central and Eastern parts of the country. **High school education** provides an extended curriculum for four years (two at junior high and two at high school proper). In addition to basic literacy and numeracy, the system seeks to impart a sound understanding of Bhutan's cultural heritage, and familiarise students with information technology. Although there are now elite fee-paying schools in Bhutan, the state system provides free education and free textbooks up to high school level. **Higher education** is provided in a five-year degree programme (two years at junior college and three at undergraduate level), but the country's only university, Sherabtse College in Kanglung, is overstrained. Many graduates opt to study overseas in India or elsewhere. Vocational training for those who do not go on to higher education is provided by the Royal Institute of Management in Thimphu and the technical institutes at Kharbandi.

Tourism

Since the introduction of social, economic and political reforms from the 1960s onwards, Bhutan has begun to play a more active role in international bodies, including the regional SAARC meetings. At the same time, outside visitors have been welcomed in Bhutan in increasing numbers, starting from the present king's coronation in 1974, and the infrastucture for satellite and internet communications is now in place. Initially when tourism was introduced to Bhutan, there were quotas restricting access to 2,000 persons a year. Nowadays there are no quotas, but numbers are limited by the all-inclusive pricing system that encourages wealthy visitors and discourages individual budget travellers. The annual number of visitors rose to 7,600 in 2000 but fell to 5,249 in 2002, following the events of 9/11. With so few visitors, revenue from tourism is not yet a significant contributor to the national economy, but this is about to change as international chain hotels, like the Amman and Como hotel groups, provide more and improved facilities. Indian tourists are also expected to visit in increasing numbers, since they benefit from special conditions and fares, and do not have to pay the US dollar rate. For information on the rules and regulations for tourism in Bhutan, and a list of local tour agencies, see page 15.

Land and environment

Location
Bhutan lies between 89° and 92° east and 27° and 28° north. The Indian states of Sikkim, West Bengal, Assam and Arunachal Pradesh occupy the entire 605-km length of its western, southern, and eastern borders respectively, while the Dromo, Khangmar, Lhodrak and Tsona counties of Tibet lie to its north, forming a 470-km border. The area of the country is only 46,500 sq km. In general, the elevation of the land ranges from more than 7,000 m in the north to less than 300 m in the south.

Traditional geography
As in Tibet, the great mountain barriers of Bhutan are traditionally conceived in animistic terms, as sacred abodes of local deities who were eventually bound under an oath of allegiance to Buddhism by the great master Guru Padmakara during the eighth century. In the south-east of the country, close to the Assamese border, is the densely forested mountain abode of the mighty countryside divinity **Jowo Durshing**. In the east, close to the Dakpo area of modern Arunachal Pradesh, is the majestic

The Great Himalayan Range: the highest peaks in the world

The Great Himalayan Range is paralleled to the south by two minor latitudinal ranges, the southernmost being the Outer Himalayan range of the Shiwaliks (274-760 m); followed by the Inner Himalayas (4,600 m, valleys at 900 m) of Kashmir, and the mid-mountain belts of Nepal and Bhutan. Further north the Great Himalayas comprise nine of the 14 highest peaks in the world. The most prominent peaks are (from west to east): Nanga Parbat in Pakistan-controlled Kashmir (8,126 m), Gangotri (6,726 m), Kamet (7,756 m), and Nanda Devi (7,817 m) all in north-west India, Nemo Nanyi (Gurla Mandhata, 7,728 m) in far-west Tibet, Dhaulagiri (8,172 m), Annapurna (8,078 m), Manaslu (8,160 m) and Himal Chuli (7,898 m), all in west Nepal; Ganesh Himal (7,411 m), Langtang (7,250 m), and Shishapangma (Gosainathan, 8,012 m), all bordering Central Nepal and west Tibet; Jowo Tseringma (Gauri Shangkar, 7,148 m), Jowo Guru (Menlungtse, 7,181 m), Jowo Oyuk (8,153 m), Jomolangma (Everest, 8,848 m), Lhotse (8,501 m), and Makalu (8,463 m), all bordering east Nepal and west Tibet; Kangchendzonga (8,598 m), **Jomolhari** (7,313 m) and **Kulha Kangri** (7,554 m), all of which border Sikkim or Bhutan and Southern Tibet; and finally Phulahari (7,410 m) and Namchak Barwa (7,756 m), which divide Arunachal Pradesh from Southern Tibet.

mountain abode of **Jomo Remati**, a region known for its special milch cows. In the north-east, near the Tibetan border and Lhodrak county, there is the hidden land of **Khenpajong**, the sacred abode of Genyen Jora Rakye, which was a region of impenetrable jungle and rocky mountains, inhabited by savages and wild beasts. In the central region, protected by this hidden land, are **Kurelung** and **Bumthang**, sacred abodes of Kyebu Lungtsen, foremost of gods and demons, and **Mangde**, the sacred mountain abode of Muktsen. To the west are the forested mountains and ravines of **Dechen Phuk** in upper Thimyul, where the protector deity Genyen Chenpo Jagpa Melan resides. To the south is **Mount Tarkar**, the sacred abode of Thangkar Jinying, which has its peak pointing towards Tibet and its base in the Indian plains. Further west are the majestic mountain peak of **Dongkar La** in Paro, sacred abode of Lhatsen, and **Ha**, the alpine abode of Tsengo Chenpo Khyungdud. All of these senior-most divinities have their numerous mountain retainers (*ridren*) frequenting the lesser peaks, which are similarly conceived in animistic terms.

Terrain and rivers

In the **north**, separating the country from Tibet, lies a relatively narrow chain of glacial mountains belonging to the Great Himalayan range, with several peaks over 7,000 m, most of them unclimbed and unexplored, even now. From west to east these peaks include: **Jomolhari** (7,314 m), the most famous and picturesque; **Jichu Drakye** (6,974 m); **Matsen Gyelpo** (Bh. Masangang, 7,158 m); **Terigang** (7,060 m); **Jejehangphu Gang** (7,158 m); **Gangphu Gang** (7,170 m); **Dzongaphu Gang** (7,060 m); and **Gangkar Punsum** (7,540 m), which is the highest mountain entirely within the borders of Bhutan and currently the world's highest unclimbed peak. Even higher and more imposing is the massive **Kulha Gangri** (7,554 m), slightly to the north-east, on the border with Lhodrak. Virtually 20% of Bhutan's land mass is snow-bound. Ancient seasonal trade routes traverse these snow ranges through the high passes – **Tremo La**, **Yak La**, **Phiru La**, **Monla Karchung La** and **Phode La** – while the slightly less daunting passes – **Me La**, **Nyingzang La** and **Ngonkha La** – connect Eastern Bhutan with Tsona and Arunachal.

In general, those peaks of the Great Himalayan range form a watershed between the north- and south-flowing tributaries of the Brahmaputra River. All the rivers in Bhutan flow south. Yet among them there are three that originate north of the range in Tibet: the **Amo-chu** (Torsa), which enters Western Bhutan from the Dromo (Chumbi) valley; the **Kuri-chu**, which enters north-east Bhutan from Lhodrak; and the **Tawang-chu** (Drangme-chu), which enters Eastern Bhutan from Tsona. In the far west, the **Di-chu** (Jaldakha) enters from Sikkim. All other tributaries have their sources within Bhutan. In the extreme north-west the alignment of the Tibet–Bhutan border has been repeatedly disputed by China.

The largest part of the country belongs to the mid-mountain belt or Inner Himalayan range with altitudes ranging from 1,100 to 4,000 m. Here, the so-called **Black Mountains** (running from north to south) form a watershed between Western and Central Bhutan and are crossed via the **Pele La pass** (3,369 m). The forested ridges to the west of this range demarcate the agricultural valleys of **Samtse**, **Ha**, **Paro**, **Thimphu** and **Punakha**, where the **Di-chu** (Jaldakha), the **Amo** (Torsa), the **Wang-chu** (Raidak) with its Ha, Paro and Thimphu tributaries, and the **Punatsang-chu** (Sankosh) all flow south into India. East of the Black Mountains, another forested north–south range, crossed via **Yotong La** pass (3,425 m), defines the watershed between the **Trongsar** and **Bumthang** valleys, while the **Rodong La** (4,160 m) and **Thrumzhing La** (3,780 m) passes of the **Donga Range** divide Bumthang from **Lhuntse** distict. Lhuntse in turn is divided from Tashi Yangtse by **Dong La** pass (3,900 m). The main rivers flowing east of the Black Mountains which all converge to form the **Drangme-chu** (Manas), include the **Mangde-chu** (Tongsar) and the **Bumthang-chu** of Central Bhutan, as well as the **Kuri-chu**, **Kulong-chu**, **Tawang-chu** and **Gamri-chu** of Eastern Bhutan. In the far south-east of the country, the **Bada-chu** and **Dhanasiri-chu** follow their distinct courses into Assam.

Immediately **south** of these Inner Himalayan ranges are the less precipitous valleys of **Chukha**, **Tarkarna**, **Zhemgang**, **Mongar** and **Tashigang**, which, like the areas further north, are largely populated by the Drukpa Bhutanese. In the foothills still further south, adjoining the Indian border, the land is more densely populated by Nepali-speaking peoples. This frontier was established by the British in the 18th and 19th centuries, along the base of the abruptly rising Himalayan foothills (average altitude 300-1,600 m). Here, the hills meet the plains in a series of 18 valleys, 15-30 km long, where the rivers of Bhutan cut their way through to reach the Brahmaputra River lowlands of West Bengal and Assam, thereby forming 18 'gateways' or **Duars** (Sanskrit *dvara*). The 11 western Duars form a border with the Indian state of West Bengal, while the seven to the east, as far as the Dhanasiri-chu, border the state of Assam. This is a fertile tract, formed of glacial silt deposits, where thickly forested nature reserves are interspersed with tea plantations, orchards and rice cultivation. All the motor roads leading into Bhutan from the south pass through the Duars. In the west the boundary with Sikkim was also established by the British and accepted by India; while the boundary to the east currently follows the de-facto Sino-Indian frontier.

The country is divided into 20 administrative districts or *dzongkhag*; among which Samtse, Chukha, Gelekphuk and Samdrub Jongkhar border India on the west and south. Those of Ha, Paro, Thimphu, Gasa, Bumthang, Lhuntse, Tashi Yangtse and Tashigang border Tibet on the north and east. The central districts of Tarkarna (Dagana), Tsirang, Punakha, Wangdu, Trongsar (Tongsa), Zhemgang, Pema Gatshel and Mongar lack an external frontier. Motorable roads now link the southern border towns of Phuntsoling, Sarpang, Gelekphuk and Samdrub Jongkar with the capital and central parts of the country; and there is also a lateral paved highway linking the districts of Ha, Paro, Thimphu, Wangdu, Trongsar, Bumthang, Mongar and Tashigang.

even now only accessible on ancient trekking and caravan trade routes. In all, the
motorable roads cover 3,216 km.

Geology

Origins of Bhutan's landscape

Over 100 million years ago, most of the Tibetan plateau formed the bed of the
Neo-tethys Ocean, on the southern shores of the Eurasian land-mass. The
formation of the plateau as we know it occurred during the **Cenozoic** period
(approximately 66.4 million years ago), when the drifting Indian subcontinental
plate collided with Eurasia, some 2,000 km to the south of the present
Indus–Brahmaputra watershed, which forms the continental suture. Since then, the
sub-continental plate has been continuously subducting the Eurasian plate, and
800 km of continental crust have contracted to form the Himalayas – the world's
highest mountain range and the largest concentration of continental crust on earth
(69 km thick in places). Further south, the collision created the Gangetic and
Brahmaputra basins of Northern India. The range even now continues to extend
upwards and outwards under its own weight, as the Indian subcontinental plate
moves ever northwards at a speed of about 6.1 cm per year.

Rocks, soil and minerals

The **Great Himalayan region** of north-western Bhutan, extending from the upper
Paro valley to upper Trongsar, is formed of chrystalline gneiss with granite
intrusions along the high snow range itself. Lingzhi, like the Tibetan plateau itself, is
characterised by marine sedimentary deposits, indicative of the ancient sea-bed of
the Neo-tethys Ocean. Further south in the **Inner Himalayan belt** there are layers of
sandstone with deposits of quartz, marble, dolomite and shale. Soil tends to be
thicker on the north-facing slopes, which support dense forests at lower altitudes
and grasslands at higher altitudes. Further south near the **Duars**, sandstone
predominates, interspersed with marine sedimentary deposits and limestone. Rich
alluvial soil has been deposited by south-flowing tributaries onto the Brahmaputra
plain of north-east India. Geological surveys suggest that the Himalayan region is
rich in ores, due to intrusions of granites and igneous rock. In Bhutan these
deposits include iron, which has long been mined in Paro and Punakha (see page
106), and coal, which is found further east.

Earthquake and geothermal activity

The entire region is subject to intense geological activity. Satellite photos reveal
widespread thrust faults and deep faults throughout the Tibetan plateau and the
Himalayan zone. In Bhutan the main thrust fault is considered to divide the Great and
Inner Himalayan regions, while a boundary fault has been identified, almost parallel to
the Indo-Bhutanese frontier. Earrthquakes frequently occur in the fault zones, and
some of these have been documented in recent history. The terrain has a number of
geothermal areas including hot springs, geysers and hydrothermal explosions. For
further information on the geology of Bhutan, readers are recommended to consult
Augusto Gansser's *Geology of the Bhutan Himalaya* (Springer Verlag, 1983).

Climate

Bhutan is subject to some intense variations in its weather patterns. As one would
expect to find in a county sharing its latitude with Kunming, northern Hawaii and

Background Land & environment

Mexico, sunshine and stong winds abound, but there are also great localised and seasonal fluctuations on account of the vertical mountainous zones.

Snowfall In northern Bhutan, above 4,500 m, an alpine/arctic climate prevails, with most areas permanently covered with snow and ice. Here the winters are severe and the summers generally cool. Above 3,500 m winter snow will begin to melt in March. Below 2,500 m snow will quickly melt in all seasons, which means that the central populated belt of Bhutan receives very little snowfall, although high passes can be blocked by snow in the winter months.

Rainfall The monsoon rains begin in June and last until the end of September, during which time 85% of the annual rainfall is received – usually in the night-time rather than during the day. Rivers are swollen and landslides frequently occur. Yet there is also a great variation in rainfall – less than 500 mm per year in the more arid Great Himalayan zone, increasing to 1,500 mm in the Inner Himalayan zone, and up to 5,000 mm in the southern areas bordering Assam. In the Inner Himalayan zone the windward south-facing mountain slopes are the wettest areas. However, the daily air mass exchange between highlands and lowlands often causes stormy winds, which frequently prevent rainfall in the middle portions of cross valleys so that between 900 to 1,800 m it is quite dry, requiring irrigation for farming, while higher up it is often wet. Some light rainfall also occurs in the spring, but very little in autumn, which is the high season for tourism and trekking. Mountain vistas are best in the autumn (October to mid-November), and in the spring.

Temperature In the Great Himalayan zone the temperature will range from 10°C in mid-summer to 0°C in mid-winter. In the populated mid-mountain belt of Western Bhutan, which is visited by most tourists and travellers, the range is more extreme – 30°C in mid-summer to minus 10°C in mid-winter. More specifically, from mid-March to mid-June, the range is 26°C to 5°C; in the monsoon season from mid-June to late September the range is 24°C to 15°C; and in the winter months from mid-November to mid-March, the days are generally dry, averaging 16-18°C, while the nights, early mornings and evenings have freezing temperatures. The lower winter temperatures of the mid-mountain belt are due to the early loss of evening sunshine in the north–south aligned deep valleys of Western Bhutan, while the Great Himalayan region further north has more exposure to sunshine in that season. However, in central and eastern parts of the mid-mountain belt, including low-lying parts of Punakha, Mongar, Tashigang and Lhuntse, the summers are hotter and the winters less bitter than in the western regions. In the southern foothills and the Duars plain (up to 1,500 m), the climate is sub-tropical with high degree of humidity. The temperature here will range from 35°C in mid-summer to a balmy 15°C in mid-winter.

Flora and fauna

Vegetation
Renowned for their outstanding botanical diversity, the forests of Bhutan even now cover more than 70% of the terrain. This remarkable density of vegetation, contrasting with the stark landscapes of Tibet to the north, is due to the combined effect of strong sunshine, heavy monsoon rainfall and minimal glaciation. More than 5,000 species of plants have been identified throughout the country, including 46 varieties of rhododendron, and some 600 varieties of orchid. Many of these plants are used in the rich pharmacopoeia of traditional Tibetan and Bhutanese medicine. The three vegetation and climatic zones (tropical, temperate and alpine) found throughout the sub-Himalayan countries are also apparent in Bhutan.

Tropical zone While much of the low-lying tropical forest than once defined the Indo-Bhutanese frontier has given way to tea plantations and terraced paddy fields, at elevations below 2,000 m the wet and humid climate is conducive to thick forests of giant sal, teak, banyan and chir pine, interspersed with oak, walnut and bamboo. There are numerous hanging plants, giant orchids, ferns and bamboo, as well as evergreen plants, such as liburnum, that flower in the spring.

Temperate zone At elevations between 2,000 m and 3,000 m, in the mid-mountain belt, sub-tropical vegetation gives way to the deciduous and conifer forests of the temperate zone. Here, there is a wide range of trees, including oak, poplar, birch, ash, aspen, magnolia, cherry and maple, and with conifers such as the blue pine, hemlock and larch. Many species of rhododendron, including the distinctive red-flowering *ethometho*, bloom in the spring. Above 3,000 m bamboo and blue pine conifer forests take over, alongside fir, larch, hemlock and weeping cypress.

Alpine zone Abobve 3,500 m, the birch and blue pine forests gradually give way to alpine juniper, dwarf rhododendrons, low shrubs and seasonal wild-flowers: edelweiss, gentians, primulas, delphiniums, forget-me-nots and irises, as well as the revered national flower of Bhutam, the blue poppy. Mosses and lichens are also found, above 4,000 m, along with a variety of aromatic herbs, which are used in traditional medicine. However, it is only in north-eastern Bhutan, bordering on the Lhodrak region of Tibet, that the forest penetrates the otherwise bleak north side of the Great Himalayan range.

Wildlife

The great variation in terrain and vegetation throughout the three climatic zones has given rise to a corresponding variety of mammals, reptiles, butterflies and birds. More than 165 special of mammals have been idientified, along with 675 species of birds. The **Duars plain** is a natural habitat of the rhesus monkey and the Assamese macaque. The sub-tropical region of the **Manas National Park** offers free range to the Indian elephant, the wild water buffalo, the one-horned rhino, wild boar, jackals, wild dogs and various species of wild cats, including the Bengal tiger, the Asiatic golden cat and the clouded leopard. The forests of the **southern foothills** and lower lying regions of the mid-mountain belt provide a unique habitat for the long-tailed golden langur, which is exclusively found in Bhutan. Forests also offer concealment for a variety of deer, including the sambar, the barking deer and the rare musk deer, which secretes an important ingredient used in the manufacture of perfume. The **forested mountain gateways** to Eastern Bhutan, such as Pele La and Trumzhing La, are a habitat of the nocturnal red panda, while the Himalayan black bear and various species of antelopes frequent the **temperate forests** of the mid-mountain belt. Many of the ungulates found in the **northern parts of Bhutan** are common to the high-altitude pastures of Tibet. They include the yak, the Himalayan tahr, the Tibetan gazelle, and the rare and protected *bharal* or blue sheep (*Pseudois nayaur*). The **blue sheep** have thick sheep-like horns and goat-like legs, with dark stripes on the flanks. They prefer plateaus for grazing and have a split lip that enables them to pull grass straight out of the ground rather than crop it. Equally rare in the grassland areas of far-west and northern Tibet, the blue sheep of Bhutan has the even rarer snow leopard as its natural predator. Unique to Northern Bhutan is the takin which lives above 4,000 m. **Takins** (*Budorcas taxicolor*) are larger (over 1m at the shoulders), and short-legged. They have a shaggy dark brown coat with a lighter back; the snout is swollen and their thick horns splay out and then up and back. They live in small herds, often above the treeline, and in spite of their stocky appearance are remarkably agile on steep slopes. The winter draws them down to bamboo and rhododendron forests, from which they emerge to graze in meadows, morning and evening.

Birds Considering its small land-mass, Bhutan has a relatively high proportion of bird species. This is partly due to the diverse vertical climatic zones and protective forests within the country, and partly to the fact that Bhutan 'lies in a region of overlap between the Paleartic and Indomalayan realms' (Carol and Tim Inskipp, *An Introduction to Birdwatching in Bhutan*). This means that disparate species such as the Tibetan snowcock (*Tetraogallus tibetanus*) and the Indomalayan coppersmith barbet (*Megalaima haemacephala*) are both found in Bhutan. The country offers an important winter habitat for the protected black-necked crane (*Grus nigricollis*), which migrates from Tibet to remote valleys around **Bumthang** and **Gangteng** monastery, as well as the white-bellied heron (*Ardea insignis*), the world's second largest species of heron, which is found in the **Mo-chu** valley. Other species, such as the rare Pailas fish eagle (*Haliautus leucoryphus*), pass through Bhutan as they migrate seasonally between Tibet and Northern India. The indigenous birds of Bhutan include various species of cuckoos, woodpeckers, minivets, whistling thrushes, magpies, wagtails, choughs, kingfishers and the Eurasian hoopoe (*Upapa epops*) with its distinctive black and white striped wings. There are also indigenous species that are rare elsewhere, such as the rufous-necked hornbill (*Aceros nipalensis*), found in the southern sub-tropical forests, and Blyth's tragopan (*Tragopan blythii*), which is found in the low-lying forests of Eastern Bhutan. Among the best areas for bird-watching are the forests of the **Black Mountains** (near Pele La), and the **Dochu La** pass between Thimphu and Punakha. Trekking in Northern Bhutan offers the prospect of observing the lammergeier (*Gyps himalayensis*), the Tibetan raven (*Corvis corax*), and the blood pheasant (*Ithaginis cruentus*). Carol and Tim Inskipp's publication (see above) includes colour photographs and descriptions of many of the most significant birds found in Bhutan.

Ecological issues and wildlife conservation

As a late economic developer, Bhutan has chosen to implement a policy of sustainable growth and development, which imposes strict limitations on the exploitation of its rich natural resources. Through the National Environment Commission, the Ministry of Agriculture and the Department of Forestry Services, the government is seeking to regulate and reduce the rural consumption of firewood and end the slash-and-burn agricultural methods (*tseri*) of the indigenous Monpa tribal groups. There are checkpoints on all motor roads, monitoring illegal poaching and lumbering, but the long and open Indian border provides easy access for traffickers and terrorist insurgents alike. Conservation of Bhutan's internationally recognised biodiversity is also a primary concern for the indigenous Bhutan Trust Fund (www.bhutantrustfund.org) and the Royal Society for the Protection of Nature (www.rspn-Bhutan.org), as well as for the World Wildlife Fund (www.wwfbhutan.org.bt) which has been active in the country since 1977.

Wildlife sanctuaries Although the Buddhist ethos of Bhutan instinctively inclines the population towards the preservation of animal life, there are over 20 protected species that have been offered further protection by the 1995 Forest and Nature Conservation Act. Most of these have already been mentioned (see page 257). Conservation issues are at the forefront of government policy in Bhutan. There are currently nine protected conservation areas that together amount to almost 26% of the land-mass of the country. With the exception of the **Black Mountains National Park** and the **Trumzhing La National Park**, the other seven are all located in remote regions, bordering Tibet in the north and India in the south and east. The largest of these is the **Jigme Dorje National Park** (4,329 sq km), which encompasses the entires Himalayan border zone, including the northernmost parts of Paro, Thimphu and Punakha districts, as well as virtually the whole of Gasa district, bordering on Khangmar county of Tibet. Management of this national park has to take into account the agricultural and nomadic practices of its indigenous inhabitants, and the culture of the Laya community in particular, while protecting endangered species such as the blue sheep and snow leopard that are found in the Great Himalayan zone. The park has recently become an important area for trekking activities, and there are management guidelines in place to encourage the sound practices of ecotourism. Further west, bordering Dromo county in Tibet, the **Torsa Strict Nature Reserve** (644 sq km) occupies an uninhabited forested area of Ha district, in the mid-reaches of the Amo-chu valley. In the extreme north-east of the country, bordering the Lhodrak and Tsona counties of Tibet, the **Bomdeling Wildlife Sanctuary** (1,300 sq km) was established to protect a breeding sanctuary of the black-necked crane, as well as the snow leopard, blue sheep, musk deer and other endangered species in the north of Tashi Yangtse district. In the east of the country, bordering Arunachal Pradesh, the **Sakteng Wildlife Sanctuary** (650 sq km) is a region of temperate pine and rhododendron forest, supposedly inhabited by the 'abominable snowman' (Tib. *migu*, Nep. *yeti*). Bordering Assam in the south-east of the country, the **Khaling Wildlife Sanctuary** (273 sq km) is a natural habitat for the Indian elephant, the gaur and other protected species. The well-known **Royal Manas National Park** (1,023 sq km), which borders Assam to the south, is the oldest of Bhutan's nature conservation areas, founded in 1966, and is the best area for observing wildlife. The one-horned rhino, Bengal tiger and golden langur can all be seen here, but access has been restricted since Assamese insurgents infiltrated into the area in the 1990s. The **Black Mountains National Park** (1,400 sq km), which includes the winter habitat of the black-necked crane in Phobjika valley and virgin forest further south, now offers the best prospects for bird-watching and for spotting bears, tigers, wild boar, leopards and red pandas.The **Phibsoo Wildlife Sanctuary** (278 sq km), bordering West Bengal, and located between Phuntsoling and Sarpang, conserves a natural giant sal forest and its wildlife (similar to that of the Royal Manas National Park). Lastly, the **Thrumzhing La National Park** (768 sq km), which occupies the Ura–Mongar border area, protects temperate forests of fir and pine, which are the natural habitat of the red panda and rare species of birds.

Culture

People and language

Bhutan has the lowest population density of any country in South Asia. The overall population in 2004 was estimated at 740,000. Most people live along the southern border and in the high valleys of the mid-mountain belt, particularly along the east–west trade route that passes through Thimphu and Punakha. There are two main population groups in Bhutan: the **Drukpa** (approximately 67%) of Tibetan and Monpa origin who inhabit the mid-mountain belt, and the **Lhotsampa** (approximately 30%) of Nepalese origin who inhabit the southern borderlands. The remaining 3% of the population comprise indigenous tribal groups, such as the Toktop, Doya and Lepcha of south-west Bhutan, and the Santal who migrated there from Northern Bihar.

Altogether 19 languages and dialects are spoken in Bhutan. Among the two larger groups, the Drukpa include within their numbers speakers of eight indigenous Tibetan dialects, which have been identified by the linguist George van Driem, including the dominant **Ngalong** of Western Bhutan who speak the dialect now known as Dzongkha, the official national language. Other Tibetan dialects are spoken in remote parts of the country: **Chocha Ngachakha** in the Kuri-chu valley of Lhuntse district, **Drokpa** (Bh. Brokpa) and **Dakpakha** in Merak, Sakteng and adjacent areas of Tashigang district, **Layakha** and **Lunakha** in the nomadic areas of Gasa district, and **Lakha** and **Droke** (Bh. Brokkat) in parts of Bumthang.

Auspicious symbols and insignia of royal dominion

The motifs of the eight auspicious symbols (*tashi tagye*) and seven insignia of royal dominion (*gyelsi nadun*) are often found in temple murals, and sometimes they are depicted three-dimensionally in brass, and placed among the outer offerings on an altar. In village houses, the eight auspicious symbols are also frequently seen, inscribed individually or in a single combined decorative motif. They comprise the following. The eternal knot (*palbeu*) symbolises the union of discernment and compassion in the essential nature of the enlightened mind. The lotus flower (*pema*) symbolises the freedom of body, speech and mind from defilements. The umbrella (*dug*) offers protection from negatives forces and ill-health. The clockwise-spiralling conch (*dung*) symbolises the resonance of the Buddhist teachings. The wheel

(*khorlo*) represents the promulgation of the Buddhist teaching. The victory banner (*gyeltsen*) represents the triumph of Buddhism over non-Buddhist forces. The vase (*bumpa*) symbolises wealth, prosperity and longevity. The golden fish (*sernya*) represents the majesty and audacity of beings who have escaped the ocean of suffering.

The 'seven insignia of royal dominion', which are the hallmarks of a wise Buddhist monarch exercising spiritual and temporal power together, comprise the: precious wheel (*khorlo rinpoche*), the precious gem (*norbu rinpoche*), the precious queen (*tsunmo rinpoche*), the precious minister (*lonpo rinpoche*), the precious elephant (*langpo rinpoche*), the precious horse (*tachog rinpoche*) and the precious general (*magpon rinpoche*).

Background Culture

Also classified along with the Drukpa peoples are the **Monpa** of Wangdu Phodrang, Zhemgang, Trongsar and Bumthang districts who speak an East Bodish Tibeto-Burman language, somewhat related to the dialects spoken by the Monpa of Tawang (currently in Arunachal Pradesh), and the most populous group, the **Sharchokpa** of Eastern Bhutan, who have recently been identified as Lopas (van Driem, 1991), speaking a Tibeto-Burman language known as **Tsangla**.

The customs, religion and culture of the **Monpa** are fully integrated with those of the Drukpa and neighbouring Tibetans through long-standing political, economic and marital links. Many now speak Dzongkha in addition to their own language. Traditionally, both men and women wear robes with aprons, black yak-hair caps, and soft-soled leather boots with red and black stripes. Women wear white aprons, earrings, rings and bracelets. In sub-tropical parts, women and men both wear jackets – the women with long striped skirts. The slash-and-burn method of agriculture is practised here, despite government directives intended to replace it with more conservation-oriented systems. The staple diet consists of rice, maize, millet, buckwheat and chilli pepper, in addition to *tsampa* and tea. Hunting is still important in these areas where the virgin forest is dense, and species of wild boar, bears, foxes and langurs are to be found. Monpa houses are made of wood with bamboo-thatched roofs.

The **Lopa** were traditionally forest-dwelling hunter-gatherers and bamboo weavers. The traditional tribal dress of the Lopa is a sleeveless, buttonless, knee-length smock of black sheep wool with a helmet-like hat made of bearskin or bamboo/rattan laced with bearskin, and no shoes. Men wear bamboo earrings and necklaces, and carry bows and arrows, while the women wear silver or brass earrings, bracelets, necklaces and ornate waist belts. The staple diet is a dumpling made of maize or millet, as well as rice and buckwheat, in addition to *tsampa*, potatoes, buttered tea and chilli peppers. The

Sharchokpa of Eastern Bhutan are said to be descended from Lopa tribes, although they are well integrated with the Drukpa culture.

By contrast, the Nepali-speaking **Lhotsampa** of Southern Bhutan belong mainly to the Hindu high castes and to the Rai, Gurung and Limbu tribes. Few of them speak Dzongkha, and intermarriage is rare. Because of their different language and religion they have not intermingled with the Drukpa. Since 1959 immigration from Nepal has been banned and the government wishes to avoid a repetition of what happened in Sikkim, where, in 1975 the king was overthrown by the majority Nepali-speaking population (see page 246).

National dress

The national dress of Bhutan accords with the conventions of the official code of conduct, *Driklam Namzhak*, which was established by Tendzin Drugye, the first regent of Zhabdrung Ngawang Namgyel in the 17th century. Like the traditional dress (*chuba*) worn by the neighbouring Tibetans of Dromo, Khangmar and Lhodrak, Bhutanese dress is influenced by the harshness of the Himalayan climate, but there are also important differences. The men wear a long robe (*gho*), hitched up to the knees with a cumberband or sash (*kera*), which causes it to form a pouch above the waist, and a long-sleeved shirt (*togo*), with the cuffs turned back. They would either go barefoot or wear embroidered knee-length boots, according to the season. Since the time of the first king Ugyen Wangchuk, the male costume has also included shorts or longjohns, which are worn under the robe, also according to the season, along with knee-length woollen socks, and smart leather shoes or boots. The offical time for changing from socks to longjohns and vice versa is marked by the movement of the official monastic community from Thimphu to Punakha in autumn and from Punakha to Thimphu in the spring. The *gho* can be plain in colour, bold, checked or pinstriped, but not floral or effeminate. Sharp colours can be worn as long as monastic reds and yellows are avoided. The wearing of the *gho* is compulsory for schoolboys and government officials.

On formal occasions (such as attending government meetings or entering a *dzong*), Bhutanese men are additionally obliged to wear a ceremonial scarf (Bh. *kab-ne*) over their left shoulder, which on less formal occasions they might have folded over their arm. The origin of the scarf is probably to be found in the maroon *zen* worn to this day by Tibetan and Bhutanese monks. The scarf is made of raw silk with fringes at both ends, 3 m in length, but only 90 cm in width. When worn correctly the scarf will drape over the shoulder in such a way that it can easily be infurled when making gestures of respect to important officials or members of the royal family. More importantly, the colour of the scarf denotes rank and status in Bhutanese society. Ordinary citizens wear a scarf of plain white silk. The military wear a smaller version of this with a red border. Village headmen (Bh. *gup*) wear a white scarf with red stripes, and members of the National Assembly one with blue stripes. Nobles with the rank of Dasho are entitled to wear a red scarf, and members of the Royal Advisory Council a blue scarf. Senior government ministers (Bh. *lyonpo*) wear orange, but only the king and the Je Khenpo (Chief Monastic Preceptor of the official Drukpa Kagyu order) may wear saffron yellow.

Bhutanese women and schoolgirls are similarly obliged to wear a silk blouse (Bh. *wangjuk*) and a long seamless ankle-length dress (Bh. *kira*), which is folded under the right arm and then wrapped around to be fastened at the shoulders with two silver brooches (Bh. *koma*). A tightly fitting waistbelt of silver or woven cloth forms a pouch in the upper garment, similar to the pouch of the *gho*. Frequently a short-length buttonless jacket of heavier material (Bh. *togo*) is worn on top of the *kira*. The dress itself may be of simple striped machine-made cotton for everyday use or fine hand-spun cotton, embroidered with ornately patterned silk designs, for special occasions. On formal occasions and entering *dzongs*, women also wear an orange or red ceremonial scarf (Bh. *rachu*) draped over the left shoulder. The *rachu* is made of silk, with fringes at each end, 2 m long and 90 cm wide, but usually folded narrowly.

National language

Since the Drukpa share a common heritage of culture, language and religion with Tibet, the written language, here known as *cho-ke*, employs the classical Tibetan script. The colloquial language given national status in Bhutan is known as Dzongkha, the principal dialect of Western Bhutan. The **Dzongkha Development Commission** is responsible primarily for the promotion of spoken and written Dzongkha, although it also has a renewed interest in the promotion of classical *cho-ke* as well. The teaching of the national language is compulsory at all levels of education, but English is the medium of instruction. Primary education has been encouraged since the 1960s with the opening of state-funded schools throughout the country.

Architecture

Traditional **village architecture** varies according to the region. In the southern border areas and in parts of Eastern Bhutan thatched bamboo houses are constructed on stilts which (as in much of South-east Asia) offer protection from floods during the rainy season and unwelcome insects or reptiles. In the Laya and Lingzhi areas of Northern Bhutan, as well as in some parts of Central Bhutan, villages characteristically comprise a number of flat-roofed stone dwellings, while the nomads of that area, like the nomads of neighbouring Tibet, live in black yak-tweed tents (*ba*).

It is in the mid-mountain belt, however, that the most typically Bhutanese style of architecture can be seen. The houses are shingled, with sloping roofs, similar to dwellings in the Kongpo area of southern Tibet, and the thick walls are made of compacted mud, with the exception of the front side of the upper storey, which is constructed of intricately carved timbers, forming a series of shuttered windows, each with a trefoil shape. As in the distant Sertal region of far-east Tibet, this wooden structure overhangs the lower adobe wall. The lower floor of village houses will normally be used for storage and for animals. Access to the upper storey would be made by scaling a notched 'tree-trunk' ladder of the type that is still found in many parts of Tibet. The family would occupy the upper storey, where the interior walls are made of bamboo lattices covered with mud plaster. Usually there is an elaborate shrine room (*chokhang*), which may double as a guest room, and simple living quarters. The attic, immediately below the shingles is used as a drying area during the harvest season, and it provides some insulation for the living rooms below. The shingles themselves are weighted down with stones, and frequently need replacing because they lack gutters to channel rainwater. The doors and all wooden structures are made of dovetaled interlocking joints, close-fitting panels and grooves, requiring no nails. The outer walls of the houses are frequently whitewashed, contrasting with the richly painted woodwork. Sacred motifs, like the eight auspicious symbols (*tashi tagye*) are commonplace, and the exterior of the door is likely to depict a Garuda, tiger, or enlarged red phallus – said to distract and ward off malevolent forces. Lighting was once provided by oil lamps, but now by kerosene or electricity.

More distinctive than the village architecture is the grandeur of the administrative fortresses (*dzong*) that dominate strategic locations throughout the length and breadth of Bhutan (see box, page 66). There are also over 2,000 undamaged Buddhist monasteries, temples or hermitages, which are still active at the present day. The Tibetan term *gonpa* or *gon* (Bh. *goemba*), which is generally translated into English as 'monastery', in its primary sense refers to a remote place or wilderness, ideally suited for a meditative life, isolated from social diversions. Many

roads. A monastery will comprise a flagstoned courtyard (*dochal*) leading to a central assembly hall (*dukhang*) that contains many chapels or temples (*lhakhang*) within it, surrounded by various outbuildings – a kitchen (*tabsang*), sleeping quarters for monks (*khangtsang*), a retreat hermitage (*tsamkhang*) and some stupas. Larger monasteries may have other free-standing temples (*lhakhang*) and specialist colleges (*dratsang*) outside the main building.

In Bhutan an assembly hall or free-standing temple will be decorated in the traditional style. The walls will be white-washed, with an architrave of red potentilla wood below the shingles, to which decorative brass or gilded mirrors and ornate Sanskrit seed-letters are attached. The gilded roof (*sertok*) is surmounted by the wheel and deer motif, symbolising the location of Shakyamuni Buddha's first sermon in the deer-park of Varanasi, and a central gilded spire (*ganjira*). Most temples have an entrance portico replete with murals depicting the Four Guardian Kings of the four directions and the Wheel of Rebirth (*bhavacakra*) on the outer wall. Within the main gate, there are often images of the gatekeepers Vajrapani (east) and Hayagriva (west), watching over the portals, while the murals of the inner wall nearest the gate depict the protector deities. The central hall, which is of variable size (depending on the number of columns), contains the rows of seats, that are occupied by the monastic body during ritual ceremonies, with the thrones or elevated seats of the main reincarnate lamas (*tulku*) and monastic preceptors (*khenpo*) furthest from the gate.

Proceeding clockwise around the hall, the side-walls may well depict scenes from the life of Buddha Shakyamuni, or other historical figures. Eventually you will reach the innermost wall (facing the gate and beyond the thrones), against which the rows of clay or gilded copper images, sacred scriptures and reliquary stupas are positioned. These will vary according to the tradition which the temple or monastery represents, although images of the Buddhas of the Three Times are commonly depicted here. There may additionally be an inner sanctum containing the most precious images housed within the temple, with its own circumambulatory pathway. In front of the images, offerings will be arrayed on the altar (*chosham*), including water-offering bowls, butter lamps, *torma*-offering cakes, and representations of the eight auspicious symbols and the eight symbols of royal dominion (*gyelse nadun*), while donations will be left by the faithful as a meritorious action.

The liturgies associated with the protector deities are undertaken in a special, dark 'protector chapel' (*gonkhang*), often located on the upper level of the building, which may have restricted access. Here senior monks are responsible for maintaining the daily libation offerings (*serkhyem*) and the ritual sacraments honouring pledges made in respect of the protectors (*kangdze*). The appropriate liturgies are chanted to the rhythmic accompaniment of ritual musical instruments: the deep pounding of the large drum, the shrill blasts of the shin-bone trumpet and the clashing of the bell cymbals. Within the chapel there are images of the preferred protectors, sometimes flanking a central meditational deity such as Vajrabhairava or Vajrakīla – their awesomely terrifying faces frequently concealed behind silken veils. The side-walls and columns are often decorated with macabre stuffed animals and assorted weaponry including ancient swords and matchlock rifles. Graphic murals and painted scrolls may also depict the protectors and their symbolic ritual sacraments, outlined in gold with their salient facial features and fiery aureoles highlighted against a jet-black background.

Crafts

Traditional handicrafts, expensively priced, are made largely for the indigenous market rather than the tourist trade. There is little mechanisation, and no competition to encourage lower pricing. Since the 16th and 17th centuries, under the influence of

Pema Lingpa and later of Zhabdrung Ngawang Namgyel who were both accomplished artists and sculptors, Bhutan has been renowned for the excellence of its Buddhist arts and secular crafts. Different parts of the country are known for different skills and products. In particular, there are 13 officially recognised arts and crafts (*zorig chusum*), which are sponsored and maintained to high standards by the National Institute for Arts & Crafts in Thimphu:

Painting (*lhazo*) is highly stylised and conforms to the geometric proportions advocated by the classical Menri school of Buddhist iconography. It may take the form of portable painted scrolls (*tangkha*), temple murals (*debri*) or manuscript illumination (*peri*).

Metal casting (lugzo) of statues depicting Buddhist deities is carried out using the *cire perdue* method, which is also well known in Nepal, and by sand casting. Ritual bells and *vajras*, and household utensils, are also cast.

Clay sculpture (*jimzo*) of Buddhist images is highly refined in Bhutan, as is the making of *torma*-offering cakes from clay for ritual use, and adobe wall construction.

Engraving (*parzo*) of woodblocks for printing traditional loose-leaf Buddhist texts is still practised in Bhutan, as it is in parts of neighbouring Tibet. The carving of texts and mantras in stone and slate is also an important art form.

Carpentry (*shingzo*) is a major element in Bhutanese architecture (see above), from the administrative fortress and monastery to the simple village house. Joints are dovetailed, and planks are grooved together, without the use of nails. Other forms of woodwork include the making of wooden bowls, which is highly developed in Tashi Yangtse district. Some large bowls are made from single maple or giant avocado gnarls, others are smaller, lacquered or inlaid with silver.

Masonry (*dozo*) is important for the construction of fortresses, government buildings or monasteries. Fortunately, the techniques of cutting, dressing and stacking stone and slate are well preserved in Bhutan, unlike neighbouring Tibet where they have in some places already been lost.

Blacksmithing (*garzo*) is a handicraft still in demand for the production of iron swords, knives and agricultural tools. Thimphu is considered to be the best area in Bhutan for metalwork.

Gold and silver working (*serzo ngulzo*) is required for Buddhist ritual objects (offering bowls, libation bowls, butter lamps, amulet boxes, etc) and for items of personal jewellery, which is made in the Tibetan style, often inset with coral, freshwater pearl or *zi* (banded chalcedony/etched agate), and occasionally with turquoise.

Weaving (*thakzo*) of handloomed fabrics is mostly the preserve of Bhutanese women, and a skill that continues to have great demand, despite the competition from cheaper machine-made Indian imports. Some pieces are handed down as heirlooms. Each design has a distinctive name depending on its unique combination of fibre, colour and pattern. Cotton, wool, silk, yak and nettle fibres may be used to weave material in striped, banded or checked patterns. The finest brocade (*kushutara*) is woven in the Kurto region of Lhuntse district. Raw silk is produced mostly in Eastern Bhutan, woollen yarn in Bumthang, and yak-tweed products in the nomadic areas of Gasa.

Embroidery (*tsemzo*), including appliqué, is utilised for decorative work and for certain types of large painted scroll that are only displayed publicly on ceremonial occasions.

Rattanwork (*tsazo*), which is considered to be part of the indigenous Monpa or Lopa heritage of the Bhutanese, produces a number of useful household items, including small round or square food baskets (*bangchung*), alchohol containers, mats and traditional headwear. The best quality waterproof bamboo or rattan baskets are fashioned in interesting geometric designs in Khyeng.

Paper-making (*dezo*) is still maintained as a cottage industry. A strong lightweight paper is made from the bark of the daphne laurel and edgeworthia shrubs, and used for printing traditional texts, and for making greeting cards.

Leatherwork (*kozo*) for belts, straps and saddle bags for holding grain.

Secular festivals, dance and music

Non-Buddhist festivals include the traditional new year (*losar*) events and the recently introduced commemoration days indicative of the modern nation state. The former include the official new year (*gyelpo losar*) held in February/March, the agricultural new year (*sonam losar*) held in November/December, and the Nepalese new year in April. The latter include National Day (17 December); the King's Birthday (11 November) and Coronation Day (2 June). Such secular festivals are times for fun and archery contests.

Secular music and song vary, corresponding to the cultural divide between the Drukpa and Nepalese parts of the country. The instruments, rhythms, ballads and working songs of the Drukpa reflect the folk and popular culture of Tibet, while those of the Lhotsampa are close to the music of Nepal. The secular dances of the Bhutanese are similar to those of southern and western Tibet, with round dances and line dances predominating. They are characterised by intricate forward and backward steps, and by graceful arm movements. Modern popular music is a synthesis of Tibetan, Himalayan and Bollywood strands.

Religion

Tibetan and Bhutanese religious traditions may conveniently be considered in three categories – animism, Bon and Buddhism. The first concerns the control of animistic forces by bards and storytellers; the second emphasises the purity of space, funerary rituals and certain meditative practices, which may have originated in either Zoroastrianism or Kashmiri Buddhism; and the third is the means of liberation from the sufferings of cyclic existence as propounded in ancient India by Shakyamuni Buddha.

Animism and the 'religion of humans'

The earliest form of Tibetan and Bhutanese religion, which R.A. Stein has termed the 'nameless religion', is a type of animism based upon the worship of the elements and mountain deities. Aspects of this culture have survived through to the present: Incense offerings are made to appease local mountain spirits, and 'wind-horse' (*lungta*) prayer flags (see box, page 267) or cairns are affixed on prominent passes to ensure good auspices. Solemn declarations of truth (*dentsik*) and oaths are made in the presence of local deities, to invoke good fortune (*gyang-khug*); and talismanic objects or places (*la-ne*) are revered as life-supporting forces. Enemies or hostile forces can be overpowered by drawing in their life-supporting talisman in a ceremony known as *la-guk*. Many of these rituals have been absorbed into the Buddhist traditions of both Tibet and Bhutan.

Bon

The religion of Tazik (Persia) which was introduced into the Zhangzhung Kingdom of far-west Tibet and thence into Central Tibet and Bhutan during the period of the early kings is generally considered to have evolved in three distinct phases, known as 'revealed Bon' (*dol-bon*), 'deviant Bon' (*khyar-bon*) and 'transformed Bon' (*gyur-bon*). The original importance that Bon held for the Tibetan kings probably lay in its elaborate funerary rites and veneration of space. The earliest kings of Tibet are said to have been immortals, who would descend from and ascend into the heavens on a sky-cord (*mu*), but following the death of Drigum Tsenpo, the mortal kings increasingly focused upon funerary rites and rituals for the averting of death through 'ransom' (*lud*).

The **'revealed Bon'** refers to those rituals that were prevalent in Tibet from the time of Drigum Tsenpo until the time of King Lhatotori Nyentsen, in whose reign Buddhism made its first appearance. The **'deviant Bon'** included a new wave of rituals and practices derived from Zhangzhung and Brusha in far-west Tibet; and the **'transformed Bon'** refers to the synthesis which developed following the introduction of Buddhism to Tibet and its establishment as the state religion. Contemporary research into the earliest ritual and philosophical texts of Bon has been galvanised by the work of Professor Norbu in Italy. However, the Bon orders which have survived until the present are thoroughly imbued with Buddhist imagery and symbolism, and they have evolved their own parallel literature to counterbalance that of the Buddhists, ranging from esoteric teachings on ethics to highly esoteric teachings on the Great Perfection (Dzogchen). In Bhutan itself there is no evidence of any extant Bon order, but certain divinatory practices of Bon origin are said to be maintained by remote village communities.

Buddhism

Brief introduction

Buddhism evolved from the teachings of Siddhartha Gautama of the Shakya clan (known as the Buddha, the 'Awakened One'), who lived in northern India in the sixth or fifth century BC. The Buddha's teachings are rooted in a compelling existential observation: despite all persons' efforts to find happiness and avoid pain, their lives are filled with suffering and dissatisfaction. However, the Buddha did not stop there. He recognised the causes of suffering to be the dissonant mental states – delusion, attachment, aversion, pride and envy – and realised that it is possible to free oneself permanently from such sufferings through a rigorous and well-structured training in ethics, meditation, and insight, which leads to a profound understanding of the way things really are, that is, enlightenment. In this way the vicious circle of suffering, graphically depicted in the Wheel of Rebirth (see box, page 268) could be interrupted.

The Buddha was born a prince and had known great opulence but had also experienced great deprivations when he renounced his life of luxury to seek salvation through ascetic practice. He concluded that both sensual indulgence and physical deprivations are hindrances to spiritual evolution. He taught the Middle Way, a salvific path which was initially interpreted to mean isolation from the normal distractions of daily life, by living in communities devoted to the pursuit of spiritual liberation, which were disciplined but did not involve extreme deprivation. These communities, consisting of both monks and nuns, preserved and put into practice the Buddhist teachings. Initially, the teachings were preserved through oral transmission, but by the first century BC were increasingly committed to written form. Unlike other of the world's leading religious traditions, Buddhism does not rely on a single literary source (eg the Bible, Koran or Talmut), but on a vast, rich, sophisticated literary corpus. The preservation of Buddhism brought literacy to hundreds of millions in Asia.

Buddhism's path to salvation depended largely on the individual's own efforts. Its emphasis on self-reliance and non-violence appealed to the merchant class in

Prayer flags

Throughout Bhutan, as in Tibet, colourful prayer flags (*darchok*) are erected on rooftops, in courtyards and prominent places, like mountain passes and ridges which are exposed to the wind, permitting the natural power of the wind to distribute the blessings of their inscribed prayers as they flap to and fro.

Village houses will have a rooftop set of five flags, attached with five-coloured ribbons (*gondar*), dedicated to Jnananatha, an aspect of Mahakala, or to some other protector deity, dependent on their lineage. Larger flags attached to high poles (*lhadar*) and surmounted by silken parasols are raised in the courtyard of a *dzong* or monastery, invoking the triumph of Buddhism over negative forces. These tall flagpoles also have the motif of a wooden sword and wooden wheel at the top, indicative of the bodhisattvas Manjughosa and Avalokoteshvara, who respectively symbolise discernment and compassion. The flags are replaced annually during the new year ceremonies.

Other flags carry inscriptions printed from large woodblocks. At the centre there will be the motif of the 'luck horse' or 'wind-horse' (*lungta*) carrying a wish-fulfilling gemstone, and in the four corners there may be a protective animal: Garuda (top-left), dragon (top-right), tiger (bottom-left) and lion (bottom-right). These flags (*lungdar*) are printed in five colours: blue, white, red, green and yellow, respectively symbolising the five elements: space, water, fire, air and earth, and they are strung on exposed mountain passes or hilltops. Most mountain passes (*la-tse*) are marked by cairns of stones (some inscribed with mantras), to which sets of prayer flags are then attached. Sometimes an astrologer will be consulted to determine whether the colour or sequence should be altered to accord with the subject's purpose, goals and aspirations. In such cases, the subject's name, age and purpose will also be inscribed on the flag.

Instead of the 'luck-horse' or 'wind-horse' motif, other flags may be printed with the subject's preferred meditational deity. Those of the three bodhisattvas – Avalokiteshvara, Manjughosa and Vajrapani – are commonplace, as are the mantras of the female bodhisattva Tara, who protects travellers from the diverse dangers of the road. A set of 108 flags (*manidar*) inscribed with the image and mantras of Avalokiteshvara will commonly be erected on exposed places on behalf of a recently deceased person.

Wherever vehicles cross a major pass on a motor road, the passengers will invariably disembark to add a stone to the cairn, or tie a newly prepared set of prayer flags and burn incense as an offering to the spirit of the mountain, most of whom were tamed and appointed protectors of Buddhism by Guru Padmakara back in the eighth century. Some will cast paper prayer flags into the air from the bus window, rejoicing loudly in the ancient paean: 'Kyi-kyi so-so! May the gods be victorious!' (*lha-gyel-lo*).

Background Religion

India, and thus it spread along trade routes – north through Central Asia, into China and then into the Far East, Korea and Japan. It also spread south to Sri Lanka and South-east Asia: Burma, Thailand, Indo-China and Indonesia. Later, Nepal, Tibet and Bhutan embraced Buddhism at the zenith of its development in India, and it was this tradition which eventually came to permeate Mongolia, Manchuria and Kalmukya. In recent years Buddhism has also found adherents in the west.

The Wheel of Rebirth

The Wheel of Rebirth (Sanskrit *bhavacakra*, Tib. *sidpei khorlo*), sometimes known as the wheel of life or the wheel of existence, is a motif widely depicted among the vestibule murals of Tibetan and Bhutanese temples. Its graphic visual imagery symbolises the modes of suffering endured by sentient beings of the six realms along with the causes of their sufferings, which generate a perpetual cycle of mundane rebirths. The wheel is firmly held in the jaws and clutches of Yama Dharmaraja, the lord of death who presides over all cyclic existence. It comprises four concentric rings, the outermost one representing the **12 successive links of dependent origination** (Sanskrit *pratitya-samutpada*, Tib. *tendrel*) through which all forms of mundane existence come into being. The fundamental ignorance (1), propensities (2) and consciousness (3) which, as the successive resonances of a past life, continue to project their effects in a subsequent life in the following sequence: name and form (4), sensory activity fields (5), contact (6), sensation (7), attachment (8), grasping (9) and rebirth process (10), which in turn actualise birth (11) along with old age and death (12). The **second ring** depicts the actual sufferings endured by the gods (13), antigods (14), humans (15), animals (16), tormented spirits (17) and hell-bound beings (18), who are respectively dominated by pride, envy, diverse defilements, delusion, attachment and hatred; along with the corresponding Six Sages (Buddhas) who manifest in order to demonstrate the paths leading to liberation from cyclic existence. The **third ring** indicates the dynamic of the rebirth process (19): an upward momentum through the three higher modes of rebirth (gods, antigods and humans) and a downward spiral through the three lower destinies (animals, tormented spirits and hell-bound beings). The **innermost ring** (20) depicts the three primary defilements or dissonant mental states underlying the entire cycle, namely: the delusion, attachment and hatred, which are self-perpetuating. It is important to remember that, in the Buddhist view, the sufferings endured by the six realms of sentient existence are never considered to be eternal. Indeed the impermanence of all conditioned phenomena may be observed from moment to moment, as well as from death to rebirth. The wheel serves to remind its observer of the nature and causes of suffering and of the remedial actions to be followed in order to attain liberation from cyclic existence.

A Buddhist is one who takes refuge in the **Three Precious Jewels** (Triratna): Buddha, Dharma (his teachings) and Sangha (the monastic community). Beyond this, Buddhism has evolved remarkably different practices to bring about liberation, its teachings having been interpreted and reinterpreted by commentators in each new generation and in each cultural milieu. Buddhism's brilliance lies in its universality – its compelling existential appeal and, crucially, its efficacy. Historically it has appealed to peasants and to kings, to philosophers and to the illiterate, to prostitutes and murderers, and to those already close to sainthood. And though it was not its primary intention, Buddhism has transformed the cultures in its path – imbuing them with its ideals of universal compassion and profound insight.

The Buddhist teachings are broadly said to have developed in three distinct phases: (1) the sutra, vinaya and abhidharma texts (ie Tripitaka) of the **Lesser Vehicle** (Hinayana), which were maintained by the four great monastic orders founded in diverse parts of India by Katayayana, Rahula, Upali and Kashyapa; (2) the sutra teachings of the **Greater Vehicle** (Mahayana), which were maintained by the followers of Nagarjuna and Asanga; and (3) the tantras or esoteric teachings of the **Indestructible Vehicle** (Vajrayana), which were transmitted by accomplished masters such as Manjushrimitra, Indrabhuti and Padmakara. These different vehicles have their distinctive points of emphasis: the **Lesser Vehicle** holding that obscurations and defilements are eliminated by renunciation; the **Greater Vehicle** holding that enlightenment can be cultivated through compassion and insight which comprehends the emptiness underlying all phenomena, including those obscurations; and the **Indestructible Vehicle** holding that all obscurations are originally pure and transmutable into their pristine nature.

A primary distinction is made between the **sutra** texts, which emphasise the gradual or causal approach to enlightenment, and the **tantras** with their emphasis on the immediate or resultant approach.

Tibetan Buddhism

Among all the Buddhist countries of Asia, the highest developments of Indian Buddhism were preserved in Tibet and Bhutan. This was due partly to geographical proximity, partly to temporal considerations, and partly to the aptitude which the people themselves displayed for the diversity of Indian Buddhist traditions. The sparse population, the slow, measured pace of daily life and, in some sectors, an almost anarchical disdain for political involvement have encouraged the spiritual cultivation of Buddhism to such an extent that it came to permeate the entire culture.

All schools of Tibetan Buddhism maintain the monastic discipline of the **vinaya**, the graduated spiritual practices and philosophical systems based on the **sutras** and their commentaries, the shastras, and the esoteric meditative practices associated with the **tantras**. Different schools developed in different historical periods, each derived from distinctive lineages or transmissions of Indian Buddhism.

The oldest, the Nyingmapa, are associated with the early dissemination of Buddhism during the period of the Yarlung Dynasty. The Sakyapa and the Kagyupa, along with the Kadampa, appeared in the 11th century on the basis of later developments in Indian Buddhism. The Gelukpa originated in Tibet during the 14th century, but can claim descent from the others, particularly the Kadampa and the Sakyapa. Each of these schools has had its great teachers and personalities over the centuries. Each has held political power at one time or another and each continues to exert influence in its own geographical sphere, although it is true to say that not all of these schools survived in Bhutan.

NB The Mongol and Chinese custom of referring to the major schools of Tibetan Buddhism by the colours of the ceremonial hats worn by their monks has been avoided in this book because it is an absurd over-simplification, containing a number of anomalies, as the late Tseten Zhabdrung clearly pointed out some years ago in an article in *China Tibetology*.

Nyingmapa

The Nyingmapa school maintains the teachings introduced into Tibet by Shantaraksita, Padmakara, Vimalamitra and their contemporaries during the eighth century. The entire range of the Buddhist teachings are graded by the Nyingmapa according to nine hierarchical vehicles, starting from the esoteric sutras of the Lesser Vehicle and the Greater Vehicle and continuing through the classes of Outer Tantras to those of the Inner Tantras. It is the Inner Tantras known as Mahayoga, Anuyoga and Atiyoga (or Dzogchen), which are the teachings of the Nyingmapa par excellence.

Following the establishment of Buddhism in Tibet by King Trisong Detsen, the Nyingma literature was systematically translated into Tibetan at **Samye** Monastery. The tradition survived the persecution of Langdarma thanks to the activities of yogins such as Lhalung Pelgyi Dorje, Nyak Jnanakumara and Nubchen Sangye Yeshe, and the monks who preserved the Vinaya lineage in Amdo. When Buddhism was restored in Central Tibet in the late 10th century, the unbroken aural tradition of the Nyingmapa flourished at **Ukpalung** in Tsang under the guidance of the Zur family, and the various *terma* traditions (comprising teachings concealed in the past by Padmakara and his followers to be revealed for the benefit of future generations) developed their own local allegiances throughout the region. The most outstanding scholar and promulgator of this tradition was Longchen Rabjampa (1308-1363), who was also active in the **Bumthang** area of Bhutan (see page 236).

There are six main monasteries of the Nyingma school in Tibet, each of which has hundreds of branches: **Katok**, founded in 1159 by Katokpa Dampa Deshek (1122-1192); **Dorje Drak**, founded in 1632 by Rigdzin III Ngagi Wangpo (1580-1639); **Mindroling** founded in 1670 by Rigdzin Terdak Lingpa (1646-1714); **Pelyul**, founded in 1665 by Rigdzin Kunzang Sherab (1636-1698); **Dzokchen**, founded in 1685 by Dzogchen Pema Rigdzin (1625-1697); and **Zhechen**, founded in 1735 by Zhechen Rabjam II Gyurme Kunzang Namgyel. Of these, the Lhomon tradition of Katok was established at **Taktsang** in Paro during the 15th century. The others have no direct presence in Bhutan, although there are links with Mindroling and Zhechen through the teaching lineages of Pema Lingpa (1450-1521), Jigme Kundrol (late 18th century), and more recently through the extraordinary influence of the late Dudjom Rinpoche II (1904-1987) and the late Dilgo Khyentse Rinpoche (1910-1991).

Kagyupa

The Kagyupa school maintains the lineages of the Indian masters Tilopa, Naropa, and Maitripa, which emphasise the perfection stage of meditation (*sampannakrama*) and the practice of the Great Seal (*Mahamudra*). These were introduced to Tibet by Marpa Lo-tsawa (1012-1096) and Zhang Tselpa (1122-1193). Marpa, who lived in the **Lhodrak** area bordering Bhutan, had four main disciples including the renowned yogin Milarepa (1040-1123), who passed many years in retreat in the mountain caves of **Labchi** and adjacent Himalayan valleys. Milarepa is one of a select group of Tibetan masters revered for their attainment of buddhahood within a single lifetime. His biography and songs are classic texts, available in English translation, but it was his principal student, Gampopa (1079-1153), who founded the first monastery of that school at **Daklha Gampo** in the early 12th century. Gampopa's principal students, Phakmodrupa Dorje Gyelpo (1110-1170) and Karmapa I Dusum Khyenpa (1110-1193), respectively founded the influential monasteries of **Densatil** and **Tsurphu**. The former was the source of the eight minor Kagyu schools, including those of **Drigung** (founded by Drigung Kyopa, 1143-1217), **Taklung** (founded by Taklung Tangpa Tashipel, 1142-1210), and **Druk** (founded by Lingje Repa, 1128-1188). Of these sub-schools, it was the last, the Drukpa Kagyu order, which eventually became the dominant tradition within Bhutan (see page 238).

Kadampa

When the Bengali master Atisha (982-1054) reintroduced the teachings of the gradual path to enlightenment into Tibet in 1042, he transmitted the doctrines of his teacher Dharmakirti of **Sumatra**, which focused on the cultivation of compassion and the propitiation of the deities Tara, Avalokiteshvara, Acala and Shakyamuni Buddha. His disciples included Ngok Lotsawa (1059-1109) and Dromton Gyelwei Jungne (1004-1064), who respectively founded the important monasteries of **Sangphu Neutok** and **Reting**. Kadampa masters from **Nenying** Monastery in Khangmar county entered Western Bhutan from the 13th century onwards (see page 235). During the early 15th century the Kadampa tradition was absorbed within the Gelukpa school.

Sakyapa

The Sakyapa tradition represents a unique synthesis of early eighth-century Buddhism and the later diffusion of the 11th century. The members of the Khon family had been adherents of Buddhism since the time of Khon Luiwangpo Sungwa, a student of Guru Padmakara. Then, in 1073, his descendant Khon Konchok Gyelpo, who had received teachings of the new tradition from Drokmi Lotsawa, founded the **Gorum** temple at **Sakya**. His order therefore came to emphasise the ancient teachings on Vajrakila, as well as the new teachings on Hevajra, Cakrasamvara and the esoteric instruction known as the Path and its Fruit. The monastery was initially developed and expanded by the so-called five founders of Sakya: Sachen Kunga Nyingpo (1092-1158), Jetsun Sonam Tsemo (1142-1182), Drakpa Gyeltsen (1147-1216), Sakya Pandita (1182-1251) and Drogon Chogyel Phakpa (1235-1280). The last mentioned built the **Lhakhang Chenmo** (1268) and, with the patronage of the Mongol Empire secured, established a network of monasteries and temples throughout Central and Eastern Tibet, comprising **Gongkar Chode**, **Jyekundo**, **Zhiwu**, **Dzongsar** and **Lhagang**, to name but a few. After the death of the Sakya hierarch Danyi Zangpo Pal (r. 1305-1322), the ruling house of Sakya split into two main branches – the Phuntsok Palace and the Dolma Palace – which have until the present shared their authority on a rotational basis. The Sakyapa school established a number of monasteries in Western Tibet from the 13th centuy onwards and maintained a close rapport with the breakaway Bhutanese state, even after the rise to power of the Gelukpa administration in Lhasa.

Other important sub-schools of Sakya also developed. Among them, **Ngor** Monastery, founded in 1429 by Ngorchen Kunga Zangpo, also established its branches in Bhutan.

Gelukpa

The Gelukpa school maintains the teachings and lineage of Je Tsongkhapa (1357-1419), who established a uniquely indigenous tradition on the basis of his Sakyapa and Kadampa background. Born in the **Tsongkha** valley of Amdo, he moved to Central Tibet and founded the monastery of **Ganden** in 1409. He instituted the Great Prayer Festival at Lhasa, and propagated his important treatises on the sutra and tantra traditions in and around the Tibetan capital. Two of his foremost students, Jamyang Choje Tashi Palden and Jamchen Choje Shakya Yeshe, respectively founded **Drepung** (1416) and **Sera** (1419), while others such as Gyeltsab Je and Khedrup Je, became the prime teachers of the new Gelukpa order. The latter was retrospectively recognised as Panchen Lama I. Another of Tsongkhapa's students was Dalai Lama I Gendun Drupa, who founded **Tashilhunpo** at Zhigatse in 1447.

The successive emanations of the Dalai and Panchen Lamas enhanced the prestige of the Gelukpa school, which swiftly gained allegiances among the Mongol forces of the north-east. Following the civil wars of the 17th century, many Kagyu monasteries were converted to the Gelukpa tradition, and the regent Sangye Gyatso compiled his *Yellow Beryl (Vaidurya Serpo)* history of the Gelukpa tradition. A few Gelukpa monasteries were founded in Western Bhutan in the years immediately following Tsongkhapa's death, but the tradition never took root there, and its slender foothold was forcibly removed following the Zhabdrung's unification of the Bhutanese state.

Others

The lineages of certain minor Buddhist traditions have also survived intact – among them the **Zhiche** ('pacification') and **Chodyul** ('object of cutting') which were expounded by the South Indian yogin Padampa Sangye and his female Tibetan disciple Machik Labdron (1031-1126). The ritual practices of the latter are particularly popular among adherents of the Nyingma and Kagyu traditions in both Tibet and Bhutan.

The **Jonangpa** tradition was founded at **Jonang Phuntsoling** in Tsang by Kunpang Tu-je Tsondru (b. 1243), and widely propagated through the writings of its great exponents: Dolpopa Sherab Gyeltsen (1292-1361), Jestun Kunga Drolchok (1507-1566) and Taranatha (1575-1634). Its teachings combined an in-depth knowledge of the *Kalacakra Tantra* and other tantra-texts of the new translation period, with a distinctive view concerning the nature of the emptiness (*shunyata*) which, according to Buddhism, is the real nature of all phenomena. The Jonangpa differentiated between mundane phenomena which are regarded as being 'inherently empty' and the attributes of the Buddha which are regarded as being 'extraneously empty' of mundane impurities. The school was persecuted – ostensibly for holding this view – during the 17th century and its adherents have only survived in remote parts of Amdo. There are no Jonangpa establishments in Bhutan, although some Drukpa Kagyu commentators do have an affinity with Dolpopa's views on the nature of emptiness.

Buddhism in modern Bhutan

Buddhism continues to play a crucial role in Bhutanese life at the present day. The **Drukpa Kagyu** school is the official order, but the **Nyingma school** is also well represented, particularly in central and eastern districts.

As explained above (see page 238), there are unique political and military circumstances through which the Drukpa Kagyu, among all the various schools of Tibetan Buddhism, came to dominate the religious life of the country. This school was founded at Druk in Central Tibet by Tsangpa Gya-re Yeshe Dorje (1161-1211), whose foremost students formed its three main branches: the Middle Drukpa school at Ralung, the Upper Drukpa school in west Tibet and Ladakh, and the Lower Drukpa school at Uri and Karpo Cho-lung. Among these, the Middle Drukpa school first reached Bhutan during the 13th century through the missionary efforts of Drukgom Zhikpo and his descendants, who established strong links between Western Bhutan and Ralung. In particular, Kunga Peljor founded a number of Middle Drukpa monasteries in Western Bhutan during the 15th century, and it was to these that during the 17th century Zhabdrung Ngawang Namgyel (1594-1651), the hierarch of Ralung monastery, fled to escape the persecution of the king of Tsang, thereby founding the Bhutanese state. In this way, the Drukpa Kagyu school gave its name to the newly emergent state of Bhutan.

There are around 6,000 monks in Bhutan, approximately half being subsidised under the authority of the Je Khenpo of the Drukpa Kagyu school, and the remainder subsisting on private patronage. Each of the larger *dzongs* houses several hundred monks. By contrast, there are only about 250 nuns. In addition to monastic Buddhism, there are also a number of important reincarnating *tulkus* who are responsible for maintaining their own distinctive spiritual lineages, whether Bhutanese or Tibetan in origin, and approximately 15,000 respected lay practitioners, known as *ngakpa* or *gomchen*. Many Nyingma temples are privately owned, and passed on through familial lines of succession from one generation to the next. All those fully engaged in Buddhist practice, whether monastic or not, are highly respected by the people and by the government, for whom they provide spiritual guidance and support through their private meditations, communal prayers, ceremonial rituals and religious festivals.

The laity, in turn, place great emphasis on the importance of making offerings at their household shrines, performing daily prayers, circumambulating stupas and temples, going on pilgrimage and sponsoring religious ceremonies. As in other Buddhist countries, there is a universal understanding of the importance of the accumulation of merit for the spiritual well-being and development of each individual in this life and in subsequent lives after death.

In Southern Bhutan, where the dominant population is Nepalese, religious ceremonies correspond to those of contemporary Hindu and Newar society in Nepal.

Buddhist festivals

There are important events in the Tibetan and Bhutanese calendar, commemorating the deeds of Shakyamuni Buddha, or the anniversaries of the great masters of the past associated with one tradition or another. In Bhutan, in addition to the standard festivals associated with the Buddha's life, the most renowned of these are the **tsechu** ('10th day') festivals commemorating the deeds of Guru Padmakara, the eighth-century master of the Nyingma school who is credited with the introduction of the most profound Buddhist teachings. On each 10th day of the 12 lunar months of the year, a particular episode in the life of Padmakara is commemorated (see box, page 114). Some of these are dramatised in the context of a *drubchen* ceremony, with masked dances (*cham*), which may last from three to five days, one of which usually but not invariably falls on the 10th day of the lunar month.

The sacred choreographic tradition of the *tsechu* probably has its origins in the Lhodrak area of Tibet, immediately to the north of Bhutan, where Guru Chowang (1212-1270) unearthed a treasure-text entitled *Spiritual Teacher: The Secret Assembly* (*Lama Sangdu*), which contains dances commemorating the deeds of Padmakara. Later, in Bhutan, the tradition of sacred masked dances was developed by Pema Lingpa and by Zhabdrung Ngawang Namgyel, whose fourth regent Tendzin Rabgye (1638-1696) inaugurated the present tradition in 1670. Since then, each regional *dzong* and its affiliated village communities adopted the custom of holding their distinct annual *tsechu* festival, coinciding with a particular slot in the lunar calendar. The dances are earnestly and purposefully performed in the prescribed manner, but comic relief and an element of spontaneity are provided by clown-like jesters (*atsara*), who tease the congregation with their comic banter, while skilfully controlling the crowd. These events provide the local populace with a wonderful occasion to dress up, gather together at the *dzong*, and enjoy themselves in a convivial, light-hearted atmosphere. It is also an occasion for them to renew their faith and receive blessings by watching the sacred masked dances, or receiving 'empowerment' from an officiating lama. At Paro, Wangdu, Mongar, Tashigang, Drametse and elsewhere, a large painted scroll known as a *tongdrol* is exhibited for a few hours in the course of the *tsechu* festival, enabling the people to throng forward to obtain its blessing on that auspicious day, since such painted scrolls are said to 'confer liberation by their sight alone' (*tongdrol*). For the festival calendar, see box, page 41.

Sacred masked dances (cham)

It is important to remember that, unlike the secular operatic tradition of Tibet, such dances are not performed in isolation as a mere spectacle, but rather in the context of an elaborate spiritual practice (*drubchen*) that will culminate in the granting of a spiritual empowerment (*wangkur*) and the distribution of feast-offerings (*tsok*). Empowerments of this type are a prerequisite for anyone practising Buddhism according to the tantric tradition of Tibetan and Bhutanese Buddhism. The feast-offerings are a skilful means of accumulating both merit and insight in a liturgical context. The actual dances are performed in different sequences in different locations, and visitors will have to consult the official programme for particuar *tsechu* events. The dancers are trained monks and laymen wearing ornate costumes, and, in some cases, impressive masks. Each episode has its distinctive symbolic meaning. In general, the dances are classified according to three distinct themes: morality plays; purificatory rites which exorcise malevolent forces; and triumphal celebrations of Buddhism, glorifying the deeds of Guru Padmakara, and so forth.

Morality plays There are three important dances in the form of morality plays, designed to instruct the audience: 1) The lewd **Dance of the Princes and Princesses** (*pho-le mo-le*), based on the legend of Prince Sudhana (Norzang), in which dancers depict two princes who return from a foreign war to cut off the noses of their adulterous princesses. 2) The **Dance of the Stag and Hounds** (*sha-ba sha-khyi*), in which the hermit saint Milarepa compassionately saves the life of a hunted stag and converts its pursuing hounds and hunter to Buddhism. 3) The **Dance of the Judgement of the Dead** (*raksha marcham*), based on the final chapter of Karma Lingpa's *Tibetan Book of the Dead*, in which the executors of the rites of the Lord of Death dramatically pass judgement on two recently deceased individuals, one evil and the other virtuous – the full text is available in English translation. See G. Dorje (trans.), and. G. Coleman and T.J. Langri (eds), *The Complete Tibetan Book of the Dead* (Penguin).

Purificatory rites Many of the sacred dances are performed in order to remove obstacles or malevolent forces through acts of exorcism. Included in this category are: 1) The **Black Hat Dance** (*shanag*), in which dancers wearing large wide-brimmed black hats, high boots and silk brocade costumes exorcise demonic forces from the dancing arena, re-enacting the assassination of the apostate ninth-century Tibetan king Langdarma. 2) The **Dance of the Lords of the Charnel Ground** (*durtro dakpo dagmo*), in which the eight great charnel grounds of ancient India are ritually guarded by two skeleton-clad dancers, thereby offering protection to the dancing arena. 3) The **Dance of the Four Stags** (*shacham*), following the teachings of Namkhei Nyingpo, in which Guru Padmakara subjugates the god of the wind element by riding his stag mount. 4) The **Dance of the Ging and Tsholing** (*ging-dang tsholing*), in which two waves of terrifying acolytes in the entourage of Padmakara successively appear to take possession of the dancing arena, clearing away obstacles that will impede the sacred vision of the paradise known as Copper-coloured Mountain (Zangdokpelri). 5) The **Dance of the Three Kinds of Ging** (*gingsum cham*), based on a revelation of Pema Lingpa, in which acolytes of Guru Padmakara wielding cudgels, swords and drums overwhelm, pierce and triumph over the infiltrating elemental spirits (*jungpo nyulema*) who obstruct the path to enlightenment. 6) The **Revelatory Dance of Bumthang** (*bumthang tercham*), which was choreographed by Pema Lingpa just before he consecrated Tamzhing temple, on the basis of his treasure-text entitled *Vajrakila: Razor of Vitality* (*Phurba sogi putri*), in order to subdue the geomantic spirit lords of the soil (*sadag*). 7) The **Exorcising Dance of Guru Drakpo** (*tungam cham*), in which Padmakara manifests in the wrathful form Guru Drakpo and utilises a ritual dagger to forcefully 'liberate' the consciousness of obdurate hostile spirits into higher realms of rebirth, exemplified by the Copper-coloured Mountain. 8) The **Protective Dance of Do-le Monastery** (*dole raksha cham*), which was first performed in 1685, according to a prophecy of Mahakala, in order to distract a water spirit obstructing the construction of a bridge over the Wang-chu below Rinchengang.

Triumphal celebrations The main part of the *tsechu* festival accords with this category. Dances here include: 1) The **Dance of the Spiritual Heroes** (*pacham*), which eulogises the precious Guru Padmakara within the Copper-coloured Mountain, following a revelation of Pema Lingpa. 2) The **Drum Dance of Drametse Monastery** (*drametse ngacham*), in which animal-masked figures in Padmakara's entourage enact the victory of Buddhism following the pure vision of Kunga Gyeltsen, a son of Pema Lingpa. 3) The elaborate **Dance of Padmakara's Eight Manifestations** (*gu-ru tsen-gye*), in which each of the eight manifestations (see box, page 114) performs an

individual dance, commemorating a specific episode in the life of Guru Padmakara.
4) The **Spiritual Song** (*choshe*) commemorating the opening of the hidden land of Tsari on the present-day Tibet-Arunachal border by Tsangpa Gya-re (1161-1211). 5) The **Lute Dance** (*dranyen cham*), in which the founding of the Drukpa Kagyu school in Bhutan is celebrated. 6) The **Dance of the Sixteen Offering Goddesses** (*riknga chudruk*), which is performed as a benediction.

Throughout the performance, the accompanying musicians visualise that the past masters of their spiritual lineage and their meditational deities become manifest as the dancers, as they mark the rhythm of the dance, playing their long horns (*dungchen*), oboes (*gyaling*), drums (*nga*), cymbals (*silnyen/babchal*), shinbone trumpets (*kangling*), conch shells (*dung*), skull-drums (*damaru*) and bells (*drilbu*). More detailed descriptions may be found in Dasho Sithel Dorji's *The Origin and Description of Bhutanese Dance Masks*, and in a small booklet entitled *Festival Guide*, which is published by the Association of Bhutanese Tour Operators.

Books

The following websites will direct readers to publishers and distributors of available English-language books on Bhutan: www.amazon.com, www.chesterbooks.com, www.wisdompubs.org, www.snowlionpub.com, www.shambhala.org, www.himalayanbooks.co.uk, and www.demon.co.uk/wisdom.com.

Contemporary fiction

Choden, K, *Folktales of Bhutan* (White Lotus, 1993). An anthology of retold traditional Bhutanese stories.
Karma Ura, *The Ballad of Pemi Tshewang Tashi* (Bhutanese Ministry of Planning, 1996). Translation of an intensely lyrical tale of valour and heroic death, reminiscent of the final scene in *Crouching Tiger, Leaping Dragon*, which is set against the background of the late 19th-century internecine conflicts between Jakar and Trongsar.
Karma Ura, *The Hero with a Thousand Eyes* (Centre for Bhutan Studies, 1995). An historical novel tracing the 20th-century modernisation of Bhutan as seen through the eyes of the royal courtier Dasho Shingkar Lam Kunzang Wangchuk (b. 1928).

Guidebooks and travelogues

Pommaret, F, *Bhutan* (Odyssey Passport, 4th edn, 2003). Written by a well-known anthropologist with specialist knowledge of Bhutan, this work has many useful insights into the cultural life of the country.
Bailey, FM, 'Travels in Bhutan', *Journal of the Central Asian Society*, (1930, vol. xvii, pp. 206-20). A sympathetic account of the coronation of the 2nd king of Bhutan in 1927, written by a visiting political officer from British India.
Hickman, K, *Dreams of the Peaceful Dragon* (Phoenix, 2003). An easy-to-read account of a 1970s trek from Bumthang to Mongar, before the completion of the central highway.
Ronaldshay, LJLD, *Travels in the Lands of the Thunderbolt* (London, 1923). A fascinating account of the Earl of Ronadlshay's 1921 expedition to Paro.
Zeppa, J, *Beyond the Sky and the Earth: A Journey into Bhutan* (Riverhead Books, 1999). An amusing and compelling account of an expatriate Canadian teacher's love affair with Bhutan.

Biography and autobiography

HRH Ashi Dorji Wangmo, *Of Rainbows and Clouds* (Motithang, 1997). Biography of Yab Ugyen Dorji, the father of the 4 present Bhutanese queens, offering an intimate account of the major events in 20th-century Bhutanese history.
Douglas, K & Bays, G (trans.), *The Life and Liberation of Padmasambhava* (Dharma Publishing, 1978). A translation of Orgyan Lingpa's 14th-century revelation

recounting the extraordinary career of Padmasambhava, who introduced the highest Buddhist teachings into Tibet and Bhutan from India during the 8th century.

Dowman, K, *The Divine Madman* (Down Horse Press, 1998). A translation of the bizarre life and spiritual songs of the Bhutanese yogin Drukpa Kun-le (1455-1529).

Harding, S (trans.), *The Life and Revelations of Pema Lingpa* (Snow Lion Publications, 2003). An account of the extensive lineages issuing from the celebrated treasure-finder Pema Lingpa (1450-1521), along with extracts from one of his revelatory teachings: *Spiritual Teacher: Ocean of Gems* (*Lama Norbu Gyatso*).

Lopon Pema Tsewang, Butters, C, et al, *The Treasure Revealer of Bhutan* (Bibliotheca Himalayica, 1995). Translation of Lopon Pema Tsewang's *Life of Pema Lingpa*, along with a synopsis of his *Collected Works*.

Yonten Dargye & Sorensen, PK, (trans.), *The Biography of Pha 'Brug-sgom Zhig-po* (National Library of Bhutan, 2001). Recounts the life of the 13th-century founder of the Drukpa Kagyu school in Bhutan.

History

Aris, M, *Bhutan* (Aris & Phillips, 1979). A classic dissertation on Bhutan's early history.

Aris, M, *Hidden Treasures and Secret Lives* (Motilal Banarsi Das, 1988). A somewhat controversial study of chronology in the biographies of Pema Lingpa and Dalai Lama VI.

Aris, M, *The Raven Crown* (Serindia, 1994). An authoritative study on the origins of the Bhutanese monarchy in the 20th century.

Deb, A, *Bhutan and India: A Study in Frontier Political Relations* (Firma KLM, 1976). Analyses the relationship between Bhutan and British India prior to the rise of the Bhutanese monarchy.

Dorji, CT, *A Political and Religious History of Bhutan* (Prominent Publishers, 1995). Summarises the lives of the major figures in Bhutanese history.

Hasrat, BJ, *History of Bhutan: Land of the Peaceful Dragon* (Education Department of Bhutan, 1980).

Hutt, M (ed), *Unbecoming Citizens: Culture, Nationhood and the Flight of Refugees from Bhutan* (OUP, 2003). A series of academic papers on issues relating to the influx of Lhotsampa refugees from Bhutan into Eastern Nepal.

Olschak, BC, *Ancient Bhutan* (Swiss Foundation for Alpine Research, 1979).

Rose, L, *The Politics of Bhutan* (Cornell, 1977).

Nature, flora and wildlife

Ali, S, et al, *Compact Handbook of Birds of India and Pakistan: Together with Those of Bangladesh, Nepal, Bhutan and Sri Lanka* (OUP, 1994). A detailed but unillustrated description of Bhutan's 675 recognised species of birds.

Diemberger, H, 'Beyul Khenbalung: the Hidden Valley of the Artemisia', in Macdonald, AW, (ed), *Mandala and Landscape* (Delhi, 1997). The sacred geography of a renowned hidden land in Lhuntse district.

Fletcher, HR, *The Quest for Flowers: The Plant Expeditions of Frank Ludlow and George Sheriff* (Edinburgh University Press, 1975). Includes the botanical surveys of Bhutan, and the discovery of the Blue Poppy in Sakteng, based on original diaries and archives.

Gansser, A, *Geology of the Bhutan Himalaya* (Springer Verlag, 1983). The most comprehensive book on Himalayan geology in Bhutan.

Green, M, *Nature Reserves of the Himalaya and the Mountains of Central Asia* (World Conservation Union, 1993). This work includes a useful chapter on the national parks of Bhutan.

Inskipp, C & T, *An Introduction to Bird Watching in Bhutan* (WWF, nd). An illustrated guide to some of the most important birds found in Bhutan.

Pradahan, R, *Wild Rhododendrons of Bhutan*. Contains colour illustrations of all the Bhutanese species of rhododendrons.

Reinhard, J, 'Khembalung: the Hidden Valley', *Kailash* (vol. 6 (1), pp. 5-35, 1978). An earlier study of the renowned hidden land in Lhuntse district.

Cultural heritage, art and architecture

Cornu, P, *Tibetan Astrology* (Shambhala, 1997). A practical integrated guide to systems of astrology and elemental divination that are also practised in Bhutan.

Crosette, B, *So Close to Heaven: The Vanishing Buddhist Kingdoms of the Himalayas* (Random House, 1995). Very readable account of Bhutanese history and culture, with a focus on contemporary issues.

Dasho Sithel Dorji, *The Origin and Description of Bhutanese Mask Dances* (KMT Press, 2001). A fascinating presentation of 26 different sacred dances, derived from different parts of Bhutan, written by a former director of the Royal Academy of Performing Arts.

Myers, D & Bean, S (eds), *From the Land of the Thunder Dragon: Textile Arts of Bhutan* (Serindia, 1994). A series of articles on the many Bhutanese varieties of cotton, silk and woollen fabrics that are hand-woven and machine-made, including rare collectors' items.

Namgyel Dorji, 'Monuments of Bhutan', *The First Colloquium on Dawn and Early History of Bhutan* (National Museum of Bhutan, 1997).

Parfionovitch, Y, Dorje, G & Mayer, F (eds), *Tibetan Medical Paintings* (Serindia, 1992). Analysis and documentation of an 18th-century series of paintings illustrating the course of Tibetan and therefore Bhutanese medicine.

Pommaret, F, 'Entrance-keepers of a Hidden Country: Preliminary Notes on the Monpa of South-Central Bhutan', *Tibet Journal* (vol. 19 (3), pp. 46-62).

Schicklgruber, C & Pommaret, F (eds), *Bhutan: Mountain Fortress of the Gods* (Serindia, 1997). A comprehensive overview of many diverse aspects of Bhutanese culture.

Dzongkha and Tibetan language and dictionaries

Beyer, S, *The Classical Tibetan Language* (SUNY, 1992). An analysis of the historical development of the Tibetan language.

Denwood, P, *Tibetan* (John Benjamins, 1999). An authoritative work on the structure of the Tibetan language.

Rinchhen Khandu, *Dzongkha-English Dictionary: Topic-Based Approach with Romanization* (Pekhang Enterprises, 1998). A thematic Dzongkha-English dictionary.

van Driem, G, *The Grammar of Dzongkha* (Dzongkha Development Commission, 1992). Written by an acknowledged authority on Dzongkha and the many other dialects and languages of Bhutan, this work offers a systematic presentation of the national language.

Buddhism

Chogyay Trichen, *The History of the Sakya Tradition* (Ganesha, 1983). A brief account of the early history of Sakya and the emergence of its influential Ngorpa and Tsharpa branches.

Dorje, G, *Tibet Handbook* (Footprint, 3rd ed, 2004). Contains detailed descriptions of monasteries and temples throughout Tibet, some of them having important relations with Bhutan.

Dorji, CT, *History of Bhutan Based on Buddhism* (Prominent Publishers, 1994). A listing of prominent Buddhist figures in the history of Bhutan.

Douglas & White, *Karmapa: the Black Hat Lama of Tibet* (Luzac, 1976). An account of the history of the Karma Kagyu school in Tibet.

Dudjom Rinpoche (trans. Dorje, G & Kapstein, M), *The Nyingma School of Tibetan Buddhism* (Wisdom, 2nd edn 2002). A detailed account of the history and philosophical developments of the Nyingma school.

Karma Lingpa (trans. Dorje, G eds. Coleman, G & Langri, TJ), *The Complete Tibetan Book of the Dead* (Penguin, 2004). The first full translation of Karma Lingpa's well-known 14th-century revelation, on Buddhist approaches to the 'intermediate' phases of life and death.

Karma Thinley, *The Sixteen Karmapas* (Shambhala, 1978). Biographies of the successive incarnations of Karmapa I.

Karmay, S, 'Dorje Lingpa and his Rediscovery of the "Golden Needle" in Bhutan', *Journal of Bhutan Studies* (vol. 2 (2), pp. 1-37). An article on a specific revelation by a renowned treasure-finder, Dorje Lingpa (1346-1405).

Kuenleg, Tshenyid Lopen, 'A Brief History of Tango Monastery', *Journal of Bhutan Studies* (2000, vol. 2 (1), pp. 130-9).

Paltrul Rinpoche, *The Words of My Perfect Teacher* (HarperCollins, 1994). The standard work on the preliminary meditative practices of Tibetan Buddhism.

Pommaret, F, 'On Local and Mountain Deities in Bhutan', in Blondeau & Steinkellner (eds), *Reflections of the Mountain* (Verlag der Osterreichischen Akademie der Wissenschaften, 1996).

Powers, J, *Introduction to Tibetan Buddhism* (Snowlion, 1995). A clear outline of the nuances of Tibetan Buddhism for beginners.

Thondup, T, *Buddhist Civilization in Tibet* (RKP, 1987). A synopsis of all the major Buddhist and secular sciences that were imported from ancient India into Tibet, and thence into Bhutan.

Tucci, G, *The Religions of Tibet* (Berkeley, 1980). An overview of the various traditions of Tibetan Buddhism.

Williams, P, *Mahayana Buddhism* (RKP, 1989). A clear account of the development of classical Mahayana Buddhism in ancient India and its early transmission to Central and East Asia.

Yonten Dargye, *History of the Drukpa Kagyud School in Bhutan* (Omega Traders, 2001). Covers the period from the 12th through to the 17th centuries.

Films

Documentaries

A number of documentaries have been partly or wholly filmed inside Bhutan. Some of these are available on DVD and VHS. *The Living Edens-Bhutan: The Last Shangri-La* (1997), *Mystic Lands- Bhutan* (1997), *Bhutan: Land of the Thunder Dragon* (2001). In the BBC documentary *Joanna Lumley in the Land of the Thunder Dragon*, the well-known sitcom star follows in the footsteps of her grandfather, Lt. Cl. JLR Weir, who was despatched to offer a knighthood to the king of Bhutan in 1931. Rare footage of the late Drukpa Kagyu yogin Lopon Sonam Zangpo can be found in Arnaud Desjardins, *The Message of the Tibetans* (1966).

Feature films

Feature films have also been made in Bhutan, including much of Bernardo Bertolucci's *Little Buddha*. Bertolucci's collaborator, Dzongsar Khyentse Rinpoche, who has an acting role in *Little Buddha*, subsequently turned his hand to film-making and he has since directed 2 widely acclaimed films of his own. *The Cup* (2000) tells the amusing tale of young monks at the Chokling monastery in Bir, India, who become obsessed with the televised 1998 World Cup finals. *Travellers and Magicians* (2003) tells the story of a young Bhutanese seeking to leave his village for the USA, and the conflicts that arise when his rose-coloured view of foreign lands clashes with traditional Bhutanese values.

Footnotes

An iconographic guide to Tibetan Buddhism

It is impossible to visit Tibet or Bhutan without being overwhelmed by religious imagery. The sheer scale is breathtaking – the Potala Palace in Lhasa alone has 1,000 rooms, housing approximately 200,000 images. It will help both your understanding and enjoyment if you can recognize some of these images.

This guide contains the names of the deities or images most frequently depicted in the Buddhist temples and monasteries of Tibet and Bhutan. Illustrations of some of these are also appended. It is important to remember that, with the probable exception of images representing the ancient historic kings of Tibet, the others are not regarded as concrete or inherently existing beings in the Judeo-Christian or even in the Hindu sense. Rather, the deities are revered as pure expressions of buddha-mind, who are to be visualized in the course of meditation in their pure light forms: a coalescence of pure appearance and emptiness. Through such meditations, blessings are obtained from the teachers of the past; spiritual accomplishments are matured through the meditational deities, enlightened activities are engaged in through the agency of the dakinis, and spiritual development is safe-guarded by the protector deities. These therefore are the four main classes of image to be observed in Tibetan and Bhutanese shrines. Among them, the images representing the spiritual teachers of the past are exemplified by Buddha Shakyamuni, Padmasambhava and Tsongkhapa; those representing the meditational deities by Vajrakumara, Cakrasamvara and Kalacakra; those representing dakinis or female agents of enlightened activity by Vajravarahi; and the protector deities by Mahakala, Shridevi, and so forth.

Temples: what to expect

Most temples have an entrance portico replete with murals depicting the Four Guardian Kings of the four directions and the Wheel of Rebirth (*bhavacakra*) on the outer wall. Within the main gate, there are often images of the gatekeepers Vajrapani (east) and Hayagriva (west), watching over the portals, while the murals of the inner wall nearest the gate depict the protector deities. The central hall, which is of variable size (depending on the number of columns), contains the rows of seats which are occupied by the monastic body during ritual ceremonies, with the thrones or elevated seats of the main lamas furthest from the gate. Proceeding clockwise around the hall, the side-walls may well depict scenes from the life of Buddha Shakyamuni, or other historical figures. Eventually you will reach the innermost wall (facing the gate and beyond the thrones), against which the rows of clay or gilded copper images, sacred scriptures, and reliquary stupas are positioned. These will vary according to the tradition which the temple or monastery represents, although images of the Buddhas of the Three Times are commonly depicted here. There may additionally be an inner sanctum containing the most precious images housed within the temple, with its own circumambulatory pathway. In front of the images, offerings will be arrayed, including water-offering bowls, butter lamps and torma-offering cakes, while donations will be left by the faithful as a meritorious action.

The guide

Acala (Tib Miyowa) one of the 10 wrathful kings (dashakrodha), forming a peripheral group of meditational deities in certain mandalas.

Akashagarbha (Tib Namkei Nyingpo) one of the eight major bodhisattvas, yellow in colour, symbolizing the buddha's sense of smell and holding a sword which cuts through dissonant emotions. See **Icon 36**.

Aksobhya (Tib Mikyopa) one of the five peaceful meditational buddhas forming the buddha-body of perfect resource (*sambhogakaya*), collectively known as the Buddhas of the Five Families. Aksobhya is blue in colour, symbolizing the purity of form and the mirror-like clarity of buddha-mind. He holds a vajra to symbolize that emptiness and compassion are without duality. See **Icon 4**.

Amitabha (Tib Opame) one of the five peaceful meditational buddhas forming the buddha-body of perfect resource (*sambhogakaya*), collectively known as the Buddhas of the Five Families. Amitabha is red in colour, symbolizing the purity of perception and the discerning aspect of buddha-mind. He holds a lotus to symbolize the purification of attachment and the altruistic intention. See **Icon 6**.

Amitayus (Tib Tsepame) a meditational deity with nine aspects, who is included among the Three Deities of Longevity, red in colour, and holding a vase full of the nectar of immortality. See **Icon 45**.

Amoghasiddhi (Tib Donyo Drupa) one of the five peaceful meditational buddhas forming the buddha-body of perfect resource (*sambhogakaya*), collectively known as the Buddhas of the Five Families. Amoghasiddhi is green in colour, symbolizing the purity of habitual tendencies and the activity aspect of buddha-mind. He holds a sword to symbolize the cutting off of dissonant emotions through buddha-activity. See **Icon 7**.

Amritakundalin (Tib Dutsi Kyilwa) one of the gatekeepers of the mandalas of meditational deities, dark-green in colour, symbolizing the inherent purity of sensory contact, and holding a crossed-vajra which subdues egotism.

Apchi a doctrinal protectress of the Drigung Kagyu school, who assumes both peaceful and wrathful forms.

Atisha (Tib Jowoje) a saintly Buddhist master from Bengal (982-1054), who introduced the Kadampa teachings into Tibet. See **Icon 93**.

Avalokiteshvara (Tib Chenrezik) one of the eight major bodhisattvas and the patron deity of Tibet, white in colour, symbolizing the buddha's compassion and sense of taste, and holding a lotus untainted by flaws. There are various forms of this most popular bodhisattva: the 11-faced 1,000-armed form known as Mahakarunika (Tu-je Chenpo, Zhal Chu-chikpa, **Icon 42**), the four-armed form (Chenrezik Chak Zhipa, **Icon 39**), a two-armed form known as Khasarpani (**Icon 44**), the lion-riding form called Simhanada (**Icon 43**), the soothing form called Mind at Rest (Semnyi Ngalso), or Jowo Lokeshvara, and the standing form called Padmapani, the last of which is usually red in colour (**Icon 33**).

Begtse a sword-wielding form of the protector deity **Mahakala**.

Bhairava (Tib Jikje) a wrathful bull-headed meditational deity (in Buddhism), or a wrathful counterpart of Shiva (in Hinduism).

Bhaisajyaguru (Tib Sangye Menla) the central buddha of medicine, otherwise called Vaiduryaprabharaja, who is blue in colour, holding a bowl containing the panacea myrobalan. See **Icon 12**.

Bodongpa Chokle Namgyel (1375-1451) one of Tibet's most prolific writers, the author of approximately 100 treatises, a product of the Bodong E college, who established his own distinctive school of Buddhism in Tibet.

Brahma (Tib Tsangpa) a four-faced protector deity associated with the world system of form (in Buddhism), the creator divinity (in Hinduism).

Buddha Shakyamuni (Tib Shakya Tupa) the historical Buddha (sixth to fifth centuries BC), known prior to his attainment of buddhahood as Siddhartha or Gautama, who is also revered as the fourth of the thousand buddhas of this aeon. He is depicted in diverse forms, seated, standing, or reclining (at the point of his decease), and with diverse hand-gestures (symbolizing past merits, generosity, meditation, teaching, fearlessness and so forth). The Jowo form depicts him as a bodhisattva prior to his attainment of buddhahood, and the form Munindra depicts him as he appears among the devas. See **Icon 9**.

Buddhas of the Five Families (Skt Pancajina/Tib Gyelwa Riknga) the five buddhas of the buddha-body of perfect resource (*sambhogakaya*; **Icons 3-7**). See listed separately **Aksobhya**, **Amitabha**, **Amoghasiddhi**, **Ratnasambhava**, and **Vairocana**.

Buddhas of the Three Times (Tib Dusum Sangye) see listed separately the Buddha of the past **Dipamkara** (**Icon 8**), the Buddha of the present **Shakyamuni** (**Icon 9**), and the Buddha of the future **Maitreya** (**Icon 10**).

Buton Rinchendrub (1290-1364) compiler of the Buddhist canon, and major scholar within the Zhalupa tradition of Tibetan Buddhism. See **Icon 109**.

Cakrasamvara (Tib Khorlo Demchok) a four-faced 12-armed wrathful meditational deity, blue in colour, in union with his consort Vajravarahi, trampling upon Bhairava and Kali, and thus representing the Buddhist transmutation of the mundane Hindu divinity Shiva and his consort. See **Icon 54**.

Chenrezi Semnyi Ngalso see under Avalokiteshvara.

Cimara (Tib Tsimara) wrathful protector deity of Samye Monastery, and foremost of the *tsen* class of doctrinal protectors, greenish red in colour.

Cintamani(cakra) Tara see under **Tara**.

Dalai Lama (Tib Gyelwa Rinpoche) revered as the human embodiment of Avalokiteshvara, the patron deity of Tibet who symbolizes compassion, the successive Dalai Lamas (see page) have, since the mid-17th century, assumed both spiritual and temporal authority in Tibet. Among them, the most significant have probably been Dalai Lama III Sonam Gyatso (1543-88; **Icon 116**), Dalai Lama V Ngawang Lobzang Gyatso (1617-82; **Icon 118**), Dalai Lama VI Tsangyang Gyatso (1683-1706; **Icon 120**), Dalai Lama

VII Kalzang Gyatso (1708-57), Dalai Lama XIII Tupten Gyatso (1876-1933), and the present Dalai Lama XIV (b 1934).

Damsi a group of nine sibling demons who have violated their commitments and are said to endanger infant children.

Dashakrodha kings (Tib Trowo Chu) a group of 10 peripheral meditational deities known as the 10 wrathful kings, comprising Usnisacakravartin, Prajnantaka, Yamantaka, Vighnantaka, Padmantaka, Mahabala, Takkiraja, Shumbharaja, Acala, and Niladanda.

Denma Tsemang one of the 25 Tibetan disciples of the precious Guru Padmakara, who was active at Taktsang in Bhutan during the early ninth century.

Desi Sangye Gyatso (1677-1705) an important regent of Tibet and author of seminal commentaries on medicine, astrology, religious history, and other subjects. See **Icon 119**.

Dharmaraja (Tib Chogyel) see **Yama Dharmaraja**.

Dharmatala one of two peripheral figures, sometimes classed alongside the group of **sixteen elders**. He is described as a layman (*upasaka*) who looked after the 16 elders during their visit to China.

Dilgo Khyentse Rinpoche (1910-1991) one of the greatest Tibetan Buddhist masters of the 20th century, representing the eclectic Ri-me tradition of Eastern Tibet and spiritual advisor to the royal family of Bhutan.

Dipamkara Buddha (Tib Sangye Marmedze) the third buddha of this aeon, also known as Kashyapa Buddha, who was the one immediately preceding Shakyamuni. See **Icon 8**.

Dolpopa Sherab Gyeltsen (1292-1361) the most influential scholar of the Jonangpa school, who was a pre-eminent master of the tantras and an exponent of the *zhentong* philosophy. See **Icon 110**.

Dorje Drakden a doctrinal protector in the retinue of Pehar, who possesses the medium of Nechung, the state oracle of Tibet.

Dorje Drolo a wrathful tiger-riding form of Padmasambhava (Icon 91). See under **Eight Manifestations of Padmasambhava**.

Dorje Lekpa a goat-riding doctrinal protector of the Dzogchen teachings, wearing a wide-brimmed hat, who was bound under an oath of allegiance to Buddhism by Padmasambhava in the Oyuk district of Western Tibet.

Dorje Lingpa (1346-1405) a great treasure-finder of the Nyingma lineage whose tradition was maintained in a familial line by his Bhutanese descendants. See **icon 126**.

Dorje Yudronma a doctrinal protectress of the Menmo class, with whom the great Nyingmapa master Longchen Rabjampa is said to have had a particular affinity. See **Icon 62**.

Drigungpa Jikten Gonpo (1143-1217) one of the foremost students of Phakmodrupa and founder of the Drigung Kagyu school, based at Drigung Til Monastery. See **Icon 101**.

Dromtonpa Gyelwei Jungne (1004-64) the foremost Tibetan student of Atisha and founder of Reting Monastery. See **Icon 94**.

Drubpa Kabgye the eight wrathful meditational deities of the Nyingma school, viz: Yamantaka, Hayagriva, Shriheruka, Vajramrita, Vajrakila, Matarah, Lokastotrapuja, and Vajramanrabhiru.

Drukchen the title of the successive heads of the Drukpa Kagyu school.

Drukpa Kun-le (1455-1529) an eccentric Tibetan yogin and Bhutanese culture hero of the Drukpa Kagyu lineage.

Dudjom Rinpoche (1904-1987) one of the greatest Tibetan Buddhist masters and scholars of the 20th century – a fountainhead of the Nyingma lineage, who has a multitude of followers in Eastern Bhutan.

Dzogchen Pema Rigdzin (1625-97) the founder of Dzogchen Monastery in Kham.

Eight Awareness-holders (Skt astavidyadhara/Tib rigdzin gye) the eight Indian lineage-holders of the eight transmitted precepts of Mahayoga, who are said to have been contemporaries of Padmasambhava, namely: Manjushrimitra, Nagarjuna, Humkara, Vimalamitra, Prabhahasti, Dhanasamskrita, Rambuguhya-Devacandra, and Shantigarbha.

Eight Bodhisattvas (Tib nyese gye) the eight major bodhisattvas, standing figures who are often depicted flanking images of Shakyamuni Buddha. See listed separately: **Manjushri (Icon 31), Vajrapani (Icon 32), Avalokiteshvara (Icon 33), Ksitigarbha (Icon 34), Nivaranaviskambhin (Icon 35), Akashagarbha (Icon 36), Maitreya (Icon 37), and Samantabhadra (Icon 38)**.

Eight Classes of Spirits (Tib lhade gye) a series of lesser spirits or demons, who are to be appeased or coerced by means of ritual offerings.

Eight Deities of the Transmitted Precepts see Drubpa Kabgye.

Eight Manifestations of Padmasambhava (Tib guru tsen gye) the eight principal forms assumed by Padmakara at different phases of his career, namely: **Saroruhavajra** (birth; **Icon 84**), **Padma Gyelpo** (kingship; **Icon 85**), **Shakya Senge** (ordination; **Icon 86**), **Loden Chokse** (mastery of the teachings; **Icon 87**), **Padmasambhava** (establishment of Buddhism in Tibet; **Icon 88**), **Nyima Ozer** (subjugation of demons; **Icon 89**), **Senge Dradrok** (subjugation of non-Buddhists; **Icon 90**), and **Dorje Drolo** (concealment of terma; **Icon 91**).

Eight Medicine Buddhas (Tib menla deshek gye) the successive buddhas revered as the precursors of Buddhist medicine, viz: Sunamaparikirtana, Svaraghosaraja, Suvarnabhadravimala, Ashokottama, Dharmakirtisagaraghosa, Abhijnanaraja, Shakyaketu, and Bhaisajyaguru. For an illustration of the last of these, who is also the central medicine buddha, see **Icon 12**.

Eight Taras who Protect from Fear (Tib Dolma Jikpa Gye Kyobma)   a group of female divinities, who offer protection from eight specific types of fear, viz: Manasimhabhayatrana (pride and lions), Mohahastibhayatrana (delusion and elephants), Dvesagniprashamani (hatred and fire), Irsyasarpavisapaharani (envy and poisonous snakes), Kudristicoropadravanivarani (wrong view and thieves), Ghoramatsaryashrinkhalamocani (avarice and fetters), Ragaughavegavartashosani (attachment and rivers), and Samshayapishacabhayatrana (doubt and carnivorous demons). See also under Tara.

Eighty-four Mahasiddhas (Tib Drubtob Gyachu Gyezhi)   a group of 84 tantric masters of ancient India, for the life-stories of which, see J Robinson, *Buddhas Lions*.

Ekajati (Tib Ralchikma)   an important protectress of the Dzogchen teachings, characteristically depicted with a single hair-knot, a single eye and a single breast.

Five Founders of Sakya (Tib Gongma Nga)   the successors of Khon Konchok Gyelpo who founded Sakya in 1073, viz: Sachen Kunga Nyingpo (1092-1158; **Icon 104**), Sonam Tsemo (1142-82; **Icon 105**), Drakpa Gyeltsen (1147-1216; **Icon 106**), Sakya Pandita Kunga Gyeltsen (1182-1251; **Icon 107**), and Drogon Chogyel Phakpa (1235-80; **Icon 108**).

Four Guardian Kings (Skt Caturmaharajaika/Tib Gyelchen Zhi)   the guardian kings of the four directions, whose martial forms are frequently depicted on the walls of a temple portico, viz: Dhritarastra (east), Virudhaka (south), Virupaksa (west), and Vaishravana (north). **Icons 123-126**.

Gampopa (1079-1153)   the student of Milarepa and source of the four major and eight minor Kagyu schools. See **Icon 98**.

Ganesh (Skt Ganapati or Vinayaka/Tib Tsokdak)   the elephant-headed offspring of Shiva (in Hinduism), an obstacle-causing or obstacle-removing protector deity (in Buddhism).

Gangteng Pema Trinle (1564-1642)   the first of the nine successive incarnations of the buddha-body of Pema Lingpa, whose residence is at Gangteng Monastery in Central Bhutan.

Genyen   a group of 21 aboriginal divinities, most of whom are identified with snow peaks.

Gonpo Maning (Skt Mahapandaka Mahakala)   a spear-wielding two-armed form of the protector deity Mahakala. See **Icon 58**.

Guhyasamaja (Tib Sangwa Dupa)   a six-armed seated meditational deity, two forms of which are recognized: Aksobhyavajra (according to the Arya tradition) and Manjuvajra (according to the Buddhajnanapada tradition). The former is light-blue in colour, embraced by the consort Sparshavajra, and has three faces, symbolizing the transmutation of the three poisons: delusion, attachment, and hatred. See **Icon 51**.

Guru Chowang (1212-70)   a great treasure-finder of the Nyingma school.

Gyelpo Ku-nga   the five aspects of the important protector deity Pehar, known respectively as the kings of body, speech, mind, attributes, and activities. See **Icons 63-67**.

Gyelwa Lhanangpa (1164-1224) progenitor of the Drigung Kagyu lineage in Bhutan and rival of Phajo Drukgom Zhikpo.

Hayagriva (Tib Tamdrin) a wrathful horse-headed meditational deity of the Nyingma school who is generally red in colour, symbolic of buddha-speech, and included among the Drubpa Kabgye. He also appears as a gatekeeper in certain mandalas, and, as the renowned tamer of the egotistical demon Rudra, is frequently positioned (along with Vajrapani) at the entrance of a temple.

Hevajra (Tib Kyedorje) a wrathful counterpart of the meditational deity Aksobhya, deep-blue in colour, who is depicted in a dancing posture, with two, four, six, or 16 arms, and in union with the consort Nairatmya. See **Icon 56**.

Huashang one of two peripheral figures, sometimes classed alongside the group of **sixteen elders**. He is described as a monk (Ch hoshang) who looked after the 16 elders during their visit to China.

Hundred Peaceful and Wrathful Deities (Tib Zhitro Lhatsok, Dampa Rikgya) the assembly of the 42 peaceful deities and 58 wrathful deities, according to the *Guhyagarbha Tantra*, the basis for the visionary account of the *Tibetan Book of the Dead*.

Jambhala (Tib Dzambhala) a protector deity of wealth, yellow in colour, frequently depicted holding a gemstone.

Jamchen Choje Shakya Yeshe a student of Tsongkhapa, who founded Sera Monastery in 1419.

Jampa see **Maitreya**.

Jamyang Choje Tashi Palden a student of Tsongkhapa, who founded Drepung Monastery in 1416.

Jamyang Kunga Sangye (1314-1347) the seventh hierarch of Ralung Monastery in Tibet, who revived the legacy of Phajo Drukgom Zhikpo in Western Bhutan.

Je Yabsesum the collective name given to Tsongkhapa (1357-1419) and his two foremost students, Gyeltsabje Darma Rinchen (1364-1431) and Khedrubje Gelek Pelzang (1385-1438), who were the first throne-holders of Ganden Monastery and thus the founders of the Gelukpa school. The last of these was also retrospectively recognized as Panchen Lama I. See **Icons 113-115**.

Jigme Lingpa (1730-98) an important Nyingmapa yogin who revealed the highly influential teaching-cycle known as the *Innermost Spirituality of Longchenpa (Longchen Nyingtig)*.

Jowo see **Jowo Shakyamuni**.

Jnananatha (Tib. Yeshe Gonpo) an aspect of the protector deity Mahakala, which is particularly revered in Bhutan.

Jowo Lokeshvara see under **Avalokiteshvara**.

Jowo Shakyamuni a form of Buddha Shakyamuni, as a bodhisattva, prior to his attainment of buddhahood.

Kalachakra (Tib Dukhor, Dukyi Khorlo) a wrathful meditational deity, blue in colour, with four faces and 12 upper arms and 24 lower arms, embraced by the consort Vishvamata, symbolizing the transmutation of the wheel of time. See **Icon 53**.

Karmapa the oldest succession of incarnating lamas recognized in Tibet, embodying Avalokiteshvara's compassion and presiding over the Karma Kagyu school. See also **Icon 99**.

Katokpa the title assumed by the first 13 hierarchs of Katok Monastery in East Tibet, founded by Katokpa I Dampa Deshek in 1159.

Khasarpani see under **Avalokiteshvara**.

Ksitigarbha (Tib Sayi Nyingpo) one of the eight major bodhisattvas, white in colour, symbolizing the buddha's eyes, and holding a sprouting gemstone of pristine cognition. See **Icon 34**.

Kubera (Tib Tadak Kubera) a protector deity of wealth, known as the 'lord of horses', black in colour, brandishing a sword and holding a jewel-spitting mongoose.

Kurukulla (Tib Rikchema) a red coloured female meditational deity in dancing posture, holding a flowery bow and arrow, symbolizing her charisma to fascinate and overpower even hostile forces.

Lagnon Tendzin Drukdra (1656-1668) the second regent of the Bhutanese state.

Lokeshvara (Tib Jikten Wangchuk) an abbreviation of **Avalokiteshvara**.

Longchen Rabjampa (1308-63) pre-eminent scholar, treasure-finder, and systematizer of the Nyingma tradition. See **Icon 111**.

Lords of the Three Enlightened Families (Tib Riksum Gonpo) the three main bodhisattvas associated with the early Mahayana transmissions, namely Manjughosa symbolizing discriminative awareness; Avalokiteshvara symbolizing compassion; and Vajrapani symbolizing power. See **Icons 39-41**.

Mahakala (Tib Nagpo Chenpo) a class of supramundane protector deities, 75 aspects of which are recognized. Among these, the most widespread are Four-armed Mahakala (Skt Caturbhujamahakala; **Icon 57**); Six-armed Mahakala (Skt Sadbhujamahakala), Gonpo Maning (Skt Mahapandaka Mahakala; **Icon 58**), Tiger-riding Mahakala (Tib Gonpo Takzhon), Begtse, and Panjaranatha (Tib Gonpo Gur; **Icon 59**), the last of which is preferred among the Sakyapa.

Mahakarunika (Tib Tu-je Chenpo) see under **Avalokiteshvara**.

Mahottara Heruka (Tib Chemchok Heruka) the wrathful counterpart of the primordial buddha Samantabhadra, is dark-brown, with three faces symbolizing the three approaches to liberation, six arms symbolizing the six perfections, and four legs symbolizing the four supports for miraculous ability, trampling upon

Mahedeva and Umadevi.

Maitreya (Tib Jampa) one of the eight major bodhisattvas (**Icon 37**) and the future buddha (**Icon 10**), whitish-yellow in colour, symbolizing the buddha's loving kindness and sight, and holding an orange bush which dispels the fever of dissonant emotions.

Manjughosa (Tib Jampeyang, Jamyang) one of the eight major bodhisattvas (**Icon 31**) who is depicted upright, whitish-green in colour and holding a lily, which symbolizes the renunciation of dissonant emotions. In a more familiar seated posture, he is one of the lords of the three enlightened families (**Icon 40**), orange in colour, symbolizing the buddha's discriminative awareness and tongue, and holding a sword which cuts through obscurations and a book of discriminative awareness. Other important forms include Manjushri Vadisimha, Manjushri Kumarabhuta, White Manjushri, and the five aspects which appeared in the visions of Tsongkhapa.

Manjushri (Tib Jampel) see **Manjughosa**.

Manjuvajra (Tib Jampei Dorje) a form of the meditational deity Guhyasamaja, according to the tradition of Buddhajnanapada.

Marici (Tib Ozerchenma) the red goddess of the dawn, who is propitiated for the removal of obstacles.

Marpa (1012-96) Marpa Chokyi Wangchuk, the student of Naropa and first Tibetan exponent of the Karma Kagyu lineage, whose disciples included Milarepa. See **Icon 96**.

Maudgalyayana (Tib Maudgal bu) one of the two foremost students of Shakyamuni, who passed away before the Buddha's parinirvana. See **Icon 14**.

Migyur Tenpa (1613-1680) the third regent of the Bhutanese state, who consolidated Drukpa control over Central and Eastern Bhutan.

Milarepa (1040-1123/1052-1135) the great yogin and ascetic poet of the Kagyu lineage, who was the student of Marpa and teacher of Gampopa. See **Icon 97**.

Mipham Tenpei Nyima (1567-1619) father of Zhabdrung Ngawang Namgyek, founder of the Bhutanese state.

Nairatmya (Tib Dakmema) female consort of the meditational deity Hevajra, symbolizing selflessness or emptiness.

Ngagi Wangchuk (1517-1554) prince of Ralung who established a Drukpa Kagyu presence in Central and Eastern Bhutan.

Ngawang Chogyel (1465-1540) the 14th hierarch of Ralung Monastery who extensively propagated the Drukpa Kagyu lineage in Bhutan.

Ngawang Drakpa (1506-1530) the 16th hierarch of Ralung who consolidated the Drukpa Kagyu lineage in Western Bhutan.

Ngok Lotsawa Lekpei Sherab founder of the Kadampa monastery of Sangpu Neutok and a major student of the 11th century Bengali master Atisha.

Ngorchen Kunga Zangpo (b 1382) who founded the monastery of Ngor Evam Chode in 1429, giving rise to the influential Ngorpa branch of the Sakya school.

Nivaranaviskambhin (Tib Dripa Namsel) one of the eight major bodhisattvas, reddish-yellow in colour, symbolizing the buddha's ears, and holding a wheel of gems because he teaches the Buddhist doctrine. See **Icon 35**.

Nyatri Tsenpo the first king of the Yarlung Dynasty. See **Icon 77**.

Padmakara (Tib Pema Jungne) the form assumed by Padmasambhava at the time when he and his consort Mandarava were burnt at the stake in Zahor, but miraculously transformed their pyre into a lake. See **Icon 81**.

Padmapani see under **Avalokiteshvara**.

Padmasambhava the form assumed by Padmasambhava (ie Guru Rinpoche) while establishing Buddhism in Tibet. See **Icon 88**.

Panchen Lama the emanations of the Buddha Amitabha, ranking among Tibet's foremost incarnate successions. Among them, Panchen Lama IV Chokyi Gyeltsen (1567-1662; **Icon 117**) was an important teacher of Dalai Lama V.

Panjaranatha (Tib Gonpo Gur) see under **Mahakala**.

Paramadya (Tib Palchok Dangpo) a major meditational deity of the Yogatantra and Mahyoga class.

Pehar an important protector deity within the Nyingma and Geluk traditions. See also **Gyelpo Ku-nga**.

Peling Sungtrul title of ten successive incarnations of the buddha-speech of Pema Lingpa, based at Lhalung in Southern Tibet and Mongar in Eastern Bhutan.

Peling Tuk-se title of the nine successive incarnations of Pema Lingpa's spiritual son Dawa Gyeltsen (b. 1499), based at Tamzhing Lhakang in Bumthang.

Pema Lingpa (1450-1521) a great treasure-finder from Bumthang and Bhutanese culture hero of the Nyingma lineage. See **icon 127**.

Pema Totrengtsal the form assumed by Padmasambhava while manifesting as the meditational deity Vajrakumara to subdue the demons of the Kathmandu valley at Yanglesho (Pharping).

Phadampa Sangye the 11th-12th century South Indian yogin who propagated the Chodyul and Zhiche teachings in the highland region of Western Tibet.

Phajo Drukgom Zhikpo (1184-1251) progenitor of the Drukpa Kagyu lineage in Bhutan.

Phakmodrupa Dorje Gyelpo (1110-70) student of Gampopa and progenitor of the eight lesser branches of the Kagyu school, including the Drigungpa, Taklungpa and Drukpa branches. See **Icon 100**.

Phakpalha the title of the principal incarnate lama of Chamdo Jampaling Monastery in Kham, which was founded between 1436-44 by Jangsem Sherab Zangpo.

Prajnaparamita (Tib Yum Chenmo) the female meditational deity embodying the perfection of discriminative awareness, golden yellow in colour, and holding emblems such as the book, sword, lotus, vajra and rosary, which are indicative of supreme insight. See **Icon 48**.

Rahula (Tib Za) an important protector deity within the Nyingma school, depicted as a dark brown or black multi-headed semi-human semi-serpentine figure. See **Icon 61**.

Ratnasambhava (Tib Rinchen Jungne) one of the five peaceful meditational buddhas forming the buddha-body of perfect resource (*sambhogakaya*), collectively known as the Buddhas of the Five Families. Ratnasambhava is yellow in colour, symbolizing the purity of sensations or feelings and the equanimity or sameness of buddha-mind. He holds a gemstone to symbolize that his enlightened attributes are spontaneously present and that he fulfils the hopes of all beings. See **Icon 5**.

Rechungpa (1084-1161) a yogin who, like Gampopa, was one of Milarepa's foremost students.

Remati (Tib Magzorma) an aspect of the protectress Shridevi, who rides a mule and holds a sickle or a sandalwood club and a blood-filled skull. She is propitiated in order to overwhelm internal passions and outer disruptions due to warfare.

Rinchen Zangpo (958-1055) the great translator and contemporary of Atisha whose centre of activity was in Far-west Tibet and the adjacent areas of Spiti and Ladakh.

Sakya Pandita see under **Five Founders of Sakya**.

Samantabhadra (Tib Kuntu Zangpo) the male or subjective aspect of the primordial buddha-body of actual reality (*dharmakaya*), blue in colour, symbolizing the ground of buddha-mind or luminosity. See **Icon 1**.

Samantabhadra (bodhisattva) (Tib Jangsem Kuntu Zangpo) one of the eight major bodhisattvas, reddish-green in colour, symbolizing the buddha's nose, and holding a corn-ear of gemstones because he fulfils the hopes of beings. See **Icon 38**.

Samantabhadri (Tib Kuntu Zangmo) the female or objective aspect of the primordial buddha-body of actual reality (*dharmakaya*), blue in colour, symbolizing the ground of phenomenal appearances or emptiness. See **Icon 1**.

Samayatara (Tib Damtsik Dolma) a wrathful female meditational deity, consort of the Buddha Amoghasiddhi.

Sarvavid Vairocana (Tib Kunrik Nampar Nangze) see under **Vairocana**.

Seven Generations of Past Buddhas (Tib Sangye Rabdun) the seven buddhas of the immediate past, in sequence: Vipashyin (**Icon 11**), Shikhin, Vishvabhuk,

Krakucchanda, Kanakamuni, Kashyapa, and Shakyamuni.

Shakyamuni   see **Buddha Shakyamuni**.

Shakyamuni Aksobhyavajra (Tib Shakya Tupa Mikyo Dorsem) the aspect of Shakyamuni Buddha depicted in the Ramoche Jowo image, which was originally brought to Tibet from Nepal by Princess Bhrikuti in the seventh century.

Shakyashri (1127-1225) the great Kashmiri scholar who visited Tibet in his later years, influencing all traditions.

Shantaraksita (Tib Zhiwei Tso/Khenpo Bodhisattva) a monastic preceptor of Zahor, who officiated at Nalanda Monastery prior to his arrival in Tibet at the invitation of King Trisong Detsen. He ordained the first seven trial monks in Tibet and was responsible for the construction of Samye Monastery, which he modelled on Odantapuri Monastery in Magadha. See **Icon 82**.

Shariputra (Tib Shari-bu) one of the two foremost students of Shakyamuni, who passed away before the Buddha's parinirvana. See **Icon 13**.

Sherab Wangchuk (r. 1744-1763) the long-serving 13th regent of the Bhutanese state.

Shridevi (Tib Palden Lhamo) a major protectress and female counterpart of Mahakala, who has both peaceful and wrathful forms, the latter being a ferocious three-eyed form, dark-blue in colour, and riding a mule. Remati (see above) is included among her aspects. See **Icon 60**.

Simhanada (Tib Senge Ngaro) see under Avalokiteshvara.

Simhavaktra (Tib Senge Dongma) a lion-headed meditational deity, who is the female aspect of Padmasambhava, dark blue in colour and holding a vajra-chopper and skull cup, which symbolize that she dispels obstacles to enlightened activity.

Sitatapatra (Tib Dukar) a female umbrella-wielding meditational deity, depicted with a thousand arms, who is propitiated in order to remove obstacles.

Six Ornaments (Tib Gyen Druk) the six great Buddhist commentators of ancient India, viz: Nagarjuna and Aryadeva who developed the Madhyamaka philosophy; the brothers Asanga and Vasubandhu who developed the Yogacara, Cittamatra, and Vaibhasika philosophies; and Dignaga and Dharmakirti who developed a systematic Buddhist logic. See **Icons 69-74**.

Six Sages of the Six Realms (Tib Tupa Druk) six buddha aspects said to appear respectively in the six realms of existence in order to teach the way to liberation from sufferings, respectively: Munindra (among the gods), Vemacitra (among the antigods), Shakyamuni (among humans), Simha (among animals), Jvalamukha (among tormented spirits), and Yama Dharmaraja (among the hells).

Six-armed Mahakala (Tib Gonpo Chak Drukpa) see under **Mahakala**.

Sixteen Elders (Tib Neten Chudruk) a group of elders (*sthavira*) and contemporaries of Shakyamuni Buddha, who were traditionally assigned to promote the Buddhist teachings in the world throughout time, and who have been particularly venerated in Chinese Buddhism, where they are known as arhats (Ch lohan). See **Icons 15-30**.

Sonam Gyeltsen of Nyarong progenitor of the Katokpa lineage of the Nyingma school in Bhutan.

Songtsen Gampo the seventh century unifying king of Tibet who made Lhasa the capital of his newly emergent nation and espoused the Buddhist teachings, revered thereafter as an emanation of the compassionate bodhisattva Avalokiteshvara. See **Icon 79**.

Taklung Tangpa Tashipel (1142-1210) a foremost student of Phakmodrupa Dorje Gyelpo, who founded the Taklung Kagyu sub-school and the monastery of the same name in 1178. See **Icon 102**.

Tangtong Gyelpo (1385-1464) the Leonardo of Tibet, renowned as a mystic, revealer of treasure-doctrines, engineer, master bridge-builder, and the inventor of Tibetan opera. See **Icon 112**.

Tara (Tib Dolma) a female meditational deity, who is identified with compassion and enlightened activity. There are aspects of Tara which specifically offer protection from worldly tragedies and fear of the elements (see above, **Eight Taras who Protect from Fear**), and an enumeration of 21 aspects of Tara is well-documented. Among these the most popular are Green Tara (Tib Doljang; **Icon 49**), who is mainly associated with protection, and White Tara (Tib Dolkar; **Icon 46**), who is associated with longevity. In addition, the form known as Cintamani (cakra) Tara is a meditational deity of the Unsurpassed Yogatantra class.

Tendzin Drugye (1591-1656) the first regent of the Bhutanese state.

Tendzin Rebgye (1638-1694) the fourth regent of the Bhutanese state, a charismatic monk and blood relative of Zhabdrung.

Thirty-five Confession Buddhas (Tib ltung-bshags-kyi lha so-lnga) a group of 35 buddhas associated with the specific practice of purifying non-virtuous habits, in which the names of each are invoked in turn (usually in conjunction with physical prostrations).

Thousand buddhas of the aeon (Tib Sangye Tongtsa) the thousand buddhas of the present aeon, whose names are enumerated in the *Bhadrakalpikasutra*. Among these Shakyamuni Buddha was the fourth, and the next to appear in the world will be Maitreya.

Three Ancestral Religious Kings (Tib Chogyel Mepo Namsum) the three foremost Buddhist kings of ancient Tibet, namely Songtsen Gampo who unified the country and espoused Buddhism in the seventh century (**Icon 79**), Trisong Detsen who established the spiritual practices and monastic ordinations of Buddhism in the eighth century (**Icon 83**), and Tri Ralpachen who sought to end Tibetan militarism and lavishly sponsored Buddhist activity in the ninth century (**Icon 92**).

Three Deities of Longevity (Tib Tselha Namsum) see respectively **Amitayus** (**Icon 45**), **White Tara** (**Icon 46**), and **Vijaya** (**Icon 47**).

Thubpa Gangchentso see under **Vairocana**.

Thubwang (Skt Munindra) see **Buddha Shakyamuni**.

Tiger-riding Mahakala (Tib Gonpo Takzhon) see under **Mahakala**.

Tonmi Sambhota the seventh century inventor of the Tibetan capital letter script (*uchen*). See **Icon 80**.

Trailokyavijaya (Tib Khamsum Namgyel) a peripheral deity, sometimes assuming a peaceful guise alongside the eight standing bodhisattvas, and sometimes in a wrathful form alongside the Dashakrodha kings.

Tri Ralpachen see under **Three Ancestral Religious Kings**.

Trisong Detsen see under **Three Ancestral Religious Kings**.

Tsangma (Prince) a member of the Tibetan royal family who during the ninth century fled from persecution to Bhutan, where his descendants formed a ruling elite in the eastern parts of the country.

Tsangpa Gya-re Yeshe Dorje (1161-1211) the first Drukchen (head of the Drukpa Kagyu school). See **Icon 103**.

Tsering Che-nga five female protector deities associated with the snow peaks of the Everest Range, viz: Miyowa Zangma, Tingi Zhelzangma, Tashi Tseringma, Drozangma, and Drinzangma.

Tseringma see under **Tsering Che-nga**.

Tsongkhapa (and his foremost students) see **Je Yabsesum**.

Twelve Subterranean Goddesses (Tib Tenma Chunyi) a group of 12 protector goddesses of the earth, who are associated with specific mountain localities, such as Kongtsun Demo, the protectress of Kongpo; and Machen Pomra, the protectress of the Amnye Machen range.

Twelve Tenma see **Twelve Subterranean Goddesses**.

Twenty-five Tibetan Disciples (Tib Jewang Nyernga) the Tibetan disciples of Padmasambhava, including King Trisong Detsen, Yeshe Tsogyel, Vairotsana, Nubchen Sangye Yeshe, Nyak Jnanakumara, and so forth.

Twenty-one Taras (Tib Dolma Nyishu Tsachik) see under Tara.

Two Gatekeepers (Tib gokyong nyi) in most temples the gates are guarded on the inner side by large images of Hayagriva (west) and Vajrapani or Acala (east).

Two Supreme Ones (Tib Chok Nyi) the ancient Indian Vinaya masters, Gunaprabha and Shakyaprabha, who are sometimes classed alongside the Six Ornaments. See **Icons 75-76**. Note that some traditions identify Nagarjuna and Asanga as the Two Supreme Ones and, instead, place the Vinaya masters among the Six Ornaments.

Ucchusmakrodha (Tib Trowo Metsek) a wrathful aspect of the meditational deity

Hayagriva, in which form the spirit of rampant egotism (Rudra) is tamed.

Usnisavijaya (Tib Tsuktor Namgyel)   a three-headed multi-armed wrathful deity, who is the first and foremost of the **Dashakrodha kings**.

Vairocana (Tib Nampar Nangze)   one of the five peaceful meditational buddhas forming the buddha-body of perfect resource (*sambhogakaya*), collectively known as the Buddhas of the Five Families. Vairocana is white in colour, symbolizing the purity of consciousness and the emptiness of buddha-mind. He holds a wheel to symbolize that his teachings cut through the net of dissonant emotions. See **Icon 3**. Among other aspects of Vairocana are the four-faced form Sarvavid Vairocana (Tib Kunrik Nampar Nangze; **Icon 50**) in which all the peripheral buddhas are embodied, and Muni Himamahasagara (Tib Thubpa Gangchentso), in and around whose body all world systems are said to evolve.

Vairotsana   one of the 25 disciples of Padmasambhava, revered as a major translator of Sanskrit texts and a lineage holder of the Dzogchen tradition.

Vaishravana (Tib Nam-mang To-se)   the guardian king of the northern direction, who, like Jambhala and Manibhadra, is associated with wealth, and wields a banner and a jewel-spitting mongoose in his hands.

Vajradhara (Tib Dorje Chang)   an aspect of the buddha-body of actual reality (*dharmakaya*), appearing in a luminous form complete with the insignia of the buddha-body of perfect resource (*sambhogakaya*). He is dark blue in colour, seated, holding a vajra and bell in his crossed hands. See **Icon 2**.

Vajrakila (Tib Dorje Phurba)   a wrathful meditational deity of the Nyingma and Sakya schools in particular, and one of the **Drubpa Kabgye**. He is depicted dark-blue in colour, with three faces, and six arms, and wielding a ritual dagger (*kila/phurba*) which cuts through obstacles to enlightened activity.

Vajrakumara (Tib Dorje Zhonu)   an aspect of the meditational deity Vajrakila. See **Icon 52**.

Vajrapani (Tib Chakna Dorje)   one of the eight major bodhisattvas and one of the lords of the three enlightened families, blue in colour, symbolizing the buddha's power and sense of hearing, and holding a vajra because he has subjugated sufferings. There are various forms of this bodhisattva, among which the standing peaceful form (**Icon 32**), and the two-armed wrathful form, raising a vajra in the right hand and a noose in the left (**Icon 41**) are most frequently depicted.

Vajrasattva (Tib Dorje Sempa)   an aspect of **Aksobhya** (**Icon 4**) who may appear in a blue form or a white form, holding a vajra in his right hand and a bell in the left, symbolizing purification and the indestructible reality of skilful means and emptiness.

Vajrasattva Yab-yum (Tib Dorsem Yabyum)   the meditational deity **Vajrasattva** in union with his female consort.

Vajravarahi (Tib Dorje Phagmo)   a female meditational deity who is the consort of Cakrasamvara, generally red in colour and with the emblem of the sow's head above her own. See **Icon 55**.

Vajravidarana (Tib Dorje Namjom) a peaceful meditational deity, seated and holding a crossed-vajra to the heart with the right hand and a bell in the left.

Vajrayogini (Tib Dorje Neljorma) a female meditational deity, red in colour and with a semi-wrathful facial expression. There are several aspects, including the one known as Kecari, the practices of which are associated mainly with the Kagyu school.

Vijaya (Tib Namgyelma) an eight-armed three-headed meditational deity, who is one of the **Three Deities of Longevity**, white in colour and holding a small buddha-image in her upper right hand. Statues of Vijaya are often inserted within Victory Stupas. See **Icon 47**.

Vimalamitra (Tib Drime Drakpa) a Kashmiri master and contemporary of Padmasambhava who introduced his own transmission of Dzogchen in Tibet, and was responsible for disseminating the *Guhyagarbha Tantra*.

Virupa one of the Eighty-four Mahasiddhas of ancient India who was a progenitor of the profound instructions set down in the *Path and Fruit* teachings of the Sakya school.

Yama Dharmaraja (Tib Shinje Chogyel) a proctector deity favoured by the Geluk school, dark blue in colour and bull-headed, and brandishing a club and a snare. He is identified with Yama, the 'lord of death'. See **Icon 68**.

Yamantaka (Tib Zhinje-zhed) a wrathful meditational deity, with red, black and bull-headed aspects who functions as the opponent of the forces of death. Practices associated with Yamantaka are important in the Nyingma and Geluk schools.

Yamari (Tib Zhinje) see **Yamantaka**.

Yangdak Heruka (Skt Shriheruka) a wrathful meditational deity associated with buddha-mind, from the Nyingma cycle known as the **Drubpa Kabgye**.

Yeshe Tsogyel one of the foremost disciples and female consorts of Padmasambhava, formerly the wife of King Trisong Detsen.

Yutok Yonten Gonpo (1127-1203) renowned exponent of Tibetan medicine.

Zhabdrung Ngawang Namgyel (1594-1651) the revered founder of the Bhutanese state.

Zhamarpa the title given to the successive emanations of Zhamarpa Tokden Drakpa Senge (1283-1349), a student of Karmapa III. The monastery of Yangpachen in Damzhung county later became their principal seat.

1 **Samantabdhara** with **Samantabhadri**
(Tib. *Kunzang Yabyum*)

2 **Vajradhara** (Tib. *Dorje Chang*)

3 Buddhas of the Five Families: **Vairocana**
(Tib. *Nampar Nangze*)

4 Buddhas of the Five Families: **Aksobhya-
Vajrasattva** (Tib. *Mikyopa Dorje Sempa*)

5 Buddhas of the Five Families: **Ratnasambhava**
(Tib. *Rinchen Jungne*)

6 Buddhas of the Five Families: **Amitabha**
(Tib. *Opame*)

7 Buddhas of the Five Families:
Amoghasiddhi (Tib. *Donyo Drupa*)

8 Buddhas of the Three Times: **Dipamkara**
(Tib. *Marmedze*)

9　Buddhas of the Three Times: **Shakyamuni**
(Tib. *Shakya Tupa*)

10　Buddhas of the Three Times: **Maitreya**
(Tib. *Jampa*)

11　**Vipashyin** (Tib. *Namzik*), first of the
Seven Generations of Past Buddhas
(*Sangye Rabdun*)

12　**Bhaisajyaguru** (Tib. *Sangye Menla*),
foremost of the Eight Medicine Buddhas
(*Menla Deshek Gye*)

13　**Shariputra** (Tib. *Shari-bu*)

14　**Maudgalyayana** (Tib. Maudgal-bu)

15　Sixteen Elders: **Angaja** (Tib. *Yanlak Jung*)

16　Sixteen Elders: **Bakula** (Tib. *Bakula*)

Footnotes An iconographic guide to Tibetan Buddhism

17 Sixteen Elders: **Ajita** (Tib. *Mapampa*)

18 Sixteen Elders: **Rahula** (Tib. *Drachendzin*)

19 Sixteen Elders: **Vanavasin** (Tib. *Naknane*)

20 Sixteen Elders: **Cudapanthaka**
(Tib. *Lamtrenten*)

21 Sixteen Elders: **Kalika** (Tib. *Duden*)

22 Sixteen Elders: **Bharadvaja**
(Tib. *Bharadvadza*)

23 Sixteen Elders: **Vajriputra**
(Tib. *Dorje Moyibu*)

24 Sixteen Elders: **Panthaka** (Tib. *Lamten*)

25 Sixteen Elders: **Bhadra** (Tib. *Zangpo*)

26 Sixteen Elders: **Nagasena** (Tib. *Luyide*)

27 Sixteen Elders: **Kanakavatsa** (Tib. *Serbe'u*)

28 Sixteen Elders: **Gopaka** (Tib. *Beche*)

29 Sixteen Elders: **Kanaka Bharadvaja**
(Tib. *Serchen*)

30 Sixteen Elders: **Abheda** (Tib. *Michedpa*)

31 Eight Bodhisattvas: **Manjushri**
(Tib. *Jampal*)

32 Eight Bodhisattvas: **Vajrapani**
(Tib. *Chakna Dorje*)

33 Eight Bodhisattvas: **Avalokiteshvara**
(Tib. *Chenrezik*)

34 Eight Bodhisattvas: **Ksitigarbha**
(Tib. *Sayi Nyingpo*)

35 Eight Bodhisattvas: **Nivaranaviskambhin**
(Tib. *Dripa Namsel*)

36 Eight Bodhisattvas: **Akashagarbha**
(Tib. *Namkei Nyingpo*)

37 Eight Bodhisattvas: **Maitreya**
(Tib. *Jampa*)

38 Eight Bodhisattvas: **Samantabhadra**
(Tib. *Kuntu Zangpo*)

39 Lords of the Three Enlightened Families:
Four-armed Avalokiteshvara
(Tib. *Chenrezik Chakzhipa*)

40 Lords of the Three Enlightened Families:
Manjughosa (Tib. *Jampeyang*)

31 Eight Bodhisattvas: **Manjushri** (Tib. *Jampal*)

32 Eight Bodhisattvas: **Vajrapani** (Tib. *Chakna Dorje*)

33 Eight Bodhisattvas: **Avalokiteshvara** (Tib. *Chenrezik*)

34 Eight Bodhisattvas: **Ksitigarbha** (Tib. *Sayi Nyingpo*)

35 Eight Bodhisattvas: **Nivaranaviskambhin** (Tib. *Dripa Namsel*)

36 Eight Bodhisattvas: **Akashagarbha** (Tib. *Namkei Nyingpo*)

49 Meditational Deities: **Green Tara**
(*Droljang*)

50 Meditational Deities: **Sarvavid Vairocana**
(Tib. *Kunrik Nampar Nangze*)

51 Meditational Deities: **Guhyasamaja**
(Tib. *Sangwa Dupa*)

52 Meditational Deities: **Vajrakumara**
(Tib. *Dorje Zhonu*)

53 Meditational Deities: **Kalacakra**
(Tib. *Dungkor*)

54 Meditational Deities: **Cakrasamvara**
(Tib. *Khorlo Dompa*)

55 Meditational Deities: **Vajravarahi**
(Tib. *Dorje Pamo*)

56 Meditational Deities: **Hevajra**
(Tib. *Kye Dorje*)

ༀ། །དཔལ་མགུན་ཕྱག་བཞི་པ་ཡེ་ཤེས་མགོན་པོ་ནི །

57 Protector Deities: **Four-armed Mahakala** (Tib. *Gonpo Chak Zhipa*)

ༀ། །མགོན་པོ་ལས་ཀྱི་མགོན་པོ་མ་ནིང་ནི། །

58 Protector Deities: **Mahapandaka Mahakala** (Tib. *Gonpo Maning*)

59 Protector Deities: **Panjaranatha** (Tib. *Gonpo Gur*)

60 Protector Deities: **Shrivi** (Tib. *Palden Lhamo*)

ༀ། །གཟའ་བདུད་ཆེན་པོ་རཱ་ཧུ་ལ་ནི །

61 Protector Deities: **Rahula** (Tib. *Za*)

ༀ། །སྔགས་སྲུང་རྡོ་རྗེ་གཡུ་སྒྲོན་མ་ཆོས། །

62 Protector Deities: **Dorje Yudronma**

63 Five Aspects of Pehar: **Kuyi Gyelpo**

64 Five Aspects of Pehar: **Sung-gi Gyelpo**

65 Five Aspects of Pehar: **Tukyi Gyelpo**

66 Five Aspects of Pehar: **Yonten-gyi Gyelpo**

67 Five Aspects of Pehar: **Trinle Gyelpo**

68 Dharmaraja (Tib. *Damchen Chogyel*)

69 Six Ornaments and Two Supreme Ones: **Nagarjuna** (Tib. *Phakpa Ludrub*)

70 Six Ornaments and Two Supreme Ones: **Aryadeva** (Tib. *Phakpa Lha*)

71 Six Ornaments and Two Supreme Ones: **Asanga** (Tib. *Thok-me*)

72 Six Ornaments and Two Supreme Ones: **Vasubandhu** (Tib. *Yiknyen*)

73 Six Ornaments and Two Supreme Ones: **Dignaga** (Tib. *Choklang*)

74 Six Ornaments and Two Supreme Ones: **Dharmakirti** (*Chodrak*)

75 Six Ornaments and Two Supreme Ones: **Gunaprabha** (*Yonten-o*)

76 Six Ornaments and Two Supreme Ones: **Shakyapraha** (*Shakya-o*)

77 Three Early Tibetan Kings: **Nyatri Tsenpo**

78 Three Early Tibetan Kings: **Lhatotori Nyentsen**

79 Three Early Tibetan Kings: **Songtsen Gampo**

80 Tonmi Sambhota

Footnotes An iconographic guide to Tibetan Buddhism

306

ༀ། །པདྨ་འབྱུང་གནས་ལ་ཕྱག་འཚལ་ལོ། །

81 Founders of the Nyingma School:
Padmakara (Tib. *Pema Jungne*)

ༀ། །མཁན་པོ་བོ་དྷི་སཏྭ་ལ་ན་མོ། །

82 Founders of the Nyingma School:
Shantaraksita (Tib. *Khenpo Bodhisattva/
Zhiwatso*)

ༀ། །ཁྲི་སྲོང་ལྡེ་བཙན་ལ་ཕྱག་འཚལ་ལོ། །

83 Founders of the Nyingma School:
King Trisong Detsen

ༀ། །མཚོ་སྐྱེས་རྡོ་རྗེ་འཆང་ལ་ཕྱག་འཚལ་ལོ། །

84 Eight Manifestations of Padmasambhava:
Saroruhavajra (*Tsokye Dorje Chang*)

ༀ། །ཤཱཀྱ་སེང་གེ་ལ་ཕྱག་འཚལ་ལོ། །

85 Eight Manifestations of Padmasambhava:
Pema Gyelpo

86 Eight Manifestations of Padmasambhava:
Shakya Senge

ༀ། །བློ་ལྡན་མཆོག་སྲེད་ལ་ཕྱག་འཚལ་ལོ། །

87 Eight Manifestations of Padmasambhava:
Loden Chokse

ༀ། །པདྨ་འབྱུང་གནས་ལ་ཕྱག་འཚལ་ལོ། །

88 Eight Manifestations of Padmasambhava:
Padmasambhava

ༀ། ཁྲིམ་ཡེ་མྱུང་ལོང་ཉི་མ་འོད་ཟེར་ཅན། །

89 Eight Manifestations of Padmasambhava:
Nyima Ozer

ༀ། ཁྲ་སྐྲོག་གམ་པམ་ སེང་གུ་ན་མཐར་ ཡིང་སྒྲ་སྒྲོག །

90 Eight Manifestations of Padmasambhava:
Senge Dradrok

ༀ། ཁྲོ་བོ་གཏུམ་པོ་དྲག་པ་ གསང་གཉིས་རྡོ་རྗེ་གྲོ་ལོད། །

91 Eight Manifestations of Padmasambhava:
Dorje Drolod

ༀ། ཁམས་བཟང་རྒྱལ་ཛིལ་གགམ་ པ་རལ་པ་ཅན་གྱི་ལ། །

92 King Ralpachen

ༀ། ཁ་དམ་བཅུ་རྒྱུ་ པ་ཇོ་བོ་རྗེ་ རྒྱལ་བ་མཚོ། །

93 Founders of Kadampa School: **Atisha**
(Tib. *Jowoje*)

ༀ། ཁྲ་ད་མ་ཆི་སྐྱུ་ པ་འབྲོམ་སྟོན་རྒྱལ་བའི་འབྱུང་གནས། །

94 Founders of Kadampa School: **Dromtonpa**

ༀ། ཁ་དམ་བ་ཛོ་ གནས་ངོ་རྡོ་ཀྲུན་ལེགས་པའི་ ཤེས་རབ་ལེགས། །

95 Founders of Kadampa School:
Ngok Lekpei Sherab

ༀ། ཁྲ་ཛིན་རྙིང་པོ་ སྒྲུབ་རྒྱུད་མར་པ་ འཇིགས་བྲལ། །

96 Founders of Kagyu School: **Marpa**

ཨཿ ཁབ་པའི་རྒྱལ་པོ་རྗེ་བཙུན་མི་ལ་རས༔

97 Founders of Kagyu School: **Milarepa**

ༀ ཆོས་རྗེ་དགེ་བཤེས་སྒམ་པོ་པ་ལ་མོ་རྣམ་པོ་ཆེ༔

98 Founders of Kagyu School: **Gampopa**

ཨཿ དཔལ་ལྡན་དུས་གསུམ་མཁྱེན་པ་ཆེན་པོ་ལ་ན༔

99 Founders of Kagyu School:
Karmapa I, Dusum Khyenpa

ༀ ཕག་མོ་གྲུ་པ་རྡོ་རྗེ་རྒྱལ་པོ་ལ་མོ་རྣམ་པོ་ཆེ༔

100 Founders of Kagyu School:
Phakmodrupa Dorje Gyelpo

ༀ འབྲི་གུང་སྐྱོབ་པ་འཇིག་རྟེན་མགོན་པོ་ལ་ན༔

101 Founders of Kagyu School:
Drigungpa Jikten Gonpo

102 Founders of Kagyu School:
Taklung Tangpa Tashipel

ༀ གཙང་པ་རྒྱ་རས་ཡེ་ཤེས་རྡོ་རྗེ་ལ་ན༔

103 Founders of Kagyu School:
Tsangpa Gya-re Yeshe Dorje

ༀ རྗེ་བཙུན་ས་ཆེན་ཀུན་དགའ་སྙིང་པོ་ལ་ན༔

104 Five Founders of Sakya: **Kunga Nyingpo**

࿈ ཀྱེ་རྫོགས་ལམ་ལོག་བལ་དུ་བསམ་ཏེ་མི་རྒྱལ། །

105 Five Founders of Sakya: **Sonam Tsemo**

࿈ ཀྱེ་རྗེ་བཙུན་ཀྱི་བུ་གྲགས་པ་རྒྱལ་མཚན་གནས། །

106 Five Founders of Sakya: **Drakpa Gyeltsen**

࿈ ཀྱེ་ས་སྐྱ་པཎ་ཆེན་ཆོས་ཀྱི་རྒྱལ་པོ། །

107 Five Founders of Sakya: **Sakya Pandita**

࿈ ཀྱེ་འཕགས་པ་རི་གྷུ་རྣམ་རྒྱལ་ལ་ཕྱག་འཚལ་ཆོས། །

108 Five Founders of Sakya:
Drogon Chogyel Phakpa

࿈ ཀྱེ་བུ་སྟོན་པ་ཐམས་ཅད་ཀྱི་སྐུ་རིན་པོ་ཆེ་ལ་ཕྱག །

109 Buton Rinchen Drub

ཨ་ཁུ་ཤེས་རབ་པོ་ནག་པར་རབ་རྒྱལ་མཚན་ཅན་དུ་ནི། །

110 Dolpopa Sherab Gyeltsen

࿈ ཀྱེ་ཀློང་ཆེན་པ་རབ་འབྱམས་ཀུན་ཏུ་ཆེན་པ། །

111 Longchen Rabjampa

࿈ ཀྱེ་ལཅགས་ཟམ་པ་གྲུབ་པའི་དབང་ཕྱུག་ཐང་སྟོང་རྒྱལ་པ། །

112 Tangtong Gyelpo

310

ༀ། །དགའ་ལྡན་ནེན་ཙོང་ཁ་པ་བཙུན་དུ།

113 Founders of Gelukpa School:
Tsongkhapa

ༀ།།འདའམས་གཅུག་ཚོ་དར་རྒྱས་རིན་ཆེན་ལ་ན།

114 Founders of Gelukpa School:
Gyeltsab Darma Rinchen

ༀ།།མཁས་གྲུབ་རྒྱ་བོ་དགེ་ལེགས་དཔལ་ལ་གསོལ་བ་པ།

115 Founders of Gelukpa School:
Khedrubje Gelekpel

ༀ།།བསོད་ནམས་རྒྱ་མཚོ་འདང་འདར་རྒྱ་ཆེན་ལ་ན།

116 Masters of the Gelukpa Tradition:
Dalai Lama III Sonam Gyatso

ༀ།།བཟང་པོ་མཆོག་ལེགས་བྱུང་བར་རྒྱུ་མཚོ་ལ་ན།

117 Panchen Lama IV, Lobzang Chogyen

ༀ།།ངག་དབང་བློ་བཟང་རྒྱ་མཚོ་ནི་ལ།

118 Dalai Lama V, Ngawang Lobzang
Gyatso

ༀ།།ཕྲ་དེང་སངས་རྒྱས་རྒྱ་མཚོ་ལ་ན།

119 Desi Sangye Gyatso

ༀ།།ཚངས་དབྱངས་རྒྱ་མཚོ་ལ་ན།

120 Dalai Lama VI, Rigdzin Tsangyang
Gyatso

121 Dhritarastra, Guardian King of the East

122 Virudhaka, Guardian King of the South

123 Virupaksa, Guardian King of the West

124 Vaishravana, Guardian King of the North

125 Zhabdrung Ngawang Namgyel

126 Dorje Lingpa

127 Pema Lingpa

Concordance of Bhutanese place names

Footprint text	Variant spellings
A	
Agya Ne	Aja Ney
Amo-chu	Amo Chhu
B	
Babesa	Babisa
Bartsham	Gonpa
Bartsham Goemba Bongde	Bondey
Bongde Lhakhang	Bondey Lhakhang
Bonte La pass (4,890 metres)	Bhonte La
Bu-le	Bulay
Bumdeling	Bomdeling
Bunarkha	Bunakha
C	
Chamkhar Lhakhang	Chakhar Lhakhang
Chamkhar-chu	Chakhar Chhu
Changlingmethang	Changlingmithang
Chendebji Chorten	Chendebji Chhoeten
Cheri Dorjeden Gonpa	Cheri Goemba
Chime Lhakhang	Chimi Lhakhang
Chizhing	Pchishing
Chodrak hermitage	Choedrak Goemba
Chokhor Rabtentse Dzong	Chhoekhor Raptentse Dzong
Chokhor valley	Choskhor
Chorten Karpo	Chhoeten Karp
Chorten Kora	Chhoeten Kora
Chorten Lhakhang, Paro	Chhoeten Lhakhang
Chudzom	Chhuzom
Chudzomsa	Chhuzomsa
Chukha	Chhukha
Chukha Dzong	Chhukha Dzong
Chu-me valley	Chhume/ Chumey
D	
Dang-chu	Dang Chhu
Dechen Choling	Dechenchoeling
Dechenphuk hermitage	Dechenphu
Dewathang	Deothang
Dochu La	Dokyong La/ Dojong La
Doksum	Duksum

Domkhar Tashicholing	Domkhar Trashi Chholing
Dopshari	Dopchari
Draipham	Draifam
Drak Karpo cave hermitage	Drug Karp
Drakteng	Bjakteng
Drametse Urgyen Choling	Dramitse/ Dametsi Ugyenchhoeling
Dramphu (Tsirang)	Damphu
Drangme-chu (Nepali: Manas)	Drangme Chhu
Drena	Bjena
Dri, upper Ha	Bji
Drimednang	Bjimenang
Drizam	Bjizam
Droka	Bjoka
Dro-le Gonpa	Drolay Goemba
Drubthob Gonpa	Drubthob Goemba
Druk Choding (Tsongdu Naktsang)	Druk Choeding
Drukpa Kun-le	Drukpa Kunley
Dumto	Dumtoe
Dumtsek Lhakhang	Dumtse Lhakhang
Dung-chu	Dung Chhu
Dur Hot Springs	Duer Tsha Chhu
Dzoma	Zoma
Dzongchung ('small fortress').	Dzong Chhung
Dzongdrakha Gonpa	Dzongdrakha Goemba

G

Gamri-chu	Gamri Chhu
Gangchen Nyizergang	Gangchen Nyezergang
Gangteng Sangak Choling	Gangte Goemba
Gangzur	Phaling
Gasa Tashi Tongmon Dzong	Gasa Trashi Thongmoen Dzong
Gaton	Gatoen
Gedu-chu	Gedu Chhu
Gelekphuk	Gelephu/ Geylegphug
Genyekha	Geynikha
Getsa	Gaytsa
Goktong La (4,640 metres)	Gokthong La
Gunitsawa	Gunyitsawa

H

Ha	Haa
Ha chu	Haa Chhu
Humrel	Humral

J

Jagothang	Jangothang
Jamo-chu	Dhanasiri
Jangchulakha	Jangchhu Lakha
Jari La pass (4,747 metres)	Jhari La

Jemalangtso Lake	Jimilang Tsho
Jili La (3,810 metres)	Cheli La

K

Kawangjangsa	Kawajangsa
Khangku Lhakhang	Kahangkhu Lhakhang
Kharchu Dratsang	Namkhei Nyinpo Goemba
Khasadrachu	Khasadrapchhu
Khenpajong	Khenpalung
Khyinyel	Khaine
Kizam	Kizum
Kunga Lhakhang	Kuenga Lhakhang
Kunga Rabten Palace	Kuenga Rabten Phodrang
Kunzang Drak	Kunzangdra Goemba
Kuri Zampa	Kuri Zam
Kuri-chu	Kuru Chhu
Kurje Lhakhang	Kurjey Lhakhang
Kurto	Kurtoe
Kuruthang	Khuruthang
Kyerchu Lhakhang	Kichu Lhakhang

L

La-me Gonpa	Lamay Goemba
Laya(k)	Laya
Lhading	Hadi
Lhakhang Karpo	Lhakhang Karp
Lhodrak Se Lhakhang	Lhobrak Seykhar Dratshang
Lhongtso	Hongtso
Lhundrub Rinchentse Phodrang Dzong	Lhuentse Dzong
Lhuntse	Lhuntshi
Lingmithang	Lingmethang
Lingmukha	Limukha
Lingzhi Yulgyel Dzong	Lingshi Yugyel Dzong
Lirgang-chu	Lirgang Chhu
Lobesa	Lobeysa
Lunanang	Lunana
Lungchudzekha Gonpa	Lungchuzekha Goemba
Lungtenphuk	Lungtenphu

M

Mangde-chu	Mangde Chhu
Mebartso	Membartsho
Metsinang	Metshina
Minje	Menji
Mongar	Monggar
Monka Nering Senge Dzong	Singye Dzong
Mt Gang Bum (6,840 metres)	Kang Bum
Mt Gangchentak (6,840 metres)	Gangchhenta
Mt Gangkar Punsum (7,541 metres)	Gangkar Puensum

Mt Gyelpo Matsen (7,158 metres)	Masang Gang
Mt Jomolhari (7,313 metres)	Mt Jhomolhari
Mt Kulha Gangri (7,554 metres)	Kulha Kangri
Mt Dzongophu Gang (7,100 metres)	Zongophu Gang
Mutigtang	Motithang

N

Nikar-chu	Nikka Chhu/ Nikkarchu
Nyimalung Gonpa	Nimalung Goemba
Nyizergang Chorten	Khamsm Yuelley Namgyal Chhoeten

O

Orgyan Pelrithang, palace	Ugyen Pelri
Orgyan Tsemo	Ugyen Tsemo

P

Pangri Zampa	Phanri Zampa
Pema Gatsel	Pemagatshel
Petsheling Gonpa	Petsheling Goemba
Phobjika valley	Phobjikha
Phokpe Gonpa	Phokpey Goemba
Phuntsoling	Phuentsholing
Punatsang-chu (Sankosh)	Puna Tsang Chhu
Pungtang Dechen Dzong	Punakha Dzong

R

Raksatreng Tso	Raphstreng Tsho
Rangjung Osel Choling	Rangjung Wodsel Chholing
Rangthang Aung	Rangthang Woong
Rinchenzo La pass (5,220 metres)	Rinchen Zoe La

S

Samdrub Jongkhar	Samdrup Jongkhar
Samtse	Samchi
Senge Dzong	Singye Dzong
Shapa	Shaba
Sherabtse College, Kanglung	Sherubtse
Sherichu	Sherichhu
Simtokha Dzong	Sinmodokha/ Simtokha Dzong
Sipsu	Sipsue
So	Soe
Somdrang Gonpa	Sombrang Goemba

T

Tachogang Lhakhang	Tamchhog Lhakhang
Tagbab	Taba

Taktsang hermitage	Taktshang Goemba
Talakha Gonpa	Talakha Goemba
Taleda Gonpa	Dalay Goemba
Talo Gonpa	Talo Goemba
Tamzhing Lhundrub Choling	Tamshing Goemba
Tango Gonpa	Tango Goemba
Tarkar Tashi Yangtse Dzong	Daga Trashi Yangtse Dzong
Tarkarna	Dagana
Tashi Chodzong	Trashi Chhoe Dzong
Tashi Yangtse Dzong	Trashi Yangtse Dzong
Tashigang	Trashigang
Tashigang Dzong	Trashigang Dzong
Tashigang nunnery	Trashigang Goemba
Tashigang town	Wengkhar
Thadranang Gonpa	Thadra Goemba
Thangbi Lhakhang	Thankabi Goemba
Thangkhabe	Thangbi
Tharpaling Jangchub Choling	Tharpaling Goemba
Thekchok Kunzang Chorten	Thekcho Kunzang Chhoeten
Thombu Zhong	Thombu Shong
Thowa Drak	Thowada Goemba
Thujedrak hermitage	Thujidrag Goemba
Toktokha	Toktoka
Trekar Lhakhang	Prakhar Goemba
Tridangbi	Thri Dangbee
Trinlegang	Thinleygang
Trongsar	Trongsa
Trupang Palace	Thruepang Phodrang
Tsaluma	Tsaluna
Tsatsam Chorten	Sasum Chhoeten
Tsenkharla Dzong	Tshenkarla
Tsento	Tshentop
Tsimalakha	Tshilakha
Tsimazham	Tsimasham
Tsirang	Chirang

U

Ugyen Choling	Ugyen Chhoeling
Ura Gaden Lhakhang	Ura Geyden Lhakhang

W

Wang-chu (Raidak)	Wang Chhu
Wangchuk Dynasty	Wangchuck Dynasty
Wangditse Gonpa	Wangditse Goemba
Wangdu	Wangdue/ Wangdi
Wangdu Choling Palace, Jakar	Wangdichhoeling
Wangdu Phodrang Dzong	Wangduephodrang Dzong

Y

Yangchenphuk	Yangchhenphu
Yangthang Gonpa	Yangthang Goemba
Yele La pass (4,930 metres)	Yeli La
Yongla Gonpa	Yonglek Goemba
Yonphu Gonpa	Yongphu Goemba
Yusupang	Oesepang

Z

Zhemgang	Shemgang
Zhemgang Dzong	Shemgang Dzong
Zhongar Dzong	Shongar Dzong
Zug-ne	Zugney

Glossary

A

abhicara The wrathful rites that compassionately liberate evil beings into higher realms of rebirth

abhidharma A class of Buddhist literature pertaining to phenomenology, psychology, and cosmology

All-surpassing Realisation (*thogal*) A meditative technique within the Esoteric Instructional Class of Atiyoga, the highest teachings of the Nyingma school, through which the buddha-body of form (*rupakaya*) is manifestly realized

amban A Manchu ambassador of the imperial Qing dynasty

Anuttarayogatantra The unsurpassed yogatantras, which focus on important tantric subject matters, such as 'inner radiance' and 'illusory body'

Anuyoga The eighth of the nine vehicles of Buddhism according to the Nyingma school, in which the perfection stage of meditation (*sampannakrama*) is emphasized

apsara Offering goddess, celestial nymph

argali (*Ovis ammon Hodgsoni Blyth*) A type of wild sheep

Arpacana Mantra The mantra of the bodhisattva Manjughosa (*Om Arapacana Dhih*), the recitation of which generates discriminative awareness (*prajna*) and intelligence

Atiyoga The ninth of the nine vehicles of Buddhism according to the Nyingma school, in which the resultant three buddha-bodies (*trikaya*) are effortlessly perfected, and the generation and perfection stages of meditation are both effortlessly present

Avatamsakasutra The title of the longest Mahayana sutra (excluding the Prajnaparamita literature)

B

bahal A Newari temple

bangrim The terraced steps of a stupa, symbolising the bodhisattva and buddha levels

beyul A hidden land conducive to meditation and spiritual life, of which there are several in the Hiamlayan region, such as Pemako in southeast Tibet, and Khenpajong in northeast Bhutan

Bhadracaryapranidhanaraja The title of an important aspirational prayer which is part of the **Avatamsakasutra**

bharal A species of blue sheep (Tib nawa; Pseudois nayaur Hodg)

bindu The finial of a stupa, symbolising the buddha-body of actual reality (*dharmakaya*). The term also refers to the generative fluids of human physiology (according to Tibetan medicine and tantra), and to the seminal points of light appearing in the practice of **All-Surpassing Realisation**

bodhicitta (Tib jangchub sem) The enlightened mind which altruistically acts in the interest of all beings, combining discriminative awareness with compassion

bodhicitta vow The aspiration to attain full enlightenment or buddhahood for the benefit of all beings

bodhisattva (Tib Jangchub Sempa) A spiritual trainee who has generated the altruistic mind of enlightenment (*bodhicitta*) and is on the path to full buddhahood, remaining in the world in order to eliminate the sufferings of others. Ten successive bodhisattva levels (*bhumi*) are recognized

Bodongpa An adherent of the Bodong tradition, stemming from Bodong Chokle Namgyel

body of light The rainbow body of great transformation, in which the impure material body is transformed into one of light, through the practice of the **All-Surpassing Realisation**

Bon An ancient spiritual tradition, predating the advent of Buddhism in Tibet, which is considered by scholars to be of Zoroastrian or Kashmiri Buddhist origin, but which has, over centuries, assimilated many aspects of indigenous Tibetan religion and Buddhism

border-taming temple (Tib Tadul Lhakhang) A class of stabilising geomantic temples, reputedly constructed by King Songtsen Gampo in the border regions of Tibet

buddha   A fully enlightened being who has destroyed all obscurations and manifested all realisations.

bumpa   The bulbous dome of a stupa

C

calm abiding   (Skt shatipathana, Tib zhi-ne) A state of mind characterized by the stabilisation of attention on an internal object of observation, conjoined with the calming of external distractions to the mind

Caryatantra   The name of a class of tantra and the fifth of the nine vehicles according to the Nyingma school. Equal emphasis is placed on internal meditation and external rituals

caterpillar fungus   (*Cordiceps sinensis*) A medicinal plant used in the treatment of general debility and kidney disease

cave hermitage   (Tib zimpuk/ grubpuk) A remotely located mountain cave utilized as a hermitage for meditative retreats

chaitya   A chapel within a large temple, also used as a synonym for **stupa**

cham   Religious dance

chang   Barley ale or fortified wine (occasionally made of other grains)

charnel ground   A sky burial site, where human corpses are dismembered and compassionately fed to vultures

chimi   An elected representative

Chod (yul)   A meditative rite ('Object of Cutting') in which the egotistical obscurations at the root of all delusions and sufferings are compassionately visualized as a feast-offering on behalf of unfortunate spirits or ghosts, often frequenting **charnel grounds**

chorten   See **stupa**

Chosi Nyiden   The name given to the combined spiritual and temporal form of government maintained in Tibet from 1641 to 1951, and in Bhutan until 1902

chu   river

chuba   Tibetan national dress, tied at the waist with a sash. For men it takes the form of a long-sleeved coat, and for women a long dress, with or without sleeves, which may be shaped or shapeless

chulen   The practice of subsisting upon nutritious elixirs and vitamins extracted from herbs and minerals, undertaken for reasons of health or as a spiritual practice

D

dadar   An arrow employed in longevity empowerments, marriage and fertility rites, and during harvest festivals

de'u   Enigmatic riddle of the Bon tradition

debri   Mural paintings, frescoes

desi   The title of the regents of the Dalai lamas (in Tibet) and of the Zhabdrungs (in Bhutan), who often wielded considerable political power, particularly during the minority years of the incarnation under their charge

dharma   (Tib cho) The theory and practice of the Buddhist doctrine, including its texts and transmissions

discriminative awareness   (Skt prajna/Tib sherab) The faculty of intelligence inherent within the minds of all beings, which enables them to examine the characterisrtics of things and events, thus making it possible to make judgements and deliberations

district-controlling temple   (Tib Runon Lhakhang) a class of stabilising geomantic temples, reputedly constructed by King Songtsen Gampo in Central Tibet, forming an inner ring around the central Jokhang temple

dochal   A flagstone courtyard

dogar   Tibetan opera

Drepung Zhoton   the Yoghurt festival held at Drepung one day prior to the start of the operatic Yoghurt festival of Norbulingka

dri   femrale of the yak (*Bos grunniens*)

Drigungpa   An adherent of the Drigung sub-order of the Kagyu school of Tibetan Buddhism

Driklam namzhak   The Bhutanese national code of conduct and etiquette

drokpa   nomad

dronglhan   urban districts

drubchen   The ritual enactment of the activities of a cycle of meditational deities, consequent on the union of the meditator with the deities in question

drubchu   A sacred spring, said to have been brought forth from the ground through the meditative prowess of one of Tibet's great Buddhist masters

drubkhang   Meditation hermitage

Drubtab Gyatsa   ('Hundred Means for Attainment') A cycle of short meditative practices contained in the Kangyur, which were translated into Tibetan by Bari Lotsawa

Drukpa Kagyupa An adherent of the Drukpa sub-order of the Kagyu school of Tibetan Buddhism, which predominates in Bhutan

drung story

dukhang The assembly hall of a large monastery, in which the monks affiliated to the various colleges will congregate

dungpa A sub-district

Dzogchen Great Perfection, a synonym for **Atiyoga**

dzong County (administrative unit in Tibet), fortress, castle

E

eight attributes of pure water coolness, sweetness, lightness, softness, clearness, soothing quality, pleasantness and wholesomeness

eight auspicious symbols (Tib tashi tagye) umbrella, fish, conch, eternal knot, vase, wheel, and victory-banner, and flower

eight stupas symbolising the major events of the Buddha's life Eight styles of stupa reliquary, respectively symbolising the Buddha's birth, victory over cyclic existence, enlightenment, teaching, descent from Tusita (after teaching his late mother), resolution of schism, performance of miracles, and final nirvana

empowerment (Skt abhiseka/Tib wangkur) A ritual performed by a Buddhist master, which is an essential prerequisite, empowering prospective trainees into the practice of tantra by activating the potential inherent in their mental continuum

emptiness (Skt shunyata/Tib tongpanyi) The absence of inherent existence and self-identity with respect to all phenomena, the ultimate reality underlying all phenomenal appearances

enlightened mind See **bodhicitta**

enlightenment stupa (Tib jangchub chorten) One of the eight types of stupa, this one symbolising the Buddha's enlightenment

eternal knot (Skt srivatsa/Tib palbe'u) One of the **eight auspicious symbols**, and one of the 32 major marks of a buddha's body, sometimes rendered in English as 'heart-orb' since it is found at the heart of the Buddha

extensive lineage of conduct The transmission of Mahayana Buddhism which Asanga received in ancient India from Maitreya, and which emphasizes the elaborate conduct and spiritual development of the bodhisattva, in contrast to the 'profound lineage of view', which Nagarjuna received from Manjughosa

extraneous emptiness (Tib zhentong) The view that buddha-attributes are extraneously empty of mundane impurities and dualities, but not intrinsically empty in a nihilistic sense

F

Father Class of Unsurpassed Yogatantras One of the three subdivisions of the Unsurpassed Yogatantras (*Anuttarayogatantra*), according to the later schools of Tibetan Buddhism, exemplified by tantra-texts, such as the Guhyasamaja and Yamari

four classes of tantra See respectively: **Kriyatantra**, **Caryatantra**, **Yogatantra** and **Anuttarayogatantra**

four harmonious brethren (Tib tunpa punzhi) An artistic motif symbolising fraternal unity and respect for seniority, in which a partridge, rabbit, monkey, and elephant assist each other to pluck fruits from a tree

G

gakhyil A gemstone emblem comprising two or three segments

Ganden Tripa Title given to the head of the Gelukpa school of Tibetan Buddhism

gandharva (Tib driza) Denizens of space or celestian musicians who subsist on odours

garuda A mythological bird normally depicted with an owl-like sharp beak, often holding a snake, and with large powerful wings. In Buddhism, it is the mount of Vajrapani, symbolising the transmutative power that purifies certain malevolent influences and pestilence.

Gelukpa An indigenous school of Tibetan Buddhism, founded in the 14th century by Tsongkhapa, which, from the 17th century onwards, came to dominate the spiritual life of Tibet and Mongolia

generation stage of meditation (Skt utpattikrama/Tib kye-rim) The creative stage of meditation in which mundane forms, sounds, and thoughts are gradually meditated upon as natural expressions of deities, mantras, and buddha-mind

geshe (Skt kalyanamitra) Spiritual benefactor (of the Kadampa tradition), philosophical degree of a scholar-monk, a scholar-monk holding the geshe degree

gesture of calling the earth as a witness to past merits (bhumisparshamudra) The hand-gesture of the Buddha utilized during the subjugation of Mara through which he touched the ground, calling the goddess of the earth (Sthavira) to bear witness to his past merits

gewok County level administration, a block of villages

gho The national dress of Bhutan, worn by men

gomang chorten A multi-chapelled walk-in stupa

gomchen Experienced meditator

gongma king

gonpa Monastery

Great Prayer Festival (Tib Monlam Chenmo) A festival held in Lhasa during the first month of the lunar calendar, instituted by Tsongkhapa in 1409

Great Seal (Skt mahamudra/Tib chakya chenpo) The realisation of emptiness as the ultimate nature of reality (according to the sutras), and the supreme accomplishment of buddhahood according to the tantras). The term also refers to the dynamic meditative techniques through which these goals are achieved

Greater Vehicle (Skt Mahayana/Tib Tekpa Chenpo) The system or vehicle of Buddhism prevailing in Tibet, Mongolia, China, Korea, and Japan, emphasising the attainment of complete liberation of all sentient beings from obscurations and sufferings (rather than the goal of the Lesser Vehicle which is more self-centred and lacks a full understanding of emptiness). The Greater Vehicle includes teachings based on both sutra-texts and tantra-texts

Gu-ge style The artistic style prevalent in Far West Tibet (Ngari) and adjacent areas of northwest India (Ladakh, Spiti), exhibiting Kashmiri influence

gup A village headman

gyaphib A Chinese-style pavilion roof

gyelpo losar Official Tibetan New Year, held at the beginning of the first month of the lunar calendar, which normally falls within February or early March

H

harmika The square section of a stupa, above the dome, on which eyes are sometimes depicted

I

incarnation (Tib yangsi) The human form taken by an incarnate lama (tulku) following his decease in a previous life

Industructible Vehicle (Skt Vajrayana/Tib Dorje Tekpa) The aspect of the **Greater Vehicle** emphasising the fruitional tantra teachings and meditative techniques concerning the unbroken mental continuum from ignorance to enlightenment. It includes the vehicles of **Kriyatantra, Caryatantra, Yogatantra, Anuttarayogatantra, Mahayoga, Anuyoga** and **Atiyoga**

Inner Tantra The three inner classes of tantra. See under **Mahayoga, Anuyoga** and **Atiyoga**

Innermost Spirituality of Vimalamitra (Bima Nyingthig) The title of a collection of esoteric instructions belonging to the **man-ngag-de** (esoteric instructional) class of **Atiyoga**, which were introduced to Tibet from India by Vimalamitra during the early 9th century, and later redacted by Longchen Rabjampa in the 14th century

J

Jatakamala A stylised account of the Buddha's past lives as a bodhisattva, in Sanskrit verse, composed by Ashvaghosa, and translated into Tibetan

Jonangpa An adherent of the Jonang school of Tibetan Buddhism

K

kab-ne The ceremonial shawl worn by Bhutanese men

kadam (-style) stupa A small rounded stupa, the design of which is said to have been introduced into Tibet by Atisha during the 11th century

Kadampa An adherent of the Kadam

school of Tibetan Buddhism, founded by Atisha in the 11th century

Kagyupa An adherent of the Kagyu school of Tibetan Buddhism, founded in Tibet by Marpa during the 11th century

Kangyur An anthology of the translated scriptures of the sutras and tantras, the compilation of which is attributed to Buton Rinchendrub

Karma Gadri A school of art, which evolved in Kham, integrating Tibetan iconography with Chinese landscape themes and perspective

Karma Kagyu A sub-order of the Kagyu school, founded by Karmapa I during the 12th century

kashag The official name of the pre-1959 Tibetan cabinet

khang A house or building and sometimes an abbreviation for lhakhang (temple)

khatvanga A hand-emblem, held by Padmasambhava and several wrathful deities, comprising a staff skewered with a stack of three dry skulls and surmounted by an iron trident

Khyenri A school of painting associated with the 16th century master Jamyang Khyentse Wangchuk

kera Cumberband

kira The waistband of a Tibetan or Bhutanese **chuba**

koma A broach

Kriyatantra The name of a class of tantra and the fourth of the nine vehicles according to the Nyingma school. Greater emphasis is placed on external rituals than on internal meditation

kumbum A stupa containing many thousands of images, and often multiple chapels, sometimes known as 'Tashi Gomang' stupa

kunzang khorlo (Skt sarvatobhadra) A type of geometric poetry in the shape of a wheel, the lines of which read in all directions

kyang The Asiatic wild ass (*Equus hemionus Pallas*)

L

la Mountain pass

la-do A stone assuming the function of a life-supporting talisman (*la-ne*)

la-guk A rite for summoning or drawing in the life-supporting energy or talisman of another

la-shing A tree assuming the function of a life-supporting talisman (*la-ne*)

labrang The residence of an incarnate lama within a monastery

lam road

Lama Chodpa A text on the practice of guruyoga ('union with the guru'), written by Panchen Lama IV

lama Spiritual teacher (Skt guru)

Lamdre A unique collection of meditative practices related to the meditational deity Hevajra, which are pre-eminent in the Sakya school, outlining the entire theory and practice of the **Greater Vehicle**

lamrim (Skt pathakrama) The graduated path to enlightenment, and the texts expounding this path

Lato style A localized and less cosmopolitan style of Tibetan panting, associated with sites in the highland region of Western Tibet

latse Top of a mountain pass, the cairn of prayer flags adorning a mountain pass

Lesser Vehicle (Skt Hinayana/Tib Tekmen) The system or vehicle of Buddhism prevalent in Sri Lanka, Thailand and Burma, emphasising the four truths and related teachings through which an individual seeks his own salvation, rather than the elimination of others' sufferings

lhakhang Buddhist temple

lhamo Female deity (Skt devi)

Lhotsampa The Nepali citizens of southern Bhutan

life-supporting talisman (Tib la-ne) An object imbued with a sympathetic energy force, said to sustain the life of its owner

Ling Gesar The legendary warrior king, who is the hero of Tibetan epic poetry

losar Tibetan New Year

lumo Female naga-spirit (Skt nagini)

lung-gom A set of meditative practices in which the vital energy (lung) of the body, including the respiratory cycle, is controlled and regulated

lungta Tibetan mantras printed on cloth for use as prayer flags, which are activated by the power of the wind, or on paper as an offering to local mountain divinities, in which case they are tossed into the air on a mountain pass

lyonpo   minister (Tib. lonpo)

M

Madhyamaka   The philosophical system of Mahayana Buddhism based on the Middle Way, which seeks to comprehend, either by means of syllogistic reasoning or by reductio ad absurdum, the emptiness or absence of inherent existence with respect to all phenomena. A distinction is drawn between the ultimate truth, or emptiness, and the relative truth in which all appearances exist conventionally

Mahamudra   See **Great Seal**

Mahayoga   The name of a class of tantra and the seventh of the nine vehicles according to the Nyingma school, emphasising the generation stage of meditation (*utpattikrama*)

man-ngagde   (Skt upadeshavarga) The innermost class of instructions according to **Atiyoga**

mandala   (Tib kyilkhor) A symbolic two or three dimensional representation of the palace of a given meditational deity, which is of crucial importance during the generation stage of meditation

mani (-stone) wall   A wall adorned with stone tablets engraved with the mantras of the deity Avalokiteshvara, embodiment of compassion

Mani Kabum   The title of an early Tibetan historical work, said to have been concealed as a terma-text by King Songtsen Gampo in the 7th century, and to have been rediscovered during the 12th century by three distinct treasure-finders (*terton*)

mani prayer-wheel   (Tib dungkhor) A large prayer wheel containing mantras of the deity Avalokiteshvara, embodiment of compassion

mantra   (Tib ngak) A means of protecting the mind from mundane influences through the recitation of incantations associated with various meditational deities, thereby transforming mundane speech into buddha-speech. Mantra also occurs as a synonym for tantra

mantra vows   The various commitments maintained by those who have been empowered to practise the tantras

mantrin   (Tib ngakpa) A practitioner of the mantras, who may live as a lay householder rather than a renunciate monk

-me   The lower part of a valley

meditational deity   (Skt istadevata/Tib yidam) A peaceful or wrathful manifestation of buddha-mind, which becomes the object of a meditator's attention, as he or she seeks to cultivate experientially specific buddha-attributes by merging inseparably with that deity

momo   A Tibetan dumpling

monk   (Skt bhiksu/Tib gelong) One who maintains the full range of monastic vows as designated in the Vinaya texts

Monpa   Native inhabitants of Bhutan and the related peoples of Arunachal Pradesh and Southern Tibet

Mother Class of Unsurpassed Yogatantras   One of the three subdivisions of the Unsurpassed Yogatantras (*Anuttarayogatantra*), according to the later schools of Tibetan Buddhism, exemplified by tantra-texts, such as the Cakrasamvara and Hevajra

Mt Potalaka   Abode of the deity Avalokiteshvara, said in some sources to be located in South India

mu   A 'sky-cord' of light on which the ancient 'immortal' kings of Tibet were said to leave this world at the time of their succession

mumo   A female mu spirit, said to cause dropsy

muntsam   Meditation retreat in darkness

N

naga   A powerful water spirit which may take the form of a serpent or semi-human form similar to a mermaid/man

Nagaraja   King of naga spirits

nagini   Female water spirit

Namchu Wangden   A series of vertically stacked letters symbolising elemental power and buddha-attributes

Namgyel Chorten   See **Victory Stupa**

nectar   (Skt amrita/Tib dutsi) The ambrosia of the gods which grants immortality, metaphorically identified with the Buddhist teachings

New Translation Schools (*Sarmapa*) Those maintaining the Buddhist teachings which were introduced into Tibet from India from the late 10th century onwards, and which are contrasted with the Nyingma school, representing the earlier dissemination of Buddhism. The New Translation Schools include those of the Kadampa, Kagyupa, Sakyapa, Jonangpa and Zhalupa

ngakpa See **mantrin**

nine (hierarchical) vehicles (Skt navayana/Tib tekpa rimpa gu) According to the Nyingma school of Tibetan Buddhism, these comprise the three vehicles of pious attendants (*shravaka*), hermit buddhas (*pratyekabuddha*) and bodhisattvas, which are all based on the sutras; as well as the six vehicles of Kriyatantra, Caryatantra, Yogatantra, Mahayoga, Anuyoga, and Atiyoga, which are all based on the tantras. Each of these is entered separately in this glossary

Northern Treasures (Tib jangter) The terma tradition derived from Rigdzin Godemchen's 14th century discoveries in the Zangzang area of Northern Tibet

Nyang Chojung Taranatha's history of the Nyang-chu valley

nyenmo A plague-inducing demoness

Nyingma Gyudbum The anthology of the Collected Tantras of the Nyingmapa, most of which were translated into Tibetan during 8th-9th centuries and kept unrevised in their original format

Nyingma Kama The anthology of the oral teachings or transmitted precepts of the Nyingma school, accumulated over the centuries

Nyingmapa An adherent of the Nyingma school of Tibetan Buddhism, founded in Tibet by Shantaraksita, Padmasambhava, King Trisong Detsen, and Vimalamitra

nyung-ne A purificatory fast (*upavasa*)

O

offering mandala A symbolic representation of the entire universe, which is mentally offered to an object of refuge, such as the Buddha or one's spiritual teacher

Outer Tantra The three outer classes of tantra. See under **Kriyatantra**, **Caryatantra** and **Yogatantra**

P

pagoda A distinctive style of multi-storeyed tower, temple or stupa

Pala style Bengali style of Buddhist art

pandita Scholar, a Buddhist scholar of ancient India

Parinirvanasutra The sutra expounding the events surrounding the Buddha's decease

Path and Fruit See **Lamdre**

penma (*Potentilla fructicosa*) A type of twig used in the construction of the corbels of certain Tibetan buildings for aesthetic reasons, and to provide a form of ventilation

perfection stage of meditation (Skt sampannakrama/Tib dzog-rim) The techniques for controlling the movement of vital energy (*vayu*) and **bindu** within the central channel of the body through which inner radiance (*prabhasvara*) and coemergent pristine cognition (*sahajajnana*) are realized. It is contrasted with the **generation stage of meditation**

Phakmodrupa The dynasty of Tibetan kings who ruled Tibet from Nedong during the 14th-15th centuries

phurba A ritual dagger, which is the hand-emblem of the meditational deity Vajrakila/Vajrakumara, penetrating the obscurations of mundane existence

pilgrim's circuit (Tib khorlam) A circumambulatory walkway around a shrine or temple, along which pilgrims will walk in a clockwise direction

place of attainment (Tib drub-ne) A sacred power-place where great spiritual masters of the past meditated and attained their realizations

Prajnaparamita A class of Mahayana literature focussing on the bodhisattva paths which cultivate the 'perfection of discriminative awareness'

prayer flag A flag printed with sacred mantra syllables and prayers, the power of which is activated by the wind

prayer wheel A large fixed wheel (*dungkhor*) or small hand-held wheel (*tu-je chenpo*), containing sacred mantra-syllables or prayers, the power of which is activated by the spinning motion of the wheel

profound lineage of view The transmission of Mahayana Buddhism which

Nagarjuna received in ancient India from Manjughosa, and which emphasizes the profound view of emptiness, in contrast to the 'extensive lineage of conduct', which Asanga received from Maitreya

protecter shrine (*gonkhang*) A temple or chapel dedicated to the class of protector deities (Skt dharmapala/Tib chokyong)

puja Offering ceremony

Q

qan A Mongol chieftain or king

qutuqtu The Mongol equivalent of **tulku** ('incarnate lama')

R

rabde Monastic body, Buddhist clergy

rainbow body (*ja-lu*) The buddha-body of great transformation, in which the impure material body is transformed into one of light, through the practice of the **All-Surpassing Realisation**

Ranjana (*lantsa*) The medieval Sanskrit script of Newari Buddhism from which the Tibetan capital letter script (*u-chen*) is said to have been derived

Ratnakuta An important section of the Mahayana sutras, which, along with the Prajnaparamita literature, largely represent the second promulgation of the Buddhist teachings

reliquary (*dung-ten*) A stupa containing buddha-relics or the relics/embalmed remains of a great spiritual master

residential college/unit (*khangtsang*) The residential quarters of a large monastic college, often inhabited by monks from one specific region of the country

Ringpungpa The dynasty of Tibetan princes who usurped the power of the Phakmodrupa kings during the late 15th century and ruled much of Tibet from Rinpung in Tsang, until they themselves were usurped by the kings of Tsang, based in Zhigatse

ritual dagger See **phurba**

rongpa villager

runon See **district controlling temple**

S

sacred outlook (*dak-nang*) The pure vision through which all phenomenal appearances, including rocks and topographical features, may assume the forms of deities

Sakyapa An adherent of the Sakya school of Tibetan Buddhism, founded by Gayadhara, Drokmi, and Khon Konchok Gyelpo in the 11th century

sand mandala A two-dimensional representation of the palace of a given meditational deity, made of finely ground coloured powders or sands

sangha The Buddhist monastic community (Tib gendun)

self-arising (object/image) (*rang-jung*) A naturally produced object or image, emerging of its own accord from stone, wood, and the like, in which great sanctity is placed

self-arising seed-syllable A (*A rang-jung*) a 'naturally produced' seed-syllable A, indicative of **emptiness**

self-arising terma stone (*rangjung terdo*) A 'naturally produced' stone, said to have been discovered as **terma**

serdung A reliquary stupa made of gold

Seven Trial Monks The first Tibetan monks ordained in the 8th century by Shantaraksita

sexagenary year cycle (*rab-jung*) The cycle of 60 years on which Tibetan chronology is based (rather than centuries). This system was originally adopted in Tibet from the Kalacakra Tantra, and each year of the sixty years was later given a distinctive name combining one of the 12 animals and one of the five elements of the Chinese system

Shambhala A mysterious hidden land, often identified with Central Asia, where the Kalackra Tantra was disseminated, and from where, it is said, messianic kings will emerge during the next millennium to subdue tyrannical empires on earth

Shangpa Kagyu A branch of the Kagyu school which originated from the Tibetan yogin Khyungpo Naljor of Shang rather than Marpa

Sharchokpa The indigenous inhabitants of Eastern Bhutan

shastra A treatise or commentary elucidating points of scripture or science (Tib ten-cho)

shen   A type of Bon priest

sign of accomplishment   A sign or intimation of success in spiritual practice

six-syllable mantra   The mantra of the bodhisattva Avalokiteshvara (*Om Mani Padme Hum*), the syllables of which respectively generate com- passion for the sufferings endured by gods, antigods, humans, animals, ghosts, and denizens of the hells

sky-burial site   (*dutro*) See **charnel ground**

sok-shing   The central pillar of a building or the wooden axis inside an image, which acts as a life-support

sonam losar   The agricultural new year, held one month prior to the official new year (in Bhutan and parts of Tibet)

stone footprint   The imprint of the foot of a great spiritual master of the past, left in stone as a sign of yogic prowess

stupa   (Tib chorten) The most well-known type of sacred monument in the Buddhist world, symbolising the buddha-body of reality (*dharmakaya*), and holding the relics of the Buddha or some great spiritual master.

Sukhavati   The buddha-field of Amitabha, the meditational buddha of the west

supine ogress   An anthropomorphic description of the dangerous terrain of the Tibetan landscape, which King Songtsen Gampo tamed by constructing a series of geomantic temples

sutra   (Tib do) The discourses of the Buddha, belonging to either the **Lesser Vehicle** or the **Greater Vehicle**, which were delivered by Shakyamuni Buddha, and which expound the causal path to enlightenment in a didactic manner, in contrast to the **tantras**

Sutra of the Auspicious Aeon   (*Bhadrakalpikasutra*) The title of a sutra enumerating the thousand budhas of this 'auspicious aeon', of whom Shakyamuni was the fourth and Maitreya will be the fifth

swastika   (Tib yungdrung) A Buddhist symbol of good auspices, included among the thirty-two excellent major marks of a buddha's body. The inverse swastika is also a Bon symbol

syllable A   The seed-syllable inherent in all syllables, which is indicative of **emptiness**

T

tadul   See **border taming temple**

talismanic object/place   (*la-ne*) See **life-supporting talisman**

tangka   Tibetan painted scroll

tangka wall   (*goku*) A large wall located within the grounds of a monastery, on which large applique tangkas are hung during specific festivals

Tengyur   An anthology of the translated scriptures on the Indian treatises on Buddhism and classical sciences, the compilation of which is attributed to Buton Rinchendrub

tantra   The continuum from ignorance to enlightenment

tantra-text   (Tib gyud) Canonical texts delivered by the buddhas, which emphasize the resultant approach to buddhahood, in contrast to the causal or didactic approach of the **sutras**

teaching gesture   (*dharmacakramudra*) The hand-gesture of the Buddha utilized during the teaching of the Buddhist doctrine

terma   (Skt nidhi) The texts and sacred objects formerly concealed at geomantic power-places on the Tibetan landscape during the 7th-9th centuries, in the manner of a time capsule, which were later revealed in subsequent centuries by the treasure-finders (*terton*) appointed to discover them. Other termas, known as gong-ter, are revealed directly from the nature of buddha-mind

thread-cross   (Tib do) A wooden framed structure crossed with many layers of coloured threads, used as a device for trapping and exorcising evil forces or demons

three approaches to liberation   (Tib namtar gosum) As expounded in the **Greater Vehicle**, these are: emptiness, aspirationlessness and signlessness

three buddha-bodies   (*trikaya*) The buddha-body of actual reality (*dharmakaya*) or emptiness underlying all phenomena; the buddha-body of perfect resource (*sambhogakaya*) whose light-forms appear in meditation to advanced level bodhisattvas; and the buddha-body of emanation (*nirmanakaya*) which manifests materially in the world to guide living beings from suffering

three roots   (Skt trimula/Tib tsawa sum) The spiritual teacher (*lama*) who confers blessing, the meditational deity (*yidam*) who confers spiritual accomplishments, and the dakini (*khandroma*) who embodies enlightened activity

three world systems   (*tridhatu*) Those of desire, form and formlessness

three-dimensional palace   (*vimana*) The celestial palace of a given meditational deity

thukpa   soup, noodle soup

Tishri   The title of imperial preceptor to the Mongol Yuan emperors

-to   The upper reaches of a valley

togo   Jacket

tongdrol   Liberation by sight, an object conferring liberation by sight

torana   Stucco halo of an image, arched pediment above a gateway

torma   (Skt bali) Ritual offering-cake

tratsang   A college within a large monastery

treasure chest   (Tib terdrom) Container in which terma are concealed and from which they are subsequently discovered

treasure   See **terma**

treasure-finder   (Tib terton) The prophesied discoverer of a terma-text or terma-object

treasure-site   (Tib terka) Locations in which terma are concealed and discovered

tsamkhang   Meditation hermitage

tsampa   The staple Tibetan food consisting of ground and roasted barley flour, which is mixed with tea as a dough

tsangla   An East Bodish language, spoken by the Sharchokpa of Eastern Bhutan

tsha-tsha   Miniature votive terracotta image, sometimes inserted within a stupa

Tsechu   The tenth day of the lunar month, associated with the activities of Padmasambhava, and on which feast-offering ceremonies are held. These may assume the form of grand religious dance performances, for which reason, in Bhutan, the term refers to **cham** festivals

tsewang   Longevity **empowerment**

tshe-chu   Water-of-life spring

tsuklakhang   large temple (Skt vihara)

tulku   Incarnate lama, emanation, buddha-body of emanation (*nirmanakaya*)

tummo   The name of a yogic practice of the perfection stage of meditation in which an inner heat is generated within the body to burn away all obscurations and generate the coemergence of bliss and emptiness

Tusita   A low-level paradise within the world-system of desire (*kamadhatu*) where the future buddha Maitreya is presently said to reside

Twelve Deeds of Shakyamuni   The 12 principal sequential acts in the Buddha's life, viz: residence in Tusita paradise, conception, birth, study, marriage, renunciation, asceticism, reaching the point of enlightenment, vanquishing demonic obstacles, perfect enlightenment, teaching and final nirvana at the time of death

U

Uchen   The Tibetan capital letter script

udumbara lotus   A huge mythical lotus, said to blossom once every 500 years

utse   Central tower within a dzong

V

vajra   (Tib dorje) The indestructible reality of buddhahood, a sceptre-like ritual object symbolizing this indestructible reality, or skilful means

vajra and bell   (*vajragantha*) A set of ritual implements, respectively symbolising skilful means and discriminative awareness

Vajra Guru mantra   The mantra of Pasmasambhava (*Om Ah Hum Vajra Guru Padma Siddhi Hum*)

vajradhatu   (Tib dorje ying) The indestructible expanse of reality

Vartula   The Indic script from which the cursive Tibetan U-me script is said to be derived

Victory/Vijaya Stupa   (Tib namgyel chorten) One of the eight types of stupa, this one symbolising the Buddha's victory over mundane influences

vihara   A large Buddhist temple

Vinaya   (Tib dulwa) The rules of Buddhist monastic discipline, the texts outlining these rules

W

wangjuk   Blouse

wheel and deer emblem   A motif

symbolizing the deer park at Risipatana (*Sarnath*) where the Buddha gave his first teaching, turning the doctrinal wheel in a deer park

wheel of rebirth (Skt bhavacakra/Tib sidpei khorlo) A motif depicting the sufferings of the various classes of sentient beings within cyclic existence and the causal processes which give rise to their rebirth

wind-horse See **lungta**

Y

yaksa A type of malevolent mountain spirit

yangdul lhakhang The remote group of 'further taming' geomantic temples, reputedly constructed by King Songtsen Gampo, outside the line of the 'border-taming temples'

Yogatantra The name of a class of tantra and the sixth of the nine vehicles according to the Nyingma school. Greater emphasis is placed on internal meditation than upon external rituals

Yoghurt festival See **Zhoton**

yogin (Tib neljorpa) A male practitioner engaged in intensive meditative practices

yogini (Tib neljorma) A female practitioner engaged in intensive meditative practices

Z

Zangdok Pelri style A mode of temple construction symbolising the three-storeyed palace of Padmasambhava

Zhalupa An adherent of the Zhalu tradition, associated with Zhalu Monastery (founded 1040)

Zhidag A type of local divinity

Zhije The meditative technique of 'pacification' introduced to Tibet by Phadampa Sangye

Zhoton The Yoghurt operatic festival, held at Norbulingka in Lhasa in August

zi A species of etched agate or banded chalcedony, highly valued in Tibet

Zikpa Ngaden Tsongkhapa's five visions of diverse aspects of Manjushri

Dzongkha phrasebook

There is no scope here for a detailed presentation of the Dzongkha language, and readers are referred to the following publications: George Van Driem, *The Grammar of Dzongkha* (Dzongkha Development Commission, 1992) and Rinchhen Khandu's *Dzongkha-English Dictionary: Topic Base approach with Romanisation* (Pekhang Enterprises, 1998). For more general background on Tibeto-Burman languages, the following sources are highly recommended: Stephan Beyer, *The Classical Tibetan Language* (SUNY, 1992), and Philip Denwood, *Tibetan* (John Benjamins, 1999).

The basic word order of both Dzongkha and Tibetan is Subject- Object- Verb. Dzongkha is similar to the Tibetan dialects of Tsang but there are many elisions and vowel changes.

Vocabulary

Welcome	Bjon pa lek so (Dzongkha)
	Bjon pa ya (Mangdep)
	Jhon shun (Sharchop).
Goodbye	Le shim be bjon na (Dzongkha)
	Sho go wa (Bumthap)
	Lekpo shuk cho (Sharchop).
Thank You	Ka drin che (Dzongkha)
	Kadrin che wai (Bumthap)
	Kadrin che wa la (Sharchop).
Excuse me	Gom ma tre (Dzongkha)
	Tsek pa ma sai (Bumthap)
	Gom ma tre chow la (Sharchop).
Honorific suffix (Personal names)	La.

Nga	I	**Ga che be**	why
Nga chi	we	**Di**	this
Chod	you, singular	**Phi di**	that
Chod tshu	you, plural	**Di tso**	those
Kho	he	**A hyi**	that one
Mo	she	**Ah ya**	up there
Kho tshu	they	**Ah ma**	down there
Ga	who	**La**	to, in, at, for
Ga gi	whose	(Oblique particle used following a noun).)	
Ga lu	to whom		
Ga chi	what		
Ga te	where		
Gati le	from where		
Gnam	when		
Ga de be	how		
Ga de che mo	how much		

Selected nouns

Buildings

Khang	building	**Gon khang**	protector chapel
Droen chim	hotel/guesthouse	**Tsam khang**	meditation hermitage
Za khang	restaurant		
Ja khang	tea house	**Tshong khang**	shop
Chim	home	**La zo tshong khang**	handicraft shop
Cho sham	household shrine	**Dra tsang**	monastic school
Dzong	district fortress	**Lob dra**	school
Dum ra	park/garden)	**Le khung**	office
Goem ba	monastery	**Tro wa**	picnic
Lha khang	temple)	**Gur**	tent

Food and beverage

Toh/Zhego	food	**Cha gog**	garlic
Thu ni	drink	**Lam bend a**	tomato
Zau	puffed rice	**Do lom**	aubergine
Sib	beaten rice	**Tsong**	onion
Ne	barley	**E ma**	chilli
Kaf chi	roasted barley	**E ma dat shi**	chilli with cheese dish
Ge za	maise		
Jou	buckwheat	**Tshe lu**	orange
Moen ja	millet	**Ngang la**	banana
Thup	noodle soup	**Kong tse**	pineapple
Mo mo	steamed dumplings	**Tar go**	walnut
Chum	rice	**Kham**	peach
Kep ta	bread	**Guen drum**	grape
Sha	meat	**chu goen**	papaya
Lang sha	beef	**Nga ri kham**	apricot
Lu sha	lamb	**Tsa**	salt
Nga sha	fish	**Om**	milk
Nga kam	dried fish	**Dat shi**	cheese
Phag sha	pork	**Zho**	Yogurt
Bja sha	chicken	**Do**	Butter milk
Gong do	eggs	**Ja**	tea
La pu	radish	**Chang**	barley wine
La pu maap	carrot	**A rak**	rice wine
Kew a	potato	**Phob**	cup
Yung do	turnip	**Thu-em**	spoon
Sha mo	mushroom	**Da pa**	wooden bowl
Gop	onion		

Travel

Ja	north	**Ga ri**	car
Lho	south	**Yak**	yak
Nub	west	**Bon gu**	donkey
Shar	east	**Ta**	horse
Bo na	centre	**O la**	ravine
Nam dro thang	airport	**Ne kor**	pilgrimage
Lung kor	train	**Yul**	native place

Gye om	guest	Lam	road
Nep	host	Lam ka	trail or roadway
Ko ra	circumambulation	Ma khu	oil
Ta shel	tourism	Sa ma khu	kersosene
Dru	boat	Ga ri ma khu	petrol

Terrain

Ri	hill	La/ La tse	mountain pass
Gang ri	mountain	Bje thang	desert
Gang rue	glacier	Gyel khab	country
Tsho	lake	Dzong	district castle
Chu	river, water	Dzong khag	district, province
Tsha chu	hot spring	Dung khag	sub-district
Zam	bridge	Ge wog	county, village block
Thang	plain	Gup	village head man
Dra phu	cave	Chi mi	town representative
Nag tshe	forest	Throm	town
Pamg tshe	meadow	Yu ka pa	villager
Pang	grassland, meadow	She	farm
Tsam drok	pasture	Drok pa	nomad
Me to	flower	Tse ma na	forest
Shing	tree	Pang	grassland, meadow

Weather

Charp	rain	Thew	dust
Se ra	hail	Lung ma	wind
Khau	snow	Druk ke	thunder
Kha rue	avalanche	Sa yom	earthquake
Ba mo	frost	Khe	ice
Sa mu	fog, mist	Nim	sun

People

Mi	people, humans	A cho	elder brother
Ke pho ja	man	Puen	relative
Am shu	woman	No chu	younger sibling
a lo	child	Map	husband
Bho tsho	son	Am shu	wife
Bhum	daughter	Lo pen	sir
Aiah	mother	Aum	madam
Apa	father	Rinpoche	precious incarnation
Agey	old man, grandfather	La ma	spiritual teacher
		Ngak pa	mantrin
An gey	old women, grandmother	Ge long	fully ordained monk
		Gom chen	hermit
A sha	uncle	Mang mi	police, soldier
Aum chum	aunt	Am chi	doctor
A ni	nun	Drung he	official
Tshow	nephew	La	work
Tsam	niece	Lo pen	teacher

| sha ro | friend | Jams chi | enemy |

Countries

Boe	Tibet	Druk yel	Bhutan
Ja nak	China	Sog po	Mongolia
Gha ga	India, Nepal	Chi lip	foreigner
Dre jong	Sikkim		

Cardinal numbers

Chi	one	Ngab chu	fifty
Nyi	two	Ngab chu nga chi	ifty-one
Sum	three	Druk chu	sixty
Zhi	four	Druk chu re chik	sixty-one
Nga	five	Duen chu	seventy
Druk	six	Duen chu don chi	seventy-one
Duen	seven	Jyeb chu	eighty
Jye	eight	Jyeb chu jye chi	eighty-one
Gu	nine	Gu chu	ninety
Chu	ten	Guchu gu chi	ninety-one
Chu-chi	eleven	Ja	one hundred
Nyi shu	twenty	Nyi ja	two hundred
Nyi shu tsa-chi	twenty-one	Tong	one thousand
Sum chu	thirty	Thri	ten thousand
Sum chu so chi	thirty-one	Bum	hundred thousand
Zhib chu	forty	Saya	million
Zhib chu zhe chi	forty-one		

Ordinal numbers

| Dhang pa | first | Sum pa | third |
| Ney pa | second | | |

Money

Nguel khang	bank	Ti through	currency
Ngul trum	Bhutanese currency	Druel choe Nguel dzin	
Nuel chang	cash	travellers' cheque	

Body parts

Zu	body	Kha	mouth
Cha	hair	So	teeth
Gu to	head	Laap	arm
Mig to	eye	Kaam	leg
Nam cho	ear		

Selected adjectives (usually following noun)

Hoem	blue	Jan khu	green
Karp	white	Nap	black
Serp	yellow	Bom	big
Marp	red	Chung ku	small

Bar ma	average	**Jug tshu**	fast
Reem	long, tall	**Go le bei**	slow
Thun ku	short	**Ga tog to**	happy
Tha reem	far	**choe wa**	sad
Tha thun ka	short, near	**Gong bom**	expensive
Jha sheem	beautiful	**Gong chung ku**	cheap
Jha reem	pretty	**Dey tog to**	well
Tsok pa	dirty	**Dey tog to mai**	not well
Tsang ma	clean	**Yep**	right
Tsarp	new	**Yon**	left
Nyinm	old	**Tsa tum**	hot
Jam tog to	easy	**Khuem**	cold
La kha	difficult		

Verbs

Most Dzongkha verbs have four tenses; present, past, future and imperative. There are two types: those which have different written forms for each of these four tenses (although when spoken they sound identical), and others which differentiate tense by adding a suffix particle to the verbal stem. In such cases, the suffixes **Yi**, **Chi**, and **Nu** are added to the stem to form a past tense, **Ni** or **Ong** is added to form a future tense, **Do** or **De** is added to form a present tense, and **Zhig** is added to form an imperative. Here is a short list of some commonly used verbs:

To come

Yong-do	present
Yong-nu	past
Yong-ni	future
Yong-zhig!	imperative

To go

Song-do	present
Song-chi	past
Song-nu	future
Song-zhig!	imperative

To arrive

Hue-do	present
Hue-chi	past
Hue-ni	future
Hue-zhig	imperative

To sit

Doe-do	present
Doe-chi	past
Doe-ni	future
Doe zhig!	imperative

To sit (hon.)

Zhuk-do	present
Zhuk-ni	past
Zhuk-do	future
Zhuk zhig!	imperative

To sleep

Nyel-do	present
Nyel-chi	past
Nyel-ni	future
Nyel zhigl!	imperative

To eat

Za-do	present
Za-chi	past
Za-ni	future
Za!	imperative

To eat (hon.)

Zhe-do	present
Zhe-chi	past
Zhe-ni	future
Zhe-zhig!	imperative

To buy

Nyo-do	present
Nyo-yi	past
Nyo-ni	future
Nyo-zhig!	imperative

To do/ work

Be-de	present
Be-chi	past
Be-ni	future
Be zhig!	imperative

To offer

Phuel-de	present
Phuel-nu	past
Phuel-ni	future
Phuel zhig!	imperative

To meditate

Gom	present
Gom	past
Gom	future
Gom!	imperative

To study

Lab	present
Lab	past
Lab	future
Lab	imperative

Examples

Meeting a stranger

What is your name?	Cha gi min ga chi mo?
My name is Yonten	Nga gi min yon ten yin
Which country are you from?	Cha gi yul ga te le mo?
I am from India	Nga ja gar le yin
How old are you?	Cha gi lo ga te chi mo?
I am fifty one	Nga nga chu nga chi yin
Are you married?	Chey nyen chap chi ka?
Yes I am	Yin, Nga gi alo sum yo
Do you like Bhutan?	Cha druk yel lo ga ye ga?
Yes I do	Ga wa la

Shopping

How much is that painting?	Thang ka do gong da te chi mo?
Six Hundred Ngultrum	Ngul trum druk ja hin
It is too expensive,	
please reduce the price	Gong bom e be, a tshi chi phab nga
Can you pay five hundred?	Che gi nga chu tro e suk ga?
Yes I can	Tro e suk la

Travelling

Yesterday I went to Cheri Monastery	Kha tsa nga che ri goem ba la nga jo hin.
I visited the red temple	Nga lha khang marp nga jo hin.
Tomorrow I will leave for Bumthang	Nar ba Bum thang nga jo he hin.
Can I buy a bus ticket to Jakar here?	Nga le nga ja kar gi passey ngong tub ga?

Eating

Where is the Peljorling Restaurant?	Pel jor ling za khang ga te hin na?
It is on the east side of this road	Lam ka di gi shar kha to lo hin
Do you serve vegetarian dumplings?	Sha meap mo mo tsong tub ga?
Where is the toilet?	Charp sa ga te mo?

Health

I have altitude sickness	Nga sa to wei ney yoe
Where is the hospital?	Men khang ga te yoe?
Where is the pharmacy?	Men tsong se ga te yoe?

Telling time

What is the time?	Cho tso ga te chi mo?
It is two thirty	Cho tso nyi da che ka hin
When will the train leave from Delhi?	Lung kor delhi ney nam le jo mo?
At ten to eight	Cho tso jye ma dum le karma chu.

Index

Complete title listing

Footprint publishes travel guides to over 150 destinations worldwide. Each guide is packed with practical, concise and colourful information for everybody from first-time travellers to travel aficionados. The list is growing fast and current titles are noted below.
Available from all good bookshops and online at www.footprintbooks.com

(P) denotes pocket guide

Latin America and Caribbean
Argentina
Barbados (P)
Bolivia
Brazil
Caribbean Islands
Central America & Mexico
Chile
Colombia
Costa Rica
Cuba
Cusco & the Inca Trail
Dominican Republic
Ecuador & Galápagos
Guatemala
Havana (P)
Mexico
Nicaragua
Peru
Rio de Janeiro
South American Handbook
Venezuela

North America
Vancouver (P)
New York (P)
Western Canada

Africa
Cape Town (P)
East Africa
Egypt
Libya
Marrakech (P)
Morocco
Namibia
South Africa
Tunisia
Uganda

Middle East
Dubai (P)
Israel
Jordan
Syria & Lebanon

Footnotes Complete title listing

Credits

Footprint credits

Editors: Sophie Blacksell and Angus Dawson
Map editor: Sarah Sorensen
Picture editor: Claire Benison

Publisher: Patrick Dawson
Editorial: Alan Murphy, Sarah Thorowgood, Claire Boobbyer, Felicity Laughton, Laura Dixon, Nicola Jones
Cartography: Robert Lunn, Claire Benison, Kevin Feeney, Angus Dawson, Shane Feeney, Melissa Lin, Peter Cracknell
Series development: Rachel Fielding
Design: Mytton Williams and Rosemary Dawson (brand)
Advertising: Debbie Wylde
Finance and administration:
Sharon Hughes, Elizabeth Taylor, Lindsay Dytham

Photography credits

Front cover: Prayer Wheels Kychu in Paro (Alamy)
Inside: Photo Library and Powerstock
Back cover: Black Hat Dance (Powerstock)

Print

Manufactured in Italy by LegoPrint
Pulp from sustainable forests

Footprint feedback

We try as hard as we can to make each Footprint guide as up to date as possible but, of course, things always change. If you want to let us know about your experiences – good, bad or ugly – then don't delay, go to **www.footprintbooks.com** and send in your comments.

Publishing information

Footprint Bhutan
1st edition
© Footprint Handbooks Ltd
October 2004
ISBN 1 903471 32 X
CIP DATA: A catalogue record for this book is available from the British Library
® Footprint Handbooks and the Footprint mark are a registered trademark of Footprint Handbooks Ltd

Published by Footprint

6 Riverside Court
Lower Bristol Road
Bath BA2 3DZ, UK
T +44 (0)1225 469141
F +44 (0)1225 469461
discover@footprintbooks.com
www.footprintbooks.com

Distributed in the USA by

Publishers Group West

Acknowledgements

This first edition of *Footprint Bhutan* builds upon the short Bhutan chapters that were previously published in earlier editions of the *Tibet Handbook* (1996 and 1999). Much of the fieldwork was undertaken in the autumn of 2001 at the conclusion of a series of seminars on translation methodology which I had the pleasure of conducting in Thimphu. Thanks are due to the gracious hospitality of those who facilitated that visit: Dasho Tashi Phuntsog of the National Assembly, Dasho Senge Dorji of the Dzongkha Development Commission, Dasho Sangye Wangchuk of the National Commission for Cultural Affairs, Lopon Lungtaen of the Institute for Language and Cultural Studies, and Tulku Pema Wangyel of the Centre d'Etudes de Chanteloube in Dordogne. I am also indebted to my friend Mr Karma Khorko, director of the Bhutan Travel Service and manager of the Pedling Hotel, who is a close associate of Gangteng Tulku. Karma and his staff generously offered assistance while I was engaged in fieldwork in Bhutan, and also provided other source materials on inaccessible parts of the country. Subsequently while I was writing this book, Karma would frequently send through informative updates, which have all been included.

I would also like to express my gratitude to Jakob Leschley and Eric Schmidt—old friends and colleagues at the seminar on translation methodology, who enthusiastically provided information on a few sites that I was unable to visit personally; and also to all those students who participated in the seminar and personally assisted my fieldwork— Sangye Wangdi and the others. Lopon Pema Tsewang's *History of Bhutan*, written in classical Tibetan, has proved to be an invaluable source, as have the scholarly works of the late Michael Aris. Sonam Tobgay's information on river rafting and kayaking was previously published in the Druk Air in-flight magazine Tashi Delek (Oct-Dec, 2001). Robert Bradnock and Francoise Pommaret, an esteemed colleague and acknowledged expert on Bhutan, both contributed to the Bhutan chapters contained in earlier version of the companion *Tibet Handbook*. Iconographic line drawings are reproduced from Dr Lokesh Chandra's *Buddhist Iconography* (Aditya Prakashan, New Delhi, 1988). Wisdom Publications kindly gave their permission to reproduce the hagiographies of Tangtong Gyelpo, Dorje Lingpa and Pema Lingpa, contained in our translation of Dudjom Rinpoche's *The Nyingma School of Tibetan Buddhism* (Boston, 1991).

Finally, thanks are due to my family who have had to put up with my long periods of abstraction while working on the book; and to all the dedicated editorial staff at Footprint Handbooks: to Sophie Blacksell and to Kevin Feeney of the mapping department in particular. For lack of time, it has not been possible to include all the maps and ground plans of temples and dzongs at our disposal, but we will endeavour do so in future editions.

The health section was written by Dr Charlie Easmon, MBBS, MRCP, Msc Public Health, DTM&H, DoccMed, Director of Travel Screening Services. Additional material was supplied by Dr David Snashall, Senior Lecturer in Occupational Health, United Medical Schools of Guy's and St Thomas' Hospitals and Chief Medical Adviser to the Foreign and Commonwealth Office, London.

Map symbols

Administration

- ▫ Capital city
- ○ Other city/town
- International border
- Regional border
- Disputed border

Roads and travel

- Motorway
- Main road
- Minor road
- ---- 4WD track
- ...... Footpath
- ⊶▪ Railway with station
- ✈ Airport
- ➡ Bus station
- Ⓜ Metro station
- ---- Cable car
- ++++ Funicular
- ⚓ Ferry

Water features

- River, canal
- Lake, ocean
- Seasonal marshland
- Beach, sand bank
- ⋇ Waterfall

Topographical features

- ◯ Contours (approx)
- ⌂ Mountain
- ◸ Volcano
- ⇁ Mountain pass
- Escarpment
- Gorge
- Glacier
- Salt flat
- Rocks

Cities and towns

- Main through route
- Main street
- Minor street
- Pedestrianized street
- Ⲉ ⲓ Tunnel
- → One way street

Steps

⊨ Bridge

Fortified wall

Park, garden, stadium

● Sleeping

⊘ Eating

❶ Bars & clubs

⊚ Entertainment

Building

▪ Sight

✝✝ Cathedral, church

卍 Buddhist temple, monastery

🛕 Hindu temple

⚼ Meru

🕌 Mosque

⌂ Stupa

✡ Synagogue

Ⅰ Tourist office

🏛 Museum

✉ Post office

Ⓟ Police

Ⓢ Bank

@ Internet

♩ Telephone

🏪 Market

✚ Hospital

Ⓟ Parking

🛢 Petrol

⚐ Golf

Ⓐ Detail map

◁ Related map

Other symbols

⁘ Archaeological site

◆ National park, wildlife reserve

✤ Viewing point

△ Campsite

⌂ Refuge, lodge

🏰 Castle

🐟 Diving

🌳🌲🌴 Deciduous/coniferous/palm trees

⌂ Hide

🍇 Vineyard

⚗ Distillery

🚢 Shipwreck

✕ Historic battlefield

Map 1

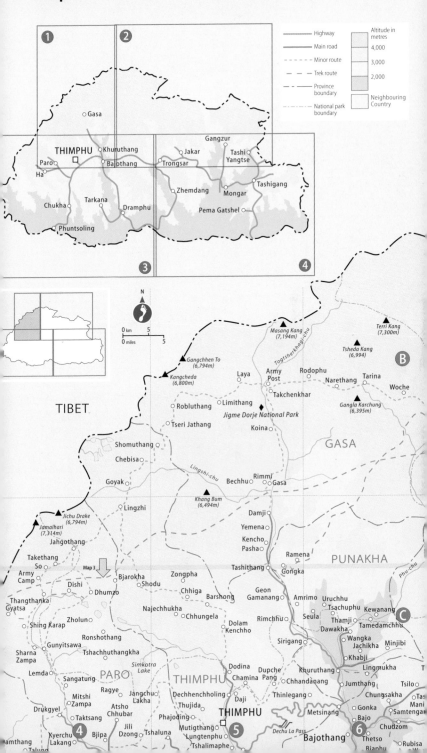

Highway	
Main road	
Minor route	
Trek route	
Province boundary	
National park boundary	

Altitude in metres
- 4,000
- 3,000
- 2,000

Neighbouring Country

① ②

Gasa

THIMPHU ・ Khuruthang
Paro □ ・ Bajothang
Ha ・

Tarkana
Chukha ・ ・ Dramphu

Phuntsoling ・

Gangzur
・ Jakar ・ Tashi
Trongsar ・ Yangtse

Zhemdang ・ ・ Mongar ・ Tashigang

・ Pema Gatshel ・

③ ④

N

0 km 5
0 miles 5

Masang Kang
(7,194m) ▲

Terri Kang
(7,300m) ▲

Gangchhen To
(6,794m) ▲

Kangcheda
(6,800m) ▲

Togtsherkhogi-chu

Tsheda Kang
(6,994) ▲

B

Laya ・ Army Post ・ Rodophu

Takchenkhar ・ Narethang ・ Tarina ・ Woche

TIBET

Robluthang ・

Tseri Jathang ・

Limithang ・

Jigme Dorje National Park

Koina ・

Ganga Karchung
(6,395m) ▲

GASA

Shomuthang ・

Chebisa ・

Goyak ・

Lingshi-chu

Bechhu ・ Rimmi ・
Gasa ・

Jichu Drake
(6,794m) ▲

Lingzhi ・

Khang Bum
(6,494m) ▲

Damji ・

Yemena ・

Kencho Pasha ・

Ramena ・

Gongka ・

PUNAKHA

Phu-chu

Jamalhari
(7,314m) ▲

Jahgothang ・

Takethang So ・

Army Camp

Map 3 →

Bjarokha ・ Zongpha ・

Dishi ・ Dhumzo ・ Shodu ・

Chhiga ・ Barshong ・

Tashithang ・

Geon Gamanang ・ Amrimo ・ Uruchhu ・
Tsachuphu ・ Kewanang ・

C

Thangthanka Gyatsa ・

Shing Karap ・ Zholun ・

Najechhukha ・ Chhungela ・

Dolam Kenchho ・

Rimchhu ・ Seula ・ Thamji ・
Dawakha ・ Tamedamchhu ・

Ronshothang ・

Gunyitsawa ・

Tshachhuthangkha ・

Sirigang ・

Wangka Jachikha ・ Minjibi ・

Khabji ・

Sharna Zampa ・

Lemda ・

Sangatung ・

PARO

Simkotra Lake

Dodina ・

Dupche Pang ・

Khuruthang ・

Chhandanang ・

Lingmukha ・

Jumthang ・ Tsilo ・

Mitshi Zampa ・

Ragye ・

Jangchu Lakha ・

Dechhenchholing ・

Chamina ・ Daji ・

Thinlegang ・

Chungsakha ・

Tas Mani

Drukgyel ・

Taktsang ・

Atsho Chhubar ・

Jili Dzong ・

Phajoding ・

Thujida ・

THIMPHU

THIMPHU □

Metsinang ・

Gonka ・

Bajo ・

Samtengang ・

Chudzom ・

amthang

Kyerchu Lakang ・

④

Bjipa ・

Tshaluna ・

Mutigthang ・

Lungtenphu ・

Tshalimaphe ・

⑤

Dechu La Pass

Bajothang

⑥

Thetso ・

Bianhu

Rubisa

THIMPHU

PARO

TIBET

ksamlung
Khenpa Taska
Hindang Gangiung
Saidu

o Dogsar
Thomthom
Wamdrang
o Naling
Jasibi
o Thunbi
o Dungkhar

Senge
Dzong
Rangmoteng

LHUNTSE

Duksammani o

o Shingphei

Kulong Chu

Tshikang o

◆ Kulong Chu
Wildlife
Sanctuary

Ne o
o Shawa
Rotpa o
o Thesa
Zhamling o
Jangchholing o
Khoma o
Gangzur

Denchhung
Langkhar o
o Todrang
Pangkhar o

TASHI
YANGTSE

soka

Khoma-chu

mling
gyen Choling
ng
Phokpe

Kusmphe o
Tangmachu o
o Minje
Menjabi o
Pemi
Bu-le
o Gonda
Pangsime o
Zenkhar
o Wambur
Shingkhar
Shomi o
o Domkhar

o Taupang

Bumdeling o
Bechamang
Tshaling o
Tashi
Yangtse

Rapting
o Belleng

Tongsang o

Chagidemet

Marshing o

o Phikti

4

5

6

Map 3

For a different view of Europe, take a Footprint